COASTAL BRITAIN

—— ENGLAND & WALES ——

Celebrating the history, heritage and wildlife of Britain's shores

STUART FISHER

ADLARD COLES

LONDON · OXFORD · NEW YORK · NEW DELHI · SYDNEY

ADLARD COLES
Bloomsbury Publishing Plc
50 Bedford Square, Londonm WC1B 3DP, UK

BLOOMSBURY, ADLARD COLES
and the Adlard Coles logo are trademarks of
Bloomsbury Publishing Plc

First published in Great Britain 2019

Some material within this book has been reproduced from
Inshore Britain (Imray Laurie Norie & Wilson Ltd, 2006)

Copyright © Stuart Fisher, 2019

Stuart Fisher has asserted his right under the Copyright, Designs and
Patents Act, 1988, to be identified as Author of this work.

A catalogue record for this book is available from the British Library.

Library of Congress Cataloguing-in-Publication data
has been applied for.

ISBN: PB: 978-1-4729-5869-3;
ePub: 978-1-4729-5872-3; ePDF: 978-1-4729-5873-0

2 4 6 8 10 9 7 5 3 1

Typeset in 9pt Bembo
Printed and bound in China by C&C Offset Printing Co

Bloomsbury Publishing Plc makes every effort to ensure that the
papers used in the manufacture of our books are natural, recyclable
products made from wood grown in well-managed forests.
Our manufacturing processes conform to the environmental
regulations of the country of origin.

To find out more about our authors and books visit
www.bloomsbury.com. and sign up for our newsletters.

Contents

One of the best known British lighthouses, Beachy Head.

3

Fortifications and sunbathers at Point, guarding the entrance to Portsmouth Harbour.

Acknowledgements

P6 from *Marmion* by Sir Walter Scott.
P8 from *Marmion* by Sir Walter Scott.
P12 from *Marmion* by Sir Walter Scott.
P25 Anon.
P28 from *The Life & Ballads of Robin Hood, the Renowned Sherwood Forester*, Anon.
P33 Anon.
P37 from *The High Tide on the Coast of Lincolnshire* by Jean Ingelow.
P44 from *You Can't Take That on the Train* by Roger Watson.
P48 from *Ode on the Death of the Duke of Wellington* by Alfred, Lord Tennyson.
P51 from *Windy Old Weather*, Anon.
P59 from *Jimmy & Nancy of Yarmouth*, Anon.
P66 from *The Lowestoft Boat* by Rudyard Kipling.
P76 by RE Banyard.
P83 by Polly Clark & David Simpson.
P95 from *Dirty Father Thames* by *Punch*.
P101 from *The Yarn of the 'Nancy Bell'* by Sir William Schwenck Gilbert.
P106 from *Dover Beach* by Matthew Arnold.
P114 from *The Tight Little Island* by Thomas Dibdin.
P121 from *Mid-Ocean; or, the Rover* by AP Herbert.
P130 from *Cupid's Garden*, Anon.
P139 from *The First Quarrel* by Alfred, Lord Tennyson.
P143 from *The Thanksgiving in Boston Harbor* by Hezekiah Butterworth.
P157 Anon.
P161 from *The Isle of Portland* by AE Housman
P172 *She Sells Seashells on the Seashore* by Terry Sullivan.
P179 Anon.
P190 from *The Harbour of Fowey* by Sir Arthur Quiller-Couch.
P208 by C Jones.
P222 from *Featherstone's Doom* by RS Hawker.
P227 from *Sonnet XVI* by Robert Southey.
P232 from *The Rime of the Ancient Mariner* by Samuel Taylor Coleridge.
P236 from *The Song of the Western Men* by RS Hawker.
P244 from *Ode to Swansea* by Vernon Watkins.
P274 from *The Bells of Aberdovey* by Charles Dibdin.
P279 from *Men of Harlech* translation by Thomas Oliphant.
P288 from *At Banavie* by Robert Southey.
P298 from *Holyhead Journal* by Jonathan Swift.
P302 from *The Sands of Dee* by Charles Kingsley.
P308 from *Get Yer Wack* by JB Jacques.
P313 from *The Lion & Albert* by Marriott Edgar.
P320 from *Nature & the Poet* by William Wordsworth.
P322 *There was an Old Man of St Bees* by Sir William Schwenck Gilbert.
P328 from *Lochinvar* by Sir Walter Scott.
Every effort has been made to trace authors.
Bloomsbury are happy to correct any error or omission in future editions.

Photographs
Becky Fisher
p134 bottom left,
p134 bottom right,
p146 bottom
Sue Woodman
p267 top
All other photos by the author.

By same author
Rivers of Britain
British River Navigations
Canals of Britain
The Canal Guide

Legend for maps

———— Canal or river
▬▬▬▬ Motorway
———— Other road
———— Railway

▨ Open water or sea

▨ Inter-tidal zone

▨ Built-up area

▨ Woodland

Scale 1:200,000.
North is always at the top.

Introduction

Surely, for its size, no other country can offer such a variety of coastline. We have some of the oldest rocks in the world and we have material which has been added since yesterday. We have jagged reefs which have claimed countless ships, high cliffs covered with colonies of seabirds or pitted with caves as well as muddy estuaries with profuse wildfowl visible to those who move in and observe quietly, those in boats likely to have much closer encounters with wildlife than those on land. There are great sweeps of sandy beach covered with holidaymakers, waters where recreational boat users of all sorts are out in their hundreds and there is also industry, with some of the world's largest commercial shipping.

The water itself offers great variety, from sheltered creeks to famous surf beaches. Currents around the coast can be challenging and the intertidal zone can run out for many kilometres in places.

One thing beats going to the coast and looking at the sea: being on the sea and looking at the land.

This book has been researched initially by paddling round Britain by sea kayak over a period of years. This has allowed greatest flexibility in going where I wanted when the conditions were suitable and not having to worry about running aground or bumping the occasional rock. Other small craft offer similar advantages while larger craft trade accessibility to the shoreline for comfort and facilities.

I have tried to stay within a kilometre of the high water line as far as possible, as a result of which I have often gone far up estuaries. People rounding Britain do not usually encounter the Severn and Humber bridges, for example.

Different people want different things from the coast. Near the end of the Lleyn peninsula we asked our landlady if she didn't find the noise of the low jets from RAF Valley to be annoying but she said that it would be a more lonely place without these manifestations of civilization. It is people who live in noisy cities who seem to worry most about peace and quiet in the countryside.

Generally, the wildlife encounters have been fantastic. Many times I have passed complete cliff faces covered with birds. I have had fulmars within a metre of my head as they checked me out for fish. I have been followed off the premises at close quarters by seals on numerous occasions and have had a dolphin hunting around me off Aberystwyth as an onlooker onshore was beside himself with envy.

The most difficult logistical problem was to paddle round three sides of the Wash rather than just cutting across, a line which takes more than one tide and where drying banks run out as much as 12km. I took a break overnight by turning up into the Witham, followed porpoises through a field of ragwort at the top of a spring tide near the Welland and ended up doing some sandbank walking on the east side of the Wash rather than waiting in King's Lynn for a further tide.

I found a wonderfully warm rockpool for a dip on the south Cornish coast in August. I nominate Lee Bay near Ilfracombe in Devon for my best, unexpectedly attractive, small inlet find.

There could be long days on the water in the summer. I put in a 17 hour paddle from the Gower peninsula to beyond Pendine, taking in the estuaries. I bivvied half under a blackberry bush at the back of the beach in my sleeping bag, feeling I deserved a long night's sleep, only to be rudely awoken a few hours later by a young lady stripping off completely in front of me to go for an early morning swim in the otherwise deserted cove.

There were several noticeable changes during the fifteen year extent of my initial circumnavigation. Naturists were rare when I started but now they are on many secluded or not so secluded beaches as soon as the sun comes out. There has also been an explosion of sit-on-top kayaks and paddleboards for hire on beaches, allowing casual holidaymakers to get afloat.

A welcome change has been the slight reduction in the many firing ranges around our coast in recent years, even if most of them are well run.

Where I had anticipated problems was trying to cut through Dover harbour. The harbour police were reluctant to connect me to the port controller at first but he could not have been more helpful, advising when it was clear to proceed, even coming out of his office in person to wave me through.

Busy commercial estuaries such as the Tees and Stour generally proved easy to cross with care as the fairways are narrow and clearly marked. The most difficult ones I found were Portsmouth Harbour and Southampton Water. I crossed due west from Southsea, by which point craft were fanning out in all directions. Off Calshot the problem was simply the speed at which the Isle of Wight launches travel. Hopefully, they are used to looking out for small craft in these waters, the most crowded with recreational boats in the world.

Is there anything I would have changed with the benefit of hindsight? I would very much like to have been able to pick the best weather, mark it up on my calendar and go when the time was right rather than going out in less than perfect conditions and having the weather improve once I went home, going home without going on the water at all because of an overoptimistic forecast or, more likely these days, staying at home and missing fine weather because of a forecast which announced good weather one day at a time.

It was a journey which has also brought home some of our history. I hadn't appreciated how many castles were built by Edward I, for example, often in places that were not for the defence of the residents.

A journey of this kind and length holds a wealth of memories. The sheer variety is revealed on the following pages.

Stuart Fisher
April 2019

Thank you

I wish to pay thanks to the following:

Willie Wilson of Imray Laurie Norie & Wilson took on this project in the first place with an unpublished author and allowed me a remarkably free hand in the layout of the book.

Peter Cornes, Terry Hailwood and the Revd Canon Jeremy Martineau offered updates to the original text.

This will be one of the last books for Janet Murphy of Adlard Coles, my commissioning editor, prior to retiring to spend more time on the sea herself. It has been a privilege to work with her on several books, during which time she, too, has given me a free hand. She has to her credit an extensive catalogue of books which have helped a generation of nautical authors and been enjoyed by untold numbers of readers.

I have worked with editor Jonathan Eyers on several books. We each have a fair idea of how far we can push the other even before we start, which results in a relaxed working relationship.

Last but not least, this book would not have happened without the practical support of my wife, Becky, who sat at many a remote spot around the coast, waiting for me to appear in the distance. Also to sons Brendan and Ross, who tested the play value of many beaches at a time when junior school teachers agreed that they were learning more on what were, effectively, geography field trips than they would have done sitting in classrooms.

1 Cheviots

*Day set on Norham's castled steep,
And Tweed's fair river, broad and deep,
And Cheviot's mountains lone*
Sir Walter Scott

The position of the border between England and Scotland has fluctuated over the centuries. Currently, it is not at its most obvious, being some 6km north of the Tweed on a section of coast with a rocky shoreline and no road access. Parking behind Ladies Skerrs near the Magdalene Fields Golf Club at the northern end of Berwick is the first time the shore can be reached with any ease although walkers are kept back from the edge of the crumbling cliffs. A sea water bathing pond is sited at the high water mark.

Berwick-upon-Tweed is one of the oldest towns in Britain, having been founded in Saxon times, its name coming from the Old English bere-wic, a corn farm, and was the only crossing place of the Tweed from 1153, being at the height of its prosperity during the reign of Alexander II. As well as having had a long history, it has also had a complex one, changing hands between the Scots and English 14 times from 1482. The town walls to resist artillery and the gun emplacements were started in 1558 and were Elizabeth I's most expensive construction project. The Tudor fortifications are the best preserved of their age in northern Europe. There are also remains of the earlier walls of Edward I including the Black Tower and the Bell Tower to warn of enemy approach. Ravensdowne Barracks of 1717 were among the earliest to be purpose built and now give an insight into the life of an 18th century foot soldier, the history of border warfare, the Kings Own Scottish Borderers Museum and a selection from the Burrell art collection. The ditches and ramparts remain. Holy Trinity Church, near the medieval church, rebuilt in 1650, was the only new church constructed during Cromwell's rule. There

is a 1750 Guildhall with a 46m spire and a butter market at ground level while there is an 18th century jail high above the ground. A ghostly fight was recorded from the border in 1604. One of Robin Hood's alibis was as a Berwick citizen. Sir Walter Scott's *Redgauntlet*'s Trumbull was based on Berwick smuggler Richard Mendham and Henry Wynd was waiting for a new Berwick jerkin in *The Fair Maid of Perth*. Confusion resulted in Berwick's being at war with Russia for many years, having been mentioned specifically in the declaration at the start of the Crimean War but not in the subsequent peace treaty.

Edward FitzGerald visited by smack from Sussex in 1861. An unexpected piece of culture arose when hotel receptionist Marjorie Ellison finally allowed a regular visitor to paint her portrait in the 1950s after he had pestered her a number of times. She later binned the pictures as amateurish and immature. Fortunately, someone else read the signature, that of LS Lowry.

The most notable structure in Berwick is the 657m long Royal Border Bridge of 1847–50 by Robert Stepehenson, 28 arches up to 38m above the Tweed in a curve of which only the top is visible from the sea 2km downstream. Berwick is a small commercial and fishing port with 460m of quays. The Tweed floods from HW Dover −0250 and ebbs strongly from HW Dover +0330, affected by freshets. It can be dangerous on the ebb, especially with freshets, and there is a bar. There can also be salmon nets out from mid February to mid September. Protecting the northern side of the estuary is a long pier with a 13m white round stone tower lighthouse with red cupola and base.

From late July to September the estuary has one of the largest flocks of swans in the country, together with goldeneyes, red breasted mergansers, pochard and other wildfowl in winter plus a few terns.

On the south side of the estuary Tweedmouth has its own small fishing fleet and the Mouth of the Tweed Festival and Tweedmouth Feast in July. Spittal has a

Dunes make their appearance from Scremerston.

One of the refuges for those on foot who get the tide wrong.

drying sandy spit which is liable to much alteration, especially after westerly gales.

A discoloured stream at Huds Head drains the disused Scremerston coalmines. Cliffs are 30m high at Redshin Cove but they gradually give way to a dune coast, one declining outcrop being topped by a pillbox and some nice lava rolls issuing onto the beach. Cocklawburn Beach has a dangerous undertow on the ebb. 18th century limekiln remains have lime loving plants on the spoil and cowslips on the dunes in the spring. A nature reserve is located behind the last of the rock outcrops at Far Skerr and then there are just dunes behind Cheswick Sands, treacherous currents for swimmers, reported unexploded bombs and a golf course. A couple of dunes form high tide islands with views inland to the Cheviots.

Crossing Goswick Sands, with its wrecks, needs to be done within a couple of hours of high tide for there to be sufficient depth for even the smallest boats.

In the vicinity of the causeway to Holy Island the deepest water is in the channel taken by South Low when the tide is out, identified by the more westerly of the two refuges.

Distance
13km from Berwick-on-Tweed to the causeway

OS 1:50,000 Sheet
75 Berwick-upon-Tweed

Tidal Constants
Berwick:
HW Dover +0340,
LW Dover +0320
Holy Island:
HW Dover +0350,
LW Dover +0320

Sea Area
Tyne

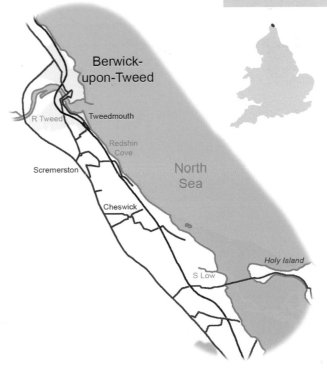

2 Holy Island (Lindisfarne)

Then from the coast they bore away,
And reach'd the Holy Island's bay.
The tide did now its flood-mark gain,
And girdled in the Saint's domain:
For, with the flow and ebb, its style
Varies from continent to isle;
Dry shod, oe'r sands, twice every day
The pilgrims to the shrine find way;
Twice every day, the waves efface
Of staves and sandall'd feet the trace.
As to the port the galley flew,
Higher and higher rose to view
The Castle with its battled walls,
The ancient Monastery's halls,
A solemn, huge, and dark-red pile,
Placed on the margin of the isle.

Sir Walter Scott

Pitted rock in Coves Haven.

Holy Island or Lindisfarne lies off the Northumberland coast at the end of the Great Whin Sill and within sight of the most northerly point in England. It is only an island for three hours every tide, Goswick Sands and Holy Island Sands forming it into a peninsula at other times. A road runs across on a causeway, covered during the upper half of the tide, and a 46m long bridge accompanied by a refuge crosses South Low which flows at all times.

Vehicle tracks across the sand show that current routes often emulate the pilgrims' way which used to cross to the island. Tides around the island are swift. If setting off to circumnavigate the island it would pay to leave from the Harbour and come up with the tide to reach the western end at the top of the tide in order to get sufficient depth of water.

A double line of anti tank blocks on the mainland is the only sign of recent military activity. The RAF had a training base here during the Second World War but were evicted afterwards despite their wish to stay.

Goswick Sands are so flat that any debris such as old logs shows up very clearly, as do lines of posts. Views up the coast are extensive and reach beyond Berwick to the lighthouse on St Abb's Head.

The only building visible on the west end of the island is a castellated house on the Snook. The whole of the west end consists of sand dunes and a host of plants thrive along with the ubiquitous marram grass, viper's bugloss, hound's tongue, gentian, campion, common centaury, sea aster, sea thrift, dune helleborine and an Australian import, pirri pirri bur, although the island has few trees and shrubs. It is an environment where rabbits, frogs, lizards, foxes and weasels breed. The dunes end abruptly against a rockface at Back Skerrs. Three headlands dominate the east end of the north side of the island, Snipe Point, False Emmanuel Head and Emmanuel Head, the latter surmounted by a 15m pyramidal beacon on top of the 3m cliffs. The beaches on the east end of the island are entirely of coarse broken rock but it is not difficult to land, even on the headlands. Snipe Point has a horizontal stratum of rock running out to sea and this has settled into a series of waves.

From Coves Haven round as far as Sheldrake Pool, seals are numerous close inshore, being attracted by the rocks. Ships are also attracted and this section of the northeast English coast is considered to be its most dangerous. Particularly so are the Farne Islands. Inner Farne is visible to the southeast and a series of constructions on others lead out in a line to the Longstone lighthouse. Also prominent is Bamburgh Castle.

Turning Castle Point brings into view the two needles, Old Law East and West beacons at Guile Point. It also brings the boater right up to Lindisfarne Castle which is visible from both the north and east coasts and stands by Hole Mouth on a steep prominence which contrasts sharply with the raised plateau of the rest of the island.

The island was probably used as a military camp and safe harbour by the Saxons trying to subdue Celtic resistance but the castle was not built on its vantage point until 1549. The smallest fortress in Northumbria, it had gun emplacements. The Stuarts seized it in 1715. It fell into disuse after 1819 until it was bought in 1902 by Edward Hudson, founder of *Country Life*. Sir Edward Lutyens converted it into a private house and it is now looked after by the National Trust, its 17th century English and Flemish oak furniture and collection of Ridinger and other prints being in an environment which has been described as romance without period.

Next to the castle are three sheds resembling upturned boat hulls.

Near the castle are limekilns that were used from 1860

The bridge across South Low. At high tide it is covered.

until 1920. Although the island is based on a dolerite dyke cooling in vertical towers, it has shale, sandstone, limestone and coal, the last two enabling the industry to exist.

Most of the 200 residents live at the back of the harbour in Holy Island at Steel End and are claimed to have an accent close to Danish. The harbour is busy in the herring season from June to September, having five working fishing boats. A dozen people are involved in farming but most are in tourism, the island drawing 50,000 visitors each year, possibly explaining why such a small community should need four public houses.

The island was given to Bishop Aiden by Bernicia when he arrived from Iona in 634 and the following year it became the first diocese in England. Cuthbert became Prior of Lindisfarne in 664 and Bishop of Lindisfarne from 685 to 687. When he was exhumed in 698 his

Boat shaped huts are found at various places on the island.

The distinctive location of Lindisfarne Castle.

body showed no signs of decay. His canonization brought thousands of pilgrims to the island.

A monastery was built in the village but was the subject of the first recorded Viking attack on England in 793, the monastery being destroyed and most of the monks killed, blamed as retribution on the evil lives of King Æthelred and his officials. A Danish attack in 875 resulted in the flight of the monks with the body of St Cuthbert. A Benedictine priory was built to replace it in 1082 and its remains dominate the centre of the village.

Another survivor is the monks' recipe for honey mead and this is now made in the village, as are assorted wines.

The 13th century church of St Mary the Virgin stands behind the remains of the priory. Turner painted it in 1830 but most of its art lies inside. Overshadowing the examples of villagers' needlework is a copy of the early 8th century *Lindisfarne Gospels*, the original of which is in the British Library. This is one of the most important and beautifully produced handwritten books in the world.

Outside the church is the Petting Stone, over which brides are required to jump to ensure a happy marriage.

The remains of the chapel and the stone cross on Hobthrush Island are hardly noticed. Also known as St Cuthbert's Island, the islet is only cut off at higher

Large limekilns on the shore below Lindisfarne Castle.

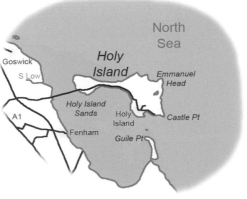

Preparing to circumnavigate Holy Island. Guile Point stands across the Harbour.

Lindisfarne Priory dominates the centre of the village.

stages of the tide but it was to this point that Cuthbert withdrew. St Cuthbert's beads are found here in the form of stone lilies, fossilized bones.

He also gave his name to Cudda's or eider ducks, found around the island and in the Lindisfarne National Nature Reserve which occupies the shallow area of sand and mud flats and saltings which lie between the island and the mainland, forming Holy Island Sands and Fenham Flats with the tide out.

No less than 250 species of bird have been recorded here and there are 44 resident breeding species including mallard, arctic tern, fulmar, shag, guillemot, kittiwake and puffin. Visitors, mostly in the winter between November and February, include wigeon, brent and greylag geese, dunlin and bartailed godwit. The noise varies between the screams of single birds to a deep booming cacophony which could drown out the sound of the Vikings landing.

There is little noise from the A1 and the East Coast Main Line from Edinburgh to London which run along the coast. The backdrop of the Cheviots can make nonsense of weather forecasts, often producing thick weather in the vicinity.

The island's road skirts the high water mark on the south side, indicated by wooden posts, on its way to the mainland. Unless the tide is reasonably high this will not be seen by the boater who will be finding a route through the dead leads to try to locate Black Low from which South Low branches off and works its way back to the causeway.

Hobthrush Island, retreat of St Cuthbert.

Distance
Holy Island is 5km long and lies 1km off Beal with causeway access

OS 1:50,000 Sheet
75 Berwick-upon-Tweed

Tidal Constants
Holy Island:
HW Dover +0350,
LW Dover +0320

Sea Area
Tyne

3 Northumberland

They passed the tower of Widderington,
Mother of many a valiant son;
At Coquet-isle their beads they tell
To the good Saint who own'd the cell;
Then did the Alne attention claim,
And Warkworth, proud of Percy's name;
And next, they cross'd themselves, to hear
The whitening breakers sound so near,
Where, boiling through the rocks, they roar,
On Dunstanborough's cavern'd shore;
Thy tower, proud Bamborough, mark'd they there,
King Ida's castle, huge and square,
From its tall rock look grimly down,
And on the swelling ocean frown;

Sir Walter Scott

Fenham Flats form a shallow lagoon, muddy at the edges but suitable for lion's mane and moon jellyfish and plenty of birdlife, as indicated by the hide at Lowmoor Point. This is Lindisfarne National Nature Reserve territory. There are streams entirely below the high water mark, including Cathangings Letch and Stinking Goat, between which is the remains of a windpump on the end of White Hill.

Views eastward are dominated by Lindisfarne Castle and by the two leading marks at Guile Point. A break in the dunes at Ross Point may be used by small craft but there is only 80mm depth of water at the top of spring tides. A notice warns about disturbing nesting shorebirds on the inside of Old Law. This pass is between dunes covered with marram grass, ragwort and rosebay willowherb.

The section of coast to Snook Point at North Sunderland is the most dangerous stretch of coast for shipping north of the Humber, but no problem for craft close inshore except when affected by strong winds. Flows south run to 2km/h.

Budle Bay, the mouth of the Waren Burn, mostly dries. It is a nature reserve, especially for wintering seabirds which seem not to be concerned about waterskiing or the two lots of caravans and the golf course along the south side.

The 9m white tower of Black Rocks Lighthouse

Rich saltmarsh with black silt at low tide at Fenham.

overlooks the Harkness Rocks surf break which has tank traps in the dunes at one end.

Bamburgh was the birthplace of Grace Darling, whose father was keeper of the Longstone lighthouse. In September 1838, when she was 23, she and her father rowed out in a coble to rescue 9 survivors of the SS *Forfarshire* who were clinging to Big Harcar rocks, a rescue which caught the public imagination and has helped to attract funds for the RNLI since then. The Grace Darling Museum in the village includes the coble. Grace died three years later from tuberculosis and was buried in St Aiden's, the churchyard with a monument designed to be seen from ships at sea. Staniland was moved to paint the scene.

The church includes a beam from a wooden church of 635. St Aiden died here in 651. Remains of a 13th century Dominican friary including part of a church are found in the village, together with the 13th to 15th century church to St Aiden with a fine 13th century crypt.

A lesser claim for Bamburgh, where the B1342 gives way to the B1340, is that it is home to the Northumbrian sausage.

Bamburgh's most conspicuous asset is the castle, one of the finest in England, standing high on a rock above the beach and surmounted by cannons. There was a wooden fort by 546. King Ida lived here in the 6th century and, after his wife died, married Bethoc the Witch, who was jealous of his daughter, Margaret, turning her into the Laidley Worm, which lived on Spindlestone Haugh and forced villagers to bring food, according to one version of the story. Her brother, Childe Wynde, returned from his travels and went to kill the dragon but recognized her voice, kissing her and breaking the curse. The queen was then changed into a toad which reappears every seven years to seek innocent maidens. A 7th century gold plaque showing the beast is on display in the castle. A 47m Anglo Saxon well survives on a headland which has been inhabited for at least two millennia. The castle was later destroyed by the Vikings. It was rebuilt in the 11th century in the present red stone by Henry I but includes an 8th century wall. It was used by King Oswald to rule Northumbria and Sir Thomas Malory's *Le Morte d'Arthur* claims it is one of the possible sites for Sir Lancelot's Joyous Gard where he eloped with Queen Guinevere. After surviving several sieges it was the first English castle to fall to gunfire in 1464 during the Wars of the Roses. Restoration was again begun in 1704 by Lord Crewe, Bishop of Durham. In 1716 it was the home of Dorothy Forster, who made a daring raid on Newgate Gaol to rescue her brother, Tom. It was once more restored in 1894–1905 by Lord Armstrong with a teak hammerbeam roof, an excellent collection of arms, artwork, china, furniture and Armstrong industrial exhibits including aviation. The castle was used by Roman Polanski for filming *Macbeth* in 1972 and for *Robin of Sherwood* in 1985. In *The House of Elrig* Gavin Maxwell describes collecting rare bird's eggs on the Farne Islands from a rented flat here. This section of coast has been suggested as the setting for much of the action in James Fenimore Cooper's *The Pilot*, featuring John Paul Jones, the first sea novel.

The B1340 follows the coast to Beadnell, passing a pillbox and vandalized lookout point, the last outcrop of the Great Whin Sill. There are between 15 and 28 islands off this stretch of coast depending on the state of the tide, but landing is only permitted on Staple and

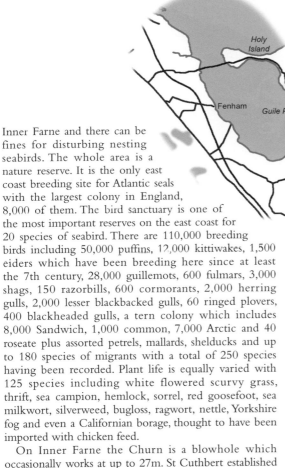

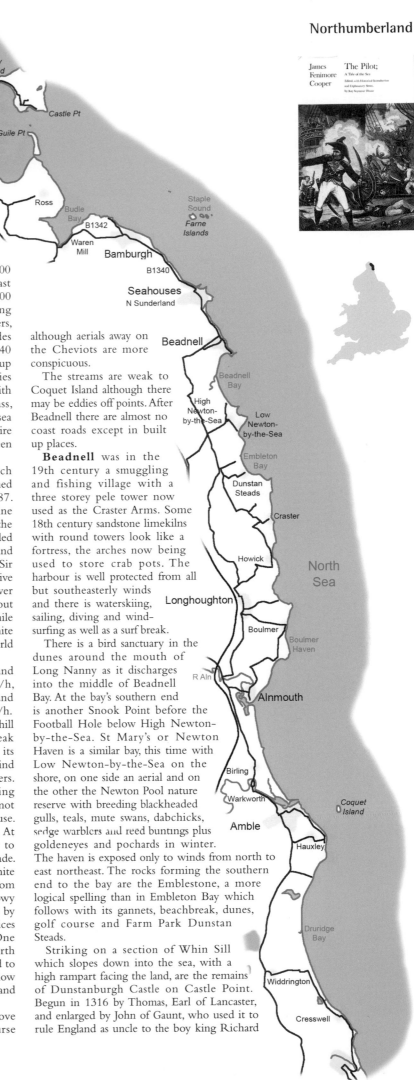

Inner Farne and there can be fines for disturbing nesting seabirds. The whole area is a nature reserve. It is the only east coast breeding site for Atlantic seals with the largest colony in England, 8,000 of them. The bird sanctuary is one of the most important reserves on the east coast for 20 species of seabird. There are 110,000 breeding birds including 50,000 puffins, 12,000 kittiwakes, 1,500 eiders which have been breeding here since at least the 7th century, 28,000 guillemots, 600 fulmars, 3,000 shags, 150 razorbills, 600 cormorants, 2,000 herring gulls, 2,000 lesser blackbacked gulls, 60 ringed plovers, 400 blackheaded gulls, a tern colony which includes 8,000 Sandwich, 1,000 common, 7,000 Arctic and 40 roseate plus assorted petrels, mallards, shelducks and up to 180 species of migrants with a total of 250 species having been recorded. Plant life is equally varied with 125 species including white flowered scurvy grass, thrift, sea campion, hemlock, sorrel, red goosefoot, sea milkwort, silverweed, bugloss, ragwort, nettle, Yorkshire fog and even a Californian borage, thought to have been imported with chicken feed.

On Inner Farne the Churn is a blowhole which occasionally works at up to 27m. St Cuthbert established a cell on the island in 676 and died here in 687. The Convent of Durham set up a small Benedictine monastery in 1255 and a tiny chapel was built on the cell site in 1370, restored in 1845. Other visitors included the Vikings, who made attacks in the 8th century, and Bartholomew, who was a hermit here about 1150. Sir John Clayton built a light tower in 1669 as a speculative venture, a forerunner of the 13m white round tower which is the 1800 Inner Farne lighthouse. Further out there are towers on Staple Island and Brownsman while the Longstone lighthouse, a 26m red tower with a white band, was built in 1826, damaged in the Second World War and repaired in 1952.

Staple Sound flows southeast from Dover HW and northwest from HW Dover +0600 at up to 7km/h, 9km/h near the islands with overfalls, whirlpools and turbulent water. In Inner Sound the flow eases to 6km/h.

Near the lookout a wreck has been left on Greenhill Rocks. The St Aidan's Dunes run to the surf break at **Seahouses**, a fishing village which has turned its attention to holidaymakers, their caravans lined behind the beach. Fishing cobles bring in crabs and lobsters. Kippers were first made here in 1843 by smoking herrings, the colour having to come from oak chips, not dyes. Swallow Fish is the last traditional smokehouse. There is a Marine Life Centre & Fishing Museum. At the point where carboniferous limestone gives way to millstone grit, the village was involved in the lime trade. The new harbour was built in 1889. It has an 8m white lighthouse tower and a detached breakwater. Away from the holidaymaker front, North Sunderland is less showy and offers better value. The Lodge, in particular, used by divers and anglers, offers five star food at two star prices in a licensed restaurant awash with diving finds. One service no longer available in the village is the North Sunderland Railway which was closed in 1951. It used to take 20 minutes for the 6km journey to Chathill, so slow that passengers were able to jump out, pick flowers and get back in again, but quicker than today.

Curlews search the rocks off Snook Point. Above the 9m cliff is an aerial in front of the golf course although aerials away on the Cheviots are more conspicuous.

The streams are weak to Coquet Island although there may be eddies off points. After Beadnell there are almost no coast roads except in built up places.

Beadnell was in the 19th century a smuggling and fishing village with a three storey pele tower now used as the Craster Arms. Some 18th century sandstone limekilns with round towers look like a fortress, the arches now being used to store crab pots. The harbour is well protected from all but southeasterly winds and there is waterskiing, sailing, diving and windsurfing as well as a surf break.

There is a bird sanctuary in the dunes around the mouth of Long Nanny as it discharges into the middle of Beadnell Bay. At the bay's southern end is another Snook Point before the Football Hole below High Newton-by-the-Sea. St Mary's or Newton Haven is a similar bay, this time with Low Newton-by-the-Sea on the shore, on one side an aerial and on the other the Newton Pool nature reserve with breeding blackheaded gulls, teals, mute swans, dabchicks, sedge warblers and reed buntings plus goldeneyes and pochards in winter. The haven is exposed only to winds from north to east northeast. The rocks forming the southern end to the bay are the Emblestone, a more logical spelling than in Embleton Bay which follows with its gannets, beachbreak, dunes, golf course and Farm Park Dunstan Steads.

Striking on a section of Whin Sill which slopes down into the sea, with a high rampart facing the land, are the remains of Dunstanburgh Castle on Castle Point. Begun in 1316 by Thomas, Earl of Lancaster, and enlarged by John of Gaunt, who used it to rule England as uncle to the boy king Richard

Bamburgh Castle, one of England's finest.

Looking out from the coast to the nearer of the Farne Islands.

Seahouses, not at its best at low tide.

II in the 14th century, it changed hands several times and suffered major Yorkist gunfire damage during the Wars of the Roses. It has been a ruin since 1538 with an impressive gatehouse tower and immense open bailey surrounded by a long wall with towers. The tidal moat was cut out of rock. The harbour provided protection for Henry VIII's navy in 1514 and has since silted up. It was painted by Turner and is now an important wildlife habitat for birds. The reefs at Castle Point can be surfed. One vessel which failed to pull off before the break is a wreck at Cushat Stiel. Along the coast behind are a column of people walking between the castle and Craster.

Little Carr, with its white conical concrete beacon, helps protect the entrance to Craster harbour. The harbour was built in 1906 to export the hard whinstone for London kerbstones, but it is now used by leisure craft and cobles landing lobsters and crabs. It was England's

The dramatic silhouette of Dunstanburgh Castle.

kipper smoking capital, smoking 25,000 fish per day, the herrings being gutted by Scottish fishwives who lived in Kip Houses which were only suitable for sleeping, giving rise to the expression 'having a kip'. The herrings are now brought from western Scotland rather than being caught locally. The Craster Tower and a settlement are legacies from earlier years. Wreckage of a steel ship close inshore includes a boiler and pieces of metal which would be uncomfortable if met in surf.

Cullernose Point is a seabird colony, above which is 58m Hips Heugh and then Howick where the First World War gardens have over 600 rhododendrons. Howick Hall was owned by Earl Grey, whose 1832 Reform Act set up our present system of democracy. On a diplomatic mission to China he saved the life of a mandarin who sent him some tea scented with oil of Bergamot in thanks. Earl Grey tea is now the world's most popular blend. The Greys also had a Victorian bathing house.

Rumbling Kern is a dolerite gully in which heavy seas resonate at low tide. There is a settlement site in a wooded valley. **Longhoughton** Steel begins 3km of reef with a break in the centre forming Boulmer Haven, a natural harbour with fishing cobles and toilets. A heron standing quietly, watching, is repeating an activity from the days when this was a smuggling village. In 1977 RAF staff were amongst those who recorded a pair of UFOs some 5km out to sea at a height of 1.5km for the better part of two hours. Boulmer is always the first reporting station on the shipping forecast. The reef ends with Seaton Point where there are caravans, overfalls and reef breaks but Marsden Rocks, in front of the golf course, form another area of reef which has claimed a ship.

The village of Craster.

England's second oldest golf course is at **Alnmouth**, a resort behind the dunes protected by tank traps. Fishing and recreational craft are faced with the width of the River Aln and the position of the bar changing and there is a surf break. Past changes have been greater and the Saxon cross and Church Hill were cut off when the river moved its course in a storm in 1806.

The millstone grit gives way to coal measures although this is not obvious at first as the dunes sweep on round Alnmouth Bay, only a caravan area above Birling Carrs breaking up the curve. Behind another golf course in

Coquet Island and its lighthouse.

a bend in the River Coquet, however, is Warkworth. The early 12th century Grade I church of St Lawrence is on the site of an 8th century church. It was built by King Coewulf of Northumbria with the longest nave in Northumberland at 27m and a vaulted roof with diagonal ribbing to prevent fire damage during the border troubles, but 300 villagers were massacred in the church by the Earl of Fife in 1174.

Also from the 12th century with a 15th century cruciform keep is Warkworth Castle, used by the 1st Earl of Northumberland, Henry de Percy, and his son, Sir Henry Percy or Harry Hotspur, who was born here, to plot treason and rebellion to put Henry IV on the throne although Hotspur later became the king's enemy. Shakespeare used it as much of the setting for his play. The keep has 8 towers, fine medieval masonry, a maze of chambers, passageways and stairways and a keep restored and made habitable again in the 19th century.

The old course of the river has waders and ducks but Warkworth Harbour has been extended with a marina at **Amble**. Use of the fishing port involves negotiating the bar off the entrance with a dangerous short sea over the Pan Bush shoal when a sea is running, although surfers may appreciate small surf in the entrance and north of the breakwater. There is a wreck off the entrance and an RAF boat was lost with many drowned a few years ago. At one time concrete ships were built here. Another unconventional visitor between 1989 and 1994 was Freddie the dolphin, who was very friendly towards swimmers. There is an 8m light tower on each breakwater. A cemetery is located on the front at Amble. The port was built to export coal, there having been 80 mineshafts between Amble and Hauxley, now all closed.

Also founded on coal is the 6ha Coquet Island off Amble. Landing is not permitted on this RSPB nature reserve, owned by the Duke of Northumberland, which has 4,000 common, 1,000 Arctic, 1,200 Sandwich and 300 roseate terns, 600 eiders in their most southerly breeding colony on the east coast, puffins, oystercatchers, gulls and guillemots. It was occupied in Roman times, jewellery and coins having been found. In the 7th century there was a small Benedictine monastery and chapel where Elfreda, Abbess of Whitby, persuaded St Cuthbert to accept the offer of the bishopric of Lindisfarne from Egfrith, King of Northumbria. A cell was established here by the Dane St Henry the Hermit, who had a vision to become a hermit, so avoiding the arranged marriage his parents were planning. He grew his own food and performed miracles, dying in 1127. Charles I had the island garrisoned in the Civil War but the Scots captured it in 1645. The 22m white and grey tower of Coquet lighthouse dates from 1841, the keepers' cottages being built onto the chapel and hermit's cell.

Coquet Road and then Coquet Channel flow strongly to the south from HW Dover −0040 and north from HW Dover +0520, the flows then becoming weak to Blyth. When Hauxley Point rocks are dry the flow is more in a northwest to southeast direction.

At High Hauxley there is an opencast mine while a lake at Low Hauxley is now a nature reserve with hides and thousands of birds, especially dunlins, curlew sandpipers and other migrants.

Bondi Carrs is a reefbreak. The shoreline is rather unusual, dunes over a thick layer of soft clay at the start of the 9km sweep of tank trap and dune backed Druridge Bay. Much of the land around the bay is restored opencast coal workings, but the power generation looked likely to resurface when it was proposed as a nuclear power station site. Ladyburn Lake forms the centrepiece of Druridge Bay Country Park at Broomhill with redbreasted mergansers, smew and other diving ducks in winter, scoters, kestrels, lapwings and others.

The restored Radar site workings form Druridge Pools nature reserve with breeding waders and wildfowl, this being on a wildfowl migration route. Behind the pools are a 14th century chapel and preceptory hostel for passing pilgrims at Low Chibburn, this previously being on a pilgrim migration route. Much of the bay offers a beachbreak.

Cresswell Ponds have good winter wildfowl and little gulls in summer, when the farm trail is also popular and crowds throng the beach. There is parking at Cresswell but care is needed when landing as the tank trap blocks are below the high water line.

Jellyfish beached at Low Hauxley.

Distance
58km from the causeway to Cresswell

OS 1:50,000 Sheets
75 Berwick-upon-Tweed
81 Alnwick & Morpeth

Tidal Constants
Holy Island:
HW Dover +0350,
LW Dover +0320
North Sunderland:
HW Dover +0340
LW Dover +0330
Craster:
HW Dover +0400
LW Dover +0350
Alnmouth:
Dover +0400
Amble:
Dover +0410
Coquet Road:
HW Dover +0420
LW Dover +0410

Sea Area
Tyne

Low Hauxley's unusual formation of dunes over clay.

Tyneside

4

Monk-Wearmouth soon behind them lay,
And Tynemouth's priory and bay;
They mark'd, amid her trees, the hall
Of lofty Seaton-Delaval;
They saw the Blythe and Wansbeck floods
Rush to the sea through sounding woods;
Sir Walter Scott

A marked change comes after Cresswell as industry or post-industry can no longer be ignored. Cresswell Tower and the caravan site on Snab Point are forgotten as **Lynemouth** comes into sight with its 420MW power

Newbiggin Rocket House, now the lifeboat station.

Cobles by the beach at Newbiggin.

Couple, the UK's first offshore sculpture, at Newbiggin.

station. Even the River Lyne is lost in the industrial jungle. The beach is black with coal dust and sea coal is still collected from the shore.

There is a golf course on Beacon Point, beyond which is Woodhorn with the tower of a windmill and the Grade I St Mary's church, the earliest church in Northumberland, over 1,200 years old, now a museum with Saxon and medieval tombstones close to the Woodhorn Museum & Northumberland Archives and the 610mm Woodhorn Narrow Gauge Railway.

Aerials before and after **Newbiggin-by-the-Sea**, at the end of the A197, mark a measured distance for boats to check their speeds. Newbiggin Point, given its charter by King John, has St Bartholomew's church amongst the caravans which is losing its graveyard to the sea so that human bones may be found in the water. There is an inshore rescue boat in the oldest station in the British Isles, formerly the 1866 Rocket House, near which cobles are stored. Surprisingly, each seems to have its own tractor for launching and so there are lots of old tractors lined up along the front rather than a few being shared. In the Middle Ages it was a large grain port but now there are only the cobles and leisure craft, the worst of the weather being fielded by a detached stone breakwater although enough waves get in to keep surfers and kitesurfers happy. In 1920 the concrete tug *Cretewheel* was wrecked here. Despite the black coal dust on the beach, Newbiggin remains a resort but has been reported to have the lowest coastal house prices in England. Sean Henry's 5m bronze *Couple*, mounted on a new breakwater, is the UK's first offshore sculpture.

Northumberland fishermen thought it was unlucky to mention pigs except by metaphor. This particularly applies in Newbiggin on Fridays. Another distinctive user of words was John Braine who lived here in the 1950s while writing *Room at the Top*.

Terns and herring gulls live in Newbiggin Bay. More caravans top the low cliffs as the River Wansbeck is crossed by the A189 and discharges over its bar into the bay at what can be a beachbreak, beyond which is the Cambois former industrial site.

The River Blyth, named after the Old English blipe or merry, discharges through the harbour at **Blyth**, the biggest town in Northumberland, large enough to have two markets per week and its own dialect, Pitmatic. It was a 19th century coal exporting and shipping port and still handles coal, together with timber, paper products, general cargoes and bauxite which is stored in three large red conical hoppers at North Blyth. The harbour wall has kelp below. Each of the piers has a lighthouse on the end. The harbour suffers scend with south-southeasterly winds and there are wavetraps inside the east pier. The harbourmouth needs frequent dredging. When the new harbour was constructed in the 1880s the High Light of 1788 was left in the residential streets. Another redundant light is on the wooden lightship in the South Harbour which is now the headquarters of the Royal Northumberland Yacht Club. The flood tide starts at HW Dover +0420. According to Robert Westall's ghost story *The Watch House*, one of its exhibits was the nameplate from the *Cactus* of Blyth.

There is a sheltered beachbreak next to the harbourmouth.

Flows are weak to Sunderland and the coast low and sandy to Seaton Sluice. The B1329 follows the coast to South Beach and then the A193 takes over to Whitley Bay. Mile Hill is no higher than 18m.

Approaching Seaton Sluice, **Seaton Delaval** Hall was designed in 1718 by Sir John Vanbrugh, his last and most elegant project with antique furniture, pictures and oriental porcelain despite being burned out twice. It was funded by spoils taken from Barbary pirates by

The distinctive harbour wall at Blyth with a wind farm beyond.

The lighthouse on St Mary's Island is now a museum.

Admiral George Delaval. One of the Delaval family used to buy electors in parliamentary elections by firing golden guineas from a cannon into the crowd. On the bank of the Seaton Burn, which helps to shape surf at the beachbreak, Starlight Castle is a folly built overnight in the 1750s. Seaton Sluice was a serious venture, however, built in 1660 by Sir Ralph Delaval as a coal and salt exporting harbour. The sluice was held closed at low tide and horses used to plough the silt before the sluice was opened and then the silt washed away. In the 18th century the village had the largest bottle making factory in England.

Rock cliffs with ledges extend to St Mary's Island. Hartley, on the Northumberland/North Tyneside boundary, overlooked by a caravan site and half a dozen aerials, has a reefbreak on the top half of the tide with onshore winds and a northerly swell which can produce waves 600mm higher than at Tynemouth.

A causeway runs from Curry Point to St Mary's, Bait or Bate's Island. Originally it was a monk's place of solitude with a chapel and a cemetery for drowned or plagued sailors but the chapel light acted as a lighthouse and this function was subsequently taken over by the 37m white tower lighthouse which now stands on the island. This acts as a museum of the history of the island and its wildlife from 1897 to 1984. The island is a SSSI for roosting shorebirds. There is a wreck just south of the island and divers make considerable use of the area.

The shore is sandy to **Whitley Bay** where there is a beachbreak, best on the top half of the tide during storms. The Old English hwit leah or white glade is now a resort with a jazz festival and Spanish City dome, a fine example of an early reinforced concrete building by Hennebique. Most of the buildings along the front are tall and elegant. The former fishing village of Cullercoats, home of Charles Kinraid in Elizabeth Gaskell's *Sylvia's Lovers*, with its Smuggler's Cave now merges into one built up area. In 1749 it was described as the best fishmarket in the north of England. It had smugglers and wreckers and still has interesting geological features in the cliffs, Blue Reef Aquarium sealife centre with sharks, rays and eels, Dove Marine Laboratory, the British Navtex transmitter and the odd wreck. Rocks and ledges to Tynemouth are interspersed with sandy beaches. Long Sands have a beachbreak, best at high water near the outdoor pool although the point break can be bigger. King Edward's Bay has a sheltered beachbreak but is plagued by whistle blowing youngsters in lifeguard T shirts, hardly the **Tynemouth** Volunteer Life Brigade, set up in 1864 as Britain's first life brigade, whose timber watch house, setting for *The Watch House*, contains lifesaving exhibits and relics from shipwrecks. In 1974 their rescue of the *Oregis* started before she hit Battery Rocks.

On the headland are the substantial remains of a Benedictine priory founded in 1090 on a 7th century monastic site within which St Oswin, St Osred and several kings are buried. Two presbytery walls still stand full height and there are splendid roof bosses in the chantry chapel which was fortified. Christopher Marlowe's *Edward the Second* describes how the king's enemies tried to catch him frolicking here with Gaveston and it was from here that he fled by boat after Bannockburn. A Gate Tower was added by Robert de Mowbray during the border wars at the time of Richard II. After the dissolution of the monasteries Henry VIII retained it as a castle. Underground chambers beneath the gun battery from the two World Wars were mostly dismantled in 1956, but there is a monument

to Lord Collingwood with cannons from the *Royal Sovereign*, the ship he commanded at Trafalgar. Hornblower reported to him in CS Forester's *Hornblower & the 'Atropos'*. The area featured in the work of American artist Winslow Homer. It has become the end of the Coast to Coast cycle route.

Cresswell
Lynemouth
Woodhorn
Beacon Pt
A197
Newbiggin-by-the-Sea
A189
N Seaton
R Wansbeck
Cambois
R Blyth
Blyth
B1329
A193
Seaton Sluice
Hartley
Seaton Delaval
St Mary's Island
Whitley Bay
Cullercoats
Tynemouth
R Tyne
S Shields
Marsden Bay
North Sea
A183
Whitburn Colliery
Cleadon
Whitburn
Roker
Monkwearmouth
R Wear
Sunderland
A1018
Ryhope
B1287
Seaham
Easington
Easington Colliery
Horden
Blackhall Colliery
Blackhall Rocks

The Watch House
ROBERT WESTALL

King Edward's Bay with priory remains.

A race can form past the ends of the piers, each topped by a lighthouse. Inside the North Pier the Black Middens surf break can sometimes be one of the best in Britain with a left barrel over a boulder reef on the bottom half of the flood. The flood starts at HW Dover +0030 to 2km/h and the ebb runs from HW Dover +0630, the ebb being substantially longer when the River Tyne is in spate, crossed from North Tyneside to South Tyneside.

The South Pier is the longer at 1.6km. Built 1855–95, it contains 3,000,000t of stone and was designed by James Walker. South of the Tyne the geology moves from the coal measures to the post-Carboniferous.

South Shields developed on fishing and shipbuilding, being badly bombed during the Second World War. It has a beachbreak which may be better at the cliff end and has urban breeding herring gulls.

The A183 follows the coast to Sunderland and the shore is mostly sandy to Lizard Point. From Trow Point to Lizard Point is a SSSI.

Marsden Bay's cliffs are unstable with frequent collapses of the interesting magnesian limestone formations. In the centre of the bay was a large arch, part of which collapsed in 1996, resulting in a causeway out to it, but it remains a nature reserve with kittiwakes, cormorants, fulmars, guillemots, razorbills, terns, blackheaded gulls and even gannets. The Grotto, facing it, is a hotel at the foot of the cliff with a lift down to it. It was built into caves as a smugglers' tavern, enlarged in 1782 by ex-miner Jack the Blaster and further enlarged to form an inn with all facilities. On dark and windy nights the groans of Jack the Jibber may be heard, a smuggler who shopped his partners to the customs men but they escaped and left him to die in a bucket suspended halfway down the cliff.

The disused Souter Point lighthouse on Lizard Point is

Marsden Bay with the lift serving the Grotto, the stack in the bay after the arch collapsed and Souter lighthouse.

a 23m white and orange striped tower. Built in 1871, it was the world's first reliable lighthouse, the first with an AC power supply. It only failed twice in 117 years, once mechanically and once when the keeper fell asleep.

Ledges continue to Whitburn Bay, together with some smaller arches around the Whitburn Colliery area, where lion's mane jellyfish swim off the rocks.

The Razor Blades are three left reefbreaks which work on the upper half of the tide and there is a sheltered beachbreak at **Whitburn**.

Lewis Carroll often stayed in Whitburn. He gained inspiration from the locals, and his statue appears in the library. Cleadon is a village located near two windmills.

South Tyneside becomes Sunderland. Beach begins again at South Bents, off which there is a wreck and surf breaks here and further south in Whitburn Bay. The local geology is interesting, particularly to boats out of control.

The River Wear discharges into the sea at **Sunderland** between two long curved piers. Outside the northern Roker pier are the sheltered Cats and Dogs break and a memorial to the Venerable Bede. On the end of the pier is Roker Pier lighthouse, a 23m white tower with three red bands, faced by a disused lighthouse on the southern pier. This early Christian settlement, which takes its name from the Old English sundorland, a satellite part of an estate, became a medieval fishing port with a charter from 1154 with docks from at least 1382 and then grew on coal exporting from the 16th century, especially in the 19th century. Colliery vessels returned from London in 1665 with the plague. The world's largest shipbuilding centre, there were 65 shipyards by 1840. The docks still handle coal, petroleum products and general cargo but recession hit Sunderland hard, notwithstanding its elevation to city status. Sunderland Museum & Art Gallery chronicles the city's role in merchant shipping and has equipment from Sunderland lighthouse, the Roker lighthouse of 1903 being moved here from the harbour in 1976. Another noteworthy venue is St Andrew's church of 1906/7 by ES Prior with many

fittings by the Arts & Crafts Movement. The latest attraction is the National Glass Centre in a purpose built glass building, covering 1,300 years of the use of glass in the city. Perhaps the Shadows' *Alice in Sunderland* added to its fame. This is another place with urban breeding herring gulls.

The river floods from HW Dover −0130 and ebbs from HW Dover +0430. Along the coast, flows are weak to Tees Bay. The A1018 follows the coast briefly.

A railway also follows the coast to Seaton Carew, initially through the tank farms of Hendon and then out past the 112m Tunstall Hills or Maiden Paps.

Ryhope Engines Museum is in the Victorian Gothic Ryhope Pumping Station with its 49m chimney, designed by Thomas Hawksley. Two beam engines of 1868 are sometimes in steam although the six Cornish boilers were replaced with Lancashire models in 1908. The engines pumped 3m³/min from 43m and 77m deep wells to supply Sunderland, one of them being used for dewatering during construction.

The B1287 emerges from under the railway to pass over a burn and the Sunderland/Durham border, then follows the coast to Seaham, north of which there is a surf break. It passes Seaham Hall, now a hotel and spa, where Lord Byron married Anne Isabella Millbank in 1815, and edges past fine beaches.

Seaham, at a break in the 15–18m limestone cliffs, has harbour breakwaters like a miniature version of Sunderland, built 1828–44 as a commercial coal exporting port by Lord Londonderry for his mines and still privately run. Coal is tipped 12m down chutes from lorries. There is a 10m white metal light column with black bands. In 1862 the lifeboat capsized and was lost with all hands including four people previously picked up from a fishing boat.

In appearance, the Durham coalfield resembles

Sunderland seen from Whitburn Bay.

Hawthorn Hive, one of the wooded denes of the Durham coalfield which can serve as emergency exit routes.

The Durham coalfield seen from Blackhall Rocks.

Waves break onto the beach at Blackhall Rocks.

the coast between Aberdeen and Stonehaven, a plateau with steep cliffs except where ravines are crossed by railway bridges. The crumbling 20–30m magnesian limestone cliffs have coal waste, intercepted by denes which give emergency escape routes on an otherwise inaccessible stretch of coast. Landscaping above ground hides the legacy of collieries which run out under the sea for up to 8km.

Dawdon Colliery of 1899 had shafts to 520 deep. It broke European mining rate records in the 1970s but closed in 1991. A white arch faces the shore and Liddle Stack on Chemical Beach is an Eiffel Tower shaped pillar with an arch at its base.

Kinley Hill is marked with a tower and then comes Beacon Hill, at 85m the highest point on the County Durham coast. Hawthorn Hive or landing place is crossed by a high brick railway arch of 1905. A waterfall drops down the cliffs beyond **Easington Colliery** of 1899, closed in 1993, and black sand on the beaches is further evidence of years of coal working. An explosion in 1951 is recalled by 81 trees to represent the dead miners. At **Easington** and **Horden**, the former colliery villages stand in rows on the cliffs, but Horden also has the largest and least spoiled of the denes and the Castle Eden Dene nature reserve with what is believed to be original woodland, the Eden argus butterfly, roe deer and a requirement to keep to approved footpaths. A 10 arch railway viaduct crosses the dene.

Approaching the Tees, the beaches become cleaner but the water colour changes to a polluted brown although seals still live here.

After the former Blackhall Colliery, operational from 1909 to 1981, there is a nature reserve on the cliffs at Blackhall Rocks, the rocks themselves being covered in mussels and the site of a wreck. Oystercatchers pick through the delicacies washed up on the beach. Steps lead up to a limited area of parking where a layer of broken windscreen glass suggests the criminal element are frequently active.

Hartlepool seen from a cave at Blackhall Rocks.

Distance
59km from Creswell to Blackhall Rocks

OS 1:50,000 Sheets
81 Alnwick
& Morpeth
88 Newcastle
upon Tyne
93 Middlesbrough

Tidal Constants
Coquet Road:
HW Dover +0420
LW Dover +0410
Blyth: Dover +0430
R Tyne Entrance:
HW Dover +0440,
LW Dover +0420
Sunderland:
Dover +0420
Seaham:
Dover +0430
Hartlepool:
Dover +0440

Sea Area
Tyne

Connection
River Tyne – see RoB p148

23

5 Cleveland

Next fishy Redcar view Marske's sunny lands,
And sands, beyond Pactolus' golden sands;
Till shelvy Saltburn, cloth'd with seaweed green,
And giant Huntcliff close the pleasing scene.
Anon

Blackhall Rocks are the most interesting part of the Durham coalfield coast, a profusion of arches and caves in the limestone, some of complex shapes with multiple exits and various ledges and internal walls, the sort of place where those on foot can easily become cut off by the tide.

This section of coast now comes under Tees & Hartlepool Port Authority control. Beyond Crimdon Park Durham gives way to Hartlepool at the Crimdon Beck. Terns, fulmars, blackbacked gulls, common gulls and guillemots patrol the water.

Beyond the golf course at North Sands is West View, which seems almost to be a snub to the former Steetley Magnesite works to the east which extracted magnesium from sea water. The A1049 arrives from behind the works, passes a cemetery and the 1830 Grade II Throston Engine House, used for loading coal wagons, and heads for the Headland at Hartlepool.

The Headland is a limestone outcrop which forms a migration watchpoint, protected by a Russian cannon captured at Sebastopol in 1854, the 1315 town wall to keep the Scots out, a seawall which produces large clapotis with northeasterly winds and two lighthouses, of which the 1926 Heugh lighthouse is a 13m white metal tower. St Hilda was an early abbess here and St Hilda's Grade I Early English church of 1189–1293 was built by the family of Robert the Bruce on the site of a 7th century monastery founded by St Aidan. Tidal eddies form off the harbour entrance. Men collecting sacks of coal off the beach and wheeling them away on bikes may seem like something out of the Depression but the sight has been much more recent.

Hartlepool takes its name from the Old English heorot eg pol, stag island pool. Its capture was one of the few successes of the Northern Rising of 1569. The harbour which once sheltered the Crusade fleet now handles forestry products, coal and fish. Hartlepool was an active port, a small fishing village by the start of the 19th century and the third largest port in England and a major shipbuilding centre by the 1880s after the east Durham coalfield opened and the railway arrived. Hartlepool Maritime Museum features the local maritime history, fishing, shipbuilding and tools, ship and engine models, marine engineering, nautical instruments, a rebuilt fisherman's cottage, a ship's bridge and a gas powered lighthouse lantern. The three masts of the frigate HMS *Trimcomalee* of 1817, the oldest British warship afloat, can be seen in the Hartlepool's Maritime Experience in the marina where there is also the paddle steamer *Wingfield Castle*, a coble and displays charting the history of Hartlepool.

Long Scar is a reef in the centre of Hartlepool Bay, formed by a petrified forest, and there are various other reef and beachbreaks for surfers. During the Napoleonic Wars in the early 19th century a French privateer was said to have been wrecked there, the only survivor being a shivering monkey in a military uniform. Such animal uniforms were not unusual at the time but the local fishermen believed the monkey to be a French spy, held a court martial and hanged the poor creature. Alternatively, perhaps the victim was a powder monkey, a boy with the job of carrying gunpowder to the gunners.

More recent residents have included Compton Mc-Kenzie, author of *Whisky Galore*, Ridley Scott, director and producer of *Alien*, *Blade Runner* (inspired by Teesside's industrial skyline) and *Thelma & Louise*, Sir Edward Mellenby, who discovered vitamin D deficiency causes rickets, and Reg Smythe, the *Andy Capp* cartoonist.

The A178 follows the bay. The Staincliffe Hotel begins the housing of the resort of **Seaton Carew** with its fire signal basket and clocktower. To some people it is now Seaton Canoe after the fraud case in which John Darwin was supposed to have been drowned from his canoe but several years later turned up in Panama after all the life insurance policies had been claimed by his wife, Anne.

Beyond the built up area, Seaton Sands have a wreck, dunes and a golf course. Here the Ekofisk oil pipeline lands, destination the Tees Bay industrial complex which looms ahead with a skyline of structures, aerials and columns of various colours of smoke. There is a 1.2MW nuclear power station, oil terminal, chemical works and the transporter bridge across the Tees, the only one in England still working. The RSPB said there was a major threat of oil pollution but 22,000 waterfowl enjoy the environment in the winter, including 3,800 knots, 300 sanderlings and flocks of shelducks in one of the most important sites in the north of England, regardless of present pollution.

The North Gare breakwater ends almost due west of the South Gare breakwater, the latter with a 13m white tower lighthouse. Tees & Hartlepool is the UK's second busiest port. Despite the heavy shipping traffic, Tees Mouth is easier to cross than some major estuaries because the fairway is narrow and clearly buoyed, lying close to the South Gare breakwater.

Three hundred metres upriver from the lighthouse is the Gare surf break with fast hollow rights onto a boulder dump, excellent but potentially dangerous.

The river divides Hartlepool from Redcar & Cleve-

Blackhall Rocks

West View's pier is a dominant feature on the approach to Hartlepool's Headland.

land. Cleveland is Viking for cliff land although the cliffs are conspicuously absent from this coast, unlike the neighbouring counties with their high cliffs.

The Tees floods from HW Dover −0040 and ebbs from HW Dover +0300 at up to 6km/h, freshets decreasing the duration and rate of the flood and increasing the duration and rate of the ebb. Off the entrance, flows begin southeast at HW Dover +0140 and begin northwest at HW Dover −0430 at up to 4km/h. Flows then run parallel to the coast at up to 3km/h to Whitby. On the east side of the entrance is the Teesside Wind Farm.

Along the front of the former steelworks are Coatham Sands with surf during onshore winds. Having the Redcar steelworks and blast furnace as neighbours and the Everest gas pipeline landing might be factors to be ignored by seals and cormorants, even by surfers and golfers, but it would not not have seemed the ideal place for a caravan site.

The 16th century fishing village of **Redcar**, its name taken from the Old English hreod, reed, and Old Norse kiarr, marsh, has now become a resort. The Tees & Hartlepool Port Authority relinquishes control as reefs break up the shoreline. There is a wreck on Salt Scar, the remains of a boiler southwest of High Stone and a wreck on the Flashes. Lion's mane and compass jellyfish float in the shallows. Surf forms on outer and inner scars with an inshore swell. The Zetland Lifeboat Museum & Redcar Heritage Centre houses the oldest surviving lifeboat, shallow, self draining and in oak with a cork covering at first. She saved 500 lives while in use between 1800 and 1887, including 27 in three launches one day in 1830, and has displays on rescue, local marine life, fishing, a fisherman's cottage and an aquarium, all housed in the former lifeboat house of 1877. Restoration of the sea defences in 2012 included the first use of Dycel concrete mattresses for this purpose and a suction pad lifter to position them. The six storey Redcar Beacon, a cylindical tower wrapped with spiralling mesh, was built at the same time and claimed to be Britain's first vertical pier.

Redcar Beacon, Britain's first vertical pier.

The Saltburn Smugglers Heritage Centre in fishermen's cottages covers 18th century smuggling.

Skelton Beck descends through wooded glens while other water descends more sedately, being used to power the Saltburn Cliff Lift, the oldest tramway of its kind in Britain, dating from 1884 with such features as stained glass windows. There is also the 381mm gauge Saltburn Miniature Railway in the town.

The surf break is the most popular in northeast England but the waves lose much

Racehorses are exercised on the sands, there being a horse racecourse in the town.

The railway follows the coast to Saltburn-by-the-Sea and the A1085 follows behind the dunes, known as the Stray, to **Marske-by-the-Sea**. All this section of coast can be surfed with onshore winds.

In Marske, the spire remains of St Germain's church, most of which was demolished in 1960. Close by is the 1779 grave of Captain Cook's father, who died unaware that his son had been killed six weeks earlier.

The Cleveland Way footpath now follows the coast to Filey Brigg. A pier was necessary for **Saltburn-by-the-Sea** to become a Victorian resort. The Old English sealt burna, salt stream, suggests the town is much older.

of their power on the flat beach. Fast and powerful rights may be taken off Saltburn Scar at Penny Hole although the flat rock platform is the most sheltered part of the beach with the wind from the southeast.

Now beginning in earnest are the cliffs of the North York Moors with marked horizontal strata, rich in fossils, particularly ammonites and

Hunt Cliff and Boulby Cliff beyond end the North York Moors.

belemnites, to Ravenscar. The cliffs run 30–180m high to Sandsend with heavy landslips. The North Yorkshire & Cleveland Heritage Coast stretches from Saltburn to Scarborough. From 1600 to 1870 the cliffs were the site of significant alum workings.

Flows start southeast at HW Dover +0200 and northwest at HW Dover –0410.

Hunt Cliff is the uncompromising start to this section of coast, 110m high, dark red and nearly perpendicular. At the top it continues to rise to Warsett Hill, 166m high, a venue the Romans chose for a signal station.

In 1535 a sea man was caught off Skinningrove and held for several weeks, during which time he would eat only raw fish and communicate in shrieks although he was courteous to visitors, especially maidens. Eventually, he escaped back to the sea.

Skinningrove was chosen as a steelworks site with the village built for iron mines at the head of the valley. Kilton Beck, which discharges near the pier, is stained brown by iron ore waste. The Cleveland Ironstone Mining Museum explains the industry.

Two shorebreaks work on the lower half of the tide, giving rights off Hummersea Scar, a set of flat rocks with a channel cut through to form a harbour for the alum industry. Disused quarries are located at the top of the cliffs as the coast becomes the edge of the North York Moors National Park to Sandsend. Also on top of the cliffs is an Earlier Neolithic funerary area tumulus, a radio aerial and 213m high Rockhole Hill. The cliffs here are 180m high but at Boulby Cliff they increase to 200m. An intrusive feature is the Boulby Mine, the deepest potash mine in Europe.

Staithes is the jewel of this coast, the fishing village with its drying harbour nestling in a gap in the cliffs. On the east side Easington Beck separates Redcar & Cleveland from North Yorkshire, drains down from Scaling Dam Reservoir and enters the harbour through a channel where a cat's cradle of ropes moor the boats and make it very difficult for boats to enter or leave. Facilities include toilets near the Cod & Lobster. Parking is not permitted except for residents. This village is where Captain Cook worked as a boy in William Sanderson's general store which has since been lost to the sea although some of it has been incorporated into Cook's Cottage. Captain Cook & Staithes Heritage Centre has a 1745 street scene of Sanderson's haberdashery shop, fishermen's warehouse and cottage, chandler's and ale house. Painter Dame Laura Knight had her studio here.

The harbour entrance can be difficult or even too rough to get in. There are three surf breaks on the lower half of the tide, north of the harbour having impressive lefts, south of the harbour also having quite good lefts and the Cove being one of the best breaks in Britain, fast, hollow and powerful.

Black cliffs reach 90m at Old Nab and the serious fossil coast begins at Port Mulgrave which has ruined piers, a drying harbour and a tunnel at the foot of the cliff which carried a narrow gauge railway to take iron ore from Dalehouse to Jarrow.

The sea can break across the entrance to Runswick Bay with onshore winds, but it is more sheltered than the rest of this coast in northerly swells. There are impressive lefts at Cobble Dump and three right reef breaks which work on the lower half of the tide. Outer Reef can have 5m rideable waves, Middle Reef can have waves of moderate size and Innermost Reef can be sheltered with long rides after easy paddles out. The Hob Holes near Innermost Reef were home to a hobgoblin who could cure whooping cough. There is also a beachbreak in the middle of the bay. An earlier Runswick slipped into the sea in 1682 but the present one is on firmer ground and is popular with artists.

Staithes at low water, where Captain Cook acquired his love of the sea.

Staithes is sheltered by the cliffs..

Above Kettleness is the Goldsborough Roman signal station, the best preserved on this coast with a square tower in an 8,000m² fort with 1.2m thick walls, overwhelmed and burned by the Saxons in the 5th century, two skeletons being found in the ruins. Red Cliffs are 90m high and have been excavated for alum, for which a boiling house remains. There were also alum works between 1615 and 1867 at Overdale Wyke, which has a wreck. More recent remains in a field are a Victorian station which was part of the former coastal railway.

A further alum boiling house remains at Sandsend, the start of a significant break in the cliffs to Whitby with a slipway next to a carpark, making a convenient place to land except when the parking becomes overcrowded in the summer.

Distance
49km from Blackhall Rocks to Sandsend

OS 1:50,000 Sheets
93 Middlesbrough
94 Whitby
& Esk Dale

Tidal Constants
Hartlepool:
Dover +0440
Staithes:
HW Dover +0500
LW Dover +0450
Whitby:
Dover +0500

Sea Area
Tyne

6 North Yorkshire

Cliffs and more cliffs

The fishermen brave more money have
*   Than any merchants two or three;*
Therefore I will to Scarborough go,
*   That I a fisherman may be.*

Anon

The Caves surf break at Sandsend has lefts up to 1.5m at mid tide with decent northerly swells but is sheltered from the west. There are good beachbreaks along the sandy beach which edges Sandsend Wyke but these close out at the top of the tide. The A174 also follows the shore to **Whitby**.

Piers protect the mouth of the River Esk, around which there are wrecks. The first Cistercian monastery and abbey, now ruined, were founded by St Hilda in 657 and the dates for Easter were established here by the

Sandsend Wyke, looking towards Whitby.

The mouth of the Esk at Whitby.

Synod of Whitby in 664. Sightings of a shrouded St Hilda have been reported from the choir on sunny summer mornings. Also well established was that St Hilda tackled a plague of snakes, driving them over the cliff where they coiled up and petrified to form the snakestones. Regardless of the facts, some local ammonite species have the scientific name Hildoceras. Caedmon, the first English poet, lived here until his death in 680. Robin Hood and Little John were said to have overwintered here. Robin found refuge disguised as a fisherman or he may have come to Whitby to help the abbot repel the Danes. The town has produced a 9m pliosaur. The name comes from the Old Norse name Hviti, meaning white, and Old Scandinavian by or village. The abbey

was destroyed by the Vikings in 867, refounded in 1078 and rebuilt in the 13th century, the work visible being 12th to 15th century, the three-tiered choir and north transcept. Just 199 steps lead to part of the 12th century Grade I St Mary's church, restored in the 18th century. The central tower collapsed in 1830.

Whitby was a whaling and shipbuilding port in the 18th century, the ships built including the colliers *Endeavour*, *Discovery* and *Resolution* in which James Cook circumnavigated the globe, and it was from here that he set out to claim Australia for Britain. HM Bark *Endeavour* returned here in 1997, the 40% size replica incorporating a small piece of wood from the original vessel which has been to the moon with American astronauts in the intervening period. Cook's statue is on the West Cliff. The Whitby sea was compared with Sydney Harbour in DH Lawrence's *Kangaroo*.

Whitby became a herring and kipper port in the 19th century, was developed as a resort by railway promoter George Hudson and is now a commercial, fishing and recreational port. In December 1914 the abbey and coastguard station were shelled by two German warships after they had shelled Scarborough. This was a misguided attempt to draw part of the British fleet here as the Germans did not feel able to take on the whole British fleet but which resulted in anger serving to recruit civilians to fight the Germans.

Whitby's jet industry, from the fossilized monkey puzzle tree, has been active since Queen Victoria made jet popular by wearing it as mourning jewellery for Prince Albert. Amber is also found. John Wesley was a frequent visitor and opened the Methodist chapel in 1788. Whitby Museum features jet, fossils, natural history, model ships, Captain Cook and the Scoresbys. The Captain Cook Memorial Museum is in the house of Quaker shipowner John Walker, with whom Cook was apprenticed.

Headless horses are sometimes seen pulling a coach. Whitby is where Count Dracula was said to have landed in England, Bram Stoker having found the name in the library while on holiday. Scott set some of *Marmion* in the town. In Elizabeth Gaskell's *Sylvia's Lovers*, which exposed the activities of the press gangs and their effect on the whale industry, it was Monkshaven and the Esk became the River Dee. Lewis Carroll set *Wilhelm Von Schmitz* here.

To land involves passing over the bar. The ebb runs at up to 9km/h with freshets and there can also be 9km/h flows across the harbourmouth. Cliffs extend to Scarborough, mostly a rocky ledge backed by a steep bank. Beyond the aerial, swells break heavily over the Scar. The coastline as far as Robin Hood's Bay was used for filming *Carrington* in 1995.

From Saltwick Nab the coast is once again part of the North York Moors National Park as far as Long Nab. Black Nab on the east side of Saltwick Bay has many wild flowers and insects, herring gulls, cormorants, fulmars, another aerial and the remains of an alum boiling house. The 13m white octagonal tower of Whitby High lighthouse stands on the 73m cliffs soon after its fog siren, known as the Whitby Mad Bull or Hawsker Bull, which can be heard 16km away.

Ness Point or North Cheek has a rock platform which uncovers with the tide at the entrance to Robin Hood's Bay at the end of the B1447. The honeycombed cliffs are part of an eroded dome with the centre being 2km out to sea. The cliff is receding at 60mm/year behind sandstone reefs from between which the clay has been washed. In 1975 a 12m seawall, the highest in Britain, was completed after several houses were lost to the sea. The village has narrow precipitous streets in a ravine. The nearest parking is a considerable distance away up a 30% hill. The village was first recorded in 1538.

In the 18th century the village was used for smuggling. King's Beck discharges through a tunnel with interconnecting passages and many houses have inter-connecting doors covered by cupboards. It was where Sylvia and Philip Hepburn were to spend part

of the day after getting married in *Sylvia's Lovers* and Pauline had a jaunt here with Miss Verney in Compton Mackenzie's *Guy & Pauline*. These days it is noted for its crabs. It is the end of the Coast to Coast Walk from St Bees Head. Others who have come here are artists, including Leo Walmsley who lived here from 1894 to 1913 and incorporated the village into a number of his books as Bramblewick. In 1986 it was used for filming Charles Dickens' *David Copperfield*. Many come for the June folk music weekend.

In 1881 the crew of the brig *The Visitor* were rescued despite the village being unable to launch its small lifeboat in a storm. The larger Whitby lifeboat was dragged 13km over the snow for the rescue.

There is a beach break. Cliffs are particularly rich in 150–185,000,000 year old fossils to Ravenscar.

Mill Beck enters the sea at the Boggle Hole where there is a youth hostel in the old mill. The next stream runs down past Stoupe Brow where there are the remains of another alum boiling house. Further up the hill are tumuli and Robin Hood's Butts.

At Old Peak or South Cheek there is a turreted tower nestling on the edge of the cliff. Further back is a radio mast and between them a golf course and Raven Hall, built in 1774 on the site of a Roman signal station. In

1890 there were plans to build a resort but the developer went bankrupt. Today the hall is a hotel.

The Peak Alum Works produced a tenth of Yorkshire's output in the 1820s, refined alum being taken from an artificial harbour to Newcastle, Hull and London, extensive remains still existing. The cliffs have the appearance of cliffs that have been subject to heavy slippage. The Ravenscar Coastal Centre features the geology and history of the Yorkshire coast and has a rockpool aquarium. A coastguard lookout hut stands above a wreck site. The 110m cliffs, now of shale and clay laid down in estuarial conditions rather than the marine cliffs further north, have scrub oakwood with wood vetch.

War Dike runs back from the top of Beast Cliff although the only beasts of today are to be found in the Staintondale Shire Horse Farm with everything from Shetland ponies upwards. However, blackbacked gulls can be beastly to other birds. Hayburn Wyke, from the medieval wic or dairy farm, is where Thorny Beck's waterfall drops to an area of beach.

Long Nab is followed by Cromer Point along with its Sailors' Grave. The last point before Scarborough is **Scalby** Ness Rocks. The Sea Cut was opened to pass Scalby Mills and discharge near the point in 1804, collecting floodwaters from the upper River Derwent to protect land further downstream. The Scarborough Sea Life Sanctuary has seals while the bay has surf breaks. A cable car runs behind North Bay and there is a North Bay Railway while the A165 is to run parallel to the coast to Reighton. In the distance a prominent windmill stands on the skyline.

North Bay also has Peasholm Park where naval battles are fought between large model ships, canoes and other boats are for hire and there are Japanese gardens.

One of the most conspicuous landmarks on the coast is the headland topped by **Scarborough** castle, surrounded by a semicircle of cliff with a road around its base. The headland was used in the Bronze Age, from when a fine sword has been found. The Romans had a signal station on the site in the 4th century, overcome by the Saxons in the 5th century. The Vikings came in 965 and named the town after its founder, Thorgils Skarthi, the hare lipped. Harald Hardrada burned the

town in 1066. The castle was built in 1158 by William le Gros, Earl of Aumâle. It has a three storey rectangular stone keep and buttressed walls. It was seized by Henry II, improved by King John

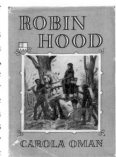

Dracula

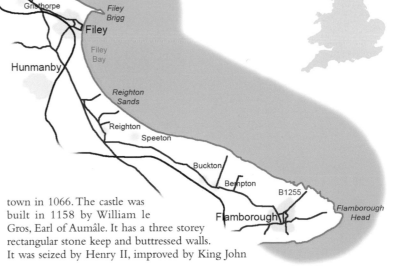

The estuary of the Esk at Whitby with the abbey above.

Whitby Mad Bull and the lighthouse just visible on the cliffs.

in the 13th century, sheltered the Earl of Cornwall in 1312 and was attacked by the Scots under Robert the Bruce in 1318. *Edward the Second* claims Gaveston escaped by sea to Scarborough. The castle was captured by Sir Thomas Stafford in 1557, proclaiming himself Protector but being executed when it was retaken. It was attacked by cannons in the Civil War, during which it changed hands several times, and was used for political prisoners including Quaker founder George Fox in 1665/6. Richard III's ghost is said to appear on the battlements. In December 1914 it was the first of the ports to be shelled by two German warships, resulting in the recruiting slogan 'Remember Scarborough', and came under fire again in the Second World War. A Scarborough warning, no warning at all, predates this. The latest controversy is over various issues related to seawall enhancement. Robin Hood was said to have led the crew of the *Blithe* in the capture of a French ship, after having himself tied to the mast so that he could shoot his arrows straight.

On a quieter note, spa water had been discovered in 1620 and stored in a cistern from 1698. In 1738 the Spa was destroyed by an earthquake, a storm badly damaged its wooden building in 1836, the Grand Hall was destroyed by fire in 1876 and the waters are now unfit to drink. The conspicuous Spa Bridge of 1827 by Outhett is a rare four spanned cast iron 27m high structure with 20m arches on ashlar columns carrying a 6.7m carriageway drive. While Scarborough is the most important resort on Britain's east coast, in 1660 it was probably the first fashionable resort in Britain, developed after Dr Wittie suggested naked sea bathing by both sexes. George Crabbe suggested it as a destination for *The Mother*.

The visitors needed somewhere to stay and the Grade II★ Grand Hotel was the biggest brick building in Europe in 1867 when constructed. It has 365 rooms, 52 chimneys, 12 floors and 4 turrets to represent the days, weeks, months and seasons of the year. It is now a Butlin's holiday centre.

The 12–13th century St Mary's church was restored in the 19th century and Anne Brontë is buried in the churchyard, the town having influnced her *Agnes Grey* and *The Tenant of Wildfell Hall*. Michael Seaton had taken one of the Buckleys on a flight over the town in Agatha Christie's *Peril at End House*. Billy Parkin had been a tannery apprentice here in Ken Follett's *Eye of the Needle*. Susan Hill was born here. Its more recent literary associations relate to Alan Ayckbourn's theatre. Scarborough was used for filming *A Chorus of Disapproval* and *PC Penrose*. Genuine horror filmsets are to be found in Terror Tower. Other historical material is in the Three Mariners Inn which was a smuggling den but is now a museum with a selection of fishermen's jerseys, all blue but each port having a different stitching pattern which helped with identification of bodies washed up. Near Scarborough Art Gallery is the Rotunda Museum with the William Smith geology collection.

The Old and East Harbours are on the south side of the headland with the lighthouse. The harbours are a yachting and angling centre. Speedboats take customers for trips round the North Bay, but they are noisy enough for there to be plenty of warning that they are coming. Surfers find rights off the headland and lefts off the East Pier with a big swell. The northgoing stream is strong off the harbour from HW Dover +0420 to HW Dover −0110 but streams in South Bay are barely perceptible.

Near the bathing pool a semicircle of rock supports the toe of the cliff where a hotel fell into the sea. Perhaps it was helped by the vibration of the motorcycle events on Oliver's Mount above.

More surf is to be found in Cayton Bay below the A165 where Bunkers is the best beachbreak in the area with lefts and rights. Pump House is usable on the upper half of the flood tide between the rocks for 1–1.5m surf although there is a strong rip for anything larger. It gives long rides but can close out. For 1.5m–4.5m surf, Point break is one of the longest lefts on the east coast, dangerous but cleaning up even in messy conditions.

Cliffs run out to Filey Brigg, Lebberston Cliff, Gristhorpe Cliff, Newbiggin Cliffs and North Cliff. On top are large areas of caravan park but guillemots and razorbills nest undisturbed on the cliffs and North Cliff Country Park is a bird migration watchpoint.

The cliffs run into what is almost an arête, finishing with an old coral reef which is likely to produce difficult water at all times as it is exposed to wind from any direction. There is a race off the end and the northwesterly flow runs eastwards along the southern side at up to 3km/h. Any misadventures will be watched by the crowds of people drawn to the rocks, whose sightings in the past have included a monster with long neck and several humps. The Romans chose the location for a signal station because of its visibility. Walkers come here because it is the end of the Cleveland Way, Britain's second long distance footpath, opened in 1969, and the start of the Wolds Way and Centenary Way.

Filey Bay provides a contrast with barely perceptible currents and a sweep of sandy beach which is used for everything from sand yachting to donkey rides. The bay can have sheltered surf when Cayton Bay is blown out.

Filey was five glades from the Old English leah. It is a resort with white hotels and refined Victorian terraces, paddling and model boating pools, golf course, miniature golf and Filey Museum featuring the lifeboat, fishing and rural and domestic life in a 1696 farmhouse. This old fishing port with its Coble Landing lands crabs and lobsters in the summer and cod and haddock in the winter, along with codling and mackerel.

St Oswald's church has Norman pillars and doorways and a 13th century effigy of a boy bishop. A windmill is another landmark beyond the town. It was the loss of a toy dog on a family holiday which led to Tolkien's first children's book, *Roverandom*.

Holiday villages with large caravan sites follow, Primrose Valley Holiday Village at **Hunmanby** Sands with a surf break and Reighton Sands Holiday Park at Reighton. Speeton has the Grade II★ St Leonard's Church with a funnel shaped belfry built by the Danes.

The Speeton Hills meet the coast here at the end of the Wolds and there is a change of character as North Yorkshire gives way to the East Riding. High vertical chalk cliffs run unbroken as far as North Landing, Speeton Cliffs, Buckton Cliffs, Bempton Cliffs and North Cliff merging into each other in a line without respite for 8km, although

Robin Hood's Bay welcomes tourists but not their cars.

Reefs between Robin Hood's Bay and the Boggle Hole.

there is chalk shingle when the tide drops. On top is an unusual sloping edge formed by a layer of softer boulder clay. Nothing is seen of the earthwork on Buckton Cliffs, the aerial on Standard Hill or Danes Dyke, an earthwork which cuts right across Flamborough Head, a ditch in which flint arrowheads have been found so it is pre-Iron Age, at least 2,000 years old. A visitor centre on the

Scarborough hides behind its headland, topped by the castle, a headland which has seen millennia of military activity.

Filey Brigg, seen from the south, is extended by low reefs which always offer plenty of interest.

The seabird laden chalk cliffs extend to Flamborough Head.

120m Bempton Cliffs does not do them justice. They have to be seen from below to appreciate the 200,000 seabirds with 33 species breeding including kittiwakes, fulmars, guillemots, razorbills, puffins and gannets, this being the only gannetry in England and the only one in mainland Britain, part of the largest seabird breeding colony in England. Seals and porpoises join the fishing parties.

Caves are located around the inlet of Thornwick Bay where the cliffs do an effective job of hiding the holiday centre above. Also well hidden is the entrance to North Landing, used by cobles and small crab and lobster vessels which are winched up onto wooden beams on the steeply sloping face next to the former lifeboat slip, the lifeboat now having been moved to South Landing. The sea can be a luminous turquoise and it is a delightful spot at the end of the B1255, although getting close with a vehicle to load boats can be difficult. There is only a steep single track road down the cliff from the large carpark above, a road used by the local fishermen with no parking area available. Onshore seas can break heavily onto the beach.

Flows start south from Dover HW and north from HW Dover +0600 at up to 6km/h.

Distance
60km from Sandsend
to North Landing

OS 1:50,000 Sheets
94 Whitby
& Esk Dale
101 Scarborough

Tidal Constants
Whitby:
Dover +0500
Scarborough:
Dover +0520
Filey Bay:
Dover +0530
Flamborough Head:
Dover +0540

Sea Area
Tyne

The old lifeboat slipway at North Landing.

Holderness

7

Hornsea steeple, when I built thee,
Thou was 10 miles off Burlington,
10 miles off Beverley, and 10 miles off sea;
Anon

From North Landing the 46m chalk cliffs continue. There are breeding seabirds, especially gulls, and puffins, guillemots, razorbills and cormorants.

On top of the cliffs a golf course, aerials and tower remain hidden, but there is a fire beacon basket at Selwicks Bay at the end of the B1259 and then the 27m white round tower of Flamborough Head lighthouse. At the head there can be turbulence close inshore with flows strongest close to the cliffs, especially when the tide is on the turn. Along the coast there is no slack and eddies can form on both sides of the head. Flamborough Head is the northeastern extremity of a band of chalk which sweeps round the south of England to Lyme Bay, the cliffs after High Stacks dropping away in height because of the dip of the chalk strata. Flamborough Steel is a rocky ledge extending 400m from the cliffs along the southern side of the head. From here the coastal waters become steadily muddier.

The Flamborough Head Heritage Coast continues past a tumulus. It was off this point in 1779 that the American navy had one of their first successes as John Paul Jones in the *Bonnehomme Richard* captured the *Serapis* and *Countess*, recorded in Thomas Carlyle's *The French Revolution*. It was not all bad news, however, and Captain Reason of the *Serapis* was knighted for allowing the Baltic convoy to escape in the course of the engagement.

Fishermen used to keep one boat at North Landing and another at South Landing so that there was always one ready for the prevailing conditions. The inshore lifeboat has recently been moved from the former to the latter.

A nature trail runs below the Mesolithic Beacon Hill site. **Flamborough** has the remains of a 14th century fortified manor and relics of Constable's family. Just before another golf course is the southern end of Danes Dyke, probably an Iron Age earthwork. The village may have been named after Kormak Fleinn, the Arrow.

The most notable building in Sewerby is Sewerby Hall, a Georgian mansion with fine panelling and cantilevered oak staircase on the site of a medieval manor. Dating from 1751, it has putting, bowls, croquet, archery, aviaries, zoo, playpark, ponds and 20ha of gardens and parkland, walled gardens, art gallery and displays on archaeology and local aviator Amy Johnson. There is a Beside the Seaside exhibition. Sewerby also has the Bondville Miniature Village.

Holderness was a large bay filled with boulder clay, forming a pre-glacial raised beach at the 30m level from where the chalk ends at Sewerby. Erosion left a line of former cliffs running inland to Hessle.

That line is now broken by the resort of **Bridlington** at what was the site of a mere. Prominent on the front is East Riding Leisure Bridlington with a fairground, flumes, swimming and surf pools, served by a road train along the esplanade. Bridlington Harbour Museum features the harbour's history from 1777, the great gale of 1871, Bridlington Bay seabed finds, the RNLI, air sea rescue, fishing, seabirds and egg climbers. There is John Bull's World of Rock, Park Rose Pottery with 5ha of parkland and Bridlington Birds of Prey & Animal Park. Bridlington Priory was a 14th century priory church. In the oldest remaining biography in English, Margery Kempe visited her confessor, who lived here. Sir George Ripley, who died in 1490, was a Canon of Bridlington and wrote the *Compound of Alchemy*. The town was used as Walmington-on-Sea for the *Dad's Army* film.

The harbour has trawlers, cobles and recreational boats but largely drains to mud at low tide although there are plans for a marina. Fish caught include codling, plaice, cod and haddock and it is England's leading shellfish port. A notable 20m Bridlington trawler was the *Pickering* which had experienced many strange events on board and on which a shadowy figure had been seen. The boat was exorcised in 1987 and everything returned to normal. The resort has watersports including windsurfing, scuba diving and yacht racing with a Royal Yorkshire Yacht Club regatta in mid August. A lifeboat station and a maritime rescue sub-centre keep an eye on things.

At Hilderthorpe the longest beach in Britain begins, backed by dark brown cliffs of clay 9–12m high to

Selwicks Bay with Flamborough Head lighthouse.

Kilnsea. Flows along the coast run to 2km/h with eddies at Bridlington but the velocity increases to 6km/h by Spurn Head, by which point the flow is 1½ hours later. The flows are removing the land faster than at any other point on the British coastline, claiming 12ha/year as the coastline moves inland at 1.7m/year.

The site of Hilderthorpe Village is before a golf course and caravan site, then the site of Wilsthorpe Village at the edge of Carnaby Moor and, protected by the first of various sets of tank traps, the site of Auburn Village.

Barmston Beach Holiday Park is a caravan site and East End has two plus a picnic area. Between the two the Barmston Main Drain discharges although not obvious from the sea.

Skipsea with its castle site was another mere, followed

Flamborough Head and South Landing seen from Bridlington.

Bridlington harbour.

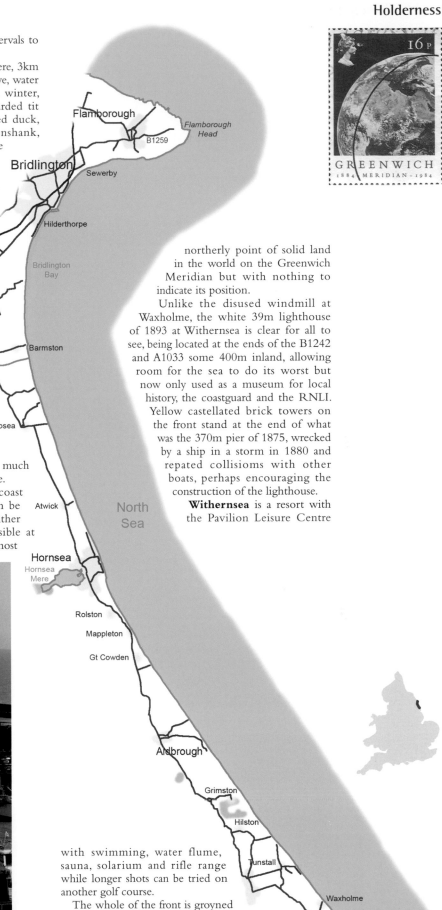

by another golf course and more caravans at intervals to Atwick.

The one large mere remaining is Hornsea Mere, 3km long and a nature reserve with wigeon, goldeneye, water rail, coot, bearded reedling and cormorant in winter, reed and sedge warbler, reed bunting and bearded tit in summer, mute swan, mallard, pochard, tufted duck, shoveler and gadwall all year and ruff, greenshank, wheatear and whinchat in passage. This is the largest lake in Yorkshire and has boating and big pike despite the angling. **Hornsea**'s Old English town name refers to the horns or corners on the lake. Hornsea Freeport was Britain's first factory outlet and discount shopping centre, set in 11ha of parkland with classic cars, adventure playground, model village, birds of prey and butterflies. Hornsea Museum shows tools and trades in a former 16th century farmhouse. There is also bowling. The Marine Hotel is on the front. The promenade is protected by groynes all along the front.

Mappleton, with its windmill, is between Rolston and Great Cowden, both with firing ranges no longer in use although lookout towers remain on the cliffs.

Aldbrough is losing 5m per year of its frontage and steps down to the beach have to be rebuilt each season. Low Farm perches close to the edge, in danger of becoming lower. Notwithstanding, BP are storing North Sea gas in huge caverns beneath the fields, not particularly intrusive and much less visible than conventional gasholders would be.

The only wooded area on this section of coast comes at Grimston, where old moats will soon be having their contents emptied by the sea. Neither Admiral Storr's Tower nor the church are visible at Hilston. Beyond Tunstall the coast forms the most

northerly point of solid land in the world on the Greenwich Meridian but with nothing to indicate its position.

Unlike the disused windmill at Waxholme, the white 39m lighthouse of 1893 at Withernsea is clear for all to see, being located at the ends of the B1242 and A1033 some 400m inland, allowing room for the sea to do its worst but now only used as a museum for local history, the coastguard and the RNLI. Yellow castellated brick towers on the front stand at the end of what was the 370m pier of 1875, wrecked by a ship in a storm in 1880 and repated collisioms with other boats, perhaps encouraging the construction of the lighthouse.

Withernsea is a resort with the Pavilion Leisure Centre

with swimming, water flume, sauna, solarium and rifle range while longer shots can be tried on another golf course.

The whole of the front is groyned and can suffer a heavy shore dump at high tide, when cliffs can make it difficult to land elsewhere. Northerly swells bring lefts for surfers. An inshore lifeboat was inaugurated in 1999. Although not at the best point for rescue conditions, it has easy takeout conditions on land. There is some parking between the lifeboat station and a toilet block.

Withernsea lighthouse, safe from coastal erosion.

Distance
54km from North Landing to Withernsea

OS 1:50,000 Sheets
*101 Scarborough
107 Kingston upon Hull*

Tidal Constants
*Flamborough Head:
Dover +0540
Bridlington:
Dover +0540
Bull Sand Fort:
Dover −0440*

Sea Areas
Tyne, Humber

Entrance to what was once the pier at Withernsea, alas, no longer.

Humber

8

'For evil news from Mablethorpe.
Of pyrate galleys warping down;
For shippes ashore beyond the scorpe,
They have not spared to wake the towne:
But while the west bin red to see,
And storms be none, and pyrates flee,
Why ring 'The Brides of Enderby'?'
Jean Ingelow

From Withernsea the coast continues southeast past another caravan site with further soft brown cliffs. At high tide there is a dump at the foot of the cliffs and it does not take much of an onshore wind to throw the broken water higher than the cliffs. At Holmpton a farm perches on the edge of the cliffs, half a red brick barn having already been lost over the brink.

Beyond Dimlington High Land, 40m high, is the rather better protected Easington gas terminal which was the first destination for North Sea gas and still hosts pipelines from the Amethyst, Ravenspurn, Rough and West Sole gas fields. The water tower and disused windmill are not seen from close inshore, just large blue frameworks around tanks. Experiments continue with storing gas by pumping it back under the North Sea. Aerials around the terminal are conspicuous over a large area.

Easington itself, at the end of the B1445, is a village of sea cobble houses and a 14th or 15th century thatched red brick barn. It has pillboxes but these cannot provide protection from the sea. A straight road runs southeast from the village to end abruptly at the clifftop with a line of bollards. Along this coast 29 villages have been lost to the sea. So far 4 of them have had their names revived for use by North Sea gas fields. Caravans claim the clifftop.

Coastal waters pass to Associated British Ports control before Kilnsea, formerly a mere and now primarily a visitor centre for Spurn Head, Yorkshire's final fling. Spurn Head, 6km long, is a prime example of a spit. In

1399 Henry IV landed at Ravenspurn, since lost to the sea, on his way to depose Richard II. Edward IV also landed here in 1470 in his fight back against Henry VI.

Fossils on the beach include corals and ammonites. With sand hills 6–10m high, it is sometimes only 50m

A road to nowhere at Holmpton.

Collapsing cliffs at Holmpton.

Easington North Sea gas terminal.

A large windfarm off Kilnsea.

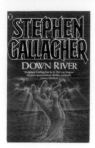

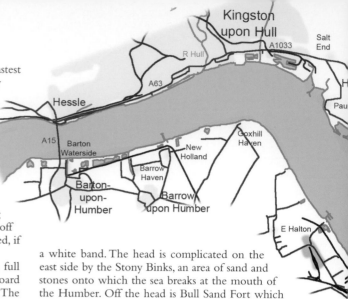

wide and is moving at 2m per year, one of the fastest rates of coastline change in the world. About every 250 years the sea succeeds in breaking through, as it did in February 2017, the spit now being an island every high water and being approachable only by four wheel drive vehicles at lower water. A new spit has formed parallel to it four times since 670. Some heavy staging marks the point where the tarmac road suddenly disappears into the sand and a new road of concrete blocks has been laid on the west side. A military railway was also laid along the spit, lifeboat crews travelling along it on sail powered trolleys which they had to take off the track when they met a train. Spurn Head featured, if not by name, in Stephen Gallagher's *Down River*.

This is one of only three lifeboat stations with full time crews because of the inaccessibility. Crews board from the west side of the head where there is a pier. The first lighthouse here was a coal fired one of 1427. Others followed and then there was Smeaton's 27m tower of 1771–6, founded on sand and later shored up with timber before being demolished in 1895. One of the two disused towers remaining is that of Thomas Matthews, a 39m Staffordshire blue brick structure painted black with

A break in the road running along Spurn Head.

The Spurn Head lighthouse.

The lifeboat walkway at Spurn Head.

a white band. The head is complicated on the east side by the Stony Binks, an area of sand and stones onto which the sea breaks at the mouth of the Humber. Off the head is Bull Sand Fort which guards the entrance.

The spit is a national nature reserve and a seabird sanctuary with a bird observatory for migrants plus oystercatchers, blackbacked gulls, terns, cormorants and the wildfowl and waders of the estuary in general. The Humber has 130,000 winter wildfowl including 31,000 knots, 4,000 curlews, 5,200 redshanks, 27,000 golden plovers and 24,000 lapwings. The RSPB said the area was at risk of permanent damage from pollution, port expansion and cockling. Geoffrey of Monmouth suggests the estuary was named after Humber, King of the Huns.

Birds like mud and at any time there is 2,000,000t of it in suspension in the estuary from five major rivers which drain a quarter of England. The Hawke Channel runs close to the head with strong tidal streams which change suddenly. Tidal streams in the river are rapid and irregular, affected by up to an hour by spates and wind direction. Flows are weaker outside the channels. At high water the tide reaches to Kilnsea and inshore of the **Patrington** Channel, but at low tide it is mostly dry north of a line from Spurn Head to Hawkin's Point, exposing Kilnsea Clays, Easington Clays, Skeffling Clays, Trinity Sands with their wreck and Sunk Island Sands where shelducks and great crested grebes join the wildfowl. A monument on the shoreline and another behind it on the Winestead Drain are on the Greenwich meridian. Of Sunk Island 31km^2 has been reclaimed with dykes and banks.

Sunk Channel is continuously dredged but depths in the Humber are subject to frequent change with moves of buoyage and strong tidal streams. Large vessels use the fairway and must not be obstructed.

At Hawkin's Point there is a measured distance. Gradually the bank of silt builds up until it is a kilometre wide at low tide all the way to Paull through Foulholme Sands. At low tide it is not possible even to see Stone Creek which discharges **Keyingham** Drain, just the vast expanse of mud used by seals, herring gulls and the odd very noisy hovercraft.

Paull Roads lead up past Paull Holme with the remains of two manor houses. Two lighthouses precede another disused one of 1836 at Paull where there is also a battery and a viewpoint in front of the aerial. A 5km tunnel being built under the river to Goxhill will contain a high pressure gas main, the world's longest gas pipeline in a tunnel inserted as a single string. It will be 35m below the seabed after tides exposed an earlier pipe.

Hedon Haven leads to **Hedon**, now 3km inland but formerly a flourishing port. Earlier, the Humber discharged due east to the sea. Hedonism is not an obvious association at this time. Its place has been taken by Salt End oil jetties which are on the outside of the bend where the East Riding becomes Kingston upon Hull, even without them the most difficult part of the estuary for large vessels to negotiate. Behind the jetties is a large tank farm and works. This is also below the flightpath into Humberside International Airport at

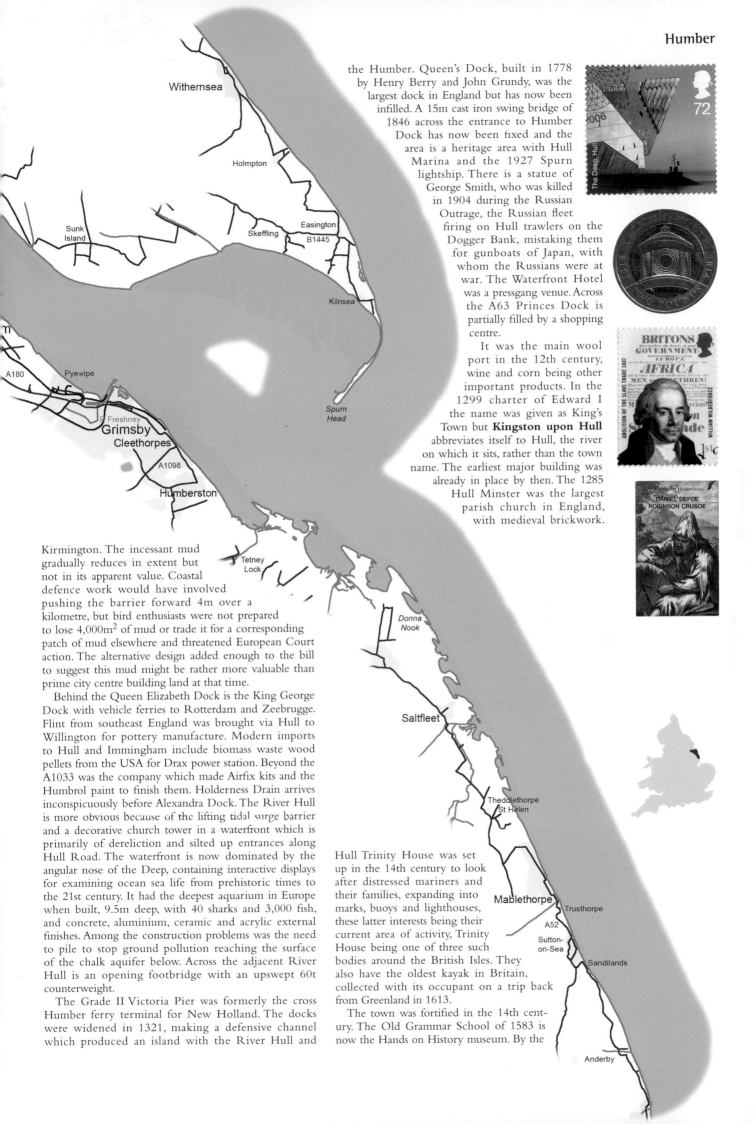

the Humber. Queen's Dock, built in 1778 by Henry Berry and John Grundy, was the largest dock in England but has now been infilled. A 15m cast iron swing bridge of 1846 across the entrance to Humber Dock has now been fixed and the area is a heritage area with Hull Marina and the 1927 Spurn lightship. There is a statue of George Smith, who was killed in 1904 during the Russian Outrage, the Russian fleet firing on Hull trawlers on the Dogger Bank, mistaking them for gunboats of Japan, with whom the Russians were at war. The Waterfront Hotel was a pressgang venue. Across the A63 Princes Dock is partially filled by a shopping centre.

It was the main wool port in the 12th century, wine and corn being other important products. In the 1299 charter of Edward I the name was given as King's Town but **Kingston upon Hull** abbreviates itself to Hull, the river on which it sits, rather than the town name. The earliest major building was already in place by then. The 1285 Hull Minster was the largest parish church in England, with medieval brickwork.

Kirmington. The incessant mud gradually reduces in extent but not in its apparent value. Coastal defence work would have involved pushing the barrier forward 4m over a kilometre, but bird enthusiasts were not prepared to lose 4,000m^2 of mud or trade it for a corresponding patch of mud elsewhere and threatened European Court action. The alternative design added enough to the bill to suggest this mud might be rather more valuable than prime city centre building land at that time.

Behind the Queen Elizabeth Dock is the King George Dock with vehicle ferries to Rotterdam and Zeebrugge. Flint from southeast England was brought via Hull to Willington for pottery manufacture. Modern imports to Hull and Immingham include biomass waste wood pellets from the USA for Drax power station. Beyond the A1033 was the company which made Airfix kits and the Humbrol paint to finish them. Holderness Drain arrives inconspicuously before Alexandra Dock. The River Hull is more obvious because of the lifting tidal surge barrier and a decorative church tower in a waterfront which is primarily of dereliction and silted up entrances along Hull Road. The waterfront is now dominated by the angular nose of the Deep, containing interactive displays for examining ocean sea life from prehistoric times to the 21st century. It had the deepest aquarium in Europe when built, 9.5m deep, with 40 sharks and 3,000 fish, and concrete, aluminium, ceramic and acrylic external finishes. Among the construction problems was the need to pile to stop ground pollution reaching the surface of the chalk aquifer below. Across the adjacent River Hull is an opening footbridge with an upswept 60t counterweight.

The Grade II Victoria Pier was formerly the cross Humber ferry terminal for New Holland. The docks were widened in 1321, making a defensive channel which produced an island with the River Hull and

Hull Trinity House was set up in the 14th century to look after distressed mariners and their families, expanding into marks, buoys and lighthouses, these latter interests being their current area of activity, Trinity House being one of three such bodies around the British Isles. They also have the oldest kayak in Britain, collected with its occupant on a trip back from Greenland in 1613.

The town was fortified in the 14th century. The Old Grammar School of 1583 is now the Hands on History museum. By the

The old lighthouse at Paull.

Hull waterfront with the River Hull tidal surge barrier and the Deep.

16th century the port had whaling expertise and Hull remained Britain's main whaling port until the mid-19th century. The port saw increased trade with the Continent in 1665 when London was closed down because of the plague. In 1877 it became the first city to have a public hydraulic power supply. Wilberforce House, Jacobean with oak panelled 17th century rooms, 18th century staircase with rococo plaster ceilings and Victorian parlour, was the birthplace of William Wilberforce in 1759 and has displays on slavery which he helped to abolish, Hull silver, dolls, toys and Victorian military costume. Other museums abound. The Ferens Art Gallery has Frans Hals, Ruisdael, Canaletto and 19th century Humberside marine paintings and contemporary art. There is a Streetlife Museum of Transport and a Maritime Museum with Hull's maritime heritage, models, paintings and the world's oldest planked boat outside Egypt, dating from 1500 BC. The Hull & East Riding Museum has fine mosaics, ancient civilizations and the Hasholme boat. The University of Hull Art Collection features British prints, paintings, drawings and sculpture of 1890–1940 with the Thompson Collection of Chinese ceramics.

In 1998 a 6m high chalk cylinder sculpture weighting 65t and entitled Two Sisters was positioned off Minerva Pier by floating crane. It took a month to dissolve, an operation which cost £50,000. Hull is also into trails, the Fish pavement sculpture trail by Gordon Young leading through the city with fish from A to Z. Kingston upon Hull Ale Trail includes 35 public houses. Stevie Smith was born in Hull and her aunt was the Lion of Hull in *Novel in Yellow Paper*. By the Minerva is an old public toilet which must be the best kept in the country, well worth a visit. Also of note is Hull Paragon station with a roof of five spans on cast iron columns to emulate those of larger stations.

Hull, the city from which Robinson Crusoe began his fictional journey, has produced more tangible travel history by building the *Bounty* and England's first steam packet. A statue of local Amy Johnson marks her solo flight to Australia in 1930. The same year Catherine Cookson took a planned Christmas holiday here despite finally being given a date of December 23rd for a long awaited hospital operation. It set up its own independent telephone system.

It was claimed that John Paul Jones escaped from Hull after being imprisoned for murdering his carpenter but this is dubious. It is the UK's foremost deep water fishing port and business includes building materials, vehicles and machinery. The port has a total of 13km of docks including the Albert Dock, lying inside St Andrews Quay which runs along the waterfront for 4km, where the tide floods to 9km/h and ebbs to 7km/h. The *Janet Coombe* paid a visit during her maiden voyage in Daphne du Maurier's *The Loving Spirit*. The *Hoplite* had dropped off some fortunate passengers here on her way from Melbourne to Newcastle in *The Watch House*.

At Gipsyville aerials mark where the Hull to Doncaster railway joins the shore on the far side of the A63 just before Kingston upon Hull gives way to the East Riding again.

Commercial boats fill the entire channel as they tranship in **Hessle** Haven, little more than a stream, off which the flow can increase to 11km/h. Christian mystic Margery Kempe was captured in the 15th century for a £100 reward and accused of being a Lollard as she was about to cross the Humber on the ferry here and faced opposing sides in the city, one of them wanting her imprisoned. There are Georgian houses but the Grade I All Saints church is late 13th century, Hull being in the chapelry of Hessle until 1661. On the shoreline is a fire signal basket and a viewpoint over the river although a better view is obtained from the bridge.

The Grade I Humber Bridge carries the A15 with 30m of clearance. When opened in 1981 its 1.41km main span was the world's longest and it was the world's first major suspension bridge to use hollow concrete piers. The 156m high towers support a total of 44,000km of 5mm diameter high tensile steel in the suspension cables and diverge 36mm to allow for the Earth's curvature. The deck height means that it has been used for over 220 suicides. Most Hull traffic still arrives from the M62 rather than over the bridge.

The bridge crosses from the East Riding to North Lincolnshire where Barton Waterside is linked by Barton Haven to **Barton-upon-Humber**, a market town. St Peter's church has a 10–11th century tower with some of the finest Anglo-Saxon architecture in England and finds have thrown new light on medieval diet and diseases. St Mary's parish church, in turn, has Transitional Norman, Early English and later architecture with a medieval wine merchant brass and monuments. Baysgarth House Museum is beyond the windmill. The red brick Georgian houses have left a legacy in the Clay Pits which were dug along the shoreline for several kilometres for brick and tile clay and now form a nature reserve. The Barton-upon-Humber to Habrough railway runs dead straight for 6km to New Holland, then turns sharply and runs almost straight again for a further 11km to Ulceby.

Barrow Haven, fed by the Beck from the direction of **Barrow upon Humber**, passes a windmill or two and the Castles, Norman motte and bailey designs.

New Holland pier is visited by large vessels but in front of an aerial towards Goxhill Haven the only vessels are the craft dumped on the mudflats to rot, snipe now being their main company. Stone groynes protect Skitter Ness as the estuary turns southeast.

Skitter Beck becomes East Halton Beck. At Skitter Haven or East Halton Skitter in Halton Marshes it discharges, the last respite before the industrial part of this side of the estuary.

The oil terminal with its North Killingholme Haven tank farm is next to flooded pits occupied by wildfowl at the start of Killingholme Marshes. Lighthouses precede South Killingholme Haven between Whitebooth Road and an oil refinery with its flare stacks.

After passing from North Lincolnshire into North East Lincolnshire, **Immingham** Dock is the UK's busiest cargo port, with piers extending out into the estuary. Immingham Gas Terminal, Immingham Bulk Terminal for coal and iron ore, Western Jetty, Eastern Jetty and Immingham Oil Terminal are all part of the complex. The ebb runs up to 13km/h and the flood to 7km/h, in addition to which there can be significant clapotis off ship hulls

The Humber Bridge had the world's longest main span.

Rotting boats near Goxhill Haven.

by Knell, Tudgay and Carmichael, photographs, folk life and local history and there is a Time Trap Museum in Grimsby Town Hall cells. Alfred Enderby traditional fish smokers continue one of the older arts of the fish trade.

The railway arrives past a football stadium to run along the shore to its **Cleethorpes** terminus, a shore with a wreck and with fish nets staked out on the sand. Sand at last means that Cleethorpes is a Victorian resort which developed from the village of Clee after the railway arrived but it takes its name from the Old English claeg, clay, and Old Scandinavian thorp, farm. The pier has a disco, bars and restaurant. The A180 becomes the A1098 which passes sands which flood quickly. Urban foxes cross the road at night to feed on seabirds on the beach. This is a migration route with grey plovers, dunlins and knots plentiful. Entertainment is also plentiful with a Leisure Centre, Discovery Centre & Boating Lake with estuary exhibition, aquarium and observatory, Jungle Zoo, Moon

Industrial coast between Immingham and Grimsby.

to add to the interest. Immingham Dock handles dry and liquid bulk cargoes, chemicals, fertilizers and general cargo, the centre of the Humberside chemical and petroleum industries. The dock of 1906–12 was a major Edwardian engineering project by Sir John Wolfe Barry, an 18ha basin with 2.8km of docks and 270km of railway track. Earlier, it was the site from which the Pilgrim Fathers sailed to the Netherlands in 1620.

A factory chimney at Pyewipe looks out over mudflats which have collected various wrecks.

A thousand years ago Grim, a Dane, landed at the mouth of the River Freshney to sell his fish, thus becoming the first fish merchant in the town which bears his name and had the world's largest fish market, dealing in skate, flatfish, scallops and cod, **Grimsby**. The church of St James was originally built in 1110 and the town received its charter in 1201, the first town in England to do so. The docks were begun in 1800, John Rennie designing the lock with hidden brick arches like a viaduct because of the poor ground conditions, a concept repeated by James Rendal in building the Royal Dock in 1846–8. The dominant feature of the lower estuary is the Dock Tower, a 94m folly modelled in 1852 by JW Wild on the Palazzo Publico in Sienna. It contains water tanks for hydraulic operation of dock gate and crane, one of William Armstrong's earliest applications of hydraulic power. The Fish Dock of 1934 and the commercial port cover 55ha and handle Danish dairy products and bacon. Already the UK's busiest car importer, capacity was increased in 2013 with a new jetty to handle ships carrying 3,000 cars, with 1.2km² of parking space ashore. Small inshore seine net trawlers have replaced the larger trawlers of the past. Grimsby Fishing Heritage Centre features 1950s Grimsby, trawlers at war, life on board, an Arctic trip and the *Ross Tiger*. The Welholme Galleries have ship models, paintings

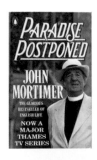

Bulk carrier moored at Immingham Dock.

Grimsby Dock Tower dominates the estuary.

on the Water, Fantasy World and Deep Sea Experience. The promenade has illuminations and the 3km 1948 Cleethorpes Coast Light Railway, one of Britain's oldest seaside miniature railways, with steam, a 1956 diesel engine and the Signal Box Inn, claimed to be the smallest pub on the planet. The meridian is marked by a stainless steel bar in the seawall. A souvenir model diver present from Cleethorpes earned undeserved significance in John Mortimer's *Paradise Postponed*.

In 1956 hundreds of people, including the RAF, watched by telescope and radar a UFO more than 20m

Cleethorpes pier and beach.

in diameter hovering at a height of 16km for an hour until two fighters were sent to investigate.

Haile Sand Fort with its cormorants stands off the **Humberston** Fitties holiday camp as North East Lincolnshire becomes Lincolnshire. Landmarks all but disappear for many kilometres if the tide is out, exposing up to 2km of sand with sandhills to Gibraltar Point and the former sea cliffs at the 30m level well inland around the position of Louth.

The Louth Canal emerges onto Tetney High Sands but any discharge reaches the sea at Cleethorpes when the tide is out. Little terns breed in Tetney Marshes and an oil pipeline runs out past several wrecks to serve the Tetney Monobuoy.

There is a disused airfield between Northcoates Point and Horse Shoe Point, the latter used for cockle digging.

Donna Nook is a firing range named after a wrecked ship. It extends 10km seawards and is in use when red flags are flying or red lights show. There is a control tower on the shoreline with orange targets on each side. Grainthorpe Haven to Saltfleet is a nature reserve with 250 species of bird recorded, common and grey seals resting on the sands and moon jellyfish in the water.

This is where a family were cut off by the tide in the 1990s. The father swam with his five year old daughter to raise the alarm and the mother was rescued at midnight after being kept afloat by the seals pressing around her to give her support.

Beyond the limit of Humber Port control Sand Haile Flats, Samphire Bed and the saltmarshes are a migration watchpoint.

Saltfleet Haven is one of the few natural harbours in Lincolnshire, fed by South Dike, Mar Dike and Great Eau although difficult to locate from offshore, where there are Saltfleet Overfalls. **Saltfleet** has a disused windmill and notable gardens. Stevie Smith recalled holidays here in *Novel on Yellow Paper*.

The Saltfleetby–Theddlethorpe Dunes are a nature reserve with sea buckthorn scrub, natterjack toads, reed buntings, sedge warblers and hen harriers. It is also the bombing range for RAF Wittering.

Theddlethorpe St Helen is marked by an aerial. It was where Paul Morel and Clara Dawes took breaks and swam in the sea in *Sons & Lovers*.

Mablethorpe is from the Old French name Malbert. Mablethorpe, Trusthorpe and Sutton on Sea run along the A52 by the coast for 6km yet, amazingly, are virtually invisible from the water. Sutton was damaged in the 1953 floods and they don't intend it to happen again. All that can be seen is a high bank topped with beach huts.

First comes a gas terminal which serves the Pickerill and other North Sea fields. Donkeys and a beach train in the summer, together with a fire signal basket, give a clue that a town has been reached although a holiday camp at North End, next to the Seal Sanctuary & Animal Gardens, is the only definite sighting. Mablethorpe is a resort with promenade and illuminations, Mablethorpe Miniature Railway, paddling pool, crazy golf, fairground, Embassy seafront theatre, sailing, golf and Olde Curiosity Museum with 4,500 glass lampshades. Groynes now provide protection but a white strip offshore is the remains of a village taken in the Middle Ages. Between 1827 and 1843 Tennyson stayed on occasions at Marine Villa, now called Tennyson's Cottage.

Trusthorpe has masts and the Trusthorpe Overfalls further out while the resort of Sutton on Sea also has a beachbreak and radio masts. Beyond Sandilands is one positive mark, a tall dolphin about a kilometre out to sea. By this point the Sea Bank has moved inland with a golf course in front of it and then the Moggs Eye picnic area.

At the northern end of some recent houses at Anderby Creek there is a path through to a carpark and toilet where a parking charge needs to be paid at the small shop.

Distance
146km from Withernsea via Hessle to Anderby Creek

OS 1:50,000 Sheets
*107 Kingston upon Hull
113 Grimsby
122 Skegness & Horncastle*

Tidal Constants
*Bull Sand Fort:
Dover –0440
Paull:
HW Dover –0450,
LW Dover –0440.
Kingston upon Hull:
HW Dover –0450,
LW Dover –0440
Humber Bridge:
HW Dover –0440,
LW Dover –0420
North Killingholme:
HW Dover –0500,
LW Dover –0450
Immingham:
Dover –0500
Grimsby:
Dover –0450
Inner Dowsing
Light Tower:
HW Dover –0500,
LW Dover –0450
Skegness:
HW Dover –0450,
LW Dover –0440*

Range
Donna Nook

Sea Area
Humber

Connections
*River Hull – see RoB p152
River Trent – see RoB p162
Louth Canal – see CoB p302*

Haile Sand Fort.

9 The Wash

Eastern England's most technical water

Last summer we decided
(That's the missis, kids and me)
We'd have a week in Skeggy
Where there's sun and sand and sea.
Roger Watson

Anderby Creek is at the end of the Main Drain with Anderby Drainage Museum and the world's only cloud observation platform. It would have been at the end of the Alford Canal which was planned to link Alford with the coast but it was never built. Mudbanks at the mouth can be treacherous. There is a picnic area and dunes continue south to Gibraltar Point, blackbacked gulls striding between the groynes. More picnic areas follow at Wolla Bank and Chapel Six Marshes. **Chapel St Leonards** has Willoughby High Drain discharging to the south of Chapel Point but, like Mablethorpe, the town is seen mostly as a collection of beach huts with the Golden Palm Resort inconspicuous.

Things are different at the resort of **Ingoldmells** with Fantasy Island and Funcoast World including the Splash subtropical waterworld, one of Europe's largest, the site of Butlin's first holiday camp in 1936. Inland from Ingoldmells Point is a tower up and down which screaming punters are carried at various speeds, a large pyramid surrounded by the Millennium Roller Coaster, the largest looping rollercoaster in Europe, and a tent structure which would put any other tent to shame. There are donkeys on the beach and jet and water skiers on the sea. At the back of the A52 is Skegness Airfield and a windmill while Hardy's Animal Farm is tucked in there somewhere.

Masses of caravans and a golf course fill the gap until amusements announce arrival in **Skegness**. Named as Skeggi's headland after an Old Scandinavian man, Skegness was a fishing village until Lord Scarborough drew up plans to develop it into a resort in the mid 19th century, one of the first British town plans. The pier was added in 1881 but was badly damaged in 1978 and only 188m remains. The town's line that 'Skegness is so bracing' is hardly a selling point for today's holidaymaker but it has been around too long to shake off. Indeed, the jolly fisherman of railway advertisements has been employed since 1908 and now has his own statue. The poster is mentioned a couple of times in John Hadfield's *Love on a Branch Line*. Tennyson stayed in Skegness in later years at Enderby's Hotel, now the Vine. There are the obligatory promenade and illuminations, Natureland Seal Sanctuary, funfair with big wheel and rollercoaster, gardens, theatres, ballrooms, swimming pools, bowling areas, boating lakes, Village Church Farm museum with its Victorian interior and Skegness Model Village. It had a zoo (where a lion ate the Revd Harold Davidson of Stiffkey, better known as the Prostitutes' Padre, who was

performing in its cage). A fire signal basket stands on the shore, starfish abound in the shallows and there can be surf, especially in the autumn.

Skegness is the last community before Hunstanton, whether going straight across the Wash or round the coast. Initially there is a golf course behind the dunes, giving way to Gibraltar Point National Nature Reserve, 6km² of sandhills, rough grazing, fresh and saltwater marshes, beach and foreshore with a nature trail, bird observatory, field station, sea buckthorn scrub, little terns, ringed plovers, oystercatchers, dunlins, knots, herons, kingfishers, short eared owls, cormorants and wildfowl generally plus natterjack toads. A red lorry rigged out as a safari vehicle drives loads of punters noisily along the beach. In January 2016 two sperm whales were stranded here with others at Skegness, Wainfleet and Hunstanton.

Wainfleet Road becomes Wainfleet Swatchway beyond Gibraltar Point where the Steeping River discharges as a mud rapid through Wainfleet Harbour. Beside the Boston Deeps the tide drops to reveal up to 5km of silt. The RSPB/WWF say the Wash is one of the world's most threatened sites for birds because climate change could raise the sea level, presumably changing surrounding farmland to more mud. The depths are subject to constant change, navigation is difficult as there are few features and it is often misty. Flows can be up to 6km/h inshore, mostly in the channels, possibly with eddies along the sides, and levels, rates and durations are affected by northeasterly and southwesterly winds. The ebbs from the major rivers are usually longer than the floods and may be up to 15km/h with spates.

Some 2km inshore is the Sea Bank which ran for 72km towards King's Lynn, much of it remaining, probably having been in place by the time of the *Domesday Book*.

Between Wainfleet Sand (mud) and Friskney Flats seals bask on the banks.

St Guthlac's church has a window dedicated to the saint holding a whip reputed to have been given to him by St Bartholomew. As long as he held it the village would remain free of rats and mice.

Strong northeasterly winds can give a considerable sea in the Boston Deeps, especially at the northeast end on the top half of the tide.

Wrangle has a coastguard station from where, presumably, they can see the sea from time to time. Wrangle Flats and Butterwick Low are littered with wrecks. Freiston Shore with its windmill is about a kilometre inland from Freiston Low and is good for birdwatching, including avocets, shelducks, brent geese and waders, although in the 18th century it was known for its fine bathing beaches. The coastal defences have been breached deliberately to flood more farmland for them. Freiston itself

The pier and assorted white knuckle rides at Skegness.

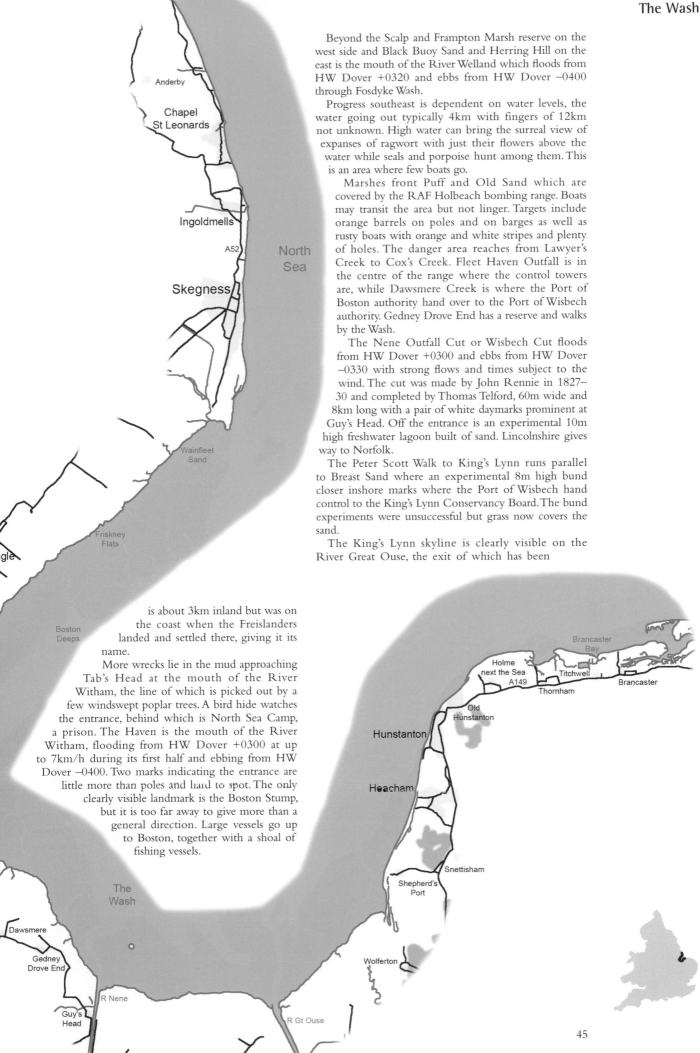

Beyond the Scalp and Frampton Marsh reserve on the west side and Black Buoy Sand and Herring Hill on the east is the mouth of the River Welland which floods from HW Dover +0320 and ebbs from HW Dover −0400 through Fosdyke Wash.

Progress southeast is dependent on water levels, the water going out typically 4km with fingers of 12km not unknown. High water can bring the surreal view of expanses of ragwort with just their flowers above the water while seals and porpoise hunt among them. This is an area where few boats go.

Marshes front Puff and Old Sand which are covered by the RAF Holbeach bombing range. Boats may transit the area but not linger. Targets include orange barrels on poles and on barges as well as rusty boats with orange and white stripes and plenty of holes. The danger area reaches from Lawyer's Creek to Cox's Creek. Fleet Haven Outfall is in the centre of the range where the control towers are, while Dawsmere Creek is where the Port of Boston authority hand over to the Port of Wisbech authority. Gedney Drove End has a reserve and walks by the Wash.

The Nene Outfall Cut or Wisbech Cut floods from HW Dover +0300 and ebbs from HW Dover −0330 with strong flows and times subject to the wind. The cut was made by John Rennie in 1827–30 and completed by Thomas Telford, 60m wide and 8km long with a pair of white daymarks prominent at Guy's Head. Off the entrance is an experimental 10m high freshwater lagoon built of sand. Lincolnshire gives way to Norfolk.

The Peter Scott Walk to King's Lynn runs parallel to Breast Sand where an experimental 8m high bund closer inshore marks where the Port of Wisbech hand control to the King's Lynn Conservancy Board. The bund experiments were unsuccessful but grass now covers the sand.

The King's Lynn skyline is clearly visible on the River Great Ouse, the exit of which has been

is about 3km inland but was on the coast when the Freislanders landed and settled there, giving it its name.

More wrecks lie in the mud approaching Tab's Head at the mouth of the River Witham, the line of which is picked out by a few windswept poplar trees. A bird hide watches the entrance, behind which is North Sea Camp, a prison. The Haven is the mouth of the River Witham, flooding from HW Dover +0300 at up to 7km/h during its first half and ebbing from HW Dover −0400. Two marks indicating the entrance are little more than poles and hard to spot. The only clearly visible landmark is the Boston Stump, but it is too far away to give more than a general direction. Large vessels go up to Boston, together with a shoal of fishing vessels.

The breached Freiston Shore coastal defences and footpath.

straightened as the Lynn Channel. Flood in the Lynn Channel begins at HW Dover +0300 and the ebb is from HW Dover –0330. Flows are strong and times subject to the wind.

There are more substantial banks up the east side of the Wash. Bulldog Sand lies on the former line of the Babingley River and this leads to Peter Black Sand off Dersingham, where the emphasis should be placed on Black rather than Sand. Herring gulls and others search for food. Wolferton Creek runs up the coast to clear Ferrier Sand, passing Shepherd's Port where Snettisham Scalp is a bird reserve with access restricted by the RSPB, having common terns in summer and waders and wildfowl in winter.

Heacham can have up to 2km of Stubborn Sand offshore to disperse the scent from Norfolk Lavender, England's only lavender farm. The Peddars Way may be pre Roman and forms the northern end of a track which includes the Ridgeway and runs right across southern England to Lyme Regis. Heacham stands on a former coastal railway line and has attractive Queen's Cottages almshouses by the 13th century St Mary the Virgin church. Native John Rolfe went to America and returned to live here with his bride, the native princess Pocahontas, a marriage which brought peace between the natives and the settlers in America. Stevie Smith recalled holidays here in *Novel on Yellow Paper*.

East Anglia acts as a groyne, collecting material moving south down the east coast, the coast building from Hunstanton to Weybourne. Now the water clears, perhaps for the first time since north of the Tees. Edmund landed in 855 to become king of the Angles. He prayed on the beach and a clear spring gushed forth. The location is also marked by

the Grade II remains of St Edmund's chapel of 1272. As the only west facing Victorian resort on the east coast of England, development of **Hunstanton** was initiated by Henry Styleman Le Strange from 1843. Growth continued, particularly after the arrival of the railway in 1862, although the name is from the Old English man Hunstan. As hereditary Lord High Admirals of the Wash, the Le Stranges could claim anything from the sea as far as a man could ride at low tide and then throw his spear. This still applies to all oysters and mussels from the beach, there being a bank of mussels and the wreck of the 1907 trawler *Sheraton* at St Edmund's Point. Tope, dabs and flounders are also amongst the sea's harvest. The pier was built in 1870, damaged in 1939 and 1950s fires and lost in a storm in 1978 with a further fire in the remains in 2002.

Hunstanton's most distinctive feature is its striped cliff, light grey marl on top of brown carrstone, 18m high and packed with fossils including plants, sea urchins, cuttlefish and shark teeth. Above is a disused white lighthouse of 1840, replacing one of 1665, and a fire signal beacon. It closed in 1922, having been used during the First World War as a naval watchpoint. Christmas Day sees an annual swim for the hardy and Hunstanton Kite Festival & Classic Car Rally takes place in August. As a resort it has a funfair, Hunstanton Sea Life Sanctuary with seal rehabilitation, Alive Oasis Sports & Leisure Centre with aquaslide, whirlpool spa, bowls, squash, table tennis, racket ball, rollerskating, cafeteria and bar, deckchairs, pony rides, pitch and putt and crazy golf. Activities on the water include sailing, powerboat racing, water skiing, windsurfing and jet skis yet there are still jellyfish and fulmars as part of the local environment. Amphibious landing craft used in Vietnam are now used for sea tours. Winter birdwatching is popular and there are many

Smaller targets in the Holbeach Firing Practice Area. The experimental reservoir lies on the horizon to the right.

Kite surfers in profusion beyond the striped cliffs at Hunstanton on a breezy day.

nature reserves in the area. *Barnacle Bill* and *Dad Savage* are two films which have been shot in Hunstanton and there is also a carnival.

There are beach huts at the former fishing village of Old Hunstanton as dunes begin. Old Hunstanton Hall is a moated Tudor mansion, owned by the Le Stranges from the Conquest until 1949. The Neptune Inn was used to store seized contraband until the 1880s, after which it was a coaching inn. The A149 runs parallel to the coast to Cromer while the Norfolk Coast Path passes Hunstanton Golf Club, which has hosted the English Amateur Championships and often the Oxford and Cambridge varsity tie, and follows to Cromer.

In 1998 the 2049 BC Bronze Age Seahenge circle of 55 oak posts, with a large inverted central oak tree used for religious ritual at Holme next the Sea, became public knowledge, the best such example in Europe. The posts were removed to Lynn Museum for preservation despite widespread protest but two concentric rings of a larger 2400 BC site 100m away have been retained. The village is surrounded by reserves. Holme Bird Observatory of 1962 consists of 2km^2 of dunes and saltmarsh with hides and over 50 species of plant including sea bindweed, sea lavender, bee and pyramid orchids and sea buckthorn. It has recorded over 320 species including wrynecks, hoopoes, ospreys, sooty shearwaters, collared flycatchers, red rumped swallows and 21 species of warbler. In addition they have recorded 363 species of moth. Permits

are needed for entry to the reserve. The coast is an AONB to Mundesley and there are sandhills to Wells.

Gore Point has a wreck. Behind the dunes is Broad Water and then Harbour Channel at Thornham where there is a ruined church tower. The port's last granaries were swept away in the 1953 floods. A whale taken at Thornham in 1488 was 20m long and 3.7m high.

Harbours to Cromer have entrances which are masses of broken water with strong winds from the northern half of the compass, worse with a southeastgoing swell after gales.

Marshes on this coast are the best in Britain and contain 9,000 year old trees like a petrified forest.

Behind Brancaster Bay is Titchwell with its cross. The 1780 seawall was felled by the 1953 tidal surge but not repaired. Reedbeds, fresh water, brackish marshes, saltmarsh and beach make up the 1.7km^2 RSPB nature reserve where there are avocets, marsh harriers, terns, ringed plovers, bearded reedlings, brent geese, shore larks and wildfowl and waders, watched from hides.

There is a golf course at Brancaster, to which Atwood was alleged to have taken young men for weekends in Robert Harris' *Enigma*. The village is noted for its mussels and is where the Romans built the Branodunum fort in about 300 as the northernmost of their forts to defend the Saxon shore. The beach floods quickly so visitors are cleared from Wreck Sands with a siren. Marram grass and barbed wire are features of the shoreline.

Distance
*99km from Anderby
Creek to Brancaster*

OS 1:50,000 Sheets
*122 Skegness
& Horncastle
131 Boston
& Spalding
132 North West
Norfolk*

Tidal Constants
*Skegness:
HW Dover −0450,
LW Dover −0440
Clay Hole:
HW Dover −0450,
LW Dover −0440
Tabs Head:
HW Dover −0500,
LW Dover −0410
Lawyer's Sluice:
Dover −0440
Old Lynn Road:
Dover −0440
Wisbech Cut:
HW Dover −0440,
LW Dover −0340
West Stones:
HW Dover −0440,
LW Dover −0400
Hunstanton:
HW Dover 0110,
LW Dover −0420
Brancaster Bar:
HW Dover −0430*

Range
Holbeach

Sea Area
Humber

Connections
*River Nene −
see RoB p166
New Bedford River −
see RoB p173*

The wind blows a sandstorm along the beach in front of the dunes at Brancaster.

10 Scolt Head Island

Mighty Seaman, tender and true,
And pure as he from taint of craven guile,
O saviour of the silver-coated isle,
O shaker of the Baltic and the Nile,
Alfred, Lord Tennyson

Scolt Head is part of the distinctive coastline of northern Norfolk, formed over the last millennium. Partly saltings and partly sand dunes, its position is exposed. There is no land between here and the North Pole. Formed over the last millennium, it belongs mostly to the National Trust who bought it from Lord Leicester in 1923 with money raised by local naturalists. The extreme eastern tip was purchased by Norfolk Naturalists' Trust in 1945. In 1953 the Nature Conservancy Council took a 99 year lease on the island and it now acts as an important nature reserve with breeding colonies of common, Sandwich, Arctic and little terns, ringed plovers, oystercatchers, blackheaded gulls and some waders. Redshanks and Arctic skuas have been seen and the island is an ornithologist's paradise. A nature trail has been laid out on the island and a boat takes people out to it during appropriate months. However, there is no access to the west part of the island from May to July and all the terneries are out of bounds from mid April to mid August so that breeding birds are not disturbed.

The west end of the island is a textbook example of a spit which is steadily growing along the outside of Brancaster Harbour. The island is moving westwards and landward, the laterals showing former western ends of the island, in contrast with the Brancaster golf course ridge which has grown eastwards.

For a circumnavigation of the island, launching of portable craft is cleaner and more convenient at the west end of Brancaster's golf course than at Brancaster Staithe.

The shallow water can be deceptive and often catches out people who visit the wreck of the *Vina* on the end

Scolt Head Island stands off the mouth of Brancaster Harbour.

Brancaster Staithe at high water but it can be very muddy once the tide drops.

Scolt Head forming a true island for once as Norton Creek reaches maximum depth at the top of a spring tide.

Looking over Trowland Creek towards Burnham Overy Staithe, an area of saltmarsh divided by tidal creeks.

of the spit, the corroded silhouette jutting out of the sand in three separate places. The 1,021t cargo vessel of 1894 was used as a Second World War aircraft bombing target, including for determining the size of bombs to be used for D-Day. Two submerged Covenanter tanks are reminders that this was also a Second World War tank firing range. Shells are still found occasionally and should be reported but not touched.

Passing the golf course brings the more sheltered but faster flowing waters of Brancaster Harbour with the run south past the golf course up to Brancaster Staithe.

Brancaster Marsh, which surrounds Mow Creek, is largely an area of tall rustling reeds. With the tide out,

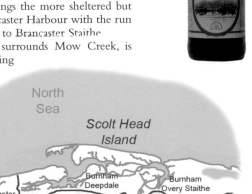

The mouth of Burnham Harbour with Scolt Head Island to the left and Gun Hill to the right.

Burnham Overy Staithe is a popular sailing centre.

the sandy bed is covered by a thin layer of mud. Tides in Brancaster Harbour can be strong, up to 13km/h.

The harbour, home of Brancaster Staithe Sailing Club, is a busy place in season with power and sailing boats in profusion.

Anti-smuggling measures were in place against armed Dutch boats by 1710 but a boat taken in 1832 was carrying 2.5t of tobacco and 3,000l of brandy.

Brancaster Harbour's channel is constantly changing, as are the many sailing boats which use it. Brancaster Staithe has a shellfishery begun by the Romans. Whelk sheds and mussel fishermen's huts line the waterside. Working boats land mussels which are placed in sacks and barrowed up from the water's edge.

A hut acts as the harbourmaster's office and boaters are asked to visit it before launching. It has a box on the side to receive launch fees. Inside are the rules which require all collisions, including those involving kayaks, no matter how slight, to be reported to the harbourmaster. There are also identification charts for birds and plants seen on the island. Two clocks on the outside give the times of the next two high tides.

The island is separated from other saltings by Norton Creek, these other saltings in turn being divided from the mainland by Trowland Creek. Both are shallow and it is possible to cross on foot to Scolt Head except at the highest tides. To circumnavigate Scolt Head Island it is necessary to take the narrowest part of Norton Creek at high tide, ideally at springs. The tide floods eastwards and ebbs westwards.

Norton Creek contains numerous rafts supporting trays of oysters and mussels. Along the banks, sea aster covers the saltings and Norton Creek gets shallower as it gets narrower until Burnham Harbour is reached.

A windmill stands just outside Burnham Overy Staithe. Church towers from a number of villages with the first name Burnham, homestead by the stream, might be seen. Burnham Deepdale has St Mary's church with a round flint tower from after the Conquest, a seasonal font from a single block of stone with a monthly farm

worker on each face and medieval stained glass. In the 1760s they were all under the control of the Reverend Edmund Nelson, whose son Horatio acquired a love of the sea from playing by the sandy harbour. At 12 the lad was a midshipman, destined to become the greatest seaman in history.

Burnham Overy Staithe, which declined from a busy 19th century port to become silted up by the 1920s, has a Grade II Westend Watermill 200 years old, last used in 1941, damaged by fire in 1959 and now restored. Residents of the village included Richard Woodhouse, the master of the *Cutty Sark*, from 1899 to 1926. Overy Marshes were drained in the 1630s.

The harbour, fed by the River Burn, has sailing and windsurfing with an annual regatta. Gun Hill is growing westwards and the entrance is broken with strong winds, swell or ebb when the bar can be dangerous to small craft.

The northern half of the island is quite different from the south. Instead of saltings there are dunes thrown up by storms, changing their positions from year to year with the tough marram grass fighting to hold them in place. The end of the island is a favourite spot for seabirds. The currents are confused here and surf conditions can be quite reasonable.

As well as drifting sand, the beach which forms the northern face of the island can throw up semiprecious stones, cornelian, onyx, amber and jet. The other kind of jet is present, too, with frequent sallies from King's Lynn.

The dunes are lower at the centre of the island, allowing views through to the woods on rising ground to the south and permitting southerly winds to generate offshore waves. The only building on the island shelters behind high sand dunes towards the western end of the island. Here the surf is often better than at the other end of the island, especially on a flood tide or with a northerly wind, and the birdlife is more profuse. Gulls stare indignantly at small craft but are not sufficiently annoyed to stop wading about in the shallow water, fishing for food items.

Distance
Scolt Head Island is 6km long and lies 40m off Burnham Deepdale

OS 1:50,000 Sheet
132 North West Norfolk

Tidal Constants
Brancaster Bar: HW Dover −0430 Burnham (Overy Staithe): HW Dover −0410

Sea Area
Humber

Norfolk

11

As we were a fishing off Haisboro' Light,
Shooting and hauling and trawling all night.
It was windy old weather, stormy old weather;
When the wind blows, we all pull together.
Anon

West Sands in Holkham Bay are a naturist site, behind which is Holkham National Nature Reserve, the largest coastal reserve in England with 40km² of sand, mudflats, saltmarsh and sand dunes running to Blakeney. Corsican pinewoods were planted in the mid 19th century to stabilize the dunes. Holkham Iron Age fort was built on an island in the marsh, a 2.2ha oval with bank and ditch, perhaps protection for a coastal trading station and possibly where the Iceni failed to beat the Romans in 47. The *Shakespeare in Love* shipwreck scene was filmed at Holkham and it was also used for Jack Higgins' *The Eagle Has Landed*.

A church tower and a monument break the skyline at Holkham Park, now owned by the Earl of Leicester. The monument of 1845, over 30m high with a wheatsheaf on top and presented by tenants, is to a former owner, the agricultural reformer Coke who began the farming revolution on his own in the first half of the 19th century, changing from rye and wheat and introducing new livestock breeds, increasing crop and livestock yields, and still was able to invent the bowler hat in his spare time. Holkham Hall is a Palladian mansion of 1734–60, one of Britain's most stately homes, designed by William Kemp with contributions by Rubens, Van Dyck, Glaude, Poussin, Gainsborough, Raphael and Reynolds. It has a Bygone Museum with vintage cars, traction engines, a Victorian kitchen, laundry, pump room, 1900 harness room, brewery tapping room, shoe shop, tools, history of farming, pottery, art gallery, Holkham Nursery Gardens in a 2ha 19th century walled garden, 12km² deer park designed by Capability Brown, lake and beach. In Edwardian times it was known for its large wildlife shoots. In *The Diary of a Country Parson* James Woodforde records being invited by the Cokes with the great and good of Norfolk to a ball and supper at Holkham to commemorate the centenary of the Glorious Revolution of 1688.

The Run, the mouth of the harbour at **Wells-next-the-Sea**, is subject to frequent change with a bar which is roughest with northerly winds. Water skiers, sailors and beach huts greet arrival at the lifeboat and National Coastwatch station, behind which is a sheltered inlet near to the carpark. The flood runs from HW Dover +0140 and the ebb from HW Dover −0440. A klaxon warns when the flood starts. The name notes local springs. In October 1880 the lifeboat capsized on the bar with the loss of 11 of the 13 crew. The lifeboat station was moved from the town to its present position in 1895, reducing a pull of up to 4km to the sea. The last horsedrawn lifeboat launch took place in 1934. At the end of the Second World War German prisoners of war tried to steal the lifeboat but were unable to start the engine.

The 260mm gauge miniature steam Wells Harbour Railway runs alongside the harbour, to complement the Wells & Walsingham Light Railway to Little Walsingham. The embankment built to reclaim Holkham Marshes was the work of the Cokes. The harbour gets its odd shape from a dyke built down the middle of the harbour, after which land was reclaimed to its west. Abraham's Bosom is a canoeing and boating lake.

Wells is a commercial and fishing port with whelk and shrimp boats and handles fertilizers, animal feedstuffs, cockles and skate. It has been a port for at least 200 years. James Woodforde took a short trip from here in a small boat in 1779 and proved himself not to be a sailor. The Stone quay was built in the mid 19th century when it imported coal, timber, salt, rape and linseed and exported barley and malt for Guinness. Wells Maritime Museum features fishing, the port, the coastguard, lifeboats, wildfowling and bait digging. The church of St Nicholas of 1879 replaces one of 1640 burnt down after a lightning strike. There is a carnival in August in this village of flint cottages which was used for filming part of *Dad Savage*.

At low tide 2km of Bob Hall's Sand is exposed beside the Run while at high tide there are various channels through the marshes, particularly East Fleet and Stonemeal Creek which continues as Cabbage Creek when the tide drops, crossing a nature reserve

The tower mill at Cley next the Sea.

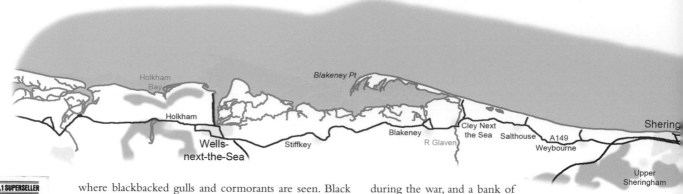

where blackbacked gulls and cormorants are seen. Black Shuck, a jet black dog as big as a calf, possibly the Devil, was said to haunt the area, convenient for keeping the public away from smuggling operations. Stewkey Blue cockles are gathered from Stiffkey Marshes with their sea lavender. The marshes and Blakeney Point are included in Blakeney National Nature Reserve, an area used for military training for both World Wars. *The Eagle Has Landed* was set in this part of the country.

The River Glaven has been silting since the 17th century, blocked off by shingle, and finds its way to the sea through Blakeney Harbour, the entrance of which is difficult with strong onshore winds and which can have a series of races off it. The River Stiffkey also feeds the harbour further west. Blakeney is noted for its flint cottages and windmill. The church acted as a lighthouse and there is a Watch House, at one time used by the Guides. The 14th century guildhall remains have a brick vaulted undercroft. Sailing is popular and the harbour has the largest fleet of sharpies in England. In the 13th century it was one of Britain's leading ports and by the 16th century it had an Icelandic fishing fleet but its downfall was to be the lack of a railway connection.

Blakeney Point is a 6km spit protecting the harbour and growing thrift, sea lavender and samphire. One of several hides is conspicuous on the point where common, little and Sandwich terns nest and oystercatchers, plovers, redshanks and rare migrants are seen. Landing is not permitted during the breeding season. As many as 500 common and grey seals rest up on the point where they are visited by a flotilla of noisy sealwatching tour boats, the owners of which object to others approaching. There is the wreck of the *Hjordis*, sunk for target practice

during the war, and a bank of protected mussels off the point.

The bank of shingle and sand does not just form the spit but continues to Weybourne, a 12km wall up to 10m high and 20m wide with a high tide dump. The coast is building eastwards and Cley next the Sea is now a good kilometre away from it, although in the Middle Ages it was an important seaport with a custom house and Dutch gables which suggest there was trade with the Netherlands. The landmark is a 15m high 1819 tower mill which was used as a flour mill until 1917 and has been a guesthouse since 1983, complete with sails but no machinery. Other notable buildings in the village of Georgian houses and flint cottages include the Made in Cley pottery with jewellery in a Regency shop with contemporary fittings, Knucklebone House with cornices and panelling made from sheep's vertebrae and a smokehouse for kippers. The George Hotel has a boules pitch, a stained glass window of the saint and his adversary and a brass lectern in the bar on which birdwatchers can record their sightings. The 2.6km^2 of Cley Marshes Nature Reserve was the first reserve in the country, set up in 1926, with access by permit. There are rare migrants, bearded tits, bitterns and common terns and in winter shore larks, snow buntings and wildfowl. Naturalist Richard Mabey grew up here. A 4km bank round Blakeney Marsh and a 3km bank round Cley Marsh were built 3.6–5.4m high, 1.8–3m wide at the top. Begun in 1522 by Sir John Heydon, they were extended in 1630 by van Hasedunch and completed in 1649 by Simon Britliffe, lord of the manor at Cley. They were overwhelmed and breached in 1742, 1897 and 1953, each time being rebuilt and strengthened. A road runs across

The soft cliffs make their first appearance at Sheringham.

the marshes beside the river to Cley Eye where there are a gun emplacement, parking, toilets, a café and the Grade II stone remains of Blakeney Chapel, built in at least 1586 but probably not a chapel. In 2007 a decision was made to allow coastal defences to collapse. In 2014 the crash of a USAF helicopter, which struck pink footed geese disturbed by the previous helicopter, spread live ammunition across the marsh.

There are yellow horned poppies at Salthouse where there is a risk

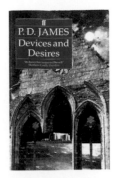

Dad's Army and *Love on a Branch Line*. Also known as the Poppy Line, it has steam and diesel engines and a model railway. The 1887 line by William Marriot, resulting in the change of Sheringham from a fishing village to a resort, was closed in 1924, restoration starting in 1965.

Soft chalky cliffs begin with agate, quartz and cornelian on the sandy beach and extend to Happisburgh. Sandy beaches extend much further. On top is a golf course and, behind that, Upper Sheringham. The church was mentioned in the *Domesday Book* but the more significant church related building to be constructed there was the Grade II★ Sheringham Hall, built in 1812 for Abbot Upcher and his wife, Charlotte, by Humphrey Repton. It is landscaped with rhododendrons, azaleas and woodland, the only man made structure visible in the 3.1km² Sheringham Park being a temple. Coastwatch use a former coastguard lookout.

Silingham became Siringham then **Sheringham**. Scira's people, the Scirings, were forgotten as it became a resort of flint, Edwardian and Victorian buildings with a promenade and a carnival week in August. There is a Splash Leisure pool with giant waterslide and wave pool, Sheringham Museum with local history and the lifeboats,

of unexploded mines. Approaching Weybourne there is a pillbox and an area with security fencing and aerials. The Muckleburgh Collection is Britain's largest working military collection with sixty armoured vehicles and guns, the home of the Suffolk & Norfolk Yeomanry Museum with its history from 1759 and more recent exhibits from the Falklands and Gulf War plus lifeboats and a Harrier.

Weybourne with its 17th century brick and flint cottages was garrisoned against the Spanish fleet in 1588 and was defended with pillboxes until 1958. Gold coins found on the beach in 1940 were thought to be from a 1st century BC tribe. The Romans built a pottery kiln and there is a Saxon church tower, the remains of an Augustinian priory of about 1200 and a ruined windmill. Dunes are eroding fast and a house stands on the brink at Water Hill. Offshore are flounders, bass, whiting and cod. The setting for PD James' *Devices & Desires* was strongly influenced by this coast.

Any whistle is likely to come from the 8km North Norfolk Railway as a train approaches, used in filming

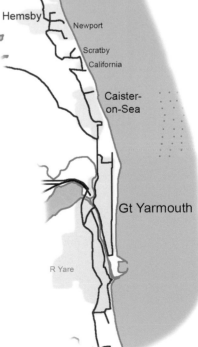

The pier at Cromer with its new lifeboat station on the end.

the remains of a priory and a cannon in Gun Street. Sheringham Art & Sculpture Trail is nautically inspired. The Two Lifeboats hotel refers to the *Augusta* and *Duncan* which took the crew off the Norwegian brig *Caroline* in 1882. Deckchairs are hired to the holidaymakers who paddle between the rock groynes. In the late 1800s the Norfolk whelk fishery was developed here for bait and for London shellfish appetites. Fishing vessels still work off the beach, the lobster and 50t/year crab catch now being sold locally. Sheringham shares a May Crab & Lobster Festival with Cromer, including the world pier crabbing championships and lifeboat demonstration. The Potty Morris Festival in July is based around the Lobster Inn.

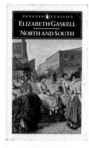

A 35km² windfarm's 88 turbines stand on Sheringham Shoal, 17km offshore. Sloping boarding at the high tide mark protects the soft cliffs. Beeston Hill of 63m, also known as Beeston Bump, had one of nine Second World War listening posts which established the positions of German ships and passed on their messages to Bletchley Park for decoding. A 10m tower on top had twin wooden skins with gravel between for protection from bullets. In 1915 Sheringham had a Zeppelin attack, Britain's first aerial bombing.

On top at Beeston Regis in a field is All Saints church with a 15th century choir screen. There is a Beeston Regis Nature Trail. At West Runton is Roman Camp, the highest point in Norfolk at 102m, plus the Hillside Animal & Shire Horse Sanctuary with native ponies, horsedrawn farm machinery and gypsy caravan, a children's farm and riding. In 1990 the cliffs revealed most of a 650,000 year old, 4.6m high, elephant skeleton. East Runton's cliffs are topped by a caravan site while crab boats are hauled up on the beach by tractor and

there is a popular surf break. The Coastwatch lookout building had to be abandoned because of erosion in the 2013 storm surge.

Lobster pots are laid and fishing and crab boats are also launched off **Cromer** beach by tractor but with a beachbreak each side of the pier. The Rocket House Café and restaurant suggest that lifeboats did the same but the lifeboat station, with the *Ruby & Arthur Read*, is built at the end of the pier beyond the Pavilion Theatre. Opened in 1999, it presumably ended what was the last traditional end of pier show in the country. The Gangway approach road has granite setts set with their corners raised to help horses grip. The former lifeboat station has been moved to Southwold as a museum. The Henry Blogg Museum has his 1935–45 lifeboat, *HF Bailey III*, which rescued 818 people, together with the medals of Henry, who received more awards than any other coxwain, plus photographs and models. Off the coast is the early 20th century wreck of the *Fernbo*, rescued by Blogg. Cromer Museum, in a late Victorian fisherman's cottage, also features lifeboat services with local history, fishing, bathing, archaeology, geology and natural history. Unlike Blakeney, the coast here is eroding. The sea took Shipden, leaving the village of Cromer (from the Old English crawe mere, crow's lake), established 2km inland, on the coast at the end of the Cromer Ridge by the 18th century. As he returned to challenge Henry VI, Edward IV put a boat ashore here to establish the level of support he could expect. Surfers are now using the resort. It has another windmill. The 49m knapped flint Perpendicular church tower of St Peter & St Paul is the tallest in Norfolk and served as a daymark before the 14m lighthouse was built 800m inland in 1866. The fishing village became a resort with the coming of the

Looking back towards Mundesley, the toe of the cliffs protected by a line of boarding in addition to groynes.

Bacton Natural Gas terminal is largely hidden from the sea.

railway but those already coming here for the sea bathing included the Barclays banking family. There are Amazona Zoo, Fun Stop Corner children's indoor adventure centre, tennis, putting, squash, cricket, deckchairs and a carnival week in August. A family holiday here in Elizabeth Gaskell's *North & South* seemed to set Margaret Hale on the road to recovery. Sir Arthur Conan Doyle was believed to have thought of the plot of his *Hound of the Baskervilles* while staying here. Lord Alfred Douglas played golf here while staying with Oscar Wilde. *The Eagle Has Landed* claimed there was a Cat night bombing support device sited here but that the Germans had been informed about it. The town inspired the Norwich school of painters including Dixon, Cotman and Bright. *September Song* was filmed here.

The A149 turns south. The eroding chalky cliffs with their fossils have been subject to extensive landslips to Happisburgh because of groundwater in the cliffs, although this does not stop fulmars nesting all along this coast to Great Yarmouth and herring gulls being resident. An undersea forest is present as far as Winterton-on-Sea. Beyond the groynes Foulness takes its name from the large pieces of chalk lying beneath the surface. Tidal streams follow the coast at up to 5km/h. The 18m white octagonal lighthouse of 1833 replaces the first one built by Sir John Clayton which remained unlit until 1719 because of lack of funds and was then made unsafe by a massive landslip. A searchlight close by gives a narrow vertical beam for 10 minutes per hour to show the cloudbase.

The resort of Overstrand has the Pleasaunce gardens laid out by Gertrude Jeckyll. The poppies inspired Clement Scott's poem *Garden of Sleep* which led to the Poppyland craze of the late 19th century. There are 30m

cliffs and low tide surf at Trimingham but there is no access from the beach as far as Mundesley as the cliffs are dangerous.

Radio masts stand back from the cliffs, there is a radar golfball and the church at Sidestrand was moved in 1880 when the sea got too close. A water tower behind Cliftonville is a landmark from further out. **Mundesley** appeared in the *Domesday Book* under its Anglo-Saxon or Norse name of Muleslai. It has become a fishing village with cod, sole, eels and skate, boats being tractor launched off the beach from near a line of beach huts. These days it is a resort with promenade, deckchairs and holiday camp. Mundesley Boat Day for the independent lifeboat is in August. The old coastguard lookout point has become Mundesley Maritime Museum on the coastguard and the village's history. Nelson and animal artist Briston Riviere stayed here and William Cowper wrote the hymn *God Moves in a Mysterious Way* after watching a storm over Happisburgh. Golf and horse riding are available.

Mundesley mill has gone although its overshot millwheel remains on the River Mun, believed to be the only one of its kind in Norfolk.

Stow Mill was built in 1827 by James Gale, whose son, Thomas, was the miller for 45 years. It has sails but no machinery and contains an exhibition of milling.

The long thatched barn at Paston was built by Sir William Paston in 1581. The Grade I St Margaret's church has Paston family monuments and 14th century wall paintings. *The Paston Letters* described life during the Wars of the Roses.

Much more conspicuous on the cliffs, especially from the east, is the Bacton Gas Terminal with pipelines from the Hewett, Leman, Camelot and other North Sea gas fields and some high masts.

The line of artificial reefs to protect the coast at Sea Palling.

Marram grass binds the dunes at Horsey Corner. The concrete seawall is hidden from on top.

The dunes run on southwards from Horsey Corner.

Rock protects the crumbling California Cliffs.

Groynes, a sloping sea wall, a wreck and low tide surf front the village of Bacton. At Keswick is the gateway to Broomholm Priory, now a farm as prophesied by Mother Shipton. Founded in 1113, the priory had part of the True Cross which could cure leprosy and bring the dead back to life, as referred to by Chaucer in the *Reeve's Tale*.

Walcott reaches to Ostend with holiday camps, a pillbox, another aerial and low tide surf. Happisburgh, named after Haep, has caravans and a fire beacon, also groynes which have recently been supplemented with substantial new sea defences although the sea continues to eat metres into the cliffs each year. A hand axe and Palaeolithic flints have been revealed, the 650,000 year old flints being the oldest in Britain. Footprints revealed briefly in 2013 before being washed away were believed to be of a Homo antecessor group, made over 800,000 years ago, the oldest human footprints outside Africa and the fourth oldest ever found.

All Saints church has a 34m tower, possibly as a beacon, and a 15th century font with the four Evangelists, angelic musicians and men carrying clubs. Many shipwrecked sailors have been buried with anchors for gravestones and there is a mound with 119 men from HMS *Invincible*, wrecked in 1801 on her way to join Nelson in Copenhagen. Also buried is Jonathan Balls, an arsenic poisoner who murdered a dozen people, mostly relatives, and then himself by accident, being buried with plum cake, Bible, poker and fire tongs to handle the eternal flames. At Well Corner the ghost of a smuggler murdered in a dispute over booty comes from the sea into the sands. From the 1800s he was seen regularly to empty a sack into the well. The well was excavated to reveal a torso and a sack containing a head and legs. It was one of the places claimed as the home of the Haselbury girl recorded in song.

There were so many wrecks that in the 19th century Trinity House used explosives to clear them. The inshore rescue boat has retreated inland and the last of a line of houses not already taken by the sea was demolished after the 2013 storm surge. A lighthouse of 1791 has a white 26m tower with three red bands. Britain's only privately owned lighthouse, it is in the middle of a field and was the high light to a lower one demolished in 1883 when cliff erosion made it unsafe. In the 1860s it was used in experiments to make coal gas during the day to be stored and burnt at night.

Dunes start 9–12m high, gradually declining to Winterton Ness. In 1953 they were breached by the sea at Sea Palling. They now have a concrete seawall which cannot be climbed, only the occasional gap allowing access. A church at Eccles on Sea was overwhelmed by dunes which then moved inland, exposing it to the sea, causing the tower to collapse in 1895. The foundations can still be seen on the beach after a scouring tide. From Eccles to Waxham a straight line of artificial reefs 1.7m high have been placed 300m offshore. The rock island line's boulders have large wire loops attached and each reef has an Environment Agency notice banning landing

Curlews fly over the marram grass covered dunes and the beach at Sea Palling is used by naturists and for jet ski hire.

From Waxham to Winterton-on-Sea is an AONB while, less than 2km inland, a line of windmills stand in the rather different landscape of the Broads. Waxham was attacked by 1,100 Flemish in 1440, of whom 800 were killed or drowned. The Hall at Waxham is now a farmhouse, accompanied by a magnificent barn, the largest in East Anglia, which has been supported by the Prince's Trust. It is haunted by the ghosts of six members of the Brograve family who met sudden deaths in major battles over the centuries, all called together by late 18th century owner Sir Berney Brograve to dine and drink until they vanished at midnight. There is a derelict church and a Tudor wall with turrets and a gatehouse.

From Warren Farm at Horsey Corner the dunes to 17m high are topped by marram grass and continue almost unbroken to the start of Great Yarmouth. Initially the groynes continue, as does the seawall which was built after the dunes were breached at Horsey in 1938. This used to be an exit from the Broads and the sea may still want to get back to the Hundred Stream.

While there are few landmarks on the coast it hides a totally different landscape beyond the dunes, the Broads. From Warren Farm, with its skylarks to answer the terns on the sea side of the dunes, it is not far to two windmills including the well preserved Horsey Mill. The thatched Saxon All Saints church in Horsey has a round tower with a 15th century octagonal belfry. Winterton Ness is just 2km from the head of the River Thurne at West Somerton, a river which flows westward before finally discharging its waters at Great Yarmouth.

The sea probably reached the former cliffs near the Winterton Dunes National Nature Reserve as late as the 18th century. Winterton-on-Sea is a village better known than some, if not by name, as it has been used for some of the BBC's *Dad's Army* sequences and it was the 1930s Cape Cod in the film *Julia*. Holy Trinity & All Saints church has a 40m tower, a significant landmark, while most of its inside is made from ships' timbers and fittings and there is a Fisherman's Corner. This is not surprising. In 1725 Daniel Defoe wrote that most buildings between Winterton and Yarmouth were built from wreck timber. These days there is a little more variety in the building. By the beach are separate thatched round houses based on South African rondavels. Behind the village are two rows of wind generators while on Scroby Sands is one of Britain's largest offshore windfarms. There are many fewer wrecks there now so the lighthouse with its black banded round white tower is disused. Wreckage was not just on the shore. The 300 year old Fisherman's Return had its windows permanently boarded up because so many bodies were thrown through them when the fishermen did return ashore. Theirs have not been the only unwelcome boats, tank traps being seen in the dunes at strategic points, although many submarine cables have been landed in the village.

Flows run to 5km/h from here to Yarmouth with a strong southerly flow at high water and a strong northerly

The Britannia Pier packed with amusements at Great Yarmouth.

Distance
*102km from
Burnham Harbour
to the River Yare*

OS 1:50,000 Sheets
*132 North West
Norfolk
133 North East
Norfolk
134 Norwich
& the Broads*

Tidal Constants
*Burnham
(Overy Staithe):
HW Dover −0410
Wells Bar:
Dover −0440
Blakeney Bar:
HW Dover −0430
LW Dover −0420
Cromer:
HW Dover −0420,
LW Dover −0350
Winterton-on-Sea:
HW Dover −0400,
LW Dover −0320
Caister-on-Sea:
HW Dover −0300,
LW Dover −0240
Gorleston:
HW Dover −0220,
LW Dover −0210*

Sea Areas
Humber, Thames

Connection
*River Yare –
see RoB p185*

at low water. Along this section of coast the tidal constant changes very rapidly, over 3 hours between here and Southwold. Winterton Overfalls form 6km off the coast beyond the Cockle Gateway.

Hemsby and Newport look over Hemsby Hole but there is nothing to indicate the whereabouts of the new port itself. Hemsby is a resort and has holiday camps, as does California, part of Scratby named after its tavern. This section of coast has unstable sand cliffs with rocks placed at the bottom. Three bungalows at Newport were taken by the 2013 storm surge.

It is **Caister-on-Sea**, however, which claims to have invented the holiday camp although the name from castra, a camp, was probably less of a fun place, the town having been founded in the 2nd century, one of the chief towns of the Iceni. Footings of 3rd century buildings show it was once a Roman commercial port, possibly with a fort, at what was the mouth of the Bure. Fun these days includes an ice cream van on the beach. Caister Point is perhaps the most insignificant point in the country on a map, slightly more visible when looking along the shore. Sandbanks 24km offshore act as breakwaters but give a short choppy sea and waves break heavily on Caister Shoal, inside Caister Road. There are also a couple of placed reefs, older than the ones at Sea Palling. The town begins with a radio mast and a water tower and ends with a golf course as the coast turns low and sandy to Great Yarmouth. Behind the golf course is a helicopter base serving the North Sea platforms, next to Yarmouth greyhound and motor racing stadium. Beside the golf course is a horse racecourse, formerly a barracks run by Capt Manby who invented lighthouse flash signatures and the line throwing rescue mortar.

Great Yarmouth is primarily a resort with 24km of beaches. The North Beach, backed by the Imperial Hotel and others, is reasonably restrained. The serious fun begins with the Britannia Pier which has slides, a roundabout and a wigwam among other items at its seaward end and any amount of amusements thereafter. *Love on a Branch Line* contrasts its garishness with Arcady fair. Further south there are an assortment of eyecatching features, notably the Pleasure Beach and a prominent blue rollercoaster plus log flume, go karts, ghost train and more. The Sea Life Centre is one of the largest with shark tank, rays and Lost City of Atlantis. Treasure World has diving for treasure. There is Merrivale Model Village. There is also a jetty and the Wellington Pier with its pavilion. Henry James' *English Hours* did not like the cockneyfication of the seafront or the overflow of black minstrelsy.

Yarmouth takes its name from the River Yare and grew rich in the Middle Ages on herrings, vast shoals of which gathered off the town each autumn. This led to successive arguments with the Cinque Ports and then the Dutch over herring rights and reached the point where the Cinque Ports attacked the Yarmouth fleet while escorting the king to Flanders in 1297, resulting in the burning of 29 ships and the killing of 200 men. The town's coat of arms has three herrings. The Yarmouth Free Herring Fair every autumn was one of the greatest medieval trade fairs. Thomas Nashe wrote about the Yarmouth fishing in *Lenten Stuff* in 1597. The Yarmouth bloater, the cold smoked herring, was invented in 1836 and the herring peaked before the First World War with over 1,100 drifters but overfishing destroyed the stocks and the last drifter was sold in 1963. In *The Snow Goose* Paul Gallico makes reference to a Yarmouth drifter used in the Dunkirk evacuation. The town hall has a golden drifter weathervane. Fish found today include dab, sole, cod, whiting, bass and spined weaver.

Margery Kempe sailed from here on her pilgrimage to the Holy Land in 1414. James Woodforde made several journeys here and reports in *The Diary of a Country Parson* of being shown over a Sunderland collier and drinking

with the crew, of the deaths in the 1789 storm and of the landing of the Prince of Orange and his family here and in Harwich in 1795. The port saw increased trade with the Continent in 1665 when London was closed down because of the plague but suffered from the plague itself, brought by colliery vessels which had visited London. The town has now become a North Sea gas and oil exploration base. Nelson landed here after the Battle of the Nile in 1798 and sailed to and from the Battle of Copenhagen in 1801. The 43m Norfolk Naval Pillar of 1819 has 217 steps and is topped by Britannia facing, some think oddly, away from the sea. It commemorates Nelson, who was given freedom of the town, and is located alongside Yarmouth Roads just inside Yarmouth Port Limit. Near the monument was set Peggoty's hut in *David Copperfield*. More drama on the beach in 1900 resulted in Herbert Bennett being hanged for murdering his estranged wife with a bootlace, much evidence pointing to his guilt. Eleven years later another woman was strangled on the beach with a bootlace.

Built 1261–1400, the town walls are one of the most complete sets in England, including the North West Tower. There are some notable old buildings. The flint Tolhouse Gaol Museum dates from the 13th century, one of the oldest municipal buildings in England, used as a courthouse and jail. The Elizabethan House Museum in a merchant's house of 1596 has contemporary panelling, a 17th century Flemish window of a Dutch buss, Lowestoft porcelain, 18/19th century drinking glasses, Victorian toys, a Tudor bedroom, a Victorian kitchen and displays of 19th century domestic life. It was said to have been used for plotting against Charles I by owner John Carter, a friend of Cromwell. The daughter of a later owner fell in love with a young man who was sent to sea to get rid of him, where he was drowned by a crew member. The daughter saw his ghost and drowned herself. The ghosts of the pair were seen floating beside the ship and the guilty crew member confessed, the father dying of a broken heart.

The Old Merchant's House is a 17th century town house with splendid plaster ceilings, local original architectural and domestic fittings and 17th and 19th century ironwork. The Grade II★ Customs House dates from 1720. Great Yarmouth Minster was the largest parish church in England although not the only one to make the claim. Great Yarmouth Exhibition Galleries have their place and Anna Sewell House is the birthplace of the author of *Black Beauty*. The town supplied twice as many ships as any other town for Edward III's siege of Calais. There will be something, somewhere, on the Norfolk Giant, Robert Hales, who died in 1863 aged 43, 2.34m high and weighing 203kg. The filming of *Keeping Up Appearances* recorded some of the town more recently.

Just south of Nelson's Monument and an aerial is a power station with a cooling water outfall structure in the sea off the South Beach. The geography of the area has changed significantly over the years. The spit used to reach to Gunton but in Roman times it was an island. The present river mouth was cut in the 16th century and has been maintained since then. The Great Yarmouth Outer Harbour was added in 2012 with a new port area north of the river entrance. The seabed off Yarmouth is subject to frequent change and is where Robinson Crusoe suffered his first shipwreck, eventually landing north of Winterton Ness, and about which warning was given in *Redgauntlet*.

Flows begin south at HW Dover +0600 and north from HW Dover −0020 at up to 5km/h. In addition, the river is ingoing from at HW Dover +0540 at up to 4km/h and outgoing from HW Dover −0030 at up to 11km/h although the ebb can be continuous for eighteen hours with heavy rain and wind can also have an effect. There is a slack period at local HW +0130 and at local LW +0200.

Cobholm Island

12

Then said the father, 'A trip on the ocean
Jimmy shall go in a ship of my own.
I'll consent that he shall have my daughter
When to fair Yarmouth again he returns.'
Anon

Tides flood south and ebb north. The whole of the east coast here is popular with holidaymakers during the summer but is quiet in winter. **Gorleston** has sand cliffs with a concrete wall at the back of the beach to complicate a high tide beachbreak. The whole of this section of coast has heavy groynes protecting it but large blocks of concrete with steps formed in them stand well forward of the cliffs in places, showing how the sea has eaten back behind this former sea wall.

It is an ill wind that blows nobody any good or, in this case, waves. Hopton can have quite decent surfing conditions at times. At Corton on the B1385, masonry is included in some of the cliff falls, showing that the coastline is still moving inland remorselessly. Naturists and windsurfers enjoy Corton's beach but somebody who didn't was a 17th century exciseman caught by smugglers, who rammed his head down a rabbit hole and drove a stake between his legs to secure him while they handled a cargo. There are a windmill and the remains of a ruined church but the prime businesses today are holiday camps, caravans and the Pleasurewood Hills Theme Park with log flume, chairlift, two railways, pirate ship, sealions and waveswinger.

Progress can be gauged approaching Lowestoft as markers on the shore measure off a nautical mile.

At Lowestoft Denes along the North Beach large mature hotels and guest houses replace the small private houses seen so far. The Scores are steep alleyways down the cliff. Much of the Beach Village was lost in the 1953 storm surge. Lowestoft Maritime Museum covers the fishing fleets and tools, sailing, lifeboats, shipbuilding, a drifter cabin, commercial models of 1880–1960 and marine paintings by Don and Harry Cox.

The lighthouse is on the coastal site with the longest continuous use, chosen 400 years ago. The present 18m tower was operational from 1874 with paraffin, then gas, then electricity from 1936. The Lowestoft lighthouse now has a range of 45km. The high and low lights of 1609 had lanterns added after the locals complained about flying sparks.

The Royal Naval Patrol Service Museum at Sparrow's Nest, named after landowner Robert Sparrow, based in the depot for crews of minesweepers, drifters and trawlers from 1939 to 1946, features naval documents, uniforms, models and a trawler wheelhouse mockup. The landmark from Gorleston has been a wind turbine, tallest in the UK, the 126m Gulliver, an unromantic structure marking the most easterly point in the British Isles, Lowestoft Ness. In 1609 Trinity House built their first lighthouse here.

From here to the harbourmouth at Lowestoft the shoreline is protected with concrete tripods. When approaching from the north the mouth of the harbour seems so insignificant that the true entrance appears to lie somewhere between the South Pier and the decorative Claremont Pier.

However, appearances can be deceptive and that narrow harbourmouth protects a busy harbour which should not be entered unless the harbour is at a quiet period. A yachting harbour on the right is followed by the trawl basin and the not unpleasant smell of fresh fish.

Lowestoft takes its name from the Old Danish man Hlothver and the Old Scandinavian toft, farm. The resort area of Lowestoft was laid out in the second half of the 19th century by Sir Samuel Morton Peto who built the railway so that fish could be delivered fresh to Manchester, a man whose other designs included the Houses of Parliament and Nelson's Column.

Lowestoft was notorious in 1664 for the case in which Amy Duny and Rose Cullender were hanged as witches with subsequent implications for the Salem witch trials of 1692 in the USA. Mostly, it has been a place of the sea, however. It was the birthplace of Sir Thomas Allen, who struck the first blow in the defeat of the Dutch here in 1665 and tackled Algerian pirates in 1669. Sir John Ashby, also born here, commanded the Blue Squadron at the victory of La Hogue in 1691.

The harbour was opened in 1831 and the town became prosperous after the mid 19th century by exploiting the Dogger Bank. Duncan Pike's desperate boast in Susan Hill's *The Albatross* was that he had seen the trawlers at Lowestoft. In *Love on a Branch Line* there is suspicion that *Susie* might be a Lowestoft chorus girl, actually a traction engine. *Guy & Pauline* refers to Lowestoft china and Sabine Baring-Gould's *Mehalah* has undue concern over Lowestoft soup dishes. Edward FitzGerald shared with fisherman Posh, Joseph Fletcher, the cost of their boat, *Meum & Tuum*. Benjamin Britten was born here in 1913.

Three thousand drifters came to Great Yarmouth and Lowestoft every autumn and before the First World War there were seven hundred drifters working out of Lowestoft. There are plaice, cod, dab, dogfish and brill, but there are now less than fifty deep sea trawlers as the town's fleet yet it remains a busy fishing port and fishmarket and Birds Eye Walls remain the town's biggest employers.

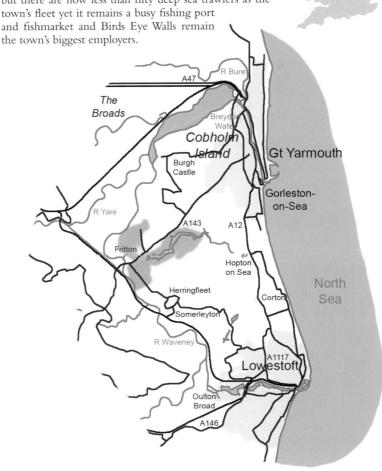

59

Lowestoft Ness and its direction and distance indicator.

Gulliver, the unromantic marker of Britain's easterly point.

The entrance to Lowestoft harbour in a summer haze.

In 1916 the town was bombarded by eight German battle cruisers.

A son of the town was anti-Puritan satirist Thomas Nash while Benjamin Britten was born here in 1913.

A hotelier suggested that the port could operate a hovercraft service across the North Sea to bring in more business. In *The Annals of Imperial Rome* Tacitus describes the North Sea as the roughest in the world, which may have been the case as far as the Roman knowledge of oceans went.

The inner harbour and Lake Lothing are approached straight ahead under the lifting bridge. Lake Lothing is the main industrial port with rig supply vessels, shipbuilding and coastal freighters. Scrap steel and paper bales line the quay with the A146 running parallel and it is only towards the western end that the risk of obstructing the movement of a large vessel lessens and pleasure craft moorings are met. In amongst these is a test structure used for dropping lifeboats into the water from considerable heights.

Just before Mutford Lock are a swing railway bridge, a sunken vessel of some size and a lifting road bridge. Mutford Lock in **Lowestoft** is adjacent to the A1117 crossing and was constructed in 1831 to cut through a neck of land. Although it is only opened on limited occasions, it has to cater for tide differences in either direction and so has eight gates, a set of four in diamond formation at each end.

Swing railway bridge at the west end of Lake Lothing.

The built up end of Oulton Broad.

The pioneering Somerleyton swing railway bridge.

The water is tidal on both sides although at significantly different times on the tidal cycle. There are times when a falling tide on one side makes a level with a rising tide on the other and all gates could be opened briefly.

The scenery is very different on the two sides of the lock. On the west side is Oulton Broad. Launching is not possible from the Wherry Hotel to the right of the lock, the left bank of the lock is private according to the British Transport Commission notice and use of the harbour further left again could incur the fee chargeable to all vessels. It may be that the BTC would not object to bona fide craft being carried past the lock over their property as they ceased to exist under that name in 1962. Tom Dudgeon received a telegram here in Arthur Ransome's *Coot Club* and the Wherry Hotel was used by the *Teasel*'s crew.

The east end of the broad is populated by ducks which march around in armies, begging for food, but which refuse to stand up to get out of the way of pedestrians. The area is pleasantly rural with even the toilets thatched. The Grade II brick and flint Lowestoft Museum in Nicholas Everitt Park has Lowestoft porcelain and a millennium of local history while marine and archaeological exhibitions stand nearby. The broad has powerboat racing. In 1956 Sir Christopher Cockerell used the broad to test his first working hovercraft.

Oulton Dyke leads north to join the tidal River Waveney which forms the Norfolk/Suffolk boundary from here to Breydon Water.

The River Waveney offers an environment for simply being alone with the water, the sky and a line of reeds down each bank. In winter the reeds are harvested in sheaves for thatching, the stubble being burned back to encourage new growth. The hand harvesting leaves a line of reeds at the water's edge, those growing just out of reach from the dry land.

At Somerleyton the railway crosses one of a pair of swing bridges, the other being at Reedham. These were the first swing railway bridges and are each 42m long with double tracks. Repairs to the bearings in 2010 needed handmade parts.

Somerleyton Staithe marks Somerleyton, a mid 19th century village with ornamental cottages built by railway engineer and developer Samuel Morton Peto. The village is best known for the Grade II★ Somerleyton Hall & Gardens.

By now streams have become strong and tidal flows

The arched bridge across the river at St Olaves.

Herringfleet Mill stands behind the reeds by the river.

Pleasure craft on the River Waveney at St Olaves.

Remains of the Roman Burgh Castle.

are a major factor in progress. The Landspring Beck arrives unobtrusively. On the other bank is the Grade II★ Herringfleet Mill, built about 1820, the last surviving smock drainage mill in the Broads and the last full size working mill in the county. It has four sails and a braced tailpole with hand winch, octagonal with tarred weatherboarding and a boat cap, clinker built in three dimensional curves and tapers. The external 4.9m x 230mm scoop wheel lifts water 3m to the river. It is still operated sometimes.

The Herringfleet Hills arrive suddenly on the right. Rearing to a height of 20m, they seem relative mountains in this flat area, some of which is below sea level. Pillars remain from another swing railway bridge and a signal box on the disused line has been converted to a house with its own mooring.

The New Cut bears left to the River Yare just before St Olaves, a village with a fine street of 17th century houses and the remains of a 14th century Augustinian priory. The old Bell Inn and a grocery store front the river opposite

a couple of marinas and the village is finished off with a miniature windmill after the A143.

The river curves back in a loop, almost meeting the New Cut again.

In this area it is common for overhead wires to be lifted well clear of shipping on high pylons but the ones here are unusual in that they are rectangular and have no arms, unlike the more usual tapered structures.

After skirting Fritton Marshes, the river passes the Scots pines of Waveney Forest, a major feature in a landscape generally flat and devoid of trees.

Trees do not reappear until the Roman Burgh Castle, a scrappy hamlet of caravans, ship repairers and the Fisherman's Inn. A line of greengage trees runs parallel with the river near the castle.

Burgh Castle itself is in a remarkably good state of repair with three of the four walls of this trapezoidal fort built in 297 still intact. Gariannonum was one of a line of forts built up the east coast to resist the Saxons who were less subdued here than in the south.

The A47 crosses the northeastern end of Breydon Water on a lifting bridge.

The lifting bridge in Great Yarmouth with the Elizabethan House beyond.

The lighthouse in Gorleston.

Passing the round towered church of St Peter & St Paul, the Waveney joins the Yare at the southwest end of Breydon Water.

The lake is a nature reserve and its most characteristic residents are cormorants which stand on top of the poles lining the navigation channel with their wings outstretched in a vertical cruciform, faces to the wind, in order to dry their feathers. One of the fairway marks was the downfall of the *Margoletta* in the *Coot Club*. The lake would probably be of more interest to wildlife were it not for its sloping concrete sides. A windpump behind the southern levée is typical of those used by kestrels as nesting sites.

A pier and the A47 Yarmouth by pass bridge at the east end of Breydon Water are the only warning of the dramatic change that takes place on turning the corner. Suddenly the countryside becomes **Great Yarmouth** in a few metres. The River Bure leads in from the rest of the Broads.

A notice forbids hire craft from going any further and this should apply to smaller craft unless they can be sure that they will not get into difficulty in the fast currents and they will not interrupt the movements of the many commercial ships in the narrow and busy final 5km to the sea.

This final run is filled with industrial activity and interest, ancient and modern. Just beyond the bascule bridge carrying the A12, on the right is a magnificent thatched warehouse with a wherry weathervane.

Yarmouth has been one of the largest herring ports in the world. In medieval times it was famous for smoked red herrings because shoals of herrings congregated off the coast each autumn. In the 19th century the coming of the railways meant that many more people could buy the Yarmouth bloater. The peak came in 1913 with a thousand vessels operating out of the port but use of the drifters as wartime minesweepers and overfishing of stocks in peacetime have destroyed the industry. The port saw increased trade with the Continent in 1665 when London was closed down because of the plague.

However, instead of bewailing its loss, Yarmouth has turned to other industry. Since the 1960s it has become a base for first the offshore gas industry and then the oil industry. A run down to the South Denes passes rig supply vessels, small fishing boats, new minesweepers under construction, a lightship, the Yarmouth lifeboat and continuous industry with names familiar throughout the offshore world. One of the less likely names was the Turmeric steel fabrication yard. The name originally belonged to two women running an ailing domestic business. The whole firm was bought as being quicker than registering a new name. The yard was to turn out some sizeable structures for the North Sea oil industry.

The Ferry Boat Inn may offer services required but this is not a wise place to stop.

The final turn east out into the North Sea at the Brush involves passing a jetty which can obscure until the last moment large vessels turning into the rivermouth.

Distance
Cobholm Island is 66km long and lies 40m off Lowestoft with road access

OS 1:50,000 Sheet
134 Norwich & the Broads

Tidal Constants
Gorleston:
HW Dover −0220,
LW Dover −0210
Lowestoft:
Dover −0140

Sea Area
Thames

Connections
River Waveney –
see RoB p187
River Yare –
see RoB p185
River Bure –
see RoB p178

The harbourmouth at Great Yarmouth, overlooked by the coastguard station.

13 Haddiscoe Island

The tallest drainage windmill in Norfolk

This island is a relatively recent arrival. In Anglo-Saxon times the area was all part of a broad estuary with several outlets to the sea. Then, in medieval times, the land rose, producing areas of marsh flanking the River Yare and the River Waveney but even now much of the surrounding land is below sea level.

The low lying nature of the land makes it susceptible to any wind but that same wind was seen as a power source for pumping excess water from the low lying areas up to the rivers. As a result numerous windmills were built and most remain, in various states of repair.

Finally, the peninsula between the two rivers was severed from the surrounding area in 1832 when the New Cut or Haddiscoe Cut was dug from Reedham to St Olaves. Surprisingly, the dead straight New Cut connects to a point south of St Olaves, on the way passing very close to a loop of the River Waveney which could have reduced the length of the cut by a third and saved a bridge. It was used by the barge *Welcome* in Arthur Ransome's *Coot Club* to avoid the bridge at St Olaves.

The waters around the island are tidal, tides setting from the Reedham end of the New Cut. Road access is most convenient from the A143 at St Olaves and this suggests launching about low tide to get the maximum benefit from the tide, down one river with the slack and back up the other with the flood.

Parking is conveniently available where a piece of approach road to the former low level bridge remains next to its high level modern day counterpart. The foundations for both project into the New Cut, reducing it to half its normal width and providing the only feature in its straight 4km length. The former low bridge used to open, the keepers collecting payment with a net on the end of a pole.

The jetty of the former Bridge public house makes a convenient launch point.

On the right the island has been sheet piled adjacent to the water and a concrete beam runs along the top of the bank, marking further flood defence works.

The Norwich to Lowestoft railway has been constructed on the southwest bank of the New Cut but just before Reedham it curves away to the left before crossing the River Yare on a swing bridge.

Little is seen of the attractive thatched village of Reedham as the route now turns right onto the River Yare.

The church tower at Wickhampton is visible over the reeds and nearer but less obvious are a pair of green lids enclosing units which replace an older sewage works.

Boat traffic can now be heavier because, in addition to all the holiday cruisers, the river is used by coastal freighters going up to Norwich. In the winter, when things are quieter, shelducks and oystercatchers may be seen and even common seals may come ashore and rest up beside the river in Reedham Marshes, launching themselves back into their safe element like tree trunks just in front of the approaching boat. Swans are common but they are used to boats and the river is wide so there are no problems.

One of the mills in the marshes has arms but from there can be seen the fully restored Berney Arms mill, its white sails and rotating cap mounted on a tarred brick body. At 21m high, it was built in 1870 as Norfolk's tallest drainage windmill.

Red and green posts mark the navigation channel from Berney Arms as it leads out onto Breydon Water, a large lake which acts as a nature reserve, and the higher buildings of Great Yarmouth appear on the skyline. The 8km/h and 11km/h speed limits are lifted on the lake but a speed restriction is reimposed on the River Waveney although many boats seem to take little notice of it. The washes they throw up add to any windblown waves, at their largest at this corner of Breydon Water. Floating seaweed is a reminder of the proximity of the sea.

The return along the River Waveney is described in the previous chapter, this time going with the river flow.

After turning back onto the New Cut, a marina entrance is passed before arriving back at the A143.

The New Cut slices towards Reedham.

The New Cut meets up with the River Waveney.

Berney Arms mill seen from the Roman walls of Burgh Castle.

Distance
Haddiscoe Island is 6km long and lies 40m off St Olaves with road access

OS 1:50,000 Sheet
134 Norwich & the Broads

Tidal Constants
Gorleston:
HW Dover −0220,
LW Dover −0210

Sea Area
Thames

Connections
River Waveney –
see RoB p189
River Yare –
see RoB p184

14 North Suffolk

Suffolk's small coastal broads

In Lowestoft a boat was laid,
  Mark well what I do say!
And she was built for the herring trade,
  But she has gone a-rovin', a-rovin', a-rovin',
  The Lord knows where!

Rudyard Kipling

Lowestoft's East Point Pavilion Visitor Centre with Niblets café in an Edwardian style building at the south side of the entrance to Lake Lothing is themed on a North Sea gas exploration rig.

Flows south begin at HW Dover −0610 and north at HW Dover +0010 at up to 5km/h, flow and levels being affected by the wind. Claremont Pier was built in 1903 out into Lowestoft South Roads, in all a total length of 204m. The Centre for Environment, Fisheries & Aquaculture offices overlook the beach. Initially the beach is in front of such establishments as the Hotel Hatfield and the Jolly Roger plus the obligatory fire beacon. Low cliffs and beaches follow to Southwold and the Suffolk Coast Path continues to Felixstowe.

There is a water tower as Lowestoft merges into Pakefield and the church of St Margaret and All Saints which, until 1748, was two churches in one with two parishes and two rectors. It was restored after being badly damaged in the Second World War. Pakefield also has a holiday camp. Stevie Smith recalled holidays here in *Novel on Yellow Paper*. Pakefield Hall brings a break in the built up area.

Kessingland has the standard fire beacon and holiday camp. African wildlife is to be found in Africa Alive! There is an ancient forest on the seabed. Finds of Paleolithic and Neolithic implements show this has long been a popular resort. In 1745 customs officers watched five cargoes being unloaded by smugglers but made no arrests because of the large numbers present. The *Elizabeth Henrietta* beached in 1810 and the crew got ashore on lines but the captain refused and was lost. A further beaching in 1875 was the landing of a 3.6m shark. The village had a lifeboat until 1936. Sir Henry Rider Haggard was born here, bought the Grange and was visited by Rudyard Kipling.

Offshore banks close with the shore at Benacre Ness, where the Hundred River or Latymere Dam discharges. The coast is eroding so trees may be found in the sea.

Claremont Pier at Lowestoft, now past its best.

Multiple lines of electric fences keep the public away from Benacre Broad.

From here to Southwold the sea is eating into the ends of several ridges of deep honey-coloured sand separated by low lying land, some of which contains small broads, a coast joined by the Suffolk Coast & Heaths Path. A number of submarine cables were landed on this easy section of coast. Largest of the broads is Benacre Broad, overlooked by a large hide for twitchers. Others are kept away from areas of the beach used for nesting by little terns by multiple lines of electric fences. Natural England have closed to the public several square kilometres of land to the west of here which they have designated a conservation area.

The former medieval port of Covehithe's 15th century St Andrew's Grade I church became too large to maintain so villagers built a smaller thatched one inside the roofless and windowless shell of its predecessor in 1672. It contains a medieval font.

Covehithe Cliffs lead to Covehithe Broad, a reedy lagoon with much birdlife amongst the dunes. Beyond Easton Broad are 10m high Easton Cliffs, off which jellyfish are found.

Southwold, from the Old English *suth wald*, place in the southern forest, was a prosperous 11th century fishing port with one of the oldest charters in England, dating from Henry VII in 1489 and celebrated in late May or early June at

67

The seafront at Southwold with the lighthouse just visible.

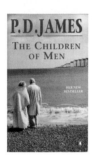
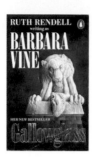

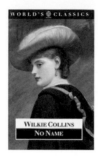

the Charter Fair, opened by the mayor's taking the first ride on the merry go round. It became Gordon Brown's chosen holiday destination. The 15th century Grade I Perpendicular church of St Edmund has a magnificent screen of about 1500, many wooden angels in the roof and Southwold Jack, an earlier oak figure of a man at arms with sword and Wars of the Roses equipment, who strikes a bell with his axe when a cord is pulled to signal the start of a service or the entry of a bride at a wedding.

Guncliffe Hill was used as the site the six 8kg guns provided by Charles I in the 1630s to protect against Dunkirk privateers. These were replaced in 1745 by George II. The guns were 150 years old at the time so it should be no surprise that a local ghost is a headless gunner after one of the guns exploded.

During the First World War they were bombarded by the Germans so the guns were then hidden away during both World Wars.

This is Pevsner's most delightful of English seaside towns, with a mixture of Dutch influence, Georgian, Regency and Victorian houses with red brick and flint fishermen's cottages round open firebreak greens, the layout the results of a fire in 1659.

At the end of the A1095, Southwold is almost an island, being circled by the Buss Creek which is named after herring busses. Arguments with the Dutch over herrings led to the Battle of Sole Bay in 1672 when

130 Dutch ships under de Ruyter faced 150 English and French ships. Following instructions from Louis XV, who wanted the English and Dutch fleets to destroy each other, the French sailed away before the start. The outcome was as they had hoped, bloody but indecisive. The battle is recalled in Broadside ale brewed in the town by Adnams, the oldest brewery in Suffolk, the largest employer in the town, still pulling some drays with Percheron horses. There was brewing here in the 14th century, Ernest and George Adnams buying the brewery in 1872 but George meeting a bitter end when eaten by a crocodile in Africa. The British Free Fishery was founded here in 1750. The current catch includes flatfish, sprats and cod.

The lighthouse with its 32km range was built in 1887 and features in the *Grandpa in My Pocket* TV show. The 190m pier was destroyed progressively by a wartime mine and storms in 1934, 1955 and 1979. Its restoration was completed in 2002 with an amusement arcade. Its landward end is set about with beach huts and in the tarmac are a couple of hoofprints which, it is suggested, represent a relatively recent visit by the Devil.

In *The Children of Men* PD James describes a Quietus here, a mass suicide of the elderly, theoretically voluntary. Paul Garnet and Nina Apsoland have a day out together here in Barbara Vine's *Gallowglass*. Wilkie Collins set a significant part of *No Name* in the town. George Orwell lived from 1930 to 1933 in his parents' house and taught here, writer Neil Bell was born in the town and Southwold was Hardborough in Penelope Fitzgerald's *The Bookshop*. There are literary and arts festivals. For retired seamen there is the Southwold Sailor's Reading Room along with ship models, local history, archaeology and natural history. The town also has the Southwold Railway and a whipping post.

Blackbacked gulls wait on the groynes for food and a ghostly war widow waits at the upstairs window of a restaurant in the town.

Alfred Corry Lifeboat Museum has been set up in the former Cromer lifeboat station by the River Blyth which has been re-erected here to house the *Alfred Corry*, one of the oldest lifeboats in existence, a boat which was rowed and sometimes used under sail. The river used to discharge at Dunwich with a long spit, but a new entrance was cut in 1590. It produces fast currents with an ebb of up to 9km/h which can produce a confused sea at the entrance with an onshore wind. The gravel bar changes position off the entrance piers and there can be heavy surf. Slack is at local HW +0030. A protective mole on the north side of the entrance was rejected as it might have further stripped Walberswick's beach.

There is a carpark serving Walberswick beach near the end of the B1387 but it is locked at 7pm over weekends in the summer to deter campers.

Distance
18km from Lowestoft to Walberswick

OS 1:50,000 Sheets
134 Norwich & the Broads
156 Saxmundham

Tidal Constants
Lowestoft:
Dover −0140
Southwold:
Dover −0100

Sea Area
Thames

South Suffolk

Walberswick is sometimes referred to as Hampstead-on-Sea for its superior atmosphere. Holiday homes are located in former quayside sheds of what was a prosperous fishing and shipbuilding village, taking over as Dunwich declined in the 13th century. Its popularity with artists is not new, English impressionist Philip Wilson Steer having lived in Valley Farm. Charles Rennie Mackintosh also had a house here. The British Open Crabbing Championships are held here annually. Birdwatchers are another group who flock here and not just for the skylarks by the beach. The village and shore, together with the Suffolk Heritage Coast, are displayed in the Heritage Coast Centre on the Green. Maggie Hemingway set *The Bridge* in the village.

In the mid 1700s black drummer Tobias Gill drank here because he was banned from public houses in Blythburgh where his regiment were quartered as he was badly affected by drink. He was found drunk beside the dead body of local girl Ann Blackmore on the way back to Blythburgh and was hanged for rape and murder. A phantom coach pulled by headless horses and whipped by a black driver is sometimes seen in the lane.

A windmill stands beyond Corporation and Redland Marshes on the far side of the Dunwich River which joins the River Blyth at Walberswick. Until 1590, when the new exit to the River Blyth was cut, it flowed south to discharge at Dunwich.

A Roman settlement and then an Anglo-Saxon city, Dunwich had 5,000 inhabitants and nine churches in Norman times and was the fifth busiest port in England, the most prosperous town in Suffolk. Beaches used to be protected by piling them with brushwood weighted by stones. In January 1326 the port was inundated, losing 400 houses and three churches. The town lost 400m of coast in 400 years although it is now fairly stable. The Franciscan Grey Friars had their first monastery washed away 12 years after building it in the 14th century, a wall and two gatehouses remaining from a later attempt. The 1832 church of St James with the remains of the earlier All Saints and the Leper Hospital have just one grave remaining although human bones project from the eroding cliff. Shadowy figures of residents of the city are sometimes seen on the clifftops, lights come from the priory, the sound of monks chanting has been heard and the bells from a dozen churches are claimed to ring from under the sea on stormy nights.

Dunwich Museum illustrates the city from Roman times and features the local wildlife, the locality having many birds, butterflies and insects among the heather and gorse. The sea has produced plaice, dabs, sole, cod and smuggling.

Writers have been attracted here. *English Hours* calls it desolate and exquisite. Paul Garnet had been born here in *Gallowglass*. PD James lived in Dunwich, setting several Adam Dalgleish stories in the vicinity. *Unnatural Causes* is set in Minsmere and also in Dunwich, Dunwich Heath becoming Monksmere Head with Minsmere as Monksmere. Larksoken power station is based on Sizewell and the

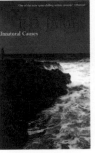
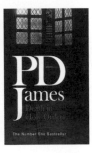

Dunwich is now no more than a small village on the sandy cliffs.

Sizewell nuclear power station is a distinctive landmark.

Half timbered houses in the fantasy village of Thorpeness.

The magnificent Moot Hall by the beach in Aldeburgh.

Black Dog, a phantom which is seen at night and causes depression, is well known in the area and has particular associations with Blythburgh and Bungay. Her book *Death in Holy Orders* is set south of Sizewell. Algernon Swinburne wrote lines about Dunwich and Henry James wrote about the village in *English Hours*. Dunwich was visited by keels from Iceland in *A Dream of John Ball* by William Morris. Edward Thomas wrote his biography of Richard Jeffries in a Dunwich Heath coastguard cottage. John Seymour's post-Crash novel *Retrieved from the Future* was based in the area and Dunwich was described in *The Bridge*.

Cliffs to the south of Dunwich are topped by Dunwich Heath, the remains of the Suffolk Sandlings heathland with bracken, heather, gorse and silver birch, inhabited by kestrel, partridge, red legged partridge, skylark, stonechat, meadow pipit, pied wagtail, linnet, goldfinch, redpoll and yellowhammer, joined by migrant warblers and wildfowl in the winter and by stone curlew, cuckoo, nightjar, swallow, sand martin, lesser whitethroat, willow warbler, wheatear, whinchat, tree pipit and yellow wagtail in the summer plus breeding heathland birds. The effect is somewhat spoiled by all the caravans dotted along the edge, by a line of cottages (off which is a historic wreck site) with a large and conspicuous hide added in the end and by many cars glinting in the sunshine in the RSPB's carparks.

Minsmere Level has been their prime site since 1947, 10km² of nature reserve, perhaps the best in Britain, marsh, lagoon, reedbed, heath, scrub, woodland, meadow and island. Access is restricted. Over 340 species of bird have been recorded, a third of them nesting, the greatest variety of any reserve in the country, including avocet, nightjar, woodcock, nightingale, marsh harrier and a third of the UK's breeding bitterns. In the autumn there are many waterbirds, even spoonbill and purple heron. Residents include heron, water rail, kingfisher and bearded reedling. Winter visitors include red throated diver, scoter, eider and hen harrier and summer visitors include garganey, gadwall, shoveler, redstart, red backed shrike, Cetti's, reed, sedge and grasshopper warblers and corn bunting while spotted redshank, little stint, black and bar tailed godwits and ruff are birds of passage. Over 1,000 butterfly and moth species include the Minsmere common underwing, not found elsewhere in Britain.

The cliffs end before the Minsmere River passes a windpump and old chapel site to discharge into Minsmere Haven at the Sluice.

The most conspicuous feature on the coast is Sizewell nuclear power station. The Magnox Sizewell A was in production from 1966 to 2006. Sizewell B of 1995 with its white dome is the only British PWR nuclear station, using 120,000m³/h of seawater for cooling, the warm water attracting fish and anglers. Towers off the coast are used as nesting sites by gulls and cormorants, which will not have too far to go for meals, and there are terns in the vicinity.

This smuggling village once handled 36,000l of gin in a single night. Its beacon was last used in 1918 by British warships to get bearings prior to bombarding Zeebrugge.

Sizewell Hall is used as a Christian conference centre, a grand structure, but is to be upstaged. South of Thorpe Ness, where large holes are formed in the shingle by wind and tides, is a pillbox on the sand cliffs and then the unique village of Thorpeness at the end of the B1353, planned in 1910 by barrister, dramatist and author Glencairn Stuart Ogilvie as a self catering village for those wanting to experience the Merrie England lifestyle, this being a project which was to fail. The houses are mostly of concrete although disguised as Tudor, Elizabethan, Jacobean, 18th century East Anglian tarred weatherboard and the like. An 1824 post windmill, used to house displays on the village and Suffolk Heritage Coast, was moved from Aldringham in the 1920s to pump water to the House in the Clouds, a water tower disguised as a seven storey clapboarded house. The Meare is a 26ha boating and wildlife lake with a *Peter Pan* theme, JM Barrie having been a regular visitor, and it also hosts the Thorpeness Regatta & Fireworks in August.

John Seymour

Aldeburgh is from the Anglo Saxon aldburh, old fort, or the Old English Alda's fort. In the 16th century it was a prosperous fishing port. Lobster pots are laid off the beach and catches are sold straight from the boats drawn up on the beach amongst the sea holly, rest harrow, sea kale, sea pea and horned poppy. Thus, the fish and chips in the village are claimed to be the best in the world. A giant scallop shell sculpture on the beach by Maggi Hambling is dedicated to local resident Benjamin Britten.

The village was put on the map by Britten who, in 1948, with singer Peter Pears, started the Aldeburgh Festival each June in the Jubilee Hall before moving it to Snape Maltings. The Moot Hall, a magnificent half-timbered herringbone brick and stone building of 1520–

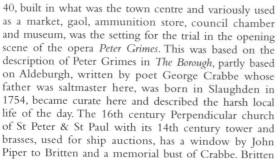

40, built in what was the town centre and variously used as a market, gaol, ammunition store, council chamber and museum, was the setting for the trial in the opening scene of the opera *Peter Grimes*. This was based on the description of Peter Grimes in *The Borough*, partly based on Aldeburgh, written by poet George Crabbe whose father was saltmaster here, was born in Slaughden in 1754, became curate here and described the harsh local life of the day. The 16th century Perpendicular church of St Peter & St Paul with its 14th century tower and brasses, used for ship auctions, has a window by John Piper to Britten and a memorial bust of Crabbe. Britten and Pears are buried in the churchyard, as is Elizabeth Garrett Anderson, England's first woman doctor and, in 1908, the first lady mayor.

In 1645 the Witchfinder General, Matthew Hopkins, was paid the significant sum of £6 for his gruesome services in clearing the village of witches. It was to become a village with two towers belonging to rival gangs trying to be the first to spot shipwreck cargo. By the early 19th century it had become a respectable resort and many of the remaining houses are 19th century with Flemish gables. Seven of the crew of the lifeboat were drowned in a capsize in 1899 while returning through surf. The beach produces amber and the Amber Shop is the largest and oldest in Britain. Behind the beach is a boating pool watched over by a statue of the terrier of Dr Robin Acheson, the doctor from 1931 to 1959, whose dog liked to watch model boats being sailed. The firebeacon is modern and there is an Olde Marine Regatta & Carnival with fireworks.

Seafront House is where the opera *Billy Budd* was written and EM Forster stayed and was involved in writing the libretto. The village has long been popular with writers. *No Name* was set in the village in 1862. Ghost and mystery story writer Montague Rhodes James visited regularly, especially from 1922 to 1936, setting *A Warning to the Curious* on the beach. Susan Hill visited in the 1960s and set the ghost story *The Woman in Black* and other novels in the surrounding villages. Aldeburgh

The dog which liked to watch model boats.

is Heype in *The Albatross* and it also inspired her to write *Strange Meeting* and *The Bird of Night*. Barbara Vine, usually writing as Ruth Rendell, had a house here and based Nunthorpe in *No Night is Too Long* on the village although its location was given as north of Aldeburgh, perhaps Thorpeness. Aldeburgh was Owlbarrow, Kathleen Hale's holiday home for Orlando the Marmalade Cat. Freya and Logan Mountstuart rented a house here for a couple of months in William Boyd's *Any Human Heart*. There is a spring Literary Festival.

A number of submarine cables land at Aldeburgh. The village is at the end of the A1094 and at the end of Orford Ness, a 16km spit which is growing at 15m per year. This is the largest vegetated spit in Europe with shingle, saltmarsh, mudflat, brackish lagoons and grazing marsh, important for breeding and passage birds, and shingle flora with many rare species. Blackbacked gulls from the sea and shelducks from the river fly over and there are hares. Aldeburgh is almost at the end of the River Alde, later the River Ore, which comes within 100m of the sea here.

Aldeburgh is also the start of a line of 102 Martello towers built in the 1880s to protect the coast against Napoléon, 47 of which survive. Based on the tower at Cape Mortella (meaning myrtle) in Corsica which had stood up well to a British bombardment, a tower was usually slightly egg-shaped in plan, used 700,000 bricks, had doors high up which were reached by removeable ladders and had an 11kg gun and two 140mm howitzers. The first tower is unusual in being larger and quatrefoil in plan. In 1801 Nelson took command of protecting the coast from here to Beachy Head while a French invasion was threatened.

Flows begin south–southwest from HW Dover –0550 and north–northeast from HW Dover +0020 at up 6km/h.

Plaice, sole, flounders, bass and cod are found off the 4–5m high gravel ridge of Sudbourne Beach, which has produced amber and bloodstones and which anglers are allowed to use but off which others are kept, initially because of a SSSI with nesting birds including avocets and then because of military interests, being a secret military site from 1913 to 1993, used by the Royal Flying Corps, RAF and Atomic Weapons Research

The first Martello tower at Aldeburgh begins the line of defences.

Orford Ness lighthouse with erosion protection.

The Suffolk Coast & Heaths Path skirts Oxley Marshes and follows the coast to Felixstowe, passing another four Martello towers before Bawdsey, where there is a Second World War gun emplacement.

Bawdsey Cliff stands 12–15m high with the former of RAF Bawdsey on top. There have been a number of slips and rabbits dig in the exposed material. The beach looks attractive from offshore but close up it is as dirty as they come with jagged pieces of broken glass everywhere and a thick layer of decaying polystyrene cups along the beach, together with other debris. In the 18th century it was used by smugglers Margaret Catchpole and William Lauder, as recorded in the Rev Richard Cobbald's partly factual novel.

A radio tower stands along from Bawdsey Manor, started in 1886 for Sir William Cuthbert Quilterbut in a fantasy of Victorian, Gothic, Flemish, Tudor and Oriental styles with a dragon shaped weather vane. It was here that Robert Watson-Watt developed radar before the Second World War, to prove of major importance in winning the Battle of Britain. It has a museum but is mostly used for social functions.

Cliffs and grassy banks surround Woodbridge Haven,

Establishment for the first radar experiments and for atomic weapons teasting during the Cold War. The numbers and positions of experimental radio masts on Lantern Marshes varied and were used for the USAF's Cobra Mist. From 1967 to 1970 they were used for over the horizon radar for early warning of ballistic missiles but it not only failed to work properly but also interfered with ship's radios. Some conspicuous structures remain, including a number of high masts which served a transmission station for the BBC's World Service. There may still be unexploded ordnance on the spit. There have also been claims of UFO sightings here.

Flows are strongest at Orford Ness itself and there are overfalls off the ness on the ebb and a wreck beyond them. There have been lighthouses at the ness since 1627 when 32 ships were lost in one night. The disused 30m white lighthouse tower with red bands was built in 1792, at one time Trinity House's most powerful at 30,000,000 candelas.

In the 16th century the spit ended at Orford but it now extends another 8km along Orford Beach. Orford Haven entrance is dangerous in strong onshore winds, especially with a strong ebb on a spring tide, and is turbulent near the bar. The offshore flow begins southwest at HW Dover –0550 and northeast from HW Dover +0050, the flood into the River Ore beginning at HW Dover –0500 and the outgoing flow from HW Dover +0120 at up to 11km/h.

There is a SSSI around the entrance. A different form of wildlife is associated with Hollesley Young Offenders Institute, the residents of which included Brendan Behan in 1958, who wrote about it and about swimming at Shingle Street in *Borstal Boy*. Amber may be found on the gravel beach at Shingle Street where there is parking, sometimes in appropriately deep gravel. Never revealed was the reason why the village had to be evacuated on one occasion during the Second World War. It was blamed on a failed German invasion but the destruction of the Navigation Inn by a bomb developed by Porton Down may have had more to do with it.

Felixstowe from the heavily slipped cliff at Bawdsey.

the mouth of the River Deben, dangerous in strong onshore winds, especially with a strong ebb on spring tides, with a further complication that the bar shifts. Flows begin inwards from HW Dover –0620 at up to 7km/h and outwards from HW Dover +0040 at up to 9km/h. There is a summer passenger ferry across to Felixstowe Ferry, a venue guarded by the Walton Castle Roman fort site and by a pair of Martello towers now with a golf course between them.

Felixstowe is met with tiers of brightly painted beach huts, a sight to be seen regularly from here southwards. The water comes under the control of Harwich Haven Authority before Cobbald's Point. Felixstowe, from the Old English for Filicia's meeting place, is an Edwardian resort of gabled houses with gardens and parks, a water clock, waterfall, grotto, arboretum and Italian garden. The German Empress Augusta made it fashionable after an 1891 visit, Wallis Simpson waited here for the divorce of Edward VIII

Brightly painted beach huts at Felixstowe. There are many more to come further south.

Landguard Fort on the right, the radar scanner and the cranes of Felixstowe.

and other visitors included Kaiser Wilhelm II and TE Lawrence. Alan Jacobson, Mr Suffolk, lived here, as did novelist Robert Greenwood. *Novel on Yellow Paper* refers to the beach and describes the North Sea ferries. Jennifer Coombe's family had a holiday here in *The Loving Spirit*. and Paul Gernet promised daughter Jessica a trip here in *Gallowglass*. Rita, a former Miss Felixstowe, was shown to be the daughter of a bad loser in the ankle competition in *Love on a Branch Line*. Old pier remains cover at low water but there is a much larger affair in the centre of the shallow bay. There are a couple of Martello towers among the buildings, one housing a coastguard station, and the remains of an old fort near low water. The Fludyers Hotel is prominent but not so much as a pink construction on the shore. Charles Manning's Amusement Park and a Quasar game are among the local entertainments. Dominating the skyline are the cranes of Britain's leading container port which faces onto Harwich Harbour behind the A154, one of the largest container ports in Europe, handling 4,000,000 containers per year. The UK's ninth busiest port, it is the busiest of those not handling fuel. The harbour was protected by Landguard Fort, first built in 1543, attacked unsuccessfully by the Dutch in 1667, the last invasion in England, and rebuilt in 1744. In 1763 the governor caused furore by using the chapel over the gateway for a dance, employing the altar as a bar. The fort was modified in 1875, 1890, 1901 and 1914 and used until 1956. The Ravelin block next to the fort houses the Felixstowe Museum which features the fort. A nature reserve with restricted areas for ground nesting birds and overlooked by hides occupies much of the area to Landguard Point, although a large mast bearing a radar scanner is a prominent landmark. Frederick Marryat's *Frank Mildmay; or the Naval Officer* refers to the gunner here as having no powder. St Andrews Spit extends from the point with a wreck on it off the point.

Flows run southwest from HW Dover −0600 at up to 2km/h and northeast from HW Dover +0050 at up to 3km/h. Flows into the harbour, the mouth of the River Orwell and the River Stour, and the ebb flows are up to 2km/h. Occasional isolated waves, the better part of a metre high, can be thrown up by container ships. It was the route taken unintentionally from Pin Mill to Flushing in Arthur Ransome's *We Didn't Mean to Go to Sea*. In addition to all the container ships there are car ferries from Harwich to Cuxhaven, Turku, Esbjerg, Gothenburg and Hoek van Holland plus many pleasure craft. The Harwich Deep Water Channel is on the east side of the harbourmouth close to Landguard Point, is relatively narrow and is clearly buoyed in an area which sees extensive bed movements.

Crossing the harbourmouth takes boats from Suffolk to Essex with the Essex Way running along the front of **Harwich** (from the Old English herewic, army camp) past a line of figures cut in the chalk. Edward III marshalled a fleet here in 1340 to defeat the French at Sluys, the opening major sea battle of the Hundred Years War. It was a royal naval dockyard from the 17th century when Samuel Pepys was MP. Drake, Frobisher, Hawkins, Cavendish, Nelson and Raleigh sailed from here, it was home to Christopher Jones, master of the *Mayflower*, and Charles II sailed the first pleasure yacht from here. It was also where 6,000 Spaniards were to be landed in 1571 to replace Elizabeth with Mary, Queen of Scots if the Ridolfi plot had succeeded.

In 1753 Joseph Pain arrived just in time to stop 16 year old son Tom signing up with Captain Death on the privateer *The Terrible*, his first bid for the sea. Turner is thought to have painted *Snow Storm* after having himself strapped to a mast for four hours to experience it. Daniel Defoe's Moll Flanders stole luggage in Harwich and took it to Ipswich while waiting for the heat to die down on her activities in London.

Dovercourt was a resort from the 1850s with a boating lake and a 3km promenade. Two disused leading lights of 1863 on cast iron tubular legs are the last surviving pair of iron light towers on the British coast. They were superseded by buoys in 1917. The landward one resembles one illustrated in Nellie L Yates' child's religious book *Sylvia*. This suggests her Havendock might have been Harwich.

There is limited amount of parking near a boating lake. The beach is of sand and this is where *Hi-de-hi* sequences were filmed by the BBC.

The Harwich Deep Water Channel leading into Harwich Harbour is busy but relatively narrow so it can be crossed quite quickly.

Leading lights including the last surviving cast iron light towers on the British coast at Dovercourt.

Distance
54km from
Walberswick to
Dovercourt

OS 1:50,000 Sheets
156 Saxmundham
169 Ipswich
& the Naze

Tidal Constants
Southwold:
Dover −0100
Aldeburgh:
HW Dover −0010,
LW Dover −0020
Orford Ness:
HW Dover,
LW Dover −0010
Orford Haven Bar:
HW Dover +0020,
LW Dover +0010
Bawdsey:
HW Dover +0030,
LW Dover +0010
Felixstowe Pier:
HW Dover +0040,
LW Dover +0020
Harwich:
HW Dover +0050,
LW Dover +0030

Sea Area
Thames

Connections
River Alde −
see RoB p193
River Deben −
see RoB p196
River Orwell −
see RoB p199
River Stour −
see RoB p201

16 Tendring Peninsula

Sunshine holiday beaches among remote marshland

We've wallowed in the Wallet,
awash with sodden deals,
And slipped from Southend jetty,
the sou'easter at our heels.
Stern winter had his will of us
on black December days,
Our kedge is on the Buxey
and our jib is off the Naze.
RE Banyard

Dovercourt to Brightlingsea is called the Sunshine Coast, the driest in England. The town is quickly left behind and the coast soon becomes one of typical Essex saltmarsh, the beach well coated in shells and a heron picking about. Seawalls move in and out past sections of marsh, protected in turn by the occasional pillbox.

Beyond Crabknowe Spit is Pennyhole Bay, at the back of which are the Walton Backwaters with a multitude of creeks and hundreds of islands, described by Arthur Ransome in *Secret Water*. Hamford Water (Secret Water) divides Pewit Island (Peewitland) from Horsey Island (Swallow Island) and Stone Marsh (Flint Island).

From Stone Point there is a continuous beach, off which is the Medusa Channel, named after Nelson's frigate of 1801 when a local man piloted him out through it after winds prevented him from departing through the usual channel. There is a nature reserve reaching to a sewage works. Harwich Haven Authority is left behind.

Typical Essex marsh shoreline near Dovercourt.

The Naze Tower with the Naze at high water. A slip is taking place with suitcase sized lumps of soil falling in the photograph.

Beach huts stretch away into the distance at Frinton.

The Naze is at the start of the greater Thames Estuary. Flows begin southwards at HW Dover −0600 and northwards from HW Dover +0020 at 3km/h peak flow although tidal flows may be overridden by tidal surges.

The Naze itself consists of 20m of crumbling red sandstone cliff with many Ice Age fossils of primeval bird skeletons, crabs, shark teeth and reversed whelks, topped by grass and gorse. The brown brick octagonal Naze Tower on the summit was built in 1720 by Trinity House, the most massive and highest unlit beacon on the British coast. Originally 27m high with 113 steps, it has been reduced to 25m. In transit with Walton Hall it leads through the Goldmer Gat, giving a safe passage to the inside of the Gunfleet Sand bank which dries 7km offshore

Dovercourt

North Sea

The Naze

Walton-on-the Naze

Frinton-on-Sea

B1033

B1032

Brightlingsea

Mersea Island

St Osyth

R Colne

Point Clear

A133

Holland-on-Sea

Clacton-on-Sea

Jaywick

Colne Pt

Thames Estuary

Clacton pier has the largest area of any pier in Europe and is packed with amusements for holidaymakers.

parallel with the coast. Around the tower is a nature reserve and nature trail with little terns nesting, migrating birds and the Essex skipper and painted lady butterflies in summer. There is a picnic site and the point was used for settlement in the Iron Age. The beach produces black copperas stones, a source of ferrous sulphate which has been used for tanning, dying and ink making. Meanwhile, old pillboxes capsize into the sand.

Ten metre cliffs continue to Frinton-on-Sea but the front seems to be one long line of beach huts. **Walton-on-the-Naze** became a resort in the 1830s, renowned for its candied sea holly which was supposed to be an aphrodisiac.

The coastguard station is the Maritime Rescue Sub Centre for the whole of the Thames Estuary. The adjacent house now contains a museum on the maritime, seaside, urban and geological aspects of the area.

A Martello tower was built away from the front where it could watch over the head of the Walton Channel.

The pier is the second longest in the country at 790m and the fourth pleasure pier to be built. When constructed in 1895 it did not reach the sea at low water so it had to be extended. At the shore end it is 46m wide with the remains of an earlier pier underneath, while on top are tenpin bowling, giant wheel, Pirate Pete play area and other holiday entertainments. A spur to its construction was the arrival of the railway in 1867.

Brill, cod, dabs, haddock, hake, whiting and sole are found in the sea here.

The beach huts are built on stilts at the foot of the Greensward, an expanse of sloping green bank behind the beach at **Frinton-on-Sea** at the end of the B1033. The name from the Old English frithen tun means protected village or fenced settlement. Developed in the 1890s by Sir Richard Cooker, Frinton is the only British resort of any size without a public house. It retains a quiet, unspoilt 1920s/30s atmosphere with broad treelined esplanade and red brick houses. Beyond the Copperas Ground is the Wallet where flows southwest run to 3km/h and northeast to 4km/h. Some of the pirate radio stations of the 1960s operated off this section of coast. Paul Garnet had to drive Nina Apsoland here in *Gallowglass*.

Low lying land occupied by a golf course is fronted by a substantial seawall which winds past Sandy Point and Chevaux de Frise Point to Holland Haven, where the Holland Brook discharges at a country park and nature reserve.

Below a radio mast is a jet ski base. A café beside the water and a fire basket begin 6km of continuous built up holiday beach or 11km of beach in total, beginning with Holland-on-Sea and the B1032.

Clacton-on-Sea is the capital of the Tendring pen-insula and the Essex Sunshine Coast although there is enough wind for the Gunfleet windfarm to be built 6km offshore. Named after Clacc, an Old English man, Clacton is at the end of the railway and A133 and developed after 1860 with a promenade, seafront gardens and Victorian and Edwardian houses but is unashamedly a holiday town. Its centrepiece is the pier, the largest in Europe at 2ha. Built in 1871, it was extended to 360m in 1893 and carries a Seaquarium, arcades, rides, sea lion show, roller skating, dodgems, Reptile Safari and ice rink. Found around it are a road train, the Magic City play centre, lido and bowling. Also found was what appears to be a yew spear tip about 400,000 years old, the world's oldest wooden artefact.

The landing strip seems a bit small for Clacton Airshow. Other annual events are Clacton Classic Car Show and Clacton Jazz Festival. Jennifer Coombe's mother looks here for a holiday in *The Loving Spirit*. It has been used for filming BBC *Eastenders* sequences. More Martello towers follow including one with a coastguard station and a zoo in a dry moat.

A golf course gives a short break before Jaywick and Seawick and then St Osyth Beach continues to Lee-over-Sands at Colne Point. Rock groynes project at intervals where 100,000t of rock and 500,000m^3 of sand were placed from January to March 1999, dredged from 45km offshore to avoid disturbing holidaymakers and nesting terns. As St Osyth is 3km inland it must be fairly desperate to put its name to a beach. The beach is effectively zoned, firstly jet skis and all manner of small and noisy craft racing round in small and noisy circles. Then it is the naturists and the naturalists with their hides, presumably averting their gaze and their binoculars from their neighbours. Offshore are blackheaded, blackbacked and common gulls, oystercatchers and cormorants. The nature reserve consists of 1.6km^2 of saltings and shingle with brent geese, sanderlings, curlews, redshanks and little terns, an area restricted to their own members.

The Colne Bar at the end of the estuary of the River Colne consists of banks of mussel shells. Point Clear is fronted by caravans and chalets. On St Osyth Stone Point on the other side of Brightlingsea Reach is the first Martello tower of the east coast line. It was used by the Royal Navy as HMS Helder during the Second World War. Built in 1810, it now forms the East Essex Aviation Society & Museum with parts a P51D Mustang and a Tempest recovered from the sea and displays from both World Wars. Flows run in to 2km/h and out to 3km/h.

A tower with a conical top stands at Westmarsh Point by **Brightlingsea**, another yachting centre.

The Mersea Stone marks the corner of Mersea Island.

Distance
33km from Dovercourt to the Mersea Stone

OS 1:50,000 Sheets
(168 Colchester)
169 Ipswich
& the Naze

Tidal Constants
Harwich:
HW Dover +0050,
LW Dover +0030
Bramble Creek:
Dover +0050
Walton-on-the-Naze:
Dover +0040
Clacton-on-Sea:
Dover +0100
Brightlingsea:
Dover +0110

Sea Area
Thames

Connection
River Colne –
see RoB p204

Mersea Island

To the Romans it was Maris Insula and to the Saxons Meres–ig, the isle in the mere, yet it is less an island than a section of Essex marshes isolated by channels. Only 21m high, it consists mostly of London clay, some of it over 30m deep, sand and gravel outcropping at the ends. There are some glacial chalk boulders on the beaches in the south although the alluvial mud is more conspicuous in the north. In places there are Red Hills, heaps of burned soil from Celtic salt workings. High sea walls surround much of the island, even though they sometimes pull back from the shoreline.

The Danes had a camp here in 894 and in the 17th century it was settled by French Hugenots island.

The Mersea Stone is, in fact, just shingle although more solid than most of the surrounding landscape. It was important for the defence of Colchester so Henry

Off the first part of the south coast are grids of posts, most too close together to allow even a kayak through. This is now the holiday shore with low sand cliffs in front of the 14ha Cudmore Grove Country Park with its visitor centre and picnic area. It is also a coast with at least three caravan parks.

The Mersea Flats dry out to 2km offshore at the Cocum Hills where an east cardinal mark is placed near the wreck of the *Moliette*, a three masted concrete schooner with a noteworthy history. After running through Southend pier she was moved here and used on the shore as a scandalous nightclub, raided by the police with some customers preferring to dive into the sea rather than be recognized. During the Second World War she was placed out on the edge of the drying flats and used as a target. Somebody later dredged up the brass shell

The strange dry land fleet at West Mersea. L'Espérance *has the light blue hull, overlooking Besom Fleet.*

VIII built a large triangular blockhouse in case the French attacked. It was occupied successively by the Royalists and the Roundheads in the Civil War, was refortified against the Dutch and was demolished in the 18th century. Barbed wire, gun emplacements and mines were then prepared in case of a visit by Hitler and there is still the risk of unexploded ordnance. Some pillboxes remain.

cases which were used to fund the building of a bungalow of the same name on the island.

Other catches include sprats, cod, herrings and shrimps.

East Mersea had a priory related to the Priory of Cluny. The tower of the thousand year old St Edmund's church has a turret in the corner and is near a moat. It has an 1848 grave of a 15 year old girl, covered over with an iron

A path of oyster shells through the marsh.

Old barges used as pontoons for the fishing fleet.

A slip beside a piled Essex weatherboarded building.

Weatherboarded cottages as City Road joins the Lane.

The Strood with the footways just covered.

cage to deter body snatchers. Baring-Gould, well known for his hymn *Onward Christian Soldiers*, was vicar here for a decade from 1871 but didn't like the place, the people, the climate, the mosquitoes or the smell, as indicated in *Mehalah*, in which Waldegrave Decoy is visited by George De Witt and spiteful Phœbe Mussett. Three years after he left, the rectory had to be pulled down following an earthquake with its epicentre near Wivenhoe.

The remaining part of the coast with its sea defence wall hides wind generators and sewage works before arrival at West Mersea.

West Mersea is the island's only built up area, where there are also toilets and the Country Kitchen Café. Beach huts line the front. Windsurfers, kite surfers, jet skis, powerboats and sailing craft mean it can be busy on the water and the whole of the southeast side of the island has a buoyed inshore area where swimmers have precedence. 15km/h speed limits surround the island.

The lower tower of the church of St Peter & St Paul dates partly from 1046 when it served the parish and the small Benedictine priory but includes some flat bricks from a Roman villa previously on the site. It was given to Rouen abbey between the 11th and 15th centuries. By it is the Mersea Island Museum with local and natural history, social and marine exhibits, the RNLI, oyster production, fishing equipment, fossils and minerals. Duck punts were built here and one is on display with a punt gun. There is a 1920s fisherman's cottage. Down from the church is the ruin of the King's Hard.

Now a resort, it is the main sailing centre on the Blackwater. There are many Georgian houses.

Beyond Besom Fleet is Cobmarsh Island with traces of a medieval fort. In the complex area of channels Mersea Quarters receives flow from Mersea Fleet and Thorn Fleet with Packing Marsh Island between them, Little Ditch and the Salcott Channel. Flows pass over the Quarters Spit into Virley Channel. Between Little Ditch and the Salcott Channel is Sunken Island. In the early 1800s a boatload of excisemen were found here with their throats cut.

There are gulls, cormorants, herons, mute swans, mallards, grebes, eiders, black brents, oystercatchers and, in the winter, greylag geese, blackheaded gulls and wigeon, a good area for overwintering birds.

The River Blackwater is ingoing to 3km/h and outgoing to 4km/h.

Besom Fleet is overlooked by a surreal fleet of residential boats parked in saltings, only getting their hulls wet at the top of the tide. One with a blue hull parked prominently near the water is *l'Espérance* of 1891 which belonged to pianist Semprini, who must have formulated his *Semprini Serenade* for the BBC while watching other craft come and go. Another is approached from the road along a path of oyster shells.

Some old barges are used as pontoons for the largest inshore fishing fleet between Lowestoft and Brixham. There used to be a huge fleet of cutter rigged oyster smacks with their vertical stems and low sterns for handling the catch. Some restored ones are still to be found here.

It was for the oysters that the Romans took an interest in Mersea. West Mersea Natives can still be bought from stalls and the old oyster pits for holding catches are in use yet. In Victorian times winkles were also supplied. The Company Shed was the headquarters of the Tollesbury & Mersea Oyster Co. There is now a fishmonger and seafood café. They serve mackerel, herring, oysters, crab, shrimps, lobsters, mussels and cockles, implements to get into them as necessary and Tobasco to season them. Customers bring accompaniments and drinks. Across the road, the Coast Inn and others cater for more conventional tastes.

There are various slips, one accompanied by an old wooden building on piles above the water. There are also toilets and free parking but the latter is limited and is quickly filled by sailors.

West Mersea Yacht Club is the busiest yachting centre on the Blackwater with a week long regatta in August while Dabchicks Sailing Club caters for less affluent sailors.

In 1990 the lifeboat stationed here was called to a more unusual rescue, a taxi broken down on the causeway. When they arrived, guided by the vehicle's lights below the surface, the two occupants were on the roof, which was already 300mm underwater.

Opposite, the Lane leads up between weatherboarded cottages to City Road, which does not even boast surfacing.

After a caravan site, Strood Channel leads into surrounds which ought to be quieter but are not because the noisy brigade like to race up and down when the tide is in. The Strood Channel needs to be taken at high water on spring tides to ensure the mud is covered.

There are wrecks on the Mersea side and also on Ray Island which is normally attached to the mainland by Bonner's Saltings, a nature reserve with stunted blackthorns. Permission is required to land on it. Mehalah, in the book of that name, lived here with her widowed mother in a house later burned down by Elijah Rebow although there are no buildings on it now.

Around the marshes there is still wildfowling using punt guns between Sep 1st and Feb 20th, these large guns spraying flocks of birds with shot.

The B1025 crosses the Strood Channel on the Strood causeway, built by the Romans. This covers at the tops of spring tides on several afternoons each month and again in the small hours, the night time depths being greater. There is little difference between the jetskis and motorbikes crossing, noise, speed and spray. The cars range from those which switch on their wipers and blast through and those which stop and then proceed cautiously, some even turning back. Buses are undeterred and offer the novelty of saltwater paddling pools for customers at no extra cost. Road signs warn of dangers if the water is over the footways and it can be half a metre over on a high spring tide. On each side of the road is fencing of reconstituted plastic, probably not sufficiently rigid for anyone thinking of climbing along it but solid enough to require climbing over for anyone portaging across the road.

Beside the road to the north of the channel is a small wind pylon with contrarotating blades which catch the sun, to the distraction of drivers and boaters alike. A couple of pillboxes guard the crossing.

While both sides of the Strood offer a sea of silt most of the time, the east side is little used even with the tide in. This is the quietest and most remote part of the island's coast, saltings with grass and sea aster divided up by numerous muddy channels.

To the south at almost the highest point on the island is Barrow Hill or Grim's Hoe, topped by a tumulus 100m in diameter with oak and holly growing on it. It was

The mysterious Barrow Hill on Mersea Island's highest point.

Looking from the Strood towards Fingringhoe Marsh at high tide, the mud covered and a jigsaw of saltings and channels, excellent for waterfowl.

Sheep graze on the levée holding the Pyefleet Channel in check.

excavated in 1912 and revealed a brick vault containing a lead casket, inside which was a green glass urn with cremated bones, said to be two Viking brothers who had been fighting over the same girl. With a full moon it is claimed that the clashing of swords and the wailing of the girl can be heard. Mehalah was listening for the sounds when her house was burnt down by her lover. In fact, it is thought to be the remains of a regional native ruler co-operating with the Romans. There was another such tumulus in West Mersea.

Garish oilseed rape can draw attention to Fingringhoe Ranges to the north. When in use, a red flag should be flying. There is a lookout hut on the north shore of Pyefleet Channel and firing should stop for passing craft although there is always the risk of finding unexploded ordnance. Despite this, it was the favourite mooring for yachting cartoonist Mike Peyton.

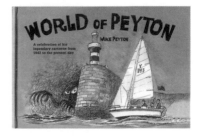

Grids of posts near the mouth of the Pyefleet Channel.

Withies mark the fairway for larger boats. The tide ebbs at quite a rate and an opposing easterly breeze from Brightlingsea Creek can kick up steep waves. The middle of the channel has oysterbeds with grounding not permitted, the oyster season being opened by the Mayor of Colchester in a boat.

Pewit Island still has lapwings around it, together with reed warblers, skylarks, cuckoos and snipe on the surrounding land. The small community of East Mersea produces wheat, barley, oats, rape, pigs, sheep and poultry. In the past it was better known for wildfowling and smuggling. *Mehalah* tells of a deserter who was hanged here after murdering a farmer with his spade in an attempt to rob him but was then trapped on the island.

Pyefleet Channel discharges into the River Colne opposite Brightlingsea Creek and just below Geedon Creek where it splits round Rat Island. Flows run out to 3km/h and in to 2km/h. On the Mersea shore are the remains of the wreck of the SS *Lowlands*.

An oyster smack moored in Pyefleet Channel as it joins the River Colne.

Distance
Mersea Island is 8km long and lies 100m off Peldon with road access

OS 1:50,000 Sheets
168 Colchester (169 Ipswich & the Naze)

Tidal Constants
Brightlingsea: Dover +0110
West Mersea: HW Dover +0110, LW Dover +0120

Sea Area:
Thames

Connections
River Colne – see RoB p204
River Blackwater – see RoB p207

The wreck of the SS Lowlands. *Westmarsh Point and Brightlingsea lie beyond.*

Dengie Peninsula

When Saint Cedd sailed down from Lindisfarne
With thirty monks they built this barn;
A church of stone from the Roman wall.

Othona stone, Roman bricks, mortar and wood.
They built it strong on solid ground and saw that it was good;
And all the while the sea heaps shells against the fortress wall.
Polly Clark and David Simpson

Radio Caroline broadcasts from above the nuclear power station at Bradwell.

Across the Blackwater, Bradwell nuclear power station, built on a former airfield, was in use from 1962 to 2002 with the first pair of full size Magnox reactors in Britain, from 2015 becoming the first UK rector site in care and maintenance.

Pillboxes on the shore face each other across the Blackwater and an unplanned defence measure is 12ha of compressed and broken cockle shells which form Bradwell Shell Beach. Leading to Sales Point, a line of 11 sunken barges form a wavebreak which covers at high water.

A black weatherboarded house outside the seawall at Tip Head was occupied by Walter Linnett, the last professional wildfowler, punt gunner and eel spearer until well after the Second World War. Haunted by the ghost of an old seaman, it is now used as a bird observatory, local birds including herons, cormorants, terns and herring and blackbacked gulls. Another hide is damaged and disused. Close by is a nature reserve.

The Romans built their Othona fort here, bricks and stone being reused to build St Peter's on the Wall chapel in 654 by St Cedd, who came from Northumberland as a missionary to the East Anglians. It has been a cathedral and a barn from the 17th century to 1920, now being used by the Othona Society for nondenominational services, one of the oldest places of worship in England. Looking like a barn, it has served as a navigation mark over the centuries on this section of coast which has few landmarks.

The St Peter's Way walk is round the Bradwell Marshes while St Peter's Flat and

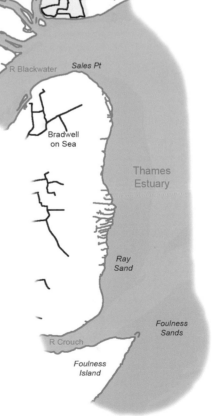

A line of sunken steel barges act as a breakwater off the Bradwell Marshes.

St Peter's on the Wall chapel, a site used earlier by the Romans.

Dengie Flat offshore offer some shallow conditions. Wrecks lie about the flats and between Sandbeach and Marshhouse Outfalls there is another line of barges, this time 16 of them. Saltings and mudflats ending with a hard clay shelf make up the Dengie Flat SSSI with 24,000 birds including knots, teal, shelducks and, especially, brent geese. The RSPB said they were threatened by sea level rise and shellfisheries.

Before Grange Outfall, Crouch Harbour Authority takes control, the occasional seal occupying the water in an area generally devoid of people.

Ray Sand on the north side of the River Crouch is extended along the Whitaker Channel by Buxey Sand for 16km. There is a 700m gap at low water but there is no corresponding gap on the south side of the rivermouth where Foulness Sands run out for 9km. Flows start into the estuary at HW Dover −0430 at up to 5km/h and out from HW Dover +0130 at up to 6km/h.

Distance
19km from Mersea Island to Foulness Point

OS 1:50,000 Sheet
168 Colchester

Tidal Constants
West Mersea:
HW Dover +0110,
LW Dover +0120
Bradwell-on-Sea:
Dover +0110
Holliwell Point:
HW Dover +0120
LW Dover +0130

Sea Area:
Thames

Connections
River Blackwater –
see RoB p207
River Crouch –
see RoB p210

Looking across a rare patch of sand at Holliwell Point as water drains towards the River Crouch.

Foulness Island

Foulness Island off the Essex coast holds much for the boater with an interest in wildlife, particularly birds. Its name derives from the Old English fugla and naess meaning wild birds promontory, indicating that it has only become an island in recent times. This applies to New England Island and Havengore Island, too, which have, even more recently, been rejoined to Foulness Island by the construction of dams.

Foulness is known for its different forms of flight. The prolific birdlife has already been mentioned. For some years it was under discussion and public inquiry as one of the proposed sites for London's third airport. Direct rail and motorway links to London were planned for the site, which would have covered the island and have involved much reclamation from the Maplin Sands, not unprecedented as much of Foulness itself has been inned from the sea over the years.

The final form of flight is brought about by the Ministry of Defence who purchased the island in 1915 and who also own Potton Island and Rushley Island. Foulness is QinetiQ's MoD Shoeburyness military firing range and the public are not admitted to the island, excepting the couple of hundred civilians who live there and farm the soil which Arthur Young, in 1814, described as being the richest in the county.

Timing a trip in the area needs to take into consideration the fact that the channel between Foulness and Rushley Island and the mainland can dry out at low tide, that the Maplin Sands can dry out for up to 7km from the high water mark and that Foulness Sands can be exposed for up to 11km from Foulness Point, quite apart from the range.

High tide not only gets the deepest water but also gives the best views over the tops of the levées. From the top of the levées there are extensive views over the flat cornfields, broken only by occasional trees and a fortification tower looking eastwards from behind the levée. Cattle are pastured on the levées.

Crouch Harbour Authority hands over to Port of London Authority at Foulness Point. The most active part of the range is at this end. Normally, artillery shells bury themselves completely in the sand although it is possible for the sand to be washed off from time to time. This area is teeming with birdlife. A third of the world's population of brent geese winter off Essex, 100,000 of them off Foulness Island. Perhaps they are protected from other predators and do not consider the risk of being hit by shells but they were enough of a hazard to stop the third London airport being built on the 91km^2 of Maplin Sands. Flocks of oystercatchers wheel noisily but most of the birdlife congregates at the northeast end of the island. Banks of edible cockle shells are found towards this point, indicating the spot from which are taken over 60% of all cockles sold in Britain.

The sight of birds apparently standing on the surface is an indication that the tide has won. The birds are standing on the bed. The sandy mud is flanked along its northern edge with a bank of cockle shells and then deeper water faces the boater on the run up the River Crouch.

A large flock of oystercatchers wheel around at the northern end.

The north coast of Foulness with masts visible across the island.

Although it has some prominent lattice masts and observation cabins, these need to be seen on the charts as the Ordnance Survey do not mark military installations on their maps, simply showing what was there before the military took over.

On Foulness a dilapidated selection of lattice pylons, gantries and old buildings lie scattered at random across the horizon in military fashion, quietly rusting. A tower in the northwest corner looks like a church tower but is

Gulls circle over the Crouch/Roach confluence.

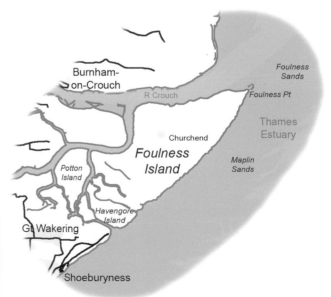

Havengore Bridge onto Foulness Island.

Assorted military masts on Foulness.

Distance
*Foulness Island is
10km long and lies
100m off Samuel's
Corner with restricted
road access*

OS 1:50,000 Sheets
*(168 Colchester)
178 Thames Estuary*

Tidal Constants
*Holliwell Point:
HW Dover +0120
LW Dover +0130
Burnham-on-Crouch:
Dover +0120
Havengore Creek:
Dover +0100*

Range
Shoeburyness

Sea Area
Thames

Connections
*River Crouch –
see RoB p210
River Roach –
see RoB p211*

not marked on any of the maps or charts, unlike the less obvious spire of the disused one at Churchend. Further back, the gas holder and buildings of Great Wakering are seen with the tower blocks of Southend just visible through the haze on the skyline.

Most levées are lined with slabs and their covering of knotted wrack can make launching difficult below high tide level unless the boater uses feet to feel for the joints between the slabs. At times the tang of seaweed can be surpassed by the smell of guano from the many birds in the area.

An early morning or late evening trip often brings a better selection of birdlife. The incessant twittering of skylarks serenades the launch while a heron might flap lazily past.

If the water is calm, passage will throw up a gentle swell which will cause jellyfish to just break the surface. These are generally the harmless moon jellies, recognized by their four purple rings on an otherwise transparent body. A hare might be seen surveying the new arrival from the top of the levée before darting for cover in the grass.

A turn into the River Roach after a glimpse of the masts of dinghies moored at **Burnham-on-Crouch** leads into a narrower channel. Around the feet of levées mud is being deposited. Its appearance is claylike and it seems fairly solid until touched, when it reveals a black organic content and considerable tenacity. In the 19th century it was described as 'an idyllic paradise of wild life, with swans reflected in the still blue waters of the fleets; as the sea lavender bursts into flower, a purple glow would steal over the marshes, and creek and pool were royally fringed with sea aster.' The sea aster is still one of the first plants to move onto the reclaimed mudflats, its fleshy leaves providing a cover of greenery for the wildlife.

Pleasure and fishing boats are moored here with access apparently being made from Foulness Island.

Oystercatchers rush past in flocks while herring gulls announce their presence with their familiar cries rather than with speed. Terns drop like stones to the water to take small fish. Shelducks flap around with pretended broken wings, trying to attract the boater away from their broods of growing ducklings.

A further left turn up the Middleway brings progressively narrower water channels and the reappearance of **Great Wakering** and its gas holder. All of these creeks

are silting up or have been dammed, particularly New England Creek and Shelford Creek, so that Havengore Island and New England Island are now linked to Foulness and all are inaccessible, being controlled by the Ministry of Defence. This is emphasized to the east of Yoke Fleet with an assortment of observation posts, water towers and other buildings including two high lattice masts on the east side of Foulness. Taking care not to turn into Shelford or New England Creeks, a further turn is made into Narrow Cuts, the shallow channel between Rushley Island and Havengore Island, leading through to Havengore Creek which is crossed by a bridge replacing a former bascule bridge. The bridge is the only road link with Foulness Island and has military control points on it. There are obstructions between its supports and suspended from the bridge so that it is not passable even by craft which would otherwise be small enough to pass under it. It will only be lifted within two hours of high water, when the range is not in use, during daylight hours.

The range has outer and inner areas. Because high velocity explosives are fired, craft need to stay out of the Outer Sea Area when it is active, resulting in a long diversion for boats trying to get into or out of the River Crouch. However, it is the only range in the country where small craft are required to go far out to sea, 8km, even when the range is not active, with obvious safety implications. Any boat found within the Inner Sea Area at any time is subject to penalties and confiscation. The Inner Sea Area reaches from Fisherman's Head, 3km from the northern end of the island, to Shoebury Ness. Detouring round the Inner Sea Area involves being out of contact with land for 27km. The buoys defining the edge of the area are up to 13km apart, not visible from one to the next because of the curvature of the Earth.

Emergence onto the Thames Estuary brings a strange sight in the form of a line of apparently sunken ships of modern design. These are actually at the Great Nore anchorage and are simply hull down below the horizon because of the distance. Hills can be seen on the Kent shore. Some 8km south of Havengore Creek, the lattice structure of Maunsell Fort can be seen in the middle of the estuary while, 5km away, a measured mile is marked out.

Exit from Havengore Creek is onto the centre of the Inner Sea Area, boats being required to turn southwest towards Shoebury Ness. Some range staff are concerned about the safety implications of this policy and they should be contacted before attempting to navigate in the area.

The Broomway is 300m beyond the high water mark, a public bridleway crossing Havengore Creek and running parallel to the coast for 9km, a walk along it described by Richard Macfarlane in *The Old Ways*. It existed by 1419 and was the only route on foot to Foulness until 1932. It has produced the incident of a sailing barge colliding with a horsedrawn coal cart. It is named after the wooden brooms marking the route. Mackerel leap just off the shoreline, which is embanked marshland to Shoebury Ness, some fine salt marshes. Burial urns, pottery, barrows and red hills show it is an area which has long been occupied.

The observation box at Asplins Head overlooks a set of supports which once carried an overhead pipeline and now rust within a circular protective wall which is submerged at high tide.

Several of the most prominent towers are close to the southeast shore, which suffers from the shallowness of the water. The towers and buildings have a discarded look, an appearance belied by a more recent radar scanner on top of one and by several futuristic rooms on stalks along the coastline. A set of supports which once carried an overhead pipeline now rust within a circular protective wall which is submerged at high tide.

Potton Island

The northwest side of Potton Island with the tower blocks of Southend beyond.

Potton Island is in the middle of an area of islands, creeks and marshland to the north of the Thames Estuary. The channels dry out over the bottom of the tide.

Opposite Potton Point, where the River Roach passes from Potton Island to Foulness Island, is a spread of mudflats alongside Devil's Reach, which is popular with wildfowl. The whole area is rich in wildlife, especially wildfowl, and seabirds find this a little more sheltered than the Maplin Sands. Canada geese, shelducks, oystercatchers and cormorants are among the commoner varieties although large numbers of other birds overwinter here.

Paglesham Pool marks the far end of Wallasea Island, the northern bank of the River Roach at this point, and attention is drawn to it by a prominent pillbox at the confluence. There are oyster beds just above this point.

A sunken barge in the channel leads into the moorings by Paglesham slipway. Perhaps the easiest launch point is from the boatyard at Eastend on the north side of the River Roach as the Ministry of Defence control access to the island itself. The boatyard welcomes all boats but charges for use of the slipway. There is a toilet and limited parking.

The boatyard is the dominant feature of the shoreline, surrounded by moored pleasure craft and the wooden skeletons of former piers projecting out into the soft mud. The landscape is flat, the highest points on Potton being on the levée which surrounds it completely. The

Mouth of Potton Creek at the northwest end of Potton Island.

The causeway across to the island at low water.

The northwest corner of Potton Island seen across the River Roach.

The bridge across to Potton Island and the lookout post.

Sutton's Boat Yard near the southern end of the island.

Moorings around the southern end of Potton Island with plenty of mud exposed.

Distance
Potton Island is 3km long and lies 100m off Barling Marsh with restricted road access

OS 1:50,000 Sheet
178 Thames Estuary

Tidal Constant
Havengore Creek: Dover +0100

Sea Area
Thames

Connections
River Roach – see RoB p211

main intrusions into the skyline are the clump of trees at Eastend with the inevitable flock of rooks circling around them and the tower of Paglesham church, visible behind.

Another church to rise above the marshes is the spire at Barling. A line of poplar trees, a gas holder and a few tower blocks in Southend-on-Sea complete the list of items which break the horizon of tidal defences. These defences are concrete faced on Potton's Paglesham Reach shore but at water level there are banks of compacted mud and clay, etched by the water and covered with a fine coating of green weed. Patches of wrack float in the water where there are stones and gravel and occasional bands of shells are exposed in the clay. It is an unusual shoreline, suitable for rabbits to run free.

The Violet discharges at Barling Ness and has moorings for a small number of fishing boats. When it divides, Barlinghall Creek feeds down from Barling Hall on the right and Potton Creek curves away to the left.

Cows graze around the farm buildings at Great Potton and a causeway leads across to it. This is soon followed by a swing bridge with a guard post at one end. While

frequent notices surround Potton Island, forbidding landing, they now also appear on the mainland bank. The occasional observation post or set of handrails on steps leading up from water level onto a largely deserted Potton Island give it a somewhat sinister atmosphere.

Sutton's Boat Yard brings light relief with cranes and boats under repair, pleasure craft from **Wakering** Yacht Club moored in the channel and a slipway down on the far side of Mill Head.

The banks now support sea aster with its fleshy leaves and blue flowers in summer, a crisp brown carpet in winter.

Moorings continue ahead in the channel which separates Rushley Island from the mainland. Across it may be seen the bridge which controls access to Foulness.

The Middleway now leads northwards, still with the occasional boat moored where there is sufficient depth. A large hanger sized building is passed on Potton and then Narrow Cuts come in between Rushley Island and Havengore Island, the main channel leading through to the Thames Estuary.

The largest building on Potton Island, from the Middleway.

Southend-on-Sea

21

The Broomway returns to land at **Wakering** Stairs.

Essex gives way to Southend-on-Sea. Beyond Pig's Bay a 2km long obstruction runs out but there are gaps which allow boats through. The tide goes out a further kilometre and at low tide firing can take place parallel to the shoreline way out on the sands.

At **Shoeburyness** there is less clay than there was because the Romans set up a pottery kiln at Shoebury.

From Shoeburyness, Shoebury Ness itself is quickly reached, the start of Sea Reach with the Yantlet Dredged Channel and the Southend and Warp Deep Water Anchorage beyond the West Knock daymark. The other side of the 2km of flats, the channels are now used by many large commercial vessels. Pier remains stand around the ness. The Danes had a camp at Shoebury in 893, used as a base for raiding across the country. The artillery barracks of 1858 were used to test Armstrong guns against ironsides. This part of the range has been closed and now forms Gunners Park with a SSSI.

A proposal for the Thames Gateway would have three new islands, a 9km barrage and bridge leading from the ness to Sheerness and the Isle of Grain and a connection from one island to the south end of Southend pier.

Southend-on-Sea, the south end of Prittlewell, is the largest town in Essex, a resort and the nearest seaside town to London. Average pay in Southend is the lowest in the country so 20% of working residents commute to London. A radio mast as the B1016 comes alongside begins 11km of front. Beyond Shoebury Common and Thorpe Bay is Southend Flat, an extensive mooring for small craft, and beach huts in plenty. There is a marine activities centre and Southend Sea Life Adventure aquarium, fish in the sea including cod, flounders, bass, eels, mullet and tope.

Southend is best known for its pier, the longest pleasure pier in the world at 2.1km. Built in 1830 for passengers, it was rebuilt in 1889 in iron and extended in 1927. Horsedrawn trains were replaced by 910mm gauge electric trains. Buildings at the seaward end have been burnt out four times, the most recent in 2005 with a replacement culture centre building in 2012, and the pier has been hit by over a score of large vessels, including an 800t coaster which cut through in 1986, marooning two anglers. Dr Prentice made his fatal departure from here in the *Elsie Davidson* for D-Day in Nevil Shute's *Requiem for a Wren*.

There are lifeboats stationed at both ends. Southend Pier Museum features the pier, the railway and the disasters. Nelson stayed in Royal Terrace. Adventure Island has over forty rides including Viking Boats, Raging River Log Flume, Tidal Wave, Vortex, Queen Anne's Revenge pirate galleon, rollercoaster and big wheel. The Grade II Kursaal ballroom of 1901 has multiple tenpin bowling with roller and ice skating. There is the Victorian Cliffs Bandstand, RollaCity, illuminations from mid August to early November, fireworks every Saturday from mid September to October, London–

Southend Classic Car Run, Southend Jazz Festival in August and the Southend-on-Sea Barge Match. Some 4.5km^2 of parks mostly date from 1900 to 1930. With all this there are still boarded up hotels and increasing

Military scrap rusts in Pig's Bay. Beyond is the protective boom.

numbers coming here to retire, perhaps the very same Mods and Rockers who used to come at bank holidays for running fights along the front. Finding a purse containing seven guineas allowed Sydney Chaplin with brother Charlie and their mother a much needed day's holiday here. The town has been used for filming *Killing Dad* and for BBC *Eastenders* sequences. There is Mr B's Space Chase Quasar for

Kursaal
1ST

kids. Chalkwell Park rose garden faces out onto Chalkwell Oaze. The City or Crow Stone marks the northern limit of the River Thames.

Leigh-on-Sea, settlement in a glade, was a cockle and whelk fishing village using bawleys or boiler boats, collecting cockles from Maplin Sands and also sprats, whitebait and brown shrimps, leading to boatbuilding. Cockles and jellied eels are still on sale near the beach of cockle shells. This is probably where the Essex pilgrims boarded the *Mayflower*. When the Peterboat Inn was rebuilt in the late 19th century it was found to have many smuggling cellars underneath. Weatherboarded houses front the cobbled high street. Tennis players David and John Lloyd and author John Fowles were born here. Leigh Heritage Centre on Leigh Creek and Leigh Folk Festival add to the folklore.

Between Leigh Sand and Marsh End Sand, an area where waterskiing is permitted and where cormorants, oystercatchers and blackbacked and herring gulls will be found at times, Ray Gut separates Southend-on-Sea from Essex.

The elm trees in the name of Two Tree Island blew down in the 1960s. It has brent geese and other winter wildfowl, separated by Hadleigh Ray or Oyster Creek from Canvey Island.

The beach at Southend.

Distance
17km from Havengore Creek to Two Tree Island

OS 1:50,000 Sheet
178 Thames Estuary

Tidal Constants
Havengore Creek:
Dover +0100
Southend:
HW Dover +0120,
LW Dover +0130
Benfleet Creek:
HW Dover +0140,
LW Dover +0130

Sea Area
Thames

Range
Shoeburyness

Southend Pier, the world's longest pleasure pier despite many attempts to shorten it or burn it down.

Canvey Island

22

Hadleigh Ray (or Oyster Creek) leads up between **Canvey** and Two Tree Island but not until Smallgains Creek has been passed, home for many sailing boats. Further out, catamarans, trimarans, yachts and cruisers are the order of the day.

The line past Bargander Sand involves passing the pier off Smallgains Creek, the name originally coming from small grains because of the poor harvests. The route heads towards the prominent water tower on Round Hill at **South Benfleet**. For the first time since Bridlington there are hills, occupied by the flint Hadleigh Castle, seen on the north side of Hadleigh Marsh. Built from 1230 by Henry III as defence against the French and

by chimneys beyond the town and the masts of moored dinghies.

Hadleigh Marsh is used as a refuse tip and northerly winds blow the smell of refuse across the creek. Water skiers use this reach so it pays to keep to the edge of the channel.

The green roof of the **Benfleet** Yacht Club is another prominent landmark among the rocking masts of Benfleet Creek which precede a boatbuilder's yard and the Benfleet barrier, one of a series of lifting flood barriers protecting low lying areas.

Both the B1014 and railway follow the creek

After the 1953 floods

Boats in Benfleet Creek await the return of the tide.

expanded for Edward III, curtain walls and two towers remain. It is backed by cornfields with housing keeping to the hilltop, unlike the castle, which began to slip from its escarpment. The Salvation Army bought it in 1891 to house poor Londoners, who worked in market gardens and brickworks until 1914. The castle was painted by Constable and written about by Arthur Morrison. The country park was the 2012 Olympic mountain biking venue.

Heading up into Benfleet Creek, there are numerous leads into the marshes on the island side, made more confusing by the lines of moored yachts in the navigation channels, not a problem in 893 when the Danes had a camp with many ships, defeated by Saxon forces.

A curiosity of the marshes was that men brought up in the area were healthy but wives brought down from higher ground did not feel so good and soon deteriorated so that getting a new wife was an annual occurrence for many men in the 18th century and some outlived dozens of wives.

Estuarine birds include blackheaded, herring and other gulls but flocks of starlings maintain the land element in Natural England's reserve in the estuary. Aircraft climb from London Southend Airport and bank away while radio controlled biplanes zip around over **Hadleigh**.

The scenery is a contrast of horizontal and vertical lines, the horizontal of the marshes and the hilly ridge cut

for a short while until it becomes the narrow East Haven Creek. Wrecks litter the entrance to further leads, an outfall reveals the whereabouts of a sewage works which has been smelled from time to time, a flare stack peers above the skyline to hint at what is to come and a single pillbox hints at what might have come.

Elder bushes help break up the otherwise exposed western end of the island while sea aster takes over

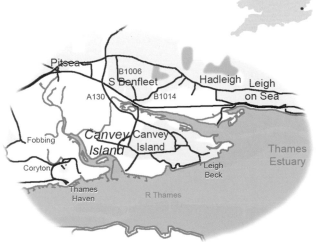

The Benfleet barrier.

Moorings as South Benfleet rises on the right bank.

at ground level, the skeletons of small crabs deposited amongst its fleshy leaves by the receding tide. Shelducks, oystercatchers and plovers fly overhead while the skylark twitters continuously, almost invisible as he hovers over the marsh.

East Haven Creek is reduced to ditch proportions on the outside of the bend under the A130 bridge. With the tide in, this is not obvious and small powerboats sweep down the creek in the centre of the channel. Low water shows where their propellers have carved grooves through the soft mud. The creek can be forded at low tide, mud permitting.

Vange Creek, the name from fen district, drains **Pitsea** Marsh, reckoned as one of the country's leading tips for hazardous waste. Warning notices advise water users to keep out and sprinklers play on the built up debris. Domestic refuse litters the surface of the water but the smell is drowned out by the scent of black mustard, cow parsley and other flowers in profusion along the edge of the creek. A tidal barrier across the southern end of East Haven Creek is matched by another at Fobbing Horse.

Holehaven Creek is another water skiing area, this time with a ski jump. A fire tug anchorage is located here. At high tide it is possible for small craft to run through the vegetation on the west end of Lower Horse island and cut the corner at Shellhaven Point, passing under the pipe jetty. Canvey received the world's first consignment of liquified natural gas in 1959.

The Dutch under Van Gent attacked Hole Haven in 1667, firing buildings and stealing sheep. The attack only lasted three hours, leaving the invaders plenty of time to go on and give their attentions to Queenborough the same day.

Clipping the corner of Canvey Island involves passing the shiplapped Lobster Smack, a popular inn and the

East Haven Creek without water but with keel gouges in silt.

The pipe bridge crossing Hole Haven dwarfs even the storage tanks at Ca

island's oldest, once notorious for prize fighting. It is thought to have been the model for Sluice House in Charles Dickens' *Great Expectations*. Beyond it is a tank farm. Although the Holehaven Anchorage (from holy haven) is for tankers, the jetties are constructed so that small boats can go under them and pass inshore, avoiding any conflicting movements.

A degaussing range was situated off Thorney Bay, a popular creek with holidaymakers where deep golden sand is exposed. From here, the tourists take over with the Labworth Café (a reinforced concrete structure resembling the deck of the *Queen Mary*, the only building designed solely by Ove Arup) and other accoutrements of a seaside resort. Dr Feelgood were a local band, formed in 1971 and with a first album *Down by the Jetty*.

A small wall cuts off part of the estuary in a paddling pool. A couple of hundred metres out from here runs a line of withies.

The island has a substantial concrete seawall with heavy flood doors around it, an item constructed since January 31st 1953 when the floods drowned 58 people on the island. The 12,000 population of those days has now risen to 33,500, living at the eastern end of the island, but the seawall hides most of the buildings. The island has sunk 6m in the last 2,000 years, mostly in the 2nd century. In 1630 Cornelius Vermuyden built the first wall round it, linking together five islands, and received a third of the resulting island in payment. Some 200 of his workers settled there and one of their thatched houses faces a prominent road junction in the centre of the island.

The barrier on East Haven Creek.

The Thames Estuary spreads out in front of the island, many large ships lying at anchor. The former Chapman light was mentioned in Joseph Conrad's *Heart of Darkness*. Nearby is the Chapman Explosive Anchorage while the other side of the river has a caravan site glinting in the sun at Allhallows. Southend pier is visible to the east but

The Lobster Smack, probably Dickens' Sluice Inn.

Holiday chalets nestle up to oil storage tanks and tanker discharge pipes in the Thames Estuary.

Canvey Island's sea bathing pool.

PS Great Western 1838

this drops below the horizon on launching small craft.

In 1838, sailing down the Thames after fitting out, the *Great Western* suffered a fire without major damage. However, a charred wooden ladder gave way and Brunel fell 6m, being badly injured and having to be put ashore on Canvey. The ship was beached on Chapman Sand and floated off on the next tide. As a result of the delay, the ship failed by a few hours to be the first to cross the Atlantic under continuous steam.

The beach is somewhat sparse and the character of the area changes as the seawall turns north. Towards Canvey Point the area is one of muddy saltings covered with weed which gives the requisite sea smell.

Canvey Point (sometimes known as Deadman's Point) is dominated by Southend-on-Sea along the skyline.

Distance
Canvey Island is 8km long and lies 40m off South Benfleet with road access

OS 1:50,000 Sheet
178 Thames Estuary

Tidal Constants
Benfleet Creek:
HW Dover +0140,
LW Dover +0130
Thames Haven:
HW Dover +0140,
LW Dover +0130

Sea Area
Thames

Looking up the estuary from Leigh Beck with the houses largely hidden behind the uncompromising seawall.

Thames

The mouth of
Britain's best
known river

23

Filthy river, filthy river,
Foul from London to the Nore
What art thou but one vast gutter,
One tremendous common shore.
Punch

in *Great Expectations*, is no longer an island. Grain, at the end of the B2001, takes its name from the Old English *greon*, sand or mud depending on the size of the grains. It became a malarial area when infected by troops returning from abroad during the First World War. Offshore is the 1855 Grain Tower, a Martello tower but

A delivery of containers to the Thames Gateway port.

In Sea Reach the fairway is on the north side and craft are required to be at least 60m from berthed tankers and jetties. Flows are strongest on the north side of the channel, ingoing to 6km/h and outgoing to 7km/h.

Shell Haven had been named by Henry VIII's time. Shell did not arrive until 1912, by which time the Cory brothers had had a small refinery here for forty years at Coryton. Shell closed their refinery in 1999. Beyond is the 6km² Dubai Ports' DP World London Gateway, Europe's largest logistics site, taking the world's largest container ships, up to 200,000t, 400m long and carrying 18,000 containers. Sailor Tristan Jones described this as by far his most depressing mooring in a lifetime at sea.

As the river turns from the south there is a container terminal behind Mucking Flat. Power station chimneys at Tilbury break the skyline.

Crossing the River Thames from Thurrock to the Medway shore brings very different conditions, the Blythe Sands mud draining for a kilometre from a sloping seawall protecting the Kent marshes, farmland divided up by Cliffe Fleet, Salt Fleet, a peripheral channel and numerous smaller ditches, an area threatened to become suburban sprawl and possibly a new airport. Egypt Bay had smugglers and is particularly good for saltmarsh plants while there are breeding and wintering birds on the Halstow Marshes. St Mary's Bay has a white beach composed entirely of broken shells, contrasting with the adjoining mud below high tide level. Herons find it a quiet environment in which to fish. Offshore, in still conditions, narrowboats make a run for the Medway, strangely small in front of the commercial shipping.

A water tower stands on the ridge above the pillbox, sea of caravans and dinghy park at Allhallows-on-Sea. At one time Allhallows was proposed for development as Europe's leading holiday destination.

The Yantlet Beacon is a daymark indicating the mouth of Yantlet Creek where Thames sailing barges used to serve the wharf. Just beyond the beacon is the London Stone, marking the end of the River Thames and the Medway Approach Area limit.

The former Yantlet Demolition Range had to have the least satisfactory management of any range around the British coastline in recent years.

The Isle of Grain, where Pip encountered Magwitch

Yantlet Creek flows across Allhallows Marshes.

much modified. It was at Nore Station in 1732 that the first light vessel was moored.

A proposal for the Thames Gateway includes 1–2km of new saltmarsh off the Isle of Grain and the first 3km of beach on Sheerness, assuming the locals prefer more marsh to their beach, also a barrage and bridge from Shoeburyness.

Medway gives way to Kent here

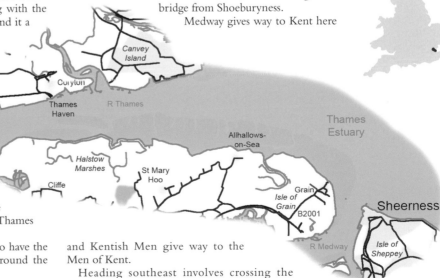

and Kentish Men give way to the Men of Kent.

Heading southeast involves crossing the narrow and well-buoyed Medway Approach

Yantlet Beacon daymark.

The London Stone marks the end of the River Thames.

Channel leading out past the Great Nore anchorage, scene of the Great Mutiny which spread from Sheerness in 1797 with important implications for Melville's *Billy Budd, Sailor* and was included by Frederick Marryat in *Frank Mildmay; or the Naval Officer* and *The King's Own*. In *A Ship of the Line* CS Forester explains how it was the best place for the Royal Navy to make up crews by seizing crewmen off inbound merchant ships. A white light every 7 seconds at Garrison Point warns of a large vessel movement in the Medway or its approaches, but any such movement should be easily visible in plenty of time in good weather conditions. The ebb starts at HW Dover with a strong eddy northeast of Garrison Point during the ebb. Strong southwesterly winds can cause low water to stand for up to an hour and a half and strong northwesterly winds can cause a stand of up to two hours before low water. Heavy rain reduces the rate and duration of the flood and the converse applies for the ebb. A radio mast stands on Garrison Point above the car ferry jetty for Flushing.

Distance
23km from Canvey Island to the Isle of Sheppey

OS 1:50,000 Sheet
178 Thames Estuary

Tidal Constants
Thames Haven:
HW Dover +0140,
LW Dover +0130
Yantlet Creek:
Dover +0120
Sheerness:
Dover +0120

Sea Area
Thames

Connections
River Thames –
see RoB p235
River Medway –
see RoB p242

The Grain Tower defends the mouth of the Medway.

Isle of Sheppey

24

Situated at the mouths of the Thames and Medway, Sheppey has always held an important strategic significance for England and yet has always been the island of sheep, too. Ptolemy mentioned its strategic

the 17th century Old House at Home, selling food and ales from the wood, and public toilets.

Along the banks of Loden Hope and Long Reach the mudflats are littered with empty oyster shells. Pylons

A tug uses its fire cannons off Sheerness.

defensive position in 161. To the Romans it was Insula Ovinium and, to the Saxons, Scaepige, both meaning island of sheep. The Danes first visited England in 835, capturing Sheppey, which they did again in 852 and 1004, and the Dutch invaded in 1667. Various kings have lived here. It now houses 32,000 people on the north side and still the marshes on the south side are left to the sheep.

The River Medway from Garrison Point brings the boater past the old naval docks, now surmounted by a radar scanner. A red and white striped block at the base bears the name Medway Radio in fading letters, a legacy from the heyday of pirate radio.

The naval dockyards were laid out in 1665. Samuel Pepys wrote in his diary that he had been 'to **Sheerness**, where we walked up and down, laying out the ground to be taken for a yard, to lay provision for cleaning and repairing ships and most proper place it is for the purpose.' Most of the present docks were laid out by Rennie but the Royal Navy went in 1960, the docks now being commercial. Behind, where the A249 and A250 end, the nearest area of Sheerness is still known as Blue Town from the fact that most of the houses were decorated with Royal Navy paint.

The docks are now the scene of considerable activity and small craft may have to heave to while tugs manœuvre large freighters in and out. There is a Ro-Ro car ferry service to Flushing and Japanese boats land large numbers of import cars and vans, this being Britain's largest car handling terminal. In the other direction go a daily train load of Minis from Oxford. An 1860 iron framed boat store, 64m x 41m x 16m high, reaching for four storeys, was the first multistorey iron framed building and, thus, the precursor to the skyscraper. It was unbraced but had stiff joints for stability.

The BBC's *Wings* series by Barry Thomas opens with a German Taube over Sheerness on Christmas Eve 1914.

The 1855 Grain Tower sits in the centre of the rivermouth.

Turning into the Swale, Deadmans Island is passed on the right. This was the burial place for sailors who failed to survive the quarantine period for incoming ships. Queenborough Harbour now is a safe haven for pleasure craft but it was here that the English fleet assembled before going out and beating the Spanish Armada. A number of old buildings remain in what was once called Bynne but was renamed Queenborough by Edward III in honour of his wife, Queen Phillipa. Handy for the B2007 and harbour are

stride between the Swale and Chetney Marshes, leading back to Kingsferry Bridge over what is still called Ferry Reach.

The 1960 Kingsferry Bridge connecting the island to the mainland has a centre section lifting road and railway clear of shipping using the Swale, the only one of its type in the UK, a 1.27km long high level road viaduct of 19 spans being opened in 2006 to remove the delays caused by the bridge's opening although it has safety issues and, in September 2013, was the scene of a 150 vehicle accident, the worst ever in Britain. There is parking space and a slipway down into the water. At times the area might be crowded with water skiers who are allowed to operate west of the bridge. At such times there may be a caravan serving snacks here.

Much of the shoreline of Sheppey shelves only gently and is muddy, a very tenacious clay. North of Fowley Island the Swale has a number of leads which peter out at the east end at low tide and so there is something to be said for not travelling westwards up the Swale on the lower part of the tide. A possibility is to run eastwards with the ebbing tide and then use the flood to run up the Thames Estuary. The difficulty this throws up is the great expanse of flats on the northeast coast, a problem which is less acute at neap tides.

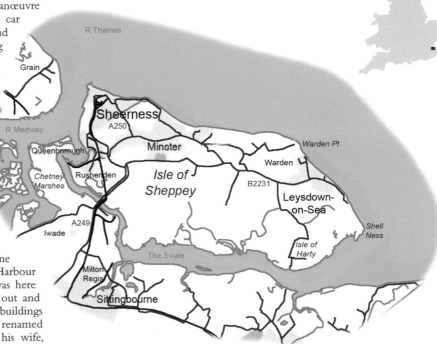

Queenborough Harbour, looking west towards the Medway.

The lifting Kingsferry road and railway bridge and the Swale road bridge.

Levées are seen frequently in the area. The southern half of the island runs with levées and creeks which once divided it into three separate islands.

Just east of the bridge is an anchorage for pleasure craft. Soon after on the mainland side is Ridham Dock, bringing in timber biomass. Milton Creek hides next to it behind a group of islands known as the Lilies and is headed by **Sittingbourne** and fronted by works producing, among other things, concrete culverts. Milton Creek is the destination for many larger boats using the Swale and the buoyage is set for inbound ships from both the east and the west. Thus, boats passing along the Swale find the buoyage reverses at this point. A hulk lies opposite Milton Creek.

All around the island is silt laden because of the washing away of the London clay of which it consists. The sea never has the salt water smell.

At Elmley Ferry a causeway crosses the Swale although there is still nearly 3m of water cover in the centre at low tide. Stone revetment has been used to protect the shoreline in places and the land is not always as flat as might be expected. Few buildings are seen. King's Hill Farm is noticeably isolated.

Two of the main waterways splitting the island are Windmill Creek and Capel Fleet. They meet by Flanders Mare saltings, an area rich in birdlife and overlooked by an ornithologists' hide on Spitend Point. Curlews and oystercatchers are seen and the air is filled with the screams of the ever wheeling flocks of gulls.

The Grade II Ferry House Inn is conveniently close to the water and was at the northern landing point for a ferry for **Faversham** which ceased operation in 1979. There has been a public house on the site since Elizabethan times. Other than a couple of farms, the only other building to be seen is the church of St Thomas the Apostle, built in 1216.

Boats moored by the Kent shore tend to be working boats and fishing boats will be seen travelling up and down the Swale. The Swale Smack & Sailing Barge Match takes place at this end of the Swale and features the traditional sailing vessels of the Thames Estuary.

The Harty marshes were once the scene of salt workings, a Roman tile kiln has been found near Shell

A Thames sailing barge leaves the Swale.

Ness and Oxford's Ashmolean Museum has a complete Bronze Age foundry from the Isle of Harty.

Shell Ness has a national nature reserve and there is a naturist area.

Rounding Shell Ness, the water becomes less calm and a beam sea develops to add to problems caused by shallow water when waves are coming up the estuary. The mud shore becomes more weathered and then gives way to gravel and the small shells which give the area its name. A fortification point fronts the first of the buildings.

The seabed is very flat here and, after landing during an ebb tide with breaking waves, there can be a real dilemma on relaunching as the water retreats rapidly. The shore has the consistency of soft clay but the tenacity of paste glue.

At low tide the Columbia Spit can extend 4km northeast from Shell Ness. At the end lies one of the two beds which produce the oysters for which **Whitstable** is famous. Ships risk having to pay damages if they run aground here.

Running northwest from Shell Ness is a shanty town of holiday huts. When James II was trying to escape to France his boat ran aground here and was boarded by local fishermen who treated the king in less than royal manner.

Groynes line the shore and show the longshore drift to be against the boater. Later, concrete seawalls make their appearance.

Standing behind one group of huts is Muswell Manor. Here, in 1901, J Moore-Brabazon, later Lord Brabazon of Tara, formed a ballooning club. The Short brothers joined it five years later and six Wright biplanes were built at a factory nearby. All the significant aviation pioneers flew from here and it was the start of the Royal Flying Corps, later the Royal Air Force.

Holiday huts, caravans and amusement arcades become thick on the ground at **Leysdown-on-Sea** at the end of the A2500. Beyond are the first of the clay cliffs which form the northern side of the island. They contain many slips and mudslides and much of Warden, including the church, has already been claimed by the sea. King Cnut lived at Shurland for a time. If it was here that he proved he did not have the authority to command the sea to stop then he is still making his point as the sea steadily advances inland.

Caravans saturate the hill on the side of Warden Point and here can be found one of the few pieces of woodland

The bank of brilliant white shells near Shell Ness.

on the island. Through the woods, on occasions, gallops the ghost of Sir John Sawbridge who lived in Warden Manor in the 17th century and who was said to have led the gang conducting the smuggling which was rife then. He is on his way to supervise the unloading of a cargo. From the manor a lost underground passage is thought to run to Shurland Hall.

Beyond Warden Point another caravan site tops the cliffs at East End. The beach is littered with boulders, some of stone, some of rounded balls of clay.

Slippage of the clay cliff at Warden.

Wind farm in the Thames Estuary off Sheppey.

Beacon marking the line of obstructions at Royal Oak Point.

Unusual flint and concrete barrel construction at Minster.

Royal Oak Point is marked by a line of sunken barges, this line being continued with other obstructions for larger ships. Further out, large vessels pass up and down the Thames Estuary or wait at the Great Nore anchorage for their turns to dock. The masts of a substantial modern ship break the surface at one point.

At **Minster** an area of cliff has been battered back and extensively laid with French drains and a concrete seawall. Perhaps this will be the pattern for the whole of this coast in the future if the Environment Agency's policy of taking no action is overcome. Many fossils are in the material being lost to the sea. Minster Abbey, the parish church of St Mary & St Sexburga, was founded in 664 by Sexburga, the widow of Saxon king Earconbert of Kent.

The shallows were a feature after the Norman conquest, too. At that time the island had been divided up between four Norman barons. One of these was Robert de Shurland. Lord Robert had a violent temper and, when he came upon a group of mourners arguing with a priest who was refusing to bury a corpse until he had been paid, slew the priest. On reaching home he considered the implications of his act and decided to go to the king before the story reached him. The king's ship was moored conveniently off the coast at the time and Lord Robert rode his horse, Grey Dolphin, a great distance out through the shallow water to reach the king's ship. The king was so impressed with this feat that he granted Lord Robert a pardon. On returning to shore he met the Witch of Scrapsgate, to whom he refused alms and who foretold that the horse which had just saved his life would later claim it. To break the curse he butchered his horse on the spot. Some time later he was walking along the beach with a friend when he found the skeleton. He related the tale, giving the skull a kick as he passed. The bone punctured his foot and he died from blood poisoning soon after.

Scrapsgate is marked now by a set of dinghy masts in a compound behind the beach. The beach becomes more sandy and beach shelters are frequent although the local pastime of setting fire to them has reduced their numbers. A new seawall has been constructed at the back of the beach. The Ship on Shore pub includes construction of concrete barrels after the 19th century *Lucky Escape* sank in a gale, ruining her cargo of barrels of cement. A funfair and fortifications precede Sheerness.

Distance
The Isle of Sheppey is 17km long and lies 200m off Iwade with road access

OS 1:50,000 Sheets
178 Thames Estuary (179 Canterbury & East Kent)

Tidal Constants
Grovehurst Jetty:
HW Dover +0120,
LW Dover +0130
Hartyferry:
Dover +0120
Whitstable Approaches:
HW Dover +0130,
LW Dover +0110
Sheerness:
Dover +0120

Sea Area
Thames

Connection
River Medway –
see RoB p242

The beach at Sheerness.

Isle of Thanet

'Twas on the shores that round our coast
From Deal to Ramsgate span,
That I found alone on a piece of stone
An elderly naval man
Sir William Schwenck Gilbert

From the former Harty Ferry crossing point on the south side of the Swale the Graveney Marshes form the South Swale Nature Reserve with large numbers of wildfowl and waders including brent geese. From the mussel banks of the Pollard Spit there are shallow flats and sands in front of the coast to North Foreland. The Seasalter Co dealt in smuggling from 1740 to the mid 19th century, signalling the all clear with brooms showing from chimneys. The Saxon Shore Way follows the coast round the Oaze and Whitstable Bay and then the coast becomes built up from Seasalter and buoys marking a 15km/h speed limit are placed 300m offshore all the way to Reculver. A windmill is conspicuous on

the top of Duncan Down and a golf course less so on the shore. **Whitstable** was a port for Canterbury. The name is from the Old English Witon stapol, pillar of the council of wise men. In *Goldfinger* Ian Fleming described Whitstable, Herne Bay, Birchington and Margate as 'the cheap bungaloid world of holiday lands'. The world's first passenger steam railway, the Crab and Winkle line, served this route from 1830 to 1952.

Whitstable harbour manages to squeeze in some large vessels for its small size, just 680m of quays. The town is a yachting centre as well as a resort. It has been known for its oysters since Roman times and has the largest oyster hatchery in Europe. Smuggling included brandy, gin, tobacco, lace and Napoleonic French prisoners. The Whitstable Oyster Company may call their best oysters Royal Whitstable Natives. There is a Whitstable oyster festival. A wood panelled cinema is set in an old oyster warehouse and other attractive buildings include weatherboarded fishermen's cottages and black tarred boat sheds. The world's first diving helmet was invented

Where everyone of significance landed

Herne Bay with the pier remains, the second longest until 1978.

Whitstable Harbour with vessels docked.

The twin Reculvers towers act as an important shipping landmark.

The River Wantsum, formerly the Wantsum Channel dividing the Isle of Thanet from the mainland and carrying shipping.

here and the marine associations continue with the Whitstable Barge Match, waterskiing and small surf break. Residents have included horror film actor Peter Cushing.

The agreeable waterfront continues with Whitstable Castle surrounded by trees at Tankerton and also the Hotel Continental with architecture which would seem appropriate for the Low Countries. A hill is equipped with a ship's mast and cannons. A peculiar local feature is Whitstable Street, a narrow stone causeway which runs out into the sea for 700m at low tide and collects shells. A Tudor wreck at Tankerton has been excavated.

Beach huts line the shore towards Swalecliff where herring and blackbacked gulls hang about Long Rock. At the end of the seawall at Hampton, used by powerboats, a line of rocks run out to sea, submerging as the tide rises. Beyond the Hampton Inn is the Sea Cadets' TS Triumph.

Herne Bay, from the Old English hyrne, corner, was a fishing village with cod, bass and skate and was used by the North Kent smuggling gang but became a resort in the 1830s. In the winter of 1962/3 the sea froze for 400m beyond the end of the pier. This was the town's central feature, the second longest in the country at 1.2km until damaged by storms in 1978 and demolished the next year, leaving the ornate pierhead standing well offshore and the root of the pier developed as the Pier Sports Centre with roller skating, squash and a dancehall. The pavilion replaces the grand Pier Pavilion of 1910 which burnt down in 1970. There are original items surviving, notably the ornate 24m clocktower of 1837. The Seaside Museum Herne Bay features this Victorian resort, the pier, the archaeology and the fossils. With its high sunshine levels, Heron's Leisure Centre can make maximum use of such items as the flume and beach pool. Seafront gardens and a bandstand complete what a traditional resort should have. The Dolphin Hotel and Divers Arms add further coastal associations. BayFest takes place in August. John Nivers, in Lewis Carroll's *The Blank Cheque*, wanted to go on holiday to Herne Bay

Much further offshore in the middle of the Thames Estuary are the Maunsell Sea Forts on Shivering Sands and Red Sands, 13 of the original 21 forts remaining like so many balls on posts on the horizon.

Earth cliffs 30m high, initially as a green bank, extend to Reculver from Beltinge where there is a prominent water tower.

Reculver was important because it guarded the northern end of what was formerly the Wantsum Channel, separating the Isle of Thanet from the mainland. The Romans built their Regulbium fort here in the 3rd

century to resist the Saxons, some walls remaining. The ghostly crying of children is sometimes heard on stormy nights and babies' skeletons were found beneath the foundations in 1966 so this could be an example of ritual live burial sacrifice. In 669 King Egbert of Kent founded a monastery inside the fort, destroyed by the Vikings in the 9th century. The site of a 7th century church by St Augustine was used as the site for the 12th century church of St Mary which was demolished in 1809 and a new one built at Hillborough, after the sea washed away most of the fort and threatened the church. The Reculvers or Two Sisters are twin towers which remain, having been restored without their spires by Trinity House as a shipping landmark. The spires were originally added in the 16th century for Frances St Clare, the Benedictine abbess at Davington, after being shipwrecked with her sister, Isabel, who died from her injuries, as a memorial and landmark. Both are buried under the towers. The North Kent gang were also active here and it was where Goldfinger lived and had his Thanet Alloys smuggling base. The site is now part of a country park with a sea of caravans. It is a bird migration watchpoint.

Barnes-Wallis tested his bouncing bomb here. The Copperas Channel, Gore Channel and South Channel lead past the Margate Hook bank, heading on to the larger Margate Sand, both of which dry at low tide.

The embankment across the old Wantsum Channel is reinforced by stone groynes at intervals. On the other side from a mussel bank is the much diminished River Wantsum.

Plumpudding Island is also part of the mainland these days, crossed by the Wantsum Walk which is also a popular cycle route. Minnis Bay faces Margate Hook and is popular with kite surfers. The Minnies are drying ledges which continue round to Pegwell Bay. On top of these are chalk cliffs, the first chalk since Flamborough but very different now, low and in manicured blocks with neatly rounded edges, a massive seawall supporting a promenade around the bottom and built up on top. Indeed, virtually the whole of the cliff line of Thanet seems to be built up.

It begins with Birchington, claimed to be the largest village in Kent. The medieval church of All Saints has the 1882 grave of Victorian artist Dante Gabriel Rossetti.

Greenham Bay has the risk of rockfalls while in Epple

Bay it is more likely to be golf balls. Westgate on Sea is red brick Victorian and Edwardian with landscaped gardens on a promontory but mostly the buildings seem to be more like low rise tower blocks. St Mildred's Bay lies between ledges and beyond Westbrook the Nayland Rock ledges occupy most of the bay with its beachbreak so that it is almost possible to miss **Margate** harbour. Its 20m stone tower lighthouse on the end of John Rennie's 250m stone pier of 1815 allowed steamboats to bring holidaymakers from London before the railway was built. *The Snow Goose* makes reference to the *Kentish Maid* excursion scow used in the Dunkirk evacuation and *Kangaroo* compares Sydney with Margate. The Nivers family did not enjoy their holiday here in *The Blank Cheque*. Mr Nyttleton had been staying here with his family in Hardy's *Desperate Remedies*. In *Tom Tiddler's Ground* by Dickens and others, Miss Pupford's Parisian accented assistant had never been out of England except in the pleasure boat *Lively* off Margate.

Margate is from the Old English mere gate, sea gate. Margate Promenade Pier was damaged in storms in 1978 and has now been demolished. This Cinque Port limb was the target for the Armada, from where they were to assist Spanish troops to invade from Flanders. The 16th century Tudor House is its oldest building remaining. The resort was helped when Benjamin Beale invented the bathing machine here in 1753. The Old Town Hall is the Local History Museum covering the seaside, maritime matters, police and town silver. The Theatre Royal Margate is the country's second oldest. The Dreamland Margate amusement park, the UK's first amusement park, was founded in 1920 with log flume, Bounty Ship swingboat, dodgems, 61m wheel, oldest operating roller coaster in the UK and more, claimed to be the largest seaside leisure complex in the south of England. JMW Turner and Tracy Emin lived here and the Turner Contemporary art gallery is sited overlooking the harbour, including their work and Rodin's The Kiss.

The B2051 climbs away from the A28 past the Ship Inn towards Cliftonville where the jaded

air of Southend and the retirement hotels is repeated. The tidal swimming pool was one of the last built. The cliff railway has been dismantled and the road train now cuts short its route, yet there are still some interesting finds, like one of the world's smallest theatres, the Tom Thumb, in what was a double garage and a nearby Italian restaurant where the proprietor believes that the meal should be correct and the conversation stimulating. Margate Caves were discovered in 1798 and used as a dungeon, a church and by smugglers, the passages to the sea now having been sealed. The 2,000 year old Shell Grotto dug out of the chalk, discovered in 1835, was thought to be the only underground temple in the world, covering 190m^2 with 4,600,000 shells.

Palm Bay with its promenade fronts Cliftonville where TS Eliot had a mild nervous breakdown while staying. Jetski World Safaris are located alongside for those who want their own.

Long Nose Spit runs out as a ledge in front of Foreness Point. Streams run southeast at HW Dover +0440 to HW Dover −0450, are weak and irregular until HW Dover −0120, run northwest until HW Dover +0040 and then are turbulent for the rest of the cycle.

Botany Bay, the first of seven bays to Dumpton Gap, known as the Jewels in Thanet's Crown, has high water surf. The 18th century Battle of Botany Bay took place between the revue men and smugglers with fatalities. At the far end of Botany Bay, named after where convicted smugglers were sent, there is an old fort site above an arch at White Ness. Now private residences, the 1760s Kingsgate Castle at the back of Kingsgate Bay occupies an imposing position on top of the cliff at Hackemdown Point. A local resident was Frank Richards, author of *Billy Bunter*. The B2052 is now running along the cliffs. Joss Bay is a surfing venue, named after Joss Snelling, head of the Callis Court gang, still active and fined at 89 but presented to Queen Victoria as a

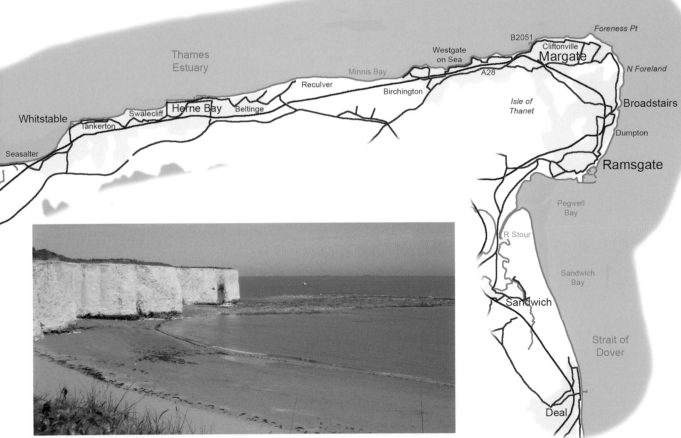

White Ness overlooking Kingsgate Bay.

Broadstairs with Bleak House, where Charles Dickens wrote David Copperfield, *using local characters.*

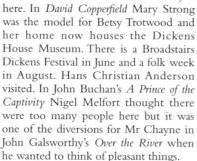

noted smuggler. A smugglers' tunnel leads down to the beach and high tide surf.

North Foreland, where the Thames Estuary gives way to the Strait of Dover, is marked by the 26m white octagonal tower of 1790, the coal of which was replaced by 18 oil lamps because the glass could not be kept clean. There has been a light here since 1499, the current one with a range of 32km, the last to be automated by Trinity House. Beneath it in 1665 was a four day battle when the English beat the Dutch fleet. The 39 steps down to Stone Bay with its high tide surf gave John Buchan the title of his novel, part of which he wrote while his wife was convalescing here in 1914.

Cliffs increase in height to 37m to Ramsgate and flows are southwest from HW Dover +0420 and northeast from HW Dover −0140.

A prominent building in **Broadstairs** is the castellated Fort House, summer home of Charles Dickens where he wrote *David Copperfield*, renamed Bleak House in 1853 after he published this book. Wilkie Collins also stayed here. In *David Copperfield* Mary Strong was the model for Betsy Trotwood and her home now houses the Dickens House Museum. There is a Broadstairs Dickens Festival in June and a folk week in August. Hans Christian Anderson visited. In John Buchan's *A Prince of the Captivity* Nigel Melfort thought there were too many people here but it was one of the diversions for Mr Chayne in John Galsworthy's *Over the River* when he wanted to think of pleasant things.

The broad stairs in the name were stone steps built down the cliff to the shore in 1434. The harbour and pier were once owned by Henry VIII and the York Gate portcullis arch dates from the same time. In the 18th century it was a shipbuilding centre and it was a smuggling centre during the Napoleonic wars. The Crampton Tower Museum features the work of Victorian railway engineer Thomas Russell Crampton and includes a Broadstairs–Canterbury stagecoach. A weekly firework display takes place over Viking Bay and the Customs House water gala has been running for over a century. Viking Bay and Louisa Bay, Dumpton Gap and beyond all have surf.

Mark on the entrance to Ramsgate Harbour.

The Italianate greenhouse of 1805 in the grounds of the home of Admiral Lord George Keith, in the King George VI Memorial Park at East Cliff, includes a vine imported from Corsica for Queen Caroline who liked grapes.

The corporate Cinque Port of **Ramsgate**, named from the Old English hraefn, raven, was built after a bad storm in 1748 and completed in 1750 by John Smeaton, Samuel Wyatt and John Rennie. In 1754 Jacob Steel added a striking staircase up the cliffs, since called Jacob's Ladder, and a drydock followed in 1791. The lighthouse on the West Pier was one of the first to have a revolving light, powered by a weight dropping within the tower and needing to be rewound each day. The lifeboat was also one of the first, operational from 1802, and holds the record for the number of lives saved because of its proximity to the Goodwin Sands, the graveyard of ships. Ramsgate was also noted for its trawlers, as mentioned in *Hornblower & the 'Atropos'*. George IV landed in 1820 and was well treated by the town, resulting in the regal designation, and it was also a regular holiday destination for the young Princess Victoria. The Royal Harbour is commercial but contains two marinas. Outside is the Western Marine Terminal, Port of Ramsgate, which has operated cross Channel services since 1981 to Dunkirk and Ostend and now has 3,300 sailings per year including high speed catamarans. A ferry movement is indicated by an orange flashing light on the East Pier, not the North Breakwater which extends it and outside which is surfing. Wellington sailed from here to Waterloo and St George the Martyr church has a stained glass window to the 82,000 men who landed from Dunkirk, nearly a quarter of them in Ramsgate. *The Snow Goose* refers to a Ramsgate motorboat being strafed at Dunkirk. There are 6km of Second World War tunnels 20m below the town. It was a 19th century resort. Susan, the Nivers' maid, chose this as a holiday destination and Lewis Carroll's *The Black Cheque* and his *The New Belfry of Christ Church, Oxford* gave a backhanded insult by reporting that two builders of bathing machines in Ramsgate had based designs on that structure.

The 19th century Clock House has become the Maritime Museum covering maritime and navigation exhibits, Goodwin Sands wrecks, the RNLI and the restored drydock, the resort, port and archaeology. The Clock House set Ramsgate Mean Time until 1848. Regency villas are frequent. Those brought up here include Gothic Revival leader Augustus Pugin and actress Brenda Blethyn. Van Gogh taught art here in the 19th century. West Cliff Hall has historic cars, motorcycles and cycles, a model village houses 6,000m^2 of Tudor houses and there is a local museum in the library. Ramsgate is a town of 19th century terraces and at Westcliff there is a boating pool.

The award-winning A253 approaching the port was built by the innovative technique of using something like a giant chainsaw to cut 200mm slots 5m into the chalk, filled with concrete before further excavation took place, a technique which saved money and the demolition of 11 houses.

Sand builds up in the harbour entrance after north-easterly gales. There is an eddy off the South Breakwater with a northeastgoing stream and strong flows across the entrance, but streams are then weak to Deal, flowing southwest from HW Dover +0600 to the next HW Dover −0100 and northeast from Dover HW to HW Dover +0500.

The cliffs end at Pegwell. Pegwell Bay has a hovercraft slip which served the first international hoverport with a service to Calais from 1968. The EU's withdrawal of duty free allowances made it uneconomic. William Boyce's picture of Pegwell Bay was one that Francis Croft was keen to acquire in *The Bird of Night*.

According to Sellar & Yeatman's spoof history, *1066 & All That*, Thanet was the place where all invaders of note landed, not particularly helpful as it was probably still an island at the time. However, Ebbsfleet probably saw two significant landings. In 449 Jutland chieftains Hengist and Horsa, meaning stallion and horse, arrived with the Saxons and a banner showing a prancing white horse, now the badge of Kent. In 1949, the 1,500th anniversary, the *Hugin* replica was sailed from Denmark and is now on display at Cliffs End. St Augustine's Well is near where St Augustine landed in 597, celebrating his first mass in the presence of King Ethelbert, the site marked in 1884 by St Augustine's Cross. The Spanish Armada had also intended to land here. Two golf courses are fronted by a nature reserve and Pegwell Bay Country Park. The estuary of the River Stour has flows inwards from HW Dover −0450 and outwards from HW Dover +0200.

From Shell Ness, where there are fish traps, beacons and a wreck, the shore is followed by the combined Stour Valley Walk, White Cliffs Country Trail and Saxon Shore Way, overlooking the drying mud and sand of Sandwich Flats.

Richborough was a Roman port. Eight centuries ago **Sandwich** was a coastal port. TH White, in *The Once & Future King*, claims Arthur and Sir Lancelot landed here

A Stour estuary channel mark.

Sandown Castle is now little more than a rockery

from France after fighting the Romans. Other users are said to have included Thomas à Becket avoiding Henry II and Richard the Lionheart heading to the Crusades. Now it is 3km inland but the history does not go away. On misty nights a Roman might be seen fighting a Saxon on the shore. During the Second World War soldiers on defence watch saw a cohort of Romans march into the sea.

King Alfred captured 16 ships off the mouth of the Stour but was beaten by a much larger Danish force. The first recorded sea battle was in 851 when Athelstan and Ealhhere defeated a Danish fleet off Sandwich. The Danes occupied Sandwich in 1006, King Swein of Denmark first landed here in 1009 and Cnut landed some hostages here five years later and mutilated them before sailing for Denmark. The town was plundered by 25 Viking ships in 1048 and Tostig occupied it in 1066, the Danes under Asbiorn being beaten back a couple of years later. The Battle of Sandwich took place in Sandwich Bay on St Bartholomew's Day in 1217. The French were led by the English traitor Eustace the Monk, who was able to turn his ship invisible by magic. Stephen Crabbe of Sandwich found the ship, perhaps with a little magic of his own, and cut off Eustace's head, making the ship visible again. The English won and the hospital or almshouses in Sandwich, which treated the wounded, was renamed St Bartholomew's after the victory, a name it retains. Edward III's fleet of 1,100 ships gathered off the town prior to the siege of Calais. The mayor wears black in memory of the 1457 attack by French from Honfleur. An original Cinque Port, it was visited by Elizabeth I in her process of 1573. A daily evening curfew bell is still rung. Sandwiches have a less noble origin, the local earl originating them as convenience snack for long gambling sessions.

Along the back of the bay are the finest dunes in southeast England with a nature reserve and growths of bedstraw broomrape, golden samphire, yellow horned poppy and 95% of Britain's lizard orchids. A bird observatory is surrounded by the Prince's, Royal St George's (Royal St Mark's in *Goldfinger*), which has hosted the British Open and the Walker Cup and was described by Fleming as the 'greatest seaside course in the world', and Royal Cinque Ports Golf Links, hosting the Halford Hewitt Challenge Cup, said to be the world's largest golf tournament, for 640 former public schoolboys. It also has tolls on the road on each side.

A shingle beach at the back of the South Downs is unbroken except for the Sandwich Bay Estate until arrival at the Sandown Castle site, the start of **Deal**, approached up a steep gravel beach and over some large rocks.

The buttresses of Sandown Castle date from the 16th century but little now remains, more a glorified rockery than fortifications. The rocks forming the beach defences are a greater obstruction to getting to and from the water and may be reinforced by a high tide dump and a line of anglers after cod, codling, whiting and flatfish. Larks serenade the dilemma.

Distance
57km from Harty
Ferry to Sandown
Castle

OS 1:50,000 Sheets
178 Thames Estuary
179 Canterbury
& East Kent

Tidal Constants
Hartyferry:
Dover +0120
Whitstable
Approaches:
HW Dover +0130,
LW Dover +0110
Herne Bay:
Dover +0120
Margate:
HW Dover +0050,
LW Dover +0100
Broadstairs:
HW Dover +0040,
LW Dover +0110
Ramsgate:
HW Dover +0030,
LW Dover +0010
Richborough:
HW Dover +0020,
LW Dover +0030
Deal:
HW Dover +0020,
LW Dover +0010

Sea Areas
Thames, Dover

Connection
River Stour −
see RoB p246

26 Strait of Dover

Britain's front line and the world's busiest waters

The sea is calm tonight.
The tide is full, the moon lies fair
Upon the straits; on the French coast the light
Gleams and is gone; the cliffs of England stand,
Glimmering and vast, out in the tranquil bay.
Come to the window, sweet is the night-air!
Only, from the long line of spray
Where the sea meets the moon-blanched land,
Listen! you hear the grating roar
Of pebbles which the waves draw back, and fling,
At their return, up the high strand,
Begin, and cease, and then again begin,
With tremulous cadence slow, and bring
The eternal note of sadness in.

Matthew Arnold

Fishing boats work off the beach in Deal and the Deal Rowing Club are also able to get their rowing boats afloat. The 300m pier of 1957 was built for larger craft, Britain's only postwar pier of its kind. Some 40,000 men, nearly 400 transport ships and over 200 men of war gathered here in 1809, the largest British force ever, to attack the Scheldt. Buried in the churchyard of St George's church of 1709 by Sir Cloudesley Shovell is Nelson's Captain Parker. Nelson himself stayed in the Royal Hotel to meet Lady Hamilton and Queen Victoria and Winston Churchill often stayed. William Penn sailed from here in 1682 to found Pennsylvania. The 1854 Deal Timeball Tower was used so that boats could set their timepieces to GMT for navigational purposes, the ball dropping at 1pm. One of only four working ones left in the world, it is now controlled electronically from Greenwich. The building contains a museum of maritime communications and telegraphy alongside the A258. There was a thriving naval yard from 1703, one of the most important in England, and the centre of the town was used by smugglers in the 18th century, Deal boats often having false keels and hollow masts to assist them. Flogging Joey was Capt William McCulloch's 19th century coastal blockade, his HQ here in an attempt to stop smuggling.

The Grade II town hall of 1803 is in front of Deal Maritime & Local History Museum. This was a non-corporate member of the Cinque Ports. The first Royal Marine barracks were built here in 1794. Deal Maritime Local History Museum contains model and full sized boats, figureheads, cannons and compasses. The 18th century buildings and Deal Maritime Folk Festival recall the era but the stone marking where Julius Caesar landed in 55BC to begin the Roman conquest of Britain takes more imagination. This was probably the Dorobellum where, Geoffrey of Monmouth says, Cassivelaunus consulted his princes on how to resist Caesar. In Daniel

Deal has the only post war pleasure pier in Britain.

Deal's timeball tower is one of only four working ones left in the world.

Hiding behind boats on the beach, Deal Castle was Henry VIII's largest coastal defence.

Defoe's imagination this is where Gulliver began most of his travels. In Old English times it was a dael or valley.

Beyond the Downs are the Goodwin Sands, the Ship Swallower, 19km x 8km, 6km off, but moving towards the coast. These have claimed innumerable vessels, including Goldfinger's trawler, and about which warning was given in *Redgauntlet*. Nevertheless, the Goodwins did not prove an adequate defence. Deal Castle, built in 1539, was Henry VIII's largest coastal defence and is the largest castle on the south coast and one of England's best Tudor artillery defences. With a circular central keep, six gun bastions, six lower crescent shaped bastions and a dry ditch, it had 119 guns and now features a coastal defences exhibition. It changed hands twice during the Civil War.

Strong flows begin south at HW Dover +0420 and north at HW Dover −0150.

Walmer was another non-corporate Cinque Port with a Tudor rose castle built in the 1530s by Henry VIII near the shore. It fell to the Parliamentarians in the Civil War in 1642, being recaptured briefly by the Kentish army in 1648. The original Wellington boots are here, Wellington being resident from 1829 until his death here in 1852, sleeping on a camp bed in a spartan room, according to *The Once & Future King*. It was the residence of the Lord Wardens of the Cinque Ports from 1708 and was visited by the late warden, the Queen Mother. The Beauchamps lived in the castle, recorded as the Flyte family in Evelyn Waugh's *Brideshead Revisited*. The castle has an 18th century panelled interior and the most notable garden is the Queen Mother's Garden, laid out for her 95th birthday, but most of the garden is as designed by Pitt the Younger in 1795 with a moat garden, woodland walk, boxed yew hedge and croquet lawn. Poet Robert Bridges was born here. Trinity House almshouses of 1958 replaced those in London's Mile End Road.

A swimming area at Oldstairs Bay and some eccentric seaside architecture are among aspects of **Kingsdown**. This is where

the Downs (land rather than sea) are severed and the white cliffs begin in earnest. Occasionally, a white golf ball may come down off the course on Hope Point. More to the point, it could be a fall of chalk, leaving chalk debris in the sea. Otherwise it is just those uncompromising white cliffs glistening in the sun and the throb of ship engines out in the Strait of Dover although it might have been something more sinister in *Moonraker*. The constriction in the Channel pushes the wind up a force. This is the world's busiest shipping lane, complicated by the cross-Channel traffic. The Dover Strait Traffic Separation Scheme acts as a dual carriageway for ships, complete with central reserve and an Inshore Traffic Zone. The authorities are not keen to see small craft crossing.

Being the nearest point to the Continent has had major military implications over the centuries. This is Britain's front line, the first place to be visited by successive invaders. Pillboxes occur at strategic positions and the granite obelisk of the Dover Patrol Memorial is a reminder of a wartime job which was very exposed.

The resort of **St Margaret's at Cliffe**, by St Margaret's Bay since Victorian times, was a fishing village which has been the normal setting out point for cross Channel swimmers, not now

encouraged, this being just 35km from Cap Griz Nez in France, visible on a clear day, close enough to shell across the Channel in both World Wars. The first channel swimmer may have been Jean-Marie Saletti who escaped off a prison hulk and swam to Boulogne in 1815. Captain Matthew Webb made the first official crossing in 1875. Double and triple crossings have been undertaken. Surfers often use the beach. The black pebble beach is served by an ice cream seller and by toilets, having a holiday park close by. St Margaret of Antioch church has a window to the memory of the 1987 Zeebrugge ferry capsize victims. Successive residents in the same holiday house at the north end of the bay were Noel Coward and Ian Fleming, who used the cliffs for the Moonraker silo and would have used the bus service to London, the 007. Around the bay are found ivy and carrot broomrapes. St Margaret's Museum has maritime and Noel Coward exhibits and a Bronze Age skeleton. Above the bay the Pines Garden has 2ha of trees, shrubs, flowers, a grass labyrinth, a lake, a Romany caravan, a bronze Churchill statue of 1972 by Oscar Nemon and the Pines Calyx, claimed to be one of Europe's most sustainable and healthy structures, an events space. Blackbacked gulls, cormorants and jellyfish ignore a hole cut in the chalk cliff face and propped with a brick pillar, suggesting some military purpose in the past.

South Foreland is where the east coast really turns

St Margaret's Bay, starting point for cross Channel swims.

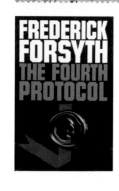

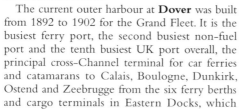

to become the south coast, described in the evening in Thomas Hardy's *A Pair of Blue Eyes*. On top are a Grade II white smock windmill of 1929 and a 21m white castellated lighthouse tower of 1843 which was the first to be lit electrically and was used in 1898 by Marconi for the first ship to shore radio transmission and also used by Faraday.

The Dover Harbour Limit includes Fan Bay and Langdon Bay with wrecks at the bottom of the cliffs, including Britain's earliest known wreck from about 1100BC. Divers have recovered 352 French bronze swords, axes and other Bronze Age implements from the bed of the bay, presumably the site of a wreck. On the cliffs, about which Vera Lynn sang, are wild cabbage, a memorial, aerials, the Langdon Battery and the maritime rescue co-ordination centre.

The current outer harbour at **Dover** was built from 1892 to 1902 for the Grand Fleet. It is the busiest ferry port, the second busiest non-fuel port and the tenth busiest UK port overall, the principal cross-Channel terminal for car ferries and catamarans to Calais, Boulogne, Dunkirk, Ostend and Zeebrugge from the six ferry berths and cargo terminals in Eastern Docks, which has the UK's longest illuminated sign, 88m x 650mm. From the first of these came the Dorn family in their camper with a surprisingly dense ball in the children's toy cupboard in Frederick Forsyth's *The Fourth Protocol*. *The Eagle Has Landed* claimed there was a Mouse night bombing support device sited here but that the Germans had been informed about it. The Western Docks have a cruise terminal. It is the only Head Port of the Cinque Ports which remains a significant harbour. A buoy laid off the harbour in 1977 was the first to feature the new IALA buoyage system A, which has red buoys on river right.

Port control is on the end of the 900m Eastern Arm. A floating current meter should not be touched as it has a 75m radius exclusion zone but it is a useful guide to what

The old South Foreland lighthouse on Dover's white cliffs.

the current is doing as it passes. Each entrance has inward and outward flows in different places at nearly all times, giving turbulence in addition to anything resulting from ferries' manoeuvring. The Southern Breakwater is 1.3km long. The large walls are hit by swells from the west and result in significant reflected waves in rough conditions.

Dover takes its name from the River Dour or from the British Celtic dobra, water. Dover Museum has a Bronze Age boat of oak and yew which, at 3,550 years old, is probably the world's oldest seagoing boat, thought capable of carrying a significant load across the Channel. The museum also has a Roman section and a 1940s air raid street scene. To the Romans Dover was Portus Dubris, the headquarters of the Roman northern fleet, Classis Britannica. A Roman mansion of about 200 is one of the best examples in Britain with painted frescoes and hypocausts and now with an exhibition of Roman Dover. Some 37m^2 of painted plaster was saved when the Romans demolished it in 270 and left it under the ramparts of a fort extension, the most extensive area of Roman painting to have been found north of the Alps. The Roman pharos of about 45 is one of two lighthouses they built in Dover. Originally 24m high, 12m of Roman flint rubble in tufa ashlar with mortar and tile reinforcing make it one of the highest remaining Roman structures in Europe. The current top is 15th century, forming the belltower of the Anglo Saxon church of St Mary in

Eastern Docks are a hive of activity. The French coast is just visible on the horizon.

Dover Castle, Britain's oldest, strongest and one of the largest,

Castro with 13th century two seater sedilia and double piscina in the chancel, greatly restored in the 19th century.

These structures are within the walls of Dover Castle, described as the Key to England. Count Eustace of Boulogne failed to take it from William I after not waiting for reinforcements to arrive. The Danes were beaten back in 1068. It is England's oldest, strongest and one of its largest fortresses, covering 32ha with a large irregular outer bailey. An 1180s three storey square keep and curtain with square open backed wall towers and barbicans by Maurice the Engineer for Henry II are the finest of their kind. There is a 13th century outer curtain wall with D-plan wall towers. The castle stands prominently above the town and has been garrisoned continuously since Norman times. It has Queen Elizabeth's Pocket Pistol, a 7m ornamental gun given to her by the Dutch. It was where Churchill watched the Battle of Britain and was the nerve centre for Operation Dynamo, where he planned the successful Dunkirk evacuation of 338,000 members of the British Expeditionary Force and French troops with Vice Admiral Ramsay after 45,000 had been considered a theoretical maximum. The castle has an Iron Age fort and has the only underground barracks in Britain, while 60m below the castle are the warren of secret wartime tunnels which form Hellfire Corner, complete with hospital. The town failed to keep out the plague in 1665 but fell to the Parliamentarians in the Civil War without a shot being fired. Exhibitions include a replica 12th century royal palace, a display of the unsuccessful 1216 siege by Prince Louis, Henry VIII's court in the keep, a model of the Battle of Waterloo, armour, cannons, the history of the Princess of Wales' Royal Regiment, spy equipment and a nuclear bunker.

Sir Gawain was killed in a battle here or at Richborough, fighting with Sir Lancelot and King Arthur

against the Arthur's son, Sir Mordred, after he had usurped the throne in their absence in France. *Le Morte d'Arthur* describes how his damaged skull remained on show in a chapel in the castle. The castle has been used for installing the Lord Warden of the Cinque Ports, has been used for filming Zefirelli's *Hamlet* and, not surprisingly, has a ghost. It was also used for filming *The Other Boleyn Girl* and *Those Magnificent Men in their Flying Machines*.

On the cliffs is a memorial to Louis Blériot, where he landed after flying the Channel in 1909, and there is a statue to Stewart Rolls who flew the Channel both ways in a single flight the following year. The *Wings* series has Triggers' flight being issued with car inner tubes in case of ditching during their flight from here to Amiens. Another statue celebrates Captain Matthew Webb. Gerald of Wales returned here from France in 1189 and had his vow to the Third Crusade cancelled as he was thought to be of more use back in England following the death of Henry II. In 1213 King John met Pandulf, the papal legate, and handed him the crown of England and Ireland, receiving it back five days later. Margery Kempe managed to sail to Dover despite the efforts of other passengers to avoid her company. The Duke of Suffolk was beheaded on a boat in 1450 and his body laid on the beach, possibly with his head on a pole. Tom Paine was searched here in 1792 as he left Britain for the last time, embarking for Calais minutes before Government officials arrived with an arrest warrant. Dover features in Ian Fleming's *Casino Royale*, *Diamonds are Forever* and *Chitty Chitty Bang Bang*, Charles Dickens' *The Uncommercial Traveller*, Graham Greene's *Travels with My Aunt* and Alexandre Dumas' *Les Trois Mousquetaires*, saw the Vikings under Asbiorn repelled in Charles Kingsley's *Hereward the Wake* and a Limehouse tug and barges bringing troops back from Dunkirk in *The Snow Goose*. Strong watched Altamont depart on his foreign

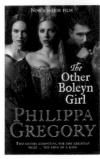

tour in Thackeray's *Pendennis*. John Geste, boarding a cross Channel steamer in Percival Christopher Wren's *Beau Geste*, preferred Devon to Kent. A Jack of Dover was a fool.

In 1670 Charles II conducted the secret Treaty of Dover whereby he promised Louis XIV to declare war on the Dutch, convert to Catholicism and to make England Catholic again.

The 12th century church of St Mary the Virgin, largely rebuilt in the 19th century as the number of burials under the floor was making it unstable, has had major connections with the Lords Warden of the Cinque Ports.

There is a Victorian Old Town Gaol museum.

At the entrance to the Eastern Docks the A2 and A20 meet, a significant traffic terminus although it is a rare major UK port without a connecting railway station. Siegfried Sassoon's *Memoirs of an Infantry Officer* refers to a First World War hospital train from Dover and John Hilliard returned this way from the front in *Strange Meeting*. Harvey Lawson and Francis Croft departed from here for Venice in *The Bird of Night*. *Eye of the Needle* claims a false oil dock was built here to foil the Germans. Further along the seafront is a panel taken from the German Battery Todt near Calais by Allied troops in 1944.

There is also the Stade, the fishermen's beach, across which not all Dover sole pass. To its west is the Wellington Dock with the restored *Sorceress* in which Edward VII had meetings with Lillie Langtree. Dover beach was Jordon's Sand in Dryden's *Absalom & Achitophel*.

On the Western Heights are the foundations of a 12th century Knights Templar church, extensive 18th to 19th century fortifications, parts of a moat around a former 19th century fort, the Citadel and the Grand Shaft, a triple spiral staircase connecting Victorian barracks with the town, plus a current young offender institution.

To the west of the harbour is the 110m Shakespeare Cliff which takes its name from a passage in *King Lear*. Running through the cliff in twin high Gothic arch cuts visible from the water is the Shakespeare Cliff Tunnel of 1.3km, 3.7m wide x 8.5m high, separated by a 3m pier because of the poor ground conditions. Shakespeare beach is the start point for official cross Channel swims. Passing below is the Channel Tunnel, opened in 1994 with the world's longest section of undersea tunnel, 50km long with two 7.6m diameter running tunnels and a smaller service tunnel. Near it are false starts in 1881, 1882 and 1972.

If the Samphire Hoe Country Park looks like a slightly landscaped pile of Channel Tunnel spoil retained in vertical sheet piling, there can be no accusations of deception. It is crossed by the Saxon Shore Way and North Downs Way long distance footpaths.

The final major rail tunnel is the 1.8km Abbot's Cliff Tunnel of 1840–4 where the cliff was close to the high water mark. It included a number of shafts driven in from a road at the base of the cliff with the spoil being tipped into the sea. In the process the

Lydden Spout gushed forth and was incorporated into the design.

Abbot's Cliff has the best of the listening ear devices. Others were set up at Hythe, Dymchurch, Greatstone and Denge. They were used to detect the sound of approaching enemy aircraft but climatic conditions made them unreliable and they were replaced by radar. Sculptures of them have been erected. At Capel-le-Ferne on the B2011 above East Wear Bay is a Battle of Britain memorial. The Wing building, shaped like a Spitfire's wings, contains the Scramble Experience and a large propeller is sculpted on the ground outside. The bay was much used by smugglers.

Below this is the Warren, an unstable area of chalk on gault clay which is slipping seawards, slips having been recorded since 1765, ten of them having interrupted railway traffic since 1844. It took its present form in 1915 when a 3km section moved 50m seawards, resulting in closure of the railway for 4 years. The upper part is known as Little Switzerland and there is a caravan site above the shore. Steady Hole was the scene in 1856 of the murder of two teenage girls from Dover by a soldier from Shorncliffe Camp, subsequently hanged for the crime.

There are more Martello towers before Copt Point which has a visitor centre and where submarine power cables land so the wreck off the point was probably not appreciated. There are surf breaks on each side of the point.

Although there are the remains of a Roman villa on East Cliff, **Folkestone**, named after the Old English man Folca, was a fishing village which was attacked by Olaf and 93 ships in 991 and later became a Cinque Port, then a cross-Channel ferry port. Telford's harbour work of 1808–20 was unusual in that slabs up to 2t each were laid at 45° on broken stone. The town became a resort from the 1840s and the 450m South Pier was added in the late 19th century. It was where Georgie and his staff were sent to take a week's break, avoiding the Contessa di Faraglione, in EF Benson's *Mapp & Lucia*. It was also the setting for HG Wells' *The New Accelerator*. Richard Somers left the port when taking a break in Italy in *Kangaroo*. Ferries were still operating from Ostend at the time of *The Fourth Protocol*, a German Hanomag lorry arriving with a nuclear bomb part built into one of its exhaust pipes.

It was unusual for a resort in not having a seafront. Instead there are the Leas, a 1.6km long clifftop lawn and gardens promenade, the town's gardening produce having included a 231g strawberry in 1983. To get up and down, a 30m high 40° water powered cliff railway was installed in 1885, the first on the south coast, restored in 2010. The lower terminal has its ticket office, waiting room, pump room and offices listed.

A second lift was added in 1890 but was taken out of use in 1960 after an accident, by which time there was already a decline in demand. The other rail related structure just visible from the sea is the yellow brick Foord Viaduct of 1843. By Sir William Cubitt, it is 230m long with 19 arches up to 24m high and was the only major structure on the South Eastern Railway between Dover and London. As at Folkestone Warren, any train other than the Golden Arrow pulled by a boxy Merchant Navy or Battle of Britain class steam engine crossing this viaduct just does not look right.

St Mary & St Eanswythe's church is part 13th century on the site of a 7th century Saxon nunnery. Also old, the high street is steep and cobbled. The town has an 1895 bandstand and a statue of William Harvey, who was born here in 1578 and discovered the circulation of blood. The Creative Quarter is an arts base and chef Phil Vickery was born here.

Flows start southwest at HW Dover +0320 at up to 3km/h and the other way from HW Dover −0200

The Shakespeare Cliff and Samphire Hoe with steep approach road tunnel and railway tunnel.

The heavily slipped Folkestone Warren.

at up to 4km/h, at which time an eddy forms in the harbourmouth.

There is a picnic site before Mill Point and, after it, the Mermaids Café Bar for those who prefer to be served.

A 5km parade, esplanade and sea wall run to Hythe, passing a castle built in the 1530s by Henry VIII and a Martello tower with a Bofors gun.

The A259 comes alongside at **Sandgate** and is to stay fairly close until St Mary's Bay. Fishermen's and coastguard cottages are squeezed in below the cliffs at Sandgate and HG Wells built himself a house here. It was in this district that Noël Coward set his *Blithe Spirit*. The Royal Military Canal begins, moves away from the coast, leaving room for a golf course, and adds to the defences of the Martello towers which now become more frequent. *Novel on Yellow Paper* tells of an unfortunate encounter here.

Hythe, Old English for wharf, was a port from Roman times but silted up in the reign of Charles II and is now playing fields. It was a Cinque Port and is now a resort. In 1786 Lionel Lukin converted a Northumberland fishing boat as the first shore based lifeboat. The town received its charter from King Ethelred in 732. St Leonard's church of 1080 has a 13th century chancel and a crypt containing 2,000 skulls and 8,000 thigh bones from the 13th and 14th centuries plus relics of the Battle of Waterloo, one of two surviving English ossuaries. The Mackeson brewery was in Hythe from 1669.

Folkestone's cliff railway up to the Leas.

111

WILLIAM HARVEY
1628 BLOOD CIRCULATION

The best preserved of all the Martello towers at Dymchurch.

Large numbers displayed in the vicinity of two Martello towers are part of the Hythe Ranges. Range safety craft may allow transit of the area. *Eye of the Needle* reports the capture of two incompetent spies in the dunes. The ranges are the start of Romney Marsh with sheep grazing, for which the first of the drainage sluices discharges between Dymchurch Redoubt and a holiday centre. For 5.6km Dymchurch Wall follows, a huge embankment which may be Roman. Further work was done on it in Henry VIII's reign. Rennie was consulted in 1803 and it was faced in the 1820s and 1830s with Kentish ragstone from Hythe, in 1892, in the 1930s with Welsh granite, in the 1960s and in 2011. This does not make it a pleasant place to land in surf but it protects Romney Marsh and Dymchurch with 13,500 houses up to 2.3m below high water level. Of the protecting Martello towers, a 10m one with 4m thick walls in **Dymchurch** is perhaps the best preserved of all, has an 11kg gun and was used as a lookout point for smugglers in the 19th century and as an observation point for the 1940 Dunkirk evacuation. The Day of Syn is an annual smuggling fête based on the 18th century fictional smuggler and vicar, Dr Syn. The Norman parish church of St Peter & St Paul dates from 1150. A 1574 courtroom with the Law of the Levels was used by the Lords of the Level of Romney Marsh, who controlled the marsh drainage. These days amusement arcades and funfairs for holidaymakers seem to be more the village's way of life.

St Mary's Bay with its holiday camps is where Edith Nesbit, author of the *Railway Children*, used to live next to the railway. New Sewer, one of the marsh's major drainage channels, discharges through a sluice here. A golf course separates the sluice from Littlestone-on-Sea, marked by a prominent brick water tower. Littlestone and Greatstone were banks of shingle at the mouth of the River Rother until the Great Storm of 1287 switched the estuary to the other side of Romney Marsh and left the port of Romney as an inland village. **New Romney**, the capital of Romney Marsh, was a Cinque Port and the usual meeting place for the Portsmen's Court of Brotherhood & Guestling. St Nicholas' medieval church has a 30m tower which was used as a shipping landmark. Greatstone remains a high tide surfbreak.

The village is also the headquarters of the Romney, Hythe & Dymchurch Railway which runs along the coast for 22km between Hythe and Dungeness. Built for a millionaire racing driver, it is the world's smallest public railway, the 380mm gauge trains being to a third scale. Opened in 1927, it was used during the Second World War to move troops and goods. The longest train had 54 coaches. Trains run at 40km/h with steam and diesel engines. Even if not visible from the water, the smoke is seen and the American style horns heard. The railway headquarters also has two model railways and a toy and model museum.

Romney Sands are actually quite silty and a section of 1944 Mulberry Harbour built for the D-Day landings is stranded here. Covered in barnacles and mussels, it has two ladders on the landward side which give access to the top. Weak flows follow the coast.

A continuous line of houses extends through Greatstone-on-Sea to Lydd-on-Sea. Behind a holiday camp is Lydd Airport with light aircraft mostly landing parallel to the coast.

Fishing boats of reasonable size are winched up on the beach which is now of shingle. In the 19th century the locals wore shingle shoes made of wood which acted like snowshoes but that did not stop 55,000l of brandy being landed here by smugglers in one week in 1813. Dungeness has the most extensive area of shingle in Britain, one of the largest in the world, growing eastwards with north–south ridges.

The Pilot Inn at Dungeness has its large screen TV rigged up not to football but to the Automatic Indentification System, allowing customers to follow the complex shipping activity in the Strait of Dover, although it has been known to be particularly interesting on April 1st.

A section of D-Day Mulberry Harbour on Romney Sands.

The railway turns in a loop near the point and there are some huts made from old railway carriages. Dominating this part of the coast are the nuclear power stations. Dungeness A was used 1965–2006, becoming a store of nuclear waste with the B station also with a limited lifespan.

The deep water and Inshore Traffic Zone come close to this point which is also susceptible to sudden fogs. The beach is steepest with fastest currents at the corner. The death toll was 1,000 per year here in 1615 when the first of five successive lighthouses was built. The 1862 light was one of the first in England to be electrically powered although it was later changed to oil. The 1904 light was superseded in 1961 when the new power station blocked the sightline. The latest one is a 43m slim black cylinder with white bands, built for automatic operation in case a nuclear emergency required its evacuation. It was off Dungeness that the SS *Great Eastern* burst a water jacket in 1859, scalding the stokers. It was over Dungeness that *633 Squadron*'s Mosquitoes joined 146 American B17s in Operation Rhine Maiden.

The change in direction of the coast is such that a change in sea state is likely, with the added complication of significant numbers of anglers with lines out round the point.

Beyond several square kilometres of gravel on what is recorded as Denge Beach, on which Halfway Bush is sufficient of a landmark to be indicated on the OS map, Denge Marsh has gravel pits and a 5km² RSPB nature reserve, to which public access is prohibited. This is a migration point for waders and warblers with 270 species having been recorded including lapwings, herons, swans, little terns, firecrests, stone curlews and various ducks.

Fishing boat on the beach at Dungeness.

The coastline is low to Hastings and the 8km which front **Lydd** Ranges are featureless. There is a range safety craft. Vessels may pass through but should follow instructions. In West Road Kent gives way to East Sussex before coastguard cottages and the aerial of the range lookout at Jury's Gap mark the return of the road. There is some parking space next to the lookout's hut.

Whether that remains the case has yet to be seen. The coast is eroding but may not be protected as this could damage plants in a Special Area of Conservation. Not providing protection could result in Lydd Ranges being flooded, which could be even more important than the plants.

Dungeness nuclear power stations and old and new lighthouses.

The lookout point at Jury's Gap.

Distance
64km from Sandown Castle to Jury's Gap

OS 1:50,000 Sheets
179 Canterbury & East Kent
189 Ashford & Romney Marsh

Tidal Constants
Deal:
HW Dover +0020,
LW Dover +0010
Dover
Folkestone:
Dover –0010
Dungeness:
HW Dover –0010,
LW Dover –0020
Rye Approaches:
Dover

Ranges
Hythe, Lydd

Sea Area
Dover

Connection
Royal Military Canal
– see CoB p97

27 East Sussex

Keeping out Napoléon but not the Normans

Then a very great warman, called Billy the Norman,
Cried 'Hang it! I never liked my land;
It would be more handy to leave this Normandy,
And live on yon beautiful Island.'
Thomas Dibdin

Dolphins also fish while birds hunting for food include blackheaded gulls, oystercatchers, cormorants and turnstones. Rye Harbour Nature Reserve forms a major part of a 7km² SSSI with shingle ridges, saltmarsh, grazing marsh, arable fields and gravel pits. It has one of the finest examples of shingle vegetation in Britain with

Cliff End and the cliffs return after Romney Marsh.

A bungalow poised ready to fall over the cliff at Fairlight Cove.

From Jury's Gap at the end of the Jury's Gut Sewer Broomhill Sands lead along the back of Rye Bay to Camber Sands, the only sand dune system in the southeast, where Pontins have a holiday camp.

Dunes are studded with Second World War pillboxes, bunkers and gun emplacements which protected the entrance to the River Rother and now give shelter to a golf course. The sands have produced a 47m oak wreck, possibly the *Avon*, lost in 1852. The sands have been used for filming Normandy landings and even as the Sahara Desert.

Seas break heavily onto the bar with southwesterly winds, attracting windsurfers and board and kite surfers, the river channel being protected by training walls which cover at half tide and militarily by a pillbox. Flows inwards start at HW Dover −0520 at up to 9km/h and outwards less strongly from HW Dover.

Streams in the bay are weak but there is the added complexity of many gill nets. The whole coast from here to Selsey Bill is a scallop fishing ground.

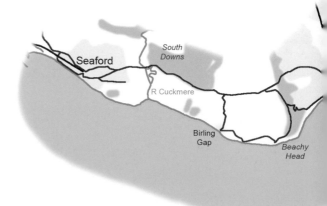

rare wildflowers, dragonflies, other insects and frogs with good wildfowl in winter and terns breeding in summer.

The geography of this area is changing fast. Camber Castle, built in Tudor times to defend the mouth of the Rother, is now nearly 2km from both the river and the sea. Rye Harbour, 2km seawards of **Rye**, is well over a kilometre from the sea. Winchelsea Beach is over a kilometre from the old sea cliffs at Winchelsea, at the foot of which is the Royal Military Canal running behind Pett Level and ceasing its military defence duties at Cliff End where there are dragon's teeth Second World War concrete blocks. A large white house has been built to look like a castle. On Hog Hill a windmill is conspicuous.

was subdued by King Offa of Mercia on his way to Bexhill in 771. In the 9th century the locals rose against the sleeping occupying Danes but they were woken by a cockerel, as a result of which the locals played cock-in-the-pot on Shrove Tuesday until the 19th century, throwing sticks to break a pot, the winner taking the cockerel inside. The town had its own mint in Saxon times, run by the Dunk family who still live here. In 1287 much of the town was washed away in a great storm. It declined from a major port to a fishing town with many attacks by the French between 1337 and 1453 in the Hundred Years War, the remains of the town walls dating from this time. It became a Cinque Port, probably

Fishing boats drawn up on the beach at Hastings.

The shoreline is a well groyned steep beach, the level horizon broken only by the buildings of Winchelsea Beach.

The 1690 wreck of the 70 gun warship HMS *Anne* at the approach to Cliff End has a 75m radius exclusion zone round it. The area also has the remains of a sunken forest.

One source for material being deposited around Rye Bay is Fairlight Cove where erosion is resulting in houses being lost over the cliffs. Many fossils have been revealed here, including dinosaurs. Some

the original one. There was smuggling in the 19th century but it became one of the first resorts. A description of *Gala Day* opens *Private Parts* by Fiona Pitt-Kethley of St Leonards. *English Hours* thinks it less of a dull Brighton than as somewhere with its pictorial side hidden behind all the entertainments

Hastings has two cliff railways. East Hill Cliff Railway of 1903 is the steepest in Britain. It leads from the Stade, Saxon for landing place, where Europe's largest fleet of beach launched fishing boats are got afloat over rollers. Tall black huts were used from 1750 for drying nets because they were charged rent according to their frontage. These huts are unique and some are featured at a fishing museum in a former Victorian fishermen's church with the 1912 lugger *Enterprise*, the first horse capstan, model fishing and lifeboats and figureheads. The fishermen's beach has squid, octopus, cuttlefish and surfers. The Shipwreck & Coastal Heritage Centre is Britain's only specialist shipwreck museum and has finds from 3,000 years of wrecks, including the *Anne* and *Amsterdam*. Blue Reef Aquarium has the live denizens of the deep, seen from an underwater tunnel. Also here

57,000t of Boulogne limestone protection has been installed and 56 drains to dry out the silty clay. The rocks are frequented by blackbacked and herring gulls. Dinosaur footprints can be found at low water. On the west side of the village Covehurst Beach, used by naturists and others, is protected by gorse bushes below a white lookout tower. The tower of Fairlight's Victorian St Andrew's church is hidden by the cliffs. On the shore is Lover's Seat where the girl concerned waited for her sweetheart to be rowed ashore from his ship. This part of the coast is the 2.1km² Hastings Country Park with woodpeckers, linnets, greenfinches and redpolls, forming part of the High Weald AONB.

Hastings was named after Haest's tribe. The town

is the Stade Family Fun Park including Swan Lake. The Old Town was the original fishing village, Dante Gabriel Rossetti being a subsequent resident. Henry James also lived in the town and it was the setting for *Foyle's War*, filmed here by ITV. Catherine Cookson could not come to terms with living here, however, as she did for much of her adult life, initially working as a workhouse laundry manager, before returning to northeast England. Oscar Wilde, in *The Decay of Lying*, thought the Channel here looked too often like Henry Moore grey pearl. The lifeboat station, begun in 1858, is located near a ruined detached harbour arm. The 15 year old Princess Victoria's party on holiday here and at St Leonards were met with decorations, bands and crowds and presented with a basket of fish by local fisherman but also had a nasty accident when one of their horses played up and their landau came close to overturning.

The A259 runs along the front. Despite the appeals of the people of Hastings and of motorists alike for a bypass, it has been refused. Pelham beach has sea creature landmarks to help children locate themselves.

The West Hill Cliff Railway of 1891 runs through a brick tunnel and a natural cave. St Clement's Caves contain over 4,000m^2 of sandstone passages and caves, used by smugglers, as a Second World War air raid shelter and for presenting Smugglers Adventure. St Clement & All Saints church has a 1066 brass rubbing centre. A Flower Makers' Museum has had the biggest exhibition of flower making tools in Europe since 1910 and further entertainment comes with Treasure Island and its boating lake. The Old Town Hall Museum of Local History in the Georgian building of 1823 has the history of Hastings, the battle and the Cinque Ports, maritime history and John Logie Baird who invented television locally.

The ruined Hastings Castle, begun in 1066, was the first Norman castle in Britain, built of earth and wood by the Count of Eu. It covered 4.5ha. A stone replacement was mostly taken by the sea in 1287. It features an 11th century siege tent and the Battle of Hastings. The Grade II★ circular St Mary in the Castle Regency former church hosts jazz breakfasts. One of the most significant churchmen was St Thomas à Becket who was dean here.

The 280m long pier of 1872 by Eugenius Birch, on cast iron columns, has been restored after being largely destroyed by arsonists in 2010, having survived a fire

Marine Court at St Leonards, stacked like the decks on a liner.

The Modernist De La Warr Pavilion on the front at Bexhill.

116

in 1917. Near the end is the Conqueror's Stone where William ate lunch after landing from France. His every move seems to have been documented. Turner produced ten paintings of Hastings. The Museum & Art Gallery features the round the world voyage of the *Sunbeam* in 1876/7 plus fish, seabirds, maritime paintings, pottery, ironwork and ceramics and the Jerwood Gallery opened in 2012, containing the Jerwood Collection including works by LS Lowry, Sir Stanley Spencer, Walter Sickert, Maggi Hambling and Prunella Clough.

There is the world's oldest chess congress at the end of the year and Hastings Week with craft fairs, sports, Norman archery and poetry competitions around October 14th, the anniversary of the battle. An unlikely local resident was Archie Belaney, who was better known as the 'Red Indian' environmentalist Grey Owl.

St Leonards was built in the 1880s by James Burton as a new town and included the Mercatoria area for a market and Lavatoria Square for washerwomen. There is a promenade and the 1930s Marine Court was built to look like an ocean liner with sun decks. Many members of royalty have stayed in the Royal Victoria Hotel. The parish church replaces one of Adrian and Sir Giles

Gilbert Scott destroyed by a flying bomb in 1944. Robert Tressell's *Ragged Trousered Philanthropists* was based on the town.

From here the railway runs along the front to Pevensey. There is a Hastings Half Marathon for runners. A local runner was Alan Turing who, during the Second World War, used to run over 60km from London to meetings at Bletchley Park, where his group cracked the German secret codes.

At Bulverhythe there are dinosaur footprints at low tide and there is a 100m radius exclusion zone round the 1749 wreck of the Dutch East Indiaman *Amsterdam* near Bopeep Rocks, also visible at low springs, its cargo having included 27 chests of guilders. The nursery rhyme, written for the daughter of the landlord of the Bo-Peep public house in the 18th century, is not as innocent as it seems. Sheep were smugglers and tails were casks of French brandy.

Bexhill, from the Old English byxe, box, was founded in 772 and burned to the ground by William the Conqueror as a warm up for the Battle of Hastings. The Bexhill Stone in the side of the tower of St Peter's church is evidence of its Saxon origins. A Cinque Port

The pier at Eastbourne.

Departure from Eastbourne as chalk grassland leads up onto the South Downs.

Beachy Head with one of the best known British lighthouses and the Belle Tout lighthouse beyond.

and a garrison town for George III's German Legion, it was developed fully in the 1880s by Lord De La Warr. In 1935 the De La Warr Pavilion was built by the B2182 along the front and 3km long promenade and is a Grade I Modernist building restored with its arts centre, theatre, exhibitions, bars and restaurant. The town has a museum, a bandstand and Bexhill Roaring 20s Edwardian festival in May with 9 days in period costume. Agatha Christie chose the front for her second venue in *The ABC Murders*. Avis Parsons had spent holidays in Bexhill as a

child in Susan Hill's *Cockles & Mussels*. Obelisks mark the start and finish of the world's first international motor race in 1902, remembered each year with the Bexhill 100 classic and vintage car rally.

Offshore, Jenny's Stool and My Lord's Rock draw attention to the shortage of self respecting mineral samples in the area. The coast continues low to Beachy Head. This Jewel of the South Coast was the first place to permit mixed bathing. Now there is naturist use between the beach huts at the end of the town and Norman's Bay.

building a fortress with ditch and bank inside. It was besieged by Simon de Montfort in 1264, was given to John of Gaunt in 1372, provided defence against the Armada and was used again in the Second World War, over the years having been progressively upgraded. Kipling gave an alternative local history in *Puck of Pook's Hill*.

Meanwhile, the Martello towers have begun again on the modern shoreline at Norman's Bay, the first of this set being prominent.

Gravel pits in the Crumbles area have been converted to the Sovereign Harbour with berths for over 800 boats. Two green buoys off the entrance mark a First World War wreck within sight of the Martello tower near Langney Point which has been converted to a lighthouse. The harbour name comes from the Royal Sovereign Shoals 8km offshore, guarded by the Royal Sovereign lighthouse which was towed out and sunk on site after construction in Newhaven, the first lighthouse to be designed with an integral helicopter deck from the start.

Eastbourne was a village until 1877 but was developed by the Duke of Devonshire in a decade to become the Empress of Watering Places, visited by holidaymakers and by politicians for their party conferences and possibly with the oldest population in Britain. Cyril Connolly, at school with George Orwell and Cecil Beaton, describes the former St Cyprian's school, which he calls St Wulfric's, in his *Enemies of Promise*. Gavin Maxwell, at the same school a decade later, uses the same name in *The House of Elrig*, in which he describes an ecstatic moment racing across Beachy Head on horseback, contrasted the following week when another pony lay down in the Eastbourne traffic and rolled on him. John Hilliard and David Barton both had former ties with the town in *Strange Meeting*. Jane Austin's unfinished *Sanditon* was thought to have been based on the town or on Worthing and Elixabeth Gaskell completed *Sylvia's Lovers* here. In *A Prince of the Captivity* Nigel Melfort dislikes the horrible band in green jackets.

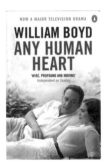

First come all kinds of entertainments. The Sovereign Centre has four pools, flume and wave machine, Fort Fun has Formula Fun go karts, there is miniature golf, a boating lake, a ride on miniature steam and diesel railway for well over a kilometre, a Butterfly Centre, Treasure Island children's play area and galleon, crazy golf and the Redoubt in an 1804 moated Napoleonic tower containing a museum with the military history of Sussex, the Cinque Ports, Martello towers, naval events, Sussex sailors, battlements and gun emplacements. The 5km front is followed for much of the way by the promenade, flowerbeds and the Dotto road train. The 300m pier of 1872–88 was badly damaged by fire in 2014. Military bands give concerts from the bandstand. England's first RNLI museum has the most comprehensive official collection of lifeboats in a building in memory of actor William Terriss, who was murdered outside a London theatre. The Wish Tower, named after the Saxon wisc, marshy place, is a Martello tower with an exhibition of puppets. For road users, parking is very expensive and can only be paid in cash. A battle between 400 smugglers and the coastguard in 1833 left four officials dead but the smugglers left without their cargo.

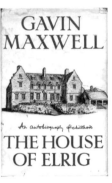

A mat is unrolled across the beach but it is not reachable for six weeks in the summer because a line of orange buoys off the beach marks an exclusion zone for craft. Other delights of Eastbourne include the Musgrave Collection with coins from the Romans onwards and mini sculptures, paintings and Victoriana, the How We Lived Then museum of shops and social history, Eastbourne Heritage Centre, the Grade II Winter Garden, petanque and sailing. EM Forster was

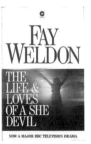

Waller's Haven drains Hooe Level to Norman's Bay and Pevensey Haven does the same for the Pevensey Levels to Pevensey Bay.

The Roman fort of Anderitum was built with 760mm thick walls on a 4ha site on the shoreline in 300 on a peninsula in marshland, with water on three sides, where it commanded the harbour entrance. It was unusual for a Roman fort in being oval. On 28th September 1066 the Normans landed at Pevensey, now over a kilometre inland. The fort sheltered the invading French, William

The Seven Sisters stretch away from the Birling Gap towards Seaford Head.

Distance
*57km from Jury's
Gap to Seaford*

OS 1:50,000 Sheets
*189 Ashford &
Romney Marsh
198 Brighton
& Lewes
199 Eastbourne
& Hastings*

Tidal Constants
*Rye Approaches:
Dover
Hastings:
HW Dover,
LW Dover −0030
Eastbourne:
HW Dover −0010,
LW Dover +0020
Newhaven:
HW Dover −0010,
LW Dover*

Sea Areas
Dover, Wight

*Connections
River Rother –
see BRN p253
Royal Military Canal
– see CoB p101*

at school here and the town was used for filming *Waiting for God*. It was used by Logan Mountstuart and Freya Deverell for their witnessed adultery to end his previous marriage to Lottie in *Any Human Heart*.

Tumuli define the end of the town as chalk cliffs begin to rise again, chalk reefs forming the Pound, and the South Downs Way ascends to Beachy Head Countryside Centre. Between Eastbourne and Seaford is a Heritage Coast.

Beachy Head, described during a dazzling dawn in *A Pair of Blue Eyes*, takes its name from the French *beau chef*, beautiful headland, and originally extended to Boulogne where the chalk cliffs continue. Beachy also means shingly or stony. At 162m these are the highest chalk cliffs in England and are a favourite spot for suicides. They are at the end of the South Downs, designated as a national park in 2009 from here to Winchester. In the 1860s a vertical series of echinoderms taken from the cliff helped to confirm evolution theory. Since Margate the sea has been attacking the ends of the strata, but it now goes with the trend. This is also the longest stretch of chalk cliffs in Britain. On top are field systems and evidence of Stone Age cultures between 8500 and 4000 BC with earlier human activity going back nearly 250,000 years, before the English Channel cut through. Vegetation includes sea lavender, hoary stock, round headed rampion, sheep's fescue and quaking grass, carnation sedge and fragrant, common spotted, pyramidal, bee and early spider orchids in some of the best remaining grassland in Sussex. It attracts such butterflies as red admirals, painted ladies, large and small marbled whites, clouded yellows and Adonis and chalkhill blues. It is a migration watchpoint for butterflies and birds. Peregrine falcons, skylarks, meadow and rock pipits, wheatears, spotted flycatchers, nightingales, linnets, stonechats, jackdaws, herring gulls and cormorants are all seen. The winds here are predominantly along the line of the English Channel.

The 1902 Beachy Head light, a 43m white round tower with a red band, was built of Cornish granite at the foot of the cliffs where it was more often below cloud level. A race runs off the light. It replaced the 17m Belle Tout lighthouse of 1834 which was built 30m from the cliff edge so that any boat unable to see it was getting dangerously close inshore. During the Second World War the disused light became a target for the Canadians to practise against and it was featured in *Dick Barton at Bay*, as the High Tower in *The Life & Loves of a She-Devil* and an episode of the BBC *Doomwatch* scientific fiction series

when it was supposed to have attenuated the sound of an aircraft flying over. The Channel is still getting wider at 500mm/year and when the lighthouse was only 4m from the edge the 850t grey tower was slid 17m back onto a new basement in 1999. The difficult task involved cutting a trench round the outside and jacking against this, action which could equally have brought down more of the cliff face instead of moving the tower. Erosion continues and the 60m high Devil's Chimney outcrop fell in 2001. The Iron Age settlement and tumuli nearby were formerly 2–3km inland. Falling Sands beach below is more used to falling chalk. In 1801 Nelson took command of protecting the coast from Orford Ness to here while a French invasion was threatened.

Cottages are falling over the cliff at the Birling Gap, used for filming *Brighton Rock*, where access to the beach is down a staircase tower. Fishing boats are winched up a nearly vertical slope. This is thought not to have prevented a Viking attack.

Went Hill Brow, Baily's Hill, Flat Hill, Flagstaff Point, Brass Point, Rough Brow, Short Brow and Haven Brow are of progressively increasing height and, with English idiosyncrasy, are known as the Seven Sisters. Rabbits play around the obelisk and tumuli. Below, in 1747, 30 Spanish crew were drowned when the *Nympha Americana* ran aground. This area must have been the setting for *The Adventure of the Lion's Mane* although it is astonishing that the name meant nothing to Sherlock Holmes or any of the locals except the victim.

The Cuckmere is the only Sussex rivermouth with no port. In the 16–18th centuries this assisted the smugglers, especially the Alfriston gang who operated from Cuckmere Haven. Today the river flows through the Seven Sisters Country Park and is followed by the Vanguard Way. The Environment Agency propose to turn 46ha of the estuary into marsh and allow the collapse of the three coastguard cottages, one of which featured in the film *Atonement*. A heron might move out onto the sea rocks in search of booty. *The Old Ways* describes the escape of an eel from a cormorant here.

The Hope Gap sees autumn migrants after berries. There are willow warblers, blackcaps, redstarts and even hoopoes and ortolan buntings while fulmars and gannets are seen off the 86m high chalk cliff streaked with rust. A settlement and a golf course are on top while a waterski lane is accepted on the sea. Sheet piling protects an outfall pipe running into the sea at **Seaford**, near where it may be possible to land on a steeply shelving gravel beach, behind which there is parking.

West Sussex

I too have dreamed, on Brighton Pier,
A wild piratical career,
But I would sooner milk a cow
Than be a jolly pirate now.
AP Herbert

massive sets of steps cut into them. In 2014 a Ford Focus left the road and fell 24m to the rocks, clearing the walkway, the driver receiving only minor injuries.

The water is clear and lobster pots are laid to Brighton, somehow too artificial an environment for them or for the blackheaded and herring gulls and oystercatchers.

Newhaven breakwater seen from Seaford.

Facing Seaford Bay at the Cinque Port of **Seaford** is the 103rd and last of the Martello towers, containing Seaford Museum. Seaford was at the mouth of the River Ouse until the great storm of 1579 and had tide mills.

Newhaven was the new port which developed after the river shifted in the storm. A pier with a lighthouse and tide gauge is sheltered by an 1878 concrete breakwater, 850m long with a 14m lighthouse tower, the fairway running close to the breakwater. Cross-Channel paddle steamers began a service to Dieppe in 1847 and car ferries continue today. This was the route used by Sherlock Holmes while trying to avoid Professor Moriarty in *The Adventure of the Final Problem* and by Alan Duncan, anxious to escape England, in *Requiem for a Wren*. Anton Zelewski arrived as a foot passenger on the *Cornouailles* from Dieppe with a box of what appeared to be cigars in *The Fourth Protocol*.

The entrance is guarded by Newhaven Fort, listed as an Ancient Monument, which was garrisoned until 1956. On display are 1860s Victorian barrack rooms, underground tunnels, cliff ramparts and big guns. Flows run into the river from HW Dover −0450 and out from HW Dover +0100 at up to 4km/h.

From Friars' Bay the chalk cliffs become like those around the Isle of Thanet rather than those on the rest of the south coast. They are trimmed and have an Undercliff promenade along the bottom. At intervals there are

In 1915 businessman Charles Neville designed Anzac-on-Sea, named after the Australian and New Zealand troops stationed nearby and renamed **Peacehaven** at the end of the First World War. An odour free sewage works behind the housing has the largest grass roof of its kind in the UK. This is as far as Pinkie Brown and Rose got on a bus trip into the country in Graham Greene's *Brighton Rock*. A monument to George V marks the meridian and there is also a fire beacon on the cliffs. The A259 has been edging towards the top of the cliffs, which it reaches after Telscombe Cliffs, also reached by a tornado in 2006, and runs parallel with the coast to Bognor. Below the cliffs much of the coast is used by naturists as far as Brighton Marina, Brighton having had the first naturist beach in Britain.

East Sussex gives way to Brighton & Hove and Saltdean gives way to the flint houses of Rottingdean after the White Horse Hotel and the black Rottingdean smock windmill of 1802. Sir Edward Burne-Jones lived in the village and the Copper family have made the village known throughout the folk singing world. The Grange, now with antique toys, is an 18th century vicarage remodelled by Sir Edwin Lutyens. The Gardens are where Rudyard Kipling wrote *Kim*, the poem *Sussex* and many of his *Just So Stories*. A stone head built into the wall grants wishes if the nose is stroked in the correct

Manicured cliffs topped by the meridian marker at Peacehaven.

Break in the cliffs at Rottingdean.

The end of Brighton Marina's western arm.

way. In the 1890s the village name was brought up market for the top girls' finishing school of Roedean and the yellow brick St Dunstan's Training Centre for the Blind was opened in the 1930s.

Along the shore the groynes of 1907 were the first to be made in reinforced concrete and are now showing their age but that does not dissuade surfers.

At the foot of the 30m chalk cliffs the 1,200 berth **Brighton** Marina was built between 1971 and 1979. 1.1km and 600m arms were constructed by having a 1,200t crane placing 110 12m diameter concrete caissons weighing up to 625t each and partly filled with sand.

At 31ha, it is the largest man made marina in Europe and the inner basin is reached via the largest non-commercial lock in Europe. It

has bowling, a Walk of Fame and Brighton's largest cinema.

The wall of cylinders produces irregular clapotis with a sea of any size. On the west side divers are required to keep 200m away because of a historic wreck. Some anglers interpret this as meaning this 200m zone is for their own exclusive use.

Running west from the marina is Volks' electric railway of 1883, the world's oldest public electric

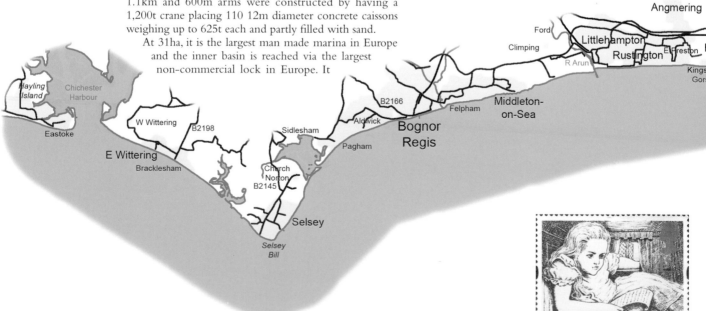

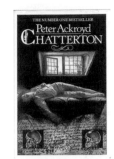

Beyond Brighton's Palace Pier are the British Airways i360 and remains of the West Pier.

line. The 2km 830mm gauge line was designed by Magnus Volks who, in 1896, added the 5km Brighton & Rottingdean Seashore Electric Tramroad powered by an overhead cable. This ran on 7.3m legs on a track in the sea. It was nearly destroyed by a storm 4 days after opening, but was rebuilt and eventually abandoned after 4 years as being too unreliable. Concrete blocks to hold the tracks are still visible in the rocks.

The fishing village of Brighthelmstone, named after the Old English man Brihthelm, saw sea bathing from 1641 when it was pronounced to be medicinal, but it was not until the 18th century when it became one of the world's earliest resorts because of the patronage of the Prince of Wales, later George IV. He took a villa for a year for Mrs Fitzherbert and himself while in dispute with his father, travelling down from London on the roof of a public stagecoach. It has been called London by the Sea, the place Londoners traditionally went for a naughty weekend, and is claimed to be England's loveliest and liveliest seaside city, the city status being bestowed in 2001, and also Europe's gay capital.

The area near the marina is Kemp Town, named after lord of the manor, Thomas Kemp. It has produced an elephant's tooth. Lewis Carroll lived in Sussex Square off Lewes Crescent, the opening chapter in *Alice's Adventures in Wonderland* being inspired by the tunnel between two gardens. Actress Dame Anna Neagle lived in Lewes Crescent itself and Brighton had one of the first film studios. Frederick Marryat wrote his first two books, *Frank Mildmay; or the Naval Officer* and *The King's Own*, while living in Brighton. Madeira Drive, along

French steamers, painted by Constable and Turner but destroyed by a storm in 1896.

In 1995 the inshore lifeboat carried out a very difficult rescue from under the pier, when two girls from a beach party were recovered in the middle of the night in gale force conditions, during which the boat ripped its port side on metalwork and lost much of its buoyancy.

Brighton's most striking building is the distinctive Royal Pavilion, described as lachrymose in Peter Ackroyd's *Chatterton*, converted from a farmhouse in 1787 to a neoclassical villa and then, in 1815–22, made into the most exotic palace in Europe, an oriental domed seaside palace with Chinese decoration and Indian exterior. The Chinese Room has the UK's largest chandelier, 9.1m and weighing 1t, made in 1818. John Nash was the only architect using cast iron at the time and he also used laminated timber ribs and prestressed timber beams here. Victoria was not keen on Brighton, especially the Pavilion. In the grounds is an oak in which Charles II is said to have hidden after the Battle of Worcester, subsequently sailing to France from Shoreham in 1651. The nearby Brighton Dome for the performing arts is in a former stable block of 1803 which accommodated 44 horses and their grooms. The mood was summed up by Rex Whistler's painting of *The Prince Regent Awakening the Spirit of Brighton*, a nearly naked prince lifting the veil of a sleeping girl. There is a Prince Regent Swimming Complex with four pools and a waterslide, the Grade II Theatre Royal Brighton and Brighton Museum & Art Gallery with important Art Nouveau and Art Deco collections. In 1991 the Brighton Bottle Orchestra performed on 444 miniature Gordon's gin bottles and *Pendennis* refers to listening to the band of the Heavies.

Not all liberal thinking was appreciated, however. In Meeting

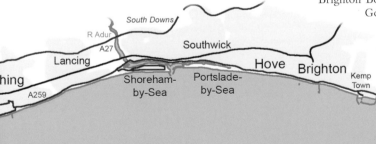

the front, has been the finishing point for the Veteran Car Run which has taken place in November since 1896, the Historic Commercial Vehicle Run in May and the London to Brighton Stock Exchange Walk in June, all of which begin in London. At the end of the drive is the oldest aquarium in Europe in the Victorian architectured Sea Life Brighton but it has the largest underwater tunnel in Europe with sharks, stingrays, octopuses and seahorses amongst its exhibits.

The UK's second most visited leisure facility is the Grade II Victorian Brighton Palace Pier of 1899, 536m long with a 58m head and outsides of the pavilions to echo the Royal Pavilion. It has a funfair, mechanical slot machines and music blasting out over the sea. It stands just east of and replaced the 1823 342m chain pier for

House Lane the ghost of a monk disappears through the wall of the Friends' Meeting House, apparently having been bricked in after running away with a local girl. George Orwell uses the old ladies of Brighton as the antithesis of the poverty stricken workers of the north of England in *The Road to Wigan Pier*.

The Lanes are a maze of 17th century streets and alleyways with small shops, leading down to the Artists' Quarter studios in the Victorian seafront arches and the Fishing Museum. The meeting between Edwin

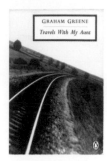

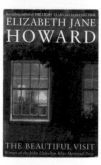

Clayhanger and Hilda Cannon and a description of the city and the front were featured in *Clayhanger*, part of which Arnold Bennet wrote in the Royal York Hotel, which he called the Royal Sussex. Brighton was the first destination for Henry Pulling and Aunt Augusta in *Travels with my Aunt*. In the *Wings* series it was where Will Farmer first saw future wife Molly Grayson. Here Charlotte Stant accepted the proposal of Adam Verver in Henry James' *The Golden Bowl*. Driving to Brighton in a motor car with Agnes was Arthur's highest ambition in Elizabeth Jane Howard's *The Beautiful Visit*. The area has been used for filming *Only Fools and Horses* and for *Brighton Rock*, set in Brighton by Greene and filmed here by the Boulting brothers who lived in Hove. It is a Regency seafront with large hotels used by political parties for their conferences. It would seem to be fairly safe Tory territory as Sir Cooper Rawson polled 75,205 for the Conservatives in 1931, the greatest number of votes ever achieved by anyone. The Grand Hotel was bombed in 1984 by the IRA during a Conservative Party conference. Oscar Wilde's De Profundis says Lord Alfred Douglas insisted on being sent to the Grand Hotel by him.

Offshore are lanes for powerboats. At midnight on May 17th a ship has been seen at times to capsize on a reef. It was that of Lord Manfred, returning after placing St Nicholas' belt on the tomb of the Blessed Virgin at Byzantium in the 14th century to fulfill an initially forgotten vow. St Nicholas of Myra's church was subsequently built by his father, the 4th Earl de Warrenne, to remind people to honour their vows. Under a plinth in the church are buried a knight and his horse, both in full armour, the horse galloping round the churchyard on moonlit nights.

The Grade II Middle Street synagogue is one of the finest in Europe with abstract stained glass and ornate brass and ironwork. Churchill Square was declared the Best Designed UK Shopping Centre in 1999. There are surf breaks between the piers. On the beach is the Ellipse Brighton with outdoor theatre, concerts, dances, beach volleyball, basketball, paddling pool, sandpit and new works of art. The British Airways i360 tower, 161m high with a viewing deck, is the world's first vertical cable car, most slender tower and tallest moving observation tower. This is near the West Pier, destroyed in two arson attacks in 2003. The country's only Grade I pier, it was opened in 1866 as Birch's best work. At 340m long with a 94m head, it had elegant wrought ironwork, further damaged in a 2016 storm and now just an island skeleton of rusty metal.

All of this is the setting for the three week Brighton Festival in May, England's largest. There is surf after southwesterly winds with pier legs for added slalom interest. In 1806 an 11m basking shark weighing some 8t was washed ashore.

Moving west, the 1820 terraced Grade I Regency Town House is becoming a heritage centre while the King Alfred Leisure Centre was one of the first on the south coast.

Despite the name derived from hufe, Old English for a hovel, **Hove** sees itself as the more refined extension of Brighton and Constable painted the beach in 1824. Brunel was here for part of his school education. The Hove Museum is in a Victorian villa with a film gallery, contemporary craft, childhood room and 18th century furniture. The beach becomes shingle to Bognor with a 5m raised beach to Worthing. To decoy the Germans, *Eye of the Needle* reported that an armoured division would be moved here.

A fire beacon at **Portslade-by-Sea** locates a large boating pool which has been isolated at the head of the **Southwick** Canal, a non tidal eastern basin of Shoreham Harbour. The chimneys of the 420MW Shoreham Power Station mark the progress from Brighton & Hove to West Sussex and the point where foam is discharged into the sea. The beach is used by naturists and the Hotpipe break by surfers.

The westgoing stream begins at local HW −0200 for six hours at up to 4km/h.

The Eastern Arm and Southwick Canal were part of the River Adur until the new harbour entrance was established in 1817–21, a triangular pier being built opposite the entrance in 1826 at Telford's suggestion to help flows and reduce sedimentation. Even so, the harbour silts rapidly following dredging. A disused lighthouse of 1846 faces the rivermouth at Southwick but the lifeboat station was rebuilt in 2011. A Victorian fort was constructed in 1857 when a French invasion was expected.

The harbour entrance is protected by two breakwaters and a bar shifts in the entrance after prolonged westerly winds. There are flows up to 4km/h at the entrance.

Shoreham-by-Sea is on a long peninsula and is named after the Old English scora, a steep hill. Until 500 years ago the River Adur flowed straight out to sea near Lancing church and had the River Arun as a tributary. Shingle pushed the mouth of the Adur eastwards while the Arun broke through to the west in several places. It is used as another Quietus location in *The Children of Men*.

Shoreham Airport is Britains' oldest licensed airport and has an Art Deco terminal building, D-Day aviation museum, Second World War blister hanger, Horsa glider, Spitfire and air sea rescue gallery. In 2015 a Hawker Hunter in an air display crashed onto the A27 with a number of fatalities after failing to pull out of a loop. In the *Wings* series it was where Alan Farmer turned his Avro northeast on his triangular course exercise.

Lancing merges into Worthing which continues into Ferring with no break obvious from the sea. **Worthing**, named after the Old English man Weorc, was just a few fishing cottages and a smuggling centre but became the biggest resort in west Sussex from the end of the 18th

Worthing's Victorian pier is a very respectable structure, even if outclassed by Brighton.

Littlehampton's East Beach Café and its steel shell.

Littlehampton's timber breakwater at the mouth of the River Arun.

century, encouraged by Princess Amelia, the delicate younger sister of the Prince Regent. It features Regency housing and inter war elegance with a long seafront. Oscar Wilde wrote his *Importance of Being Earnest* here and used the name of the town for his main character. The town's churches and Dr Augustus Fagan's sanatorium feature in Evelyn Waugh's *Decline & Fall*. The town also boasts Elisabeth Frink head sculptures while the Museum & Art Gallery covers archaeology, geology, local history and bathing costumes. It has the second oldest population in the UK, average 43. The major feature on the seafront is the 290m Victorian pier with a pavilion at the end.

Goring-by-Sea's English Martyrs Catholic church has a 1993 replica of the ceiling of the Sistine Chapel.

Beach huts around **Ferring** are all that break up the

line of housing behind the beach through Kingston Gorse, East Preston, Rustington and Littlehampton, completing what is effectively a 16km run of housing. Ecclesden windmill is on the Downs behind Kingston Gorse at **Angmering**. Birdlife is limited but there are terns, blackbacked and herring gulls and swans. Between Worthing and the River Arun a chalk anticline continued southwards but it has been shortened and the top 240m removed, which does much to reduce its impact on the landscape. **Rustington** is a village with a medieval church of St Peter & St Paul and flint cottages plus a modern sports centre. In this village Sir Hubert Parry wrote the setting to Blake's *Jerusalem*.

Littlehampton was another fishing town which became a resort but in *A Prince of the Captivity* Nigel Melfort disliked a man who made ugly faces. The books which make up Osbert Lancaster's *The Littlehampton Saga* were set around the River Arun. The Little was only added in the 15th century to distinguish it from Northampton and Southampton. Along the promenade are bathing huts. The East Beach Café, facing a beachbreak, has drawn much attention for its interesting steel shell. A pumping station feeds a long sea outfall. When the latter was built in the early 1970s four boreholes were put down along its line to sample the seabed. Two hit wartime mines.

On the east bank of the Arun is the prominent Harbour Park funfair. There is a commercial and yachting port on the river. In the Middle Ages it was used for unloading Caen stone for major Sussex buildings. A white over a red flag on a pilot boat indicates a large vessel movement is due. A training wall running out from the lighthouse covers at half tide. The open structure

Butlin's distinctive holiday camp at Bognor Regis.

The inconspicuous entrance to Pagham Harbour.

timber breakwater extends on the west side of the harbourmouth to protect shipping. With a westerly wind blowing, dry sand can be blown through it in a veritable sandstorm. The pierhead has a tide gauge. Overfalls form on the bar with winds from force 5 between southeast and southwest against ebbing spring tides. Flows go in from HW Dover –0400 and out from HW Dover +0100 at up to 11km/h, being affected by heavy rain, important as there is a 12km/h speed limit and speed cameras, although the flow would not explain the 63km/h clocked by one speedboat.

To the west of the river, dunes and a golf course put a stop to housing for a while. North of Climping is the former Ford Aerodrome. Further inland beyond the Arundel to Chichester line there are former raised beaches at the 30m level.

In fact, Atherington did have more building along the front but medieval houses and the church were taken by the sea.

The 1849 St Nicholas' church in **Middleton-on-Sea**, a First World War seaplane base, replaces another church taken by the sea. Unusually, the houses along the front include some thatched ones and this section of coast is now protected by a line of rock islands. Patches of loose bootlace weed proliferate.

There is an 11km unbroken front of houses through Felpham and Bognor. Felpham has flint walled cottages and was the home of William Blake, about as far as he could get both geographically and in environment from his dark satanic mills. There are toilets, a seafront café and some shelter for landing if the wind is from the west but parking is limited.

Aldingbourne Rife separates Felpham from **Bognor**, of which the most prominent structure is the tented roof on Butlin's holiday camp, from another building of which colourful slides emerge.

Late 18th century architecture was by London hatter Sir Richard Hotham who wanted to call it Hothampton, but Queen Victoria called it 'dear little Bognor' and the royal opinion took precedence. Her family had come here for two months when she was a girl and she had enjoyed walking and riding on the beach as well as sea bathing. The name derives from the name of the Old English woman Bucge and ora, meaning shore. George V added the Latin Regis for 'king's' while recovering from a lung operation in Aldwick in 1928. It was one of the first seaside resorts to be favoured by royalty. There is a pier and the 2km seafront including the B2166 has a road train and one of the star attractions has to be the International Bognor Birdman competition in August. It was where Nicholas Fanner had been in military intelligence during the war in *Paradise Postponed*. Janet Prentice was able to try shooting for an aircraft off the town in *Requiem for a Wren*.

Accompanied by housing to the resort of Pagham, the shingle beach continues to Selsey Bill. Bognor Rocks and Barn Rocks run southeast in two lines, the former having a wreck at the inshore end at Aldwick. The Grade II Barton Manor is the oldest inhabited house in the UK.

The one break in the beach comes at the exit of Pagham Harbour, a 4km^2 nature reserve with strong streams in the entrance. There are 200 bird species here including terns, shelducks, curlews, redshanks and oystercatchers. Red admirals and other butterflies and

A conspicuous tower on a house at Selsey Bill acts as a landmark.

Bracklesham is not keen on dogs anywhere.

Distance
78km from Seaford to Hayling Island

OS 1:50,000 Sheets
197 Chichester & the South Downs
198 Brighton & Lewes

Tidal Constants
Newhaven:
HW Dover −0010,
LW Dover
Brighton:
HW Dover −0010,
LW Dover
Shoreham:
HW Dover −0010,
LW Dover
Worthing:
HW Dover,
LW Dover −0010
Littlehampton Entrance:
HW Dover,
LW Dover −0010
Bognor Regis:
HW Dover,
LW Dover −0010
Pagham:
HW Dover +0010,
LW Dover −0020
Selsey Bill:
HW Dover +0020
LW Dover −0100
Chichester Harbour Entrance:
HW Dover +0020
LW Dover +0040

Sea Area
Wight

Connections
River Ouse
(East Sussex) −
see RoB p250
River Adur −
see RoB p253
River Arun − see
RoB p256
Chichester Channel −
see RoB p259

moths are present with plant life including spartina grass, sea purslane and glasswort. The harbour is silted up but Sidlesham was a working port until the mid 19th century.

There is an earthwork at the southern corner of the harbour at Church Norton where St Wilfrid's church is named after the first Christian missionary to the south Saxons who landed here in the 7th century. It is the 13th century chancel of a large church, the rest of which was moved to the centre of Selsey.

Lines of moorings at Selsey lead to a fire beacon and an RNLI lifeboat station of 2017 although a naval officer was awarded a silver medal in 1838 for rescuing three men from a sloop. It is a coast where lobsters, crabs, whelks and cockles are found and, in 1956, four boys found a rhinocerous skeleton. Selsey is claimed by Piscator in *The Compleat Angler* to have a Shelsey cockle species. Important in Saxon times, Selsey is a quiet resort today.

Selsey Bill is a low sharp point where the coast has eroded more than any other in Britain in the 20th century. The site of Selsey cathedral of 680–1080 is now some 2km offshore. Flows run eastwards from HW Dover +0600. Fast currents come right to the shore with a race close inshore and an eddy on the corner so sharp that a stopper can be formed like that beside a jet into a weirpool. Further out there is a mark on the Mixon, from where it can dry most of the way back to the bill, leaving just a narrow passage through. For larger boats the Outer Owers, further out, are the most dangerous shoals in the English Channel. An interesting half timbered tower on a house near the bill is a useful mark for shipping. The heavily groyned beach sees oystercatchers picking about between cuttlefish bones and terns are present. Towards the west of Selsey is the Grade II Medmerry windmill. **Selsey** is old English for seal island and it is still all but an island at the end of the B2145. Golfball sized hailstones in 1998 preceded the second tornado to hit Selsey in a decade, damaging 20% of its houses.

West Sands Holiday Park is the second largest in Europe of its kind. Adjacent, 110m of the sea defences have been removed and 1.8km² of farmland flooded to create more salt marsh, the largest open coast managed realignment in Europe.

On the other side is Medmerry Park holiday village at Bracklesham at the end of the B2198. Off Bracklesham is the 1706 wreck of the 54 gun *Hazardous*, renamed after being captured from the French, with a 100m radius exclusion zone around her.

Around 2–3km out is the probable site of a Roman station served by the road, Roman coins having frequently been washed up on the beach. Some 6km of surf beach, better at low water and heavily used by windsurfers and kite surfers, stretch past East Wittering and West Wittering to the entrance to Chichester Harbour. **East Wittering** has a Grade II windmill and the tower of Cakeham Manor House as a nautical mark. There is a wreck onshore at East Wittering and two cardinal marks out on the East Pole Sands locate wrecks used as targets. West Wittering is marked by the spire of its 11th century church of St Peter & St Paul and is where the Rolls Royce design team were moved when their leader developed cancer. It is a prime venue for windsurfers.

East Pole Sands can dry out for a considerable distance, as can West Pole Sands on the other side of the harbourmouth and over which large standing waves can develop at the inshore end at Eastoke Point near high water. The fairway is on the west side of the entrance but the banks are subject to great change and there is risk of the sea breaking through at the Hinge and cutting off East Head, which ran southwest into the English Channel until the 18th century. An annual sandcastle contest has been banned by conservationists as disturbing to a wildlife habitat. Waves break heavily with any swell and can break right across the entrance, being dangerous with a southerly wind against a strong ebb. Conditions are quietest from local HW −0300 to local HW +0100. Flows are ingoing for seven and a quarter hours to 5km/h and outgoing for five and a quarter hours to 12km/h. The entrance is best avoided with any swell during the ebb. Chichester Harbour has over 10,000 craft exceeding 3m long.

29 Hayling Island

Hayling Island offers a largely sheltered circumnavigation in an area seething with pleasure craft in the summer but quieter in the winter when the island is occupied only by its 17,000 residents.

The channel separating the island from the mainland dries out for the bottom metre at spring tides and there are strong tidal flows at the southeast and southwest corners of the island. Thus, there is much to be said for running north up one side of the island on the last hour of the flood and returning down the other side on the first half of the ebb. The entrance is best avoided with any swell during the ebb.

The RNLI have an inshore lifeboat beside the eastern entrance to Chichester Harbour, at one time competing against a privately owned RIB which was beating them to casualties. Black Point, also known as Sandy Point, has Hayling Island Sailing Club. The next headland to the west is the site of a boatyard with yachts up on the slips. Lines of moorings lead up the Emsworth Channel, leaving the built up area behind.

Saltings line the channel. Posts mark Mill Rithe which leads up to further moorings and boatyards. A barn is prominent in what is a farming area, broken up by belts of trees through which the stumpy spire of St Peter's church, North Hayling, is just visible. On the other side the disused airfield covers most of Thorney Island, in the 1980s used to house Vietnamese refugees. It is where Alan Duncan had his first operational posting in *Requiem for a Wren*. **Emsworth** has houses and the swaying masts of the boats moored in Emsworth Yacht Harbour.

Travelling up the Sweare Deep involves passing the entrance to Northney Marina on the island. Beyond the spire of St Thomas a Beckett church to the northwest of Conigar Point are the Grade II★ remains of Warblington Castle, its tower lacking one side but still standing to its full height. The black Grade II Langstone windmill tower and tidemill, now residential, stand on the shore to its west.

At low tide, the Wadeway public footpath crosses the channel to the Ship Inn from the island although a navigation channel was dredged through it in 1821. Normal access is via the A3023 over the 29 span 290m Langstone Bridge and to its west the piers of the old railway bridge remain. It was considered essential for the island to be served by rail if it was to become a second Brighton. After the first railway was washed away it was successfully established at a further attempt and the first train arrived on the branch from **Havant** in 1867, terminating just north of West Town. The line is now used as the Hayling Billy coastal path and cycle track. Meanwhile, the road bridge was demolished in a storm at the beginning of January 1877.

Passage between the piers of the old railway bridge leads into Langstone Harbour. Langstone was the port of Havant and had a boat train service to St Helens on the Isle of Wight.

The north side of the harbour is overlooked by Ports Down while tower blocks in Portsmouth break the skyline and a chimney marks the harbourmouth, a point which would not, otherwise, be obvious on the far side of Langstone Harbour. Long Island, Baker's Island and South Binness Island are all nature reserves. Cormorants and oystercatchers may be seen in the area. The Hayling Island coastline used to be the site of oyster beds but now a protective wall of rubble has been bulldozed out over them to form a new marina.

A large part of the Langstone Channel is designated as an area permitted for water skiing from April to September and windsurfers launch from Stoke. A number of Royal Navy Mk 5 rafts have threats about not landing or mooring on them.

Large ships including dredgers use the Langstone Channel and things become very congested around the harbourmouth, not helped by the various structures lying around.

A metal fabrication is bounded by four green cones and a D-Day Mulberry Harbour section lies with its back broken nearby.

Hayling Island Sailing Club at Black Point.

The Sweare Deep with Thorney Island beyond.

The Royal Oak and Langstone windmill and tidemill.

Langstone bridge and the Ship.

The piers of the old railway bridge mark the northern limit of Langstone Harbour.

The passenger ferry from Portsea approaches Hayling Island.

The rip from Chichester Harbour, seen from Eastoke Point.

The Chichester Bar marker.

Distance
Hayling Island is 7km long and lies 300m off Havant with road access

OS 1:50,000 Sheets
196 The Solent & Isle of Wight
197 Chichester & the South Downs

Tidal Constants
Chichester Harbour Entrance:
HW Dover +0020,
LW Dover +0040
Northney:
HW Dover +0030,
LW Dover +0040
Portsmouth:
Dover +0020

Sea Area
Wight

Connection
Chichester Channel – see RoB p259

A ferry connects Portsea Island with Hayling Island. In the 19th century a thousand passenger ship, the SS *Hayling*, was set up to operate the service. It also carried Portsea tramcars which were to continue to Westfield but the ship ran aground on a sandbank. After it took 11 days to refloat her, the idea was abandoned. The entrance is best avoided with any swell during the ebb. Gulls ride the fastest line of the flow and then fly back to do it again. The Ferryboat Inn is situated at the Hayling Island landing.

The shoreline now becomes sandy with some shells. Both sides of each harbour have spits and at low water springs the East Winner can extend 2km out from the high water mark. This is the main surfing, windsurfing and jetski area. Windsurfing was invented on Hayling Island. A world kiteboarding speed record of 58km/h was set here in 2015.

The town faces Hayling Bay except at Gunner Point where there are golf links. The built up area commences with bathing huts and public toilets are strategically placed. Permanent buildings appear in the form of more substantial dwellings and a poor man's answer to Bath's Royal Crescent.

The seawall gradually makes its appearance. Blackheaded gulls circle and cuttlefish come inshore to breed in the summer but the hordes of tourists frighten away most wildlife.

Funland Hayling Island amusement parks are followed by more huts, holiday bungalows and the garish accoutrements of the seaside holiday resorts, bingo halls, amusement arcades and chip and ice cream shops.

Access can give problems if the sea is rough as there is a seawall and at the higher stages of the tide it it is necessary to launch from its sloping concrete base. If the sea is boisterous it is better to use the sand further west.

This part of the island is extensively groyned and the tide race into Chichester Harbour can cause rapids to build up around the last few groynes.

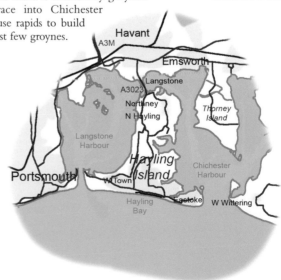

30 Portsea Island

It's down in Portsmouth Harbour
Our ship lies waiting there.
Tomorrow to the seas I'll go
If the winds blow high or fair.
Anon

Lifeboat station and Langstone Harbour.

The former Eastney Barracks were home to the Royal Marines.

Eastney pumping station chimney oversees the West Winner.

Sir Arthur Conan Doyle 1859–1930
Writer and creator of Sherlock Holmes

The critical factor on a circumnavigation of Portsea Island is to take Port Creek at the north end at mid tide as it can dry out at low tide and there is minimal clearance under the bridges at the top end of the tide. It is also worth bearing in mind that large naval vessels usually enter Portsmouth Harbour during the first half of the flood or the 1st, 2nd or 5th hours of the ebb because of eddies and strong tides in the harbourmouth at other times. The mouth of Langstone Harbour is also subject to strong tides. Small craft entering and leaving Portsmouth Harbour must do so via the Boat Channel on the west side of the entrance. Thus, the fairway has to be crossed twice. This chapter moves from the ferry between Portsea Island and the Ferryboat Inn on Hayling Island.

Portsea is connected to the mainland by several bridges. Most of it is taken up by Portsmouth, Britain's most heavily populated offshore city in the country with 200,000 residents, only central London being more densely populated, although it was recorded as having only three manors in 1086.

The entrance is best avoided with any swell during the ebb. The coastguard lookout is passed on the right, a wooden shed on top of an old gun emplacement. In 1986 John Andrews was on duty when a lightning bolt from the blue knocked him out of the door, put his equipment out of action, blew chunks out of the concrete and left him unconscious, hanging over the parapet 10m above the road. He escaped with cuts, grazes and a slight neck injury.

The West Winner bank can produce interesting surf in front of Fort Cumberland, dating from 1747. The beach behind it is popular with naturists. The Victorian Eastney Beam Engine House with its 1887 Boulton & Watt reciprocal steam pumps and Crossley gas engines is not visible. Eastney Barracks have been converted to housing. In October 1966 there was more in the wind as a tornado cut through several houses. In *Requiem for a Wren* Bill Duncan trained here and Janet Prentice first showed her firing acumen on the former Fraser Gunnery Range. Mary Holmes was from Southsea in Nevil Shute's *On the Beach*.

Before the Canoe Lake is the Cumberland House natural history. It is also near the northern end of an anti-submarine barrier which runs out to Horse Sand Fort.

The South Parade Pier on the A288 was rebuilt after a serious fire in 1904, faced by the Strathearn Hotel, Ocean Hotel and others. Beneath the pier it is possible

The small craft gate in the anti submarine barrier.

The South Parade Pier at Southsea.

to combine surfing and slalom between the cast iron piers to form a new and exciting sport with potentially interesting results.

The end of Southsea Common is dominated by Southsea Castle, built by Henry VIII in 1544 as part of the coastal defences. Accompanied by a lighthouse, it now has surrounds of sunken gardens. Its sea defences are of sloping rock although metal loops act as handles so that it would be possible to swim ashore in an emergency. The D-Day Story houses the Operation Overlord

Spitbank Fort off Southsea Castle. Beyond is the Isle of Wight.

A hovercraft arrives at the Clarence Pier with its funfair rides.

tapestry which is 83m long and took the Royal School of Needlework seven years to prepare. Adjacent is a Blue Reef Aquarium Portsmouth with 4m deep reef.

The harbour is defended by Spit Sand, ending in Spitbank Fort, one of three forts built across Spithead by Lord Palmerstone in the 1860s. One kilometre off, it is the nearest of the Spithead forts, with 4.6m thick walls, a 120m deep well, a cannon with a 38t barrel and a Victorian kitchen. It has now been restored after standing derelict as a home for seabirds for 30 years. Before it was cleaned up it had a metre of guano on the floors and vandals had also left their mess.

It was beyond this location that the *Mary Rose* capsized. The 100 gun *Royal George* overturned in 1782 with the loss of 900 lives while under repair. The cod and bass have plenty of interest to see in these waters. Some of the naval activity here is claimed in *The Maid of Sker*. vNow Spithead sees nothing more dramatic than fleet reviews.

Southsea, Hardy's Solentsea, where he set *An Imaginative Woman* at the start of *Life's Little Ironies*, became a fashionable resort after 1812 and produced a number of literary giants. Rudyard Kipling was here as a boy and HG Wells was a draper's apprentice, the experience used in *Kipps* and *The History of Mr Polly*. Local doctor Arthur Conan Doyle wrote the first of his Sherlock Holmes stories here, included reference to Fratton and Portsmouth in others and yearned for Southsea shingle in *The Adventure of the Cardboard Box*. Hornblower's family lived here, as did Lieutenant Oxbelly in Frederick Marryat's *Mr Midshipman Easy*. *Frank Mildmay; or the Naval Officer* and *The King's Own* both feature the area frequently. Portsmouth appears several times in *Les Trois Mousquetaires*, not least for the assassination of Buckingham. The resort has fashionable terraces and one of the longest seaside promenades of all.

Hovercraft operate between Ryde and the 1861 Clarence Pier. Established in 1965, this is the world's oldest hovercraft service, the only scheduled hovercraft service in Europe. It runs at 83km/h rather than a possible 120km/h because of Solent regulations. The pier

is dominated by the rides of a funfair which the pier became in the 1960s, rebuilt after being bombed in 1941. The harbour tide streams work in opposition to those in Spithead which flood west and ebb east and tides over the west part of Horse & Dean Sand are confused and irregular.

Portsmouth Harbour's benefits of a narrow deep water entrance leading to a large sheltered basin have long been recognized. A 12th century settlement received its charter from Richard I in 1194 when he built the first dock here as an embarkation point for the Crusades. In 1415 Henry V established the first Royal Navy here by commandeering ships from along the south coast in which to sail to Agincourt. Henry VII first fortified the seawalls in the 15th century. In 1495 Henry VIII added Europe's first dry

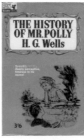

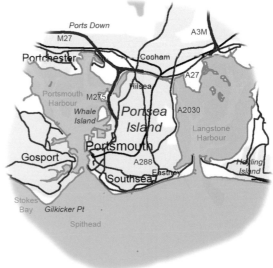

The entrance to Portsmouth Harbour with Portsmouth and Southsea on the right. To the left is the distinctive Spinnaker Tower.

dock and there has been steady development since so that **Portsmouth** is now Britain's premier naval base and the approach channel has been straightened for the new aircraft carriers based here. In 1787 HMS *Sirius* took the first settlers from here to Australia and Portsmouth also developed to suit the needs of the New World. Significant departures have included much of the D-Day fleet in 1944 and the Falklands Task Force in 1982.

Portsea's Point, inspiration for William Walton's overture *Portsmouth Point*, is dominated by the Grade I Round Tower, a first attempt at fortification in 1481. From 1540 to 1912 it was joined to another on the west side of the harbourmouth by a chain with 1.2m links, tightened by capstan to close the harbour off when necessary. It is adjoined by the 18 gun battery of 1494, the Sally Port (where Hornblower returned to English soil in *Hornblower & the 'Atropos'*), the site of King James' Gate and the Square Tower also of 1494 with its bust of Charles I. At their foot is the last beach.

Portsmouth had the unfortunate experience of electing Captain the Honourable Edward Legge RN unopposed as their MP in 1747 and then discovering that he had died in the West Indies nearly three months earlier.

It was to her family home in Portsmouth that Fanny Price was banished in Jane Austen's *Mansfield Park*. Portsmouth was where midshipman Easy first went to sea and where he later bought the captured *Joan d'Arc* for use as the privateer *Rebiera*. Angela Nivers, in *The Blank Cheque*, wanted to go on holiday to Portsmouth because of the soldiers. Thomas Griffiths Wainewright was sent here to the hulks and thence to Van Diemen's Land in Oscar Wilde's *Pen, Pencil & Poison*. Philip

Hepburn returned here from France in a transport ship of wounded in *Sylvia's Lovers*. Bill's Café's buttered buns were questioned as Portsmouth pebbles in *Eye of the Needle*.

Old Portsmouth teemed with ale houses, brothels, sailors, pressgangs, narrow lanes and pretty houses. Although 65,000 buildings were destroyed during the war, a number of half timbered and other old houses remain among the new structures, especially in Old Portsmouth.

The Still & West forms part of an attractive harbourside group around the Camber, where the Land Rover Ben Ainslie Racing team base is the centre for challenging for the America's Cup. Many emigrated from here, including 3,000 families to settle Nova Scotia in 1749.

Above them all is the 170m Emirates Spinnaker Tower which attempts to embody the spirit of sailing in Portsmouth, more recreational than military, but has been seen by some as a hypodermic needle. Its opening in 2005 was marred when the mayor became trapped in the external lift and had to be rescued by abseilers.

Gunwharf Quays, sited on what was the Royal Navy's main ordnance store, is a thriving shopping centre. It was from here that Dee Caffari set off to be the first woman to circumnavigate the globe solo in both directions.

Isle of Wight ferries terminate at Portsea and there is also a passenger ferry across the harbour to **Gosport**.

Portsmouth Historic Dockyard hosts several famous warships. HMS *Warrior*, built in 1860, was the first fully ironclad battleship and, as the fastest (with steam and sail) and most heavily armed (with 44 guns), immediately made every other warship in the world out of date. Her restorers included recreational canal pioneer Sonia Rolt.

Fortifications and sunbathers at Point.

The original harbour at Portsmouth with Wightlink ferry terminal, Ben Ainslie Racing centre, the cathedral and Southsea beyond.

Charles II's state barge, which carried Nelson's coffin in 1806, is also present and another important exhibit is WL Wyllie's lengthy nautical panorama of the Battle of Trafalgar.

Opposite Cold Harbour an aircraft carrier might be seen towering over ornate cast iron structures onshore. Dwarfed in the background is the world's longest serving ship and possibly its most famous, the flagship of the

Point's Spice Island Inn and the Still & West.

Ben Ainslie Racing building and boat stack, mural on the Bridge Tavern by the Camber and Spinnaker Tower.

The Spinnaker Tower and Gunwharf Quays shopping centre.

Statue recalling those who emigrated from Portsmouth.

The Portsmouth waterfront with HMS Warrior on the right.

HMS Warrior outclassed all other warships when launched.

The northern end of Portsmouth Harbour with HMS Warrior.

Commander in Chief at Portsmouth, HMS *Victory*. Built in 1765, she was Nelson's flagship at Trafalgar in 1805 and carried 850 crew and 104 guns. She weighs 3,500t and measures 69m x 16m. Afloat until 1922, she is now in the world's oldest drydock and restored to her 1805 period to show what life was like aboard. Princess Victoria with her party visited her when a girl. E Temple Thurston comments on her name in *The 'Flower of Gloster'*. On

collection of Tudor artefacts including the only English shawm, possibly the oldest in the world, all but one of the Tudor arrows in existence and wooden combs complete with nits. *Mary Rose* was launched in Portsmouth in 1511 under Henry VIII's instructions, his favourite ship. The 700t carrack carried 415 crew and 91 guns, the first ship able to fire broadsides. In July 1545, after firing a broadside, she sank with vice admiral Sir George Carew

landing here, Nelson was unsuccessful in using a byway in an attempt to evade the adoring crowds.

Her neighbour has also revealed a time capsule of English life with the world's most comprehensive

and up to 700 men 2km off Southsea Castle in a French attack when her gun ports dipped below the water. She was preserved in the Solent silts until her dramatic raising in 1982 to become the centrepiece of the Mary Rose

The world's longest serving ship, HMS Victory.

Museum in the dock in which she was built, the only 16th century warship displayed anywhere in the world.

François Thurot planned to burn Portsmouth and the dockyards in 1756 by entering at night in a barque stripped as low as a raft but the plan was foiled by spies in France.

To the south of Fountain Lake lie 3km of naval frontage packed with all kinds of destroyers, frigates, anti submarine ships and aircraft carriers. Here is the Grey Funnel Line in all its glory, packed in for the naval enthusiast to appreciate. Navy Days take place in August.

Tucked in at the head of Fountain Lake is the ferry port. This is the UK's second busiest passenger port although only taking a sixth of Dover's numbers.

Maryport was described as having a garnish of Portsmouth in the *Lazy Tour of Two Idle Apprentices* by Charles Dickens and Wilkie Collins. Charles Dickens set the theatre of Vincent Crummles' family in *Nicholas Nickleby* here. Wild Tom Packer in *The Perils of Certain English Prisoners* was the son of a respectable Portsmouth shipwright. Collaborator Snow White was passing on details of Atlantic convoys from the Naval Department

to the Germans in *The Eagle Has Landed*. Like Dickens, George Meredith was born in the city.

The harbour can be quite choppy with waves reflecting off the ships and landings are strictly limited.

Whale Island is largely artificial, carrying the naval gunnery establishment HMS Excellent. Janet Prentice undertook a short course here in *Requiem for a Wren*. HMS *Bristol* is moored on the south side and used for training. Generally, the northern end of Portsmouth Harbour is quiet with large areas of mudflats at low tide, expanses which are largely the preserve of cormorants and other seabirds.

Overlooking the harbour are Fort Nelson and Fort Southwick. These forts form part of a line along the top of the Downs built by Lord Palmerston in the 1860s to counter the threat of a French invasion. These forts were equipped to fire very substantial iron balls, the better part of a metre across, persumably the length of Portsmouth Harbour, some 8km. A sunny day with deep blue storm clouds inland over the Downs makes the area magic.

Dominating the northern end of the harbour is **Portchester** Castle. The outer bailey is a Roman fort, towers date from the 3rd century and most of the rest was constructed in the 12th and 14th centuries.

Aircraft carrier HMS Queen Elizabeth.

The Royal Navy's premises located around Fountain Lake.

The ferry port and the Royal Navy's base in Fountain Lake.

If the red flag is flying from the ranges at Tipner then the whole of the upper end of Portsmouth Harbour has to be considered a danger area. The flag cannot be seen from the north without approaching uncomfortably close. Before the M275 bridge is Horsea Island, a former tip site, while retired warships were dismantled at Pounds Ship Breakers on the right.

The upper arm of Portchester Lake can get unexpectedly choppy if a southwesterly wind is funnelling waves into this corner. Concrete mattresses line each bank as the creek turns past the Blue Lagoon at Hilsea Lido. Assorted

stainless steel sculptures including Richard Farrington's Jackstar welcome those arriving at Portsmouth by road.

The northern end of the M275 hides IBM's UK headquarters, one of the largest office complexes in the south of England, positioned on reclaimed land. The most northerly part of the channel is also the last to fill as the tide floods.

The A3 Hilsea roundabout with the busy A27 and the end of the M27 has low bridges with hand chains on each side and a warning about eddies at higher stages of the tide. Flow through the bridges in Port Creek, also called

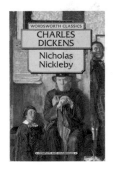

Jackstar sculpture by the M275 at Tipner.

The full extent of the headroom under the A3 roundabout bridges at low tide.

Ports Creek, Portsbridge Creek or Canal Creek, can be quite swift. Port Creek used to be narrow and winding but was dug as an alternative route to Portsmouth for the Portsmouth & Arundel Canal when the Portslade Canal part of its line across Portsea island was closed.

South of a further channel Hilsea Lines provided 18th and 19th century defence against northern approaches to Portsmouth.

A line of rusting oil drums of concrete give way to chalk bank on the left facing across to a low concrete wall. There are warnings that the water is polluted but it is not noticeably so, the more obvious human pollution being the smashed windows of the moored craft. The next bridge carries the railway which was brought from Brighton in 1847 to link with the Isle of Wight steam

packet. Before Tudor Sailing Club, Broom Channel is crossed by the A2030.

Farlington Marshes are an RSPB bird reserve, a winter feeding ground with brent geese, pintails, shovelers, teal, wigeon, curlews, dunlin, redshanks, kestrels, peregrine falcons and short eared owls.

A sea dredged aggregate wharf projects into Broom Channel, then Portsmouth Watersports Centre is across the road from the large Portchester Microtools Co. The waters are quiet except for the proximity of the A2030.

Lines of moored boats obstruct the view ahead down Eastney Lake and Lock Lake, where a section of D-Day Mulberry Harbour lies with its back broken on the left. There were more breakages in the winter of 1963 when 1.2m thick ice tore boats from their moorings.

Distance
Portsea Island is 7km long and lies 300m off Cosham with road access

OS 1:50,000 Sheet
196 The Solent & Isle of Wight

Tidal Constant
*Portsmouth:
Dover +0020*

Range
Tipner

Sea Area
Wight

Connection
*Portsmouth Harbour
– see RoB p267*

Port Creek separates Portsea Island from the mainland with the A27 alongside.

Solent

But work was scant on the Isle, tho' he tried the villages round,
So Harry went over the Solent to see if work could be found;
Alfred, Lord Tennyson

Lee-on-the-Solent with the hovercraft slipway left of centre of the picture and Solent Airport behind the houses.

The mouth of Portsmouth Harbour sees a return from Portsmouth to Hampshire. It is one of the most difficult pieces of inshore water round our coast to cross. The problem is not the fairway, close to the east shore, which carries aircraft carriers, destroyers, frigates, cargo vessels, cross-Channel car ferries and other large craft and is subject to the International Regulations for Preventing Collisions at Sea, including no use of whistles, because the narrow channel is clearly defined. The difficulty is the rest of the crossing where smaller craft spread out so that Isle of Wight car ferries, hovercraft, work boats and a mass of yachts race past. There are more pleasure craft in the Solent than there are commercial ships in the whole world so it gets a bit busy at times.

Man-of-War Anchorage is located off the entrance and large vessel movements take place on the first three hours of the flood and first, second and fifth hours of the ebb on spring tides but at all times on neaps. Flows across the entrance are to 1km/h. Off Southsea Castle the flood into the harbour is weak until HW Dover −0340 then it increases to 2km/h, while the maximum flow on the ebb is 5km/h at HW Dover +0400. Tides become increasingly complex from here to Southampton Water where there is a double high tide on springs yet neap tides are more conventional and there may be a stand of water on intermediate tides. No doubt it was all simpler when Spithead was part of the valley of the River Frome.

Fort Blockhouse is thought to be the oldest fortified site in Britain still with that use although it has been developed over the centuries.

The Royal Naval Hospital Haslar, built in 1760 as the largest new brick building in Europe, was the UK's last naval hospital and the largest military hospital in England, where patients could be landed from

Haslar Lake at any state of the tide. It precedes Gilkicker Point, the eastern extremity of Stokes Bay, the start line of the Whitbread Round the World Yacht Race, now the Volvo Ocean Race.

Razor wire surrounds the former Hasler Prison, later the Haslar Immigration Removal Centre. The Solent Way footpath leads past Fort Monckton. A stone's throw from this is the Palmerston Fort Gilkicker on Gilkicker Point, later a signal station with excellent visibility. and now housing. Spithead gives way to the Solent.

Stokes Bay begins with a golf course. It is where Queen Victoria used to embark for Osborne House on the Isle of Wight. In 1875 the royal yacht *Alberta* with the Queen on board ran down and cut through the yacht *Mistletoe* with the loss of three lives. There are the remains of an exposed pier which received boat trains from 1863 until the First World War, these days not receiving trains of any sort. Number 2 Battery is prominent by the River Alver before Browndown Point.

The B3333 runs along the front of the Victorian and Edwardian resort of **Lee-on-the-Solent** until it becomes the B3385 and

disappears inland. The village has a new beach, 20m wide over 2km in front of the Old Ship. There are buoyed jet ski and waterski areas with a passage between them for hovercraft to approach their service area at Solent Airport, the former HMS Daedalus. There is also a

Gilkicker Point with Southampton Water and Fawley power station beyond.

hovercraft museum. The airfield was a seaplane base from 1917. Royal Marines often exercise with helicopters low over the water. Elmore Angling Club made the *Guinness Book of Records* here with the biggest beach angling contest, funds going to the RNLI. A larger landing will be the British end of the 1GW IFA2 high voltage DC interconnector cable between the British and French national grids, to be completed by 2020.

Beyond **Hill Head** the River Meon enters through Titchfield Haven and the Dockyard Port of Portsmouth control passes to the Port of Southampton. In the 18th century Hillhead Harbour conducted smuggling. There is now a coastal nature reserve with bearded tits, reed warblers, water rails, bittern and wigeon, avocets breed in summer and geese, ducks and waders winter here while there are bass, mullet and cockles in the sea. The soft cliffs also give some protection to naturists in what is quite an effective afternoon suntrap.

Beyond Hook Park the River Hamble enters and from it emerge the pride of the British luxury yachting fleet. Southampton Water itself is the River Test valley drowned in the Ice Age and was the birthplace of common cordgrass which has spread right round the British coast in the 20th century. This part of Southampton Water is subject to considerable gusts when wind of any strength is from the northwest. The flood runs for nine hours and the ebb for three and a half, affected in a complex pattern by heavy rain and southwesterly winds in addition to the double high waters north of Calshot.

On the west side are **Fawley** Refinery with the Esso Marine Terminal and its flares and former Fawley power station with its 198m chimney. This part of the estuary is more simple to cross than the mouth of Portsmouth Harbour in that shipping is all going along the same track with the fairway on the Calshot side. However, notice does need to be taken of the fairways on the chart to the south, the North Channel cutting across in front of Lee-on-the-Solent but large inbound craft needing to pass close to Cowes before turning northeast into the Thorn Channel in an exaggerated S movement. A vessel over 150m long, flying a black cylinder and usually preceded by a Southampton Harbour patrol launch, has a rolling prohibited entry zone for 1km ahead and 100m to each side, much of which is a blind spot from the wheel. The sheer size of some of these craft is brought home by seeing one towering above and beyond each end of the main hangar at Calshot. The simple rule is not to start crossing if there is anything big or fast in sight. Tankers, container ships, liners and car ferries all use this water, together with many yachts. AP Herbert described the varied Southampton Water traffic in 1920 in *The House by the River*. The most important craft to spot are the passenger launches between Southampton and Cowes as these are quite small but travel very fast. If plans to develop a new container hub at

Dibden Bay are eventually successful this stretch of water will be used by container ships up to 350m long. Most of this traffic will be ship to ship so there will be a corresponding increase in smaller vessels, the number of containers handled at Southampton more than tripling.

The Calshot site has much of interest although there is no longer a Calshot Spit light vessel. One of these, in wood, is now the headquarters of the Royal Northumberland Yacht Club in Blyth harbour. A coastguard lookout point and radar scanner are on top of a tall column. For years a large Princess flying boat was moored off this point. On the other side is Calshot Castle, built in 1540 by Henry VIII with stone from Beaulieu Abbey, used until 1956 and restored as it was before the First World War with bunks and uniforms on display.

The three main buildings on the site are hangars. It was a flying boat base from 1913 to 1961 and by the 1920s carried out nearly all the maritime air training. It is the most complete surviving seaplane/flying boat base in the UK, if not the world, and includes Britain's second oldest seaplane hangar. It has been used by the navy and the RAF in the 20th century and was the site of the first Royal Naval Air Station in the UK as well as being the site of coastal artillery and anti aircraft guns. Another hangar is the Schneider Trophy hangar. TE Lawrence was based here in 1929–31, the period of the Schneider Trophy races which took place round a triangular course over the Solent and were to lead to Britain's retaining the Schneider Trophy after winning it three times in succession, in the process doing the preparatory work for the Spitfire which was to be of major importance during the Second World War.

The site's use for Calshot Activities Centre has also been important in recent years, especially for sea kayak training. There are plenty of other activities, too, the main hangar having an indoor dry ski slope, huge climbing wall and banked cycle track used by the British cycle racing team. The accommodation blocks were used by refugees from Tristan da Cunha when volcanic eruption threatened their island in the south Atlantic.

Calshot Spit is not the piece of land which runs northeast then north, but the underwater feature which is growing and which runs southeast then southwest from its end, throwing up testing water conditions to the south of the centre. Large vessels are required not to create excessive wash which could endanger those on the beach, where sea kale thrives.

There is parking around the end of the B3053 where beach huts line what an old notice proclaims to be a private beach but which is clearly used by the public. A hut on the beach sells refreshments.

From Calshot to Cornwall there is a steady regression back in time along the coast from recent sedimentary rocks to some of the oldest granite in the world. Luttrell Tower is a cylindrical brick structure on a Georgian folly

Calshot with the coastguard tower, Calshot Castle and the historic hangars now used by Calshot Activities Centre.

by Thomas Sandby, the Royal Academy's first professor of architecture, for Temple Luttrell, MP and smuggler. Marconi used it for wireless experiments. Two feet on a granite base are thought to be part of an Egyptian statue from the time of Rameses II.

Stanswood Bay is edged with rich golden sandy cliffs, topped by pines on the edge of the New Forest which continues until the Lymington River. A boathouse stands above assorted obstructions including a tide gauge while there are oyster beds further offshore.

Port of Southampton control comes to an end at Stansore Point with its mark as a free for all of telephone and high voltage cables and gas and water pipelines begins, crossing to Egypt Point at Cowes on the Isle of Wight. Three Stone Farm is named after the legend that when the island approached the mainland it was possible to leap across three stepping stones with the aid of a pole. It wasn't even an island until 9,000 years ago. Grass snakes are reported to swim across from the mainland.

Between Stansore Point and Stone Point at Lepe is Lepe Country Park, the setting for *Requiem for a Wren*,

Fawley power station chimney and the Luttrell Tower.

The pine lined sandy cliff behind Stanswood Bay.

written after being based here while working on a secret rocket launched pilotless plane for D–Day. At the back of Lepe Spit are old coastguard cottages with Solent Rescue and what looks like a small lighthouse and a boathouse. Mulberry Harbour sections were made here and there was a plan for a railway tunnel to Cowes.

Smugglers used to meet in the Ship Inn and also in the Solent Marshes, broad mudflats from here to Hurst Point, intersected by narrow creeks. A dolphin stands at the mouth of the Beaulieu River, the UK's only privately owned tidal water, the most beautiful of the Solent creeks, an entrance which can be dangerous to two hours either side of low water. It was an entrance negotiated by the *Agamemnon*, *Swiftshure* and *Euryalus* of the Trafalgar fleet in addition to many others built at Beaulieu. A causeway connects to Gull Island, which is awash at high water. In the 18th century the Bull Lake or Bull Run was cut through the end of the island but it ceased to be used in the 20th century as the island was being eroded. Boats from the Beaulieu River Sailing Club, the masts of which are seen over Needs Ore Point, now have to go round Beaulieu Spit to reach the open Solent.

Old coastguard cottages overlook a shingle bank to which they no longer have access as 3km of the shoreline has been designated the North Solent National Nature Reserve on which landing is forbidden. The bird sanctuary is home to Britain's largest colony of blackheaded gulls, 14,000 of them, plus an important breeding colony of little terns, oystercatchers and cormorants. The mudflats attract waders but the RSPB said the Solent was at risk from oil exploration.

The westgoing stream is stronger than the eastgoing stream, reaching 6km/h off Lepe Middle. The shore continues low and quiet from Great Marsh past Park Shore, Little Marsh, Thorns Beach, Durns Point and a ruined jetty to a beacon marking where a line of underwater obstructions crosses to the west of the Newtown River on the Isle of Wight.

Tidal marsh gradually widens through Pitts Deep Quay and Pylewell Point until it is 1km wide at

Dolphins stand in the Solent at Stansore Point.

The mouth of the Beaulieu River at Lepe.

Lymington Spit at the end of the Lymington River's Long Reach, which has the narrow fairway well marked from the Jack in the Basket mark so it is easy to keep clear of Wightlink's Yarmouth to Lymington car ferries. The mark may have acted as a form of nautical stocks. In 1790 HMS *Pandora* set out from here with the brief of searching the Pacific for the mutineers from the *Bounty*. HW Tilman kept *Mischief* and his subsequent Bristol Channel pilot cutters here and was given a starting and finishing gun by the Royal Lymington Yacht Club for

Coastal Britain: England & Wales

An embankment protects the Pennington Marshes and lakes.

29 species of bird including 1,300 brent geese, 2,200 wigeon and 1,300 dunlin.

The saltmarsh of Pennington Spit reaches out to Hurst Castle, the narrow low water creek of Keyhaven Lake disguising the fact that Keyhaven has fishing boats, the name possibly coming from the Saxon cy-haefenn, cow harbour. In 1901 there were plans for a rail tunnel from here to the Isle of Wight. A picnic here in *Requiem for a Wren* was the only time Alan Duncan met Janet Prentice in her life.

A 26m white round tower lighthouse stands at Hurst Point and shines over Hurst Castle, on which a former low red light was placed. The castle was constructed from 1541 to 1544 with stones from Beaulieu Abbey after the dissolution of the monasteries. Built to control the entrance to the Solent and protect Portsmouth, it was one of Henry VIII's most sophisticated, a twelve–sided central tower in a curtain wall with three semi–circular bastions. In 1648 it was the prison for Charles I for 19 days. Despite its sophistication it was quite a small structure, on a par with Calshot Castle, until 1860 when the Victorians added two long wings, making it look huge from the water. They also added two 38t guns which, together with searchlights, were not removed until 1956. Exhibits include Trinity House artefacts.

Fort Albert on Cliff End controls the other side of the gap and this is the closest the Isle of Wight gets to the mainland, just over 1km away. The constriction means fast flows and there may be heavy overfalls off Hurst Point reaching right to the shore and over the Trap ridge of sand and gravel, especially with the northeastgoing stream, with the possibility of strong eddies off the point with flows in either direction. Currents round the point can be swift. These difficulties can be avoided by using Mount Lake and portaging over Hurst Beach shingle. Ahead, the Needles and their lighthouse on the end of the Isle of Wight are prominent.

his expeditions to Greenland and the Southern Ocean. Their starting platform ensures that many sailing boats with more short term objectives set out from here and the occupants of Lymington Yacht Haven make certain of plenty of other sailing activity.

Plans for a deep water port got as far as an Act of Parliament but Oxey Marsh, behind Oxey Lake, and the Pennington Marshes with their former saltworks site remain quiet with the Lymington & Keyhaven Nature Reserve, important for plants, insects and birds with plovers, ducks, swans, egrets, winter visitors including brent geese, shelducks, teal, dunlin and lapwings, these days disturbed by no more than the Solent Way long distance footpath, as marram grass covers the marshes and saltmarsh nature reserve reaches right along this stretch of coast. It was not always so civilized. Between 1802 and 1853 Colonel Peter Hawker was reported to have killed

Distance
38km from Portsea to Hurst Castle

OS 1:50,000 Sheet
196 The Solent & Isle of Wight

Tidal Constants
Portsmouth:
Dover +0020
Lee-on-the-Solent:
HW Dover +0020,
LW Dover +0010
Calshot Castle:
HW Dover +0010,
LW Dover
Stansore Point:
HW Dover –0010,
LW Dover +0010
Lymington:
HW Dover –0020,
LW Dover
Hurst Point:
Dover –0020

Sea Area
Wight

Connection
Southampton Water – see RoB p271

The Royal Lymington Yacht Club's starting platform.

Looking back from Hurst Beach over the nature reserve towards the Solent.

Hurst Castle and lighthouse with the Isle of Wight opposite and the Needles in the distance.

142

Isle of Wight

32

And as that day, on Yarmouth Bay,
Ere England sunk from view,
While yet the rippling Solent lay
In April skies of blue,

'Pray to the Lord with fervent lips,'
Each morn was shouted, 'Pray';
And prayer arose from all the ships,
As first in Yarmouth Bay.'
Hezekiah Butterworth

It was still part of the mainland 9,000 years ago, at the end of the last Ice Age, but it is now a 381km² island with 97km of coastline, nearly half of it Heritage Coast. There were Beaker Folk present in 1900 BC. It has been Ynys yr Wyth, the isle of the channel, while resident Belgae called it Wiht, meaning raised, and the Saxons called it Whitland or Wiht-ea. Carisbrook was called Wihtgarsburh, perhaps after a Saxon king and maybe leading to the island's name. On the other hand, to the Greeks it was Ouichtis or Ictis. To the Romans it was Vectis or Vecta when they invaded in 43 under Vespasian, unusually, not leaving any roads. The Jutes settled in the 6th century. Edward I became Lord of the Isle in 1293 and Henry VI crowned Henry Beauchamp King of Vectis. From 1841 there was an honorary governor.

A miniature England, it is England's largest and most comfortable island, similar to the mainland but with less extremes of climate except for waterspouts, to which the surrounding waters are rather susceptible. EM Forster seemed to find it more attractive than its large neighbour in *Howards End*. It claims more sun than anywhere else in the country and has over half designated as AONB.

Being an island makes it distinct, however. In the 12th century it was one of the earliest places to have rabbits. The Isle of Wight wave moth is found on the cliffs and it is the only place in Britain where the square spot dart moth is found. However, *Memoirs of an Infantry Officer* refers to the Isle of Wight disease wiping out bees during the First World War.

The island is separated from the mainland by the Solent which sits above the line of an Eocene-Oligocene syncline from the centre of the island. The Solent was part of the River Frome until the sea broke through after the last Ice Age and it sank during the Bronze Age. All the island's rivers are tributaries which flow northwards. About 730 Bede referred to the Soluente, named after gannets (solan geese) or a place of muddy animals. In 1749 Dr Thomas Short of Sheffield claimed it was caused by an earthquake in 68. It is now a submarine exercise area and carries much commercial and recreational traffic.

The shortest crossing is from Hurst Point to Cliff End but it is also the most difficult and dangerous. Parking around Keyhaven and Milford on Sea seems to be geared up to the needs of daytrippers and overnight parking is forbidden. There are four unrestricted spaces in front of Keyhaven Yacht Club on a first come basis, otherwise it will be necessary to park in the village and walk back. With the tide out there is plenty of black organic silt. The Avon Water meanders through Keyhaven Lake, which is sheltered from open water.

Despite the proposal to place a boom across in 1967 if *Torrey Canyon* oil arrived from Scilly, the width restriction in the channel can result in a race to 8km/h, especially as water leaves at the eastern extremity of Hurst Point. Southwestgoing flows are stronger, from a hour before Dover high water. Northeastgoing flows run from five hours after Dover high water and there may be turbulence southeast of Hurst Point where flows from the North Channel meet those from the Needles Channel. Upwellings and standing waves add to the interest.

Cliff End is dominated by the brick block of Fort Albert, reputedly designed by Prince Albert, built in 1856 to protect Portsmouth against French attack. These days it is divided into flats and topped by rooms which might have formed urban attic studios.

There are three bays to the Needles. There is little flow in these bays with a southwesterly current but the flows work strongly round the bays with a northeasterly stream. The first is Colwell Bay which has Linstone Chine, Brambles Chine and a holiday park below a country park where Golden Hill Fort gets its name from the surrounding gorse while the chines are narrow river valleys. Fort Warden at Warden Point adds to the extensive defence arrangements at the entrance to the Solent.

Totland Bay follows with white sands, an 1879 pleasure steamer pier and an old lifeboat house, the lifeboat being moved to Yarmouth in 1924 because of the difficulty of launching when conditions were rough, the difficulty of the service being acknowledged by the fact that this was one of the first places to have a steam lifeboat. A seawall protects **Totland**, which has a clock museum.

Headon Warren, home to gorse, heather, mushrooms, thrift and the remains of Hatherwood Battery, is the

Information on Totland's old lifeboat house.

Fort Albert, part of the protection for the western Solent.

The chairlift and multicoloured sands of Alum Bay.

The Needles and their lighthouse.

The Needles look rather different from the south.

thickest layers in the country, some 460m, and exhibits some of the sharpest Alpine folding, the dip being nearly vertical on its north side, best seen from close to the cliffs. It strikes east–west, running to Culver Cliff and forming the central spine of the island. Before the sea broke through, the chalk continued to Ballard Down on the Isle of Purbeck. There can ocasionally be low tide dumping surf.

Some 80m above the sea is Palmerston's Old Battery of 1862, to oppose a French invasion and used in both World Wars, intercepting planes and torpedo boats during the Second World War. There is a 65m tunnel to a searchlight position, two original Armstrong barrels and a museum of gunnery. The New Battery of 1893 with its silos was also used for secret rocket testing from 1956 to 1971 with 27 launches of Black Knight and Black Arrow rockets.

The cliffs end with the Needles, of which three remain, Old Pepper, Wedge and Roe Hall, plus Frenchman's Cellar which is attached to the cliffs. The 30m pinnacles have been strengthened by folding of the chalk, especially on the south side of the inner one. The location is exposed, however. The largest gap used to have a real needle, the 37m high Lot's Wife, which collapsed in a storm in 1764, and a rock arch to the island fell in 1810. Jupp's high level lighthouse of 1786 was superseded by the 24m high, red banded, cylindrical, granite, Needles light tower of 1859 on the outer Needle, to which a helicopter platform was added in 1987, the low light to avoid cloud. This Needle is hollowed out to give storage space. The RAF used to abandon crew members on the middle Needle for rescue training exercises. The Needles were described briefly in *A Pair of Blue Eyes* and *The King's Own* charts the route of the *Asoasia* home past the Needles. *The House by the River* described the light as being deep green in 1920.

Wrecks in the vicinity include the 44 gun HMS *Assurance* of 1753, the 38 gun *Pomone* of 1811 (from which all were saved including two Arab stallions from the Shah of Persia for George III) and four pieces of the 1947 Greek freighter *Varvassi*.

Flows to 7km/h run around and between the Needles. In the English Channel, easterly flows run down the west coast of the island, weak at first but stronger after Hanover Point, and then run eastwards from St Catherine's Point. Westerly flows follow the route in reverse.

Scratchell's Bay forms a secluded sun trap at Sun Corner, the Downs rising to 120m at the back in a curving wall of chalk with diagonal pinstripe lines of flint. In winter it can be less attractive. In 1890 the *Irex* was wrecked on her maiden voyage, the biggest sailing ship lost on the island's shores. The crew were rescued using lifesaving apparatus from the clifftop. Around the corner, Main Bench runs 140m high with various caves, including Kitchen Parlour and Cellar, Admiral Lord Holmes reputedly entertaining

start of designated heritage coast which runs right round to St Lawrence.

Ballast is dredged from the Shingles and Pot Bank but the mineral interests are greater beyond Hatherwood Point. The east side of Alum Bay has sand cliffs in 21 colours including red iron oxide, yellow limonite and white quartz, the colours brightest when wet. The 50m high Needles Chairlift of 1971 brings tourists down off Alum Chine from the pleasure park above but the cliffs are unstable and a line of tape is intended to stop them from digging in the sand and risking collapses, the colours making it popular for preparing sand drawings. Alum was mined in the 16th century and sand was shipped to Cheshire until the 19th century from the pier,.

A stone Marconi memorial marks where the Marconi Company erected their first wireless transmitter in 1897 to send a message to a ship 29km away.

Alum Bay suffers squalls off the cliffs during gales, the south side consisting of chalk. The chalk is one of the

The island ends with Tennyson Down and the Needles.

The hidden Scratchell's Bay.

peregrines. Cormorants, shags and herring gulls also nest and there are blackbacked gulls and oystercatchers. Locals used to descend the cliffs to collect feathers and eggs and the gentry amused themselves by shooting the birds. A quicker descent was made in 1736 by Samuel Baldwyn, whose corpse was thrown over so that his wife could not carry out her threat to dance on his grave.

The 12m cross of Cornish granite serving as a daymark is Tennyson's monument of 1897. Tennyson Down is chalk turf with hairy violets, cowslips, spring gentians, orchids, betony, ragwort, heather and gorse. Alfred Lord Tennyson moved to the island in 1853, claiming the air was 'worth sixpence a pint'. Farringford Hotel was his home

guests in one and storing wine in the other although it seems unlikely that the word would not have got round about the wine. Frenchman's Hole is where a fugitive Frenchman in hiding starved to death. Bar Cave is 30m deep while Neptune's Cave is 60m. This is the most easterly nesting point on the south coast for guillemots, razorbills, puffins, ravens and

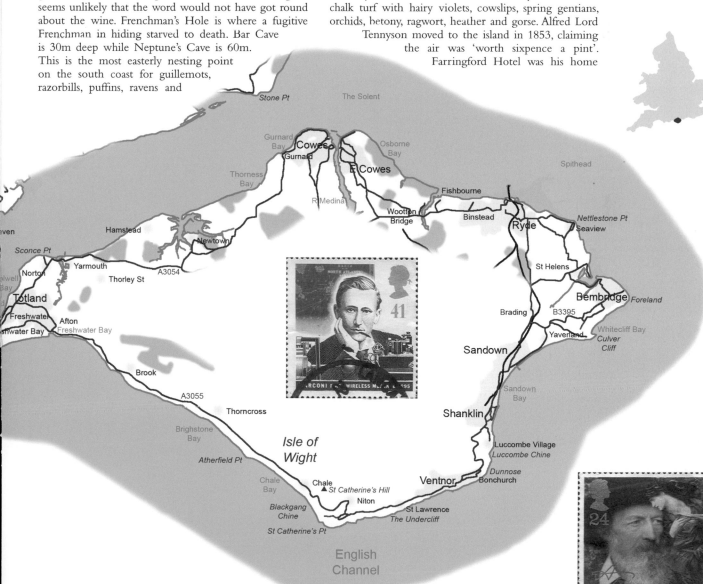

for 39 years, where he wrote *The Charge of the Light Brigade* and *Maud* and where he was visited by Kingsley, Lear, Swinburne, Dickens, Garibaldi and Lewis Carroll. In 1908 his family donated land for St Agnes' church, the only thatched church on the island, using Norfolk reeds.

Freshwater Bay has the former Palmerston Redoubt, now a residence, and a cave 9m x 40m long. It has a reef break with surf best on northerly winds, which arrive via the River Yar valley which must have continued from the south in the past as the river almost divides the island in two. The village has an esplanade and an inshore lifeboat. It also has the Dimbola Lodge museum of prints by 19th century portrait photographer Julia Margaret Cameron in two cottages joined by a Gothic tower and with a statue of Jimi Hendrix. Cameron was the great aunt of Virginia

The chalk cliffs of Freshwater Bay.

Hanover Point mark looking down to St Catherine's Point.

Extensive slipping around Blackgang Chine.

Woolf, who based her play *Freshwater* on the activities here. The A3055 arrives along the valley and rises up past Arched Rock, Stag Rock (where a stag leapt to escape hounds when the cliff was less worn) and Mermaid Rock, resulting from a 1968 cliff fall. This 19th century Military Road was partially rebuilt and opened to public use in the 1930s.

There are tumuli on the west end of East Afton Down, venue for the 1970 Isle of Wight Pop Festival where Jimi Hendrix gave his last public performance a fortnight before his death. In quieter times there is a golf course and hoary stock is to be found. Hang gliders fly on Compton Down, where chalk cliffs give way to Lower Greensand, Gault clay and Wealden beds in an anticline. Compton Chine's geological specimens include Gryphaea shells, petrified sea anemonies, silicified chalk sponges, moss agates and brown and white jasper. Dinosaurs' bones and footprints are found by Compton and Brook Bays. Compton Bay produces its best surf with southeasterly or north northwesterly winds. Flows run to 2km/h.

Fossil trees form the Pine Raft at low tide at Hanover Point, where there is a milk churn shaped mark built in the sea. Amongst those which have not benefited are a wreck in Shippards Chine and, in 1829, the East Indiaman *Carn Brae Castle*, wrecked on Brook Ledges in atrocious conditions. Brook Bay gets its best surf with the same winds which suit Compton Bay.

Coming onshore, a waterspout did slight damage in January 1971 and disappeared, to reappear a couple of hours later in London.

Garibaldi planted a tree at Brook House and African clawed toads were released in Brook in 1967.

Found below the Undercliff are Mesolithic hazelnuts, known as Noah's nuts.

The isolated Hardman Rock stands off the coast before Chilton Chine, home of Isle of Wight Pearl with 35,000 pieces of jewellery, claimed to be the UK's largest collection of pearl jewellery. A holiday camp follows before Grange Chine and Grange Farm has alpacas, llamas and water buffalo. These start the sweep of Brighstone Bay which continues past another holiday centre at Shepherd's Chine and has the first beach huts. The bay has its best surf with west to northwest winds.

An aerial and a museum back from the cliffs at Thorncross are not conspicuous from inshore, unlike the 229m transmission aerial on Chillerton Down, visible over a wide area.

Red houses on the cliffs at Atherfield Point were a

Chale with Freshwater in the distance.

coastguard station overlooking Atherfield Ledges where, in 1888, a rescue by Brook and Grange lifeboats of the Californian grain ship *Sirenia* was one of the most remarkable in the entire history of the RNLI. The boats fought horrendous conditions for two days, even a local smuggler joining the volunteers, and most of the ship's crew were rescued with most of the lifeguard crews also surviving. Flows at the point run to 4km/h.

Salt and freshwater fossils are found together, including fossil oysters, lobsters and ammonites, while mackerel are alive and well. A full length container on the beach in Chale Bay, also known as the Bay of Death or the Ships' Graveyard, did not come down the 126 steps at Whale Chine. It may have been named after a whale washed up in the 18th century or after the Wavells who owned Atherfield Farm in the 16th and 17th centuries. Chale is marked by a 15th century Perpendicular tower on a church founded in the 12th century and with many shipwreck victims buried. The village has a buttressed barn at the manor house.

Blackgang Chine, named after a smuggling gang, is one of England's most popular theme parks, in existence since 1843 despite the fight to keep ahead of its 16ha site's progressive collapse into the sea, there being extensive slippage along this coast, especially in 1994. The skeleton of a 23m whale washed up on the shore in 1842 is the largest and best preserved in Britain. It accompanies a shipwreck museum, smugglers' cave, smugglers' lugger, lifeboat, paddle steamer, coastal erosion display and Blackgang Sawmill Museum with replica Victorian water power sawmill, hedge maze, BBC *Coast* and many other exhibits. There are the bell from the *Beaumonde*, wrecked in 1883, and a cannon from an Armada vessel, just two of the 180 shipwrecks which have taken place in the vicinity since 1750. In 1724 Defoe suggested that smugglers were Blackgang's only foreign commerce. The *Volkerak* was washed onto the beach in 1951. Although her cargo of china clay from Fowey was taken off, most of the ship had disappeared within a month. Increasingly, there is a high tide dump onto the steep shingle beach on this section of coast.

An earlier important wreck on the Atherfield Ledges took place in 1317, the sailors selling the cargo of wine. Of the 174 casks, 53 were received by landowner Walter de Godeston, who was required by the Pope to build a lighthouse as a penance or be excommunicated. He had complied by 1328. The Pepperpot or St Catherine's Oratory is the remaining western tower of a chapel, an octagonal, rocket shaped, ancient monument for a priest to operate a light and say masses for those lost at sea. It stands by an aerial on top of 236m St Catherine's Hill, the highest point on the island. The light was closed down with most religious activity during the Reformation but there were so many wrecks that Trinity House had Jupp establish another in 1785, the Salt Cellar, but problems with fog resulted in abandoning work on this and moving to a lower level. The ledges have surf at low water. *Hornblower & the 'Atropos'* comments on the unbelievable green of the island as the ship manages to round St Catherine's Point in a gale.

Most of the coast itself is also moving down. In 1799 a farmhouse and 40ha fell. The steps to the shore at Rocken End were closed in 1913 after slips took the coast road and houses. At Windy Corner 250,000t followed in 1928. This shattered landscape is the only British venue for the Glanville fritillary.

In 1901 a Marconi radio message was picked up 300km away in Cornwall, more than twice the previous best distance. The wreck of the *Clarendon* with the loss of 23 lives in 1836 prompted the construction of the listed, white, octagonal lighthouse on low St Catherine's Point four years later. At 41m above the sea, its height was reduced by a third in the 19th century and it is now 26m tall with a 48km range. A fog signal was installed in 1868

but this was undermined by erosion in 1932 and replaced by a smaller version of the light tower to give the Cow & Calf. A German aircraft attacked with incendiary devices in 1943 and set fire to the engine house, killing the three keepers who were sheltering there. The following year it overlooked Piccadilly Circus, the name given to the area where 7,000 ships and 130,000 men gathered ahead

St Catherine's lighthouse is at low level.

of D-Day landings. The smaller tower was superseded by a radio beacon in 1987, the year of the great storm when the wind was recorded at 167km/h here and the incapacitated 935t *Union Mars* missed the point only because the wind direction changed. A light range and experimental station and automatic weather reporting station were added in 1991.

Flows run eastwards from five hours twenty minutes after Dover high water and westwards from twenty minutes after Dover high water at up to 9km/h although currents are weaker inshore. The offshore race can be violent. With strong flows there are eddies near land, an eddy forming west of the point on westerly flows. HM Submarine *Swordfish* was lost off the point in 1940, its remains being found in the 1980s.

Reeth Bay is the most practical landing point on this section of coast although vehicle access is not permitted down the approach road. Surf is best with southwesterly to westerly winds.

Niton was noted for its daytime inactivity, a sure sign of smuggling.

From Reeth Bay the coast is again subject to slips. Reedmace growing on the hillside behind the beach is an indication of the water content of the soil. Puckaster Cove is where Charles II landed in 1675 and, whether by design of otherwise, it is a section of coast not easy to reach on foot except along the beach. There was probably less choice for the East Indiaman *Three Sisters*, lost with three crew in January 1799 when overcome by rain and snow. The inaccessibility of this section of coast also suits naturists.

Binnel Point at the end of Binnel Bay has various pieces of wall of a former harbour. Poet Alfred Noyes became a resident.

Two masts stand above St Lawrence, a 13th century village with an 1197 church which, at 7.6m x 3.4m, was the smallest in England until extended in 1842. A row of former coastguard cottages stand by Woody Bay.

At 13ha, the Isle of Wight Rare Breeds & Waterfowl Park is one of the UK's largest collections of rare farm breeds. The Royal National Hospital for Diseases of the Chest was open from 1869 to 1964. The patients laid out measured walks for other patients. The site is used for the Ventnor Botanic Garden with 9ha in the Undercliff growing 3,500 species of subtropical trees and shrubs, described as the Madeira of England, and with the UK's largest wild colony of wall lizards introduced. Queen Victoria planted the Chinese fan palm. The brown turkey fig was planted in 1869 for hospital patients. There is also a Museum of Smuggling History from 1297. Steephill has a castle built in 1835 with gardens claimed to be the best in the British Isles. The town has its own sunny microclimate but also weaver fish with poisonous spines.

Ventnor Bay has its best surf at low water because

Ventnor beneath St Boniface Down.

of a high tide dump. Beach huts begin again but it would be hard to miss **Ventnor** as its name is spelled out prominently in various places. It is another unstable venue, having a Blue Slipper layer of wet Gault clay at the bottom, causing seaward landslides. In the 18th and 19th centuries two thirds of the fishermen and some of the farmers were smugglers but it developed into a resort and Victorian winter health retreat on a series of terraces, complete with Winter Gardens, a lift and, formerly, two railway stations. Admiral Hobson was born here. Tennyson, *Punch* contributor the Revd James White, Carns Wilson who was Mr Brocklehurst in *Jane Eyre*, Carlyle's friend John Sterling, Macaulay, H de Vere Stacpoole and painter William Gray were resident. Visitors included Winston Churchill, Karl Marx, Gandhi, Thackeray, Richard Doyle, John Leech, Elizabeth Sewell, Elgar and painter Thomas Miles Richardson. In *English Hours* Henry James noted it had not been subject to too much cockneyfication, Bonchurch was simply delicious and the Undercliff was the prettiest place in the world. Bertha and Francis Horton honeymooned here in *The Loving Spirit*. Its climate was promoted by Sir James Clark. The 1955 pier was damaged in the 1987 storm and closed and the last of the three piers was destroyed by fire in 1993. Offshore is St Catherine's Deep, a disused explosives dumping ground.

Ventnor merges into the 13th century village of Bonchurch, named after St Boniface, who was present

and after whom the Norman church of 1070 is named. Rising high above is St Boniface Down, covered with holm oak, gorse, tumuli, radar scanners and telecoms aerials. Swinburne lived in the village as a youth and is buried here. Charles Dickens started *David Copperfield* while on holiday here and had Sophronia and Alfred Lammle walking in meaningful conversation on Shanklin sands in *Our Mutual Friend*. A skateboard ramp and Bonchurch Pottery serve less academic holidaymakers. Tetrapods protect the seawall by

Much of the coast at Dunnose has slipped into the sea.

Horseshoe Bay while Monks Bay is said to be named after monks of Lyra Abbey in Normandy who landed here.

The Landslip at Dunnose is the site of major slips in 1810 and 1928, now softened with oak and hazel and used by herring gulls. In 1878 it was where HMS *Eurydice* was lost with all but two of her 366 crew. Returning from the West Indies, she was hit by an ice storm and the crew, who were already celebrating their homecoming, were too drunk to lower the sail.

A flight of 300 steps lead down Luccombe Chine to Luccombe Bay, where a cliff fall revealed smugglers' caves and a 1910 landslide destroyed a fishing community, Luccombe Village being separated from the bay by nearly vertical cliffs 30–50m high.

Shanklin Chine was used by smugglers but in 1545 is where they ambushed French raiders and killed their leader, Chevalier d'Eulx. It opened in 1817 as the island's earliest tourist attraction and has a nature trail with rare flora and fauna including chipmunks, an aviary, a 14m waterfall, chalybeate water which is supposed to be beneficial for the complexion, a Victorian sea water bath, illuminations, a memorial to 40 Commando, Royal Marines and a 1944 PLUTO exhibition on the pipeline running from the pier to Cherbourg to deliver 2.9l/s of fuel to troops during the Normandy landings. The cliff is heavily rock bolted in an attempt to prevent further falls. A thatched Fisherman's Cottage is now a public house.

A promenade passes such facilities as the Lazy Wave Café, toilets, unnamed beach huts, a cliff lift, a conspicuous

The cliffs of Luccombe Bay.

Thatched cottage below a heavily rock bolted cliff at Shanklin Chine.

Beach huts below a pitted cliff at Shanklin.

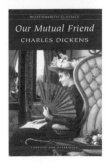

clocktower, an amusement arcade and the Journeys End Café. The pier was breached during the War and did not survive the 1987 storm.

Shanklin is a fishing village which became a Victorian and Edwardian resort, not least because it often has the UK sunshine record although a storm off the town in August 1975 produced 45 lightning flashes per minute. Despite being the start of the Dockyard Port of Portsmouth control, its beaches with groynes are far from naval in appearance. Flows run to 4km/h in the bay. There are various surf breaks.

Keats wrote *Otho the Great, Lamia* and part of *Hyperion* in Shanklin, living here for a long period, and suggested it be called Primrose Island. Ironically, Keats Green mostly has hydrangeas. Dickens set some of *Our Mutual Friend* here, Wilkie Collins had Magdalen Vanstone recuperate here near the end of *No Name*, Austen visited and Longfellow stayed in 1868 and wrote the inscription which is not his greatest verse. Kilvert objected to having to wear a bathing costume in 1874, especially as his would

not stay on and caused him injury on the sharp shingle, but he watched a girl bathing naked on a nearby beach the following year. Prendergast, in *Decline & Fall*, had bought here the cane which was used by Grimes for beating the boys.

Beyond Little Stair Point a road train might be seen on the A3055 passing over a train on what *English Hours* calls a detestable little railway. Beginning as a horsedrawn line in 1880, it became Britain's first standard gauge electric line in the 1930s, using former London Piccadilly Line coaches. Initially from Ventnor, it now runs from Shanklin to Ryde.

The join with **Sandown**, another resort with safe bathing, is seamless. The 1876 pier, extended in 1894, with its amusements survives as the island's only pleasure pier despite being damaged in the 1987 storm.

Henry VIII's Sandham Castle of 1540 was destroyed by the sea but Charles I built another which lasted until the middle of the 19th century. The French were repelled in

149

The pier stretches out from Sandown.

Red Cliff leads into Culver Cliff.

Culver Down, the east end of the island's spine.

Herons on the hillside overlooking Whitecliff Bay.

the 15th and 16th centuries, as were privateers during the American War of Independence.

Pitted red sandstone cliffs back the esplanade and such establishments as the Pioneer Café, public toilets, Strollers and the Beach Café. After the pier the establishments are very much grander, the Trouville Hotel and others. Sandham Rides with go karts and bumper boats retain a balance.

John Wilkes retired to the former Sandham Cottage. Darwin started writing *The Origin of Species* in the town and Lewis Carroll wrote *The Hunting of the Snark* here. Dinosaur Isle museum has fossils and activated full size models while there is a geology museum with 1,300 fossils in the library. Yaverland has fossils on the beach.

As the B3395 turns away from Sandown Bay, Isle of Wight Zoo claims the largest tiger collection in the UK in a granite fort. Beyond the Grand Hotel and adjacent golf course is a church which is partly Norman, next to a Jacobean manor house.

The dense clay Red Cliff section of coast follows as the green and yellow cliffs are left behind.

In November 1957 a storm grounded the 3,500t *Iano* here, the 19 crew being rescued.

Bembridge Down, 104m high, is topped by Bembridge Fort, built for Palmerston and used until the Second World War. The first wireless signal station on the south coast was built here in 1900, able to relay signals on Channel shipping movements to the Admiralty in Portsmouth. Further east is the Yarborough Monument, a 104m stone needle of 1849 to Charles Pelham, the 1st Earl of Yarborough and first commodore of the Royal Yacht Squadron. It was moved from its original location in order to allow the building of Bembridge Fort.

Whitecliff Ledge notes the change from red clay to the wall of white chalk which forms Culver Cliff, the end of which has the same flint pinstriping as Scratchell's Bay. On the cliff is the Hermit's Hole cavern. Culver comes from the Anglo Saxon cofa, cave or cove, or from culfre, dove. There are nesting ravens, falcons and many seabirds including terns. In 1564 Elizabeth I called for the apprehending of someone who had stolen some valuable hawks from the cliff. Culver Down is said to resemble a cow but that might require sufficient distance.

The expectation of coloured sand to mirror Alum Bay is thwarted by a covering of vegetation. Whitecliff Bay's low cliffs help Bembridge Airport, the runway of which is in line with the bay and the only surfaced one on the island, starting 900m from the beach. This break can produce surf to 1.5m.

Bembridge's windmill of 1700, with stone tower and wooden machinery, the only one remaining on the island, was used until 1913. Out to sea is the Nab Tower.

Long Ledge is a prelude to Bembridge Ledge which forms the eastern end of the island, the Foreland. At high water the Run extends into a sheltered channel which emerges beyond the lifeboat station, rebuilt in 2010. Flows are to 3km/h. The lifeboat took 110 people off the *Empress Queen* on the rocks in 1916 and all the crew from the SS *Wakulla* three years later. The rocks attract herons and purple sandpipers. Lobster pots are set.

Bembridge developed from a fishing village to a quiet resort, the kind of place to find England's oldest working telephone box, a K1 dating from 1921. Bembridge Maritime Museum has the maritime history of the island, shipwrecks, Trinity House, pilotage, navigation, salvage, diving equipment, pirates, sail, paddle steamers, hovercraft, ship models, HM Submarine *Swordfish* and a merman. Bembridge Heritage Centre is in a former Victorian school. The 1820s church was built by the locals and rebuilt 20 years later.

Out in the Spithead are large ships at anchor.

Edward III sailed from Bembridge Harbour or Brading Haven to invade Normandy in 1346, following the repelling of a French invasion here in 1340. Brading

Bembridge's lifeboat slipway runs out from Bembridge Ledge.

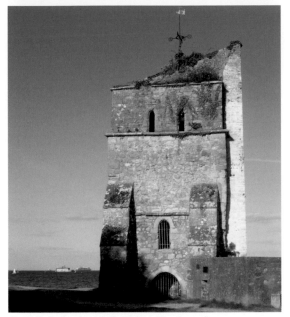

St Helen's church with St Helen's Fort beyond.

could be reached by water until land around the River Yar was reclaimed in 1878 at the second attempt, producing saltmarsh which is good for winter wildfowl and waders and allowing Bembridge to be reached by land. The harbour is a boat racing centre, home of Bembridge Redwings and Swans. In the 18th and 19th centuries it was used for smuggling. Daw Bank and Daw Passage were named after smuggler Dicky Dawes, whose sister, Sophie, married Baron de Feucheres, who took her to France where she allegedly murdered him before returning with his fortune.

There are the remains of a tidal mill and also of the 13th century St Helen's church by the Duver spit, the name being a dialect word for dunes. The seaward face is painted white as a daymark. Gorse is one of 260 plant species found in the vicinity. The island's first golf course was here with international status. Bootlace weed is found in the sea, as are swans.

St Helen's Fort is one of four remaining Palmerston Follies in the Spithead, built in 1860 to protect against the French but never used. This one is the closest to land. The French were not the only enemies and, when a pressgang ship was spotted off St Helen's in *Mr Midshipman Easy*, an escape was made past the Needles by the *Rebiera*.

The 1080s Cluniac priory was suppressed by Henry V, much being lost to the sea in 1550 although soft sandstone holystones were taken from the ruins and used for scouring the decks of ships while waiting at anchor. Priory Bay Hotel now stands on the site. It was a favoured mooring for Nelson, who took on spring water from Bembridge, maybe his last landfall in Britain ahead of Trafalgar in 1805. St Helen's Road was the scene of the 1797 Spithead mutiny.

Flows run west from two hours forty minutes before Dover high water at up to 1km/h and southwards from two hours twenty minutes after Dover high water at up to 2km/h.

Priory Bay has produced over 300 palaeolithic handaxes, suggesting there was quite an active factory here, some tools up to 70,000 years old being shown in Oxford's Pitt Rivers Museum. On Boxing Day in 1950 Seaview Bay lost one of only two suspension piers in the country, a three span pier of 1881. Numerous cables from Portsmouth land in the vicinity of Nettlestone Point. Off the point are No Man's Land Fort and Horse Sand Fort, two more of the Palmerston forts, although the Second World War barrier leading out has been removed.

Seaview Yacht Club is the source of the popular Sea View one design sailing class, which may not be sold out of the club, and also of the Mermaid.

Prawns and lobsters are caught locally but, at the other end of the scale, a blue or sei whale was killed and landed in 1888.

The 4ha Seaview Wildlife Encounter has 70 species, mostly waterfowl, a total of 2,500 birds with waterfalls up to 4.6m high.

Puckpool Point has an 8m beacon topped by a white diamond. The remains of the 18th century Puckpool Battery were converted to a park in 1928 but the sea defences have not done so well, having been damaged by tidal surges in 1905 and 1989.

Ryde East Sands reach 2km out at low tide with two distinct eastwards spurs at the outer end and 500m off Puckpool Point. The sands cover fast, leaving some deep holes. **Ryde** has 10km of beach, the Georgian, Edwardian and Victorian brown brick resort with bowling greens, tennis courts, canoe lake, swimming pools, 9 hole and crazy golf courses and road train. Prominent along the front is Appley Tower, a Victorian watchtower Gothic folly of 1875 with a shell collection. There is a promenade, Grade II Ryde Pavilion with 22 bowling lanes. The Ship Inn was where Charles II played while waiting for the tide to turn in 1662. A prominent 55m All Saints church spire of 1872 is one of Sir Gilbert Scott's best in Early English Decorated style. The Prince Consort Building with its colonnades, now a private residence, was built in 1846 by Prince Albert for Queen Victoria as the home

Nettlestone Point is the island's northeast corner.

London Underground train on Ryde Pier.

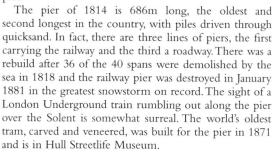

The beach at Binstead.

of the Royal Victoria Yacht Club, which allowed female members, unlike the Royal Yacht Squadron. In 1870 Empress Eugénia stayed overnight in Ryde after her flight in disguise from the Tuileries. *The King's Own* tells of Captain Capperbar using extensive navy materials and manpower on his cottage in Ryde.

A proposal has been made for an embankment–tunnel–embankment link to be made between Ryde and Portsmouth. The FastCat link to the end of Ryde pier is the latest manifestation of a ferry service begun in 1796. It can be avoided by craft able to pass under the pier itself although this still means crossing the path of hovercraft from Southsea which operate from the east side of the pier.

The pier of 1814 is 686m long, the oldest and second longest in the country, with piles driven through quicksand. In fact, there are three lines of piers, the first carrying the railway and the third a roadway. There was a rebuild after 36 of the 40 spans were demolished by the sea in 1818 and the railway pier was destroyed in January 1881 in the greatest snowstorm on record. The sight of a London Underground train rumbling out along the pier over the Solent is somewhat surreal. The world's oldest tram, carved and veneered, was built for the pier in 1871 and is in Hull Streetlife Museum.

The Solent is one of the world's busiest shipping lanes with Ryde Roads seeing much passing traffic. Flows start west an hour and twenty minutes before Dover high water at up to 5km/h and east from four hours twenty minutes after Dover high water at up to 4km/h. Plaice and flounders live on the bottom in the flow.

To Old Castle Point flows are weaker inshore and irregular with eddies near low water. A 3000 BC fish trap has been found with a submerged oak forest of similar age. The shoreline is wooded with large tree trunks

devoid of bark but with extensive sinews strewn along the beaches.

Behind a golf course is Binstead's Holy Cross church, built in the reign of Henry II to prevent the residents from bothering Quarr Abbey, where his queen, Eleanor, was imprisoned. It was one of the first Cistercian abbeys, built in 1132 and named after the Binstead quarries which were begun by the Romans and later supplied the stone for Winchester and Chichester cathedrals, Beaulieu Abbey, Winchester College and Portchester Castle. After the dissolution of the monasteries the stone was used for forts at Cowes and Yarmouth but there are the remains of an anti pirate gate and portcullis in the seawall. A pagan sheela-na-gig figure is placed over the churchyard entrance and there is a grave with a carving of the ship of smuggler Thomas Sivell and also the grave of Samuel Landor, said to be the largest man in the world in 1844 when he died.

The modern Quarr Abbey is a large building designed by Expressionist architect Dom Paul Bellot, a monk, and built by 300 local housebuilders using Flemish bricks for the Benedictines in 1908–14 for monks exiled from Solesmes by French religious laws. Many First World War soldiers convalesced here, including Robert Graves, as described in his *Goodbye to All That*. The French departed in 1922 and left 25 British monks with a church, the campanile of which can be seen over the trees from the water, one of Europe's best modern church buildings. It is built on a site which the Romans may have used for making salt.

Wootton Creek was Fugelflete or bird lake to the Saxons. The Vikings also used it, one of their bronze pins having been found. Except when it froze over in 1963, of late the creek has been the terminal for the car ferries from Portsmouth, the most expensive in the world for the distance travelled. Opposite the terminal at Fishbourne is a holiday village at Wootton and the creek is a yachting centre with a race platform off Wootton Point.

A disused jetty leads to a footpath at Woodside and thence to the road.

Northwest of Woodside is a hamlet of holiday huts with jet skis and other small craft moored off, plus a buoyed waterski area, inside which lie two wrecks.

King's Quay is where King John is alleged to have sulked after signing Magna Carta, although that is disputed. It is also where Charles I landed after escaping from Hampton Court in 1647.

Various important properties hide beyond the woods. Barton Manor was laid out by Victoria and Albert and extended by Edward VII, the 8ha including 2ha of vineyard, claimed to be one of the finest in England, a hedge maze and a water garden in what was Queen Victoria's skating rink.

The Swiss Cottage of 1853 was for the royal children to learn practical skills including cooking and gardening and is accompanied by a miniature fort designed by

The car ferry terminal at Fishbourne in Wootton Creek.

Queen Victoria's shelter below Osborne House.

Landing house on the Barton estate by the royal landing stage.

Prince Albert and built by the princes with bricks which they made for themselves. The most important building is Osborne House, designed in Palladian Italianate style by Prince Albert and Thomas Cubitt as a brightly decorated summer residence. It was the favourite home of Queen Victoria from 1845, making the Isle of Wight fashionable. It was where she spent much of her time from 1861 and where she died in 1901. It has a clock tower and a 33m flag tower. The Durbar Room of 1893 by Lockwood Kipling is ornately finished in Indian decor, showing many gifts presented to the queen. Another room is decorated with animal horns and there are terraced gardens with fountains and statues and rare trees in 1.4km^2 of grounds, the venue being used to film *Mrs Brown*.

On Victoria's private beach is a ceramic lined shelter used by her, its circular wooden bench supported on cast iron dolphins. Notices put up by Natural England and the Osborne Estate ban landing around much of Osborne Bay, because of wildlife concerns rather than privacy. There is plenty of small print on the notices, which can only be read by landing. Natural England consider it a wildlife haven and there are such birds as common gulls, egrets and curlews despite the noisy neighbours at Woodside. Victoria's bathing machine stands by the shore.

Rather larger is the landing house of 1854, originally at the head of the jetty used by the coastguards, the royal

family and guests including Napoléon III and Empress Eugenie. Osborne was a Royal Naval College preparatory school between 1903 and 1921, when it was given to the nation by Edward VII, students including the future Edward VIII and George VI. The adjacent land is now a golf course.

Norris Castle of 1795 in mock medieval style was the last Georgian castle on the island, built by James Wyatt for Lord Henry Seymour. It has tapestries from four centuries, furniture, pictures, sculpture, armour and weapons on display. Queen Victoria was unable to buy it but was allowed to use it until she built Osborne House. She installed a shower for Kaiser Wilhelm II's visits to Cowes Weeks many years before they were in common use. The grounds have been used for gymkhanas and Scout and Guide camps and refreshments have been sent down to sailors stranded offshore.

Old Castle Point refers to **East Cowes** Castle, built by John Nash and protected by a stone wall of which sections remain. He also built the church. The view of Calshot's main hangar and Fawley refinery stacks across the Solent show how Southampton Water runs well to the west.

The Dockyard Port of Portsmouth now becomes Cowes Harbour to Egypt Point. Flows in Cowes Roads may run to 6km/h. Named after the Saxon medene, middle river, the Medina, which formerly rose south of the present

The Old Castle at East Cowes.

Moorings in the estuary of the River Medina.

extent of the island, has a strong flood from six hours after Dover high water and a very strong ebb from forty minutes after Dover high water. It has the double high waters of the area, the first forty minutes before Dover high water and the second an hour later. A westgoing eddy flows across the estuary and in 1892 it was proposed to take a tunnel under the river although road traffic is still using a chain ferry service.

Two former sandbanks or cows on opposite sides of the estuary may have given the new name to Shamblord.

A 300m long breakwater protects the east side of the estuary with a 350m detached breakwater across part of the rivermouth. Inside them are a mass of moorings and boats of all sizes coming and going, in addition to three marinas providing mooring for 2,000 yachts. Ferries to Southampton may travel above 12km/h and show quick flashing yellow lights.

South of the breakwater is a hovercraft slipway leading to the hangar sized Columbine Shed with the world's largest permanent Union Flag painted across the full width of its doors in 1977 to commemorate the Silver Jubilee. The first practical hovercraft flight was from here in 1959. Saunders-Roe have constructed hovercraft, helicopters and the world's largest metal seaplane, the Princess flying boat, here although the flying boat hangar suffered damage in a fire caused by a storm in 1951. Artemis Offshore Academy is now based here. The Vestas Sailrocket 2, developed here, reached a peak speed of 126km/h in 2012.

In 1876 a tornado cut a 30m swathe through **Cowes** in seconds, even embedding a roofing tile in a yacht 800m out to sea.

A stone from the Fastnet Rock is located at Trinity church, which has a view of the start line of yacht races, as a memorial to the victims of the 1979 Fastnet Race, a more recent storm of note. The race takes place from here in alternate years.

Warship building took place in Cowes from the days of Elizabeth I and convoys were mustered here during the Napoleonic Wars. The town's shipbuilders may have been the original caulkheads, a term now applied to all islanders. John Coombes began building yachts for Cowes in *The Loving Spirit*.

Cowes is the world's most famous yachting centre despite its small size and the dearth of wind in the area. Indeed, Cannes has been called the Cowes of the Mediterranean, presumably not by the French. The first race was recorded in 1788 and popularity was assured when Edward, Prince of Wales, raced yachts here in the 1890s. The nine day Cowes Week in early August is one of the world's largest regattas and one of the world's longest running sports events, having taken place since 1826. Races round the Isle of Wight from here have taken place in June since 1824 with the first official Round the Island Race in 1851, won by the

US schooner *America* which had a streamlined hull and lighter sails, leading to the America's Cups. The Round the Island Race has the largest entry of any British sailing race. 1851 was also the start of the Admirals Cup Race series, taking place in alternate years.

William Arnold became collector of customs in the town in 1777. Unusually, he was efficient and incorruptible, putting many smugglers out of business. His son, born here, was the future Dr Thomas Arnold of Rugby School, inspiration for *Tom Brown's Schooldays*.

Its most famous sailor and boat designer was Uffa Fox, born here in 1898. A pioneer of planing dinghies, he was involved with International 14s, Flying 15s and International Canoes but was never admitted to the Royal Yacht Squadron as he was in business. In the Second World War he referred to mainland England as 'our gallant ally' and was employed to design lifeboats to be dropped to ditched airmen, secretly giving himself the brief of having them easily convertible to recreational craft in the subsequent peacetime. The town was also home to Cowes ketches and is the base for Bekens, leaders in yacht photography,.

Cowes Maritime Museum is in an old sail loft which was the home of Sir Max Aitken. Cowes is the island's designer shopping hotspot. The 80t hammerhead crane of 1912 is England's oldest remaining.

The Royal Corinthian Yacht Club, Royal London Yacht Club and Island Sailing Club are lesser sailing clubs in town. The former West Cowes Castle or cow, another possible source of the town's name, was built in 1539 for Henry VIII to protect against the French and Spanish. It is now the home of the Royal Yacht Squadron, the oldest exisiting yacht club, formed in 1815 as the Royal Yacht Club, when yachts were fitted out as men of war. This may have been the first British use of the term 'yacht', derived from the Dutch. A row of 22 small brass cannons, from founding member William IV's *Royal Adelaide*, are mounted across the front for race control and to give royal salutes. A mermaid statue also watches events. Members pay no fees in foreign ports and, apart from the Royal Navy, have the exclusive right to fly the White Ensign and of landing in front of the castle which the squadron has occupied since 1855. The latter was made easier in 2006 when a haven was established for temporary mooring, based on 16 reinforced concrete caissons weighing up to 102t each and towed from Southampton, where they were cast. Cyril Graham's parents had been drowned in a yachting accident off the island in Oscar Wilde's *The Portrait of Mr WH*.

During the Second World War the castle was used to control D-Day operations. Cowes also received a major wartime hit in 1942. The esplanade was built in 1829 to support Cowes Week.

The Best Western New Holmwood Hotel faces onto what may be an eddy to Egypt Point, the end of Cowes Harbour control. This is one of the narrowest parts of the Solent and a net was stretched across to Stone Point during the Second World War. For the same reason there are submarine gas and water pipelines and a power and telephone cable crossing area as far as Thorness Bay to Stansore Point. Flows run westwards from forty minutes before Dover high water at up to 5km/h and eastwards from five hours after Dover high water at up to 4km/h.

Gurnard was named after a local fish species although a sunfish caught in these waters in 1990 was claimed to be a result of continuing climate change. The Watersedge Restaurant and Gurnard Sailing Club are by the shore used for building by the Romans.

From Gurnard Bay westwards the flows are deeper and stronger on the island side of the Solent, running to 6km/h. Many rocky ledges run out, including Gurnard Ledge at Gurnard Head, and it is heritage coast and generally devoid of habitation until Yarmouth. Frequent dead trees complete with branches and roots are testimony to the unstable nature of the coast, slips often being only too obvious. The sea may be brown, yellow or white depending on the local soil colour. Naturists find secluded points at which to sunbathe.

Remains of PLUTO pipes are to be found by Thorness Bay, as may be young windsurfers under instruction.

From Salt Mead Ledges to the Newtown River the coast is part of the Newtown Rifle Range & TRaining Area for 3km. Even if no red flags are flying there may be indications of military exercises taking place in the area. This is where a tank driver drowns in *Requiem for a Wren*.

The Newtown River was the best harbour on the island until it silted up in the late 19th century. It was sacked by the Vikings in 1001 and by the French in 1377. In 1954 the sea broke through a 300 year old seawall. Small craft may be able to go directly from Newtown Bay to Clamerkin Lake at the top of a high tide instead of going to the rivermouth. Fishhouse Point is a bird sanctuary and landing is not permitted. Much of the estuary is a 3.2km² nature reserve with 180 bird species including passage and wintering wildfowl and waders, Canada geese, ospreys and little terns and 300 plant species including wood calamint as the various channels reach between saltmarsh, shingle, sand, pasture and woodland. The RSPB said that offshore oil exploration would put the Solent at risk. There is also a Marine Archaeological Site.

A Celtic cross set in a hedgerow facing the west side of Newtown Bay commemorates three young men drowned in the 1930s.

At Hamstead Point a concrete ramp was used for D-Day landing practice.

There is a submerged cliff off Bouldnor Cliff and a submerged forest off Bouldnor. Fossil leaves of fan palms and teeth and bones of mammals, crocodiles and turtles have been found. Bouldnor Forest, of Corsican pine and other trees, is popular with red squirrels, which benefit from the absence of grey squirrels. Part of a pier remains from an abandoned attempt in Victorian times to develop the area.

The A3054 comes to the shore at Bouldnor, the first road since Gurnard Bay, bringing buildings, beyond which are the remains of a church at Thorley and Thorley Manor. There is also a ruined jetty.

Despite being the terminal for ferries to Lymington since 1830, Yarmouth is less important today than it was in the past, being recorded in 991 and chartered from

The cannon-ringed headquarters of the Royal Yacht Squadron.

A warning to passers by.

Mermaid at the mouth of the River Medina.

1135. Of Saxon origin, it takes its name from eremue or ermud, muddy estuary, and its grid street plan from the Normans. King John came in 1206 and 1214 and Charles II was here twice, giving the town a silver mace in thanks for supporting his father, Charles I. The town hall of 1272 was used as a meat market and rebuilt in 1763. It was a rotten borough between 1304 and 1832 with two MPs and an electorate of between two and nine. The French visited in 1377 and 1524, St James' church

The rural estuary of the Newtown River.

The Waverley *swings off the pier at Yarmouth.*

Distance
*The Isle of Wight is
37km long and lies
1km off Hurst Castle*

OS 1:50,000 Sheet
*196 The Solent
& Isle of Wight*

Tidal Constants
*Hurst Point:
HW Dover −0020,
LW Dover −0010
Totland Bay:
HW Dover −0050,
LW Dover −0020
Freshwater:
HW Dover −0030,
LW Dover −0010
Ventnor:
Dover −0010
Sandown:
HW Dover +0020,
LW Dover +0040
Foreland:
HW Dover +0020,
LW Dover +0030
Bembridge Harbour:
HW Dover +0020,
LW Dover +0030
Ryde:
HW Dover +0020,
LW Dover +0010
Cowes:
HW Dover +0020,
LW Dover +0010
Yarmouth:
Dover −0010*

Submarine Areas
P1, Q1

Sea Area
Wight

being rebuilt in 1614 after their demolition job although the list of rectors runs from 1294. When the church was burned down the bells were taken to Cherbourg or Boulogne.

Yarmouth Castle of 1547, built in limestone, was Henry VIII's last coastal defence and Britain's first arrow headed castle, garrisoned until 1885. It is an ancient monument, featuring marine archaeology, excavation of a 16th century Venetian cargo ship off Yarmouth, Solent shipwrecks, ship paintings and old Yarmouth photographs. It was occupied by Parliamentarians during the Civil War but the moat was filled in by Sir Robert Holmes in 1669. The arms over the gateway are those of England and France before the union with Scotland and Ireland. Sir Robert was the Captain of the Island. He had captured New Amsterdam, now New York, in 1664 and took a cargo of gold from a Dutch vessel off the coast of Guinea, melted down to mint new coins which, thus, were called guineas. The George Hotel was the house he built himself and which was visited by Charles II. Sir Robert also captured a statue of Louis XIV which he had completed with his own head, now on show in the Grade II★ St James' church.

The 210m Grade II timber pier of 1843 finished smuggling as boats could be seen coming in the River Yar entrance. The corporation fitted gates to the pier in 1877 and locked them in the evenings and on Sundays so that there was no access from the shore. A large crowd of fishermen smashed them down so the corporation took legal action against the ringleaders but they had already divested themselves of all their possessions to relatives and friends so there was nothing further which could be done. In October 1909 50m of the pier was demolished by a barge in heavy seas. It is England's longest wooden pier open to the public but has a toll. The swing bridge is the only one on the island.

As early as 1630 the *Arbella* had sailed from here to Massachusetts. On a more mundane level, colliers from the northeast of England were visiting until 1907. The following April, 34 seamen on the *Gladiator* were killed when it was rammed by the US liner *St Paul* in a blizzard with the visibility down to 200m. A yellow buoy marks another historic wreck.

The Solent's most popular harbour, it was extended to cater for more boats before the idea of marinas had been invented. When applicable, a 'Harbour full' sign is displayed. The Royal Solent Yacht Club is based here and the Old Gaffers Festival takes place in early summer. The Boathouse fortifies those in need. Formerly, a railway line ran to Freshwater. The Master Gunner's Lodgings now house a coastal defence display.

Black Rock starboard buoy off Norton marks a deep hole over which the Fiddlers Race runs.

Victoria Pier runs out at Sconce Point, from where a tunnel to Keyhaven was proposed in 1900.

The 20ha Fort Victoria Country Park surrounds the ruin of Palmerston's 1853 fort, of which 21 arches remain on the site of Carey's earlier Sconce Fort. It houses several attractions. Fort Victoria Model Railway is the longest and most advanced in Britain, having a 143m main line with computer controlled trains in HO gauge. Nearby is the Island Planetarium and the Sunken Secrets Archaeology Discovery Centre features shipwrecks and submerged settlements. A marine aquarium has tropical and local fish, of which bass, sole and conger eels are typical.

Beyond is Fort Albert at Cliff End.

Yarmouth Castle, the first of its kind.

Fort Victoria, more defences against the French.

Poole Bay

33

If the wind is in the east,
Old Harry ledge can be a beast.
Anon

The steep shingle Hurst Beach is 2.4km long, a narrow spit which appears to be very exposed to the weather yet remains stable, albeit with some reinforcement by rubble and building materials when breaches have threatened. In December 1989 two anglers were airlifted off after being trapped for 20 hours by storm damage to the spit. Ammunition from an offshore dumping ground was washed up three times in the winter of 2004/5. In Christchurch and Poole Bays flows start west at HW Dover −0100 and east from HW Dover +0510 at up to 2km/h although speeds can be up to 7km/h at the east end of the North Channel which runs inside the Shingle Bank and North Head.

Where the bank flattens out to give some sandy beach there are slipper limpet shells, whelk egg cases and cuttlefish bones on the beach. Behind is Sturt Pond. There may not be any bones left but it is fed by the Danes Stream which still runs red from the blood of Danes slaughtered on its banks more than a millennium ago or perhaps from the iron rich soil. The Mineway bank takes its name from a track leading up from the sea, used to bring ironstone concretions up for smelting.

From here to Poole Harbour the water is edged by earth cliffs which are cut by small streams to form steep bunnies and chines, much used by 18th century smugglers, and there are frequent landslips as the sea encroaches. The groynes at **Milford on Sea** are just the first of many such defences. Likewise, the colourfully painted beach huts are the first of several such clusters.

Road access has been very limited since Calshot but the B3058 now comes close and the coast is largely built up to Poole Harbour.

The teak and steel schooner *Lamorna* was wrecked in Christchurch Bay in about 1950.

Below Hordle Cliff, Hordle beach has Second World War tank traps and a single ochre coloured building was once a light anti-aircraft gun practice range. Pillboxes are collapsing into the sea as the cliffs recede. Cutting in obliquely in front of Barton golf course, Beckton Bunny was mined during the Second World War as it offered an easy landing place.

Groynes protect **Barton on Sea**, which has always been badly affected by slips, and prehistoric reptiles are found in fossil bearing strata.

The groynes at **Highcliffe** are of rock at the end of Chewton Bunny which marks the transition from Hampshire to Dorset. Chewton Glen bridge carries the A337 over on the first reinforced concrete arched bridge in the UK, not planned as such but used to make up for the incorrect setting out of the abutments of a 36° skewed bridge, being designed to take a 20t traction engine.

A yellow buoyed area inshore along this coast in the summer marks a zone where swimmers have priority. The shore is exposed to southerly winds and large swells break a long way out, surf size declining westwards. Steamer Point takes its name from a wreck and the coastguards had their training centre above on the low cliffs at Highcliffe.

A resident of Highcliffe was Gerald Gardner, the founder of modern witchcraft. Gothic style was used in the 1830s for Highcliffe Castle for Lord Stuart. It was badly damaged in a fire in the 1960s but the dilapidated structure is Grade I and has been used for TV film settings, despite having a ghost which turns on lights.

Sculpture on the beach at Milford on Sea points towards the Needles.

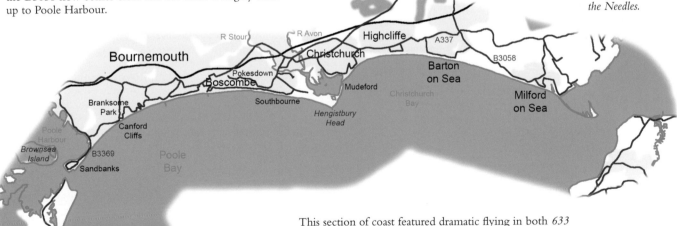

This section of coast featured dramatic flying in both *633 Squadron's* Operations Rhine Maiden and Crucible.

The Rivers Avon and Stour enter **Christchurch** Harbour, a silted up commercial port, and then discharge into the sea through the Run, a difficult stretch of water with flows inwards to 7km/h and ebb flows to 13km/h with an entrance channel which moves and a bar over which the depth changes frequently. It is a fishing and sailing centre with lobster and whelk pots on the quayside at Mudeford. A major incident on Mudeford Quay in 1784 was a bloody fight between smugglers and revenue men. Christ Church itself had its stone cross shattered and thrown 40m by a 1958 lightning strike.

Hengistbury Head with Christchurch Harbour to the right.

Dorset becomes Bournemouth here. Clarendon Rocks run out into the sea much further than the rock groynes along this section of the bay.

Hengistbury Head stands out as a conspicuous block of dark red Bracklesham beds ironstone surrounded by low land. As such, it has attracted attention and was occupied from Stone Age to Roman times. There are six bowl barrows on the head and two on low ground, one of which has yielded valuable finds. There was an Iron Age promontory fort when it guarded one of the country's busiest ports and Iron Age coins, pottery and bronze items have been found. In 1848 a coal merchant began excavating the ironstone and sending it to Lymington for processing, but the sand eroded very fast and the spit extended northwards until the Run was only 30m wide. This was not checked until 1938 when a large groyne was built southwards from the head.

Gordon Selfridge planned to return dwelling to the head with a 250 room castle with turrets but he blew his retailing fortune on two sisters and was unable to proceed with the project. Today the head is visited by 1,000,000 people per year, many by a land train. Around the head are heath, woodland, meadow, salt and freshwater marshes, dunes, rocky foreshore and shingle with a nature reserve good for small annual spring plants. Some of the plants are from Jamaica, imported accidentally with contraband by smugglers.

There is a small race at the long groyne and it can also produce surf if the wind is in the right direction. Streams run strongly over Christchurch Ledge which runs southeast nearly halfway across Christchurch Bay, a totally different direction from the growth of the spit, as at Calshot.

Now in Poole Bay, the Hengistbury Head site ends with Double Dykes, 460m long with a 5.5m central entrance gap.

The high earth cliff shoreline is continuously built from Southbourne to Poole Head. There are eight chines in the Bracklesham beds and it was the use of these by smugglers which led to the eventual establishment of the resort which claims the best weather in Britain. Outfalls, groynes and other obstructions keep larger boats out of the inshore area although boating further out includes offshore powerboat racing. The formerly sandy beach at

Bournemouth Pier without surf.

Southbourne, now covered with stones as an anti-erosion measure, occasionally dumps but the surfable waves have been killed by the stones. It has zones for swimming, for kids, no dogs, no bottles, can recycling, in fact, pretty highly regimented. There is a cliff lift, land train and Fisherman's Walk.

Beyond Stourcliff and Pokesdown is **Boscombe** with its pier, a surf venue at which has been installed the first artificial reef of giant sandbags up to 2,500t outside Australasia. Valentine tanks on the sea bed were being developed with canvas flotation collars and propellers for Second World War amphibious use but were blown up more recently as they contained live ammunition. For more gentle explosions the BBC have used the area with the UK's third oldest population, average age 42.8, for filming *One Foot in the Grave* and the Hotel Miramar was the set for *Separate Tables*. Dr Prentice had his Royal Observer Corps induction in the Royal Bath Hotel in *Requiem for a Wren*.

East Cliff has a cliff lift. Above Harry Ramsden's is the Russell-Cotes Art Gallery & Museum in a Victorian mansion with Renaissance pottery, oil paintings, watercolours, sculptures, Napoléon's table and other furniture, Japanese art, theatrical effects, a Bath chair and a marine collection with models, ships, shells and wreck items, rather a varied set of themes.

Bournemouth is largely a Victorian town from the mid 19th century, Hardy's Sandbourne where Rosa Halborough was at a high class school in *A Tragedy of Two Ambitions* in *Life's Little Ironies* and where Tess Durbeyfield stabbed Alec D'Urberville in his *Tess of the D'Urbervilles*, which was filmed here, and it was included in his *The Hand of Ethelberta*, *The Well-Beloved* and *Jude the Obscure*. In *De Profundis* Oscar Wilde says Lord Alfred Douglas was sent here by his doctor to recover from jaundice and insisted on being accompanied by Wilde. Following his illness, Gavin Maxwell tells in *The House of Elrig* of an angry adolescent winter here with his mother and his tutor with endless stories of food, *Les Carnets du Major Thompson* claiming that locals ate without moving their arms, unlike the gesticulating of continentals. In *Paradise Postponed* Henry Simcox claimed Kathmandu had the worst class system outside Bournemouth and in *A Prince of the Captivity* Nigel Melfort thought there were too many houses. Resident spy Mrs Matilda Krafft was picked up here in *Eye of the Needle*. It has 8km² of parks and gardens, including the Upper Pleasure Gardens and the Lower Pleasure Gardens, the latter having been renamed as just the Pleasure Gardens because people were getting the wrong message. The River Bourne flows down past the Vistarama Balloon, tethered 150m above the ground, through gardens to reach the sea by Bournemouth Pier, a popular and better surf venue than Boscombe but visited by pleasure steamers. The 255m

Looking west from Alum Chine towards Poole Head on a fine summer's morning.

x 34m wide structure replaced one weakened by teredo worms, of which the pierhead was demolished by a hurricane in 1867 and the rest in a storm 9 years later. By the pier at West Cliff is the Oceanarium and there are donkey rides and Punch & Judy shows on the beach and then another cliff lift. The town was also used as a Schneider Trophy sea plane race course.

Durley has the Durley Inn but no dogs, no smoking, can recycling and zones for swimming and for kids.

There can be surf at the sheltered beach at Alum Chine although the beach covers completely at high water. This is where Stevenson, as an invaid, wrote *The Strange Case of Dr Jeckyll & Mr Hyde* and much of *Kidnapped*. As well as toilets just behind the beach, the chine has two interesting footbridges. One of 1904 is a 70m steel suspension bridge with tapered steel lattice pillars which were encased in concrete in 1973 to protect them. The other is a 20m reinforced concrete arch of 1912. Bournemouth gives way to Poole.

Branksome Chine, again with no beach at high water, is a narrow gorge cut into an earlier wider valley. There are lion's mane jellyfish despite the jet skiers, waterskiers, windsurfers and surfers. Here and at Canford Cliffs Chine, Flag Head Chine, Poole Head and Sandbanks there are steep waves on southerly to southeasterly force 5/6 winds.

The soft cliffs finally end at Poole Head and the B3369 runs out along the spit which has grown from the north to affluent Sandbanks with the fourth highest property prices in the world, a bungalow having fetched £3,000,000 for demolition for its site. Sandbanks overlooks the entrance to Poole Harbour, perhaps the largest natural harbour in the world, used for at least two millennia. Poole returns to Dorset. The combined estuary of the Piddle, Frome and Corfe Rivers is used by car ferries from Poole to Cherbourg, St Malo, Guernsey and Jersey, freight vessels and 5,000 yachts. The rule of thumb is to stay out of the way of large commercial vessels. Beyond the chain ferry across the entrance is Brownsea Island with Branksea Castle in a commanding position. The 2km² island was the location of the world's first Scout camp in 1907 under Robert Baden-Powell.

Approach to the harbour is through the Swash Channel which runs between Hook Sand and a rubble training bank of 1876–1927 which extends out for a kilometre from the southeast end of Shell Bay and which covers at half tide. Flows out of the harbour are to 9km/h from HW Dover −0130 and they go in at up to 6km/h from HW Dover +0610. There is a strong rip on the northeast side of the entrance with either flow direction. Strong southerly winds give heavy seas over the bar and strong easterly winds alter the depth of the bar. South Haven peninsula is growing. In Shell and Studland Bays there are short surf waves with easterly winds of force 5.

This is the start of the South West Coast Path with a Coast Path Sculpture, featured in Mark Wallington's *500 Mile Walkies*, and the start of an AONB which extends to Bowleaze Cove.

In Studland Bay the Milkmaid Bank drying patches keep most craft away from the natural beauties on the naturist beach (designated by the National Trust). Behind the rapidly eroding beach are dunes which edge

heathland with scrub and spartina grass and the Little Sea, a nature reserve adjoining Studland Heath with common and sand lizards, smooth and grass snakes, adders, slow worms and bird hides which overlook Slavonian grebes, teal, wigeon, tufted ducks, pochard, brent geese, water rails and bar-tailed godwits in winter and nightjars, sedge, reed, Dartford and willow warblers, chiffchaffs, whinchats, stonechats, linnets, redpolls and common Sandwich terns in summer plus sanderlings, shearwaters, gannets and skuas in the autumn. The coast from here to Orcombe Point has been designated the Jurassic Coast World Heritage Site.

Crab pots are laid out from here to St Alban's Head. These are some of the warmest seawaters in Britain and Studland is a resort at the end of the B3351. Launching of craft including kayaks is charged. Beyond Redend Point are Redend Rocks and the Seven Sisters show themselves at very low tides. The church of St Nicholas of Myra dates from Norman times. In the 16th century the village was used by pirates. A circular pillbox and gun emplacement are reminders that Churchill, Montgomery and Eisenhower watched practice wartime landings from the Manor House hotel, now the Pig on the Beach. The Bankes Arms Country Inn hosts the Isle of Purbeck Brewery.

The 65,000,000 year old Ballard Down was previously connected to the Needles, the chalk dipping nearly vertically and the River Frome continuing along the syncline and through the Solent with tributaries from the north and south but is now the end of the isolated Isle of Purbeck. In the same way, Studland Bay mirrors Alum Bay on the Isle of Wight. The Isle of Purbeck features extensively in *The Well-Beloved*.

The magnificent Dorset cliff coast begins abruptly at the 60m Foreland or Handfast Point where vertical chalk cliffs have the Yards, three projections from the cliffs, caves, arches and stacks, notably Old Harry (the Devil, first climbed in 1987) and Old Harry's Wife, the top of whom broke off in a storm in 1896, a fallen woman, no doubt. The clear water is popular with shags, shelducks, fulmars, cormorants, kittiwakes, razorbills, oystercatchers, peregrine falcons, guillemots, puffins and blackbacked gulls. There are also many 20mm shell cases from Spitfire and Hurricane wartime live bombing practice raids in targets in the sea and on four tanks on the cliff top, these days with plenty of wild cabbage.

There is a strong race off the point with a southerly flow. All three east-facing bays at the end of the Isle of Purbeck have complex patterns of eddies.

The mainland cliff begins with St Lucas Leap and then has Parson's Barn above the 21m Little Pinnacle, followed by the 37m Pinnacle. The dramatic chalk cliff ends at Ballard Point, off which there is a race on the ebb.

Ballard Cliff, reaching off beyond Pinfold Cove round the northern edge of Swanage Bay, becomes cliffs of sand and coloured clay. Streams are weak in the bay, in the middle of which is Potters Shoal which is used for shrimp fishing from February to April. There are also flounders, plaice, sole, bass and mackerel. New Swanage becomes Swanage where

The chain ferry crosses the busy entrance of Poole Harbour from Sandbanks.

Old Harry and his wife and other chalk features of the Foreland.

Old Harry Rocks, Studland Bay
South-west England 2nd

Distance
*39km from Hurst
Castle to Peveril
Point*

OS 1:50,000 Sheets
*195 Bournemouth
& Purbeck
196 The Solent
& Isle of Wight*

Tidal Constants
*Hurst Point:
Dover −0020
Christchurch
Entrance:
HW Dover −0040,
LW Dover −0020
Bournemouth:
HW Dover −0030,
LW Dover −0020
Poole Harbour
Entrance:
HW Dover −0020,
LW Dover −0010
Swanage:
HW Dover −0030,
LW Dover −0040*

Submarine Area
O1

Sea Areas
Wight, Portland

Connection
*Poole Harbour – see
RoB p275*

the Tanville Ledges run out eastwards, Phippards Ledge doing the same just to the south. As further north, there is short surf with force 5 easterly to southeasterly winds. An unexplained swell often develops in the bay, even with offshore winds, possibly catamaran ferries using Poole Harbour.

It was an easterly wind which drove 120 Danish ships ashore at Peveril in 877. They raided frequently in Anglo-Saxon times but this was not one of their successes, a monument on the seafront commemorating King Alfred's naval battle victory. The church of St Mary the Virgin was built in 1859, the fourth on the site since Norman times, the lower half of the tower of 1250 remaining and thought to have been built as a refuge against pirates. The Tithe Barn is Grade II.

Swanage was Knollsea to Thomas Hardy, who lived here in 1875/6 while completing *The Hand of Ethelberta*. It was used for his closing chapters, including details of the effects of an onshore wind, and was also chosen for the honeymoon of Anna and Raye in his *On the Western Circuit* in *Life's Little Ironies*. Stockdale, *The Distracted Preacher* in his *Wessex Tales*, attended a commemoration service here. It may have been where Emma Hardy wrote *The Maid on the Shore*. It was used for Juley Munt's home in *Howards End*. Jennifer Coombe's family had a holiday here in *The Loving Spirit* and Harvey Lawson and Francis Croft finished a three hour walk here in *The Bird of Night*. In Old English times it was Swana-wic, the herdsmen's workplace.

The Victorian resort developed at the end of the A351 and the railway, which is now the 10km steam Swanage Railway and goes only to Norden although there are hopes to extend it back to Wareham again. There is a promenade, Punch & Judy, sandy beach and canoe and pedalo hire, features needed for a self-respecting resort. The Swanage Museum & Heritage Centre was established in 2001 and there is a Mowlem Theatre, recalling civil engineering contractor John Mowlem. Producing and exporting Purbeck stone and marble

The Pinnacles and Ballard Point, looking towards Swanage.

was an important industry for the town and a derelict wooden jetty exported the stone to build Salisbury Cathedral, Westminster Abbey and others. There were also some significant imports. The Wellington Clock Tower of 1854 on the shore originally obstructed the southern approach to London Bridge and was moved here in 1867. The town hall of 1883 has a façade which was designed by Edward Jermain, a pupil of Wren, and moved here from Mercer's Hall in London's Cheapside. The police station with its gaol of 1803 at the back is now a shop, presumably more secure than most. Swanage Jazz Festival takes place in July and Swanage Folk Festival in September. Swanage pier is Victorian. Windsurfing and diving are popular in the area.

The bay ends at Peveril Point which is overlooked by a National Coastwatch Institution lookout point and is backed by low cliffs, off which is a strong race with a south southwesterly stream. Taking out is straightforward in various places but it will be necessary to move across to the centre of town to get a vehicle close as the parking areas near the point seem to be privately owned and not welcoming of visitors.

Swanage Bay with Swanage itself seen from Peveril Point.

Dorset

34

The star-filled seas are smooth to-night
From France to England strown;
Black towers above the Portland light
The felon-quarried stone.
AE Housman

The 150km of Jurassic Coast from Swanage to Exmouth was declared England's first natural World Heritage Site in 2001 because of its fossils which cover 180,000,000 years, new fossils appearing after rough weather. It also includes some of the most interesting cliff scenery and other coastal geology around Britain.

At the northern end of Durlston Bay there is surf with a force 4 southerly wind and southwesterly swell. On the other hand, if conditions are settled the water can be clear to 7m as far as Weymouth and lone divers might be met, just wetsuited heads and floating torpedo buoy markers. Durlston Marine Research Area and Voluntary Marine Nature Reserve has cameras and marine hydrophones to pick up any indiscretions.

Durlston Head slopes up from a low undercut cliff to the 1.2km^2 Durlston Country Park. The Durlston Castle folly of 1890 now houses the Seventhwave restaurant. Three years earlier civil engineering contractor John Mowlem had presented the Great Globe, a 3m diameter 40t Portland stone feature. This is also the best place to see the early spider orchid.

There is a race off the head on the southwestgoing stream, which begins at HW Dover −0030 and begins northeastwards at HW Dover +0530 at up to 6km/h.

Puffins, guillemots, razorbills and cormorants like this coast. The dark limestone cliffs with extensive quarries from Anvil Point to St Alban's Head are also very popular with climbers.

A measured distance is marked out above the cliffs, the start of which is near Tilly Whim Caves which were used by smugglers. The quarry owner was George Tilly and his whim or gantry crane was used for lowering stone but could be equally effective for raising contraband.

The 12m round white Anvil Point lighthouse tower of 1881 and a dwelling are located on the end of chalk Round Down, the light only 45m above sea level to remain below orographic cloud. It was electrified in 1960 and the optic donated to the Science Museum in London.

Many of the coastal features have intriguing names with sound reasoning. Topmast refers to the loss of the sailing ship *Alexandranova* in 1882 with her 77 crew in a violent storm, following which a topmast was found on top of the cliffs. Long Hole is 6m deep. Blackers Hole has jackdaws although there used to be breeding peregrine falcons. Dancing Ledge is as big as a dance floor and has ruts for stone carts, having supplied much of the rock to build Ramsgate Harbour. After Durnford preparatory school's pool are the Pig and Whistle Cave, named after the noise made by waves, and a cannon on the cliffs.

The horizontal strata have left some large rectangular holes around Seacombe Cliff and there are a mixture of caves and disused quarries. The Romans had a number of quarries around the Isle of Purbeck and stone has been a regular export from the area since then.

Mike's Cove and Willie's Cove are separated by the cylindrical Watch Rock, on which a watch was found after a ship was lost with all her crew. In 1786 the East Indiaman *Halsewell*, on passage from Dover to Bengal, was lost here with 158 of the 240 on board.

Winspit Bottom below Worth Matravers had coastal quarries which provided stone for Allhallows school and is overlooked by the hills of East Man and West Man, each with strip lynchets. Greater horseshoe bats now occupy the quarries. Crab Hole, no doubt, was somebody's favourite fishing spot.

St Aldhelm's or St Alban's Head is unusual in that the point is neither high nor steep, so that landing on the rocks is not too difficult but then high cliffs rise up behind. St Alban's Ledge runs out for some 8km to the southwest. There is a strong race over it with a calm passage on the inside which may be only 50m wide with a mere half hour free of overfalls at the turn of spring tides. Flows west northwest begin at HW Dover −0020 and they begin east southeast at HW Dover +0540 at up to 9km/h. There are eddies on both sides of the head, especially on the west side.

It was visited in about the year 700 by the Saxon bishop St Aldhelm while waiting for winds to sail to

Durlston Head with its undercut cliff.

Seacombe Cliff and St Alban's Head.

The weed protected projecting nose in Egmont Bight.

see the Pope. On the top of the head is a Grade I 12th century Norman chapel to St Aldhelm with 1.2m thick walls, circular on top to hold a lit beacon. A radar dish monument recalls pioneering Second World War work undertaken on radar at Worth Matravers. This was the outward route taken for the Vindicator's flight in *Thunderball*.

West of the head is used as a warship exercise area with firing from the sea. Yellow DZ buoys are targets and should not be approached within 1.6km, the nearest being 4km offshore.

It seems a remote coast but there are 26,000 lobster pots from here to Portland Bill, meaning quite a lot of fishing boat inspections. From here to Kimmeridge Bay there are dark cliffs fringed by hard clay ledges.

Chapman's Pool has a long hollow reef break after a force 5 southwesterly. It is overlooked by the 50m Houns-tout Cliff, tout being Old English for lookout, the vertical face attracting birds. On Egmont Point, to the west of Chapman's Pool, is the Powder House, the remains of a gun battery position. Sir Nigel Irvine used the cliffs to contemplate claims put to him in *The Fourth Protocol*.

The cliffs are very fragmented blackstone shale to Kimmeridge, producing an unusual situation where a stream enters Egmont Bight. Normally it would have carved a valley, as it has done at higher levels. When it reaches the cliffs, however, the green vegetation growing in the water is more resistant than the rocks alone and so the water trickles down from the top of a nose projecting into the sea while cliffs have been eaten back on each side. Cliff falls are frequent and reveal fossils. There are the remains of the Freshwater Steps and the foundations of a pumphouse to pump water to a large bath at Lord Eldon's 18th century Encombe House, Hardy's Enckworth Court.

The wreck of the *Treveal* is 800m south, sunk in a gale with the loss of 36 of the 43 on board while on her maiden voyage from Calcutta. The drifter *Abide* tried to salvage the jute on board and was holed on the wreckage. In 1952 the *Glenmore* also sank on the wreckage, all of which has since been flattened. However, a barge with a cargo of stone sank 400m northwest and it can dry with some tides.

Swyre Head, at 203m, overlooks Rope Lake Head. There have been many wrecks on the Kimmeridge Ledges from here, popular with divers.

In the 1630s Sir William Clavell of Smedmore House used the oil shale as a fuel to extract salt from sea water, established an alum factory and exported his product by ship although he failed to build a stone jetty to make Kimmeridge a port. Shale mines followed in the 19th century. These days Clavell's Hard has sea cabbages, rock pipits, oystercatchers, mallards and herring gulls but no industry. All that remains overlooking Kimmeridge Bay is the 1830 Clavell Tower folly built with classical motifs and Tuscan columns by the 70 year old Revd John Clavell for astronomy but moved back 25m from the edge in 2008 as it was being undermined and in danger of collapse. Thomas Hardy courted coastguard's daughter Eliza Nicholls here.

Beside Kimmeridge Bay is the Fine Foundation Marine Centre which opened in 2001 with displays on the Purbeck Marine Wildlife Reserve, reaching from St Alban's Head to the far side of Worbarrow Bay,

162

The Clavell Tower overlooking Kimmeridge Bay.

even having a live link to a seabed camera. Here are blennies, gobies, prawns, crabs, corkwings, ballan wrasse, pipe fish, 15-spined sticklebacks, bass, pilchard, snakelocks anemones and sargassum seaweed while brittlestars, piddocks, sponges, anemones, sea fans and soft corals live in the deeper water where an underwater nature trail has been laid out for divers. Giant ammonites and other fossils are found around the bay. On the west side of the bay is an oil well with a nodding donkey which draws $1.8m^3$/day from the Kimmeridge shales through a 550m well of 1958, making it second only to Wytch Farm as a British onshore well and the world's longest continuously operational. In the 19th century there were also glass and cement works here.

Kimmeridge is known for its surf with Ledges Bay and Broad Bench giving rides of up to 1.6km under the right conditions. Broad Bench is a reef break which can give 4m waves, more after a southwesterly force 5 or 6, best in a light north to northwesterly breeze. Board surfers and windsurfers are attracted. Approach is down

vessels but a range control vessel is able to prevent loitering, which is a significant part of the pleasure in such scenery.

Charnel was an old landing site inside Broad Bench. Between Broad Bench and Long Ebb is Hobarrow Bay, a Roman industrial site. There was also a Roman settlement behind Brandy Bay, which was later used by smugglers, as the name suggests. These days goats, adders, peregrines and ravens nesting are the occupants. Tyneham Cap is a reminder of Tyneham village, beyond, which was temporarily evacuated in 1943 when the range was extended, the surviving occupants still waiting for permission to return. There is an exhibition in the 13th century St Mary's church, which may be visited when the range is not in use.

Beyond Gad Cliff and Wagon Rocks, with a conical hill on its summit, is Worbarrow Tout, just before which is an inlet with dragon's teeth tank traps, probably less effective than the rocks.

Behind Worbarrow Bay remains much of the part of Flower's Barrow which has not been eroded by the sea, 2.4km of a unique beach head fortification by Iron Age invaders of about 400 BC to control Lulworth Cove. Later, the Romans camped here

an expensive toll road, car users being charged double if carrying any kind of boat on the roof.

The pillbox and tank traps at the entrance are reminders of wartime concern, as was a German mine taken out of a fishing net in 1951. More relevant today, however, is the 28km² Lulworth Ranges which run from here to Lulworth Cove. They have been used since 1916 with tanks firing from the shore, usually to 10km out but sometimes to 19km. 70,000 high velocity shells are fired per year and anything suspicious on a beach should be reported but not touched. Red flags and lights are shown on St Alban's Head and Bindon Hill when the range is in use. Firing stops for passing

after conquering the Veniti. A Second World War gun emplacement and Allen Williams turret are more recent fortifications.

Halfway along the back of the bay is the white sandy beach at Arish Mell where landing is prohibited. Rusty military vehicles stand around on the range. There are concrete blocks across the outfall from the Winfrith Heath nuclear establishment.

Butcher's Rock, Cockpit Head, Black Rock and Mac-

Gad Cliff feels very powerful and threatening.

Worbarrow Bay with the forbidden beach of Arish Mell on the right and Mupe Rocks on the left.

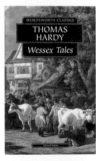

kerel Rock lead to Mupe Bay with Mupe Ledges and Mupe Rocks, used by shags and shipborne naturists, the caves formerly used by smugglers. Outside is the Bacon Hole cave used in the 19th century by smugglers. One of the most complete fossil forests in the world resulted when Jurassic trees became submerged in a swamp and covered in algae, to which sediments stuck, now visible as thrombolite algae rings.

Below Bindon Hill, Southcliff is a fine example of broken beds while Potter's Hole was a dwelling. At Little Bindon the 12th century Cistercian abbey was converted to a chapel and cottage in 1250, remodelled in 1500 and brick faced in the 18th century. Grade II★, it has 18th century sailing ships scratched in the plaster and a ceiling painted with stars and planets.

One of the most popular beauty spots on the south coast is Lulworth Cove at the end of the B3070, the prime jewel in a coast rich with geological jewels. It has attracted authors, poets and painters since the 18th century. Rupert Brooke stayed with the Neo-Pagans. Keats wrote *At Lulworth Cove a Century Back* here and perhaps *Bright Star*. To Hardy it was Lulstead or Lulwind Cove where Sgt Troy disappeared in *Far from the Madding Crowd*, where the bodies of the missing pair were found in *The History of the Hardcomes* in *A Few Crusted Characters*. In *Wessex Tales* it was where Bonaparte landed to survey the coast in *A Tradition of Eighteen Hundred & Four* and was a smuggling destination in *The Distracted Preacher* and *The Dynasts*. It was used for filming *Mansfield Park*. Between 1879 and 1955 the public came from Weymouth by paddle steamer, used by Owen and Cytherea in *Desperate Remedies*. The heritage centre features paddle steamers, smuggling, oil and local flora, fauna and history. A stone jetty enclosed an oyster

pond and the mill pond was used for washing clothes and sheep, not necessarily together, fed by a spring which also provided West Lulworth's water, now lacking its cob and thatched mill which collapsed. The Doll's House began life as a Canadian log cabin brought over on the deck of a ship, to which were added a brick skin, chimney stack and two bedrooms in the roof. The locality has also given its name to the Lulworth skipper butterfly, only found between Swanage and Sidmouth.

South Ledge had low tide impressions of fossil pine

Stair Hole with various entrances and cliffs popular with climbers.

164

Lulworth Cove attracts varied watersports as well as many holidaymakers on foot.

trees. More impressive to most visitors is the heavy swell which results from southerly winds.

Just west is Stair Hole in which there are several arches where the sea has eaten into the Lulworth crumple rock strata. This coast is very popular for geology field trips because the whole sequence is here. Stair Hole will later widen out like Lulworth Cove, lose its protective Portland stone and excavate the Wealden clays as at Worbarrow and Mupe, further widening like Man o' War, then producing a straight coast as further west, before eroding it completely as in Poole Bay.

Beyond Dungy Head, St Oswald's Bay below Hambury Tout has surf with southwesterly winds but dumps at the west end. Blackbacked gulls frequent the vicinity.

At the west end of Man o' War Cove is the best of all the Dorset coast features, Durdle Door, a 12m natural arch of Purbeck limestone, named from the Old English thirl, drill. More of *Far from the Madding Crowd* was filmed here, as was some of *Nanny McPhee*, *Wilde* and videos with Billy Ocean, Cliff Richard and Tears for Fears. Shirley Cooklin used to holiday here, as recalled in her *Knockback*. After the wonderfully named Scratchy Bottom, the protective layer of rock is reduced to a series of bovine bottom scratching subsurface rocks. The Bull, the Blind (hidden) Cow, the Cow and the Calf lead past the precipice of Bat's Head where a wave carved bat cave or mousehole at the bottom passes through from east to west. Like most of these arches and holes, it just asks to be explored, easily done at the right state of the tide.

The Warren, with 19th century navigational marks, tumuli and field systems, has guillemots nesting. Once a herd of cattle fell to their deaths here.

The cliffs at White Nothe are 50m high, white Cretaceous chalk and sandstone on Jurassic clay. On top, the coastguard cottages are the highest buildings on the Dorset coast. Now the cliffs begin to decline in height and to vary in colour. Hang gliders ridge soar. A smugglers' path passes behind the Bear, which perhaps ought to be the Bare as it is used by naturists.

Ringstead Bay has windsurfers and lobster pots. Timbers from a Spanish Armada ship wrecked here were used in the dining room of Owermoigne rectory. It was used for smuggling but made its name with Burning Cliff above the bay. From 1826 the oil shale burned for four years, the oil having a high sulphur content which produced a lot of smoke and a strong smell. Jurassic rocks

Inside Stair Hole, showing the tortured strata.

The great chalk arch of Durdle Door.

follow to Weymouth. With the fire safely out it now has a 46ha nature reserve with kestrels and green woodpeckers. A small wooden chapel is dedicated to St Catherine by the Sea. Ringstead Village itself was abandoned in the Middle Ages because of the combined effects of pirates and Black Death.

Ringstead Ledges run out from Bran Point. Wrecks on the rocks include the 1927 loss of the coal barge *Minx*. There is a bad weather anchorage further off.

Upton Fort of 1902 had two 230mm guns and was used until after the Second World War.

Osmington Mills was used by the late 18th century smuggler French Peter and now has the Smugglers Inn.

It has thatched stone cottages and a coastguard built slip which had a lifeboat during the Second World War and occasional fishing boats since then. It now has an school field study centre. Above is an 85m x 98m high white horse of 1808 on the hillside, the only English white horse to have a rider, George III.

Black Head correctly gives the change of cliff colour but is slightly concave rather than being a headland. A wreck obviously got it wrong, too, on Black Head Ledges. Beyond is Osmington where Jurassic rocks behind beaches have sand ripples and burrows fossilized.

Redcliffe Point is a more accurate description of the next coastal feature and is the limit of Port of Weymouth

166

Bat's Head with its tunnel.

control. From Bowleaze Cove a modern sea wall runs along the foot of Furzy Cliff, above which are the Grade II Art Deco Riviera Hotel and the remains of a 4th century Roman temple on Jordan Hill. Thomas Hardy used Overcombe as the setting for *The Trumpet-Major* but using features from surrounding villages. Bob Loveday of Overcombe was a *Victory* crewman in *The Dynasts*. Suddenly it gets busy as the A353 arrives on land and buoys funnel in windsurfers, waterskiers and jet skiers from Weymouth Bay over a submerged wall towards a landing with toilets. Within the areas of buoys in summer it is necessary to give way to swimmers. Surf is best at low water with southeasterly winds.

Weymouth Bay is one of the warmest, driest and sunniest areas in the country. Certainly the lion's mane jellyfish like it. The flows are mostly westgoing to 1km/h but may be negligible to the southeast from HW Dover −0510 for two hours.

The 1.4km² Lodmoor Country Park has picnic tables and barbecue stands, Leisure Ranch with Cresta Run, Rio Grande Railway, go kart circuit, bumper boats, hundreds of models in Model World, 9 hole mini golf, Sea Life Adventure Park and Butterfly Farm with one of the largest marine life displays in Europe at 2.4ha, ocean tank, cliff habitat, sand basin, fish farming, tidepool tank and intertidal deep tank, Tropical Jungle with birds and iguanas and RSPB nature reserve with hides and seamarsh birds, being good for migrating and wintering birds including bearded tits.

Melcombe Regis has a statue of George III from 1810, an ornate Queen Victoria jubilee clock of 1887 and memorials to British, ANZAC and US troops. It also has St John's church which was fully restored before being attacked by an arsonist in 2001.

Weymouth has made two notable introductions to England, firstly Black Death in 1348, killing up to half of the British population. In 1789 George III was sent there because of his health, making it the first resort by beginning the practice of nude sea bathing, not at some secluded cove but out of a bathing machine with a small orchestra playing the *National Anthem*. The Gloucester House was the Gloucester Lodge at that time, George III's summer home where Cabinet meetings were held, part of a Georgian seafront. Queen Margaret and son Prince Edward landed here in 1471. Press gangs also operated from here.

The gently sloping beach is ideal for children and, with the esplanade, offers all the facilities of a resort, a land train, Punch & Judy shows, donkey rides, swingboats, merry-go-rounds, helter-skelter, trampolines, pedaloes, sandcastles and sand sculptor in what is called the Naples of England. It was Budmouth Regis to Hardy, who worked here as an architect in 1869 and began his first published novel, *Desperate Remedies* and described it as a

'twopenny-halfpenny town' where Edward Springrove worked in an architectural practice with Owen Graye and went rowing with Owen's sister, Cytherea. Hardy had a relationship here with his cousin, Tryphena Sparks. He used the town in *Under the Greenwood Tree*, *The Return of the Native*, *The Mayor of Casterbridge*, *The Dynasts* and *Life's Little Ironies*. Mr Grove proposed to Jane Pounsett here in *The Diary of a Country Parson*. Here, the narrator describes spending a couple of days in Kazuo Ishiguro's *The Remains of the Day*. It was suggested as a destination for *The Mother*. It was used for filming *Far from the Madding Crowd* in 1967 and also John Fowles' *The French Lieutenant's Woman*. Thomas Love Peacock was born here. There is a fireworks festival barge and Weymouth hosts the Wessex Folk Festival in June and Dorset Seafood Festival in July. Angling contests also take place with a fleet of boats racing out of Weymouth Road at a set time, usually 9am.

There are fishing and recreational vessels. Three green lights indicate a vessel arriving and three red lights one departing from the 17th century harbour which was at one time a Roman port. Brewers Quay in a former Victorian Devenish brewery introduces brewing. Deep Sea Adventure includes underwater exploration and the *Titanic*.

One of Weymouth harbour's breakwaters was built in 1903 to deflect waves rebounding off the northern breakwater of Portland Harbour. Overlooking it is the Nothe, 15m high with a Victorian fort built in 1860–72 to defend Portland Harbour against the threat of Napoleonic invasion. It has been restored with the Nothe Fort Museum of Coastal Defence and has the only operational coastal defence searchlight in the country, displays of 40mm anti aircraft and other guns, weapons, Mk VIII torpedo, underground magazines, garrison life of Victorian and Second World War soldiers, Ferret Scout Car and other military vehicles and paddlesteamers and a children's assault course. It was the Look-out to Hardy,

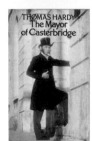

Paddlesteamer Waverley *at Weymouth pier.*

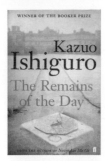

who used it in *The Dynasts*, in *The Melancholy Hussar* in *Wessex Tales* and in *Life's Little Ironies*. It was used by the BBC for filming *Beau Geste* and *Knockback*, which describes the beach in Weymouth. The Nothe has band concerts and the Nothe Gardens with picnic tables, barbecue facilities, a floodlit waterfall and Newton's Cove, which has a new promenade and seawall as part of a scheme to stop housing and a Defra laboratory slipping into the sea as Nothe Clay slides over Nothe Grits, a scheme which was difficult because the contractor could only reach it from the beach at low tide. The Mixon, an underwater ridge, runs out after the Port of Weymouth gives way to Portland Port control.

Portland Harbour is Britain's largest artificial harbour, the second largest man made harbour in the world and, in the 19th century, one of the greatest civil engineering projects undertaken in England, being 4km across. It was naval from the Crimean War until 1996. The west side is protected by land and the east side by breakwaters, on which landing is forbidden without a licence. The harbour was constructed on a Saxon stronghold in 1847–1905 by convicts awaiting transportation to Australia. In 1893 the two northern breakwaters were added to give protection against torpedo attacks. The breakwaters are of Portland stone from Verne Hill, up to 7t per block, tipped from trucks on a temporary railway built along the top. Sections of Mulberry Harbour, used for D-Day landings, can be seen on the southern side of Portland Harbour. Captain Bampfylde delivered a captured French warship to Portland Roads in *The Maid of Sker*.

The entrances have semi-circular walls faced with granite above water level. Notices require craft to keep 30m from these. Flows through the gaps reach 2km/h and there are eddies off the ends of the breakwater but there is negligible flow in the Inner Harbour. A torpedo firing point operates eastwards from the Northeastern Breakwater when orange flags fly but operates in an easterly direction so that entering the North Ship Channel avoids any conflicts.

A prison ship was located at the southern end to supplement overcrowded jails in the 1990s, recalling prison hulks of the 19th century. In *His Last Bow* Sherlock Holmes discusses an American imprisoned at Portland. There is a prohibited area to the west of the approach to the South Ship Channel but direct approach avoids this. The former naval base and dockyard are now a commercial port.

The South Ship Channel can have a nasty sea in the entrance, especially with strong westerly, southwesterly or easterly winds although winds behave unexpectedly across the harbour and increase as the wind is squeezed between Portland and the mainland. In 1914 HMS *Hood* was sunk across the entrance as a blockship and is now popular with divers. In addition, an overhead power cable hangs low across the entrance.

Weymouth and Portland were at their busiest during the Second World War when they despatched 600,000 men and 140,000 vehicles in a year. In June 1944 they were two of the main departure points for the Normany landings with embarkation for Omaha Beach, the largest invasion fleet ever assembled.

The Isle of Portland consists mostly of Jurassic Portland stone, so beloved of architects for public buildings. Portland takes its name from Porta, a Saxon pirate who seized the island in 501. To the Romans it was Vindilia and to poet and novelist Thomas Hardy it was the Isle of Slingers, those using pebbles in slings, or the Gibraltar of Wessex. It is a 7km wedge of limestone nearly 150m high at the northern end but sloping nearly to sea level at the southern end.

Above Balaclava Bay the Verne Citadel on Portland Heights was the 19th century High Angle Battery with 320mm guns with a 6km range, sited on the harbour rock excavations, used as a prison since 1950. John Hannan escaped in 1955 and hadn't been recaptured by the new millennium, the longest evasion on record. Peter Aitken was scathing about it as a prisoner in *Knockback*. St Peter's church of 1872 was built entirely by convicts with a fine floor, mosaic borders, a superb medieval style timber roof and much creative work. Before a rifle range,

The North Ship Channel leading into Portland Harbour. Portland Heights rise beyond.

The port area in Portland Harbour.

The South Ship Channel with a power cable across. HMS Hood *lies in the gap. The Nicodemus Knob shows the original cliff level.*

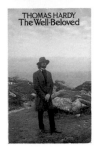

the original transportation prison remains in use for prisoners.

Less conspicuous than the masts and the white radome on the summit is the Nicodemus Knob left as a navigation mark but also showing the ground level before quarrying began. Portland stone starts grey but weathers to white, is easy to carve but is very durable and has been used for many of London's public buildings including St Paul's cathedral and all Wren's churches (Wren having controlled the quarries when MP for Weymouth), Buckingham Palace, the Monument, the Cenotaph, Somerset House, Bush House, the Bank, the Royal Exchange, the Mansion House, the Law Courts and the British Museum. It was also used for the Menin Gate First World War memorial in Ypres and large numbers of World War gravestones.

Off Grove Point, Fiddler's Race runs for seven hours from local high water. A pillbox protects the area. A derrick crane serves Durdle Pier, the first of a number to lift boats onto the rock ledges along this side of the island. Another pillbox or perhaps a hide is built of best Portland stone, well camouflaged in the area, unlike the park of caravans, and looks over clear water with bootlace weed, blackbacked gulls and cormorants. Broadcraft Quarry was Britain's first butterfly reserve, the silver studded blue not being found anywhere else in Britain, and it also has rare ivy broomrape and ravens. **Easton** was Hardy's East Quarriers. A dismantled railway previously ran close to the shoreline.

The King's Own suggests the proximity to Cherbourg made Portland Bill a major smuggling location. Portland Museum covers the navy, maritime history, shipwrecks, smuggling, convicts, Portland stone, fossils, geology, natural history, household items, Portland sheep and Thomas Hardy, being based in a pair of 300 year old cottages donated by birth control pioneer Dr Marie Stopes, which inspired Avice's cottage in *The Well-Beloved*. A convert from atheism, Stopes had to be discouraged from destroying an ancient shell with a human scratched on it as it disputed the biblical timescale. Hardy reports

that it was an island using trial marriages, a real marriage not taking place until a union had been proved fertile.

Portland Port control limit is reached by Church Ope Cove, scene of the ill advised theft of a boat at the end of *The Well-Beloved*. Above the water are the 15th century Grade I ruins of Rufus Castle, Hardy's Red King Castle or Bow-&-Arrow Castle, captured in 1142 by the Earl of Gloucester. John Penn's Grade II Gothic style Pennsylvania Castle of 1800, Hardy's Sylvania Castle, stands among the only trees on an island with generally spartan vegetation more reminiscent of Mediterranean limestone landscapes. Slightly older is St George's church of 1776, perhaps the most impressive 18th century church in Dorset with an unspoilt original interior and the graves of Mary Way and William Lano, shot by a pressgang in 1803, and of prison warder Joseph Trevitt, murdered by a convict in 1869. Almost to the 20th century, land transactions were recorded by church gift, the cutting of notches in reed poles kept in churches, the distances between the notches showing the quantity of land and being legally binding. To the north of Church Ope Cove, which was used for stone barges and smuggling, are Boy's Rocks and to the south Girl's Rocks, 150 steps up from the beach between with the Pirates Grave Yard.

In calm conditions it is possible to land in Freshwater Bay, popular with climbers although marred by a rubbish tip. A pumping station supplied water from a spring for the naval base. At Southwell the 13th century Grade II St Andrew's church remains have gravestones marked with skulls and crossbones, indicating Black Death. St Andrew's Avalanche church is in memory of those lost from the clipper *Avalanche* off Portland in 1879 en route to New Zealand and houses artefacts from the ship.

Field systems and the Culverwell mesolithic site on top of the island are outdone for interest by all the caves, derricks, disused quarries and undercut rocks along the

Church Ope Cove with Rufus Castle on the right and Pennsylvania Castle among the trees.

Freshwater Bay with one of the derrick cranes used for boat launching.

The Bill of Portland with the current lighthouse and a daymark on the southern end of the island.

Pulpit Rock with a tempting gap inside.

edge of the island, where fishing boats were entered by climbing down knotted ropes. The east side of the island is losing 300mm/year as the rocks are undercut and fall into the sea. Cave Hole is a blowhole. The Butts have the remains of the *Marguerita* lost in a gale in 1946 with a Danish crew, while an engine on the seabed is from the 1949 wreck of the *Reliance*. The area is popular with divers. Portland sea lavender is prolific here but grows nowhere else in the world. The Ledge runs eastwards from the southern part of the island with a race or shaffle over it. Hardy referred to it as the Race, off the Beal.

The 140,000,000 year old Bill of Portland is 6m high. Two lighthouses were completed in 1716 in transit to clear the Shambles bank, the higher a 41m tower. The lower was converted in 1789 to be the first to have glass lenses and Argand lamps. It is now a bird migration watchpoint observatory and from where Anne Garland watched the *Victory* in *The Trumpet-Major*. Midshipman Easy and his crew did not feel safe from a pressgang ship seen from Spithead until they reached here. The light also attracted the French so two 8kg cannons were installed. In 1906 a new 41m white round towered lighthouse was built with a red band, now Portland Bill Lighthouse Visitor Centre. The Comber family were lighthouse keepers from 1721 to 1911. There is a nearby 18m white stone beacon. Off the bill is the most difficult piece of water on the south coast of England. Southward eddies on both sides of the head cause violent disturbance where they meet east–west flows over the Portland Ledge, resulting in cathedral sized holes and noise which can be heard over a considerable distance. There is always smooth water inside the race, up to 1.6km wide, with weaker and shorter eddies off spring tides. Flows southwards on both sides of the island, used at the end of *The Well-Beloved*, can run for 9 hours in 12

at up to 19km/h, the streams weakening around Lyme Bay to 3km/h on the west side. An anticlockwise eddy on the east side begins at HW Dover +0620 to be 18km long after ten hours twenty minutes. A clockwise eddy on the west side begins at HW Dover –0150 to grow to 13km long but affects the coast further west. The best time to pass west is at HW Dover –0140 and the best time eastwards is at HW Dover +0550. Henry Knight describes the race in *A Pair of Blue Eyes*.

To Berry Head all of the water lies within the 37m contour. Winds are predominantly along the line of the English Channel but can form eddies around the bill.

Drake engaged the Spanish Armada off the point in 1588. One of the first British battleships to be torpedoed by German U-boats, HMS *Formidable*, went down off Portland Bill on New Year's Day 1915. Since 1983, children have had a more benign view with *The Adventures of Portland Bill* on television.

Heading north, the first structure of significance is Pulpit Rock, the gap between it and the main mass of island rock occupied by a wedged rock, resulting from quarrying in the 1870s. The Pom Pom Rock stack was demolished in a January 2014 storm. The location is associated with smuggling and there are several caves close by. The next 200m are known as Whitehall as it supplied much of the stone for government buildings in London's Whitehall. Near the Old Higher lighthouse, later used as a home for Marie Stopes and now a guest-house, there is a blowhole.

During an exercise in 1944 600 American soldiers and seamen were drowned off Blacknor when E-boats attacked an exercise, the guns onshore unable to respond because there were so many men in the water.

The west side of the island has disused quarries, particularly between Weston and **Fortuneswell**, Hardy's Street of Wells. Tout Quarry has become a sculpture park with over 40 sculptures in the rock face or on loose rocks. It is also a nature reserve with orchids, rock roses and other rare limestone plants attracting unique butterflies. The Spirit of Portland statue of a stoneworker and a fisherman stands on the summit above West Weare.

Chiswell, the seaward side of Fortuneswell, has been hit by storm damage repeatedly, particularly in the Great Storm of 1824 which destroyed 80 houses and damaged others. Chesil Cove has surf with a southwesterly wind. On the other side of the A354 behind West Bay is a tank farm and what was a naval helicopter base, now the sailing centre which hosted the 2012 Olympic sailing from Osprey Quay. The aircraft carrier HMS *Illustrious* sank here in a gale in 1948 with the deaths of 29 young men. There are plans to store gas in salt caverns 2.4km below the island. Immediately adjacent and facing into Portland Harbour, which was not there at the time of its construction in 1539, is Portland Castle, one of Henry VIII's finest coastal forts with 4.3m thick walls, used to defend against the French and Spanish and then used to deter piracy. In the 19th century piracy was celebrated in February by a day of residents ransacking each others' houses and taking hostages before all retiring to the public houses. It was one of the last forts to surrender to Cromwell. It was used as the private residence of harbour builder Captain Charles Manning in Victorian times. Earlier, the reeve of Dorchester asked the crews of some Norwegian ships their business and was killed for his troubles. It was also one of the places harried by Godwine in 1052. It was a seaplane station in the First World War, was used in 1944 when US troops were departing for D-Day and has been home to Wrens. It has reproduction Elizabethan armour and impressive cannons.

The sea has risen 60m since the Ice Age, when the coastline was 16km further south. Chesil Beach was Hardy's Pebble Bank. The Old English cisel is shingle. The bank is moving slowly northwards. The 13km of graded pebbles of flint, quartzite and limestone, including some chert and jasper, form part of a 29km sweep of shingle around Lyme Bay and is the most fascinating shingle structure in Britain and possibly the longest in Europe. The beach gets lower (from 13m) and narrower (from 180m) towards its western end, the depth of shingle decreasing from 15m to 11m in this direction and the size of the pebbles being carefully graded from fist size at Chesilton to pea size at Bridport, so precisely that fishermen lost in the fog can tell their location from the size of stones on the beach. Below water level the stones are graded in the opposite direction. Some of the stones have been recovered from Maiden Castle where they were used with slings. Blue clay lies below the shingle some 900mm–1.2m above low water springs. Cans or hollows on the inside of the beach are where water has seeped through and washed the bank away.

Fishing lerrets are used to catch mackerel off the bank. Occasionally the beach is overtopped by storms after strong southwesterly winds. In 1795 seven ships under Rear Admiral Sir Hugh Christian, on their way to the West Indies, were lost here with 200 men and women. In 1824 the West Indiamen *Carvalho* and *Colville* were lost with all hands in the storm which carried the 95t sloop *Ebenezer* into the Fleet on a wave. A ship was left on top of the beach in 1853. In 1872 a number of looters died of hypothermia after starting on the cargo of schnapps carried by the wrecked *Royal Adelaide*. Even whales

Chesil Beach, the head of the Fleet right and Lyme Bay left.

and dolphins may be washed up and an 18th century mermaid turned out to be a dead camel.

The beach is steep and can have heavy breakers, a dump and a strong undertow. Behind Chesil Beach the Fleet occupies what Hardy called the Waddon Vale.

Chesil Beach forms part of the West Dorset Heritage Coast but is closed to walkers for half the year. It has a diverse range of bird and animal life. Three species of tern breed on the shingle bank, being a protected breeding site for the little tern. There are bass, pollock and flatfish in the water and a line of anglers along the beach.

Red flags and lookout points on Chesil Beach, opposite Charlestown at Tidmoor Point, mark the limits of the danger area from the Chickerell firing range which operates from the camp on the north side of the Fleet but is a danger even on the open sea.

The top of the bank is littered with cuttlefish bones and fishing floats.

St Catherine's chapel of 1376–1401 on Chapel Hill has an elaborately vaulted stone roof, rare in England, and 1.2m thick walls. It may have been built as a landmark for sailors and its survival was perhaps due to its use as a tower for a maritime fire beacon. It has also been visited by unmarried women hoping their patron saint would find them husbands.

Abbotsbury Subtropical Gardens were founded in 1765 as the castle gardens. The shingle absorbs the sun's heat and Chesil Beach provides shelter so that there are enormous exotic trees, shrubs and flowers, azaleas, ancient camellias, rhododendrons, 8ha of woodland and formal gardens, 18th century walled gardens of the former Abbotsbury Castle, Victorian garden, New Zealand garden, an aviary, peacocks and rare pheasants and there is still room for some cow parsley. Abbotsbury was Hardy's Abbotsea and the hotel in Ian McEwan's *On Chesil Beach* was somewhere to the south.

Pillboxes guard the coast near Lawrence of Arabia's cottage. Between Labour in Vain Farm, back from the Old Coastguards which were visited by Thomas Hardy, and West Bexington there are chalets with caravan sites at Swyre and Cogden Beach. Carparks are easy to spot because these are the sections of beach in use, the rest being largely deserted. The French spotted West Bexington in the 15th century and burned it. In the 18th and 19th centuries their interest in it was more for smuggling.

Cogden Beach effectively brings an end to the Chesil Beach although shingle beach continues for some distance. The parking area is up towards the B3157 and just along from the Othona Community's centre.

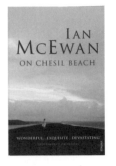

Chesil Beach forms the western edge of Portland Harbour.

Distance
79km from
Peveril Point to
Cogden Beach

OS 1:50,000 Sheets
194 Dorchester
& Weymouth
195 Bournemouth
& Purbeck

Tidal Constants
Swanage:
HW Dover –0030,
LW Dover –0040
Lulworth Cove:
HW Dover –0430,
LW Dover –0440
Portland:
HW Dover –0500,
LW Dover –0540
Chesil Cover:
HW Dover –0450,
LW Dover –0540
Chesil Beach
HW Dover –0450,
LW Dover –0540
Bridport (West Bay):
HW Dover –0510,
LW Dover –0540

Ranges
Lulworth, Chickerell

Submarine Areas
D031 N1, D026
Lulworth Inner,
X 5021B, D014
Chesil Bank,
X 5018, D012
Lyme Bay North

Sea Area
Portland

Connection
The Fleet – see RoB
p279

35 Lyme Bay

**Britain's
Jurassic
coast**

She sells sea-shells on the sea-shore.
The shells she sells are sea-shells, I'm sure.
For if she sells sea-shells on the sea-shore
Then I'm sure she sells sea-shore shells.
Terry Sullivan

From Cobden Beach the coast passes the Bronze Age Bind Barrow burial mound to arrive at Burton Beach with Burton Cliff, a deep golden colour with stratified sand, from which 400t fell in 2012. The beach has sea kale, wild cabbage, pink bindweed, white sea campion, yellow horned sea poppies and horse mushrooms. The River Bride discharges past the Saxon thatched stone settlement of Burton Bradstock and a caravan site and East Cliff with its golf course. Fossils are found along the coast to Lyme Regis. The resort of Burton Bradstock was a centre for making rope and nets with locally grown flax. These days the ropes are used for water skiing and nets including nets for Wimbledon's tennis.

The beach was used for military exercises during the Second World War. August sees the Burton Bradstock Festival of Music & Art.

West Bay's piers were rebuilt in 2004, the seawall strengthened and the beach replenished. The River Brit is too small for **Bridport** to function as a port and West Bay served this purpose, declining after the railway arrived. Quite large vessels can use West Bay to deliver timber and take away sand and gravel. Rolled pea sized Bridport gravel was used for surfacing the skid pan of the Transport Research Laboratory at Crowthorne. The harbour was in use in the 13th century and rebuilt in 1740 with many ships in the 19th century, the sluice

Burton Cliff with its marked golden strata.

Golden Cap beyond Doghouse Hill with Charmouth in the distance, seen from the Hive at Burton Bradstock.

The working harbour at West Bay.

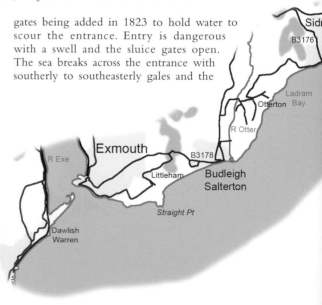

gates being added in 1823 to hold water to scour the entrance. Entry is dangerous with a swell and the sluice gates open. The sea breaks across the entrance with southerly to southeasterly gales and the bar dries. The National Coastwatch Institution lookout point was blown away in the February 2014 storms. It was where Mrs Downe and Mrs Barnet had their fatal capsize in *Fellow-Townsmen* in the *Wessex Tales*, this one also explaining about how silting overcame attempts to extend the navigation to Bridport. Schooners and naval vessels were built here until 1897 and it was used for filming *Harbour Lights*, *The Life & Times of Reginald Perrin* and the *Broadchurch* TV series, set in this area. Pier Terrace on the east side of the entrance was designed by Edward Prior, an enthusiast of the Arts & Crafts movement. The unstable cliffs have started by Eype's Mouth, eype being an Old English steep place, and there is an undertow, not that the mackerel, bass and herrings are worried. Cormorants and blackbacked gulls search for booty. A hut by the shore at Eype was the scene of the murder of *Broadchurch*'s Danny Latimer.

Below Thorncombe Beacon the coast kicks out past Great Ebb to East Ebb Cove and East Ebb and the foot of Doghouse Hill, beyond which is Seatown which can have a heavy dump, it being difficult to land or launch with a swell. This area is another noted for its fossils.

The rocks of the Corner and Western Patches protect the foot of Golden Cap, at 191m the highest cliff on the south coast, claimed to glow at night, the gorse, broom, bracken, heather and golden upper greensand at the top accounting for the name. There is a monument on the summit and the peak was used for filming *The History of Tom Jones: A Foundling* and Jonathan Swift's *Gulliver's Travels*. There is a tremendous range of birdlife to be found, including thrushes in the spring, cuckoos, swallows, grasshopper and willow warblers, chiffchaffs, lesser whitethroats and tree pipits in the summer and buzzards, kestrels, partridges, lapwings, skylarks, rooks, stonechats, goldcrests, meadow pipits, pied wagtails, linnets, yellowhammers and reed buntings all year, even mallards as a stream feeds down to St Gabriels Mouth where it runs down from the top of a nose of loose rock. There are many rare insects including bees and beetles in the undercliff. The 13th century ruins of St Gabriel's church stand back from Broom Cliff.

From Seatown to Charmouth was a favourite smuggling area and, while the soft, black, brooding Jurassic blue lias cliffs would not have been the easiest of places to land contraband, the slipped hillside above would not have been easy for revenuemen to patrol.

Worcester and was to escape to France with the help of local boatmen but news of the plan leaked out and he had to flee on horseback. St Andrew's church has the 1792 tomb of James Warden, killed in a duel with his neighbour, and the coffin of the Rev Edward Bragge which was made from his kitchen table as he had been so keen on his food. A plaque on Gwyle bridge warns vandals of the penalty of transportation. The beach huts featured in the *Broadchurch* TV series.

In 1825 the Old Lyme Road was built to avoid the Lyme Regis toll road but it had to be closed in 1924 after the Black Ven landslip, the largest coastal mudslide in Europe. Extensive stabilization has been undertaken in recent years.

It was at the Black Ven Jurassic blue lias cliffs in 1811 that 12 year old Mary Anning found a 6.4m ichthyosaur, the head of which is in the Natural History Museum in London. This began the serious hunting of fossils around Charmouth and Lyme Regis and the origin of the tongue twister *She Sells Sea-Shells*. Her later finds here included a plesiosaurus and a pterodactyl. A storm revealed an almost complete ichthyosaur on Boxing Day 2013 and it was removed over eight hours before another storm obliterated the site. The Charmouth Heritage Coast Centre features the coast, fossils (especially ammonites), local history and an 1850s cement works which ground limestone pebbles from the beach with steam powered millstones and burned them in limekilns behind. A 12m dragon's skull found on the beach in 2013 was a publicity stunt for *A Game of Thrones*. There is a 65ha nature reserve, disturbed only by the noise of geologists' hammers from behind Canary Ledges.

Broad Ledge has its best surf after a southwesterly gale but can be difficult. It played a central role in the March 1993 accident in which four school pupils out of six, paddling with a teacher and two inexperienced instructors from an outdoor centre in **Lyme Regis**, died after a catalogue of errors by various people. Britain's worst ever canoeing accident and the only fatalities ever of canoeists under instruction, it resulted in the setting up of the Adventure Activities Licensing Authority for outdoor centres.

In 774 King Cynewulf gave the monks of Lyme permission to produce salt from sea water. Lyme takes its name

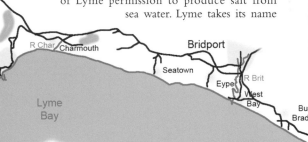

from the River Lim, British Celtic for the flooding river. The medieval port and cloth town, a significant part of which has been lost to the sea, was given its charter in 1284 by Edward I, who added Regis to the name and used the village as a base for his wars against the French. Set on seabed limestone outcrops, the 180m Cobb, probably from the Welsh for embankment, was built about 1300, the oldest remaining working artificial breakwater of its kind in Britain, William Jessop reporting in 1805 that the cliff had receded 83m since the Cobb's construction. It was repaired in Portland stone in 1825 and has been rebuilt several times, now having a main southwestern arm 270m long x 12m x 3.7m high with buildings on top and an eastern breakwater 3.7m x 5.8m high, the gap

Ducks and swans occupy the pools where the River Char enters the sea by the Beach Café. Surf is best at low water with a southwesterly wind but there may be a launching charge. Charmouth is a resort of honey coloured stone houses, thatched cottages and Regency houses. A 14th century new town by the Abbot of Forde, it was a refuge from the feudal system, allowing people to buy property and trade. The Street is part of the Dorchester to Exeter Roman road. The George was a coaching inn on this south coast route and Catherine of Aragon stayed in 1501 in a medieval hotel since given a 19th century façade. Charles II hid in what is now the Abbots House in 1651 after his defeat by Cromwell at

173

The unstable cliffs at Cain's Folly.

Looking along the front at Lyme Regis.

The Cobb at Lyme Regis, one of Britain's oldest artificial harbours.

to the shore being closed by blockwork. The first clash between Drake and the Armada occurred in the bay in 1588, assisted by five local boats. In 1644 Prince Maurice arrived with Royalist forces but the smaller Parliamentary army in the town were swelled by townswomen dressed as men and supplied by sea, so the Royalist siege failed. The Duke of Monmouth landed in 1685 on what is now called Monmouth Beach and stayed in the George Inn to raise an army to fight James II. He was defeated at Sedgemoor and a dozen Lyme men were hanged in chains on the beach where he landed. Judge Jeffreys dined in the former Great House in Broad Street the night before the hangings and his ghost still haunts the spot, perhaps chewing a bloody bone. To Thomas Hardy,

Lyme Bay was Dead-man's Bay. Although on the A3052 today, the village had no wheeled access until 1759.

Now a resort, the Pearl of Dorset, with a promenade and the Cobb Arms, it has Georgian architecture, the 16th century St Michael the Archangel's church and a town crier. It was a watering hole which attracted Jane Austen, who had a seafront cottage, and set Louisa Musgrove's fall here in *Persuasion*, which was filmed here. Local resident John Fowles set *The French Lieutenant's Woman* here and the 1980 film with Meryl Streep waiting on the end of the Cobb is the image of the village which has become famous. Martha Grimes' *The Lamorna Wink* claims there had been serial child killings here.

174

Following the 1915 sinking of HMS *Formidable*, the body of John Cowan was one of those recovered by fishermen and taken to the Pilot Boat, the cellar being used as a mortuary. The landlord's collie, Lassie, made a great deal of fuss, licking the face of the victim and keeping him warm. He later recovered. The incident resulted in Lassie books, cinema films and TV series.

Turner painted another image of the village. Lyme Regis Marine Aquarium is sited on the Cobb. A new danger of late has been the stealing of whelks from fishing boats by gulls and dropping them onto the Cobb to break them, much as thrushes do with snails on concrete paths.

Fishing boats also catch mackerel, prawns and conger eels. In addition, the harbour houses pleasure craft although the sea breaks right across the entrance with southerly or southeasterly gales. Experienced surfers find the best surf in Poker's Pool on the bottom half of the tide with a southwesterly wind.

A Dinosaurland Fossil Museum Jurassic exhibition is in a Grade I former church while Lyme Regis Museum has not only local history, lace prints and documents but also fossils from the blue lias including the ichthyosaurus which started it all. Mary Anning Day is in September and Lyme Regis Fossil Festival takes place in May, as does the Lyme Regis Jazz & Blues Festival. The Mighty Hop and Town Mill breweries are both located in the town, there having been a town mill here in 1086.

After Virtle Rock the coast passes from Dorset to Devon, a very remote section to Seaton but with a high sunshine rating and a mild climate. Coastal woodlands are rare in the southwest but are extensive from here to Seaton. Beyond Seven Rock Point is Pinhay Bay, where oystercatchers will be seen on Jurassic rocks. Whitlands Undercliff, 750mm wide, was caused by slips in 1765 and 1840. After Humble Point is Charlton Bay to which there is a path down from near the former Allhallows College. The bay leads to Dowlands Cliffs & Landslips. From Lyme Regis to Axmouth the coast is particularly prone to slipping as the iron rich red sandstone is overlain by impermeable clays topped with porous chalk and younger mudstones. On Christmas Day 1839 a 1.2km length of coast weighing 8,000,000t and involving 8ha of earth, Mesozoic chalk and cottages collapsed into the sea at Bindon Cliffs, Britain's biggest recorded landslide. Nobody was hurt as warning had been given and it was the first ever documented slip. Today it is covered with ash woods, bluebells, wild garlic, maple, beech, hazel, hawthorn, yew, rhododendrons, privet, brambles, ivy, ferns and a selection of less usual plants and insects. The year after the landslide, farmers managed to get a crop of wheat off what was called Goat Island and the *Landslide Quadrille* was composed.

Culverhole Point is usually difficult for landing and leads to Sparrowbush Ledge and Haven Cliff with the Axe Cliff Golf & Country Club on top. A shingle bank remains from falls from Haven Cliff in 14th century storms. In Roman times Axmouth was one of the busiest ports in Britain but the River Axe, protected by Triassic cliffs, silted up and the town is now 1.5km inland. The harbour entrance works were destroyed by storms in 1869–75. It was proposed to run an English & Bristol Channels Canal here from the Parret estuary near Stolford, avoiding the southwest peninsula.

The Roman Fosse Way began from here and ran to Lincoln. Fishing vessels and yachts still use the quay but a landslip in 1537 narrowed the entrance and the shifting bar of shingle dries, reducing the entrance after storms and making the mouth dangerous on the ebb. Surf in the estuary is best on the lower half of the tide with a southerly wind. There can be a dump, the best landing being at the end of the beach.

The B3172 arrived over one of the first bridges in Britain to be built of unreinforced concrete, now the oldest remaining. It has three arches but during construction in 1877 the west one settled 600mm, causing the main arch to crack right across. In 1956 timber planks on steel girders were placed across to take the load off the main span and in 1990 it was made an Ancient Monument and retired to being a pedestrian bridge, a new road bridge being built upstream.

Another transport route here is the Seaton Tramway, moved here from Eastbourne in 1970. Of 838mm gauge and using the former railway route, it has the world's only open top trams in public service. Out of season they are used as mobile hides for birdwatching trips, stopping when anything interesting is spotted.

Seaton has a beach of large round pebbles which were exported for paint blending and rubber processing. Kilvert caused scandal by nude bathing here in 1873, by which time it was out of fashion on this beach. Today the village is a resort of Victorian and Edwardian houses with a largely Norman St Michael's church and a promenade. The seawall dates only from 1980, following flooding in a violent storm, and the Tesco store is even newer, on the site of Warner's holiday camp, the first in Britain. Seaton Museum features the Jurassic coast and rock samples of different ages are used in the 18m diameter spiral Seaton Labyrinth. There is an annual arts and drama festival.

The undercliff has fossils, plants and over a hundred bird species. Crab pots are laid around Seaton Bay, which can be busy with powerboats and waterskiing.

The B3174 winds round the back of Seaton Hole to the thatched village of **Beer**, from the Anglo-Saxon bearu, grove. The Fine Foundation Centre about the heritage coast is near a Second World War gun position. Landing is difficult with a swell. Small crab and lobster

Dowlands Cliffs, site of Britain's largest recorded landslide.

boats are launched from the steep shingle beach and are pulled back up by capstan. In 1837 Jack Rattenbury, the king of the smugglers, retired after 50 years to become a fisherman and publish his *Memoirs of a Smuggler*.

Most striking is the colour change where the white Cretaceous chalk gives way unconformably to red Triassic sandstone, dominated by 130m Beer Head. There was a Stone Age settlement at Beer. In 1665 the village was hit by the plague. Shipwrecked Spanish sailors found it undefended and stayed. Flemish refugees set up the lace industry which supplied the lace for Queen Victoria's wedding dress. The Clifftop Jubilee Gardens date from 1897 and there is the 1.6km long 184mm gauge Beer Heights Light Railway, Pecorama model railway exhibition, restaurant in a Pullman car, Peco Pleasure Gardens & Exhibition, floral gardens, aviary, crazy golf and assault course. The town was also used in filming *Harbour Lights*. Beer R&B Festival takes place in October. Herring gulls and a large caravan site look down on Beer Roads.

Beer Quarry Caves have been mined since Roman times and have supplied stone for such prominent buildings as Hampton Court, Windsor Castle, the Tower of London, St Stephen's at Westminster and Salisbury, Exeter, Winchester and St Paul's Cathedrals. There has been a dramatic slip from South Down Common near Beer Head.

A high mast stands north of Beer and another back on South Down Common. From Sherborne Rocks to Sidmouth the cliffs are unstable, the subsequent lack of easy access making them popular with naturists. At Hooken Cliffs 4ha slipped 76m in 1790 and there are chalk pinnacles.

The sea dumps at Branscombe Mouth, by which is the 14th century Great Seaside farm and a selection of more recent static caravans. Flint and stone thatched cottages occupy Branscombe.

The 12th century St Winifred's church has a three decker pulpit, one of only two in Devon, and the remains of a mural showing the Devil spearing adulterers. The thatched Branscombe Forge of 1580 was begun in Norman times and there is a notable Old Bakery. In January 2007 the beach was invaded by people looting containers of BMW motorbikes and other products from the stricken MSC *Napoli* beached in a storm after being damaged off the Lizard.

Cretaceous upper greensand rests uncomformably on Triassic mudstone. The undercliff is a good place for migrant birds and there are buzzards, kestrels, rooks, stonechats, meadow pipits, goldfinches, linnets and yellowhammers plus swallows, house martins, lesser whitethroats and tree pipits in summer and the thistles attract finches in the autumn and winter.

There is the Iron Age or Roman Berry Camp fort site above Branscombe Ebb. At 152m Weston Cliff is the highest cliff on the south Devon coast despite the sandstones having been laid down in the Triassic era on the bed of a vast southwards flowing river. Weston Wild Flower Meadow has almost 100 species of flowers and grasses as well as birds, butterflies and other insects. Weston Mouth has a pebble beach and caves which were used by smugglers despite the dump. Hook Ebb Rocks precede Salcombe Mouth, again liable to dump. The 172m Salcombe Hill leads to Salcombe Hill Cliff where falls of red Triassic mudstone cause the seawater to be deep red. Above are Cretaceous upper greensand, an aerial and an observatory.

Sidmouth was a fishing village including Newfoundland cod fishing until the River Sid (Old English for low lying river) silted up in 1824 after a storm washed away protection, fishing boats now being winched onto the beach. Surf is best on the bottom half of the tide with winds between southeast and southwest, although there may be a landing charge. With choppy conditions landings are safer at the east end at high water. The town was Hardy's Idmouth.

It is a resort of Georgian, Regency and Victorian buildings with an esplanade and a row of seafront hotels,

Beer Head with its slips and the last of the chalk.

the Royal York & Faulkner, the Elizabeth, the Kingswood & Devoran, the Marine and the Riviera. The Royal Glen Hotel was Woodbrook Cottage, where Princess Victoria's parents came in 1819 while avoiding their creditors. They arrived in a snowstorm on Christmas Day. Three days later a boy shooting sparrows in the road outside fired an arrow through the glass window and pierced the sleeve of baby Victoria's nightdress. Within a month of arriving, Victoria's father, the Duke of Kent, had died of illness. A Russian eagle on a roof is a reminder that Grand Duchess Helena of Russia had a house here. In the appendix to his *Euphranor* Edward FitzGerald noted it as an example of the indolent middle classes with people lounging about, throwing stones in the sea and carrying novels. Jacob's Ladder leads from the beach to Connaught Gardens where the floral displays are especially good. In the summer there are band concerts. Sidmouth Museum features the geological, maritime and more recent history of the town. Sidmouth Folk Week is held in August. The B3176 pays a brief visit to the front. There are tennis, bowls, golf and sailing. Arthur Conan Doyle played

Branscombe Mouth, the last accesible point before Sidmouth.

cricket here with the MCC but was put off by howling dogs, later writing his *Hound of the Baskervilles*. The BBC used the town to film Agatha Christie's *Sleeping Murder* episode of *Miss Marple*.

There are two offshore rock breakwaters and Clifton Walkway with fallen rocks before Chit Rocks, near which are restored 17th century limekilns. Cliffs of Cretaceous upper greensand lying uncomformably on red Triassic mudstone front 156m Peak Hill behind the long enclosed beach past Tortoiseshell Rocks. A sequence of impressive red Triassic sandstone stacks are met, able to be explored by many small boats, rowing boats and sit on top kayaks on hire from Ladram Bay, a busy sheltered cove with the large Ladram Bay Holiday Park caravan site. The bay was at the centre of the action in HG Wells' *The Sea-Raiders*.

Crab Ledge, Brandy Head, Black Head and Danger Point are a series of points which are little more than curves in the cliffs, although one has a large circular hole with a flight of steps up to it. Brandy Head, named after its smuggling, has a Second World War observation hut which was used in tests of weapons. Off Otterton Point is Otterton Ledge which can produce surf.

The River Otter, apparently named after its wildlife, was used for the cross-Channel wool and salt trades as far as Otterton until an 1824 storm when it silted up with a bank of quartzite pebbles, some of which look like muffins, leaving only a narrow entrance. Laid down in sandstones in Brittany 400,000,000 years ago, they were transported north by vast rivers in the Triassic era and deposited in the Budleigh Salterton Pebble Beds, subsequently falling onto the beach and being washed eastwards by the sea. A fossilized rhynchosaur has been found here. The area was used for smuggling in the 18th century despite the fact that it dumps here again. The Otter Estuary Nature Reserve with mink, merlins and kites is on a marsh which was larger until French Napoleonic prisoners of war built an embankment to reclaim some of it. Arches in a brick wall are the remains of limekilns. Small lobster fishing boats are winched up the beach.

Budleigh Salterton is a 19th century resort which takes its name from the 13th century saltpans established in the marshes by Otterton Priory monks and from the glade of the Old English man Budda. It has Georgian and Regency houses and the Fairlynch Museum & Arts Centre in an 18th century thatched house, featuring the local geology and history including the Bronze Age, clothing and with a smugglers' cellar and lookout tower. There are golf, bowls and croquet and the seawall is unchanged from when, in 1870, Sir John Millais painted

Dunscombe Cliff and Salcombe Hill Cliff.

The mouth of the River Sid at Sidmouth.

Tortoiseshell Rocks with Big Picket Rock at the end.

The stacks in Ladram Bay stretching away past Sidmouth towards the cliff colour change at Beer Head.

177

Budleigh Salterton with Straight Point in the distance.

The etched cliff and naturist beach west of Budleigh Salterton.

Distance
46km from Cogden Beach to Dawlish Warren

OS 1:50,000 Sheets
192 Exeter & Sidmouth
193 Taunton & Lyme Regis
194 Dorchester & Weymouth

Tidal Constants
Bridport (West Bay):
HW Dover −0510, LW Dover −0540
Lyme Regis:
HW Dover −0450, LW Dover −0540
Exmouth Approaches:
HW Dover −0500, LW Dover −0530

Range
Straight Point

Submarine Area
D012 Lyme Bay North

Sea Area
Portland

Connection
River Exe – see RoB p281

The Boyhood of Raleigh, who was born locally at Hayes Barton near Yettington. It was also used for filming the *Sleeping Murder* episode of *Miss Marple*. Budleigh Salterton Jazz Festival is in April and Budleigh Salterton Literary Festival in September. Kate Pettigrew used it as a refuge in John L Balderston's *Berkeley Square* but it was considered inadequate as a honeymoon destination for Elvira and Charles Condomine in *Blithe Spirit*.

The B3178 visits briefly before the beach again becomes inaccessible by vehicle and is used by naturists, blackbacked gulls, cormorants and razorbills. The water is clear and there are strangely pocked red sandstone cliffs with pine trees on top. Heather and gorse grow on top of the cliffs at Beacon Hill beyond the East Devon Golf Course.

There are the caravans of the Devon Cliffs Holiday Park behind Littleham Cove. Otter Cove and a cave are the start of the Royal Marines' rifle ranges on Straight Point, marked by red flags or lights.

There is a 7m metal light mast. Oystercatchers are undisturbed.

Earth cliffs to 62m high extend to Orcombe Point from the popular beach at Sandy Bay, where there can be surf with southerly or southwesterly winds. A Geoneedle monument marks the end of the Jurassic Coast. The World of Country Life has a Victorian street, vintage cars, owls, pets, a safari deer train and goat walking.

From Orcombe Point an esplanade leads to Exmouth past the red Triassic mudstone and sandstone Maer Rocks with surf on southerly winds and past Conger Rocks, off which is a jet ski area and where windsurfers also operate. The Maer offers a carpark by various amusements for children and the largest OO gauge model railway complex in the world. The 4ha Maer nature reserve has 400 flowering plant species. The Second World War Allen Williams turret takes the form of an armed dome for defence.

Exmouth is one of the oldest seaside resorts in England. Despite its sandy beach and its safe bathing, it does have a substantial seawall to face winter storms and there is a dangerous area where the water swirls out past Pole Sands, the intertidal part of Dawlish Warren. The Point was the normal landing place for raiders, including the Celts and Romans. It was burned by the Danes under King Sweyn in 1001. One of the principal Devon ports by 1199, it sent 10 ships and 190 men to Calais for Edward III. It was Royalist in the Civil War. It was a busy port in the early 16th century and was used as a base by Sir Walter Raleigh. In the 17–19th centuries it was subject to attacks by Algerian and Tunisian pirates. The resort use began in 1720 with large scale development from 1792. Exmouth Festival is in May or June.

The River Exe floods to 7km/h and ebbs to 8km/h in the channels when banks are uncovered. The sea breaks across the entrance in south or southwesterly gales and sandbanks move. Pole Sand spit reaches nearly to Orcombe Point while the spit of Dawlish Warren reaches nearly to Exmouth and has the 2km² Dawlish Warren Nature Reserve, a low spit running from Warren Point, now half the width it was in the 18th century. It is noted for 180 bird species including blacktailed godwits, greenshanks, curlews, sandpipers, greater sand plovers, terns, great spotted cuckoos and winter migrants, amongst them brent geese with up to 20,000 birds at a time present. Plants include the sand crocus, which only opens in April when the sun is shining. There are a wind generator and a golf course.

Flows are west southwest from Dover HW and northeast and east from HW Dover −0440 at up to 2km/h. There can be surf with easterly winds. There are a visitor centre and chalets at the root of the spit, used as a sandy resort with go karts and safe beach for children. There is parking nearby but it is busy in summer. Railway camping coaches are located on a disconnected siding.

Southwest Devon

Stand each shock
Like Thurlestone Rock.
Anon

Between Dawlish Warren and Teignmouth the Paddington to Penzance railway reaches its best. The most impressive part of the South Devon Railway, it was built after 1844. Beyond the red block of Langstone Rock with its natural arch it moves out onto the foot of the Permian cliffs formed from dune sand and, with a walkway, runs 5m above the beach with a seawall which is concave to throw back waves, causing clapotis when conditions are rough. *Memories & Opinions* tells how Q, Arthur Quiller-Couch, was rolled badly while swimming here as a child. The wall was damaged badly in 2014 storms and this section of track had to be rebuilt. This is probably the most exposed piece of railway line in the country and when conditions get serious trains use only the line furthest from the water. Cross Country electrics are susceptible to heavy flying spray and rescue diesel engines have had to be stationed locally for them. Netting is secured with 57 cables which measure significant rockfalls to alert signallers in Exeter. Most of the long breakwater in Coryton Cove has been lost. As far as Holcombe a force 4 easterly will give surf at mid tide, used by board surfers around **Dawlish**. The station was rebuilt in 1875 after the previous one burned down and, again, partly in 2014. Often subject to saltwater spray, the footbridge has been rebuilt in fibre reinforced polymer to Brunel's original appearance but at a third of the weight. The A379 follows the coast to Broadsands but is only seen briefly at Torbay.

The Regency and Victorian resort of Dawlish developed during the Napoleonic Wars when travel to the Continent was prevented and is built around the Lawn, gardens with Dawlish Water running through the centre, giving the British Celtic for black stream or Devil water although it can turn red in spate. It is home to black swans, East Indian game ducks, South African shelducks and Chinese swan geese. The museum features a more sinister creature. In the snow and very hard frosts of February 1855 a 160km trail of footprints appeared over several nights from Totnes to Littleham, passing through the town. They looked as if they had been cut by hot cloven hooves and went over roofs, under hedges and through pipes, surely the work of the Devil. Dogs retreated from undergrowth where the footprints led. Dawlish Arts Festival is in June. The opening of *Nicholas Nickleby* and the death of Smike were set here and Jane Austin used the beach in *Sense & Sensibility*.

Coryton's Cove and Horse Cove are sandy. The railway passes through five tunnels, 34–46m long, Kennaway, Coryton, Phillot, Clerk's and Bishop's, the first three names being landowners, and was used for filming *The Ghost Train*. The rocks become increasingly interesting, particularly the red sandstone formation of the Parson & Clerk, the parson said to have enlisted the help of the Devil in an attempt to get to the head of the promotion queue as the Bishop of Exeter lay dying in Dawlish. The following Shag Rock is equally dramatic, a venue which attracts cormorants and blackbacked gulls. The beach tends to collect flotsam and can be difficult for landing to Sprey Point when conditions are choppy. This area is a spoil bed so there is also jetsam, in addition to which is a historic wreck with a 200m radius restricted area around

Langstone Rock at the end of Dawlish Warren.

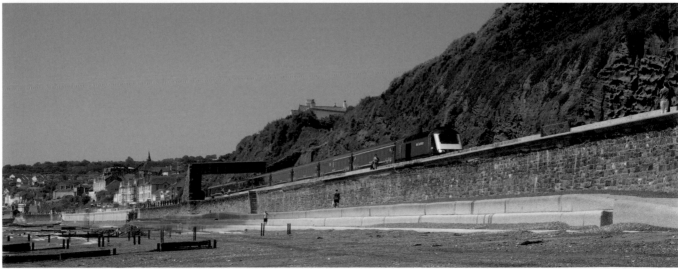

The railway runs along the front at Dawlish.

Coryton's Cove with a train emerging from one of the five tunnels on this stretch of line.

The Parson & Clerk with Shag Rock beyond.

Powerboats and jet skis offshore contrast with the relative peace of Punch & Judy shows on the sandy beach.

There is a light beacon on the low sandy Point, off which there are eddies. Surf is best on the bottom half of the tide. Spratt Sand constantly changes, as does the Bar, with the sea breaking across the entrance in southerly and southeasterly gales. The channel moves all the time, there is a small race over the pipeline across Pole Sand on the southern side of the entrance and there are swift outgoing streams to 5km/h from HW Dover +0110, ingoing from HW Dover −0510 to 3km/h. Offshore, the flows south southwest are from HW Dover −0030 and north northeast from HW Dover +0510.

There is a daymark off the Ness, the bold red sandstone headland on the south side of the estuary where Shaldon Wildlife Trust have owls, ravens, pygmy marmoset monkeys and a crocodile. The sandy Ness Cove is reached through a smugglers' tunnel. There is also a limekiln. Wednesdays from June to September are designated 1785 Day with people in Georgian costume,

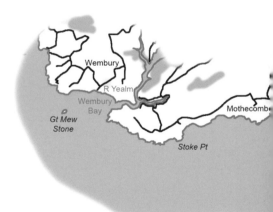

it near Church Rocks, possibly a 16th century Venetian trading galley.

Teignmouth had Saxon origins, was burnt by the Danes in 800 and was ravaged by the French in 1340 and in 1690, the last successful invasion of mainland England. The station is in French Pavilion style, notwithstanding. The town has many Georgian buildings and became a Victorian and Regency tourist centre and resort before being attacked by the Germans in the Second World War. Den Green, once used for horse racing and fish net drying, has floral displays and Keats worked on *Endymion* and *Isabella* here in 1818. The sandstone tower of St James is 13th century with an 1820 octagonal tower. The town has had a port from the first half of the 19th century with a quay from the 1930s, used by yachts. Exports include cereals, potters' clay from the River Teign (the sparkling river) and stone for sea defences, following on from the granite exported in 1831 to build London Bridge, imports including building materials, timber, coal and paper, coasters using the harbour at high water. The Grand Pier has amusements. Teignmouth Folk Festival is in June and Teignmouth Jazz Festival in November.

a farmers' market, craft fair, may-pole dancing and Punch & Judy shows. There is a music festival in June and water carnival in August.

The coast continues cliffy with vegetation on top, not to mention Shaldon Golf Course, and many secluded and

Teignmouth with its pier.

Bell Rock is reached by a group of swimmers.

inaccessible coves to Long Quarry Point. Beyond Bundle Head is Labrador Bay and then Smugglers Cove has a small wreck visible at the southern end at low water.

The waters become part of Tor Bay Harbour. Herring Cove offers limited landing in bad weather, as does Mackerel Cove. After Blackaller's Cove is Maidencombe, a private beach from which launching is not permitted.

The split Bell Rock precedes Watcombe Head and the secluded beaches seem to be used increasingly by naturists, despite the lion's mane jellyfish in the water. Brunel Manor, now a Christian retreat centre, was to be Brunel's family home. Torquay Golf Course is above Petit Tor Point, near which there was a 5,000t rockfall in 2010.

Babbacombe Bay, where Devon gives way to Torbay, and Oddicombe Beach have fine pink and white shingle and canoe hire. St Marychurch is said to be the oldest church in Devon, set up by early missionaries. More recent is Babbacombe Model Village, 2ha at 1:12 scale, and a 1926 cliff railway makes access more easy than in the past. In the 19th century there was smuggling and wrecking by luring ships onto Oddicombe and Babbacombe beaches with lanterns hung on the horns of grazing cattle. In 1853 excisemen found 153 casks of spirits. The following year Brunel helped oppose the construction of a gasworks by the shore. Onshore winds can produce a vertical eddy at the foot of the cliffs.

There is a field system on Walls Hill which slopes down to Long Quay Point where there are the remains of a quarry. The Agatha Christie Literary Trail runs to Greenway estate on the Dart, with links to 20 of her novels. She used to come here for moonlight picnics and had a romantic encounter with Amyas Boston, whose Christian name she later used for the victim in *Five Little Pigs*. The Bishops Walk was built in 1840 for the Bishops of Exeter, who lived in what is now the Palace Hotel.

Beyond the smuggling venue of Anstey's Cove and Black Head is the limestone Kents Cavern showcave, two main chambers and a series of galleries which have been inhabited by people and animals, the oldest dwelling in Britain, named because it was claimed to extend to Kent. The bones of a sabretooth tiger, cave lion, woolly rhinoceros and great cave bear have been found as well as many archaeological items including implements and tools up to 300,000 years old. There are stalactites and stalagmites, now with a sound and light show and candlelit caves. Agatha Christie's father helped fund the 1805 excavations and Hempsley Cavern appears in *The Man in the Brown Suit*.

Hope's Nose, formed of Devonian limestone, is home to Devon's biggest kittiwake colony and is a nesting place for migratory birds. Further off is a deep draught vessel anchorage, another resting place. Between the two are the Lead Stone or Flat Rock, the Ore Stone with an 8m long tunnel passing through it and, further round, the Thatcher Rock, a 40m high seabird nesting sanctuary which is thought to look as if it has a thatched roof and, in the 1930s, had two youths marooned on it for several days. East Shag rock separates Meadfoot Beach from Daddyhole Cove in the Devonian limstone, overlooked by a tower, and then the natural arch of London Bridge hides Peaked Tor Cove. Agatha Christie used to swim from Meadfoot Beach most days but mixed bathing was not allowed and men had to stay at least 50m from the ladies' bathing machines.

The resort and yachting centre of **Torquay**, named after the Cornish tor, hill, was Hardy's Tor-upon-Sea. Its inner harbour from 1870 was based on Rennie's earlier design with stone cut from Beacon Hill, which was levelled, the 1.2m square x 3 or 4m blocks

Babbacombe is sheltered from the prevailing wind.

being placed by divers. Built on seven hills, the town had its pirates but Tennyson called it the 'loveliest sea village in England' and Ruskin 'the Italy of England'. It accommodated the British fleet for long periods during the Napoleonic Wars yet it can produce a heavy sea with strong easterly or southeasterly winds. These days Tor Bay can actually be rougher than the open sea at times because of all the washes of the many powered boats, waterskiers and jet skis. Washes travel far and in many directions. It is not unusual for sea breezes to approach along the coast from both the north and the south bringing yachts under spinnakers and then to be deflected west into the bay together. Tidal streams are weak and there are 18 beaches in the bay, many with controlled areas for swimmer priority in the summer. There may also be launching charges. Surf is best on the bottom half of the tide with southerly or easterly winds or there are a wave machine and flume in the Riviera International Centre pool. A regular cargo service runs to the Channel Islands.

The English Riviera is named for its mild climate, the palm trees planted by the Victorians and the fact that it had to replace the French one in Napoleonic times. Living Coasts is claimed to be the world's only coastal zoo. Torquay Museum has 400,000,000 years of Torbay history, finds from Kents Cavern including the jawbone which is the UK's oldest recorded human bone, geology, archaeology, natural, social and local history, Celtic artworks, ceramics and Agatha Christie, the world's second best selling author, who was born in the town and set many stories in the area under fictitious place names. Marlene Tucker had bought her makeup here in *Dead Man's Folly*. The Imperial Hotel features in *Peril at End House* and *The Body in the Library*. It was also used for the summing up in *Sleeping Murder*, the final *Miss Marple* story, published posthumously. The International Agatha Christie Festival is in September and there is an Agatha Christie Mile from here to the Grand Hotel, where she honeymooned. Charlie and Leslie Titmuss also honeymooned in Torquay in *Paradise Postponed*. Torbay saw one of the last giant octopus specimens washed up dead in *The Sea-Raiders*. *De Profundis* says Lord Alfred Douglas made a stormy departure from Oscar Wilde's house here. The John Cleese BBC comedy series *Fawlty*

 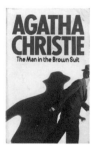    

Hope's Nose and a group of Swedish students.

The Ore Stone and Thatcher Rock at the northeastern corner of Tor Bay.

Extreme folding near London Bridge.

London Bridge at Torquay.

Between the red sandstone cliffs of Corbyn's Head, where pirate Samuel Corbyn was said to have been hanged, and Livermead Head there is a waterski approach lane. Behind, the railway reappears and the main road becomes the A3022.

The best surf at Hollicombe is on the lower half of the tide with an easterly wind. The village was used for filming *The French Lieutenant's Woman.*

The entrance to Torquay, at the heart of the English Riviera.

Towers was set here. There was also a pottery noted for its forgeries. Torbay Festival of Poetry is jointly hosted by Torquay and Brixham in October.

Torre has one of three remaining pumping stations for Brunel's atmospheric South Devon Railway from Exeter. Better known is Torre Abbey, founded in 1196 by Premonstratensian canons, the wealthiest abbey in England for four centuries, converted to a manor in 1600 and now housing the town's art gallery with an Agatha Christie room. The land may have been given by William de Brewer, lord of the manor, in thanks for the safe return of his son who went to Austria with other hostages to secure the release of Richard the Lionheart. Its tithe Spanish Barn was used in 1588 to hold 397 prisoners from *Nuestra Señora del Rosario* which foundered in the bay and from which the ghost of a Spanish woman dressed as a boy is sometimes seen in the lane. Also remaining are the 12th century entrance to the chapter house, the early 14th century gatehouse, the Palm House and grounds with golf, tennis and bowling plus a model world display including an animated circus.

Beyond Hollicombe Head is the 115 room Oldway Mansion, built by American sewing machine inventor Isaac Singer as his Victorian dream palace. It was extended by his son in the style of the Versailles Hall of Mirrors with marble grand staircase and gallery, vaulted painted ceiling, ballroom with silver mirrors, 7ha of grounds by Duchesne, Italian garden, two lakes, waterfall, rock gardens, lawns and woods. It is now used as offices by the council, the accounts doubtless done with mirrors, and was used for filming *Isadora.*

In red stone, Kirkham House is rather older, 14th century, but not as old as the church which has Saxon foundations on a Bronze Age site.

In this part of Torbay the surf is best on the lower half of the tide with winds from the east and northeast. There may be a launch fee. **Paignton** has an esplanade and a Victorian pier of 1879. It was a Bronze Age settlement, then Saxon and a fishing village built on saltmarshes and dunes until the 19th century when it became a resort with a red sandy beach safe for children. It still has crabbers and hosts Paignton Festival in July. It was used by

Fishcombe Point, Brixham breakwater and Berry Head.

the BBC for filming *Sleeping Murder*. Paignton Harbour, on the north side of Roundham Head, has pleasure craft, guided by a red 5m metal light column.

The most conspicuous aspect of Goodrington Sands are the waterslides with Spashdown Quaywest claimed to be the UK's only outdoor water park. Surf is best on the lower half of the tide with easterly winds. A steam train, complete with observation car, might be seen on the Dartmouth Steam Railway as it climbs past **Goodrington** and Saltern Cove with its caravan park. Saltern Cove's SSSI is the only one in the country to extend below low water, for a futher 380m. Hercule Poirot used the train in *The ABC Murders* and *Dead Man's Folly*.

There are country walks marked around the red sandy beach at Broadsands, where surf is best on the lower half of tides with northeasterly winds. Elberry Cove, below a golf course, has a pebble beach with a submarine freshwater spring and a waterski approach lane. It was where Sir Carmichael Clark met his death in *The ABC Murders*. Churston station featured in that book and as Nassecombe Station in *Dead Man's Folly*. Lines of large red and blue buoys stretch out across the southern side of the bay. A wooded hillside extends past Fishcombe Point to Churston Cove.

Brixham Battery was built in 1940, now the Battery Gardens and Brixham Battery Heritage Centre museum. There have been nine centuries of fishing from **Brixham**, named after the Old Englishman Boerhtsige and in existence in 1086. For three hundred years it was the premier English fishing port as a result of perfecting the Brixham trawler, which reigned supreme with up to 300 present before the First World War when steam replaced sail. Goldfinger used one and *The Snow Goose* makes reference to them being attacked in the Dunkirk evacuation. In the late 18th century Brixham was the centre for the Channel fleet and also one for smugglers. It has yachts in a marina as much as fishing vessels these days, although a 1940s trawler is popular since conversion to a replica of Drake's *Golden Hind*. There is a statue of William of Orange who landed by invitation of Protestants in 1688 with 15,000 Dutch forces to claim the throne from James II in the Glorious Revolution. Painters are attracted in numbers and the Brixham Pirate Festival takes place in May.

After a report by James Rendell in 1836, the 910m Victoria Breakwater was built between 1843 and 1916 of limestone blocks from Berry Head, faced with jointed masonry on the outside only and topped with a 6m white light tower. The slipway on the pebble Breakwater Beach was built by the Americans for the Second World War invasion of France.

Shoalstone Beach of shingle has a seawater pool near Shoalstone Point.

There is a lookout point at Berry Head. In 1967 the coastguard here reported a UFO at 500m over Brixham, domed in shape with a door in the side, which climbed rapidly and disappeared but not before it had been seen by many other people.

Berry Head has nearly vertical limestone cliffs. In a Devonian limestone quarry on top have been found arrowheads, scrapers, coins and many remains from the Stone Age, Iron Age and Romans. A fort for 1,000 men was located on the top, begun in the American War of Independence to deter attacks by the Americans and French, and Napoléon dined here, the only time he set foot on English soil. A Royal Observer Corps post was set up during the Second World War and in the late 1950s an underground Cold War monitoring station was added.

Contorted rock strata near Berry Head.

Replica Golden Hind *at Brixham.*

Britain's smallest and highest lighthouse is on Berry Head.

The white light tower of 1906 is the shortest in Britain at 5m but the highest, the light 58m above sea level on the cliff, from which a 45m shaft descends to house the pendulum which turned the light. A mast completes the major structures but Berry Head Country Park has a nature reserve with white rock rose, pelitory of the wall, navelwort, rusty back fern, rock sea lavender, goldilocks aster, honeywort, gentian, small hare's ear, small rest harrow, shags and breeding kittiwakes, razorbills, fulmars and herring gulls with zoom cameras hidden on the cliffs covering them for visitors. There are overfalls off the head, a 30m long cave and conger eels. Further off

Cave system at Durl Head.

Rock carving by P Jackson in 1933 near Sharkham Point.

Also near Sharkham Point, fine quartz intrusions into the rock.

is the point where pilots are picked up for the English Channel, North Sea and Skagerrak.

To Inner Froward Point the cliffs are 120m high. There is a tunnel through Durl Head after Cod Rock. Above St Mary's Bay are caravans and the hospital which became the home of the Henry Francis Lyte, where he wrote the hymn *Abide With Me*. A Pontin's holiday village is here plus a landslip. Surf is best on the lower half of the tide with easterly winds.

Tor Bay Harbour authority ends at Sharkham Point just before Mudstone Ledge runs out and Torbay returns to Devon.

Apart from compass jellyfish, the coast now becomes much more lonely and dramatic where huge slabs of rock have delaminated and slid away. Beyond Southdown Cliff, Man Sands, with a large limekiln, also have their best surf on the bottom half of the tide with an easterly wind before Crabrock Point, as does the pebble beach of Scabbacombe Sands, used by naturists, before Scabbacombe Head. There is an old limekiln on the beach at Man Sands.

Ivy Cove comes before the much larger Pudcombe Cove where, during his early kayak circumnavigation, Geoff Hunter twice saw a fish go 3m across the surface of the water while travelling vertically on its tail. The mood of the area is dramatic. Above are the gardens of Coleton Fishacre, designed in 1925 for Rupert and Lady Dorothy D'Oyly Carte in the Arts & Crafts tradition with luxuriant, rare and exotic plants, gazebo and water features.

Eastern Black Rock or East Blackstone stands off the cove, followed after Outer Froward Point by the guano covered Mew Stone. Inner Froward Point was the site of the Second World War Brownstone Battery. Newfoundland Cove is overlooked by a day beacon which marks the mouth of the River Dart. Castle Ledge runs out from well east of Kingswear Castle. Flows are ingoing from HW Dover +0100 until HW Dover −0520. Off the entrance the flows are southwest from HW Dover −0100 and northeast from HW Dover +0540 at up to 3km/h, but there can be a northwesterly eddy across the entrance from HW Dover +0100 until HW Dover +0540. Cruise liners enter the river. On the far side the estuary tapers out from Blackstone Point to Combe Point where the Dancing Beggars feature an arch and a blowhole.

Above Leonard's Cove is Stoke Fleming where the high St Peter's church tower forms a significant navigation mark, the church in existence by 1272, the graveyard containing railway engineer George Parker Bidder. Green Dragon landlord Peter Crowther wrote *Single-handed Sailing* in Galway Blazer, a boat he event-

The Mew Stone off Outer Froward Point.

Scabbacombe Head runs out next to Scabbacombe Sands.

Rock arch near Stoke Fleming.

Matthew's Point at the end of Blackpool Sands beach.

Pilchard Cove begins the long beach round Start Bay.

A379 storm damage in 2018.

ually lost during a transatlantic race. Blackpool Sands is a resort with pines and rhododendrons, a recently restored subtropical garden with southern hemisphere species, windsurfers, a selection of hire sit on top kayaks and what were voted the best beach toilets in England. It is not obviously a submarine cable landing point nor clear that the Bretons landed here in 1404 in order to attack **Dartmouth** but were defeated.

From Matthew's Point to Pilchard Cove at Strete is a final length of low cliff studded with caves, the beach in front used by naturists and Strete has a naturist campsite. Like Slapton, it was evacuated for the wartime training.

Slapton Sands then sweep round the back of Start Bay. A woodland walk at Strete Gate, with its steep flint shingle beach, is where the Gara ceases to have a clear watercourse and subsides into the marsh of the Higher Ley.

In Slapton the 14th and 15th century Grade I church of St James the Great has a medieval broached spire on a Norman tower. One of the great in the congregation was the wife of Admiral Sir Richard Hawkins, Lady Judith, who had two black servants to unroll a red carpet in front of her as she went to church. She died in 1629 and was buried in a tomb with a full length oak screen. There is a field centre in the village, the major feature of interest being Slapton Ley, a lagoon cut off by Slapton Sands with the A379 running in front, closed for an extended period after 5m storm waves washed away part of the road in 2018. The lagoon is a nature reserve and has a nature trail at the northern end. It is the 3,000 year old largest natural freshwater lake in the country, covering 1.1km^2, a reed fringed bird sanctuary with water lilies, yellow irises, herons, terns, mallards, great crested grebes, swans, breeding coots, a winter wildfowl roost, otters, pike and perch as well as being a boating lake. In the 16th century Slapton was reached over a drawbridge. There are two limekilns, 19th century fish cellars and a carpark in a former shipyard. The cellars were converted to the Royal Sands Hotel but this was destroyed in 1940 when a passing dog set off 6 coastal defence mines. Seven villages in the area were evacuated to allow it to be used as a practice area for American troops for the D-Day landings in 1943/4 because it resembled Utah beach. A Sherman DD tank monument remembers 746 Americans killed when 30,000 of them on Exercise Tiger from Lyme Regis were intercepted by German E-boats, more being shot by their own side, D-Day nearly being cancelled as it was feared 10 missing men may have been picked up by the Germans and interrogated, revealing the plan. A further 200 were injured. An exercise here featured in EM Nathanson's *The Dirty Dozen*.

The road was built in 1856 and has been protected in part by low profile sheet piling defences since 1918. In the winter of 2001 the sea broke through the Slapton Line and locals fought for the road to be adequately protected, fearing that the council approach of soft defences would result in the closure of the road.

The seawall in Torcross was built in 1980 after previous defences were damaged. The whole of the bay suffers a heavy dump with easterly winds. Torcross is very

Torcross with its hotel.

conspicuous from the north, particularly because of the pale hotel. Inland from Limpet Rocks is a mast.

Beesands, from bay sands, is a fishing village with shellfish processing. The Skerries Bank offshore provides protection with the sea breaking on it, especially at the southwest end in bad weather. There is an inside passage but there can be broken water all the way to the coast to Tinsey Head with strong easterly winds.

When Devonport dockyard was being extended a source of gravel was needed and it was decided to take it from off Beesands and Hallsands. Dredging started in 1897 and 650,000t was removed before protests by the local fishermen at the effects on the seabed managed to stop the work but the damage had already been done. Hallsands, built on a raised beach, began to be affected immediately but a combination of high spring tides and an easterly storm in January 1917 destroyed 29 of the 30 houses in the village, just a few pieces of wall remaining at the foot of the cliffs. The village has been rebuilt further inland and is used for waterskiing and sub aqua. A wooden sentry box was used by the mullet spotter for the village. Two radio masts stand on the top of the ridge.

Start Point, described in *A Pair of Blue Eyes*, has five 60m hillocks like a cockscomb, near the end being an 1836 battlemented Grade II lighthouse with a 28m white round granite tower with its light 62m above the water, attracting night birds. Many birds, especially migrants, come to the nature reserve. In 1989 the fog signal building collapsed because of coastal erosion.

There is a race off the point with strong streams in the area, refracted round the point. With a northeasterly flow there is an eddy close to the northern side of the point from HW Dover +0540 to HW Dover −0240. Five ships were claimed by the rocks at Start Point in a single night in 1891.

There are coloured old hard schists to Bolt Tail with dissected rock platform and 6km of raised beach, limpets, anemones, sea pinks and blue spring squill on the cliffs to Prawle Point in April. Sleaden Rocks at the west end of Ravens Cove are a favourite place for seals to haul out.

Lannacombe Bay has its best surf on the bottom half of the tide with a southerly wind while Woodcombe Sand offers the best landing in those conditions.

At Langerstone Point, Brimpool Rocks feature a number of large rockpools. East Prawle is not too far away but it is a section of coast where there are not many people.

Prawle Point is a prominent gneiss headland with Arch Rock on the end, a heavy swell and a race off it. Prawle is Old English for lookout, the lookout point operated by Coastwatch. Local birds include cirl buntings, gannets, great skuas and herring gulls.

There is a passage inside the island at high water and some carelessly parked pieces of a large Russian freighter below Signalhouse Point, being towed to the breakers when deposited here, to be subject to other breakers. Beyond Elender Cove and Gammon Head with its bluebells and ferns the porky analogies continue with the Ham Stone and Pig's Nose, near which is a historic wreck with a 300m radius restricted area. A whitewashed lookout has a conical thatched roof.

The Kingsbridge Estuary is a drowned valley without any significant rivers feeding it. Possibly it was once the estuary of the Avon, which now flows further west. The swell breaks heavily on the Bar at low water or with an easterly to southerly wind against the ebb, thought to be the inspiration for Tennyson's *Crossing the Bar*. This is where 13 of the 15 members of the Salcombe lifeboat were drowned in 1913. The ebb runs to 6km/h between a battery and Splatcove Point towards the castle at **Salcombe** and this should have added to its defensive position, although it is now a yachting centre. The entrance is best avoided with any swell during the ebb.

Sharpitor has a warm microclimate so it can sustain 2ha of rare plants and shrubs with magnolias, palms,

Remains of Hallsands, once a village of 30 houses by a beach.

Start Point, a low but strategic headland.

camphor trees, bananas, figs, flax and other subtropical species. Overbecks Museum in an Edwardian house has local shipbuilding models, shipwrights' tools, photographs, fossils, shells, birds' eggs, butterflies, handcuffs, a 19th century polyphon, precursor to the jukebox, an electrical rejuvenating machine and drawings by scientist Otto Overbeck. A transmission mast stands back from Splatcove Point.

The Great Eelstone overhangs at Sharp Tor with

Sleaden Rocks with a seal basking.

Prawle Point with its Arch Rock and lookout.

Pieces of ship on the rocks west of Prawle Point.

Gammon Head with Bolt Head across the Kingsbridge Estuary.

Thurlestone Rock, a natural arch in the centre of the bay.

Hope Cove, the first bolt hole after Bolt Head to Bolt Tail.

Model of the Herzogen Cecilie in the Ship Inn, Porlock.

its rock pinnacle and stare hole. To the west of the Range is Starehole Bay, used by divers and by waterskiers who cut close to other boats in their area. The Mew Stone, Little Mew Stone and a race are found off Bolt Head with its concrete lookout, from where dark cliffs run to Bolt Tail. Off Cove and Steeple Cove are two of the larger indentations at the foot of the Warren. In 1936 the Ham Stone claimed the Finnish barque *Herzogen Cecilie*, one of the last sailing ships to be wrecked off the British coast. In 2002 some of the beaches disappeared, together with pieces of engine lying on them.

Soar Mill Cove can offer a sheltered landing at high water but its location is hard to spot from the sea and

The thatched village of Outer Hope.

it breaks across the entrance with a southern swell.

The 120m high Bolberry Down was fortified in the Iron Age. In 1760 27 people of a crew of 800 survived when the *Ramillies* dragged her anchors and went down, one of many wrecks in this area. There is a cave in the approach to Redrot Cave. Bolt Tail is a prominent headland with another Iron Age fort.

Burgh Island with the sea tractor on the causeway.

The coast continues mostly high, precipitous and rocky to Thurlestone Rock, but the streams are weak in Bigbury Bay. Hope Cove, Hardy's Church Hope, offers a selection of sheltered landings on protected beaches remote enough for smugglers and was used in 1903 by Gladys Gradeley to finish the first west–east solo crossing of the Atlantic by a woman. In 1588 many Armada sailors came ashore from the wreck of the *San Pedro el Major* but 40 people were drowned at Hope Key in 1620. Spanish coins have been found in recent years. The village is popular with divers.

Beyond Inner Hope and Outer Hope the Great Ledge begins. Thurlestone Rock, from the Saxon torlestone, pierced stone, has a hole through but can look like a wreck and was painted by Turner. There is also a real wreck. Leas Foot Sand is sheltered and Thurlestone has a beach of coarse sand. Above Loam Castle and Butter Cove is Thurlestone Golf Course. This rocky section of coast is popular with naturists.

Popular with surfers is Bantham, one of the best surfing beaches on the south coast and in the southwest, cleaner on the flood. It is used by windsurfers, board surfers, kite surfers and kayaks. It is surrounded by marram covered sand dunes. The bay forms the eastern side of the estuary of the River Avon, the mouth of which can close out.

Much of this is applicable to Bigbury-on-Sea at the end of the B3392 where there is small to medium surf at most times, supported by the Venus Café and toilets.

A covering sand causeway runs out to Burgh Island, with a sea tractor on long legs making the crossing to and from the Pilchard Inn at high water. There tends to be clapotis where the waves meet along the line of the causeway after coming round each side of the island, presumably its cause. Murray's Rock shelters at the eastern end of Burgh Island, which is known to fishermen as St Michael's Rock as there is a small ruined chapel of 1411 to St Michael on the summit. In the 18th century this was converted to a pilchard huer's lookout, the island having an important pilchard fishery. The 1395 Pilchard Inn has a smuggler's ghost and there were 18th and 19th century smugglers, fireplace carvings showing Tom Crocker, both a smuggler and an excise officer. Wrecking went on and in 1772 the *Chanteloup* from the West Indies was wrecked on the island. The only survivor put on her jewels and swam to the shore where she was killed by the mob who cut off her fingers and ears for the jewels and buried her in the sand.

The island is a herring gull nesting site. In the 1920s Agatha Christie stayed, using it as Smugglers' Island in

Distinctive knob near Warren Point with Burgh Island and Bigbury-on-Sea beyond.

Evil Under the Sun and as the island in the book reissued as *And Then There Were None*, the all time best selling mystery novel. In 1946 it was bought by millionaire Archibald Nettlefold of GKN, not his best investment as he built a 40 room luxury Art Deco hotel with a pool and then sold it at a considerable loss. It was visited by Noël Coward, Edward and Mrs Simpson, the Mountbattens, Josephine Baker, Amy Johnson and Gertie Lawrence. The BBC filmed the *Miss Marple Nemesis* episode here.

On the north side of Warren Point, Challaborough Bay is a sandy cove with the best surf when the wind is between south and northeast. Ayrmer Cove, Westcombe Beach and other smaller inlets are relatively secluded but with persistent people on foot able to reach them. Near vertical slabs of exposed rock look almost like chalk from the distance because they reflect so much light. At sea level there are increasing numbers of reefs, the rocks becoming really vicious with sharp edged strata nearly vertical, especially around Meddrick Rocks where there is a blowhole.

After Beacon Point is the small rock fringed Ferny-combe Beach and then the mouth of the River Erme, on the far side of which is Battisborough Island, the channel inside it with angular stacks and sides so straight they appear to have been artificially cut. At Erme Mouth Mothecombe Beach is private and may only be used at weekends and on Wednesdays, there being surf at low water with moderate onshore winds and landing difficult with a heavy swell. There are two historic wrecks in the lower estuary.

Past Gull Cove, Butcher's Cove, St Anchorite's Rock, Blackaterry Point, Wadham Rocks and Ivy Island the shoreline remains rocky and inhospitable. Beacon Hill

has a ruined coastguard lookout point on top. There are many caravans behind Stoke Beach, which is sheltered from the west and southwest but exposed to the east, but footpaths to the nearest public parking require climbing a steep hillside, on which is the redundant Grade I restored 12th century church of St Peter the Poor Fisherman.

Stoke Point with its disused lookout point begins some 5km of isolated reef fringed coast, the rocks not high but not accessible, either, in any swell, the hillside rising behind. There is a ruined signal station and Warren Cottage, overlooking Hilsea and Blackstone Points, is conspicuously isolated.

Gara Point is at the end of the River Yealm, discharging into Wembury Bay, a yachting centre. In strong southwesterly winds the mouth of the bay closes out and the sea also breaks over the irregular ground within the bay. Flows are outgoing from HW Dover –0520 to 5km/h, setting north of the Great Mew Stone, and ingoing from HW Dover +0100 to 3km/h.

Wembury Marine Conservation Area operates inside a line bounded by Gara Point, the Little Mewstone, the Shag Stone and Fort Bovisand while there is a Special Area of Conservation north of the line from Gara Point to Rame Head.

There is surf at all states of the tide with northwesterly to easterly winds, best on the lower half of the tide, particularly for lefts off the slate Blackstone Rocks although surf is smaller than at Bantham.

Wembury has been occupied since Mesolithic times, as shown by flint tool finds, and has a marine centre, a 19th century Old Mill Café and St Werburgh's church which was probably built to guide sailors into the estuary. The village also has toilets and a National Trust carpark which overlooks the beach.

Patriotic rocks in red, white and blue near Toby's Point.

Distance
91km from Dawlish Warren to Wembury

OS 1:50,000 Sheets
192 Exeter & Sidmouth
201 Plymouth & Launceston
202 Torbay & South Dartmoor

Tidal Constants
Exmouth Approaches:
HW Dover –0500,
LW Dover –0530
Teignmouth Bar:
HW Dover –0500,
LW Dover –0530
Torquay:
HW Dover –0500,
LW Dover –0540
Brixham:
HW Dover –0510,
LW Dover –0530
Dartmouth:
HW Dover –0520,
LW Dover –0540
Start Point:
HW Dover –0520,
LW Dover –0530
Salcombe:
Dover –0540
River Avon Bar:
Dover –0540
River Yealm Entrance:
HW Dover –0530,
LW Dover –0540

Submarine Area
D009

Sea Areas
Portland, Plymouth

Connection
River Dart –
see RoB p285

The dead straight channel inside Battisborough Island at the mouth of the Erme.

37 Southeast Cornwall

Warships ancient and modern

O the Harbour of Fowey
Is a beautiful spot,
And it's there I enjowey
To sail in a yot;
Or to race in a yacht
Round a mark or a buoy –
Such a beautiful spacht
Is the Harbour of Fuoy!
Arthur Quiller–Couch

to Bovisand Bay which has its best surf at half tide with a southwesterly swell. Fort Bovisand was a 19th century coastal defence, now proposed for conversion to apartments. Users of the Sound include compass jellyfish.

Plymouth Breakwater, described in *A Pair of Blue Eyes*, occupies the centre of the Sound but is not connected to the land to avoid trapping silt. Designed in 1811 by Rennie, it was completed in 1841. With a crest 600mm above high water, it has no protective top wall. It defends against gales. Landing requires the permission of the Queen's Harbour Master although there are 4 stone

The Great Mew Stone, seen over the beach at Wembury.

Fort Bovisand on the right with Plymouth lost in the summer heat haze over the eastern end of Plymouth breakwater.

At Wembury divers in the clear water see sea fans and wrasse. Above them are cormorants, oystercatchers, blackbacked gulls and herring gulls as well as swallows.

Off Wembury Point the Great Mew Stone rises 60m to a sharp apex, painted by Turner. Landing is best at the northeast end at low water when there is some sand exposed but there are breaking waves in heavy weather and conditions are worst at half ebb with southwesterly winds. Residents lived rent free on the 1.2ha island in the past but had to provide fish and rabbits for the landlord. The most successful was Sam Wakeham who, with his wife and two children, took out tourists by boat and provided them with porter, tea, eggs, ham, biscuits, cabbage and rabbits. One of the visitors in 1837 was an exciseman who exposed the smuggling and found the caves and hiding places. Sam was not replaced on the island.

At Heybrook Bay a tidal causeway runs out to the quartzite Renney Rocks, on which a heron might be quietly fishing. The Shag Stone is a little further out, located by a striped mark. This forms the start of the Dockyard Port of Plymouth. Andurn Bay leads

shelters along its 1.6km length. A light beacon at the east end has a ball topmark which doubles as a shipwreck rescue centre, able to hold six people. In the centre is the Breakwater Fort with a landing pier

The lighthouse on the western end of the breakwater. Fort Picklecombe is conspicuous below Mount Edgcumbe Country Park.

on the north side while a 23m white round granite tower lighthouse is located at the west end.

The Sound, the mouths of the drowned valleys of the Plym and Tamar, is the boundary between Devon and Cornwall. **Plymouth** is 3km inland, its dome and Smeaton's Tower on the Hoe at the waterfront.

Warships and auxiliaries carry out training operations with unusual manoeuvres, especially to the north of the breakwater, using both entrances, 0730–0830 on weekdays being usual except in August. The main channel west of the breakwater has warships sometimes opening up full throttle once clear of the breakwater. On the other hand, small boats may be towed out of the way to leave a clear path for nuclear submarines. Other users include car ferries from Roscoff and Santander and increasing numbers of cruise liners. There can be a scum left on the water.

It was also the route used in 1588 by Drake to defeat the Spanish Armada, having first finished his game of bowls on the Hoe. Had he failed in his mission, Spanish admiral Don Alonso Perez de Guzman, Duke of Medina Sidona, planned to live at Mount Edgcumbe after his conquest. A horseman reporting the arrival of the Armada was to have been included in the play in *Mapp & Lucia*. The 3.5km² Mount Edgcumbe Country Park was the earliest landscaped garden in Cornwall, a Grade I historic garden, one of the most beautiful in England, impressing both Dr Johnson and Queen Victoria, with parkland, formal English, French, Italian, American and New Zealand gardens, the International Camellia Society's collection, bracken, gorse, woodland set above red cliffs, a deer park, lakes, Milton's Temple, a ruined folly, a shell grotto, chapels, an 18th century orangery, a Napoloenic battery, coastal walks and 16km of coastline, Plymouth to Whitsand being registered as

Heritage Coast. Central to this was a 1547 Tudor mansion, garrisoned for the king in the Civil War and incendiary bombed during the 1941 blitz on Plymouth. It was restored between 1958 and 1960 and is the home of the Earl of Edgcumbe, which he allowed to be used for filming *Twelfth Night*.

Fort Picklecombe at Picklecombe Point has been converted to flats, along from which is the Maker mark on the shore at the start of an area of Cawsand Bay used by waterskiers. Kingsand and Cawsand are red sandstone fishing villages, exposed to the east but sheltered to the southwest. Between them is a stream which was the national boundary between Saxon England and Celtic Cornwall, later becoming the county boundary between Devon and Cornwall until 1844. There are many pilchard cellars, mostly from the 1580s, doubtless useful for subsequent business, Cawsand having had one of the largest smuggling fleets in the West Country with 50 boats said to have been involved in 1804, bladders of brandy being smuggled into Plymouth beneath women's voluminous skirts.

Cawsand Bay has anchorages and was particularly important for this purpose before the breakwater was built, as used in *A Ship of the Line* and RD Blackmore's *The Maid of Sker*. It was used for the killing of a black cat in *The King's Own*. It was covered by a Napoleonic fort and was used in 1815 by the ship taking Napoléon to exile in St Helena, during which Drake's drum growled. The locals foiled a rescue attempt by towing his ship out to sea, action which suggests the guarding of the world's most wanted prisoner was not all it might have been.

Penlee Battery Nature Reserve is designated above vertical red strata topped by stunted trees. At Penlee Point there are breaking waves in heavy weather, worst with southwesterly winds at half ebb. Onshore are a grotto, Queen Adelaide's chapel which was a 19th century folly,

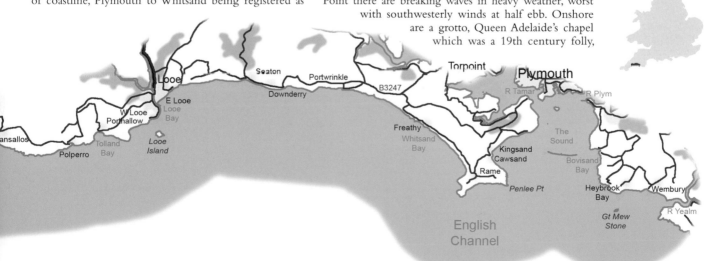

Penlee Point with Queen Adelaide's chapel folly on the skyline.

Rame Head with its chapel on top.

and a Napoleonic battery. There are two historic wrecks just west of the point, one onshore and HMS *Coronation* about a kilometre out. Cuttlefish bones may also be found washed up.

Above Lillery's Cove is the 13th century St Germanus church, lit by candles and with a stone spire. A radio mast stands on top of the 12m cliffs of Rame Head, which has breaking waves in heavy weather, worst with southwesterly winds at half ebb. This added to the impregnability of the Iron Age fort with bulwarks built across the neck of the head, a site where flint weapons were produced. A later structure is the ruined St Michael's chapel of 1397 on the probable site of a Celtic hermitage which had a blazing beacon by 1486 and a watchman to bring news of raiders or returning fleets. A National Coastwatch lookout performs a comparable function today from a lookout at the end of the Dockyard Port of Plymouth. Rame Head being beyond the point of no return, and 17 year old John Stevens had been intercepted off Plymouth while trying to get to the First World War in France.

Important though it was to mark the head, there was always a toll of shipping lost to the Eddystone Rocks out to sea. The history of the Eddystone light is one of drama. The first was built by Winstanley in 1698 and rebuilt by him the following year. He said he would like to spend a night in it in the worst possible weather. How much of his wish he got will never be known because he was in it on a November night in 1703 when it was struck by the worst night of storm ever recorded in Britain. In the morning the lighthouse and Winstanley had gone. It was followed by the Rudyard Tower of 1706 which caught fire in 1755. The 1759 Smeaton Tower was the first of modern shape, based on the trunk of an oak tree, and the first to use dovetailed stones to lock to adjacent stones to the sides, the ends, above and below. Labourers were issued with Eddystone Medals to protect them against press gangs. The lighthouse survived but the foundation became unsafe and it was dismantled and rebuilt on Plymouth Hoe in 1879 as a monument. It had such respect that it was shown on the reverse of the penny coin with Britannia and is the one structure featured on the coat of arms of the Institution of Civil Engineers. The Douglas Tower of 1832, for which Douglas was knighted, is a 49m grey granite tower with a 27km range, automated in 1982 and now with a helicopter platform on top.

Off Queener Point is a spoil dumping ground, previously used for explosives. The National Maritime Museum bought the decommissoned warship HMS *Scylla* which has been sunk off Whitsand Bay as Europe's first artificial reef, also to be a diving centre. Surf eases going westwards.

Cliffs vary between 30 and 80m in height behind Whitsand Bay, cliffs of pink, purple and green slates. Butterflies go well out to sea while mackerel, shrimps and

The Napoleonic Tregantle Fort looks down on Long Sands and Tregantle Cliff in Whitsand Bay.

mussels are found inshore. There is a wreck off Captain Blake's Point, one of many which have met their ends here. Swimming can also be difficult and there is a cross at Tregonhawke for three family members drowned in 1878. Surf is generally best on the bottom half of the tide with a fast break but at Tregantle Cliffs it works at high water.

Beyond Freathy, Sharrow Point has the Sharrow Grotto, built in 1784 by James Lugger as a cure for gout.

Tregantle Rifle Ranges are a danger area with black and white beacons at the ends but firing is supposed to stop for passing boats. The 1860s Tregantle Fort was built by French prisoners during the Napoleonic Wars, after which Tregantle Barracks were built as a national monument. It housed over 1,000 staff and more than 30 big guns. An unusual aerial takes the form of a huge horizontal ring suspended above the cliffs. Long Sands have their best surf on the bottom half of the tide with a fast break when the ranges are not in use.

A golf course leads to Portwrinkle where the Whitsand Bay Hotel was rebuilt, having been moved brick by brick from **Torpoint** in 1909. The fishing harbour was first built in 1600 for pilchard boats but it was destroyed by

a storm in 1882. There is a pier with a stone beacon to the east of the entrance and the walls of pilchard cellars can be seen. The surf works at low water on big swells with wind from the northwest but it is smaller than in Whitsand Bay.

Smuggler Silas Finny was an 18th century smuggler who shopped his colleagues after an argument. Several of them were deported and he was murdered. His ghost or gook still causes problems and some people avoid the hill between crafthole and Portwrinkle during the night.

Beyond the Brawn and the Long Stone the beach below Battern Cliffs is used by naturists. The land is also being stripped away and at Downderry the ends of seafront gardens are showing marked scour. On the B3247, Downderry developed from a fishing village, above which is an aerial and where the warm climate allows the growth of palm trees.

The River Seaton enters at Seaton where there is a café by the beach. The surf, which is smaller than in Whitsand Bay, works from low to mid tide but there can be a vicious dump in bad weather.

There are further slips at Keveral Beach. There is a bat cave, Victorian herbalists' flower garden, wild flower

Portwrinkle stands at the end of Whitsand Bay.

Working the pots near the Brawn off the Long Stone.

Holidaymakers pack the beach at Seaton.

Millendreath beach with its holidaymakers.

Flying butresses southwest of Millendreath.

meadows to encourage such butterflies as the pearl bordered fritillary and a grass labyrinth.

Colmer Rocks and Bodigga Cliff lead to Millendreath, possibly with some low tide surf, after which there are unusual flying buttresses and commoner flying black-headed gulls plus an aquarium.

Looe, Cornish for pool, is formed by East and West Looe, divided by the East Looe River below its confluence with the West Looe River. It was recorded in 1086. Until the 14th century it was one of the busiest ports in the southwest and in the 19th century was used for exporting copper ore from north of Liskeard. It was a fishing port noted for the fast luggers it built. The earliest major estuary bridge in Devon and Cornwall connected them in 1411, replaced by a Victorian one of seven arches. Victorian holidaymakers resulted in significant expansion of the village.

The Old Guildhall Museum & Gaol with the village's maritime past, smuggling, pilchard industry, lifeboat, old port, Cornish life, culture, arts, crafts and local history is housed in the Old Guildhall of about 1450. The Smuggler's Cott of about 1430 was reputed to have used Armada timbers for its reconstruction in 1595 and there are the remains of a smuggling tunnel from the quay. Looe Music Festival takes place in September and the locals apppear in fancy dress for New Year celebrations.

The two halves of the village were combined in 1593 but each continued to have two MPs until 1832. In 1852 it was visited by Wilkie Collins, who described it in *Rambles Beyond Railways*. It is still a fishing village with pleasure craft and is the headquarters for shark angling. Flows in the rivermouth are to 9km/h in either direction and a red flag is flown when conditions outside the harbour have become unsuitable or the ebb has started. At the entrance is the unique Banjo Pier with a light on

Natural rock diving platforms at East Looe.

The mouth of the East Looe River.

Looe Island stands off Hannafore Point.

a red 6m metal column. The old church tower used to be whitewashed as a sea mark. Nelson, a seal lacking one eye, was a regular visitor, now recalled by a statue. Looe Bay has surf with strong southwesterlies.

Cliffs to Falmouth are cut in killas slate. After Hannafore Point the last house at Hannafore was a Celtic monk's cell with slit windows.

Looe Island, also known as St George's, St Michael's or St Nicholas', is the largest island close to the Cornish coast. Rising to 46m and covering 9ha, it can be reached on foot on extreme spring tides. It was bombed during the Second World War by a pilot who mistook it for a British warship, the Germans reporting the sinking of the battleship *St George*. The remains of a chapel on top from at least 1139 when Benedictine monks were present are said to commemorate a visit by Joseph of Arimathea and the young Jesus on their way to Glastonbury with the Holy Grail, the chapel being under the see of Glastonbury. The presence of smugglers and treasure caves, reputedly connected by passages to the mainland, is more likely, even more so the suggestion that there were many rabbits and rats from ships wrecked on the Ranneys, but locals caught most of them in the 19th century for food. Amram Hooper was the best known resident pirate. Black Joan, the attractive sister of another smuggler, would row out to waylay excise officers to give her brother time to hide contraband. There are tunnels and a map which shows where treasure is buried. Evelyn Atkins described the venue in *We Bought an Island* and *Tales from Our Cornish Island*. Today there is a daffodil farm which has grown 15 varieties earlier than the rest of the British growers and a month ahead of Hannafore on the mainland. There is a pottery and folk craft centre but landing requires the owners' permission. They also own the foreshore rights below high water, sold in 1873 by the Prince of Wales to pay a gambling debt. Semi-precious stones on the beach include banded and moss agate, cornelian, amethyst, rose quartz, topaz and mother of pearl.

Black and white striped pairs of beacons establish a measured distance for speed trials but on a bearing significantly different from that likely to be followed

Rocks covered with lichen and thrift face the Hore Stone.

Looking across Talland Bay to Downend Point.

Polperro, the most photographed harbour in the country.

by a boat inshore, especially if crossing Portnadler Bay and turning round the Hore Stone and across Æsop's Bed into Talland Bay, which was popular with Victorian trippers from Plymouth and has been used by modern smugglers. In the 18th century Parson Dodge of Talland was a notable exorcist, including ridding Lanreath of a spectral coach and headless horses. Such was his reputation that people were afraid of meeting him driving evil spirits down to the sea at night, a benefit being that it left the way clear for his associates bringing spirits the other way, together with tea and tobacco from Guernsey. John Wesley did not approve when he visited. Privateering was also a significant trade. In the early 19th century Zephaniah Job was a ringleader, set up a local bank and rebuilt the harbour after storm damage. Smuggling resulted in the setting up of the Preventative Service, forerunners of HM Customs & Excise. The tall tower of St Tallanus' church by a prominent caravan site is separate from the Grade I church but connected by a passage, the church being noted for its fine bench ends and the graveyard for its beautifully engraved slate headstones.

There is parking behind the rocks at Porthallow and this can be important as cars are barred from Polperro and also Polruan with no road access between, making this an unnecessarily committing section. Polperro has a tram, actually a minibus, which carries passengers to and from Crumplehorn.

A granite cross on Downend Point below Brent is a war memorial while a light on a 3m white concrete pillar on Spy House Point marks the entrance to Polperro. The fishing village of St Peter's pool is sheltered by two piers, one with a light on a 3m post and both having needed replacing from time to time. It has yachts as well as crab and lobster boats with mackerel and shark fishing having replaced pilchards. Southerly or southeasterly winds or a groundswell make the entrance dangerous so it is closed by a 1978 storm gate, indicated by a black ball or a red light. The great storm of 1824 destroyed houses, breakwaters and about 50 boats. Saxons and Romans both built bridges here. Buildings include the House on Props over the water, built from timbers from the *Maverine* which sank in the harbour at the start of the

The cliff at Nealand Point threatens to fall.

A Dutch sailing vessel slips out of Polruan. Note the blockhouse, one of a pair which held a chain across the harbour at one time.

18th century. Couch's Great House of 1595 is a restaurant and the Old Watch House is also present. *Memories & Opinions* notes that Jonathan Couch, grandfather of the author, at the age of 69 married for a second time, 22 year old Sarah Roose subsequently producing him three daughters. Polperro Heritage Museum of Smuggling & Fishing past and present is based in a cottage cellar, there is a Model Village & Land of Legend and the Shell House was coated with seashells by a retired fisherman. Polperro was discovered in 1810 by Joseph Farington of the Royal Academy and has recovered from a subsequent typhoid outbreak to become the most photographed harbour in the country. Polperro Festival takes place in June.

Beyond Peak Rock there is a TV mast on Hard Head. Below Chapel Cliff is Willie Wilcock's Hole, named after a fisherman who searched a maze of tunnels behind the entrance. His spirit stills roams the passages, seeking escape, and his cries mingle with the wind on dark nights. Near the Bridges are the remains of fish drying houses.

In quiet conditions there are routes inside the reefs to the larger Larrick Rock off the overhanging cliff at Nealand Point. Some sheltered rockpools in Colors Cove can become pleasantly warm. A white painted patch on Shag Rock lines up with a white daymark above to give a leading line which, taken with Pencarrow Head and another white mark on the other side of Lantic Bay, find Udder Rock, also protected by a cardinal light pillar.

Lansallos means ancient holy place but the mood has sometimes been less respectful. The Grade I 14th century St Ildierna's church has a medieval bell broken by drunken villagers in the 19th century and the base of the pulpit is part of a pinnacle felled by lightning in 1923. There is a smugglers' cave and waterskiing in Lantivet Bay.

Beyond 80m high Pencarrow Head, Lantic Bay is surrounded by gorse, bracken and blackberries and has moorings despite being exposed to southwesterly winds and being part of a spoil dumping ground to Blackbottle Rock. Even in the 20th century it was thought that the fishing would be spoilt by mention of rabbits.

Polruan is older than Fowey and is protected on the south and west by high cliffs, on top of which are a National Coastwatch lookout, St Saviour's church tower ruin and Headland Garden where plants withstand gales in a coastal rock garden above Washing Rocks. There is a castle ruin on Polruan Point and blockhouses had a chain across the River Fowey to protect against invaders. The harbour is on the north side of the village and the boatyard, on the site of Slade's Yard, is a reminder that the village built many wooden ships, the basis of *The Loving Spirit*.

Flows run into the River Fowey from HW Dover +0030 to 2km/h and out from HW Dover −0600 to 3km/h.

In the Middle Ages **Fowey** was one of Britain's foremost ports, in 1346 sending 47 ships and 770 Fowey Gallants for Edward III's Siege of Calais and continuing with 15th century piracy against Channel shipping although Edward IV confiscated its ships because of the ongoing piracy. It is one of Britain's finest sailing centres with 1,300 moorings but is also a china and ball clay exporting port with some surprisingly large vessels using the estuary. It was Troy Town to Sir Arthur Quiller-Couch, Q.

Wreckage in Coombe Haven.

Polridmouth, Pridmouth in The King's General.

St Catherine's Castle, now a ruin, was built in D plan for Henry VIII but had a Second World War gun battery. Near it on St Catherine's Point is the 6m, octagonal, white, St Anthony's lighthouse marking the entrance which is easy for boats to miss. In Coombe Haven is a wheel and other wreckage of a boat which got it wrong.

Southground Point shelters Polridmouth but it has a heavy swell with the prevailing wind. It was there, as Pridmouth Bay, that Du Maurier's Rebecca kept her boat and may have been where part of *The Wind in the Willows* was composed by Kenneth Graham, a friend of Q, who was supposed to have inspired Ratty. Above the inlet are decoy lakes, intended to draw German bombers away from the Fowey munitions port, and beyond them is Menabilly, home of the Rashleighs and, later, Daphne Du Maurier, central to her *The King's General* and named Manderley in *Rebecca*.

The 26m daymark of 1832 on top of Gribbin Head takes the form of a red and white striped square tower. To its

Gribbin Head with its mark.

south is Sandy Cove and the Cannis rock while to its west is the beach of Platt, exposed to southwesterly winds, the sea breaking heavily on the head in bad weather.

Gribbin Head is the start of St Austell Bay and the Cornish Riviera which continues to Dodman Point. Gorse grows around the Little Gribbin. The inner part is Tywardreath Bay,

The industrial harbour area at Par.

Distance
*54km from Wembury
to Charlestown*

OS 1:50,000 Sheets
*(200 Newquay
& Bodmin)
201 Plymouth
& Launceston
204 Truro
& Falmouth*

Tidal Constants
*River Yealm Entrance:
HW Dover −0530,
LW Dover −0540
Bovisand
HW Dover −0550,
LW Dover −0540
Whitsand Bay:
Dover −0540
Looe:
HW Dover −0550,
LW Dover −0540
Polperro:
HW Dover −0550,
LW Dover −0540
Fowey:
Dover −0550
Par: Dover −0550
Charlestown:
HW Dover −0550,
LW Dover −0540*

Range
Tregantle

Submarine Areas
D009, Whitsand Bay

Sea Area
Plymouth

Connections
*River Tamar −
see RoB p290
River Fowey − see
RoB p296*

the name translating as the house on the strand, used in its English form as a title by Du Maurier and based on her house of Kilmarth, meaning retreat of Mark and built on 14th century foundations. Nearby are the remains of a chieftain's hall, possibly King Mark of Cornwall, the uncle of Tristan. The pier at Polkerris was built in the 1730s by the Rashleighs of Menabilly with pilchard salting cellars and the largest seine house in Cornwall for processing fish oil. There is a café in the lifeboat station used from 1859 to 1914 and there is a public house in a boatshed after a previous one was swept away by the sea. There is surfing on big swells but there may be a launch fee. The village has not been developed because of the powerful influence of the Rashleighs.

Par Sands, between Little Hell and Par, are brilliant white from china clay washed in and the sea is milky white. The sands are backed by dunes designated as a nature reserve and have their best surf at mid tide.

With its 370m breakwater, Par is the busiest small port in the British Isles with up to two dozen movements on one tide, not helped by Killyvarder Rock in the middle of the bay. The docks were built in the 1820s by JT Treffry on a silting up arm of the sea to serve his clay mining operation, initially with smelting works, brickworks, pilchard fishery, shipbuilding, sail lofts, granite cutting and dressing, candle making, chandlery, limekilns, blacksmith, carpentry and flourmill, from the 1940s concentrating completely on exporting china clay and importing oil and timber. The tall chimneys of the china clay drying works are prominent, receiving clay as slurry by underground pipeline, much then being driven to Fowey along a former railway line. Some of Treffry's 3km Par Canal from Pont Mills remains but it was never extended to Padstow, the plan. In front of the A3082 the Paddington to Penzance railway makes its only appearance between Teignmouth and Penzance, Par being the nearest station to the Cornish Riviera on a line where the Cornish Riviera Express was the flagship train.

From Spit Point to Fishing Point the coast is fronted by rocks with grating fronted caves in the cliffs, then comes Polgaver beach, the only accredited naturist beach in Cornwall although the designation was withdrawn in 2000, perhaps having outlived its need as many beaches are now so used. Carlyon Bay is backed by a golf course and a resort with some surf. A new housing development on the beach resulted in a row with the Environment Agency over wave protection.

It is possible to land on the beach on the west side of the harbour entrance at Charlestown, a Georgian village mostly built between 1791 and 1800. The small harbour was constructed by Smeaton for mine owner Charles Rashleigh. Protected by a four gun battery, it had lime burning, brick making, net houses, rope making, bark houses with oak for tanning, pilchard curing, a foundry and clay brought by an underground tramway. It exported copper then china clay and imported coal, timber, iron and limestone, a mix of black and white dusts gathering. It has a tidal basin and an inner wet basin. Despite the difficult entry for coasters, the gates being widened in 1976, it imported fertilizer and general cargo and exported grain and clay, used in porcelain, rubber, plastics, paint, ink, dyes and toothpaste. It has the Charlestown Shipwreck & Heritage Centre museum with the largest exhibition in the UK of diver recovered artefacts plus naval guns and anchors outside. It features village life, shipwrecks, diving from 1740, ocean liners, remote controlled boats, lifeboat equipment, the *Titanic*, the Roland Morris Collection of Nelson artefacts and Cornish mining.

It is for its sailing ships that Charlestown is best known, though, and it is not unusual to see historical sailing ships and replicas moored out in Polmear Cove. The port has been used for filming *Poldark*, *The Onedin Line*, *Voyage of the Beagle*, *The Eagle Has Landed*, *The Three Musketeers*, *Moll Flanders*, *Frenchman's Creek*, *Mansfield Park*, *Rebecca*, *Wives & Daughters*, *A Respectable Trade*, *Pandemonium* and *The Day of the Triffids*. It seems that any self respecting film including old sailing ships also features Charlestown. Parking is back behind the port after a steep climb up the road.

Charlestown with another film set under construction.

South Central Cornwall

Semiprecious stones such as agates, citrine, carnelian, chalcedony, amethyst, serpentine and rock crystal are found along this coast.

Outside Charlestown, Duporth reaches to Carrickowel Point, site of the 18th century Crinnis Cliff Battery. On the hillside above the bay are Porthpean House Gardens, noted for their camellias, primroses and violets. Lower Porthpean, with its sailing club based in old fish cellars, was a pilchard fishing centre but is now more a place of prawns in rockpools. The best surf is with southeasterly winds but there is a registration charge. Between Phoebe's Point and Gwendra Point is Silvermine Beach, suggesting previous industry, while Ropehaven implies another trade and has fulmars nesting on the cliffs in what has been designated a nature reserve. This was a former anchorage and there are the remains of a jetty.

Black Head is bold and steep, topped by an Iron Age fort site and a block of granite in memory of poet AL Rowse, who was known as the Voice of Cornwall. A stream enters the sea as a waterfall and there are wooden statues in the woods.

Sailing ship anchored off Duporth.

Beyond Gamas Point in Mevagissey Bay is Pentewan, from the Cornish pen, headland, and towan, dunes. It had an Iron Age fort. At one time the port, begun in 1818 because of congestion in Charleston, used to ship china clay, the best church building stone in Cornwall from Polrudden quarry and tin from the Pentewan valley where the works went to 15m below sea level. A new harbour was built in the 1820s but had to be abandoned after it silted up with china clay and there is now no access from the sea, no ships trading since 1940. The beach is popular with motor boats these days and, for surfing, best with the wind from the north or northwest and a huge swell, hollow at high water although there may be a charge in the summer or a locked gate to be negotiated in the winter. There is a large caravan site.

Mevagissey, at the end of the B3273, may have been a Bronze Age settlement and takes its name from its two saints, Meva and Issey. St Peter's church is on a Saxon site, mostly 13th century with a Norman font and a 16th century north aisle of Pentewan stone. The first stone pier was built in 1430 and the village developed on pilchards, curing them in the 18th and 19th centuries for Italy and then for the Royal Navy as Mevagissey Duck. In the 19th century there were experiments in smoking pilchards and large scale curing in brine, the village being the first to can in oil. Although the village pump outside the Ship Inn was used as the village water supply because there was no mains water until 1944, in 1895 it was claimed to be the first English village to have electric lights, powered by pilchard oil generators, and the South Pierhead light on its 8m white metal tower was the first in the country to be lit by electricity. It was claimed that a local fisherman would hold out a candle to check the weather. If it blew out there was too much wind for sailing; if not, there was not enough. It was a smuggling

Black Head seen from Porthtowan.

Laid back sailing off Pentewan beach with Chapel Point beyond.

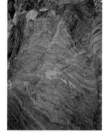

Rock strata at Porthtowan.

village, contraband mostly collected from Roscoff by cutter, and also had its wrecks. The SeaHoss is an 18th century cottage built from the recovered timbers from *The Horse*. Now it is a busy tourist resort with slate and cob whitewashed houses, shops and restaurants being established in old fish cellars. Mevagissey Feast Week is in June, Cornwall's oldest festival, since 1752. Mevagissey Museum in a 1745 boatbuilder's workshop with three ship masts as supports and ship timbers for the walls covers seafaring, boatbuilders' tools and machinery, local crafts, agriculture, mining, fishing and a Cornish kitchen with a 6 tonne granite cider press. The Wheelhouse

Mevagissey harbour at dawn.

Vault Beach leads to Dodman Point.

200

Restaurant is in a 19th century sail loft in which John Wesley was said to have preached his first sermon. There is an aquarium in an old lifeboat house and an extensive World of Model Railways. The inner and outer harbours have shell fishing and pleasure craft but there are harbour fees.

The sandy cove at Portmellon has a slip from the boatyard. Buildings have 900mm thick walls and boards to slot into gateways to keep out the sea.

Protected from the north by Chapel Point, Colona Beach has its best surf from mid to low water with an onshore wind. The cottages were built in 1930 from local stone and featured in *The House on the Strand*. It is not too accessible by land. Near Turbot Point is Bodrugan's Leap where Sir Henry Treworth of Bodrugan, a Yorkist supporter of Richard III at Bosworth who had been given land belonging to his Lancastrian neighbours, rode his horse over a cliff in 1485, pursued by Sir Richard Edgcumbe of Cothele after Henry VII became king, to reach a boat to escape to Ireland.

Compass jellyfish are in the sea around the Gwineas or Gwinges. Onshore, an earthwork and a tumulus are above the start of Great Perhaver Beach, which reaches to Gorran Haven, a 13th century village with a 15th century 34m church tower used as a shipping mark. After the Reformation the chapel was split into two floors, the Wesleyans upstairs and a fishing tackle store below, only being restored to full church use in the 1860s. The pier is below high sloping cliffs and there were limekilns as well as cellars used by fishermen. Gorran boats were some of the best in the country and their willow crab pots also sold widely.

on top and an earth bank cuts across the headland. A local clergyman installed a large granite cross in 1896 in anticipation of the second coming, used as a daymark. There have been many unexplained tragedies in the area, including the loss of the MV *Darlwyne* with 31 people in 1966. Whether these can be attributed to the race off the head or to the naval training gunfire further off is unknown.

Cliffs around Veryan Bay range between 6 and 60m in height. Porthluney Cove, used in filming *Poldark*, has its best surf on the bottom half of the tide with a southerly wind. Above is Caerhays Castle on the site of a medieval manor house which the Trevanion family had owned from the 14th century, although the 1808 conversion by John Nash was to ruin them. Owned by the Williams family from 1852, it is noted for its 24ha of gardens, perhaps the best in Cornwall, started by John Charles Williams' plant hunting

in China a century back, now with oaks, rhododendrons, huge Asian magnolias and the national camellia collection. The very valuable shrub Williamsii camellia was bred here.

A wreck sits at East Portholland while West Portholland has a limekiln on the shore and surf which is best over the bottom half of the tide with the wind from the east to southeast.

Dodman Point seen from below Boswinger.

After Pen-a-maen or Maenease Point, divers use the waters off Bow or Vault Beach while naturists use its southern end. Dodman Point has a steep east face and a sloping west one covered in gorse and bracken. The largest Iron Age fort in the southwest was sited

Portholland was as a fishing village. It doubled as Roscoff for filming Winston Graham's *Poldark*.

An easterly wind also brings the best surf at Portloe, another village with a limekiln, but there is a launching charge and a private slipway. The lifeboat was never used in 17 years as the entrance was always too bad in rough conditions, the lifeboat station eventually being converted to a church and a school. The fishing village

The sheltered harbour at Portloe.

Gull Rock stands beyond the Blouth.

Clear water and pierced rock at Nare Head.

has pilchard cellars and crab pots. The 17th century Ship Inn is claimed to make the best crab sandwiches in Cornwall. The bay beyond Manare Point was used for the TV film of *The Camomile Lawn* in 1992.

Gull Rock is a nesting place of cormorants, shags, guillemots and razorbills. It has claimed many sailing ships, including the *Hera* with 19 lives in 1914. It is accompanied by the Middle Stone and the Outer Stone, the Whelps. There are strong currents between these offshore rocks and 79m Nare Head at the start of Gerrans Bay. There is another wreck near Shannick Point where there are also egrets. The Carne Beacon tumulus may be the grave of the 5th century King Geraint or Gerennius of Cornwall who was reputed to have been rowed across Gerrans Bay in a golden boat with silver oars, buried with him although excavations have not found it. Pendower Beach, backed by bracken and gorse and also with a 19th century limekiln, has best surf with wind from the east after a persistent onshore wind.

Dingerein Castle site on the A3078 could be associated with the Iron Age King Geraint of the Britons in the 8th century, recorded in the *Anglo-Saxon Chronicles*, or Sir Geraint of the Round Table, the father of Jestyn or St Just. Porthbean Beach has surf with an easterly wind while Porthcurnick Beach, under the gaze of the National Coastwatch station on Pednvadan and the Rosevine Hotel in its own subtropical gardens, has its best surf on the bottom half of the tide with the wind between east and southeast.

Portscatho means harbour of large boats but the notable large one was the 900t *Carl Hirschberg* which arrived in the Great Blizzard of 1891, which also wrecked houses and quays. After a month the Board of Trade allowed the rocks holding it to be dynamited if a breakwater was built to replace them. There are also smaller boats. In less extreme conditions easterly winds bring the best surf. As well as the jetty this fishing village has a steep slip and 6–12m cliffs, above which rises the

Nare Head seen across Gerrans Bay from Treloan Farm.

spire of the 13th century church of St Gerendus at Gerrans. Some of *The Camomile Lawn* was also filmed here.

Roseland takes its name from rosinis, moorland isle. A signpost by the shore points to Treloan Coastal Farm, a site with caravans, camping and the first camping barn in Cornwall.

Off Greeb Point there are overfalls over the Bizzies. Birdlife includes oystercatchers, curlews, herons, fulmars, kittiwakes and blackbacked and herring gulls but red admirals and other butterflies might also be seen flying over the sea. Porthmellin Head divides Towan Beach, one of the few Cornish beaches where cowries can be found, from Porthbeor Beach which is used by divers. St Anthony faces onto the river side of the peninsula. It has palms and a 13th century church lit by a brass candelabra, with a modern door and a medieval latchet door for dogs, also allowing hens to use the belfry as a roost.

There are seals to Zone Point, off which there can be a race. After centuries of a coal burning light on St Anthony's Head the current 19m white octagonal tower lighthouse was built in 1834, an old world air of elegance not seen on every lighthouse and making it the choice for filming *Fraggle Rock*. A moated fort was built close by in 1895, to which a Second World War battery with 150mm guns was added.

The two major fortifications at the mouth of Falmouth Harbour were for Henry VIII. **St Mawes** Castle is Tudor rose in plan, completed in 1543, the best preserved of his castles, unique in having no internal changes. It fell quickly to the Parliamentarians in 1646 because they attacked from landward while all the guns face seawards. Now with subtropical gardens, it was used for filming *Poldark*.

Opposite it is Pendennis Castle of 1545, Cornwall's greatest fortress and one of Henry's finest, built on an Iron Age fort site, the end of his chain of castles to defend against the French, the penultimate garrison to be taken by Cromwell in 1646 after holding out for five months under Sir John Arundell. It includes Elizabethan ramparts, a First World War guardhouse with cells and a Second World War gun battery which was used. A gun is fired at noon during July and August.

Between the two is Black Rock, on which is a mark. Mr Trefusis of Trefusis rowed his wife out for a picnic then left her to drown but fishermen rescued her. Flows into the harbour run to 3km/h while there is 4km/h outwards with freshets.

A ria, Falmouth Harbour is the world's third largest natural harbour after Sydney and Río. It is the most westerly safe anchorage in the Channel and the first safe port after an Atlantic crossing. The Romans traded from here for tin but its heyday was with the sailing ships, the tea clippers and the windjammers. The Falmouth Packets began regular Post Office services to Spain, Portugal, America, the West Indies, the Mediterranean and Brazil. Thomas Paine's *The Rights of Man* records

the strange capture of an English packet boat from Famouth and, even more unusual, the capture of its Government dispatches, which usually stood ready to be jettisoned if necessary. In 1810 it was the last place in Britain where the Riot Act was read to mutinous crews. It was a Second World War convoy assembly point and has become a refuelling and repair port for passenger ships, cargo vessels and tankers. There are also numerous small pleasure craft.

As well as the castle, Pendennis Point has a Maritime Rescue Co-ordination Centre mast and a blockhouse. From here a wooded ridge runs northwest along the northern edge of Falmouth Bay. Falmouth Art Gallery features Cornish artists. The angular roof at the other end of the ridge is the main hall of the National Maritime Museum Cornwall, opened in 2002 with 120 small boats, an underwater window which allows the full depth of the murky water to be viewed, the only one in Europe and one of only three such windows in the world, and a 29m tower with extensive views up Carrick Roads and over the rest of the harbour. It was the point from which Sean Morley set off in 2004 to be the first person to circumnavigate all the inhabited islands in Great Britain and Ireland solo by sea kayak and the point to which Ellen MacArthur returned after her record breaking round the world sailing voyage. Robin Knox-Johnston set out from here in 1968 to win the first *Sunday Times* Golden Globe Race. Falmouth Classics take place in June and it Falmouth Oyster in October, this being one of the last places for unmotorized oyster dredging.

Falmouth, at the end of the A39, was formed by the villages of Smithike and Penny-Come-Quick, renamed by Charles II. It was developed in the 17th century by the Killigrews, who made their money out of piracy and privateering. It has many 18/19th century buildings and became a fashionable resort after the railway arrived. Residents have included Captain Andrew Blamey in *Poldark*'s *Demelza*. Famouth was also used for revictualling in *The Maid of Sker*. Its improvement of hundreds of houses by installing double glazing, central heating and other conservation measures won it the first Deputy Prime Minister's Award for Sustainable Communities.

There were many sightings in the 1970s, some more recent, of Morgawr, a sea monster like a giant seal with a long neck. This Nessie lookalike has been reported from Pendennis Point, Rosemullion Head and Parson's Beach but has probably been frightened away now by the snarling of jet skis.

The upmarket Falmouth Beach Hotel burned down in 2012 but has been rebuilt. Gyllyngvase Beach prides itself on its Queen Mary Gardens while, beyond Swanpool Point, the popular Swanpool Beach has a Swan Pool with both swans and ducks, the best surf being at mid-tide with easterly winds. A golf course tops the cliffs to Pennance Point, where there is a monument to a Home

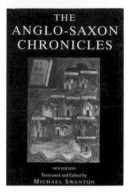

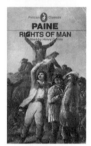

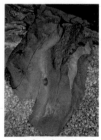

Brightly coloured rock at Newporth Head.

Looking up the estuary of the Helford River.

Guard patrolman, the cliffs running about 15m high to Rosemullion Head.

There is a wreck between Newporth Head and Maenporth, the most popular surf beach in the area with its best surf at mid tide on an easterly wind. There are caves in High Cliff.

Beyond Bream Cove, Rosemullion Head is the end of Falmouth Harbour control and also the end of the Helford River's drowned valley. The tower of the 13th century Grade II★ St Mawnan & St Stephen's church at Mawnan served as a navigation landmark and a lookout point for invaders.

Crossing the river, as swallows do, leads to the Lizard peninsula, the name a corruption of the Cornish for rocky height. Plateau heathland, it grows Cornish heath.

St Anthony-in-Meneage has the 12th century St Anthony's church founded by Normans for being spared after being shipwrecked, built from Normandy stone. To its east is Dennis Head from dynas, a fort, there being an Iron Age fortress which was strengthened by the Royalists in the Civil War and was one of the last three places in Cornwall to fall to the Roundheads. Behind it, Gillan Harbour is a yachting centre.

Nare Point is low but cliffs mostly run to 60m to Lizard Point. Relics from the four masted *Bay of Panama*, driven onto the point in 1891, are to be found in the Five Pilchards in the former fishing village of Porthallow, with a beach which is still difficult in an easterly wind.

After Porthkerris Point Porthallow has austere building defended by MoD security fencing. Beyond it the most southerly vineyard in the country was established but was prosecuted in 1998 for selling wine and cider from elsewhere as its own.

Porthoustock was the chief fishing village on the Lizard with pilchard cellars, one net taking over 4,000,000 fish. Another noteworthy landing was 9,000l of contraband brandy in one session. Fishing is for crabs and lobsters, boats being hauled up the beach by winches in wooden sheds. A beach of spoil from the active stone quarry means that it does not appear as attractive as it sounds.

A lookout is located by the Giant's Quoits megaliths on Manacle Point. From Cape Wrath to the Lizard some of our most imaginative names come from anglicizing of names in other languages. Such is the case with the Manacles, the Cornish men eglos meaning stone church. Nevertheless, their fearful reputation has been well acquired, having claimed hundreds of ships and thousands of lives as the strong tidal currents sweep between Maen Chynoweth, the Shark's Fin, the Gwinges, the Manacles, Carn-du Rocks, Maen Land and the cliffs. In 1809 200 were lost in hours with only eight survivors from HMS *Despatch* and the 18 gun brig HMS *Primrose* bringing home troops from the Peninsular War in Spain. In 1855 196 were lost from the emigrant ship *John* bound from Plymouth to Canada and in 1898 106 were lost from the liner *Mohegan*, the dead being stripped of their belongings. Some 400 victims are buried in St Keverne where the octagonal spire of St Akeveranus' church has acted as a marker for sailors for 300 years, the spire being rebuilt after a lightning strike in 1770. The peal of ten bells is one of the two largest in Cornish churches. The Manacles provide bass, caught by line.

Dean Quarries are disused but there are plans to turn them into a gabbro superquarry. Roskilly's farm manufacture ice cream behind the quarry.

Porthallow on the Lizard peninsula.

Military architecture at Porthkerris Point precedes a diving centre. Behind is the entrance to the Helford River.

Lowland Point has confused water with strong tidal streams. Small surf is to be found at North Corner with southeasterly winds. This is one of three places in Britain where the meeting of the Earth's mantle and crust can be seen, the Moho, normally 40–50km down. The green and purple cliffs at Coverack at the end of the B3294 are set off by the whitewashed cottages in this fishing and former smuggling village. One smuggler's wife used to peg a bright red shirt on the line when it was safe for her husband to come ashore with contraband. There is a shop in a former pilchard barrel salt store and there is the Paris Hotel, named after the *Paris* which grounded on Lowland

A stone quarry at Porthoustock.

The Manacles, graveyard of ships and sailors, lie offshore.

Coverack is popular with windsurfers.

Jagged rocks threaten Carrick Lûz.

Point in 1899, 756 people being saved and the ship being refloated six weeks later, again to be refloated at Rame Head after grounding there in 1914. In July 2017 the village was hit by golfball sized hailstones and flooded by intense rainfall. There is a disused slip into a sea with bass and pollock. Dolor Point has a small pier with a restaurant and bakery in a former lifeboat station, voted to supply the UK's best fish and chips. In Perprean Cove

Cadgwith provides shelter for small craft.

The Lizard lifeboat is now housed in Kilcobben Cove.

Lizard Point and its light seen across Housel Bay.

are the Oxen. Chynhalls Point has an Iron Age fort site on top and a tide race at the end while Black Head has a white coastguard lookout on top. There is another fort site overlooking the angular rocks of Carrick Lûz before Spernic Cove and the gorse and heather covered Eastern Cliff, Poldowrian Garden having a large pond, woodland, a prehistoric museum and a hut circle not far away.

Kennack Sands are a low point in the cliffs but a popular beach with interesting cliffs for all that, a nature reserve and many flowers. Daphne du Maurier taught herself to swim in a rockpool here when she was 10. The best surf is with northwesterly or northerly winds against big swells. Divers like the clear waters at other times. Beacons mark the landing point of the main submarine cables from Spain and Portugal. Goonhilly is 5km to the north.

A wheel for the 19th century Lizard Serpentine Company, which had a hundred workers making everything from ornaments to shop fronts for London and Paris, used to be powered by a stream flowing into Carleon Cove at Poltesco.

A cove beyond Kildown Point shelters England's only wood of dwarf elms. Cadgwith is windswept and the tall serpentine and whitewashed cottages have their thatched roofs held down with chains. Gig racing is based at an old lighthouse. The boats drawn up on the Stick, the beach, catch crabs, lobsters, mackerel and some red and grey mullet. There are pilchard cellars and a huer's house on the cliff, the best day's catch being 1,300,000 fish, but the last pilchards were in 1910.

Fisherman Buller and postman Hartley led singing sessions in the Cadgwith Cove Inn and later on the beach, on one notable occasion being joined by an Italian lady opera singer on holiday in the village. *Memories & Opinions* recalls how Q was invited by his senior tutor to join a reading party here and became the unexpected hero of a cricket match between Ruan Minor and Helston.

Just south of the village is the Devil's Frying Pan, a 60m hole in the cliff caused by the collapse of a large cave. Smaller caves survive near Polbarrow. Gorse backs Whale Rock and then there is a quarry. The Balk Beacon is a red and white mast at Church Cove, one of the leading line beacons to locate Vrogue Rock. Crab and lobster boats are drawn up by pilchard cellars. St Wynwallow's church, the most southerly on mainland Britain, has a chequered tower of granite and serpentine blocks, a Norman doorway, a castellated porch, wood

from the wreck of a Portuguese treasure ship and a memorial to 11 crew of the MV *Polperro* sunk in Mount's Bay by an E-boat in 1944. It was from the red serpentine pulpit in 1678 that the last sermon in Cornish was preached.

The late 19th century lifeboat house is unused, as it almost was then, the boat having only been launched once in 14 years. The 2011 lifeboat station is the fifth on the Lizard, partly built from a jack up rig because of the difficulty of land access. The 1910 rescue of 456 people from the SS *Suevic* on rocks off the Lizard by four rowed lifeboats remains the RNLI's largest ever. At Bass Point there are more Vrogue Rock transit beacons, it generally being a difficult area as the ebb runs to 6km/h over shallow ground. Overlooking it is Lloyds Signal Station, a National Coastwatch lookout.

It was from Pen Olver that the Spanish Armada was first sighted in 1588. The Jacobite *Elisabeth* was damaged off the Lizard by HMS *Lion* as the opening action of the 1745 rebellion.

Pen Olver was from where Guglielmo Marconi made radio contact with the Isle of Wight, 110km away, in 1901. His Lizard Wireless Station has been restored.

At the front of Housel Bay the Lion's Den hole results from a collapse in 1842. There has been a lighthouse above Bumble Rock since 1619, built by Sir John Killigrew, at which time most local houses were built of the timbers of wrecked ships, although there was no local help as it would stop the wrecks, of which there have been over 200 here. It was replaced in 1751 by a lighthouse with two coal fires in transit. The current light is on the eastern tower. Designed in 1874 by JN Douglass, it is one of the world's brightest with a range of 31km at a turning point on one of the world's busiest shipping lanes, usually the first object seen by inbound transatlantic shipping. It was one of the first to be electrified in 1878 and has the only large engine room surviving from that period. Christopher Coombe did not enjoy the sight in a large sea during his terrifying first voyage on the *Janet Coombe* in *The Loving Spirit*, which also reported the loss of the *Julia Moss* here with all hands.

Above Polbrean Cove a youth hostel was originally built in the 1860s as a villa for artist Thomas Hart.

In calm conditions there is a passage inside the rocks of Vellan Drang, off which there is a race in an area exposed to wind, strong tides and obstacles. A swell makes the trip exciting. Nearby is a meadow with over 200 bodies buried from the 1720 wreck of the *Royal Anne*.

Distance
63km from Charlestown to Lizard Point

OS 1:50,000 Sheets
(200 Newquay & Bodmin)
203 Land's End & Isles of Scilly
204 Truro & Falmouth

Tidal Constants
Charlestown:
HW Dover −0550,
LW Dover −0540
Pentewan:
HW Dover −0550,
LW Dover −0540
Mevagissey:
HW Dover −0600,
LW Dover −0550
St Mawes:
HW Dover −0610,
LW Dover −0550
Falmouth:
HW Dover −0600
Helford River Entrance:
HW Dover −0610,
LW Dover −0550
Coverack:
HW Dover +0610,
LW Dover −0600
Lizard Point:
Dover −0610

Sea Area
Plymouth

Connection
Carrick Roads – see RoB p301

The rocks of Vellan Drang at Lizard Point.

39 West Cornwall

The most colourful cliffs in England

At break of day on the beach there lay
Blue fainted wreckage strewn
To stand in muted witness to
The loss of the 'Solomon Browne',
To the gallant men of Mousehole
Who'd sailed out on that tide.
That those who died were heroes,
It cannot be denied
C Jones

The most southerly point on the British mainland is the nib of rock which separates Polpeor Cove from Polbrean Cove on Lizard Point and which carries a road down towards the former. Limited parking is available at the top in front of Polpeor Café, although parking and road access can be difficult everywhere in the summer. The nib is extended by the rocks of Vellan Drang.

The Lizard is an Area of Outstanding Natural Beauty, an upstanding mass of igneous serpentine, gabbro, granite and gneisses, probably Precambrian and offering the most colourful cliffs in England. It is the centre of the serpentine turning industry, which became fashionable in 1846 after Queen Victoria paid a visited to Cornwall and ordered a serpentine table. Beaches can produce such semiprecious stones as agate, citrine, carnelian, chalcedony, amethyst, serpentine and rock crystal.

Seas off the Lizard can be bad but not as bad as they will become for round the world sailors, for whom this is the timekeeper's startline. In *Hereward the Wake* an adverse easterly headwind prevents the Irish Danes from rounding the Lizard and so positions them by chance where Sigtryg, King of Waterford, can snatch the Princess of Cornwall, his fiancée, after her forced marriage to Hannibal Grylls, the King of Marazion.

Polpeor Cove's lifeboat station was in use from 1914 to 1959. Pistol Cove is where a couple of hundred soldiers were washed ashore from a wreck in the 18th century, together with many pistols and other weapons. An invasion of hounds after the bodies resulted in the local people refusing to keep dogs thereafter.

Choughs are nesting again as far as Mullion on a stretch of coast with heather, unusual clovers, tree ferns and gunneras.

Both geologists and climbers enjoy the 60m high cliffs in Kynance Cove beyond Lizard Point where there are signs of landslip. Caves, including the Dining Room and the Drawing Room, begin to appear in the serpentine and there are prominent islands, Gull

Polpeor Cove and the old lifeboat station. Note the wreck.

Mullion Island, residence of thousands of seabirds.

Rock, Asparagus Island and the Bellows which take their name from the Devil's Bellows fissure.

The National Trust imported New Forest ponies to keep the gorse in check. The high cliffs continue round the Rill (where there is a historic wreck on Rill Ledges) and Predannack Head into

Mullion Cove, where a westerley can bring in surf. Mullion Island has nesting kittiwakes, shags, cormorants and blackbacked gulls and is covered with guillemots, razorbills and other seabirds which also throng the Lizard National Nature Reserve, an area of heathland and clifftop plants.

The underlying rock changes to Old Red Sandstone, but the fishing harbour at Mullion Cove at the end of the B3296 was built of greenstone in 1895 after a storm two years earlier had wrecked most of the fishing fleet. A lifeboat was installed in 1909. A natural tunnel through the rocks is a feature here. The unfinished *Memoirs & Opinions* records the mysterious wreck of the Dutch barque *Jonkheer* at Polurrian in 1867.

The waters of Mount's Bay have mackerel, pilchards, herrings, seals and plenty of the large but harmless rhizostoma jellyfish which are rare away from the southwest. Crabs and lobsters are caught in pots marked with flags, sometimes so frequent that the sea resembles a golf course. A double ended fishing boat was developed for use in the bay.

century, has a Norman font, a wagon roof over the south aisle, some piers which are single stones and a quantity of wood from the *St Anthony*, a Portuguese treasure ship wrecked in the cove in 1526. The belltower is two centuries older and stands on the cliff edge 4m from the main building.

Dollar Cove is where a Spanish galleon went down in 1785 with 2.5t of gold coins. Dubloons and other gold coins are still sometimes found on the beach. Both

Rocks at Pedngwinian.

Pedngwinian and Gunwalloe have historic wreck sites.

Porthleven Sands reach their maximum height at the Loe Bar which blocked the River Cober with chalk derived flint shingle in the 13th century and finished **Helston** as a busy port. The Loe, which has been formed behind it, is Cornwall's largest natural freshwater lake and had to be drained at intervals by the local millers, digging through it once they had each given the lord of the manor $1^{1}/2$d in a purse to obtain permission. The flow is now controlled by a culvert at the west end. It is one of the places Sir Bedivere is reputed to have thrown King Arthur's

Between Polurrian Cove (which can have good surfing) and Poldhu Cove is a monument where the first transatlantic wireless message, 'S' in Morse, was sent to Guglielmo Marconi at St John's, Newfoundland, in 1901, the first short wave signals being sent from here two decades later. To the east and only visible from further out in the bay are the array of satellite dishes on Goonhilly Downs, formerly the world's largest satellite earth station.

Gunwalloe's Church Cove, another surfing venue, was chosen by Breton abbot St Winwaloe in the 6th century as the site for his church, the Church of Storms. The present building dates from the 15th

209

The Wheal Trewavas coppermine buildings and chimneys perch on the cliffs of Trewavas Head.

Precarious looking rock column near Trewavas Head.

Excalibur to the Lady of the Lake. There can be a strong undertow and the sea can dump heavily. On one occasion a ship was thrown right over the bar in a storm. The beach has an unusual number of exceptional waves but not such a good selection for the surfer. In 1807 Henry Trengrouse of Helston watched as 130 men of the frigate *Anson* were drowned within a stone's throw of the Loe Bar, remembered by a white cross, after which he invented the rocket rescue line.

Royal Navy helicopters based at Culdrose Airfield come and go constantly.

Opposite its notable clocktower **Porthleven** has a memorial cross to the 22 fishermen of the village drowned between 1871 and 1948 but was noted for its sailing craft. Another memorial is for Grylls' Act which allowed drowned bodies to be buried in consecrated ground without having to prove that they were Christians, prompted by the wreck of HMS *Anson*. A red ball on a mast by the clocktower shows when the inner harbour is closed by timbers in winter or during bad weather as boats have been wrecked in the harbour during storms, although boats were wrecked when the timbers failed in a February 2014 storm. It also has a 50t boulder of garnetiferous gneiss, rare in Britain so it could well have arrived on an iceberg.

The harbour was built in 1811 by Napoleonic prisoners to import mining machinery and export copper and tin. The village has toilets nearby and a pillbox overlooks the sands. The surf has a very hollow wave and is reckoned to be the wave to ride but it is not for beginners. Megiliggar rocks have claimed many ships.

The granite face of Trewavas Head is dominated by the Wheal Trewavas copper mine, the cliffs streaked with blue on the far side of the head where mine water was emptied back down the cliffs into the sea, the blue contrasting with the pink of thrift and a column of weathered rock being as impressive as the tapering mine chimneys. Porthcew can have surf.

Beyond Rinsey Head the engine house of the Wheal Prosper copper mine, closed in 1860 after undersea workings began to let in water, has been restored. In 1812 it had the prototype of what became known as the Cornish engine, which Richard Trevithick adapted that year to employ much higher pressure than used by James Watt.

Praa Sands is a fast break with a hollow wave and Kenneggy Sands can work on the bottom half of a tide with southwesterlys. Prussia Cove (Nampara Cove in filming *Poldark*), Bessy's Cove and Piskies Cove were smuggling centres, as was the King of Prussia inn. Innkeeper Bessie was involved in smuggling and the King of Prussia was John Carter, the most famous of the Cornish smugglers, who mounted guns on the cliffs around the inn (a cover for his smuggling activities), officially to protect against French privateers but actually to intimidate revenue men. A strict Methodist, he forbade swearing on his boats. In 1979 £3,000,000 of smuggled marijuana was intercepted. Today the hillside is covered with gorse and seals and ravens move around the coves.

Cudden Point has claimed more than its fair share of ships, including the 30,000t *Warspite* which was being towed to the breakers on the Clyde in 1948. Like most of the headlands, currents run rapidly around it. It was used in filming *Poldark*.

The Greeb, beyond Perranuthnoe with its rare surf on big southwesterlies, is a 400m long line of rocks only 20m wide and submerged at high tide. Also submerged at high tide is the causeway built in 1427 across to St Michael's Mount, one of the most romantic silhouettes in England, Milton's 'great Vision of the guarded mount'. Boats operate when the causeway is closed. The story of Jack the Giant Killer is based around the giant Cormoran who is said to have stolen cows and sheep to eat. One version of the story says that he was a common or garden giant who lived on the island and that Jack lured

The familiar shape of St Michael's Mount.

him into a pit which can still be seen. Another version has him as a super economy sized giant whose wife at Marazion (marghas byghan, little market) was so upset at his demise that she dropped the stone in her apron pocket and it rolled into the water to form the 90m high mount. Historical facts date from 320 BC if this was the island of Ictis, as the descriptions suggest, in which case tin was being shipped from here to the Mediterranean at that time. St Michael was said to have appeared to local fishermen here in 495 AD and there were subsequent pilgrimages by St Keane and St Cadoc in the 6th century. Edward the Confessor established it as a Benedictine chapel site in 1044, giving it to the monks of the similar Mont St Michel in Normandy in 1070. The Chevy Chase Room was the refectory and the Blue Drawing Rooms were the Lady Chapel, now with early rococo Gothic plasterwork and Chippendale chairs. A priory was built in 1135. A church established in the 13th century was destroyed in an earthquake in 1275 and rebuilt in the following century, during which a castle was added. The Earl of Oxford captured it in 1473, surrendering to Edward IV after a 26 week siege. In 1497 Perkin Warbeck attempted to depose Henry VII from here, claiming to have been one of the princes supposedly murdered in the Tower of London before being shown to be an impostor and being executed in 1499. The beacon on top of the church was used to first signal the arrival of the Spanish Armada in 1588 and the island was subsequently sold by Elizabeth I to Secretary of State Robert Cecil to raise funds to pay off her soldiers and sailors. It was used for Royalist gun running during the Civil War. Charles II stayed here on his way to Jersey when his defeat seemed imminent and the island surrendered to the Roundheads in 1646 after a long siege. Colonel John St Aubyn became military governor the following year, later buying it for his family who have lived here since 1659, modernizing it in 1760, and continue to live here although its ownership has been handed to the National Trust. The harbour was rebuilt in 1727 but it lost its trade to Penzance. These days the invaders are tourists who swarm over one of the National Trust's most visited properties and gaze down on the sea of bluebells on its east side in the spring.

Marazion Museum is in the old jail and a cell has been reconstructed. This is where Henry Francis Lyte was married while undertaking early clerical duties here. Marazion Marsh includes Cornwall's largest reedbed and an RSPB nature reserve.

Here is some of the most prolific agricultural land in the country with the Golden Acres at Gulval growing early flowers for the London market. Gulval's church dates from the 15th century.

By the shore is the terminus of the main west of England railway line from London, which helped the fishing industry not only here but also in Newlyn and Mousehole.

Penzance (holy point) is also the terminus for the ferry to the Isles of Scilly. The town was burned by Don Carlos de Amesquita in 1595 and by Fairfax in the 17th century. A pier and fort were built in the 17th century to protect against pirates. Being involved in the tin trade, it was the main coinage town between 1663 and 1838 and smuggling was also rife. However, when John Carter's tea was seized he broke into the custom house and took it back but left tea which had been taken from other smugglers, his honesty making him the obvious culprit. In the 19th century a number of children in coffins were found wedged into the roof of Market Jew Chapel, thought to have been unbaptised. Penzance had its heyday in the 19th century. It was the first Cornish resort and is the only one with a promenade, claiming the mildest all year round climate in the British Isles, and the women were said to be the most handsome in Cornwall. The Exchange has modern art and Penlee House Gallery & Museum has 19th century Newlyn art, scale models of ships, a geology of the coast, local crafts and a history of fishing, the port catching coalfish, conger eels, ling and shark. The port is one of seven Trinity House depots for buoy servicing crews. Residents have included Maria Branwell, mother of the Brontë sisters, and her older sister, Elizabeth, who brought them up after her death, probably passing on many aspects of Cornish life which later appeared in their books written in Yorkshire. Richard Somers has to report to the army here for the first time in DH Lawrence's semi autobiographical *Kangaroo. The Pirates of Penzance* was Gilbert & Sullivan's musical take on life here. The drowning of artist Egbert Caine was the last giant octopus attack in *The Sea-Raiders*. Sir Humphrey Davey was born in the town in 1778 and invented the safety lamp for tin miners. In the 19th century it had the one wheeled coach, a wheelbarrow used to carry courting young men by their mates before being tipped somewhere unpleasant. The Golowan festival in June has ten days of traditional and modern music, dance, film, theatre and street procession.

Penzance Bay and Gwavas Lake have several fixed marks on submerged rock outcrops, Ryeman, Western Cressar and the Gear, and has a submerged forest.

Large quarries overlook **Newlyn** which has a tidal observatory giving the Ordnance Survey's level datum and a base point in their trigonometrical mapping grid of the country. The firm Stevenson's have built the port up to the fourth largest fishing port in England with a canning factory. The militia were used in 1896 to settle riots after objections to east coast trawlers fishing on Sundays. Breakwaters date mostly from 1866 to 1888 but were damaged in a 1962 storm. A new fish quay was built in 1981 and a new fishmarket was opened in 1988. The new quay in the name was built in the 15th century, the town being burned by the Spanish in 1595. The song *Newlyn Town* recalls a local who became a highwayman in London before being hanged as one of the first successes of the Bow Street Runners. Shark fishing is also carried out and there is a fish festival in August, including cookery demonstrations. The Newlyn School of artists was established in the 19th century, featured in the Passmore Edwards Newlyn Art Gallery.

Standing on Penlee Point are a memorial and the lifeboat station which is remembered by the nation for the day in December 1981

The harbour at Mousehole.

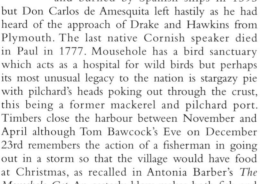

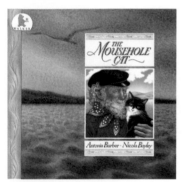

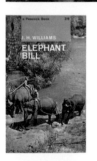

when the eight crew members of the *Solomon Browne* were lost while trying to rescue eight crew members from the *Union Star*, the coxwain being awarded a posthumous Gold Medal, the RNLI's highest honour. Mousehole, sheltering behind St Clement's Isle, is an unspoilt fishing village clustered around the Ship Inn by the harbour and was Cornwall's main fishing port until Newlyn was developed in the 19th century. It was the scene of the march of rebellious miners in *Poldark*.

Mousehole and Paul were both sacked and burned by Spanish ships in 1595 but Don Carlos de Amesquita left hastily as he had heard of the approach of Drake and Hawkins from Plymouth. The last native Cornish speaker died in Paul in 1777. Mousehole has a bird sanctuary which acts as a hospital for wild birds but perhaps its most unusual legacy to the nation is stargazy pie with pilchard's heads poking out through the crust, this being a former mackerel and pilchard port. Timbers close the harbour between November and April although Tom Bawcock's Eve on December 23rd remembers the action of a fisherman in going out in a storm so that the village would have food at Christmas, as recalled in Antonia Barber's *The Mousehole Cat*. An easterly blow makes both fish and garden molluscs inactive so the fishermen attend to their gardens. The name of the village may have come from mouz hel, maiden's brook. Several large caves in the cliff are formed in solid rock but have roofs in a stratum of loose boulders packed in soil, making them appear most unstable. Above is Kemyel Crease nature reserve. *The Lamorna Wink* is set in the area, the pub name referring to the method of being served contraband spirits. Several Newlyn School artists were based here. A holidaymaker here was George Brown, who stopped short of his boss, Harold Wilson, who used to go to Scilly.

Beyond the dramatic headland at Carn-du is Lamorna Cove below an 1861 quarry for hard granite, including stone for London's Victoria Embankment, the cove protected by a Grade II breakwater. Jimmy Williams, noted for his wartime exploits with elephants in Burma, had lived at the Menwinnion Hotel, now a care home. Derek Tangye's Minack, about which he wrote *The Minack Chronicles*, is above the cliffs before Tater-du. A claim that he and wife Jeannie were spying for Russia from here were dismissed as nonsense by those who knew them.

The first automatic lighthouse to be built in Britain was located at Tater-du (black loaf) in 1965, close by the water, following the wreck of the 500t Spanish *Juan Ferrer*, heading from Bordeaux to Cardiff but failing to round Land's End. Accompanying is the Howard's Howl foghorn. It is in a quarry of blue elvin which has been used for roadstone and replaces the granite of this coast.

Penberth is possibly Cornwall's finest fishing cove with a 17th century pilchard store and larger craft having been hauled out by a large horizontal capstan like a cartwheel. Mackerel are still caught there.

Westward, the skyline becomes fantastic with the fortified Iron Age Treryn Dinas on Cribba Head and then Logan Rock, a 66t balanced rock on top of Horrace. In 1824 it was dislodged by Lieutenant Goldsmith, a nephew of Oliver Goldsmith. Such was the public outcry that the Admiralty were obliged to bring special lifting gear from Devonport to replace it. The outcomes were that it doesn't rock as well as it used to and the bill for repositioning it nearly bankrupted Lieutenant Goldsmith, to whom it was presented.

Porth Curno has a crushed shell beach, possibly the whitest in England although nothing like the white beach at Morar in western Scotland. It can have a high tide dump but more reasonable surf on big westerly swells. The beach is the landing place for submarine cables including the first transatlantic cable and the one laid from India by the *Great Eastern* in 1870. West of the beach is the Minack Theatre, an open air amphitheatre cut into the hillside above the sea. Seating 600, it was opened in 1932. The village has an aerial and houses the Porthcurno Telegraph Museum.

St Levan, with its medieval St Levan's church, 12th century font, fine carved pews and even older, tall, Celtic cross, takes its name from the saint who landed here in the 6th or 7th century after a voyage from Wales. There is a cleft rock where he rested, striking it with his staff and predicting that the world will end when a pannier laden packhorse can walk through the gap. It has no one christened Joanna because of an argument between St Levan and a lady of that name in the 7th century over what amounted to work on the sabbath. He called her Foolish Joanna and said any other child christened with that name in the parish would be a bigger fool.

Porthgwarra is approached from its slipway by a tunnel cut through the cliffs and is popular with climbers for such pitches as Seal Slab, Pendulum Chimney and Commando Crawl. It may also be the last landing point before Sennen.

Gwennap Head has strong currents and is topped by a National Coastwatch station. Daymarks help locate

Tater-du lighthouse low on the rocks.

The irregular skyline which includes Logan Rock.

Hella Point' Red Square skyline.

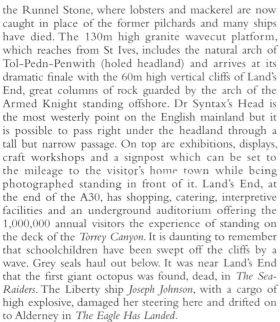

Porth Curno's white sand catches the last of the evening sun.

Land's End is protected by the Armed Knight.

The tunnel under Dr Syntax's Head.

the Runnel Stone, where lobsters and mackerel are now caught in place of the former pilchards and many ships have died. The 130m high granite wavecut platform, which reaches from St Ives, includes the natural arch of Tol-Pedn-Penwith (holed headland) and arrives at its dramatic finale with the 60m high vertical cliffs of Land's End, great columns of rock guarded by the arch of the Armed Knight standing offshore. Dr Syntax's Head is the most westerly point on the English mainland but it is possible to pass right under the headland through a tall but narrow passage. On top are exhibitions, displays, craft workshops and a signpost which can be set to the mileage to the visitor's home town while being photographed standing in front of it. Land's End, at the end of the A30, has shopping, catering, interpretive facilities and an underground auditorium offering the 1,000,000 annual visitors the experience of standing on the deck of the *Torrey Canyon*. It is daunting to remember that schoolchildren have been swept off the cliffs by a wave. Grey seals haul out below. It was near Land's End that the first giant octopus was found, dead, in *The Sea-Raiders*. The Liberty ship *Joseph Johnson*, with a cargo of high explosive, damaged her steering here and drifted on to Alderney in *The Eagle Has Landed*.

Maen Castle site stands on the cliffs.

The original Longships lighthouse (2km off, guarding Carn Brâs) was built in Sennen Cove in the 18th century and moved out stone by stone. The current one was built in 1873 and the helipad added in 1974. The keeper was kidnapped by wreckers on one occasion but the light was kept shining by his young daughter who reached it by standing on the family Bible. A keeper has been able to communicate by semaphore with his wife in their cottage at Sennen.

Fifteen kilometres off is the Wolf Rock lighthouse, one

of six that can be seen from the cliffs when conditions are good. The Isles of Scilly are also visible at times although there is no sign of the fabled land of Lyonesse which lies beneath the sea, possibly a folk memory of the drowning of Scilly at the end of the Ice Age.

The Sennen lifeboat station received a telegram from Margaret Thatcher paying tribute to the nine hours spent by the boat in rescuing crews from the 1979 Fastnet Race. A plaque in the breakwater at Sennen Cove by Colonel HW Williams, MP for St Ives in 1908, thanks fishermen for their help in raising funds for its building. Fish brought in include mullet and mackerel. Athelstan left from here to expel the Danes from Scilly.

Facilities include parking, toilets, chip shop, café, Old Success Inn. This is the only easy landing place between Gwennap Head and St Ives and even here the dump can make it impossible to get out again. The ground swell is usually present, especially with northerly and westerly winds as waves can travel 6,000km uninterrupted.

The surfing beach of Whitesand Bay is below Carn Brea hill, the hill which claims the widest sea view from the British mainland. A submarine powerline to Scilly was landed on the beach in 1988. Perkin Warbeck had landed here, claiming to be one of the murdered Princes in the Tower, was declared Richard IV and set off for London with Cornish supporters.

The coast from Sennen to St Ives is very committing as it is often impossible to land at all between the two and there would be few places to swim ashore safely in an emergency. It is possible to land at Priest's Cove where there is a slipway and a children's swimming pool in the rocks. Indeed, it is so named as the point where St Just is said to have made his landing from Ireland in the 5th century. **St Just** is the last bastion of Old Cornwall and was the Victorian centre of the tin mining industry. A 19th century tin mine stands at the back of Porth Nanven although older remains are round boulders, the Bronze Age burial chamber, Ballowall Barrow at Carn Gloose. Cape Cornwall is surmounted by the 1850 chimney of the Cape Cornwall tin mine, operating from 1836 to 1879, and the remains of St Helen's chapel. England's only cape was presented to the National Trust by HJ Heinz. Offshore are the Brisons which have claimed many ships while the Vyneck lies submerged

to the northwest of the cape, itself nearly as far west as Land's End. There are only razorbills here for company.

Porth Ledden, the next headland, is topped by the Iron Age Kenidjack Castle and a cairn circle. This pales into insignificance compared with the Botallack Mine which covers Botallack Head (dwelling on a brow) and overlooks Zawn a Bal. Used from the Bronze Age to 1914, this was one of Cornwall's richest tin mines, exporting as far as the Aegean, and peaked at 11 engine houses employing 500 men who could hear the sea moving the rocks above their heads. The beam engines of the Levant Engine House are steamed at times, having worked from 1840 to 1930, despite the 1919 lift collapse which killed 31. It inspired RM Ballantyne's *Deep Down* of 1868 and stories by Wilkie Collins.

The last working tin mine, Géevor at Pendeen, was closed in 1990 and is now a museum. From Trewellard Zawn to Pendeen Watch the sea is stained red with the tin which does seem to have some calming influence on the waves.

The lighthouse at Pendeen Watch was built in 1900 and modernized in 1926 to prevent ships mistaking Gurnard's Head for Land's End and turning in behind it. The light is visible for 43km. This is some of England's finest coastal scenery, totally unrelenting, and is popular with rock climbers, having been used as a Second World War commando training area. Off Pendeen Watch are the three rocks which form the Wra or Three Stone Oar. The cargo ship *Alacrity*, wrecked in Portheras Cove, is just one of the many this coastline has claimed over the centuries.

The coast is rich in history. Celtic fields above Whirl Pool may be the oldest human constructions still in use in England. The Iron Age Bosigran Castle, overlooking Halldrine Cove and Trereen Dinas on Gurnard's Head, is another cliff castle, the cliffs being popular with climbers.

As recalled in *Kangaroo*, DH Lawrence and his wife, Frieda, were ordered to leave Cornwall in 1917 after he had worked on *Women in Love* in Zennor for two years. Frieda was a cousin of Manfred von Richthofen, the Red Baron, and she was accused of being a spy, signalling from the cliffs. Helen Dunmore's *Zennor in Darkness* features the Lawrences' activities. There have been other strange happenings in Zennor. The 15th century St Senara's church has, carved on a bench end, a mermaid who came

The Cornish coast claims another victim, near Sennen.

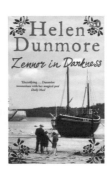

to hear the singing of chorister Matthew Trewella and then lured him back to the sea. Some years later she rose to ask a captain to raise his anchor as it was blocking the entrance to her house. The sweet singing of Matthew and the mermaid can sometimes be heard at night.

The Carracks are a set of offshore rocks which protect a heavily shoaled area between Mussel Point and Carn Naun Point and are used by grey seals. After countless headlands have been rounded, **St Ives**, at the ends of the B3306, A3074 and railway to St Erth, arrives suddenly. The Island (not an island) or St Ives Head has a National Coastwatch lookout point although the view westward is only as far as Clodgy Point. Between the two is Porthmeor Beach where surfing is restricted during the holiday season. Floating wood is joinedby cuttlefish shells. In CS Forester's *A Ship of the Line* it was one of the towns raided for crew members for the *Sutherland*.

The Wave Hub test site 16km off St Ives claims to be the world's largest and most advanced for developing offshore energy.

In 1938 the lifeboat *John & Sarah Eliza Stych* lost nearly all its crew although it was returned upright and empty.

Porthgribben Beach, with the Porthgwidden Beach Café and toilets, is the haunt of a sand sculptor in a town renowned for the sculpting in stone and bronze of Dame Barbara Hepworth, whose studio has been preserved, after she died in a fire in 1975, with a museum of her work. The Tate St Ives in the old gasworks exhibits various art while the artists' quarter drew in many who made up the St Ives school of painters and the makers of Leach pottery, Bernard Leach having been the leading modern producer. Kenneth Grahame honeymooned here. Films come together with folk and chamber music, Cornish bands and choirs, theatre and poetry in the St Ives Festival in September. The St Ives Biathlon involves running to Carbis Bay and swimming back.

St Leonard's on the landward end of John Smeaton's pier of 1770 is a fisherman's chapel on the site where St Ia arrived on a leaf or more likely by coracle from Ireland in the 6th century, apparently making a better choice of landing place than most of her fellow saints of the time although the bay can have short breaking seas. Shallow fishing boats, pointed at each end, were developed by

St Ives builders to suit the conditions. The town was one of the most prosperous of the Cornish pilchard ports in the 19th century with over 300 boats, exporting as far away as Italy. A shoal of 1905 was supposed to have been 160km long with the last great shoal of 3,000,000 fish in 1916 after which they declined quickly. The smell of fish was sometimes bad enough to stop the church clock, the vicar was reported as saying by Kilvert, who was here while a miner drowned swimming in the sea during his lunch break. An old pilchard cellar houses the St Ives Museum with local maritime history including the Hain Steamship Company which began in the port with one boat in 1840 and grew to become one of the world's largest freight companies. The huer's shelter is beyond Porthminster Point. **Carbis Bay**, overlooked by Knill's Monument, now produces mackerel, plaice, pollock and occasional surf.

The bar across the River Hayle resulted in the port of **Hayle** (heyl being Cornish for estuary) silting up in 1978 and the rivermouth is now completely closed at lower stages of the tide, has surf and has strong currents producing difficult conditions when it is covered although it exported tin from 1500 BC and the Romans sailed up to St Erth. A pillbox guarded the entrance from the west side. Beyond it, Lelant Saltings are one of the best birdwatching centres in Cornwall with cormorants, herons, kingfishers and terns breeding, widgeon, shelducks, teal, grey plovers, curlews and dunlin and unusual migrants often passing through. Rival copper miners Harveys and the Cornwall Copper Company developed alternative town centres and their two reservoirs are the country's largest sluicing operation for clearing silting. Harveys were the leading Cornish engine manufacturers. Hayle Heritage Festival has horticulture, art, dancing, traditional music and Cornish wrestling.

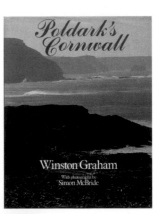

Towans or dunes form the coast for the next 5km around Upton Towans and these are backed by Atlantic Drive, the B3301, which runs from Hayle to Portreath. The towans claimed a church at Gwithian and are a location of holiday camps and the Methodist chapel of 1810 in Gwithian, named after St Gothian, the last thatched chapel in Cornwall. St Ives Bay is used by surfers at mid tide, windsurfers, kitesurfers, water skiers and canoeists. Surfing is at its best at the mouth of the Red River, a fast beachbreak which picks up most small swells, the tin staining the water and often turning the sea red around the estuary and churning up a brown froth in turbulent conditions.

Godrevy Point is dominated by Godrevy Island and its lighthouse. The area has long been one of danger. In 1649 it claimed the ship

Godrevy Island with its lighthouse.

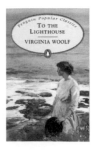

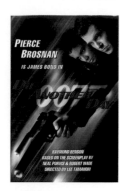

Distance
120km from Lizard
Point to Towan Head

OS 1:50,000 Sheets
200 Newquay
& Bodmin
203 Land's End
& Isles of Scilly
(204 Truro
& Falmouth)

Tidal Constants
Lizard Point:
Dover −0610
Porthleven:
HW Dover +0550,
LW Dover −0610
Penzance:
HW Dover +0550,
LW Dover −0610
Newlyn:
HW Dover +0550,
LW Dover −0610
Mousehole:
HW Dover +0550,
LW Dover −0610
Land's End
HW Dover +0550,
LW Dover −0610
Sennen Cove:
HW Dover +0550,
LW Dover −0620
Cape Cornwall:
HW Dover +0550,
LW Dover −0620
St Ives:
HW Dover −0600,
LW Dover −0550
Portreath:
Dover −0600
Perranporth:
Dover −0600

Sea Areas
Plymouth, Lundy

Submarine Areas
Mounts Bay, B1

carrying the wardrobe and possessions of Charles I, 60 people being drowned while only a boy, a dog and a few clothes were saved. It was the wreck of the *Nile* on 30th November 1854 which prompted the building of the lighthouse in 1859. The curate of Godrevy drowned here while walking his dog and has a memorial window in Godrevy church. This is the lighthouse featured in *To the Lighthouse* by Virginia Woolf whose family used to come here for holidays when she was a child, although claimed to be Skye, also inspiring *Jacob's Room* after her parents and brother had died. Unmanned since 1939 but still operating after fishermen and literary enthusiasts resisted an attempt to switch it off, it is now the preserve of gulls, oystercatchers, pipits, primroses and thrift but landing is not allowed without a permit. The area used to be good for lobsters. Kilvert reported a fight between a seal and a conger eel. Grey seals still use it and also breed at Navax Point where there are long caves which can only be reached from the sea. Fulmars, gannets, razorbills and shearwaters all frequent the coast.

The cliffs, which have claimed many ships at Hell's Mouth, rise to 75m, birds nest and the B3301 comes close occasionally but one cave that is no more is Ralph's Cupboard, now collapsed, which was used to store contraband. It was also the home of the giant Wrath who is said to have waded out to ships and eaten their crews, having the benefit of keeping the nosey public away. In 2011 200,000t of cliff face collapsed at Deadman's Cove. Crane Castle site overlooks Basset's Cove.

Porthreath pier is closed because of the number of people washed off it and the white daymark at the end was demolished in a January 2014 storm. The harbour was built in 1760 to serve tin mines and a horsedrawn tramway, the first railway in the county, was built to it in 1809. There was much trade with Swansea, the ore being traded for coal, harbour trade finally ceasing in 1960. It is now a surfing venue. Nancekuke Common's disused airfield has seen further life as a secret warfare research establishment and divers have reported hearing strange noises while exploring the seabed below the laboratories.

Porthtowan is another surfing venue with toilets, Unicorn pub and a café converted from a 19th century copper mine engine house.

The Towanroath engine house ruin above Chapel Porth is that of the Charlotte United copper mine. Chapel Porth, too, is a surfing venue but there is a bad current off the beach and a bar 1km out can cause big seas. A nature trail features buzzards, jackdaws, ravens and wrens among the local bird population.

Some of the best views in Cornwall are to be had from the 192m high St Agnes Beacon, set in an area rich in mining. Remains include the Wheal Coates tin and copper mine which closed in 1889 with shafts to depths of 180m. St Agnes Head stands 90m high with mineshafts, a large kittiwake colony, fulmars, guillemots and herring gulls breeding on its cliffs and grey seals beneath. Offshore are Bawden Rocks or Man & His Man. The Giant Bolster Festival on May Day has a torchlight procession of giant puppets on the cliffs to celebrate the tricking of a giant into killing himself. St Agnes Museum has much of nautical interest.

Trevaunance Cove's cliffs are stained a deep red from tin mining and green from copper mining. It was the world's most productive source of copper from the 17th century until 1860 when copper was found in Michigan, to where some Cornish miners emigrated and where pasties can still be bought. Ore was sent down chutes and cargoes lowered by horse powered windlasses from the clifftops. There were five harbours from 1632, the last collapsing in 1915. One pierhead remains surrounded by dressed stone rubble. Above is Trevellas Coombe, used as a setting for the filming of the *Poldark* series. A stepped line of miner's cottages are known as the Stippy Stappy. With southwesterly winds this is where many surfers shelter.

Trevellas Porth is the home of the Blue Hills mine, operational from the 1830s to 1897.

Gliding and hang gliding take place from the airfield nearby while bass and harmless basking sharks glide through the sea. Before and after Cligga Head are old mineshafts, some with conical tops which admit greater horseshoe bats. A couple fell 90m to their deaths off the cliffs in 1834 while gathering samphire. Droskyn Point has a ravine where a pilchard seiners' boat access tunnel collapsed.

St Piran, the patron saint of tin miners, was a Celtic monk who was said to have sailed from Ireland on a millstone, possibly tied round his neck or possibly a mistaken identity of a coracle. As well as performing miracles as a hermit, he accidentally discovered tin while cooking next to the rocks and smelting some. His white cross on a black field is now used as the Cornish flag. **Perranporth** (Pirran's port) on the B3285 was a tin and copper working centre in the Middle Ages. Today it is a surfing centre with sand yachting on Perran Beach in the winter, a carnival in July and the Lowender Peran Celtic festival in October. Perranzabuloe Museum covers fishing, mining and farming. Winston Graham wrote *Demelza* in a bungalow overlooking the beach.

Perran Beach is backed by mineshafts and cave dotted cliffs covered in fulmars. Gear Sands and Penhale Sands are a sweep of dunes covered by caravan sites and holiday camps under which lies buried the supposed city of Langarroc, the inhabitants of which were said to have become greedy, immoral and lazy. Also buried was St Piran's 6th century oratory, the oldest Christian building in the British Isles. Uncovered by a storm in 1831, it has now had a concrete shell built over it but has had to be buried again to keep it from the attentions of vandals. A French ship wrecked in 1764 was cleared of its cargo in a day and a half while it took the miners less time to clear a wrecked Dutch vessel of its claret a year or two later. There was a double wrecking on the beach in 1778. Parts of the dunes belonged to the Penhale Camp military training area.

Carter's or Gull Rocks off Penhale Point guard entry into Holywell Bay. Holywell is a silted up port with two sets of stepping stones across. More steps come in a flight of 15 cut into the rock at the northeast end of the bay and lead down to the well, a spring. A stream assists forming surf. It was the setting for the Korean military base in filming *Die Another Day*.

The sea can be difficult off Kelsey Head but this suits its birds of prey and the seals which breed on the Chick.

Sand from Porth Joke or Polly Joke has been used as fertilizer since the time of James II when approval was given for this use by Act of Parliament. Porth Joke was partly described as Nampara in *Poldark*.

The River Gannel discharges down the northeast side of Crantock Beach and helps shape the surf. It lies between Pentire Point West and Pentire Point East, the latter guarded by the Goose.

Fistral Bay beach, possibly Europe's best surfing beach, is used for top contests. Behind the beach is a golf course and an abandoned large red Fistral Beach Hotel.

A small beach on the west side of Towan Head has limited parking and gives a possible landing point if conditions permit near a former lifeboat station.

Legendary Aussie wave ski surfer John Christensen at Fistral.

North Cornwall

Surf can occur on all beaches as far as the River Camel when the sea is up. Towan Head has a tide race off the end and a lookout manned in an emergency. Another lookout point is the whitewashed huer's house on the headland, in use until the late 19th century when pilchards became scarce. Using a 900mm long horn, the huer's job was to signal the arrival of the fish, of major importance to **Newquay**. One catch in the 1860s filled 1,000 carts and was worth £20,000. Today the fish are bass, mackerel, pollock and shark.

Building of the harbour was approved by the Bishop of Exeter in 1439. The sea breaks heavily off the entrance in onshore gales despite the apparently sheltered easterly facing position in Newquay Bay. Pilot gigs were raced for the prize of landing pilots on incoming cargo ships and a boat from 1812 and two others from last century are preserved and used for races in the summer. Newquay became a smuggling, fishing and trading centre, trading as far as North America.

In 1875 the railway arrived, bringing minerals and clay to the harbour and later, more importantly, tourists. Newquay is Cornwall's leading seaside resort and Britain's main surfing centre with 500 hotels and 75,000 tourists at the peak of the season. Surfing is restricted with boards over 1.5m long needing to be registered. The town has 11 beaches covering 11km of coast, semitropical gardens and The Blue Reef Aquarium Newquay with local fish and shellfish. Unusually for a seaside town it is built on top of cliffs with the A3058. Surf breaks become increasingly exposed to westerly winds moving northeast. A colony of herring gulls nest on rooftops. Emma Smith was brought up here, very different from the canals on which she first made her name as an author.

Abseiling and surfing take place at Lusty Glaze. Trevelgue Head has a large Iron Age fort on top and a blowhole in the headland. Porth limekiln imported limestone from South Wales for burning, to neutralize the acidic Cornish soil.

The B3276 follows Watergate Bay, used by surfers, kitesurfers and chef Jamie Oliver's customers. In 1869 there was a riot when looters tried to prevent a steam tug relaunching a ship beached by the surf.

Griffin's Point has an Iron Age hill fort which is directly in line with one of the runways of Cornwall Airport Newquay, the former RAF St Mawgan airfield, including the Cornwall Aviation Heritage Centre. It was used for early testing of Bloodhound to 340km/h and is proposed for horizontal take off space missions by Virgin.

The church at St Mawgan has a wooden memorial to nine men and a boy who died of hypothermia in a lifeboat in 1846 after their ship sank. Mawgan Porth is a surfing venue with a chip shop, toilets, Merrymoor public house, shop and dangerous currents. The settlement there may date from as early as the 5th century.

The former airfield above Trenance is now covered with the aerials of St Eval HF transmitter station.

This is one of the most memorable stretches of coastline in Britain and includes Bedruthan Steps, a set of granite crags which were supposed to have been used as stepping stones by the giant Bedruthan. It is more likely that the steep cliff staircase, closed in the winter, was cut by wreckers. Most notable of the wrecks here was the *Samaritan* in October 1846, taking silks and cottons from Liverpool. Only two crew members survived but the ship was renamed the *Good Samaritan* by locals who dressed in its cargo for years. A memorial at the top of the steps commemorates a Derby man drowned in 1903,

his friends being saved. Best known of the Steps is Queen Bess Rock which is said to resemble a full length figure of Elizabeth I. Other features are caves which cannot be reached by land except at low tide and the site of Iron Age Redcliffe Castle at the north end of the steps. Surf works best at low water.

Beyond Park Head with its Cow & Calf rocks and seabird breeding colonies is Porthcothan Bay backed by dunes and a stream which can help produce well shaped surf but lacking a large arch demolished in January 2014's storms.

Fox Cove has the 1969 wreck of the steam tanker *Hemsley 1* and Pepper and Warren Coves divide an Iron Age fort. Treyarnon Bay has rock shelving on both sides of its entrance and a nature reserve on Trethias Island. There is a dangerous rip on the southern side. In the rocks is a natural swimming pool and surf can work away from high water.

The backing of dunes fixed by marram grass returns behind the surfing beach of Constantine Bay, the dunes hiding the location of St Constantine's ruined Grade II medieval chapel. The bay is extended northwards by Booby's Bay, also used for surfing at low tide, towards the igneous bulk of Trevose Head. This stands on the far side of the Round Hole, tumulus topped Dinas Head and Stinking Cove with the outliers of the Bull and the igneous Quies. Trevose Head is dominated by its lighthouse. Standing 62m above the sea, it was established in 1847 and has a range of 43km. In return, the beams of Hartland Point, Lundy, Godrevy and Pendeen lights can be seen from the top. Tidal flow either way is 4km/h on springs, starting northeast at Dover HW and southwest at Dover HW +0600.

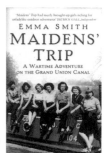

Merope Rocks, a line of needles with the occasional hole through, run east from Trevose Head and protect the lifeboat station in Polventon Bay where the **Padstow** lifeboat is based. The bay is also known as Mother Ivey's

Looking southwards from Treyarnon towards Park Head.

Treyarnon beach with the Quies on the right.

Sand dunes back the surfing beach at Constantine Bay.

The Bull and Quies off Dinas Head.

Stepper Point's daymark and Pentire Point beyond.

Bay after a formidable old lady who used to claim any wreckage. Today the most conspicuous feature is a large caravan site across the back of the bay.

Cataclews Point, with its blue Catacleuse stone outcrop, divides the bay from Harlyn Bay, overlooked by the houses of Harlyn. The village has been in use for a long time and an Iron Age cemetery has produced over a hundred cists of local slate, each grave having a crouched skeleton. Most exhibits are now in Padstow and Truro museums. The surf dumps at high tide in Harlyn Bay.

There is also surfing in Trevone Bay, the Round Hole of which resulted from the collapse of the roof of a sea cave. Razorbills, guillemots and kittiwakes nest here. A cliff collapse beyond Gunver Head has left the Butter Hole.

Largest and furthest of the offshore rocks on this section of coast is the igneous Gulland Rock off Gunver Head. Onshore is the 12m daymark on Stepper Point which also bears a National Coastwatch lookout built to view Padstow Bay and up the estuary of the River Camel, the major inlet of north Cornwall. Prominent are the houses of Polzeath and New Polzeath on a cliff, part of which slipped in the 1980s and had to be stabilized. This is a popular surfing area as there will be surf here if there is any in north Cornwall. It is biggest at low tide, though not as fast as some breaks, and 2–3m waves are common at the end of the day. Amenities include a large carpark, toilets with hot showers, supermarket, takeaway stores, chip shop and Galleon Beach Café.

Pentire Point resembles a cock's comb from the west as outcrops of rock are divided by grassy slopes. The point consists of knobbly pillow lavas. Newland, too, is a 37m igneous pillar. A small tide race runs between Newland and the point with overfalls outside Newland.

Rumps Point bears an Iron Age cliff castle which is probably the finest on the Cornish coast. The point is igneous, as are the 50m high Mouls. The area can be turbulent although it was not on the day in the First World War when Laurence Binyon landed on the Mouls from a small boat. He was moved by the solitude and tranquillity during those times of turmoil to write his Remembrance Day verse, *For the Fallen*.

A natural arch has resulted from the collapse of a sea cave in Lundy Bay, part of Port Quin Bay. Another wreck is that of the Greek freighter *Skopalos Sky*. The bay also featured a shipwreck in *Poldark*.

The little square tower of Doyden Castle is a Gothic folly, used as the Gatehouse in *Poldark*. Built in 1839 by Samuel Symons of Wadebridge, it doubled as a marker for the narrow inlet to Port Quin and as a drinking and gambling retreat. The castellated manor house of Roscarrock existed in the 11th century although it was partly rebuilt after 1880 and was used as Nampara in *Poldark*. The port's entire male population was said to have drowned in the 18th century while trying to escape from a press gang and it was again abandoned in the

The unusual profile of Rumps Point.

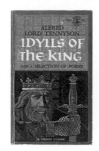

Gull Rock and the cart road down to Trebarwith Strand.

19th century after all the people and fishing boats were said to have been lost in a storm. In the latter case it is more likely that they all emigrated to Canada after the antimony mines near Droyden Point were closed.

Varley Head leads into Port Isaac Bay. Port Isaac at the end of the B3267, used as Sawle in filming *Poldark*, appears to have a welcoming message laid out across the grass facing the sea but closer inspection can show it to be the light reflecting off the windscreens of three rows of parked cars. Deception is not new to the town and there are smugglers' caves here. The town also retains its character in such narrow old streets as Squeeze-Belly-Alley. Permission is needed in advance for launching in Port Isaac and a fee is charged. Mackerel frequent the area and there are still some working fishing boats, fish

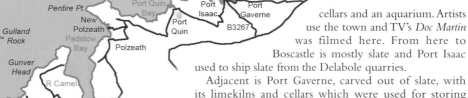

cellars and an aquarium. Artists use the town and TV's *Doc Martin* was filmed here. From here to Boscastle is mostly slate and Port Isaac used to ship slate from the Delabole quarries.

Adjacent is Port Gaverne, carved out of slate, with its limekilns and cellars which were used for storing pilchards. It also shipped slate. A tunnel through which slate was hauled has collapsed at Barrett's Zawn and there is evidence of an extensive slip on the cliffs. On top of

Sections of castle wall, a bridge and caves form an unreal landscape at Tintagel.

the cliffs a tower with slots at the top resembles nothing more than a giant concrete litter bin. Around Tregardock Beach are adders and grazing Hebridean sheep.

The prominent Gull Rock off Dennis Point marks Trebarwith Strand, Hardy's Barwith Strand, behind Port William. The sandy beach permits landing and is used by surfers. Facilities include the Port William and public toilets. In the 19th century a road was cut down through the rocks to allow access for carts to collect the shell sand for fertilizer. Carts also collected Welsh coal which had been tipped into the sea at high tide. Another high tide activity for ships was receiving slate lowered down from cliffside slate quarries on windlasses, the slate waste still being obvious on the cliffs to the north of the inlet and a tower of poorer slate has been left. The same technique of loading slate was also used at Dunderhole Point.

Surely nowhere on the English coastline is more evocative than Tintagel Head with its castle remains, best seen through a thin drizzle outside the tourist season, the remains of dark, wet, stone walls clinging to the massive bulk of the Island which isn't really an island. Tennyson's *The Idylls of the King* and *The Once & Future King* have done nothing to detract from this enchanted and forbidding spot. *Le Morte d'Arthur* has it as the base for King Mark and has the battle with the Sessoins nearby. Walter Scott mentions it in *The Betrothed* and RS Hawker in his *Quest of the Sangraal*. It was Dundagel to Hardy, who used it for his Mummers' play *The Famous Tragedy of the Queen of Cornwall*. Here Gorlois, Duke of Cornwall, kept his wife, Ygraine. Uther, the invading King of the Britons, was changed by Merlin to resemble Gorlois and seduced Ygraine. Gorlois died and Uther married Ygraine. The resulting child, Arthur, was to dwell here with his knights. Merlin's cave on the cliff face where Arthur first met Merlin seems to lack the basic mod cons which any self respecting magician should be capable of conjuring up. It has now been defaced by a large face carved into the cliff outside to represent Merlin and a tall bronze statue called Gallos has been added. Historical fact is rather stronger on the Celtic settlement founded around 400 and abandoned three centuries later, St Juliot founding a monastery in about 500. The Artognou stone found here may show this was a royal site from the Dark Ages. The castle's great hall was built in 1145 by Earl Reginald while Richard, Earl of Cornwall and brother of Henry III, contributed the wall and iron gate from the 13th century. Edward, the Black Prince, the first Duke of Cornwall, made further additions in the 14th century, in the latter part of which it was used as a

prison. The central portion had been washed away by sea erosion by the 16th century, repairs being carried out in 1852. The only other major development has been the building of a totally inappropriate large red brick Cameloot Castle Hotel right in the middle of this Area of Outstanding Natural Beauty.

Emma Hardy's *The Maid on the Shore*, about a Tintagel girl, was later used as a source of ideas by her husband.

A cliff face on Barras Nose has been eroded in such a way that it resembles the head of an elephant looking out to sea.

The Norman Bossiney Castle is a mound where the Round Table is said to be buried and from which it is claimed to rise on Midsummer's Eve. Bossiney Haven had Sir Francis Drake as its MP and has surfing, despite its inaccessibility. Lye Rock is a breeding ground for cormorants, fulmars, puffins and razorbills and seals frequent the area. Off Willapark with its Iron Age fort site are the Sisters, two large blocks of rock divided by a cleft through which it is easy to pass in a small boat if the sea is calm enough.

A more notable cleft is Rocky Valley, through which a small stream falls, the haunt of the Cornish hermit St Nectan. In this glen Arthur's knights were blessed before the quest for the Holy Grail. Its appeal is certainly not new for the ruins of a mill have cup and ring markings from the Bronze Age on them. A caravan site on the hill above is not obvious from the valley although very conspicuous from the sea.

More towering rock islands follow and rock forms become more intriguing as the rock turns to sandstone and shale. Meachard and a nearby blowhole guard the totally inconspicuous entrance to the picturesque harbour at Boscastle on the B3263, named after the former Bottreaux Castle, simplified by Hardy to Castle Boterel. With a large swell or strong onshore winds it is unusable. The inner jetty was rebuilt in 1584 by Sir Richard Grenville. The seaport thrived until the mid 19th century and the outer breakwater dates from this time when slate was being shipped. In 1941 the outer breakwater was damaged by a drifting mine and it was repaired in 1962. *A Pair of Blue Eyes* describes a steamer service which ran to Bristol. The harbour drains at low tide to leave just the River Valency, simply the Valley to Hardy, a stream which drops steeply into the village and up the sides of which 14th century cottages climb. A damaging flash flood in the valley in 2004 was very similar to a flood that had taken place in Lynmouth 52 years earlier almost to the

Meachard protects the approach to Boscastle.

The harbour entrance is hard to find and can be missed totally.

day. A new visitor centre features the flood. Land at the top is stitchmeal which has been used for over 1,000 years. Tenants grow crops on long thin stitches of land in summer and it is used as common grazing in winter. There is a Museum of Witchcraft & Magic in the village, which includes the remains of Ursula Hemp, a witch executed in 1589.

Another stream falls 36m to the sea at Pentargon Bay, Hardy's Targan Bay.

It was while working on St Juliot's church in 1872 that Thomas Hardy met his future wife, Emma Lavinia Gifford. The area around Beeny was at the centre of his thoughts, his courting and his poetry. High Cliff, Hardy's Windy Beak, is one of the highest in England at 223m and the highest point on the Cornish coast. With Beeny Cliff it was Hardy's Cliff without a Name and the setting for the episode in *A Pair of Blue Eyes* where Elfride Swancourt had to tear her clothes into strips to form a rope to rescue Henry Knight. The book noted the ferocious updraughts. From the top it is possible to see Lundy. This section of coast was given to the nation in 1959 by Wing Commander AG Parnall to commemorate his brother and other airmen lost in the Battle of Britain. No other aerial display could be more fitting for this is some of Britain's most majestic coastal scenery. It is not an area of safety, the Strangles having claimed over a score of ships in one year in the 1820s alone and even surfers avoid it at high water. It possesses magnificent cliff scenery and the rock folding becomes ever more dramatic until Samphire Rock, where the strata zigzag down the cliff face to burst forth at the bottom and emerge as a natural stone bridge, rather like a hand reaching out of a film screen.

The folded strata of Samphire Rock, flowing out into a bridge.

Cambeak, itself a heavily folded structure being eaten back by the sea and cropped by goats, is the last point before Crackington Haven, a small surfing beach overlooked by the Coombe Barton Inn. Even this haven has a sting in the tail for a sharp ridge of rock runs out to Bray's Point on the southern side of the beach, sometimes obvious, sometimes submerged and sometimes ready to damage the boats of the unwary. In 1894 seven people were lost here from the Swedish brigantine *William* and then another seven from the steamer *City of Vienna* and, six years later, the barque *Capricorna*. All are buried at St Gennys.

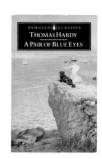

The folded strata of Cambeak.

Crackington Haven has a line of sharp rocks, below the surface much of the time.

Distance
55km from Towan Head to Crackington Haven

OS 1:50,000 Sheets
190 Bude & Clovelly
200 Newquay & Bodmin

Tidal Constants
Perranporth:
Dover −0600
Newquay:
Dover −0600
Padsrow:
HW Dover −0550
LW Dover −0540
Port Isaac:
Dover −0600
Boscastle:
HW Dover −0520
LW Dover −0600

Sea Area
Lundy

Connection
River Camel – see RoB p8

41 Northwest Devon

Literary giants and an eccentric vicar

Twine from this hour, in ceaseless toil,
On Blackrock's sullen shore
Till cordage of the sand shall coil
Where crested surges roar.
RS Hawker

Leaving Crackington Haven beneath the 130m sheer cliffs on the north side results in turning towards Dizzard Point, a cliff which has seen plenty of slips and is covered by a scrub which is England's westernmost dwarf oak wood.

A break in the cliff reveals Millook which is probably the boundary of the traditional kingdom of Cornwall as the place names change suggests, despite the present jurisdiction continuing for some distance. On rare occasions it is surfable.

Black Rock, a remarkably striking finger of rock con-

Crooklets Beach and the southern sweep of Bude Bay.

The unrelenting cliffs north of Flexbury.

Badly stacked strata at Sandy Mouth.

sidering the amount of rock around, signals the southern end of Widemouth Bay. Coming ashore here are some transatlantic submarine cables, the 6,525km New Jersey cable of 1963, the 5,195km Nova Scotia cable of 1973, the No 10/White House hotline and surfers.

Cliffs run up to Bude and passed on the way is Efford Beacon, a small grass mound.

A 6m high octagonal pointed stone tower marks Compass Point, the entrance to Bude Haven, an area of confused water resulting from the bar across it. Surf can be heavy and surfing may be restricted in summer, surfboards over 1.52m long need to be registered and a fee is charged for launching from the harbour. There is a saltwater swimming pool on the beach for those who want calmer conditions. Facing the harbour are the lock gates at the end of the Bude Canal, built in 1823 to carry beach sand to Launceston for use as fertilizer and intended to be extended to the River Tamar at Calstock, a 145km canal to cover 45km, barges returning with oats and slate for shipment. A storm damaged the sea lock gates in 1997 and 2008. The old name of **Stratton** gave Hardy his Stratleigh. There is a nature trail at the 12th century Ebbingford Manor. The town was notorious for wreckers. In the last four decades of the 19th century 47 ships were lost trying to enter the harbour with a further 85 north of Crackington Haven. Over 150 have been wrecked between here and Morwenstow. **Bude** remains the town described by John Betjeman as the 'least rowdy of British resorts' although it does rise to the occasion during the August Bude Carnival and Bude Jazz Festival week. Among those in Bude with a spirit of adventure was Sir Goldsworthy Gurney who, in 1830, built Bude Castle (now the council offices) on a raft of concrete on sand to prove that it was possible to build on shifting sand. The offices include a Heritage Centre with wrecks and other marine interests, geology and the Bude Canal. The following year Gurney began the world's first inter town steam carriage service with 19km/h carriages of his own design. Bude Light commemorates him.

The final beach is Crooklets at Flexbury where the Wrangle Point end of the beach is protected by a heavy concrete retaining wall. The beach is backed by beach huts, parking, a snack bar and the premises of Bude Surf Life Saving Club, the first lifeguard club in the country. It is heavily used by surfers. The beach was the site of the first kayak surfing contest in the mid 20th century when harbourmaster Jack Dymond asked kayak surfers to develop their surfing get together into a competition to extend the Bude season by a fortnight at the end of September.

Now the cliffs begin in earnest. Boulders litter the shore and the cliff is frequently too steep to climb. Cliffs are often exotically folded, a legacy of the Armorican period, especially at Sandy Mouth, used by surfers.

At Duckpool the landing has the added complexity of strata up on edge with pieces chipped away to produce lines of saw teeth at intervals between the boulders, hardly the best things to meet on a landing in surf but surfers use it. Daphne du Maurier had Richard Grenville viewing it from Coombe near his home in Stowe Barton in *The King's General*. To the north Steeple Point is massively landslipped, yet above this on Lower Sharpnose Point is GCHQ Composite Signals Organisation, a communications satellite ground station with a battery of enormous white radar dish aerials which are conspicuous from much of Bude Bay.

A driftwood hut was built on the cliffs by the opium

Lower Sharpnose Point with one of its radar dishes, seen from Sandy Mouth.

smoking Rev RS Hawker, the eccentric vicar of Morwenstow from 1834 to 1875, and it was here that he wrote his poems, including *The Song of the Western Men*. He also used it to warn ships of dangers from the rocks. St Morwenna was a 9th century Celtic saint and St Morwenna & St John the Baptist's church saw a number of innovations during Hawker's time. It was he who reintroduced the Harvest Festival service, condemned the plundering of wrecks and gave drowned sailors a full Christian burial rather

than simply burying them on the beach where they were washed up as was the normal practice at the time. He once dressed as a mermaid to hoax his superstitious parishioners and his vicarage had chimneys shaped like church towers. His wife was 40 years younger than him, his cat

was excommunicated for catching mice on Sunday and mourners at his funeral wore purple. Part of the church is Norman but it was founded in Anglo-Saxon times.

At Marsland Mouth the county boundary is met, scene of Rose Salterne's naked night-time fortune telling episode in the sea, with the White Witch, in Charles Kingsley's *Westward Ho!* Another hut on the north side was used by writer Ronald Duncan.

Welcombe Mouth, just to the north, was the haunt of Cruel Coppinger, a feared Dane who landed in a storm during the 18th century. He then ran a wrecking and smuggling gang for years before escaping to a waiting ship and disappearing as the revenue men closed in.

The cliffs rise to 150m at Embury Beacon and bear an Iron Age fort. Nearby fields have S shaped boundaries suggesting that they are medieval furlongs. This coast produces the best hanging waterfalls in the country and the one at Speke's Mill Mouth is among the most dramatic at a beach sought out by serious surfers. St Catherine's Tor is thought to have had a Roman villa on top. Wargery Water descends in another significant fall.

The white Quay Hotel and museum at Hartland Quay are prominent from as far away as Higher Sharpnose Point. The Wreckers Retreat bar has a three dimensional

The Quay Hotel at Hartland Quay. The quay was to the left of the buildings.

Folded strata at Hartland Quay.

The lighthouse at Hartland Point.

map of the many wrecks along this section of coast, most prominent of which was the steamship *Uppingham* in 1890. Building of the quay was authorized by Parliament in 1586 and financed by Sir Francis Drake, Sir John Hawkins and Sir Walter Raleigh, to become a significant port to the north of the present buildings. Barley and oats were exported. There is a limekiln and there were imports of coal, lime and timber as well as the lead needed to repair the roof of the 14th century St Nectan's church at Stoke, the tower of which was built 39m

Grey seal resting at Hartland Point.

high as a landmark for sailors. The quay broke up in 1887 and now little remains except the boulders on the shore, backed by strata which change from horizontal to vertical in a few metres. There is a seawater swimming pool among the rocks and a private slipway leads up to the hotel where a bar contains relics of the *Green Ranger*, a wreck in the rescue of which Hartland men played a gallant part. The hotel is the former harbourmaster's house, offices, stables, storerooms and workers' cottages. Opposite is the museum which covers four centuries of shipwreck at Morwenstow, Welcombe, Hartland and Clovelly, smuggling, coastal trades, geology and natural history.

Tower remains at the Warren were a folly. Not all wrecks were caused by the sea, a memorial recalling the hospital ship *Glenart Castle*, sunk here in 1918 by a German submarine with the loss of 153 lives.

The remains of a large freighter lie rusting on the rocks next to the lighthouse at Hartland Point, a reminder of the power of the sea. To the Romans it was the Promontory of Hercules. The 1874 lighthouse, low on the 110m high cliffs, has the strongest beam of any in Britain.

Here the coast is at its nearest to Lundy which can be seen lying 20km to the northwest.

Rounding the point into Barnstaple or Bideford Bay brings a change with the cliffs being nearly vertical until

Blackchurch Rock on the northern approach to Clovelly.

Clovelly and running parallel to the strike of the rocks rather than cutting across them as south of Hartland Point. There is a tide race off the point but tidal flows are generally weak in Bideford Bay, flooding NE and ebbing SW except between Hartland Point and Clovelly where there is a significant westerly flow on the ebb. A spherical radar scanner like a giant microphone is set on the cliffs between Barley and Shipload Bays.

A Wellington crashed in Beckland Bay in 1942. Above Windbury Point is a settlement site and the remains of the Iron Age Windbury Castle.

Mill Mouth beach was used for smuggling and has the strking Blackchurch Rock. From here the woods of Gallantry Bower cover the 110m high cliffs which reach their best at Gallant Rock where they rise almost vertically and smoothly to their full height from the water. On top is the Clovelly Court estate with the Angels Wings sculpture of 1826 like a pagoda, carved by the estate butler.

Clovelly is a lobster fishing village which had huge catches of herring in the 18th and 19th centuries. The quay was lengthened in 1826 to give extra protection to the large fishing fleet, although it still suffers from a groundswell on a westerly or southwesterly wind and sometimes from a shallow bank of stones at the harbour entrance. Steepways was the name for the village which Charles Dickens and Wilkie Collins used as the

setting for *A Message from the Sea*. It was also identified in *Westward Ho!* by Charles Kingsley, who wrote the *Water Babies* here and whose father was rector here. It was painted by Turner and Whistler and images of it were used by Wedgwood. First settled in the Iron Age, it was mentioned in the *Domesday Book* and flourished in the 13th and 14th centuries. The village is best known for its main street which follows the bed of an old watercourse and is cobbled with beach pebbles set on edge, only being passable on foot or by donkey hauled sledge, used to bring in goods from the top while refuse is removed from the bottom by boat. There is a large carpark at the top and a narrow and very steep vehicle road to the bottom where there is very limited parking, use of which may be permitted to load and unload boats. The village has an entry fee for those arriving by road.

Facilities at the bottom include the Red Lion Hotel and toilets. There a Kingsley Museum and a Fisherman's Cottage museum with a sail loft in a 1930s stone and cob house.

Merlin was said to have been born in a cave behind a waterfall near the lifeboat station.

Marie Corelli set some of *The Mighty Atom* in the village. The woods continue to Peppercombe, initially with Hobby Drive, described by Kingsley as 'a forest wall 500 feet high of almost semitropic luxuriance.' Made by Sir Charles Hamlyn, it may

The cottages of Clovelly set on their sheer and lofty cliff around the course of an old stream.

225

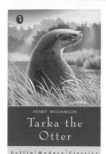

have been to provide employment during the slump which followed the Napoleonic wars. Below is a large cave which was the home in the 18th century of John Gregg and his cannibal family who were said to kill travellers and eat them, the sort of tale which would keep the public away from any smugglers who happened to be about.

The sweeping coastline is disrupted to the east of Lower Bight of Fernham by the Gore, an intertidal rocky ridge which runs out 1.2km northwards from the shore.

The bar causes problems at Buck's Mills, a tiny fishing village named after its watermill, the harbour first built in the 15th century by using gunpowder to clear the rocks. It imported limestone from South Wales in the 19th century to burn in the kilns by the shore to neutralize acidic soil. On the other hand, it was used for the early experiments on tidal power, a reliable renewable source of power which does not involve ruining the scenery and which also gives refuges for fish stocks. Big swells can produce notable surf at low water.

Below Peppercombe Castle, the remains of an Iron Age fort, the cliffs ease in height for a while although streams still drop the last 12m to the beach and cliffs turn to the bright red so characteristic of Devon soils. The brown and white bungalow was a 1920s Boulton & Paul kit, delivered by rail. Portledge estate was owned by the Coffin family for centuries, later the Pine-Coffins.

A limekiln is sited on Abbotsham Cliff. Mermaid's Pool is more likely to produce bird life, particularly curlews, oystercatchers and shags.

Kipling's Tor is a gorse covered hill to the west of Westward Ho!, a reminder that Rudyard Kipling was a pupil of the United Services College in Westward Ho! (now Kipling Terrace) from 1878 to 1882. The area was used in his *Stalky & Co*, including cliffs, Pebble Ridge and the wreck of an Armada galleon. The town was started as a holiday resort speculation in 1863, the name coming from Kingsley's novel, based around Bideford. Today it has beach huts, café, bars, hot dog and pasty stall, fast food takeaway and toilets. Surfing is popular all along the foot of the Pebble Ridge, a natural phenomenon stretching 3km north from the town and sheltering Northam Burrows Country Park and the Royal North Devon Golf Club, the first English seaside course, on low sandhills which form the burrows, the oldest still on its original site. A spit protects the Skern.

Tidal flows northwards from Westward Ho! to Baggy Point are significant on the flood. The major estuary of north Devon is that of the Torridge and Taw which discharge large tidal flows into Bideford Bay and can raise heavy seas over the Zulu Bank and Bideford Bar on the ebb with a westerly wind blowing.

The passenger ferry *Oldenburg* operates from **Bideford** to Lundy. The buildings of **Appledore** and Instow are seen on either side of the River Torridge and the hangers of RAF Chivenor on the River Taw.

Braunton Burrows on the north of the estuary are a nature reserve with marram grass, marsh orchids, roundheaded club rush, sand toadflax and sea stock. The public are kept away partly by army ranges which are operational when red flags are flying with a danger area up to 6km offshore. It is one of the grandest sand dune areas in Britain with shell sand dunes up to 30m high, hiding **Braunton**, a former busy fishing port with a history going back to the Stone Age, said to be Britain's largest village. It is here that US troops trained for the Normandy landings in 1944 because of the suitability of the venue, recalled by the American Road. Much of the activity in *Tarka the Otter* is based beyond the dunes but he did travel up the coast to Heddon's Mouth and the dunes also featured at times in *The Maid of Sker*.

Old Red Sandstone and tough Devonian slates now emerge from beneath the Carboniferous Culm Measures and there are three successive west facing sand beaches terminated by rocky headlands.

Saunton Sands are popular for surfing and end below a large white hotel block, beach huts, a pillbox and what looks like the end of a tunnel emerging onto the beach. Behind is Saunton Golf Club, which has hosted the British Ladies' and English Amateur Championships.

Saunton Down, capped with two aerials and edged by the B3231, divides the beach from Croyde Bay and has an experts' surf break on the end. The bay is again backed by dunes, with aerials on Ora Hill and parking at the north end of the beach. Croyde has perhaps the most reliable surf beach in Devon, a coastguard station, the Gem, Rock & Shell Museum featuring semiprecious stones and shells, a village of thatched and colour washed cottages and the Ruda Holiday Park.

Tide streams run north–south across the entrance to Morte Bay. While they are weak in the bay they can be 7km/h on springs at Baggy Leap where there may be a tide race or overfalls. The Salcombe smack *Ceres*, which was built in 1811 and was the oldest ship on Lloyd's Register for many years, came to grief on Baggy Point in 1936. The point, of Devonian rock, has several caves including the enormous Baggy Hole which can be reached by small boat or by the climbers who frequent the near vertical slabs on the point. The white post was a wreck point, from where a line would be fired by cannon to a shipwrecked crew if it was too rough to launch the lifeboat.

Putsborough Sand at the southern end of Woolacombe Sand has surfing. Going north, dunes gradually build up, being sown with marram grass. Woolacombe, from Wolmecoma, wolves valley, faces the sea at the end of the B3343 with nearby parking, children's playground, donkey rides, beach café and toilets, a complete resort in miniature but without brashness, and the surf is best at the northern end.

Distance
72km from Crackington Haven to Woolacombe

OS 1:50,000 Sheets
180 Barnstaple & Ilfracombe
190 Bude & Clovelly

Tidal Constants
Boscastle:
HW Dover −0520
LW Dover −0600
Bude: Dover −0540
Clovelly:
Dover −0530
Appledore:
Dover −0520
Ilfracombe:
HW Dover −0520
LW Dover −0540

Sea Area
Lundy

Range
Braunton Burrows

Connections
River Torridge – see RoB p11
River Taw – see RoB p14

The caves and slabs of Baggy Point, complete with climbers.

Exmoor

Porlock, thy verdant vale so fair to sight,
Thy lofty hills with fern and furze so brown,
Thy waters that so musical roll down
Thy wooded glens, the traveller with delight
Recalls to memory, and the channel grey
Circling it, surges in thy level bay.
Porlock, I also shall forget thee not.
Robert Southey

The coast leading away from Woolacombe passes Barricane Beach with more testing surf and Grunta Beach, named after shipwrecked pigs. Mortehoe has the attractive St Mary's church founded in the 13th century. A ridge of land covered with footpaths projects west from here to Morte Point which has been the death of many ships, assisted by wreckers in the 18th century and a tide race. Indeed, the Morte Stone alone claimed five ships in the winter of 1852. This might be said to be the starting point of the southern side of the Bristol Channel.

The tide stream between Morte Point and Ilfracombe is 6km/h on springs, starting eastwards at HW Dover +0400 and westwards at HW Dover −0520. Rockham Bay can have strong tides.

Bull Point has had a lighthouse since 1879 but a cliff fall in 1972 caused so much damage that a new automatic one was built and opened in 1975, a white round tower above the overfalls off Bull Point.

Beyond Damage Cliff is Lee Bay, a delightful inlet backed by trees and known as Fuschia Valley as it is surrounded by fuchsias and hydrangeas. There is a slipway.

An early wind generator is positioned at Higher Slade to take full benefit of the exposed position.

Passenger ferries from Lundy and South Wales operate into **Ilfracombe** and Ronald had taken the trip here on the *Lady Moira* in *One Warm Saturday* in Dylan Thomas' *Portrait of the Artist as a Young Dog*. A final landing was made here out of season in *The Maid of Sker*. This was Alfred's valley from the West Saxon Ielfred and Old English cumb, a town with a long seafaring tradition with a harbour since the 12th century. Once the fifth port in Britain, it was used by King John and by Henry III to assemble forces against Ireland and it sent six ships to the siege of Calais in 1346, only 14 years before the George & Dragon was founded. Four French men-of-war failed to attack in 1797 when the women of the town, summoned by Betsy Gammon's drum, lined up on War Hill in their red petticoats, looking like soldiers

from a distance. St Nicholas' chapel on Lantern Hill was built as a landmark for sailors in 1321 and has been a seamen's chapel and lighthouse, still showing a light today. Now Ilfracombe has only fishing vessels in the harbour which is invisible from seaward, sheltering behind the promenade pier. Heavy swells and strong tides with a short confused sea in northerly winds are a feature of the area. Hotels and colourwashed cottages abound, the town having developed in the Victorian era with the coming

A race runs off the end of Bull Point's rocks at times.

A large and distinctive sculpture guards Ilfracombe harbour.

Lee Bay is a beautiful little inlet on a coast which is generally cliffbound.

Looking east from Combe Martin past the Little Hangman and Great Hangman towards Highveer Point.

of the former railway from Barnstaple. Ilfracombe Museum has models, paintings and photographs of ships, the harbour, the coast, Lundy, minerals, natural history and archaeology and Ilfracombe Chocolate Emporium has a chocolate museum. To the east of the town an aerial stands between a fort and the 1525 watermill at Hele. Now with its 5.5m wheel restored it produces wholemeal flour. Hele Bay itself, overlooked by a golf course on Widmouth Hill, has a tide filled paddling pool. *English Hours* describes the town as a very finished little speciemn of its genus.

Rillage Point has a tide rip which develops over Buggy Pit with westerly winds.

Now begins one of the most impressive and remote stretches of cliff in England, reaching to beyond Porlock. The 300m high plateau of Exmoor with the A399 falls directly to the sea, possibly helped by Tertiary faulting. The view from Widmouth Head past Hangman Point and Highveer Point to Foreland Point with a virtually unbroken line of cliffs is breathtaking.

Water Mouth can be rough in NW winds. This inlet was used to test PLUTO, the pipeline under the ocean for supplying the Allies with fuel during the Normandy landings in the Second World War, a trial line being laid to Swansea before the English Channel was tackled. Today it is overlooked by a small holiday camp while Watermouth Castle, dating from 1825, stands at its head as a theme park with great hall, smugglers' dungeons, coloured fountain and waterfalls and various exhibitions plus older tunnels beneath.

Combe Martin is a linear village and is one of those claiming to have the longest village street in England. It follows the River Umber down from the former London Inn past the oddly shaped Pack of Cards Inn. Other features include the castle, the old poor house, St Peter ad Vincula's church (included in *The Mighty Atom*, mostly set here, by Marie Corelli who lived in the village), the Coombe Martin Motorcycle Collection (which has TE Lawrence's Brough Superior) and the 13th century silver-lead mines which were worked until the 19th century. There is a carnival in August. There are the usual facilities such as a café near the beach, overlooked by caravans and chalets. Surf is a possibility.

From here the coast is part of the Exmoor National Park although this does not prevent the intrusion of jets. Wild Pear beach is overlooked by the Little Hangman which is followed by the Great Hangman, leading away onto Girt Down. Both peaks are of resistant sandstones. The Great Hangman is 318m high, of deep red colour, from the top of which it is possible to

see Wales on the far side of the Bristol Channel. The Hangman name is claimed to follow after a thief was strangled by the rope while tying up a sheep he was stealing.

There is beach access at North Cleeve. Throughout most of this section of coast it is virtually impossible to scale the cliffs even if a landing can be made. An exception is at Heddon's Mouth where a footpath leads out beside the River Heddon past an 18th century kiln used for burning Welsh limestone to neutralize the acidic Exmoor soil. The location was used as a mooring to launch a surprise attack on the Taw in *The Maid of Sker*.

A tide race runs off Highveer Point but it may be possible to avoid it by passing inside fallen rocks if conditions are not too rough.

Martinhoe Roman fortlet and signal station, built in 50 to 60 and abandoned in 75, is on the cliffs above. It housed about 80 soldiers and had inner and outer enclosures with gates facing in opposite directions.

Hollow Brook Waterfall drops 200m in 400m. Woody Bay and Lee Bay are surrounded by oak woods, the cliffs being breeding grounds for auks, fulmars, guillemots, kittiwakes, razorbills, shags and gulls, mostly between March and July. Woody Bay has a slipway while Lee Bay has a beach landing. The latter is overlooked by Lee Abbey, built as a private house in 1850, a school for evacuated boys during the Second World War and now used as a Christian retreat centre. Onshore wildlife in this remote settlement includes dippers, herons, wagtails and mink.

A tower on Duty Point mirrors Castle Rock and other fantastic shapes along the cliffs. The

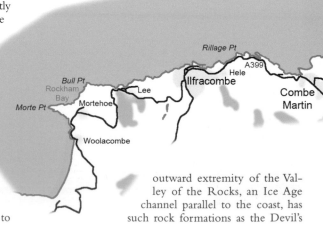

outward extremity of the Valley of the Rocks, an Ice Age channel parallel to the coast, has such rock formations as the Devil's

The cliff railway and rebuilt Rhenish tower at Lynmouth.

Cheesewring, Rugged Jack and Mother Meldrum's Cave, Mother Meldrum being the character on whom RD Blackmore based the witch in *Lorna Doone*. Some of the rocks are said to be wives of the Devil, whom he turned to stone after he returned here to his castle and found them drunk. Stone circles may have been used by Druids and there were Iron and Bronze Age residents. Stonecutter Daniel Lumb, an enthusiast of mathematics and astronomy, opened up a cleft to form a cave, entered by rolling, where he lived with his wife and family for the rest of his life. Feral goats are now present.

The Lyn & Exmoor Museum is in **Lynton**'s oldest house, which is haunted.

Lynmouth stands at the estuary of the East Lyn and West Lyn, 200m vertically below Lynton. The two are

but the most famous rescue was that of the *Forest Hall* in a gale in 1899 when it was too rough to launch the lifeboat, *The Louisa*. Instead, she was hauled overland to Porlock Bay, a journey which involved felling trees and other minor engineering works before the boat could be launched 10 hours later, saving 15 lives. There was a prosperous herring fishing and curing industry until 1607 but more recently it has been popular with tourists, the Victorians calling it Little Switzerland. Those coming for the scenery included the poets Coleridge, Southey and Wordsworth in the 19th century. RD Blackmoor is claimed to have written part of *Lorna Doone* in the 14th century Rising Sun.

It is for 15th August 1952 that Lynmouth is remembered. In one of the most violent British storms on record 130mm of rain fell in an hour with a further

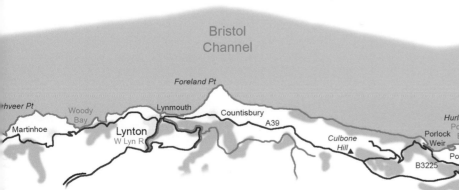

connected by a 260m working cliff railway built in 1890 at a gradient of 1:1.75. At that time it was the steepest railway in the world and the first of its kind in England, being powered by tanks each able to hold $3.2m^3$ of water, filled from the West Lyn and emptied at the bottom. It was invented by local man Bob Jones and funded by Sir George Newnes and friends. Lynmouth has a lifeboat

100mm over the next 24 hours. Descending onto the sodden moorland and swept down into Lynmouth by the two rivers, it washed down an estimated 100,000t of debris in the process, sweeping away 34 people, demolishing 60 buildings and gouging a swathe through the centre of the town. The subsequent

Cliffs to the east of Foreland Point have hanging waterfalls.

The small harbour at Porlock Weir.

appeal raised £1,336,425 from the stunned nation, a vast sum for that time. Ministry of Defence records of cloud seeding experiments taking place in southern England at the time were later found to be missing. Lynmouth has always been built on a delta of flood debris but the river bed has now been widened and the houses are not built quite so close to it. Many buildings did survive, including some old hotels near the harbour. A Rhenish tower on the harbour wall, inspired by towers on the Rhine, was rebuilt in 1954, replacing one built in 1832 by General Rawdon to supply salt water for his bath but also used as a pilchard huer's lookout. For those wishing to bathe in salt today there is a tidefilled swimming pool or the surf break.

Countisbury church of St John the Baptist to the east is a 19th century DIY job by the parishioners.

Lynmouth to Porlock is very committing in anything above a force 3 with its long run of unbroken cliffs. Countisbury Hill offers the highest sea cliffs in England at 302m and is where over 800 Vikings were killed in 878 while trying to besiege the king's thegns. Lynmouth Road runs east for 9¼ hours of each tide cycle at 3km/h on springs although the flow westwards on the ebb is barely perceptible.

Lynmouth Foreland lighthouse was established in 1900 with a range of 42km, a white round tower near the bottom of the cliff face. There are overfalls and heavy seas break over Foreland Ledge in bad weather and between the ledge and Sand Ridge in westerly gales. A channel through the rocks avoids the tide race.

Old Barrow Roman fortlet and signal station controlled Roman shipping in the Bristol Channel and watched out for trouble from the Silures in South Wales. It had the same opposite facing inner and outer gates as Martinhoe and was probably abandoned when the latter was built. The earthworks remain.

Between Foreland Point and Porlock Weir at the end of the B3225 only one house is passed, Glenthome on the Devon/Somerset border. The Sister's Fountain, marked by a 19th century cross, is claimed to have been started when Joseph of Arimathea struck his staff on the ground. Landing is possible but difficult if the weather is bad. Even so, Embelle Wood beach was used for smuggling. Woods run through to Porlock Weir except on the occasional spot where a slip has swept the cliffs bare of all vegetation bigger than grass, a frequent occurrence.

Amongst the trees is the spire of Culbone's Grade I St Beuno's church, one of the smallest churches in England at 11m x 4m with a 6.5m x 3.9m nave, dating from the 12th century or even being Saxon in parts. It seats 30 including a family box pew and is still in regular use. The name derives from Kil Beun after St Beuno, a 6th century Welsh saint, the church being founded by missionary Welshmen who crossed the Bristol Channel on rafts. There is a leper squint window and the steeple of 1810 is claimed to be the top of the steeple of St Dubricius in Porlock. The common Red name on the graves is thought to have led to the Ridds in *Lorna Doone*. The churchyard cross is Grade II★. Charcoal burners who worked in Culbone Woods were said to have been lepers who were not allowed to cross Culbone Water to approach Porlock, their hut remains still being present.

A low boulder promontory is striking because it con-

The iconic sweeping bank of pebbles at Porlock.

trasts with the incessant cliffs and gives notice of arrival at Porlock Bay, beneath which is a 5,000–6,000 year old submarine forest. Worked flints and part of an auroch skeleton have been found locally. The South West Sea Life Centre and Porlock Weir Boat Shed Museum display aspects of local life. Porlock Weir was once a busy port trading pit props for Welsh coal. Its colourwashed and thatched houses face a natural drydock, approached through a gap in the pebble bank marked with a pair of withies. The 11m tides here are used to drain the dock naturally. Pillboxes and a ruined limekiln overlook the bay. Large swell is sometimes surfed.

Dunkery Beacon is, at 519m, the highest hill adjoining the south side of the Bristol Channel. As the land slopes down to the coast it includes the notorious Porlock Hill on the A39, first climbed by car in 1901 to win a bet.

The eastern half of Porlock Bay is edged by a sweeping bank of pebbles with groynes at the Porlock Weir end, a wall of grey stones which curves round towards Hurlstone Point, hiding the thatched village of Bossington. The 8,000 year old bank has been repaired for centuries after breaches until 1990 but permission to repair a 1996 breach was refused in order to create more marsh, killing the mature oak trees on this formerly protected farmland.

The remains of a futuristically profiled coastguard lookout on Hurlstone Point stand above the water to the west where there is a strong undertow.

Between Hurlstone Point and Greenaleigh Point is another section of cliff with a landslip area in the Foreland sandstone. Selworthy Sand, between high and low tides, offers the first beach of golden sand since leaving Woolacombe. However, the cliffs have now returned, with sheep grazing precariously, and continue to Greenaleigh Point so it is not possible to climb off the beach. After the beach there are continuous boulders along the shoreline, making landing difficult.

The remains of Burgundy Chapel come as the land sweeps down from Bratton Ball to the shore for the first time with farmland and the Exmoor National Park and South West Coast Path come to an end with a nature trail.

Minehead is from the Celtic mynedd, hill, Myn-heafdon meaning the hill above two rivers, the East and West Myne. It is entered past a pair of beacon structures and a pillbox into a harbour which has a slipway but which empties to leave an expanse of silt covered sand with surprisingly angular stones everywhere. The pier was built in 1488 by Sir Hugh Luttrell and extended two centuries later by another Luttrell as the sea level dropped. The sea breaks over the pier in northerly gales while SE winds and spring tides produce a swell for three hours around high tide. In addition, there can be 7–9km/h currents yet Daniel Defoe describes it as the safest harbour on the south side of the Bristol Channel,

Selworthy Sand seen from Hurlstone Point.

despite which actress Esmé Clay drowned in a boating accident here in 1947. It was trading fish and woollen goods in the 15th century before problems with plague and raids by Welsh privateers. In the 17th century it was second only to Bristol of the Bristol Channel ports with ships going to the Mediterranean, Virginia and the West Indies. By 1716 coal was being imported from South Wales and cattle, hides and wool from Ireland with broadcloths, fish and grain being exported, herrings being a major part of the fishing activity. Trade slumped in the 19th century and it became a resort. The Inklings group of Oxford authors used it as a base for an Exmoor walking holiday. Although most development has been since the 19th century there are colourwashed 17th century cottages and records going back to Saxon times. On May Day the hobby horse, known here as the Sailor's Horse, dances through the streets, a custom dating from the mists of time. The 15th century St Michael's church on North Hill had a lantern tower to guide mariners, not to mention a chest with the arms of the Tudor vicar Robert Fitzjames (who became a bishop and built Fulham Palace) and a sculpture on the east wall showing St Michael weighing a soul while the Devil clings on and the Madonna tries to restore the balance by prayer. A reminder that alabaster was once mined in Somerset comes with the alabaster statue of Queen Anne by Francis Bird, a protegé of Grinling Gibbons, which was moved from the church to Wellington Square. Much of the town's development was undertaken by the Luttrells of Dunster, although things have now changed on the seafront with holiday amusement centres flashing batteries of coloured lights along the back of the bay.

Distance
57km from Woolacombe to Minehead

OS 1:50,000 Sheets
180 Barnstaple & Ilfracombe
181 Minehead & Brendon Hills

Tidal Constants
Ilfracombe:
HW Dover −0520
LW Dover −0540
Lynmouth:
HW Dover −0500
Porlock Bay:
HW Dover −0450
LW Dover −0530
Minehead:
HW Dover −0440
LW Dover −0500

Sea Area
Lundy

Moor Wood overlooks Minehead with its harbour wall.

43 Bridgwater Bay

Muddy waters beyond the Somerset Levels

The fair breeze blew, the white foam flew,
The furrow followed free;
We were the first that ever burst
Into that silent sea.
Samuel Taylor Coleridge

The West Somerset Railway terminus at Minehead.

Smoke issues from chimneys on both sides of the bay at Minehead. Opposite is Aberthaw power station on the Welsh coast while behind the bay is the terminus of the West Somerset Railway, the longest privately owned railway in Britain, running steam and diesel trains 37km to Bishops Lydeard.

Lying off the large holiday camp with its prominent waterslides are the Cables, a shingle reef which bears a submarine forest. Currents are swift, running at 7–9km/h close inshore on springs. Spring tides also cause a swell in the bay for 1½ hours each side of high water, giving uncomfortable conditions with strong southeasterly wind.

At low water the remains of a large fish trap can be seen among the boulders on Dunster Beach. A red pillbox fronts a golf course before lines of chalet huts stand between Dunster Beach and the Grade II★ Old Manor. At Dunster itself the Conyger Tower folly is prominent on a hilltop but the much larger Norman Dunster

Castle, Hardy's Stancy Castle (owned by the Luttrell family for 600 years), is also clearly visible. In 1645/6 the Royalists withstood a six month siege before surrendering to the Parliamentarians, one shot still being visible in the Yarn Market. The village also has a 13th century Old Nunnery, tithe barn and dovecot, 17th century watermill still operating, a medieval packhorse bridge over the River Avill, a holy well and a butter cross.

A caravan site precedes Blue Anchor, a village which takes its name from Blue Anchor Bay, in turn reflecting the tenacious blue clay which comes up when vessels weigh anchor in Blue Anchor Road. Retired boatbuilder Charles Pettican would have been happy to retire here from Wivenhoe in *Mehalah*. The B3191 follows the shore for a while.

Reefs now form the shoreline and continue as far as Hinkley Point. At the same time, cliffs begin again, bright red at first but changing to grey with a sharp dividing line, the colours merging between red and grey as far as Stoke Bluff.

Warren Bay has fishing stakes in the form of scaffolding poles driven into the bed and also a swimming pool built in the rocks just before the harbour in **Watchet**. Clapotis occurs off the west wall of the harbour, especially during northerlies. Overlooked by a little red lighthouse on the end of the wall and by a former coastguard lookout, the Grade II London Inn and public toilets, the harbour dries completely at low tide to leave an expanse of mud. This belies its importance as a port, which had a mint in Saxon times, was invaded by Vikings in 914 and now handles timber, wood pulp, paper, steel, fertilizers, animal fodder, cork, wine, cars, farm machinery and chemicals, trading with Portugal, Spain, the Azores and Pakistan. It has its own pilots and had its own boat, the Watchet flatty, built in Combwich for use on the Quantocks beaches. The present harbour was built after a storm and particularly high tide in 1900 destroyed the previous one. In *Hereward the Wake* Countess Gyda explains how they had taken fishing boats from the port to reach Flat Holm to escape the Normans. The port was used to load iron ore from the Brendon Hills to ship to South Wales during the Industrial Revolution. It was also the place where a Royalist ship was captured by a troop of mounted cavalry during the Civil War when caught on a falling tide and the place where Samuel Taylor Coleridge met an old sailor whose tales inspired him to write *The Rime of the Ancient Mariner*, a poem which received grudging acceptance from Hornblower in *Hornblower & the 'Atropos'*. St Decuman was said to have sailed here from South Wales on a hurdle, together with a cow. The quaint little Watchet Museum in the road by the top of the harbour slipway catalogues some of the port's long history. The Watchet blue cloth resembles a pale form of denim. Watchet can often be reached at low water by landing on the rocky shore to the west of the harbour when conditions permit.

There are further holiday camps both sides of St Audrie's Bay. Between them are the remains of the harbour built by Lord St Audrie in the 19th century to supply his private gasworks

The quaint Market House in Watchet, now the museum.

232

Statue of the Ancient Mariner and albatross at Watchet.

Rock pavement at the end of the Quantocks.

to 1999. The cooling water intake stands offshore, surmounted by a large structure with a crane on top. By way of contrast, the outlet water boils up from below the surface and it is easy to move through the warm water as it rises at the end of a reef having only a line of widely spaced minor obstacles marking the outfall route.

Also present between April and December are fishermen from Stolford who use mud horses as load-

with coal from South Wales. Above the stonework is the end of a sunken track which was used by packhorses to carry the coal up from the harbour.

Blue Ben and Quantock's Head form the undramatic northerly extremity of the Quantock Hills as they slope down to the sea.

East Quantoxhead has the Grade I Court House owned by the Luttrell family who owned the hamlet since just after the Norman conquest. Less longlived was the Chantry at Kilve, burned down in the 19th century, a fire thought to have been fuelled by the smuggled liquor stored in it. Another old church is St Andrew's at Lilstock. Even more ancient was a 205,000,000 year old 1m long jawbone of an ichthyosaur found near the village.

Two lookout positions top Stoke Bluff, the first being old and brick built while the second is a modern structure looking down over the helicopter practice bombing range, marked by yellow buoys and a yellow target platform 2km off Stoke Bluff. At low tide the end of Stoke Spit dries so the safety margin is reduced for passing craft. A flag is displayed on Stoke Bluff when the range is in use.

Tide streams here run at 4km/h on springs, starting west southwest at Dover HW −0400 and east northeast at Dover HW +0140. The boulder lined bay beyond has groynes and a breakwater along the back.

The most prominent feature of this coast is the Hinkley Point B nuclear power station with the 3.3GW Hinkley Point C, the world's most expensive power station, proposed. Hinkley Point A was used from 1965

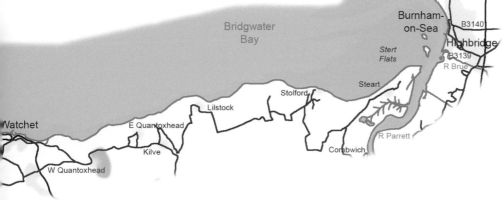

Hinkley Point nuclear power station.

Rusting buoy on Stert Island.

spreading wooden frames to go out onto the Hinkley Point nuclear power station flats to collect shrimps, prawns and the occasional salmon from their nets.

Another submarine forest leads to Stert Flats, one of Europe's outstanding wetlands with 3km of mud at low tide and site of the Bridgwater Bay National Nature Reserve. Stert Flats are the seaward extension of the Somerset Levels, themselves formerly part of the sea with the Quantocks and Mendips as cliffs. Later they became an extensive area of fenland and raised mires which were mostly drained. Two of the draining rivers entering here are the Parrett and the Brue, streams running NE and

SW at 6km/h on springs on the former with a small bore developing. The sea here becomes noticeably muddy with brown foam as waves break.

The 24km^2 of mudflats, saltings and farmland provide a feeding and roosting ground in autumn and winter and a summer moulting ground for shelducks, wigeon, whitefronted geese and other wildfowl and waders. While Wessex Water have been installing an expensive plant to clean up the Parrett estuary, the Environment Ageny have been digging up a large area of farmland on the Steart peninsula to create even more mud for birds, which cannot do any more for the power station water intakes than it does for the beaches of the resort of Burnham-on-Sea.

Stert Island probably emerged as a sandbank in the 19th century and is now noted for its wildfowl and waders. Landing is only permitted between April and October and a permit is required. The surrounding waters have codling, conger eels, skate and whiting, not to mention waterskiers and sailors from the local sailing club at **Burnham-on-Sea** where the B3139 meets the B3140. The pier has the questionable claim of being the UK's smallest.

The town dates from Saxon times but didn't really make its name until spa wells of rather dubious quality were sunk. These days a holiday camp, a regatta in August and a carnival in November are greater attractions. In the 19th century the Revd David Davies was given permission by Parliament to build a lighthouse and levy tolls on passing Bridgwater ships. The wooden lighthouse, a square structure on stilts, is no longer used except that the red line down its front lines up with the red line on the present lighthouse behind to indicate the Bridgwater Bar across the Parrett.

Almost on the previously defined line is the flat topped 137m high grassy cone of Brent Knoll. It has an Iron Age fort on the summit and was used for refuge when the Vikings raided in the 8th century.

Other distinctive landmarks include a set of aerials at

The finger of Brean Down from Uphill with the Welsh coastline visible beyond.

Fortifications on the end of Brean Down.

Weston-super-Mare with the pier to Birnbeck Island on the left and the Grand Pier on the right.

Highbridge while the silhouette of Glastonbury Tor is visible on the horizon.

Berrow has the ribs of a wrecked wooden ship on the foreshore at the top of the Berrow Flats. While there is a golf course above high water mark, lower down the activities range from horseriding to racing cars and scooters and it must be one of the few beaches with speed cops.

Beyond the holiday camp at Brean is the 13th century St Bridget's church which replaced a 6th century building believed to have been founded by Irish monks.

The first of three headlands is the 97m high Brean Down, 64ha of limestone noted for the white rock rose and other rare lime loving plants. It has a tropical bird garden and bird sanctuary established in 1912 with such birds as the skylark, jackdaw, rock pipit, peregrine falcon, gulls and autumn migrants. Such a distinctive outlier to the Mendips was bound to have attracted attention at different times. A field system is believed to be Iron Age and a Roman temple site was excavated in 1957. A fort was built near the end in 1867 when there was fear of a French invasion, housing 50 men and seven muzzle loaded cannon. In 1900 the magazine exploded and it was abandoned although it was used by an anti-aircraft unit during the Second World War. Surfers and windsurfers use the beach. It was used for filming *Elizabeth: the Golden Age.* A Severn barrage has been proposed from here to Lavernock Point, carrying a road link.

Overfalls run off to the west of Howe Rock in the direction of Steep Holm while bass, cod, conger eels and pollock inhabit the waters.

The River Axe at the foot of Bleadon Hill ends the Somerset Levels and is the Somerset/North Somerset border as it enters Weston Bay with currents up to 13km/h, where the Weston flatner working boat evolved. There is a sailing club at Uphill and also a tower on the site of a former windmill although the prominent building is a grey church without a roof. In 1769 Robert Whitworth surveyed a route for an Exeter & Uphill Canal to bypass the southwest peninsula.

Weston-super-Mare, on the other hand, has no shortage of prominent buildings, a great arc of elegant white hotels which are dazzling in the afternoon sun. The resort developed from a fishing village in the 18th century and grew rapidly after the railway arrived in 1841. Kilvert joined the naked sea bathers in 1873. Weston Park Railway and SeaQuarium Weston are on the front. The centrepiece is the 500m long Grand Pier, badly damaged by fire in 2008, restored two years later but storm damaged in 2015. There is sand yachting at the south end of the bay, water skiing and surfing. There is a swimming pool on the front and a marine lake next to Knightstone harbour which dries out at low tide. There is a carnival. Jeffrey Archer was a resident before being

provided with alternative accommodation after a court case. Humphrey Salter, in *Paradise Postponed*, thought an extra ten years of life in a Weston geriatric hospital was not sufficent reward for giving up smoking.

Worlebury Hill is covered by Weston Woods but has the gash of a disused quarry on the south side and is topped by a red water tower, an aerial and Iron Age fortifications (4ha with ramparts, ditch, multiple defences and storage pits). The end slopes down to Anchor Head. Around the end are the Dauncey's Hotel, Ocean Hotel, Cliffs Tea Rooms and Cosa Nostra Greek Taverna. Crossing to Birnbeck Island is a derelict Grade II★ pier on iron piles allowing access to a small pier used for boat trips in the summer and the lifeboat and inshore lifeboat station on the island, off which currents can exceed 7km/h on springs.

A large rope noose hangs from the pier and assorted scaffolding poles litter the seabed and extend round into Sand Bay. Conditions have changed substantially since it was named as it drains to leave an unbroken sea of deep mud, most of what little sand there is being on the road which runs past the convalescent home, Commodore Hotel and holiday camp.

In the same way, Sand Point is of rock. It marks the official start of the Mouth of the Severn and is the first coastal point from which the Severn bridges can be seen.

Behind Middle Hope Cove at the break in Swallow Cliff is Woodspring Priory, dedicated to Thomas the Martyr. A 15th century Perpendicular church surrounded by apple trees, it was founded in 1210 by William de Courtenay, a grandson of one of St Thomas à Becket's assassins. Since the dissolution of the monasteries it has been a farmhouse with chimneys in the centre of the nave.

A field system is unseen on St Thomas's Head.

The Rivers Banwell and Congresbury Yeo flow into Woodspring Bay as levées front the low marshy ground with the Blind Yeo coming in just before Clevedon. Beyond, the M5 can be seen climbing away steeply to the northeast.

Clevedon (the Old English for cliff downland) is approached past the striking bulk of Wain's Hill with its fort on top, leading into Church Hill with St Andrew's church on top and the grave of Arthur Hallam, to which his friend Lord Tennyson's *In Memoriam AHH* refers. This headland was walked by Tennyson, William Thackeray and Samuel Coleridge. The town has many Georgian, Regency and Victorian buildings. It was developed from a fishing village, where the Clevedon boat was developed as a workboat, into a fashionable resort in the 19th century by the Elton family and its features include a marine lake where rowing boats are hired. The slipway used by Clevedon Sailing Club makes a convenient landing point with parking, Fortes' Ice Cream Parlour, Royal Oak and Grade II Royal Pier Hotel close by.

Wain's Hill obscures Clevedon as it is approached from the southwest.

Distance
63km from Minehead to Clevedon

OS 1:50,000 Sheets
171 Cardiff & Newport
181 Minehead & Brendon Hills
182 Weston-super-Mare

Tidal Constants
Minehead:
HW Dover −0440
LW Dover −0500
Watchet:
HW Dover −0440
LW Dover −0510
Hinkley Point:
HW Dover −0420
LW Dover −0450
Burnham:
Dover −0420
Weston-super-Mare:
HW Dover −0420
LW Dover −0500
Clevedon:
Dover −0420

Sea Area
Lundy

Range
Lilstock

Connection
River Parrett – see RoB p17

44 Mouth of the Severn

**Mudflats,
docks and
industry**

*'We'll cross the Tamar, land to land,
The Severn is no stay, –
With 'one and all,' and hand in hand,
And who shall bid us nay?*
RS Hawker

of rock onto which it would be difficult to climb. By the secluded Ladye Bay the Lovers' Walk footpath has approached to follow the coast from Marine Parade to Portishead.

Once clear of the town, the blocks of rock gradually decline in size at the foot of Castle Hill which now has a

The pier at Clevedon with the Prince of Wales Bridge beyond.

The Bristol Channel could be a relatively recent phenomenon following a period of trough faulting in Tertiary times and formerly flowed eastwards. The Severn is sometimes referred to as Britain's back door but that must be a matter of one's perspective. It was named after the nymph Sabrina, who drowned in it, and Habren, the beautiful daughter of Estrildis, who was drowned in it with her mother on the orders of Gwendolin, the deserted wife of Locrinus, according to Geoffrey of Monmouth.

Starting from the slipway at Clevedon, passage is immediately under the graceful Victorian pier of 1869, claimed to be England's most beautiful. Formerly 230m long, it partly collapsed but restoration was undertaken.

Houses on the B3124 come right to the edge of the cliffs which are well undercut in places with evidence of some repair work. Below the cliffs are rugged blocks

golf course and, from earlier days, the remains of Walton Castle, enclosures, hut circles and field systems.

Farley is marked by the distinctive white tower of Walton Bay Signal Station and by a couple of caravan sites. On the other hand, the tank farm at **Redcliff Bay** is well camouflaged, everything grassed over and all concrete painted dark green. There were three pipelines here running out to offshore oil berths but these have now been abandoned.

A small white lighthouse on stilts at Blacknore fronts **Portishead**'s grand Nautical School, set in a commanding position overlooking the Mouth of the Severn. Merlin predicted that the Severn would discharge through seven mouths.

Above are radio masts on Portishead Down. At the back of Kilkenny Bay a park with cricket ground and golf course sweeps down to the water. Battery Point or Portishead Point is dominated by a small lighthouse with a large bell. The headland was used for defence purposes in both World Wars and in 1644 the fort was taken from the Royalists by General Fairfax. Because the fairway is close inshore this is the nearest place in the world that large ships come to public land, making it a popular viewing point.

Off the point lies the prominent Denny Island with a spoil dumping ground on the near side. Tides here are now the third highest in the world, reaching 13.7m at the spring equinox.

A wooded shoreline leads below

the Royal Inn and past the carcase of a wooden ship to the steamer pier and the entrance to the marina with 1km of quays.

The tide sets towards the bank between Portishead and Avonmouth in a southwesterly direction on the ebb and in a northeasterly direction on the flood north of Avonmouth. The flood also gives a westerly eddy close inshore in Portishead Pool.

The low marshy ground behind King Road is now disappearing although some wildlife survives. A pair of shelduck were fitted with small telemetry boxes to their tails so that their movements around the estuary could be monitored by naturalists.

The Royal Portbury Dock, opened in 1977, has container cranes and an entrance lock, 366m x 43m x 20m deep, is the longest in Britain and was the largest in the world when built. Beyond it are the silos of a molasses terminal.

Adjacent is the mouth of the River Avon, the North Somerset/Bristol border and the entrance for Bristol and the inland route to London, a route used by long lasting Severn trows with their distinctive D shaped sterns which used to serve the Bristol Channel ports and go well inland on the canal system. From this seemingly insignificant rivermouth came Cabot in 1497 to explore Canada's east coast and in 1620 the *Mayflower* emerged with the first English settlers for the USA. The oldest ship plying these waters today is the *Waverley*, the world's last seagoing paddle steamer, which makes trips to Penarth, Ilfracombe and Minehead in the summer. These days it is quicker by road and vehicles can be seen streaming over the Avonmouth Bridge on the M5 just upstream.

Avonmouth Docks, opened in 1877, have now replaced **Bristol** as one of Britain's busiest ports, despite the difficult 9km/h tidal flow across the entrance on springs. Royal Edward Dock was added in 1908 and one of its more notable buildings

The Nautical School overlooks Portishead's Black Nore light.

a premonition. The vessel had foundered off Portishead in 1867 but had been recovered on that occasion. In the midst of the industry is the Bristol/South Gloucestershire border.

Towards the northern end, Gravel Banks dry for up to 2km from the shoreline at low tide. These lead on to the English Stones and the most difficult part of the Severn for large vessels which have to negotiate the Shoots. The spring flow rate here is 15km/h and a southwesterly wind against the ebb can create great difficulties. The extensive area of boulders and weed which form the English Stones can be deceiving. In the Civil War a

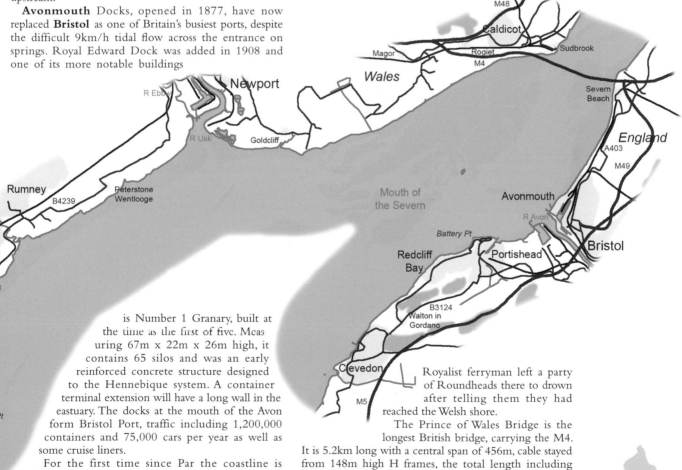

is Number 1 Granary, built at the time as the first of five. Measuring 67m x 22m x 26m high, it contains 65 silos and was an early reinforced concrete structure designed to the Hennebique system. A container terminal extension will have a long wall in the eastuary. The docks at the mouth of the Avon form Bristol Port, traffic including 1,200,000 containers and 75,000 cars per year as well as some cruise liners.

For the first time since Par the coastline is industrial with wind turbines, fuel depots, smelting works, chemical works, trading estate and gas works strung out along the A403. Stup Pill is where the 1809 trow *William* beached in 1939 after foundering at the mouth of the Avon, those lost including captain George Warren, who had been asked not to go by his wife after

Royalist ferryman left a party of Roundheads there to drown after telling them they had reached the Welsh shore.

The Prince of Wales Bridge is the longest British bridge, carrying the M4. It is 5.2km long with a central span of 456m, cable stayed from 148m high H frames, the total length including approach viaducts of 25 and 27 spans built from glued concrete segments.

The River Severn divides South Gloucestershire in England from Monmouthshire in Wales. Such birds as pigeons are happy to commute across and even butterflies cross. The shore is generally flat.

237

The old steamer pier at Portishead.

Beneath the northern end of the English Stones from Redwick to Sudbrook runs the Severn Tunnel, the longest in Britain for over a century at 7km. Built between 1873 and 1886, it used 76,000,000 bricks and was a notable engineering feat. The tunnel passes through gently dipping Triassic marls and sandstones for 2.4km and is then downthrown against Coal Measures before returning to the marls for the last 1.6km at the west end. There were many problems with inflow of water during construction and the flow broke through near the east portal, clay having to be tipped on the bed of the river at low tide to seal the leak. The Big Spring of Sudbrook proved the worst point of leakage. In 1929/30 the tunnel was grouted with 8,000t of cement, grout appearing on the surface and out of connecting fissures, many of which had obviously developed since the tunnel's construction. The concrete Mushroom in the Salmon Pool caps a leak into the tunnel. The largest pumping station supplied 70l/s of water from the tunnel to a brewery and a paper mill at Sudbrook, the crystal clear water still being used for Stella. This was the only place in the world which had six beam engines in one building.

The railway emerges from its western portal at Sudbrook to meet the Gloucester to Newport line at Severn Tunnel Junction, the railway and two sets of powerlines being the major features on a shore which is generally flat after the ivy covered rocks and the remains of a fort and church at Sudbrook, a village built for the tunnel builders, claimed to have been the first in the UK to be lit by electricity. Sudbrook Camp was built by the Silures and there is a damaged wartime lookout point.

From here the Welsh Grounds, sand and mud flats which dry up to 6km from the Welsh coast or most of

Avonmouth Dock is of vast size.

The cable stayed Prince of Wales Bridge with Avonmouth beyond.

the way to the English coast, widen out and continue until beyond Newport. Sand is firm on falling tides but can form quicksand on the flood.

The scale of the estuary is brought out by aircraft flying noiselessly down the middle.

Caldicot, site of a Roman pottery kiln, is most noticeable for Rogiet Moor Range. The coastguard suggest staying 500m offshore when the red flags are flying.

A levée begins and follows the coast all the way to Cardiff. Generally it is in good repair, faced in stone and topped with a low concrete wave wall. Because of the mud below the high water line, landing points are a problem before Penarth.

A sewage works marks Magor Pill, near which are Magor Fens, a wet meadow reserve. A vessel of 1240 designed with Viking influence, loaded with iron ore, has been recovered from Magor Pill and stored in the National Museum Wales in Cardiff. As the Gwent levels are drained there are progressively fewer wet areas and lapwings are being driven out as the ground becomes too hard for them to dig in to feed. Monmouthshire gives way to Newport.

On a totally different scale, the massive Llanwern steelworks, which Tata still use for some steel processing, covers an enormous area of ground further inland and discharges waste water to the estuary.

Gold Cliff had two large batteries of conical wire salmon putchers reaching out into the current to collect a daily harvest. This method had been used since the Middle Ages by the former Goldcliff Priory but the Environment Agency's predecessors ordered their destruction in 1992 so more salmon can now get upstream for anglers to catch. Mesolithic footprints 8,000 years old can still be found in the mud here. Also disused is another form of battery, a gun emplacement on top of the cliff. Trackways and other linear structures have been found here and parts of a boat from 1000 BC have been taken to Newport Museum & Art Gallery. Goldcliff Pill leads down from the village of Goldcliff where a mark 700mm above the chancel floor in the St Mary Magdalene's church indicates the level of the 1606 flood which drowned 22 people.

A local form of fishing is by using rowing boats to lay out nets suspended from floats that are marked with flags at the free ends. In *The Journey through Wales* Gerald of Wales suggests excavating down into the gold rock might discover honey and oil.

Gold Cliff salmon putchers in 1989, now just a few stakes.

The Usk and the Ebbw flow together into the Severn at **Newport**, a city marked by its transporter bridge (in the distance) and by the 390MW Uskmouth Generating Station (with its three chimneys, one reaching to 133m) by the confluence. Newport has two wet docks, several drying berths and a drydock. Timber, fruit and other foodstuffs and iron and steel goods including vehicles are imported while coal, vehicles, machinery, tinplate and other iron and steel goods are exported. At the entrance is the East Usk light structure, opposite the disused white West Usk light structure which resembles a large inverted water tower.

Peterstone Gout has a bird hide. The 1606 flood left its mark 2m up the wall of the church at Peterstone Wentlooge on the B4239, typical of the flooding in the area, much of which is below sea level. Peterstone Great Wharf and **Rumney** Great Wharf provide protection as far as the Rhymney River.

The Newport/Cardiff border is crossed. The Rhymney River and the largest sewage works in Europe mark the beginning of **Cardiff**, the Welsh capital, a city founded by the Romans. *Le Morte d'Arthur* claim's Arthur's forces sailed from here to attack Sir Lancelot in Beaune. The city grew into a 19th century coal and iron exporting port and was from where Scott's *Terra Nova* sailed. The name comes from the Welsh caer, a fort, on the Taff, the dark river. In 1839 the 2nd Marquis of Bute expanded the docks and linked them by rail to the pitheads and ironworks. The Taff and Ely flow into the Severn to the south of the city via the Cardiff Bay Barrage and a dredged entrance channel, which is an artificial cut through Cefn-y-Wrach, where

The Cardiff Bay Barrage and its symbol.

Penarth pier dates from the 19th century.

tidal currents run at 4km/h parallel to the coast on springs. The Cardiff Bay Barrage was bitterly opposed by environmentalists who did not want to lose this bit of the mudflats. Butetown became the tough area of Tiger Bay on the east bank of the Taff, although it is now less forbidding. The approach along the coast is past steelworks and a grain silo, with a helipad in front, cranes and a tank farm. The city is hidden. There are three wet docks, six drydocks, four oil terminals and 8km of quays, importing steel products, timber, fruit, vegetables, petroleum and chemical products, refrigerated produce and scrap metal. Coal and coke are exports. There is also equipment to handle bulk cargoes of crushed bones. Behind the Queen Alexandra Dock are the Wales Millennium Centre, the National Assembly for Wales building and the Norwegian church.

Coal was shipped from Penarth to Cape Town in the early 1850s for refuelling steam vessels heading for Australia. The *Great Britain*'s final commercial voyage, carrying coal to Panama via Cape Horn in 1886 from here resulted in her being abandoned in Port Stanley as a hulk. The Custom House has become a restaurant. Penarth Head beyond the Cardiff/Vale of Glamorgan border is 65m high, almost vertical and veined with gypsum. Having survived the winter 2014 storms, it then suffered a 150t landslide in later dryer weather. Nearby is the 200m long pier on cast iron columns with an ice

cream parlour and other facilities on concrete columns at the landward end. The century old pier was damaged by fire in 1931 and by ship collision in 1947, but it remains a notable example of pier architecture. As often happens with pier towns, **Penarth** retains its gentility despite the new buildings being erected close by and the leisure centre built on columns over the beach, if such a term can be used for a rock pavement littered with debris ranging from car tyres to a water tank, all covered with barnacles. There is an inshore rescue boat station. Facing the refurbished promenade and dinghy park are Tony's Seashore Grill, the Caprice exclusive seafood restaurant and toilets. There is a busy sailing area towards the constantly changing Cardiff Grounds bank and the Monkstone Rock light tower. The name Penarth is from the Welsh penngarth, place at the end of the promontory, although the Victorians promoted it as the Garden by the Sea resort.

A north–south eddy operates close inshore on the last two hours of the flood between Penarth Head and Lavernock Point with turbulence over Ranny Spit.

Lavernock Point with its 15m high cliffs of Sully Beds of green, grey, black and red Triassic keuper marls, with faults containing celestine and strontianite, is officially the end of the estuary of the River Severn. On top is St Lawrence's church with a plaque in the wall recalling that the world's first radio message 'Are you ready?'

Brean Down, Flat Holm and Steep Holm as seen from Penarth.

The harbourmouth at Barry Island, Sully Island connected to the mainland by a causeway at low tide.

was received here in 1897 from Marconi's transmitter positioned on Flat Holm some 5km away in the Bristol Channel.

Cliffs vary between 15 and 30m in height to Sully Bay with caravan parks on top before and after Swanbridge. Swanbridge, with red cliffs topped by pine trees, is an attractive spot after all the low ground as far as Cardiff. Sully Island is connected to the mainland by a rocky ledge during the lower half of the tide, over which strong currents flow when the tide is up. A prehistoric fort on the end of the island was later taken over by the Romans and gold and silver Roman coins have been found here.

The white Grade II* former Sully Hospital, now residential property, is prominent on the shore.

Barry, reached by the A4055, was developed at the end of the 19th century to outstrip Cardiff with docks and railway being built in 1889. The idea was to cash in on the coal boom but the industry collapsed at the end of the First World War. The docks approach is overlooked by a cast iron lighthouse with a lifeboat station inside the entrance. The 14m high dock walls were built in the dry with massive limestone blocks while away from the basins the excavation sides were battered back and left unfaced. Dewatering was with a surplus Cornish engine bought after construction of

Aberthaw power station dominates Breaksea Point.

The rock pavement at Llantwit Major.

the Severn Tunnel and the cast iron lock gates were the first ever to be operated with hydraulic rams rather than chains. In addition to the tidal basin there are three wet docks, a drydock, roll on roll off berths, a timber pond, a general cargo terminal, a bulk loading conveyor, 6km of quays and a helipad. Exports include coke, oil, resin and scrap metals but no longer coal while imports include timber, pit wood, grain, bananas and oil. The Marine Environment Research Council have a base here from which they operate the *Discovery*.

Barry Harbour is now nearly silted up. The Welsh Barri means stream running from the hill. *The Journey through Wales* suggests it is named after St Baroc, buried here, and that a crack in the rocks produces the sounds of a blacksmith's shop, even at low water.

Barry had large railway scrapyards which proved a valuable source of engines for many of Britain's steam railways. A different kind of redundancy comes in the form of four submerged forest beds found at Barry. Bendrick Rocks have revealed three toed dinosaur footprints but there are fewer left as some have been stolen.

Off Barry there is an explosives anchorage. Close inshore there can be small races off Nell's Point, which has a Coastwatch lookout, and Friar's Point. There are spring tidal flows of 7–9km/h across the mouth of Barry Harbour which continue to Breaksea Point. The Knap catches a shore break and has the remains of a Roman building. The central feature of the Porthkerry Country Park with its golf course is the magnificent 19th century viaduct carrying the Bridgend branch of the Barry Railway, just 600m from the end of the main runway of Cardiff Airport. This is a freight railway which has recently been returned to passenger use. The Bulwarks are the remains of an ancient fort.

Off **Rhoose** Point, Wales' most southerly point, pilots for Barry, Cardiff, Avonmouth, Bristol and Gloucester are met. The point has 10m high limestone cliffs with a quarry on top and Aberthaw Cement Works, flanked on each side by clifftop caravan sites.

Breaksea Point is totally dominated by the 1.6GW Aberthaw B power station, built in the 1960s. The River Thaw is crossed by a small castellated girder bridge which is painted in camouflage colours, a rather pointless exercise as the power station chimneys are clearly visible from the English coast 20km away. There may be overfalls or a race off the point and there is bound to be warm white water pouring from four cooling water discharge points, a dream find spoilt only by the amount of oil going into the sea with the water. A concrete tower off the point has a spherical top to it like a gas tank. Aberthaw Harbour itself has now silted up but stones from the beach used to be taken back to the southern coast by sailing vessels for converting to lime to treat the poor Quantock soils and it was also used in mortar for the base of Smeaton's Eddystone lighthouse.

The coast is low until Summerhouse Point although the Breaksea Ledge of limestone boulders and gently shelving rock pavement continues at intervals for a considerable distance. Spring tides to 6km/h start west between Breaksea Point and Nash Point at HW Dover –0450 and east at HW Dover +0120. The 23km of coast to Porthcawl have become the Glamorgan Heritage Coast and the brown former coastguard lookout on Summerhouse Point has now become the Seawatch Centre of the Friends of the Glamorgan Heritage Coast Association with weather and sea state forecasting, charts and the ability to listen in to ships' radio messages. The point also is the site of an old fort and there is an airfield behind at St Athan.

Over the next 8km to Nash Point the cliffs increase in height to 30m, usually with strata in a uniformly horizontal plane although one section behind Stout Bay has clearly dropped, exposing weaker strata to the waves and producing a section with rudimentary caves.

There never was a St Twit. **Llantwit Major** is a degeneration of the Welsh Llanilltud Fawr. St Illtyd came from Brittany in the 5th century and set up a monastery where St David and St Teilo were said to have studied. St Illtyd's church is over 1,000 years old with 8th century crosses and fine painted wall frescoes.

There are surf breaks around the distinctive rock pavement.

After another section of cliff, with the beginnings of caves at the back of Tresilian Bay, St Donats is dominated by its Norman castle. It was built about 1300 by the Stradling family who occupied it until 1738 when they were on the wrong side of the political fence. In 1925 it was bought by American newspaper tycoon William Randolph Hearst who used a hammerbeam roof from a Wiltshire priory to repair the medieval monastery hall and also brought in a church roof from Lincolnshire for restoration purposes. The castle has a Tudor long gallery and cavalry barracks which were built in the 16th century when a Spanish invasion was feared. In 1962 it became the United World College of the Atlantic, the world's first international sixth form college, with 360 students taken from 60 countries in the interests of promoting international understanding and harmony. It has an inshore rescue boat which patrols 23km of coast. The BBC used it as Llanabba Castle for filming *Decline & Fall*.

The undercutting of the cliffs at Nash Point draws attention to their unstable nature. There are a foghorn and two lighthouses on top, the current one built in 1830 and having an output of 144,000 candlepower which can be seen 32km away. There was once a settlement just by the point, an area where much wild cabbage is to be found.

The lighthouse on the cliff at Nash Point.

Heavy overfalls occur off Nash Point on the eastgoing stream but the Nash Passage inside Nash Sand avoids the worst of the problem. There is low tide surf.

From Nash Point to Dunraven Bay the cliffs are bold, 30–60m high, and crumbling badly.

Traeth Mawr, large beach, has 60m cliffs of flat but crumbling rock and there is another old settlement site on the clifftops. Dunraven Castle was built on Trwyn y Witch.

Dunraven Bay at Southerndown has surf and danger-ous crumbly limestone cliffs on top of which a 17th century wrecker family used to fix lanterns to the horns of grazing cattle, murdering crews and looting vessels when they were wrecked. One gang leader was said to have given up the business after recognizing the ring on a severed hand as that belonging to his son who had previously run away to sea.

Today Dunraven Bay is the first reliable landing point with vehicle access on this section of coast and has a pay carpark, toilets, ice cream kiosk and heritage centre.

Distance
101km from Clevedon via Severn Beach to Southerndown

OS 1:50,000 Sheets
170 Vale of Glamorgan
171 Cardiff & Newport
172 Bristol & Bath

Tidal Constants
Clevedon:
Dover −0420
Portishead: HW Dover −0400
English and Welsh Grounds:
HW Dover −0410
LW Dover −0430
Avonmouth:
Dover −0400
Sudbrook:
HW Dover −0350
LW Dover −0340
Newport:
HW Dover −0420
LW Dover −0410
Cardiff:
HW Dover −0420
LW Dover −0440
Barry:
HW Dover −0420
LW Dover −0500
Porthcawl:
HW Dover −0500
LW Dover −0510

Sea Area
Lundy

Range
Rogiet Moor

Connections
River Avon − see RoB p22
River Severn − see RoB p29

Surfers enjoy Dunraven Bay below the ridge of Trwyn y Witch.

45 Swansea Bay

Death by blast furnace and the first Area of Outstanding Natural Beauty

Stone-runged streets ascending to that crow's nest
Swinging East and West over Swansea Bay
Guard in their walls Cwmdonkin's
Gates of light for a bell to close.
Vernon Watkins

After Dunraven Bay, 30 to 60m high limestone cliffs, topped by the B4524, form the coast until the Ogmore River, where there are surf breaks. Southerndown is largely hidden on top but Ogmore-by-Sea is much more conspicuous in front of Ogmore Down, an area of rounded grassland.

Tusker Rock with its tidal pond lies 2km off the coast, exposed at low tide. The spines have caught ships and there are wrecks on the inside of the rock.

The Ogmore River, on the Vale of Glamorgan/Bridgend border, also has hidden danger with difficult currents in the estuary. The Ogmore River leads down from Ogmore Castle, built by William de Londres. An oval ring with a rectangular bailey, it includes a 12th century hall and chamber, a 13th century limekiln and a 14th century courthouse and guards the stepping stone crossing of the river leading to the more recent 15th century Candleston Castle, a fortified manor house, the remains of which lie at the eastern end of the dunes of Merthyr-mawr Warren, the second highest in Europe, used in filming *Lawrence of Arabia*. These days the two are separated by a sewage works.

The far end of the dunes is marked by Black Rocks after which Newton Point has a surf break on each side and more at Sandy Bay. There is an enormous holiday caravan park on the southeastern edge of **Porthcawl**, which developed to serve the ironworks and coalmines but had a new marina in 2013 and now serves leisure craft and fishing boats. Porthcawl Point is marked by a

white hexagonal lighthouse with a black base and a very strong race off the end of the breakwater which flows at 11km/h on springs. The harbour was built in the 1860s to export coal and iron ore but the development of Barry in the 1890s killed the trade and part of the old dock has been filled in and turned into a carpark. Instead, Porthcawl, which takes its name from sea kale, became a holiday resort with sailing and seven sandy beaches. Coney Beach Pleasure Park funfair behind the harbour is one of the largest and best equipped in the country. It is mentioned in *Portrait of the Artist as a Young Dog* but the town is compared unfavourably with Rhossili. The Pier Hotel is at one end of a front which stretches past a marine pool to the Seabank Hotel. There can be high tide surf off the esplanade.

In the Bronze Age the River Severn did not begin to open out into an estuary until this far downstream. The low rocky coast continues to Sker Point with low ground inland for a couple of kilometres before the hills rise steeply. Heavy overfalls can develop off Hutchwns Point. In bad weather there are heavy seas breaking over Scarweather Sands, Hugo Bank and Kenfig Patches, all of which dry at low tide.

Rest Bay only produces surf with an onshore wind. The rocks are relatively soft, despite being deeply scoured into jagged points and being covered with barnacles. The softness is emphasized by the way a house brick has worn its way down into a deep hole at one point. The bay is

Buildings along the front at Porthcawl above the rocky shoreline.

The cast iron lighthouse on Porthcawl Point.

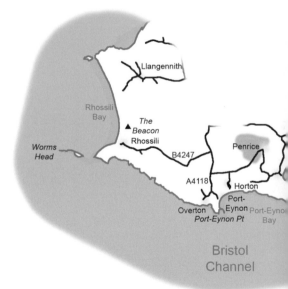

overlooked by more holes on the Royal Porthcawl Golf Course, host for Amateur Championships and the Ryder Cup, and by a water tower 3km to the northeast.

Newton to Sker Point with Sker House behind was used as the setting for much of *The Maid of Sker*. Beyond it, Kenfig Sands are only broken by the rocks of Gwely'r Misgl. Behind are Kenfig Burrows, 4km^2 of the best dune system in South Wales with the 28ha Kenfig Pool with underwater springs and a nature reserve which contains the rare fen orchid. In the 12th century a thriving community here was choked by advancing sand dunes. Only the castle ruins remain visible. It took Parliament another five centuries to get round to dissolving the Corporation of Kenfig. There are beachbreaks onto Kenfig Sands.

The inconspicuous Afon Cynffig is the Bridgend/

Port Talbot's cranes and the Tata Steel Strip Products UK Port Talbot Works at Margam, seen from Kenfig Burrows.

Neath Port Talbot border and flows down from an industrial estate and extensive railway yards. On the hillside beyond is **Margam** Country Park with its magnificent 18th century orangery, 600 fallow deer, outdoor sculptures, adventure playground, Cistercian abbey founded in 1147, castle ruins, museum of early Christian memorial stones, Iron Age fort, world's largest maze of 4,000m² and ponds, all in 3.2km² of grounds. *The Journey through Wales* tells how a young local disputed a piece of land with the monks, set fire to their best barn of grain, went mad and died and of another who hit somebody in the refectory and was killed the next morning by his enemies in exactly the same spot. It also reports that a vessel sent from this charitable abbey to Bristol to buy grain was detained by winds but that as the abbey ran out of food a field of grain ripened overnight, more than a month early.

Port Talbot has the highest level of air pollution in the UK. Trees on the hillside to the northwest have been killed by pollution from Tata Steel Strip Products UK Port Talbot Works, the largest in Britain, with its blast

through Wales Gerald and Archbishop Baldwin were delayed at the ford across the river by the tide and quicksands.

In this area the easterly stream divides at HW Dover +0410 and the northgoing branch circulates anticlockwise round the bay for 9 hours 30 minutes.

Aberavon Leisure & Fitness Centre replaces Afan Lido, the largest leisure and entertainment centre in Wales, destroyed by fire in 2009. Surfing takes place at Aberavon Sands, a resort man made from old dunes. A large twisted steel sculpture stands by Port Talbot's promenade. Behind, the land is flat for a couple of kilometres before rising steeply to 250m. The resort ends sharply with **Baglan** Energy Park and the 500MW combined cycle gas turbine Baglan Bay power station on the site of a former BP chemical works overlooking Witford Point.

The River Neath (nedd is Welsh for shining river) flows in at Baglan Bay, crossed upstream by the prominent M4 bridge at Briton Ferry and followed by the A483. In the rivermouth are training walls and fishing stakes. Marine life in the bay includes lion's mane and rhizostoma jellyfish and mackerel.

Crymlyn Burrows are sand dunes which front Crymlyn Bog, Jersey Marine saltings, a golf course, the A483, the Tennant Canal and a huge Amazon distribution centre on the site of the UK's first oil refinery, Llandarcy of 1922, where the

furnaces and cooling tower which occupies Margam Moors at the back of what have now become Margam Burrows and Margam Sands with their beachbreaks to 1.8m, best on the flood. On the foreshore is a disused metal light tower. Geoffrey of Monmouth says in his *Historia Regum Britanniae* that Margon was named after Marganus, killed here by Cunedagius.

Port Talbot was named in 1836 after the Talbot family who built the town's docks. The docks handle only iron ore and coal with three iron ore grabs. Bulk carriers of 100,000t can be handled although a throughput of 2,500,000t/year requires the visits of some 120 ships. The walls of large riprap develop near the entrance into concrete sections with large rusting hooks and a coating of slippery green weed which makes it very hard even to swim ashore in an emergency. A groundswell causes a heavy sea in the harbour entrance. The Afon Afan enters past the old docks. In *The Journey*

Neath Port Talbot/Swansea border is crossed.

Plans for a pioneering tidal lagoon in Swansea Bay to generate power were rejected by the Westminster Government in 2018.

Swansea, Amis' Aberdarcy, is overlooked by the radio mast on Kilvey Hill, part of a Pennant sandstone ridge which rises to 200m. Below these are the docks with their cranes and Trinity House building. Three wet docks handle petroleum products, iron, steel, non ferrous ores, coal and much general cargo, totalling some 5,000,000t/year with 6,000 ships visiting and a car ferry service to Ireland. There are also two drydocks. Swansea was a small harbour and fishing village at the mouth of the River Tawe before the Industrial Revolution but plentiful coal and copper ore deposits led to a smelting works being built in the 18th century and the docks being expanded to handle 10,000 ships per year. Zinc and tinplate works were added in the 19th century and Swansea was noted for its china but the industrial boom ended after the Second World War with much dereliction. Rejuvenation has been taking place with a marina with rapid action lock gates and waterfront village, art gallery, Dylan Thomas Theatre and Meridian Tower, the tallest building in Wales. Swansea Museum is the oldest in Wales. Dylan Thomas was born here and most of his stories in *Portrait of the Artist as a Young Dog* are set here, as was *Return Journey*, broadcast on BBC radio several times and included in his *Quite Early One Morning*. Also from Swansea was Taffy Jones in Henry Livings' *Nil Carborundum*. Swansea's National Waterfront Museum in glass and slate is the latest. In the Maritime Quarter, it features a Mumbles tram, fully working Abbey Woollen Mill, lightship *Helwick*, steam tug *Canning*, 500t oak trawler *Katie Anne* and an old Mumbles lifeboat. An extensive leisure centre includes an 80m hydroslide and a wave machine.

The Swansea Bike Path follows the shore on the 10km line of the railway which used to run round the bay from 1807 to 1960 by the A4067. The first farepaying passenger carrying railway in the world, it was the Oystermouth Railway until 1879 before becoming the Swansea & Mumbles Railway. Horses were replaced by steam in 1877. In 1889 it was extended to Mumbles Pier and electrified in 1928 with double deck tramcars, the largest in Britain.

The line passes the white tower of Swansea Guildhall and Singleton Park which houses a campus of Swansea University with its Taliesin Arts Centre with theatre and Ceri Richards Gallery, miniature golf course and boating lake, all below the prominent hospital tower at Cockett.

The 2.8km^2 Clyne Valley Country Park includes Clyne Castle and a branch of the Swansea Bike Path on a disused railway line which leads down to Blackspill Station of the Swansea & Mumbles Railway. It also includes the remains of the electrical substation.

Despite being sacked by the Welsh and the earlier 1180s wooden castle having been burnt, the remains of the Norman Oystermouth Castle of the Braose family stand 52m high. A more recent feature is a 30m high glass bridge by Master James of St George in 1283. Oystermouth's All Saints church has a stained glass window commemorating the 175th anniversary of the opening of the railway. In *The Journey through Wales* Archbishop Baldwin preached and signed up many of the 3,000 recruited on the journey for the Third Crusade after he and Gerald had stayed overnight in Swansea Castle. Cador, who was too old to go, offered a tenth of his wealth plus a further tenth if a penance was remitted. The book also tells the tale of 12 year old Elidyr, later to become a priest, who was befriended by a tribe of pygmies who lived underground until he tried to steal a gold ball from them for his mother, after which he was unable to find the riverbank entrance to their kingdom any more. St Illtyd had been a hermit in Oystermouth.

At the **Mumbles** the amenities include the George, Pilot and Pier Hotel and Beach Hut Café at the end of the 270m pier. *Return Journey* talks of playing Cats & Dogs in the Mermaid Café Bar & Restaurant. The land rises to 60m on Mumbles Hill and the village, which was once famous for its oyster stalls, is now better known for its open topped buses, its water skiing, boardsailing and yachting and as a setting for the TV series *Ennal's Point*.

There are slipways and small craft moorings. Wrecks lie north of Mumbles Head and there is a heavy groundswell

The pier at Mumbles.

Oystermouth Castle below Colts Hill at the Mumbles.

Threecliff Bay with the three peaks on the east side of Penard Pill.

with easterly winds, also with westerlies but this reduces with the falling tide. The spring flow northwards in Mumbles Road is only 2km/h but off Mumbles Head it is up to 7km/h and there may be a race. Middle Head is topped by a 17m high octagonal lighthouse, mentioned in *Old Garbo* in *Portrait of the Artist as a Young Dog*.

The Mixom Sands are treacherous and Limeslade bell tolls when seas are rough but there is an inside passage. Pilots for Swansea and Neath are picked up from white, red and yellow pilot vessels 3km off.

From Mumbles Head to Pwlldu Head there are broken sloping cliffs 60m high with intermittent bays. Tides run up to 6km/h off the points as far as Port-Eynon Point on spring flows which are parallel to the coast.

This expanse of Carboniferous limestone, folded almost east–west as a plateau, is the Gower, the first Area of Outstanding Natural Beauty, in 1956, a rural area within easy reach of an industrial area but pleasantly devoid of people. Extensive limestone cliffs provide a most attractive seascape as far as Worms Head and there are signs of three raised beaches.

The first inlet is Langland Bay, overlooked by a golf course and the Langland Bay Manor hotel which has silver bands and Morris dancing in the grounds in the summer. The bay was the site chosen for the first sea pollution health tests in 1988 with 400 swimmers taking part. It has, however, a strong undertow on the ebb and big surf on southerly winds.

Caswell Bay also has surfing and a strong undertow on the ebb. Amenities include beach kiosks, toilets and a telephone. A fort site tops the headland between Caswell Bay and Brandy Cove.

A stream flows down to Pwlldu Bay but then passes under the bank of boulders at the top of the beach. Pwlldu Head with its fort site on top is an overhanging bluff and then broken cliffs continue over 60m high. Breaks include the Bacon Hole and the Minchin Hole Cave which has produced one of the most important finds of southern Britain Ice Age warm fauna.

Penard Pill enters at Threecliff Bay where the Three Cliffs are a triple pointed outcrop of rock with a natural arch underneath, much used by climbers and by surfers despite the loss of the occasional swimmer in the strong flow and the noise from overhead as it is directly in line with the main runway of Swansea Airport 4km away. In the vicinity are Pennard Burrows around which are to be found a stone labyrinth, the remains of a church and a chapel, a motte, a burial chamber and the ruins of the 12th century Pennard Castle which, along with nearby cliffs, is the only British site of yellow whitlow grass which flowers in March. Strata are vertical on the sea cliffs but the ridge of Cefn Bryn looks conical from the east end. The castle was overcome with sand after the lord upset the local fairies.

Oxwich Bay has an eddy operating and is used for surfing. Rhizostoma jellyfish can be washed up in large numbers. Oxwich Burrows are a dune system with a fort site at the east end and a salt marsh behind where they have dammed the natural drainage flow. Oxwich Ponds are an interesting freshwater site with water lilies and bulrushes. Built on the Millstone Grit behind is Penrice Castle which was deserted in the 16th century by the Mansel family who moved to the more comfortable but less fortified Tudor Oxwich Castle behind its impressive gateway with the Mansel crest in the 1520s. It includes an Elizabethan long gallery.

Who Do You Wish Was With Us? in *Portrait of the Artist as a Young Dog* notes that Oxwich is not visible from the main road.

The wooded cliffs running out to Oxwich Point are a nature reserve, below which are small craft moorings amongst which mackerel swim. The point has wrecks off it and overfalls at the height of the flow in either direction.

Caves at Port-Eynon Point.

The Culver Hole at Port-Eynon Point.

The sea serpent profile of Worms Head, seen from the north.

Distance
*66km from
Southerndown to
Llangennith*

OS 1:50,000 Sheets
*159 Swansea
& Gower
170 Vale of
Glamorgan*

Tidal Constants
*Porthcawl:
HW Dover −0500
LW Dover −0510
Port Talbot:
HW Dover −0500
LW Dover −0520
Swansea:
HW Dover −0450
LW Dover −0500
Mumbles:
HW Dover −0450
LW Dover −0440
Burry Port:
HW Dover −0500
LW Dover −0450*

Sea Area
Lundy

Connection
*Tenant Canal – see
CoB p152*

Port Eynon is at the end of the A4118. Port-Eynon Bay again has an eddy, surf breaks and a backing of Millstone Grit. Horton has an inshore lifeboat.

Port-Eynon Point rises abruptly to 43m with a small stone monument on the point. On its east side are the remains of the Salt House while the west side contains the Culver Hole, a natural cleft which has been filled in with a stone wall to a height of 18m. Several openings have been left and it is thought to have acted as a medieval dovecote. The Boilers and Sumpters reef breaks flank Overton Mere.

Helwick Sands run out 11km to West Helwick as a line of shallows. Strong westerly winds against the tide cause heavy seas over the sands although the Helwick Pass gives a route through on the inside. Mewslade Bay and Fall Bay have sheltered surf.

The 30–60m high limestone cliffs continue nearly vertical to Rhossili at the end of the B4247 and a coastal reef dries up to 200m from them at low water. Caves in the cliffs were used as prehistoric dwellings and Goat's Hole Cave, Paviland, produced in 1823 one of Britain's best Cro-Magnon skeletons, about 33,000 years old, the world's first human fossil, stained with red ochre, the Red Lady, actually a headless man in his late 20s with flint implements, bone spatulae, a mammoth ivory bracelet, periwinkle pendant and 50 ivory rods. At the time the site was about 100km from the sea although his diet included fish and seafood. This cave was in intermittent use from 29,000 years ago when the temperature was dropping steadily and this was at the northern edge of the populated area. A series of forts and a settlement occupy the cliffs as far as Kitchen Corner.

A rather precarious small boat launching point exists immediately north of Tears Point, above which is a Coastwatch lookout point.

Worms Head takes its name from wyrm, the Old English for sea serpent, because of its profile, helped, no doubt, by the blow hole at the nose end. It is two islands connected at low tide by the Devil's Bridge and by a causeway to Rhossili Point. Getting the tide wrong can result in a long stay on the head, as found in *Who Do You Wish Was With Us?* The area is leased to Natural Resources Wales as a nature reserve with fine seabird colonies. The 400m wide Worms Sound lies below a further fort site which keeps lookout to the northeast near Rhossili.

Rhossili Bay has land yachting, hang gliding and surfing. It is one of the most spectacular beaches on the Welsh coast and is backed at the south end by the rounded bulk of the Old Red Sandstone ridge of Rhossili Down, rising to 193m at the Beacon and 185m at High Barrow. At the south end there are 30m limestone cliffs while at the north end there are the dunes of Hillend Burrows with their caravan site. History of different ages shows in the ribs of the 1887 wreck of the *Helvetia* at the south end of the bay, the lonely white house which used to be the rectory and the Sweyne's Howes burial chambers. *Extraordinary Little Cough* in *Portrait of the Artist as a Young Dog* features a fortnight camping here and George Hooping's running the length of the sands.

Landing is possible at Diles Lake at Llangennith Moors where a path leads through the dunes to a parking area beyond.

Rhossili Down sweeps down to the dunes of Hillend Burrows.

Carmarthen Bay

Carmarthen Bay is subject to heavy seas on westerly winds but tidal flows are generally weak in the bay.

From Llangennith with its surf the coast is flanked by the dunes of Llangennith Burrows while the sandy beach contains the ribs of the 19th century wreck of the *City of Bristol*. Some of the sand at the northern end of the beach squeaks when scuffed.

For the top two hours of the tide cycle there is a channel inside Burry Holms, an island bearing the remains of an Iron Age fort and the 6th century chapel of St Cenydd. Limekiln Point ends in Spaniard Rocks and the name may relate to the fact that 16th century gold coins from a 17th century Spanish wreck have been found at nearby Bluepool Corner. This is a magnificent little beach which the pedestrian can only reach with difficulty and which has some interesting lava flows at the back and an angular arch at the west end.

Broughton Burrows at the back of the Broughton Bay surf break and Whiteford Burrows at the back of Whiteford Sands are interrupted by Hills Tor which rises to 35m. Whiteford Burrows are designated as a national nature reserve.

Ryer's Down has buzzard, cuckoo, linnet, meadow pipit, skylark, stonechat, willow warbler and yellow-hammer.

A lighthouse on Whiteford Scar off Whiteford Point is the only wave swept cast iron lighthouse in the British Isles. Built in 1865 to replace an earlier light on timber piles which had been shortlived, it was disused from 1921. Burry Port Yacht Club, however, felt the 19m high structure with its ornate wrought iron balcony could be used to help them and so they tried installing a solar powered light in it although this did not work when there was too much guano on the solar panels and it is now unlit. Approach to the lighthouse is difficult because it is surrounded by stakes, mussel beds, quicksand and unexploded shells. Onshore is a bird hide.

The Burry Inlet and Loughor estuary are popular with migratory birds and wildfowl. The River Loughor largely drains out and around the lower end of Burry Pill there are a series of pools formed by deep ribs of sand which are then used by fish waiting for the returning tide. The pill drains Great Pill which, in turn, drains Landimore Marsh below North Hill Tor with its fort. Further east, Llanrhidian Sands front Llanrhidian Marsh, a saltmarsh which protects Weobley Castle from the north. It appears to be in an ideal position but it was attacked, captured and partly destroyed by Owain Glyndwr in 1400, being rebuilt later in the century as a fortified manor house. There are the remains of another castle at Landimore, forts at Burry Green and Llanrhidian plus Sampson's Jack and other standing stones around Oldwalls.

Approaching Salthouse Point the River Loughor has a training wall but the flow switches from one side to the other of the wall at a point marked by beacons.

All is not peaceful on the mudflats at Crofty, where cockle fishermen go out with horsedrawn carts to rake up the cockles at low tide. There has been conflict between the fishermen and oystercatchers which have been taking increasing numbers of cockles.

The river forms the county boundary between Swansea and Carmarthenshire. On its north side is the Millennium Coastal Park with its sculptures, running to Burry Port, claimed, surprisingly, to be one of Britain's most visited attractions. Beyond a new golf course is **Llanelli**, the gateway to West Wales. It developed on coal and steel and as the centre for the South Wales tinplate industry with the large Trostre tinplate works on the east side of the town, now a Tata steelworks. It is reputed to have developed the Stepney wheel, a solid spare wheel at a time when cars all had spoked wheels. The town is noted for its rugby fanaticism and *Where Tawe Flows* in *Portrait of the Artist as a Young Dog* claims that turning an empty beer glass upside down was a challenge to anyone else in a bar to a bare knuckle fight. Today the docks are in disrepair but the town has automotive products, ophthalmic glass, petrochemicals and inflatable boats. One railway which had its ups and downs is the Llanelli & Mynydd Mawr Railway which ran northwards from Llanelli along the line of the former Carmarthenshire Railway to some limestone quarries near Castell-y-Graig. The second public railway to be authorized by Act of Parliament, it closed in 1844 as an economic failure but as demand for anthracite increased it was rebuilt as far as Cross Hands in 1883.

New housing on the shore at Seaside is adjacent to a broad slipway, to which there is no vehicle access.

Coming along the shore is the main line between Paddington and Fishguard, backed by the A484.

Burry Port had a shoreline test site for early wind turbines including the prototype vertical axis model.

This is an area where the currents flow shallow but

Burry Holms with the line of the inshore passage visible.

Disused Whiteford Point lighthouse with Berges Island beyond.

very fast as the tide sweeps in and out. Boating and parascending are local activities and the harbour is used mainly by recreational craft. It was a small fishing harbour before the Industrial Revolution but was developed to serve the coal industry up the Gwendraeth valley. The Burry Port & Gwendraeth Valley Railway was built in 1869 on the line of a former canal to bring high quality anthracite from Cwm-mawr. The construction method meant that there was insufficient headroom to use standard vehicles so special rolling stock and locomotives had to be employed. The pits were worked out after the Second World War and the port closed down commercially. The town was also at the forefront of transport when the Burry Inlet was used for disembarkation after one of the first transatlantic flights, which landed off Pwll, mistaken for Southampton. There is a memorial to passenger Amelia Earhart, the first woman to cross the Atlantic in a plane, later to break records as a pilot.

The 1819 coal harbour of Pembrey, adjacent to a causeway, was disused from 1878 and silted up butit has been turned it into Bury Port Marina, marked by a light in a cupola on the end of the pier. At the far end of the harbour is Pembrey & Burry Port station, one of the last two stations in Britain to stop using cardboard tickets in 1988. St Mary's church has the graves of several shipwrecked sailors.

The 11km long Cefn Sidan Sands is one of the best beaches in Wales. Backed by 2.2km^2 of country park, the dunes of Pembrey Burrows, Ashburton golf course, parkland, nature trails, picnic sites, hot food kiosk, adventure playground, narrow gauge and miniature railways, equestrian course, pitch and putt course, craft displays, sandcastle competitions, treasure hunts, land yachting and a very gently sloping beach, it is one of the most popular attractions in Wales except during bad weather when the sea breaks heavily onto the sands.

Beyond Pembrey Forest with its Corsican pines is a disused Battle of Britain fighter airfield which has become the Welsh Motorsport

the edge of the Pembrey bombing range off Tywyn Point and also one or two wrecks around.

The Gwendraeth estuary is quieter with sparrowhawks, buzzards, curlews, herons, waders and wildfowl common, cranes and ospreys not being unknown.

At the head of the estuary is Kidwelly Castle. Built in 1274, it is one of the finest medieval castles in southwest Wales, using a walls within walls defensive system and positioned so that it could be supplied by sea if the land approach was cut off. It was begun in the 12th century with a square inner bailey and tall round curtain towers with the gatehouse being rebuilt in the 14th century. It is one of the best preserved castles in Wales and one of a line built right across South Wales which pushed the Welsh speakers northwards away from the fertile coastal area.

The main railway passes again briefly, skirting a caravan site and sweeping up beside the Afon Tywi through Ferryside, site in 1959 of the first GWR water troughs to be retired.

Opposite is Llansteffan Castle, 12th century Norman, one of the finest ruins in Wales, taken by Rhys ap Gruffydd after the death of Henry II. It has a 12th century bailey and ringwork, massive masonry defences from the 13th century at the time of the English conquests and a 15th century gatehouse. Nearby St Anthony's Well was once believed to have healing properties.

Laugharne Castle on the Afon Taf completes the trio of estuary fortifications. It was founded in the 12th century by Rhys ap Gruffydd, mostly Tudor with a small polygonal bailey and 13th century round towers. Frequently attacked in the 12th and 13th centuries, it became a mansion in 1782 and was painted by Turner. More famous these days is the boathouse in which Dylan Thomas wrote many of his plays. Laugharne forms a basis for Llareggub in his *Under Milk Wood* although he denied that its people became his characters, a matter hotly disputed and leading to much ill feeling. Cefn Sidan Sands, within sight of the boathouse, has nude bathing these days.

Beyond Ginst Point are Laugharne Burrows and Pendine Burrows, sand dunes which form Pendine range which is in use when red flags are flying, usually on weekdays.

Pendine, at the ends of the A4066 and B4314, has a telephone kiosk, the Springwell Inn, Sands Restaurant and the Beach Hotel on the end of which is a notice reminding all that it was on Pendine Sands that Sir Malcolm Campbell and Thomas Parry made their attempts on the world land speed record. The village has a Museum of Speed. In 1924 Campbell set a record of 234km/h in *Bluebird*. Three years later Parry was

Centre, Wales' premier motor circuit with autograss, karting, rallycross, motorcycle racing and scrambling. There is a watchtower in the centre and another tower on the beach towards the north end where there are a number of stakes in the water at

killed when the drive chains of his Leyland Special, *Babs*, broke. The car was buried on the spot but in 1969 it was exhumed and taken to Capel Curig for restoration.

Ladies Cave folded strata on the shore at Saundersfoot.

The beach was subsequently abandoned when its 10km length became too short for further record attempts but imagination of even faster speeds followed in *The Fight* in *Portrait of the Artist as a Young Dog.* An exception in 2018 was a mobile shed which achieved a world record 161km/h.

There are wind turbines above Pendine. Antiquities include Castle Lloyd behind Llanmiloe, a settlement on Gilman Point, chambered cairns on Ragwen Point and Top Castle at the far end of Marros Sands below Marros Beacon.

On the other hand, the 18th century Amroth Castle, on the site of a Norman castle, is a relatively modern looking building by the Carmarthenshire/Pembrokeshire border, now a holiday centre. Amroth has a shingle beach where a submerged forest, fossilized acorns and deer antlers are sometimes seen after storms and over which waders wander when conditions are less onerous. When they are more onerous there is better surf to be had at the top of the tide. There are no obvious

signs that Amroth was formerly a mining village where the coalfield reached the coast.

This is the start of the Pembrokeshire Coast National Park, Britain's smallest and only coastal national park, 583km², designated in 1952. This is the sunniest part of Wales but gales blow at least 30 days in the average year. Beyond a line from Amroth to Newgale is sometimes referred to as Little England Beyond Wales, an area where place names, church styles, spoken language and layout of communities are more typically English than in the part of Wales lying to the northeast of the line. The phenomenon dates from 1090 when Arnulph of Montgomery brought the Norman feudal system to the southwest extremity of Wales. Mainly an agricultural region, it repeats many of the geological features of the Gower with mountain limestone and Old Red Sandstone folded east–west and levelled in wave cut platforms at 60m and 120m. Following its perimeter is the Pembrokeshire Coast Path.

Beaches around Wiseman's Bridge, named after 14th century landowner Andrew Wiseman, were used for practice D-Day landings in 1943, including building an airfield in two days, watched by Churchill, Montgomery and Eisenhower. Surf is biggest at high water with windier conditions. There are the remains of 20m deep bell anthracite pits in the woods behind. There was also haematite mining, resulting in iron smelting.

At Coppet Hall Point there is a tunnel for the footpath which used to take the 610mm gauge Saundersfoot Railway running to Wiseman's Bridge. Saundersfoot on the B4316 used to export anthracite around the world, including to Dublin's Guinness brewery, the last of the mines closing in 1945. High up, St Issell's church has a 13th century Norman tower and cast iron tomb monuments and is close to Hean Castle in the woods. The trees are stunted lichen covered oaks, larches, pines and spruces, among which are dotted the holes of coal mines. The village is one of the finest yachting centres in Wales. It also has windsurfing and waterskiing with a line of buoys right across the bay from April to October with a 9km/h speed limit inside. The harbour, marked by a stone cupola on the pierhead, has an impounding dock in the corner which holds water to release at low tide to scour out the harbour entrance but it is no longer used. South of the village the rocks along the shore are heavily folded. Ivy covered cliffs lead to Monkstone Point which

Georgian and Regency houses provide a genteel air around the harbour at Tenby despite a stormy dawn.

Caldey Island and St Margaret's Island.

St Catherine's Island off Tenby.

has a passage inside at higher levels of the tide and a surf beach beyond with long rides. Cliffs of 50m continue to Tenby and on top are three masts. Now the Millstone Grit becomes limestone, seals frequent the rocks and razor shells are found on isolated beaches.

Tenby, a shortened form of Dinbych-y-Pysgod, Denbigh of the fish, is at the end of the A478 and claims four beaches including North Beach which has the distinctive Goscar Rock on the waterline. Tenby was a Viking fishing village in the 8th century, then an important fish market in the Middle Ages, shipped coal from bell pits from the 14th century and was a strategic harbour, one of the most beautiful in Britain but sacked more than once by the Welsh. The 13th century town walls are the most complete in South Wales and took 50 years to build, the Five Arches being the old South Gate. The Duke of Richmond, later Henry VII, escaped in 1471 from here to Brittany after the Battle of Tewkesbury. St Mary's Norman church, marked by its spire, dates from the 13th and 15th centuries and is claimed to be the largest in Wales. In season it has music and choral singing. Gerald of Wales held the living here for a time. Plays are performed in the De Valence Pavilion. There is a 15th century Tudor merchant's house with the original scarfed roof trusses surviving, furnishings in different periods and remains of 18th century frescoes on three interior walls. The merchant's shop is set out as in 1500. Daniel Defoe in 1724 described Tenby as 'the most agreeable town on all the south coast of Wales, except Pembroke'. Sir William Paxton developed it as a refined watering place in the 18th century and bathing machines were used from 1860. Oscar Wilde's *An Ideal Husband* refers to a violent flirtation here between Lord Mortlake and Mrs Cheveley. The Georgian and Regency harbourside with its houses of pale grey mountain limestone includes the Fourcroft Hotel and Royal Lion Hotel above the Indie Burger of more recent vintage.

The harbour is a centre for sailing and windsurfing and is overlooked by TS Tenby. At the back is a 17th century flushing sluice. Tenby Sailing Club uses a former wine warehouse. Easton House was built beside the harbour by Paxton in 1811 to house seawater baths and carries a motto in Greek to the effect that 'the sea washes away the ills of man.' More often quoted is the = sign, invented by Tudor scientist Robert Recorde who was born in Tenby and who introduced algebra to Britain. There is a 120m pier with an assortment of stakes nearby.

The 12th century castle is Norman, hence the access

to the sea, and has a museum built into it. Castle Hill also has a prominent monument. In 1644 Cromwell took Tenby under fire from both land and sea. A former lifeboat house has been converted into an indoor climbing wall.

St Catherine's Island has a fortress built in 1868 to house 11 guns and 60 men to defend Milford Haven from French attack, another of Palmerston's Follies, being restored. Recently it has served as a zoo. St Catherine was the patron saint of spinners, spinning being an important

industry in medieval Tenby. Some surf can dump onto the beach.

The gap through to the Burrows is closed at low tide and partly occupied by portable jetties to serve boats taking trippers to Caldey Island and St Margaret's Island. The buildings end beyond the esplanade. Behind the Burrows are the Whitland to Pembroke Dock railway and the A4139.

Beyond the Burrows with waves which are fast and short, Carmarthen Bay ends at Giltar Point. On the top is Penally Gallery Range which faces south and is frequently in use. Those close in to the foot of the cliffs should suffer little risk of danger from stray bullets. The headland is where Virginia Woolf decided to devote her life to literature while walking in 1904, following the death of her father, and George Eliot had been put under pressure while staying in the town to write fiction.

Caldey Sound is an eroded syncline with a 5km/h tide race running through on springs. Eel Spit runs 650m north from Caldey Island and the Fiddlers, a dangerous cross sea, breaks over it when the wind is against the tide.

Caldey Island is the Old Norse keld ey (spring island), the former Welsh Ynys Pyr. It is an area of blowholes and caves, the largest being the Cathedral Cave with a nave 92m x 12m x 18m high, lit by daylight through hidden crevices. Another cave has produced the bones of mammoth and rhinoceros, showing that the island was formerly part of the mainland. Human occupation dates back to 10,000 BC with mid Stone Age tools from Nanna's Cave, Bronze Age implements and Roman pottery being found. The Ogham Stone is sandstone with a cross, inscription in Latin and Ogham script and possibly some defaced script from earlier times. It may have been from pre-Christian sun worshippers. The 6th century Celtic missionary Pyro occupied a cell and was succeeded by Samson from Llantwit, later the first Bishop of Dol in Brittany. The inhabitants were probably killed in the 10th century by Danes. A Benedictine settlement was established in the 12th century and the ruins of the priory and the leaning spire of St Illtud's church were probably built in 1113 and occupied until

the dissolution of the monasteries in 1534. The white round tower of the monastery with its red roof was built by Anglican Benedictines in 1912 and the island has been inhabited by Cistercian Trappist monks from Chimay in Belgium since 1928. In 1958 it became the Abbey of St Samson. Today they operate a perfumery based on the island's gorse, lavender and other herbs and also make chocolate, cream and yoghurt. All the island's buildings are whitewashed. Women are not allowed to visit the monastery and no one is allowed to land on the island without the permission of the abbot.

The lighthouse at Chapel Point on the south side was built in 1828. The cliffs are said to be haunted by the ghost of the pirate Paul Jones although seals and sea birds are more tangible residents.

St Margaret's Island is a nature reserve managed by the Wildlife Trust for South & West Wales and is connected to Caldey Island by a causeway which dries at low tide. Boats from Tenby and Saundersfoot bring trippers to see the cliffs and birdlife. There are puffins and 200 pairs of cormorants, the largest colony in Wales. Limestone was quarried in the 19th century by 22 residents and an 11th century watchtower is prominently positioned.

Holes and caves in the mainland cliff face continue towards Proud Giltar. Beyond is Lydstep Haven and its beach, owned by a caravan site. The haven was the favourite place of Edmund Gosse and was also quite popular with Bishop Gower who was thought to have used the Palace overlooking the haven as a hunting lodge. It is now popular with jet and water skiers.

Shallows in the centre of Caldey Sound link back to Lydstep Point, a narrow 43m high ridge of vertically bedded limestone, steep to on the east and south sides with a nature trail on top. There is also an old fort site on the top. The cliffs lead round to Church Doors, a cove named after its tall caves, and to Skrinkle Haven. There is another ancient fort naming Old Castle Head. During the First World War the area was used to house anti-submarine airships. Tidal streams set towards the head and there can be overfalls and a short broken sea off it. The biggest danger, though, is the Manorbier range on top and lights may be shown when firing is taking place. Heat seeking missiles have been fired, dropping down off the cliffs to fly some 3–5m above the water before rising to intercept a target released by a model aeroplane. There is a helicopter landing area on the west side of the headland.

The cliffs run out to Priest's Nose on top of which is King's Quoit, a 5,000 year old burial chamber, a communal Megalithic tomb with a 5m capstone supported by two upright stones at one end.

Manorbier Bay with its reef break is backed by the massive bulk of Manorbier Castle, now a ruin. It was Norman, hence the access to the sea, and had an inner irregular bailey from about 1130 with round curtain towers, small square tower, hall and chapel and a gatehouse being added later in the century. It was used for filming *I Capture the Castle* and, in 1989, *The Lion, the Witch & the Wardrobe*. Gerald of Wales was born in the castle in 1146 and was to call it the most delectable spot in all Wales. Related to most of the Welsh princes, he was a brilliant scholar, witty and handsome. He wanted to be Bishop of St David's but Henry II prevented this for fear of a repeat of the Becket incident and a potential insurrection. Gerald debated his case three times with the Pope before resigning himself to studying and writing 17 books, notably *The Journey Through Wales*. He died in obscurity in Lincoln in 1223, never having held any high post.

The cliffs are now of Old Red Sandstone with their biggest break at Freshwater East with its weever fish and its shacks and chalets behind the dunes. Trewent Point provides protection although there is a rip tide at times off the point.

Arches through the cliffs at Stackpole Head.

Greenala Point with its Iron Age fort site is a much less obvious point. The sandstone changes back to limestone on the approach to Stackpole Quay. The harbour with its cluster of cottages was built in the 18th century to load limestone quarried from the cliffs and land coal, used in an adjacent limekiln. The Viking name is from the remains of a stack and pollr, an inlet. There is an abundance of fossils and the stump of a syncline on the rocks among the tumbling strata.

The expanse of sand backing Barafundle Bay is the last before the limestone assumes its full grandeur from Stackpole Head onwards. The head has a tide race off it but two tall arches through the head can avoid the problem above low tide. Columns resemble subterranean cave structures, caves have collapsed into blowholes, and scenery is now on a grand scale.

Church Rock, a spire of limestone, guards the entrance to Broad Haven with Stackpole Warren behind. The dam among the dunes holds back 30ha of the freshwater Fish Ponds which are crossed by various footbridges and are thick with water lilies in the summer and with wildfowl and waders in the winter. It was constructed by the Cawdors, who acquired the estate by marriage in the 18th century, yet the ponds are one of the places where King Arthur is said to have disposed of Excalibur. In 1976 an 8km² estate was given to the nation by Lord Cawdor, a descendant of the 1797 hero. Home Farm, beyond the Fish Ponds, has Stackpole Outdoor Learning Centre with activities which include canoeing, abseiling, sand yachting and bivouacking. Weever fish stings are a risk for those working what can be decent surf here.

The coast now becomes part of the Castlemartin artillery ranges, used mostly during office hours like the other ranges although night firing sometimes takes place. There is no safe landing point except at low tide between here and Frainslake Sands so this section of coastline is

St Govan's chapel on the cliff near St Govan's Head.

255

Distinctive stacks stand in Bullslaughter Bay at low water.

extremely committing. The 24km² artillery and bombing ranges are on land which once grew the best wheat in the county. There are observation towers, railways and tanks on top and firing covers a distance 20km out to sea. The army allow walkers access from the north to Elegug Stacks and then eastwards when the ranges are not in use but there has been considerable ill feeling that this fantastic coastline is not available at other times and west of Elegug Stacks may not be approached at all on land.

St Govan's Head is 37m high, bare and perpendicular with a tide race and overfalls at the foot, perhaps with common dolphins as well. Tidal streams between St Govan's Head and Linney Head start SE one hour before high water at Dover for five hours until the flow reverses. The St Gowan lightvessel is moored 10km south–south-west.

A holy well on the southwest side of the head is now dry but until recently was thought to have eye healing properties although the area is hardly ideal for those with poor eyesight. Perhaps only those with good eyesight returned safely. Nearby is St Govan's Chapel, a 13th century building almost hidden halfway down the cliff face, probably replacing a 5th century cell built by an early Christian missionary. Arthurian legend rears its head again with the suggestion that the missionary could have been Sir Gawain repenting of his licentiousness after the death of his king. The steps are said never to count the same going down to the chapel as going up but the official figure is 52. The bellcote is empty, the silver bell being claimed to have been stolen by pirates and returned by sea nymphs who hid it in a nearby rock which rings when struck but this is rather too wild an area to put the legend to the test by colliding with the rocks.

Huntsman's Leap is a 200m long by 40m deep cleft in the cliffs with a gap variously measured between 2 and 6m. The huntsman concerned is said to have been hunted by his creditors and then died of fright after looking back at what he had jumped over. Nearby is an armoured car in a delicate pale magenta colour.

Last of the more prominent crags is the Castle which takes its name from the Iron Age fort site on its top.

Bullslaughter Bay and Flimston Bay offer potential sandy landing sites at low water, the former with two prominent limestone pinnacles in the middle of the beach and an Iron Age fort site above an arch through Moody Nose at the end of the beach.

The next kilometre contains some of the best limestone cliff scenery in Britain, an absolute feast of pillars, stacks and caves. Crickmail Down has a double cave like a crypt with a blowhole and the magnificent Green Bridge of Wales is flanked by the Elegug Stacks (a degeneration of the Welsh heligog, guillemot), an Iron Age camp and the Cauldron blowhole. There are bird sanctuaries in the area with nesting places for guillemots, fulmars, kittiwakes, razorbills and shags while blackheaded gulls search for eggs.

There was once a fort on top. The scenery is only seen at its best from the sea. However, because it can only be used when the army are not present and the public are excluded from the land, it means that the next 6km of clifflined coast must be undertaken without anyone else to spot anyone in trouble if problems arise on this wild coastline.

The strata become mainly horizontal, the banding heavily marked and running for up to a kilometre at a time without any significant incursions by the sea. This is scenery on a grand scale running out as Pembrokeshire's solid rampart in almost a straight line to Linney Head. The only feature of an individual nature is Pen-y-holt Stack, looking like a slightly irregular column of giant millstones. Across Crow Sound lie the Toes and Crow Rock, over which there are overfalls.

Linney Head is perpendicular, 37m high with a flat summit on top of which are a fort site, some rusting tank remains and a large fluorescent orange letter indicating the section of the range. Below is a tide race. The tide stream from Freshwater West is almost continuously south southeast.

Wind Bay below Hanging Tar doubtless earns its name. Large waves bounce back off the cliffs and around several large rocks 100–200m away from their base, giving an unstable ride at the best of times. Beyond Blucks Pool the Pole runs out, a ridge of rock for the sea to break over before the sandy but often surf covered Frainslake Sands are reached, running up onto the dunes of Brownslade Burrows, an extension of Linney Burrows, around which tumuli are to be found.

A hut is the only survivor of a dozen built in the 1920s for boiling seaweed collected here. Once a week it was carried in baskets on women's heads to Pembroke station from where it was taken to Swansea for making into laver bread.

Freshwater West, the best surf break in Wales, is reached after passing the extensive shelves of rock which form Great Furzenip and Little Furzenip, rock over which the sea breaks heavily, not that Freshwater West itself is known for its calmness, having strong offshore currents and undertows. It has been used for filming, including for JK Rowling's *Harry Potter & the Deathly Hallows*. There is a convenient carpark off the B4319 and an immaculately landscaped toilet block with a turf roof and a telephone on the end, the effort being somewhat wasted because of the Milford Haven oil refinery chimneys showing over the hill. St Ann's Head, looking southwest from off Dale Point.

There are now considerable variations in tide stream times for small changes in position.

The air reverberates with the noise of tanks firing on Castlemartin artillery range, punctuated at times with machinegun fire or low flying jets. Yet, closer to hand, fulmars, oystercatchers and cormorants ignore the noise and rhizostoma jellyfish float peacefully in the water. Dunes behind the beach cover Stone and Bronze Age sites and the Devil's Quoit is an ancient burial chamber.

Lying between an ancient promontory fort behind West Pickard Bay and a hilltop windmill is the site of the former Angle airfield, opened in 1941 for the RAF, used for a time by the Fleet Air Arm and finally closed in 1945, the buildings now having been mainly cleared. A hexagonal stone tower follows Guttle Hole.

Sheep Island, with its caves, has a low tide connection to the Iron Age fort of about 300 BC on Studdock Point but Rat Island is usually firmly connected to East Blockhouse Point with its masts, where there was an Iron Age settlement. Between them is the huge Welcome Pit blowhole. The tower remains on the point date from 1539 to protect against the Spanish. West Angle Bay has a relocated cannon and a chimney remaining from a brickworks. The final island on this corner is Thorn Island, topped by the most dramatic 19th century fort in the area, in this commanding position overlooking the entrance to Milford Haven.

Milford Haven is Britain's best harbour and largest port, a useful link with Ireland. Founded in 1790, Nelson claimed it was matched only by Trincomalee in Sri Lanka. The name comes from the Norse, milfjord, suggesting its use may be somewhat older. The haven is the mouth of the Daugleddau and is a ria formed by a post glacial rise in sea level.

There is a confused sea off the entrance, sometimes called the Washing Machine. The flood begins at HW Dover +0130 and the ebb at HW Dover −0430, both at up to 4km/h. There are two deep water channels through the entrance but things are rather simpler to the north of Thorn Island where the channels have merged. The fairway lies between Chapel (starboard) and Stack (port) buoys but the dredged channel occupies only the southern half of the marked channel, passing to the south of South Hook south cardinal marker just up the channel. While this means that there is only a narrow channel to cross it is a busy one which allows tankers little room to manoeuvre. With vessels up to the 327,000 tonne

The Green Bridge of Wales.

Elegug Stacks in afternoon shadow.

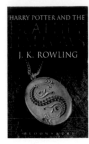

The one remaining seaweed collectors' hut at Freshwater West.

and Sandyhaven Pill offers the delights described and painted by Graham Sutherland plus egrets.

Little and Great Castle Heads both have leading light beacons and Iron Age fort sites, the beacon built on the fort site in the case of Great Castle Head. A small radar station overlooks Lindsway Bay. The remains of a First World War gun battery are sited on Watch House Point.

St Ishmael's has a motte which was the site of a Norman castle. Serving the village is Monk Haven which has a folly and was used in the Middle Ages by pilgrims heading for St David's who preferred to complete the journey on foot rather than risk the sea further west.

In Tudor times Dale at the end of the B4327 was well known as a smuggling centre. It was used by Nicolette Milnes-Walker when she set out from here to become the first woman to sail nonstop to America. Today it is one of the most photographed spots in Wales and is the third sunniest place in Britain, the early spring resulting in profuse flora. Between the white windmill ruins and the yacht moorings are Dale Flats, an area of mud and stones favoured by wildfowl and waders.

Everything from ornithology to diving is featured at Dale Fort Field Centre based on a defence fort of 1856 on Dale Point, near which is an Iron Age fort.

At the other extreme is the futuristic concrete pylon on Watwick Point, a 50m high leading light backmarker used in conjunction with another on West Blockhouse Point. The fort here was built in 1847 with six large guns, in use until after the Second World War.

Kuwait Universe the potential for causing a very expensive accident is not insignificant. Even so, expenditure on developing the haven as an international maritime park has encouraged recreational boat use as the oil companies have withdrawn their involvement. It has hosted the start of the Cutty Sark Tall Ships Race with up to 80 sailing ships.

The juxtaposition of ancient and modern is fascinating. All around extend long jetties, tank farms, flare stacks and tankers that are moored in Sandy Haven and Dale Shelf Anchorages. Five 31m high x 95m diameter concrete tanks, built at South Hook Point in 2005 for liquified natural gas from the Middle East, are probably the largest diameter tanks to have been slipformed in concrete in single operations. Defiantly in the midst of everything is the large 19th century gun emplacement on Stack Rock

Mount Sion Down with Linney Head visible in the distance. Pen-y-Holt Stack breaks the Pen-y-Holt Bay skyline.

Thorn Island with its fort on the south side of the entrance to Milford Haven.

Because Mill Bay is out of sight of potentially hostile castles at Dale and Pembroke it was used as a landing place in 1485 by locally born Henry Tudor and 2,000 men. Henry rallied the loyal Welshmen and a fortnight later beat Richard III at Bosworth and placed himself on the throne as Henry VII.

The current lighthouse is joined by a helipad and radio mast on top of the 40m high red brown plateau of St Ann's Head which forms the end of what is generally a 60m platform, heavily folded at Cobbler's Hole. An old lighthouse follows. To Wooltack Point the cliffs are mostly precipitous. West of St Ann's Head the streams begin to flow southeast at HW Dover −0140 and northwest at HW Dover +0410, even close in to the point.

Great Castle Head with its large Iron Age hill fort protects Westdale Bay with its rather more recent Gothic Dale Castle and cypresses in a garden with plants distorted by the wind. The Ritec fault runs through to Dale and continues to the Gower. There is still dumping surf with powerful lefts and rights beyond.

Dale airfield was opened in 1942 for Coastal Command, seeing frontline service with No 304 (Polish) Squadron using Wellingtons for maritime patrol until 1943, before being taken over by the Royal Navy until 1947. Many of the buildings were removed by the simple expedient of pushing them over the cliffs.

The sweep of Marloes Sands was used as a setting for filming *The Lion in Winter*. Onshore winds bring good flood tide surfing with varied breaks. On top of the cliffs of volcanic Ordovician rocks is Lord Kensington's Deer Park from the 19th century which has never had deer because of the lack of suitable plant cover. The best known wildlife were the leeches in Marloes Mere, collected by villagers in the 18th century to supply London's Harley Street physicians.

Gateholm Island is attached at low water. It has the remains of rectangular huts, which may have been a monastic settlement, and 130 hut circles which date from Roman times. This is raven and chough country, in addition to all the wildlife which emanates from Skokholm.

Skokholm takes its name from the Norse, small island in the sound, but the Vikings were not the first here for there are many traces of early and medieval settlement. From the 12th century it was managed as a rabbit warren. When initial tests with myxamatosis were carried out on the island they proved unsuccessful because the rabbits here lacked the necessary fleas which are usually present on mainland rabbits. Dale Castle Estate became the owners in 1745 and built a farmhouse and limekiln in 1760. The lighthouse was built in 1916, now accompanied by a helicopter landing site. Resident from 1927 to 1933 was RM Lockley who wrote *I Know an Island*, popularized the seals and in 1928 recovered coal,

fittings and the figurehead from the wrecked *Alice Williams*, the latter being attached by him to the rockface in South Haven.

The 97ha island has a flat top and 50m high cliffs of dark red sandstone. In 1939 it became the site of the first bird observatory in the British Isles and is now a National Nature Reserve mainly owned by the Wildlife Trust of South & West Wales. Permission to land needs to be arranged with the national park office. This nature reserve boasts 35,000 pairs of Manx shearwaters, 5,000 pairs of puffins, 7,000 pairs of storm petrels, colonies of guillemots, razorbills and kittiwakes and over 150 species recorded including cormorants, shags and the gannets which can be seen fishing as they spot their prey from on high, dive down and close their wings just before impact with the water, to emerge a few seconds later with their catches. There are grey seals and three species of dolphin. Courses held on the island include bird watching, natural history and the history of the island.

East of Skokholm streams begin east and southeast at HW Dover −0030 and west and northwest at HW Dover −0530 at up to 6km/h.

A wheel shaft off Albion Sands is from the *Albion* paddle steamer, wrecked in 1837. Her human passengers, crew and Irish whiskey were all rescued and 400 pigs swum ashore and were driven to Marloes to be butchered.

More Iron Age forts lead along to Wooltack Point but the major feature is Renny Slip with a very large cave.

Jack Sound separates Midland Isle and Skomer Island from the mainland and runs at 13km/h on springs, starting south at HW Dover −0300 and north at HW Dover +0300. There can be overfalls from the Bench to Tusker Rock with a strong eddy round Tusker Rock and a considerable overfall. Some 27km of coastline around the island and the Marloes peninsula from Gateholm Island to Martin's Haven became Wales' first Maritime Nature Reserve, the second in Britain. Harbour porpoises may be seen.

Wooltack Point with its cliffs of volcanic Ordovician rock separates Broad Sound from St Bride's Bay although a glacial meltwater channel crosses its neck to Martin's Haven, helping to protect what were the largest Iron Age fortifications in Wales. In the bay there are weak currents with an eddy parallel to the main north–south stream.

Martin's Haven forms a useful inlet with a route up a steep path to a carpark. It is an embarkation point for boats going to Skomer. Rusting winding gear and an igneous intrusion of basalt lavas with quartzite and felspar overlook the little inlet which can be a favourite spot for divers. Nearby is a Celtic ringed cross which was found in the base of a Victorian wall when it was being demolished.

Distance
120km from Llangennith via Llanelli, Ferryside and Sandy Haven to Martin's Haven

OS 1:50,000 Sheets
157 St David's & Haverfordwest
158 Tenby & Pembroke
159 Swansea & Gower

Tidal Constants
Burry Port:
HW Dover −0500
LW Dover −0450
Ferryside:
HW Dover −0500
LW Dover −0350
Tenby:
HW Dover −0510
LW Dover −05.20
Stackpole Quay:
HW Dover −0450
LW Dover −0510
Dale Roads:
HW Dover −0500
LW Dover −0510
Milford Haven:
Dover −0500
Skomer Island:
Dover −0500
Martin's Haven:
HW Dover −0450
LW Dover −0440

Sea Area
Lundy

Ranges
Pembury, Pendine, Giltar Point, Manorbier, Castlemartin

Connections
River Loughor – see Rob p37
River Tywi - see RoB p39
Afon Taf – see RoB p41
Milford Haven – see RoB p46

St Ann's Head, looking southwest from off Dale Point.

Jack Sound with Wooltack Point on the right and Midland Isle and Skomer Island on the left.

47 Skomer Island

Wales' first Marine Nature Reserve

At its southwest extremity Wales does not give way to the Celtic Sea without a struggle. Running out from almost the most westerly point in Wales is the ridge of the Skomer volcanic series which surfaces at intervals as a line of islands, getting smaller and more widely spaced as they go, Skomer Island, Grassholm Island and the Smalls. Of these, Skomer is the most accessible and has been for centuries. The name comes from the Viking Skalmey, referring to its cloven shape, and it has Iron Age field systems with further farming from the 18th century until 1939.

The most convenient launching point is Martin's Haven where there are toilets, a National Trust carpark and a National Trust shop selling guidebooks and souvenirs. There can be substantial currents through Jack Sound and Little Sound and around the whole of Skomer. They can reach 13km/h in Jack Sound. Wildgoose Race occupies much of Broad Sound and rip tides and overfalls are challenging features of using these waters.

Before launching it is worth visiting the National Coastwatch Institution lookout hut above Haven Point, both to study the tide races and to take in the panoramic view.

On the water, Tusker Rock (which can be surrounded by a strong eddy and considerable overfalls) gives a useful pointer to the speed of the current before making a commitment to Jack Sound. Midland Isle is a useful refuge although Little Sound can be lively in its own right.

Conditions will be easiest if launching is about an hour before the turn of the tide, high tide for preference as this allows access to the high and narrow caves which pass right through Skomer at each end.

Less obvious are small caves which run back under the water and which are only noticed with an explosion of trapped air as even the smallest of waves drives in. The island is a plateau with cliffs all round, often deeply eaten into by the sea so that the Neck, the eastern end, is almost severed from the main part. The narrow part connecting the two contains quartzite where sediments are rift faulted but the majority of the island consists of resistant igneous volcanic basalts from the Lower Silurian era. In the centre Skomer rises to 79m.

The difficulty in landing is somewhat academic as landing is prohibited without the permission of the wardens. The island is managed by the Wildlife Trust of South & West Wales who control this nature reserve which is also part of the Pembrokeshire Coast National Park. Complex access restrictions apply because of nesting seabirds and seal breeding. It is difficult to study the wildlife without disturbing it if on foot. There is a charge for landing, when permitted.

Jack Sound, Midland Isle and Skomer seen from the mainland.

Little Sound divides Skomer from Midland Isle.

Puffin with fish off the Mew Stone.

The Mew Stone on the south side of Skomer.

Any chance of a quiet trip is out of the question as the sky is an overwhelming mass of seabirds going about their business, landing on the sea and taking off again, investigating boats and flying in all directions in a mindboggling rush hour of activity. Some 95,000 pairs of Manx shearwaters, 6,000 pairs of puffins and 10,000 rabbits all dig burrows for nesting purposes. The rabbits were introduced about 1300 and their skins exported until the mid-1950s. There are 120 species of bird on the island, guillemots, kittiwakes, fulmars, razorbills, shags, ravens, choughs, storm petrels, short eared owls and numerous blackbacked and other gulls, including 80 pairs of predatory blackheaded gulls, while passing migrants include the golden oriole, icterine warbler, red breasted flycatcher and scarlet grosbeak. Skomer boasts 200 species of flower and fern, particularly a sea of bluebells in the spring with a complement of gorse, pink campion and thrift. Animals include the longtailed fieldmouse, common and pigmy shrews and the unique Skomer vole, a creature which is heavier and more sluggish than the mainland version and which is tame enough to be handled. The nature reserve has an international reputation. Visitors are strictly controlled and any boater presence which could disturb the birds during the breeding season is not welcomed, a problem also faced by divers who enjoy the area.

There are numerous signs of Iron Age occupation of the island with fortifications, huts and burial barrows. There is a promontory fort on the Neck, around which are areas used for grey seal pupping. Alongside is South Haven, the largest inlet and one which may be used to moor the odd yacht despite the eel grass bed which is at risk of disturbance. There are ancient field systems by the Wick, an inlet where vast flat sloping slabs of rock have been exposed.

The most dramatic part of Skomer's coastline is undoubtedly the Mew Stone, a 57m high column of rock standing alone on the south side of the island. As the mewing of gulls reverberates around it is not hard to

think of a reason for the name. The column is unusual in an area where most land is flat topped, such as Skokholm Island, with its white and red lit lighthouse, away to the south across Broad Sound, and Grassholm Island which lies to the west.

Around Pigstone Bay thick sections of rock strata lie about untidily on any surface which is vaguely flat. Underneath the finger which forms the northern edge of this bay is a narrow cleft which just allows access to the back of the Table at higher stages of the tide.

Terminating the northern arm of St Brides Bay is Ramsey Island, visible in the distance, and the bay may be dotted with freighters of some size lying at anchor.

The sea may contain moon jellyfish in the summer but the most unnerving presence is always the loud sploosh of a seal which has been following unnoticed immediately behind, satisfying his curiosity, and then diving when he loses his nerve. Skomer is a breeding ground for grey seals and they are particularly fond of the area near the Garland Stone, a 29m high conical rock on the north side, forming symmetry with the Mew Stone. Harbour porpoises may be seen here as well.

The symmetry is completed by North Haven which all but joins up with South Haven. Again, it is used to anchor the occasional boat and is the landing point for the island. At the back of the haven are the warden's house and laboratory. Naturalists and those following the island's nature trail are accommodated in an old cowshed. Farming of the island ceased in 1950 and the farmhouse was damaged by a storm four years later, becoming a ruin. A wreck off the haven is that of the Dutch coaster *Lucy*, sunk in 1967 and now popular with divers.

Also reduced to ruins is an old kiln near the Harold Stone which was used to convert limestone delivered by sea for use as a fertilizer. Surely there must be enough guano now as the thousands of seabirds continue to wheel, soar and streak across the surface of the water. Their screams continue to fill the air and they can still be heard from the mainland.

Distance
Skomer Island is 3km long and lies 1km off Wooltack Point with passenger ferry access

OS 1:50,000 Sheet
157 St David's & Haverfordwest

Tidal Constant
Skomer Island: Dover −0500

Sea Area
Lundy

The northeast coast of Skomer running out to the Garland Stone.

48 West Pembrokeshire

The southwest rampart of Wales

On the Nab Head, named from flint knapping, are the remains of the *Nymph*, wrecked in 1802, and a fort site, making flint tools and beads of jade in Mesolithic times around 5000 BC. A blowhole works east of the head. The Grade II★ St Brides Castle, now holiday accommodation, was built in 1800 as the stately home of Lord Kensington who owned St Brides, a village which seems far too small to have given its name to the bay. The village was named after the 5th century St Brigid of Kildare but there was also much influence from Brigid, the most important Celtic goddess, mistress of fire and patron of poets, whose father, Dagla, was Lord of Knowledge and greatest of the native Irish gods. The churchyard of the 12th or 13th century St Bridget's church contains early Christian tombs set in the cliffs. The cleft of St Brides Haven has rusty iron mooring rings, pumphouse and ruined limekilns. Mill Haven has a limekiln. Two Iron Age forts were sited above the cliffs before Howney Stone.

Inland from the 23m high Stack Rocks with their seals was sited Talbenny airfield. From here No 311 (Czechoslovak) Squadron flew Wellingtons on maritime patrols in 1942/3, the station closing in 1946. For most of this period there was a substantial RAF radar site at Ripperston. Goultrop Roads flow west from HW Dover −0500 and east for a much shorter period from HW Dover +0200. Overlooking them are steep hazel and oak woods, covered with lichens, gnarled by the wind and accompanied by gorse. Black bands in the cliffs are coal seams. A concrete platform is the remains of a lifeboat station.

Little Haven is a fishing village with moorings and an inshore rescue boat in the summer. It was built in the 1850s as a coal port and the whole coastline from here to Newgale is the result of the sea having cut back into coal measures. This section of coast is unstable and subject to slips.

Broad Haven is a surfing venue with a café and smaller but cleaner waves than Newgale but with weever fish. Den's Door is a stack with two arches in it. The Sleek Stone area has great rolled sheets of lava lying right next to horizontal layers which have been cut away to form arches. At Black Point an Iron Age fort has been on the move since 1944. Haroldston Bridge is an arch, followed by more landslips.

Surfing is also possible at Druidston Haven, named after a Norman, Drue. Glacial erratics lie on the sandy beach. Traces of coal seams and workings are visible but nothing compared with Nolton Haven, a coal port in the 18th century. Malator or the Tellytubby house was built underground on the clifftop in 1998 with fine sea views.

Collieries only worked between April and October each year as Lloyds refused to insure boats using the quay in the winter. The anthracite, worked from the 15th century, was of high quality, burning without a flame, but was only to be found in thin, fractured beds. There is still believed to be 230,000,000t in unworked reserves. The chimney of Trefrane Cliff Colliery, the oldest in the area, used until 1906 with undersea depths to 90m, and old shafts form the western end of the Pembrokeshire coalfield. The lane north used to be a tramway for coal tubs and the Counting House was used to check loads. The Trefân mine was closed in 1905.

Stack Rocks include the Camel off Mill Haven.

Contrasting geological features at the Sleek Stone, Broad Haven.

Newgale Sands form another surfing beach. A parking area here has toilets and the Pebbles restaurant while the Duke of Edinburgh is an alternative source of sustenance nearer to Newgale itself, replacing an earlier pub named after a duke who passed in 1882 but it was subsequently washed away. Newgale on the A487 was another coal exporting village. Its shingle storm beach is prominent and sometimes broken tree stumps complete with axe marks from 7,000 years ago are revealed. A 12th century storm not only blew away all the beach but also blew fish up into the bushes, where the locals could collect them. The bay here is used for research and oceanographic instruments, along with sea bass, may be found off the beach. Weever fish are also a risk. *The Journey through Wales* relates how hermit St Caradog's coffin was being carried across the sands to St David's when it was caught in a downpour but the silken pall covering it was not even damp.

Beyond the caravans Roch Castle may be seen which guarded the northwest end of the Landsker line, after which the native Welsh were left to their own devices. The line itself was marked by Brandy Brook but the castle was built on rock to reduce the risk of snakes, the Nor-

Exploring caves at the entrance to Solva.

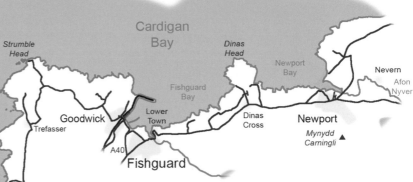

man lord whose castle it was having been told by a soothsayer that he would be killed by a snake. In fact, he died after being bitten by an adder brought in with a bundle of firewood.

The next peninsula is formed of Precambrian and Cambrian igneous and sedimentary rocks in various colours, resulting in a range of pebble colours.

Brawdy Airfield to the north of Roch and Newgale is no longer used. A motte at Pointz Castle is followed westwards by a burial chamber and settlement, further signs of ancient settlement along the coast. Sea otters might be seen.

Dinas Fawr has been worked occasionally for galena and silver while there may have been mining for copper in the vicinity in the 19th century, all small scale operations.

Solva is a magnificent spot, a little village hidden by the Gribin from passing pirates and raiders at the head of a ria drowned after the last Ice Age. There was a glacial channel on each side of the Gribin and an Iron Age earthwork at its end. Today there are yacht moorings but in the 19th century there were 30 boats supplying the village's dozen limekilns, seven of which remain, one still in perfect condition. Trinity Quay was built to prepare materials for construction of the Smalls lighthouse, which was given a trial assembly here. Wrecking was an alternative form of employment but as recently as 1979 the villagers collected thousands of planks of

Heading out of the sheltered natural harbour at Solva.

Looking along the Gribin past the Solva inlet towards Black Scar, Green Scar and the Mare.

Among stacks along the northern edge of St Brides Bay.

Malaysian mahogany valued at £200 each from a wreck. Dolphin spotting is a popular local pastime. Solfach was the Danes' name for samphire.

Off the entrance are the Mare, Black Scar and 33m high Green Scar, a prominent group of islets which give an indication of conditions in the heavy southwesterly swell following westerly storms.

A fort on the coast has been sheared by a landslip. Below it, the stream feeding Porth y Rhaw used to power a mill. St David's airfield was opened in 1943 as a Coastal Command station and used by the Royal Navy until 1960, proposed as a high powered radar base with 35 masts up to 40m high. The ruin of another mill stands above Caer Bwdy Bay, which has a notable 60m long cylinder of rolled Cambrian sandstone. A fort site stands on the headland between this bay and the following Caerfai Bay, as does a former windmill tower. Above Caerfai Bay is a park of caravans in tasteful environmental green. From the cliffs of both bays purple sandstone was quarried to build St David's cathedral. A carving on an erratic boulder dates only from the 1980s.

St David's is the smallest city in Britain and hopes to become the world's first carbon neutral city. St David was the son of St Non and Sant, Prince of Ceredigion, and was born sometime between 462 and 512, becoming the patron saint of Wales. His 6th century monastery was hidden from the view of Norse pirates in the Vale of the Roses. Boia, the local chieftain, tried to get rid of the monastery by getting his wife and maids to go around undressed and use lewd language in front of the monks. All except David fell for this until Boia and his camp were destroyed by a thunderbolt. The monastery was sacked four times by the Vikings between 982 and 989 with Bishop Abraham being killed in 1080 and a further attack in 1091. It became the site of the cathedral, built in Decorated Gothic style from 1178. The tower collapsed in 1220 and the foundations were badly shaken

The southern end of Ramsey Sound with Meini Duon, Ynys Bery, Ynys Cantwr and part of Ramsey Island beyond Pen Dal-aderyn.

in an earthquake of 1248. More recently the cathedral was wired up to study the sonic boom effects during Concorde's early test flights. The first flight was delayed by a day although claims for damages came in from the original date.

Inside, the Norman nave with its 16th century oak ceiling slopes up steeply to the high altar, behind which is a casket said to hold the bones of St David and St Justinian. The choirstall misericords are noted for their witty carvings. In the Middle Ages two pilgrimages to St David's scored equal points to one to Rome and there were calls, particularly by Gerald of Wales, for the bishop to be made a full archbishop, independent of Canterbury. *The Journey through Wales* features the first visit to Wales of an Archbishop of Canterbury, Baldwin taking mass here. The Queen has a reserved seat in the cathedral and first distributed Maundy Money in Wales from here.

Other architectural highlights include the fine fan vaulting in the roof of Holy Trinity Chapel and the Bishop's Palace of 1340 by Bishop Henry de Gower, dedicated to St Non, which included a tall arcaded parapet which served no purpose but gave an Italian style liked by the bishop, this feature being destroyed two centuries later by Bishop Barlow.

Writing from France during the First World War in *Strange Meeting*, David Barton claims there is nowhere else he would rather be than St David's.

By St Non's Bay is a well, said to have mystic powers, addressing eye and rheumatic problems. There is also a modern statue of St Non. This is the point where St David is believed to have been born in a great gale, during which the well may also have appeared, but the spot picked out by sunlight so it is to be hoped that there was rather more shelter then than now, just a rectangle of fencing on almost bare hillside. Part of a Bronze Age stone circle has the ruin of St Non's chapel in the centre.

Caves and a cliff used by climbers lead to Porth Clais,

An unusual mill tower is the central feature of TyF in St David's, which claims to be the world's first carbon neutral outdoor adventure company, based in Wales' first organic hotel.

used now for diving and moorings. Developed in Roman times and later a thriving harbour importing coal and stone for the cathedral, it is protected by a wall probably dating from the Middle Ages. Limekilns have been restored. A bridge of slate slabs crosses the head of the harbour. It was here that St David was said to have been baptized. Nobody had been organized to undertake the task but, right on cue, the bishop of Munster, Elvis, landed in Preseli at this point. *How Culhwch won Olwen* in *The Mabinogion* describes how King Arthur and his troops watched the swine and the boar Twrch Trwyth swim ashore here from Ireland after destroying a fifth of that country.

Porthlysgi Bay was named after 6th century Irish raider Lysgi. Boia was killed resisting him. The ruins of Melin Treginnis, a corn mill, are in the undergrowth. Pen Daladeryn is the most westerly point in mainland Wales. The remains of the Treginnis coper mine are on the clifftop at Penmaen melyn.

Westgoing eddies on the ebb lead from Carreg Fran to the entrance to Ramsey Sound, one of the most technical pieces of water in Wales. The west side of the sound is edged by Ramsey Island, Ynys Cantwr (Chanter's island), Ynys Bery (falcon's isle, formerly Margery Island) and others while the Bishops & Clerks form a line of smaller rocks much further out. Streams start south at HW Dover −0200 and north at HW Dover +0400 at 11km/h on springs. Eddies form on both sides of the sound and there are overfalls over the Horse rock. The major feature, though, is the Bitches on the west side, a ledge which produces heavy white water and which

hosted the first kayak freestyle world championships. In 1910 the St David's lifeboat was lost here with three lifeboat crew drowned while saving 12 people from the ketch *Democrat*. Porpoises use the sound.

Ramsey Island is either Hrafn-ey (Hrafn's island) or Hranfsaa (raven's island) in old Norse or Ynys Dewi (St David's island) in Welsh. It covers 2.6km² and the higher of its two peaks, Carnllundain, rises to 136m. St Devynog or St Devanus is believed to have set up a monastery in the 2nd century and there are said to be 20,000 saints buried here, possibly monks from the monastery although the Celtic tradition desired people to be buried as far west as possible, making the island a prime cemetery. In the 6th century it became a holy place with pilgrimages being made by St David, St Patrick and St Justinian amongst others. St Justinian, a Breton saint, is said to have set up a cell and to have taken an axe to a land bridge across the Bitches to the mainland to gain solitude. The discipline proved too rigorous for his followers who cut off his head, a well with healing water forming at that place. He returned to the mainland, either drifting with the current or walking, carrying his head.

The island was owned by bishops of St David's from early times. Since the 12th century it has been let to farmers. Rabbits, considered a delicacy, were introduced in the 13th century but they ruined the pastures. A farmhouse was built in the 18th century and a cornmill with a 4.3m wheel added in the 1890s.

In 1961 the royal family came ashore from the Royal Yacht *Britannia* for a picnic, the first time the Prince of Wales had set foot on Welsh soil. Today it is an RSPB seabird sanctuary with thousands of razorbills, guillemots, kittiwakes and fulmars although puffin and shearwater colonies have been decimated by rats. Grey seals breed in the caves and at the foot of the cliffs. Deer and goats are kept.

Rocks on the mainland here are 600,000,000 years old, some of the oldest in Britain. Boat trips from Porthstinian go round Ramsey Island. There are two lifeboat stations of 2016 and 1911 beyond the Castell Heinif site and a conspicuous pink tower above the cliffs at St Justinian. There is also a roofless 16th century chapel to the saint.

Bronze Age traders brought copper and gold from the Wicklow Mountains to Whitesands Bay, bound for Salisbury Plain. This may have been the Roman port of Menapia. St Patrick was a Roman here, had a vision of converting Ireland to Christianity and sailed from here to undertake his calling. A tablet marks the site of his chapel. Henry II landed here. The bay at the end of the B4583 has one of the finest surfing beaches in Wales but weever fish are present. Also used for windsurfing, it has a storm beach and a wreck. There is a northgoing eddy on the southgoing stream and small overfalls in the mouth of the bay.

A more significant tiderace, sometimes with overfalls, runs off St David's Head, a 30m high igneous cliff topped with an Iron Age fort with earth banks, burial chamber, settlement and field system, described by Graham Sutherland. The Coetan Arthur cromlech is a burial chamber and the Warrior's Dyke is an Iron Age settlement stone defence wall, contemporary fields still uniquely traceable. The cliffs are of particular interest for wildlife and the waters have bass, pollock and tope. This is one side of the narrowest point of St George's Channel.

From St David's Head to Penberry the cliffs are vertical. Streams in Cardigan Bay run parallel to the coast above 2km offshore, starting northeast at HW Dover −0530 and southwest at HW Dover +0100 at 4km/h although closer inshore local conditions may vary from this. All headlands are igneous intrusions with bays cut into the broken Ordovician shales between them. The conical hills of Penberry and 181m high Carn Llidi are residuals rising from the plateau. Beyond them, Dowrog and Tretio Commons are fine examples of lowland heath.

The boater is never far from a fort or a castell coch, the one before Abereiddy accompanied by a blowhole, but very much closer are the fulmars which glide past, just clearing the water, sweeping in close to the boat.

Abereiddy was a thriving slate centre from 1838 to 1930. The port was replaced by a narrow gauge tramway to Portgain. When the centre closed, either as the result of typhoid or storm waves, fishermen blasted a channel from the sea to the slate quarry which was flooded to form the Blue Lagoon, a new harbour. The beach is of fine grey slate particles, ground down by the dumping surf which is most useable at half tide. Graptolites are found in the slate. Various wrecks lie offshore on the rocks while a mark stands on Trwyncastell headland.

More quarries follow along the coast. Steps to Traeth Llyfn were cut by Second World War Italian prisoners of war but have been replaced by a metal staircase.

Porthgain, located with a small daymark after a series

Carreg Onnen, Ynys Meicel with its light and the footbridge across to Strumble Head. The race, beyond, was on spring tides.

of caves, was another slate quarrying centre with a railway from the quarries to Porthgain, crushers, bins, chutes and buildings which were last used in 1931. Slates, slate waste bricks and crushed granite roadstone were produced for use throughout Britain. The sheltered harbour, slipway and moorings are still in use and facilities include the 1743 Sloop Inn, bar and restaurant and toilet. A café is located in what was a stream powered slate cutting building. Again, the small beach is of black sand. There are marks each side of the inlet. An arch pierces Ynys-fach. A stone circle above Pwll Crochan is 20th century.

Trefin had an episcopal palace but it is the ruined watermill overlooking the beach at Aber Draw, closed in 1918, which is remembered in the poem by William Crwys Williams. Here the sea is only 3km from the source of the Western Cleddau which flows into Milford Haven.

The Neolithic Careg Sampson is the best of the area's cromlechau, a 4m capstone lifted onto seven uprights about 3000 BC by, it is said, Sampson's little finger. The Grave of Sampson's Little Finger is on Ynys y Castell, the other side of the formerly busy slate port of Abercastle. A ruined grain store, a limekiln in good condition and a cannon used as a boat mooring are all to be found here. On the west side of the port is the grave of the 1917 wreck of the *Leysian*. The first transatlantic solo sailing crossing in a fishing dory ended here more successfully in 1876 for Dane Alfred Johnson after 66 days from Massachusetts before continuing to Liverpool.

Aber Mawr, with less extreme surf than on some other beaches, was at the end of the first transatlantic telephone cable in 1873 and was the site of a pioneer submarine telegraph office which was the first source to receive news of the Casement scandal. Brunel considered it for his Irish ferry terminal and some preparatory railway and port work remains. The castell coch is a spectacular fort and there are also the inevitable limekiln.

A fisherman caught a mermaid at Aber Bach and took her home but she escaped after cursing his house with no children to be born there, which held until 1960.

Dewi Emrys wrote a poem celebrating Pwll Deri and the compliment has been returned by a memorial at Pwll Deri to Dewi Emrys. Less well remembered is the farm at Trefasser which was said to have been the birthplace of Bishop Asser, friend and biographer of Alfred the Great. Dinas Mawr, not quite an island, had an Iron Age fort.

Strumble Head is one of the most conspicuous headlands in Wales with a 1908 lighthouse on Ynys Meicel

Jumping into the Blue Lagoon.

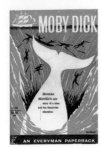

and accompanied by Carreg Onnen. Approach to the lighthouse is down steps on the cliff face and across a footbridge, not unlike that at South Stack. The steep cliffs include pillow lavas. It is a landmark on one of the transatlantic air routes, hence the frequent vapour trails on clear days. An old War Department lookout is now a bird watching post, one of the best British sites for watching migrating birds. Many rare species are spotted on their transatlantic flight path and it is also a convenient point to watch for dolphins, porpoises and basking sharks.

From Strumble Head to Pen Anglas there is a westerly eddy during part of the eastgoing stream. 2km north of Strumble Head, where there can be overfalls, there may be an 11km/h flow.

Carregwasted Point was the scene of the last invasion of mainland Britain. A landing in 1797 under the Irish American 'Colonel' William Tate of 1,400 French soldiers and released convicts was planned to start a peasants' uprising to direct attention from an invasion of Ireland by 15,000 troops and to take and burn Liverpool. It was a tactical disaster. They intended to live off the land but the French confiscated a cargo of wine from a wrecked Portuguese merchantman and got drunk. When the French saw Jemima Nicholas and the other local women approaching in their tall black hats and red petticoats they thought military reinforcements had arrived and forced Tate to surrender on Goodwick beach. Lord Cawdor, who had nearly walked into an ambush, became a hero and the Pembroke Yeomanry, now part of 562 Parachute Squadron Royal Corps of Transport (Volunteers), are the only remaining army unit to have won battle honours on British soil as a result. Eight Frenchmen were drowned, twelve were killed and one Welshwoman was shot accidentally while a pistol was being loaded in a public house. A 30m tapestry in Fishguard townhall recalls the invasion.

There is an inconspicuous memorial on the point but this is confusing as the OS map marks this but not the much more obvious obelisk on Pen Anglas. The point also has hexagonal basalt columns.

Some 400m off Pen Anglas the stream starts east at HW Dover +0530 at 4km/h and west at HW Dover −0340 at 5km/h, meaning east for 3¼ hours and west for 9¼ hours. A race runs 800m north from Pen Anglas and there can be overfalls. North northwesterly winds cause a bad swell in Fishguard Bay. Flows start east at HW Dover +0440 at 2km/h and west at HW Dover −0210 at 3km/h. On the south side outside the harbour there is little eastgoing stream but a very weak westgoing stream from HW Dover −0400 to HW Dover +0500. The first lifeboat arrived in 1822 and the station always has the most modern models.

Fishguard Harbour at **Goodwick**, from the Norse wdic meaning anchorage, is overlooked by an aerial and guarded by north and east breakwaters with light-houses but prone to seiches. using 1,600,000t of rock in the breakwaters from the Harbour Village area. The terminus of the Great Western Railway line from London and transatlantic liner terminal with vast new port installations was opened in 1906. The Fishguard Bay Hotel was built to house America bound passengers and Cunard liners including the *Mauretania* and *Lusitania* docked here until 1914 when the war curtailed plans and the trade was switched to Southampton. Today it is the ferry terminus for Rosslare, including fast catamarans.

In 1912 the first trans Irish Sea flight by Denys Corbett Wilson had taken off from here for Enniscorthy. Foodstuffs and dairy produce are imported with machinery and general merchandise going to Rosslare and Wexford. There is also container traffic and yacht moorings.

The town of **Fishguard**, from the Norse fisgard meaning fishyard, where the A40 ends at the A487, is built on the Afon Gwaun. Castle Point has an 18th century fort and three cannons built on an Iron Age promontory site following an attack by John Paul Jones. *Moby Dick* was filmed here in 1954, using a locally built whale. In the 1960s the Lower Town was used for filming *Under Milk Wood*. Arts associations continue with the Fishguard International Music Festival and the town has hosted the Royal National Eisteddfod on occasions. The Carregwasted Point invasion peace treaty was signed in the town.

Needle Rock at Aber Richard is a stack with an arch at the base. Penrhyn Ychen was used in successive World Wars for observation and artillery. There is much folding in the cliffs around Aber Bach, which is fed by a stream which used to power a mill.

Behind Dinas Cross is 305m Garn Fawr with its distinctive Maiden's Nipple rock on the summit but this is probably less striking than the wedge shape of Dinas Island, connected to the mainland by a low swamp in a former glacial meltwater channel. Pwllgwaelod, at the end of the channel, has assorted smugglers' tales and has been used for many film settings. The Old Sailors inn of 1593 used to show a light for navigation.

Dinas Island has an earthwork near the bottom and a lookout hut on the summit of the folded Dinas Head, from where it is possible to see the Wicklow mountains on a clear day. There is a nature trail but perhaps nothing to match the guillemots, razorbills and greater blackbacked gulls of Needle Rock. Sea trout and bass are the local fish.

A strong race runs 400m north of Dinas Head. From here to the Afon Nyfer is a slate coast. The far end of the meltwater channel is at Cwm-yr-Eglwys, an attractive little hamlet of colourwashed cottages. The 12th century church in the name, St Brynach's, was reduced to a bellcote in a hurricane of 1859 which wrecked 114 ships and lost part of its graveyard to a 1979 storm. This was another smugglers' cove.

Newport Bay has weak tidal streams but with onshore winds a considerable sea sets into the bay. From Aber Ysgol to the Nyfer estuary there is much wave cut platform. Cat Rock has veins of white quartz through it but the prevailing colour is black on Newport Sands where there is parking near a golf course at Cesig duon and vehicles can be driven onto the beach for loading downstream of the Bennet sandbar on the east side.

Newport was founded in 1195 after William de Turribus was driven out of Nevern by the Welsh. Court Leets still take place, as does the Beating the Bounds ceremony. The Norman lord gave burgesses the right to appoint the mayor in consultation with the Lord or Lady Marcher. Newport Castle has become a private house but the old quay and warehouses remain and Carreg Coetan, a Neolithic burial chamber, is to be found at the head of the estuary. Rising over all is 347m high Mynydd Carningli, the mountain of angels, at the east end of the Carningli Common ridge.

Distance
77km from Martin's
Haven to Cerig duon

OS 1:50,000 Sheets
145 Cardigan &
Mynydd Preseli
157 St David's
& Haverfordwest

Tidal Constants
Martin's Haven:
HW Dover −0450
LW Dover −0440
Little Haven:
HW Dover −0450
LW Dover −0440
Solva:
HW Dover −0450
LW Dover −0440
Ramsey Sound:
Dover −0430
Porthgain:
Dover −0410
Fishguard:
HW Dover −0350
LW Dover −0340

Sea Areas
Lundy, Irish Sea

The southern edge of Newport Bay running out to Dinas Head.

South Cardigan Bay

From Newport to Cemaes Head there are high slate cliffs with many slips, including at Pen-y-bâl, the haunt of every kind of seabird from oystercatcher through razorbill to cormorant. It is a rocky coast, not dramatic but off the beaten track as far as the general public are concerned. Pwll y Wrach, the witch's cauldron, is a blowhole, a deep hole where a cave roof has collapsed. Castelltreruffydd is an Iron Age fort, its location not obvious. Following a large stack, the first real inlet is Ceibwr Bay, a glacial outflow channel, site of an earlier settlement and a spot where coasters used to land cargoes. On the east side is the Pen-castell Iron Age fort site. The best of the rock formations are between Pen yr Afr and Cemaes Head where 440,000,000 year old alternating Ordovician grits and shales have been subjected to geological pressures 390,000,000 years ago to produce some dramatic folding,

finishing at Cemaes Head with a classic rounded cave roofed with thick rock strata. Cemaes Head rises steeply to 189m and has a covering of bracken.

Port **Cardigan** is the estuary of the Afon Teifi with the B4546 ending on one side and the B4548 on the other. High breaking seas may occur over the bar even in light winds, especially with the ebbing tide at full strength on springs. The southwest side of the estuary has a slip area between Penrhyn Castle and the inshore rescue boat station. Beyond this are Poppit Sands, an area of dunes, gorse and drainage channels edged with mats of sea purslane, sometimes subject to dumping surf. This is the end of the Pembrokeshire Coast National Park. The Pembrokeshire Coast Path also leaves, heading up the estuary to St Dogmaels and Pembrokeshire gives way to Ceredigion.

Magnificent folding on the cliffs at Pen yr Afr.

More folding leads to the cave at the end of Cemaes Head.

Cardigan Island as it appears when seen across Port Cardigan, the estuary of the Teifi.

The plateau site of Aberporth Range appears above the rocks of Pen-Peles, where there are square arches in the cliffs.

Tresaith nestles in a break in the cliffs.

Gwbert, on the east side of the estuary, takes its name from a wandering saint who probably landed here. There is a prominent white hotel near Craig y Gwbert.

Cardigan Island is 52m high, 16ha of Ordovician sedimentary rock, grassy and thick with bluebells in the spring, with traces of field divisions and a small pond. In 1934 the SS *Hereford* was wrecked off the island and was thought to have introduced the colony of over a thousand brown rats which finished off the former puffin colony. The island became a nature reserve in 1944 and has been owned by the Wildlife Trust of South & West Wales 1963. The rats were poisoned off in 1968 with 75kg of rat poison. To attract puffins, 200 concrete puffins were made and painted by schoolchildren to act as decoys and a number of starter homes for prospective puffins were dug in the ground. Attempts have also been made to attract Manx shearwaters by playing electronic voice noises. There are 900 pairs of nesting herring gulls, fulmars and many other seabirds. In addition, it is a seal breeding ground with bottlenose dolphins often seen on the seaward side and the WTSWW have introduced a semiwild flock of Soay sheep. A permit is needed for landing.

Mwnt is located by the sharp pyramidal hill of Foel y Mwnt. Flemish raiders were defeated in battle here in 1155. This was celebrated in the festival of the Bloody Sunday of Mwnt every year until the 18th century. Ploughs still occasionally

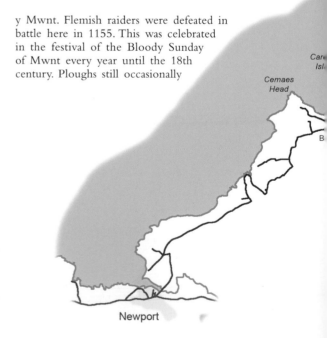

270

turn up human bones and rusty weapons. Evasion was generally considered a better policy than confrontation and the Grade I Church of the Holy Cross of 1400, on the route from Bardsey Island to St David's, was built in a hollow on the site of an earlier church, hidden from the view of raiders. It is whitewashed and constructed with a herringbone pattern used in Cornwall and probably introduced from the Mediterranean. There is an old limekiln by the beach and modern facilities include parking on the clifftop, refreshment kiosk and toilets.

West Wales Airport Aberporth and a test and research centre which is Europe's leading test facility for drones is located on top of the 130m high Pencribach table headland amidst a plethora of chimneys, pylons and towers. There was formerly live firing of rockets out to sea with a little concern that something might hit Ireland, which would have been awkward. There are buoys with scientific instruments within 1km of the headland and target buoys further out. Jets occasionally fly around to add atmosphere. Scientific instruments are also located on clifftops for some considerable distance on both sides of the centre. ParcAberporth is an associated technology park. Buildings and a walkway with assorted industrial apparatus are located near the water by Cribach Bay where there are moorings.

Aberporth on the B4333 is a fishing village, having been very successful with herring, which has become a resort surrounded by cliffs of silver grey slate. Surf is best on the bottom half of the tide.

Tresaith is also popular with holiday makers, as shown by the caravan park on a kame, and its clear waters encourage divers. It has caves and stacks but its most conspicuous feature is the glacial meltwater cut waterfall on the Afon Saith which comes straight down the steep shale cliffs onto the beach. Meaning town of seven, the name is said to come from seven difficult Irish princesses set adrift by their father, who landed here and married local farmers' sons.

A café and toilets are to be found after the low dunes at Penbryn, the beach being used as North Korea in the filming of *Die Another Day*. Caravans also back the resort

Birds Rock at the foot of New Quay Head at dawn.

mainland although the gap is frequently narrow enough for anglers to jump across. Pendinaslochdyn has a Stone Age and Iron Age fort, used from 500 BC to 500 AD, in the shape of an inverted pan, forming its top at a height of 165m, from where it is possible to see the Lleyn Peninsula and Snowdonia. There are prominent quartz veins in the rocks. Lloyd George enjoyed walking here. The Urdd Gobaith Cymru promotes Welsh language and activities to Welsh youth.

of Llangrannog, named after St Carannog, St David's grandfather, a missionary who landed here in the 6th century and of whom there is a statue on the clifftop. At the end of the B4321 with the Ship Inn in a small inlet behind dark shales in jumbled stacks, it is where ships used to unload on the beach and smugglers landed Irish salt into caves. The collapse of a cave may have caused the Carreg Bica stack or it may have been the tooth of the giant Bica, cured of his toothache by the dwarf Lochtyn, who then achieved his wish of living on an island when the giant scored along the shore with his finger.

When the tide and wave conditions are right there is a passage between the 4ha Ynys-Lochtyn and the

Cwmtydu has yet more caravans and a preserved limekiln on the shore from which smuggler Siôn Cwilt operated. Castell Bach follows.

New Quay Head is a 92m high vertical cliff with a relatively small lump known as the Birds Rock lying in the sea at its base. The horizontal sedimentary layers which follow the folded rocks on the approach to New Quay Head form tier after tier of ledges which are coloured white from the guano of rows of guillemots and other seabirds which coat the cliff. The headland is seen at its best from the water.

The effect is less attractive round the corner where a small factory built from concrete blocks on the rocks discharges dirty water down a slope into the sea.

New Quay, at the ends of the A486 and B4342 and new in the 1690s, retains its traditional seafaring character from the days when it was a fishing port and shipbuilding and repairing centre. Smuggling resulted in the development of the coastguard service. Despite having more of a Cornish atmosphere than a Welsh one, New Quay is believed to have been a model for Llareggub in *Under Milk Wood*. It was while living here in 1944/5 that he wrote its precursor, *Quite Early One Morning*, broadcast on the BBC Welsh Home Service, using some local topographical features.

The quay itself was built in 1835 and on the notice-

New Quay Head, seen from New Quay Bay. In the foreground is a roll of pillow lava, split by the sea.

board there is an old list of tolls for the landing of goods. There are pleasure craft moorings. Pollack are the local fish but a much wider choice is available from the fish and chip takeaway while other sources of sustenance include the off licence, Mariner Café, Wellington Inn, Renown Cottage and Captain's Rendezvous. There are parking and toilets before the quay.

Ina Point is named after a Wessex king who was shipwrecked here in the 7th or 8th century and later built a church, which has been replaced perhaps half a dozen times, the last in 1850.

Tide streams run across the mouth of New Quay Bay at up to 2km/h. From Ina Point to Aberaeron there are 40m high perpendicular slate cliffs with land rising behind. There are boulder beaches over the rest of this section of coast which make landing possible at any time but not without damage unless the sea is slight. At one point another waterfall cascades down the cliff.

Aberaeron, at the mouth of the Afon Aeron as the name suggests, was built by the Rev Alban Gwynne in the 18th century. A quarter of the houses are of special architectural or historical interest with a Georgian and Regency flavour, especially for retired sea captains. The triangular blade Aberaeron shovel was produced by an ironworks by the river. The hand powered Aeron Express cablecar across the harbourmouth replaced a bridge washed away by floods. New quayside buildings include Aberaeron Sea Aquarium. The former shipbuilding industry used oak from local forests. There are still fishing boats present, joined by an assortment of yachts in this resort.

Groynes protect the seafront and a harbour bar of shingle breaks up incoming waves except when it gets washed away by freshets. There can be surf north of the entrance on the ebb.

Perpendicular slate cliffs behind the beach return as far as Morfa Mawr, where there are the remains of fish traps along this coast. After this the cliffs pull back to 1km inland to leave a flat and low shore. The Afon Arth emerges from behind the groynes at **Aberarth**, formerly a busy coastal shipping port although much of it was lost to an 1846 flood. Stone had been shipped here from Bristol for Strata Florida abbey in the 12th century and there was a Cistercian corn mill from 1540. Llanddewi church of 1860 is on a 9th century site and has the only Viking hogsback gravestone in Wales.

Llansantffraid's Grade II★ church of St Ffraid has its stone tower and walls faced with purple slate, a rood

The inner basin at Aberaeron with the Afon Aeron beyond.

The harbour at New Quay.

screen from the 15th century and sailors' graves. Physician and poet Henry Vaughan was born and buried here. in the 17th century. The centre of population has now shifted, however, to Llanon on the A487 at the foot of the glacial debris cliffs, named after St Non, whom it was claimed gave birth to St David here in about 500. A wooden palisade protects the land behind the stone beach. Medieval strip farming has survived with some 140 strips. There are four limekilns and coal and beer stores but only stakes remain of a jetty at Craig-las which also handled culm and limestone and built ships.

A lane at Llanrhystud gives parking for a few cars before getting involved with the large caravan site as the high land closes back on the shore.

Distance
*58km from Cerig
duon to Llanrhystud*

OS 1:50,000 Sheets
*135 Aberystwyth
& Mychynlleth
145 Cardigan &
Mynydd Preseli
146 Lampeter
& Llandovery*

Tidal Constants
*Fishguard:
HW Dover −0350
LW Dover −0340
Port Cardigan:
HW Dover −0330
LW Dover −0300
Aberporth:
HW Dover −0330
LW Dover −0300
New Quay:
HW Dover −0320
LW Dover −0250
Aberaeron:
HW Dover −0320
LW Dover −0240*

Sea Area
Irish Sea

Range
Aberporth

273

50 North Cardigan Bay

Pretty maidens come again
Join us in a merry strain,
To all who live on land or main
Say the Bells of Aberdovey.
Charles Dibdin

Leaving the beach, a conspicuous caravan site is passed at Llanrhystud, together with the inconspicuous mouth of the Afon Wyre, sometimes with a heavy shore break at high water. After this the low shoreline is left at the Carreg Ti-pw stack and cliffs are continuous as far as the mouth of the Ystwyth. The Penderi Cliffs Nature

The unusual natural sculpting of the cliffs at Ffos-lâs near Blaenplwyf with the aerial behind.

The harbour at Aberystwyth.

Aberystwyth with the war memorial and remains of the castle on the point.

Reserve is an ancient hanging oakwood with choughs. In the vicinity of the 152m high transmission mast at Blaenplwyf the cliffs take on a rather unusual form, the boulder clay having been scoured by runs of water into shapes which resemble a line of bottles with ribs running down the outside. It is a lonely area with just cormorants and a caravan site at Morfa Bychan, a former grange of Strata Florida abbey, for company. Resident Rhys Ddu was hanged in 1408 for his part in the siege of Aberystwyth Castle. Both tidestreams set towards the coast over this length with low shingle beaches in places as the tide drops.

The Afon Ystwyth (Welsh for winding river) and Afon Rheidol meet in the harbour at **Aberystwyth**, flowing round opposite sides of the 124m high Pendinas, which has the 1852 Wellington Monument and one of the largest Celtic hill forts in Wales, Iron Age from 400 BC, on the top. The harbour no longer has shipbuilding and shipping, just fishing and pleasure boats. It almost dries out and there is a bar off the mouth over which swells break near low water and often at high water. Tidestreams are weak with 2km/h outwards on the flood and 6km/h on the ebb. Dolphins frequent the area off the harbourmouth. They are not discouraged by the discolouration of the sea by the rivers and are possibly attracted by the discolouring material or the fish feeding on it.

The diamond shaped Aberystwyth Castle was begun in 1277 as one of the first Welsh castles of Edward I although it was captured in 1408 and held by Owain Glydwr. Under Charles I in 1637 it was used as a mint by Thomas Bushell who owned the concession on the Plynlimon lead mines and who discovered a new process for refining silver. It was reduced to ruins in the Civil War in 1649 when Cromwell pounded it to rubble which was later used for housebuilding. The gatehouse remains close to the shore, where there is more surf each side of the point.

Beyond the point, on which the war memorial stands, is the building planned by Thomas Savin as a Victorian Gothic hotel in 1860. He wished to popularize Aberystwyth by building himself a railway line from Euston and offering a week's free board to each ticket holder. After spending £80,000 on the hotel the scheme failed and the building was bought for £10,000 by a patriotic committee for use as a college. The Prince of Wales (later Edward VII) was installed as chancellor and the building became part of the campus of Aberystwyth University. It was in this building that Gladstone made his last public appearance. The main campus is further inland, together with the National Library of Wales housed in an Edwardian building. The latter is one of Britain's six copyright libraries, containing over 4,000,000 books. These include the largest collection of books in Welsh or relating to Wales, old deeds, maps, 30,000 manuscripts (including the 13th century *Black Book of Carmarthen*, the oldest manuscript in Welsh) and the earliest complete text of *The Mabinogion* (the earliest Welsh prose, based on tales of the invading Irish from the 3rd to 7th centuries) founded on a collection begun by royal physician Sir John Williams who died in 1926. It contains some of the greatest Celtic treasures and is used for tracing ancestry. Joseph Parry composed the hymn tune *Aberystwyth*.

Aberystwyth is the terminal for two railways. The Cambrian Coast Railway, opened in 1863–7, goes via Dovey Junction to Pwllheli, 113km, of which 48km is subject to coastal hazards. The Vale of Rheidol Railway was British Rail's only steam narrow gauge railway, running 19km to Devil's Bridge at 597mm gauge. Built in 1902 to carry lead and zinc ore down to the harbour it now has three locomotives which haul only passenger trains.

Formerly a walled town, Aberystwyth is now a resort with the MusicFest and the Big Tribute music festivals in July and August. The largest town and shopping centre in mid Wales, it has been described as the Brighton of Wales and retains its 19th century dignity. A restored music hall, the Coliseum, contains the Ceredigion Museum which shows the area since the Stone Age. The town has a 90m long pier plus a submerged damaged portion with surfing around it. Parts of the promenade had to be rebuilt in 2014 following storm damage.

The town ends at the 148m high Constitution Hill up which runs the Aberystwyth Cliff Railway, the longest funicular railway in Europe, rising 120m in 240m. With standard gauge track plus a static electric engine at the top, it opened in 1896 and used a water balance system until 1921. The toastrack cars, each of which carries 30 people, are connected by a continuous wire rope. A 1985 Victorian style Cam-era Obscura at the top scans 26 peaks with a 360mm lens, the largest of its kind in the world, on the site of an earlier model.

From Aberystwyth to Craig yr Wylfa there are bold and rocky cliffs, varying between 6 and 37m in height, with the Dyffryn Clarach and a deep ravine at Wallog where there is a restored limekiln on an old quay.

Garreg has a folly built by Clough Williams-Ellis of the Welsh Guards in 1915 as a wedding gift to Annabel Strachey. Ellis subsequently went on to design Portmerion.

The Bells of Aberdovey, Charles Dibden's music hall song, relates to Wallog where the bells are at times said to be heard coming from the ancient kingdom of Gwyddno Garnhir, the Lord of Ceredigion, when the sea is calm or danger threatens. The gates of the village of Cantref Gwaelod had to be closed every high tide but one fateful night 1,400 years ago the drunken

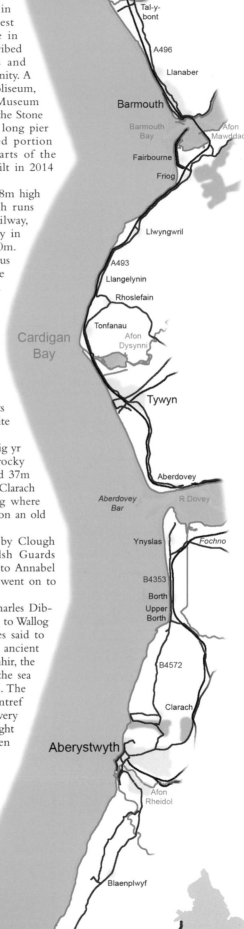

Upper Borth with Borth, Ynyslas, the Dovey estuary and Tywyn beyond.

watchman, Seithenin, omitted to do so and the sea swept in through the 13km long sea wall stretching to Mochras. Peacock's *The Misfortunes of Elphin* relates how he got ashore on one of his empty wine barrels, the only survivor. Sarn Wallog, Sarn Gynfelyn, Cynfelyn Patches and Outer Patch form an 11km ridge out to Patches buoy and are probably successive moraines of ice sheets emerging from Snowdonia during glaciation.

One quarrel between kings was settled here by the relatively civilized method of seeing who could stay seated for longest with the tide coming in. Maelgwyn was victorious. The contest is re-enacted each year with the winner being crowned King of Cors Fochno.

Spring tidal flows reach 2km/h. South of Gynfelyn they start northeast at HW Dover +0500 and southwest at HW Dover –0100. North of here they begin north at HW Dover +0430 and south at HW Dover –0130.

Company on this cliff lined section might take the form of jets overhead or jellyfish beneath. The rock strata are heavily folded on the approach to Upper Borth where there is a memorial before the cliffs come to an end as the B4572 meets the B4353.

Borth is a resort, given extra protection in 2011 by rock groynes, breakwaters and surfing reefs. The three week Borth Carnival offers Caribbean nights, donkey derbys, football, cricket and a barmen's race. There is a fortnight of water, beach and fun sports including a raft race. The fishermen's cottages are rather lost these days amongst the board surfers, wave skis, windsurfers, water skis, jet skis, parascending, tennis, crazy golf and BMX riding. Any camel seen on the sand dunes following overindulgence in the hotel should be treated seriously as such a sight is not unknown. Bass are not the only residents under the surface. At times the remains of a 7,000 year old sunken alder, birch, oak and pine forest are seen in the sands with the remains of auroch wild cattle found in peat deposits, helping give further credence to the Cantref Gwaelod legend.

Groynes line the beach past Borth & Ynyslas golf course from 1885, the oldest in Wales, to Ynyslas (Welsh for blue-green island), behind which is Cors Fochno, 6m of semiliquid peat, one of our finest lowland raised bogs. It is divided from the beach by the road, the Cambrian Coast Railway and the Afon Leri, the latter running dead straight for 4km parallel to the coast to the yachting centre and former port with rail access reached from inside the estuary of the River Dovey.

North of Ynyslas is the Dyfi National Nature Reserve which includes the Twyni Mawr and Twyni Bâch dune

systems. This large windblown sand system has such plants as bee orchid, marsh marigold, marsh heleborine, restharrow, bird's foot trefoil, marram grass and sea spurge, making an ideal habitat for rabbit, polecat, weasel and such butterflies as the large skipper, grayling, wall brown and small heath. It is particularly good for birds in the winter and its birdlife includes skylark, meadow pipit, stonechat, reed bunting, linnet, ringed plover, oystercatcher, shelduck and various gulls. An information centre explains the natural history and there is a nature trail and guided tours. The distant views range from Strumble Head to the Lleyn Peninsula and also to the Cambrian mountains and the peaks of Snowdonia.

Before the railway was built along the north side of the estuary there used to be a spur on the south side leading to a tower which is still present. Here passengers waited for the ferry to come across from Aberdovey to collect them.

Southwest winds raise a heavy sea over Aberdovey Bar off the estuary on the River Dovey, especially on the ebb when flow rates can reach 11km/h over the bar. At low tide the river channel meanders between expanses of sand.

Crossing the rivermouth brings the boater from Ceredigion to Gwynedd, the Snowdonia National Park and the A493 with Aberdovey just up the estuary. Tidal streams from here to Sarn Badrig start northwards at HW Dover +0530 and southwards at HW Dover –0130 at up to 2km/h.

Aberdovey was a busy fishing village in the 16th century and became a trading port in the 18th century but declined in the early 1800s when railways took away the coastal shipping trade. Plans to turn it into a serious rival to Fishguard and Holyhead for the Irish ferry trade never came to anything. In 1941 it was the site of the first Outward Bound course and the centre has an associated rescue post. In 1968 the old wharf buildings were renovated, the derelict coal wharf cleared and the seafront gardens created, resulting in an award from the Prince of Wales' Committee in 1972. These days it is a resort with sailing, windsurfing and water skiing. The warm climate and few frosts allow early flowering myrtle to grow here.

Dunes continue north of the estuary with a golf course immediately west of the estuary and pillboxes along the shore at intervals.

Tywyn (Welsh for sand dunes) is a resort protected by groynes and an offshore breakwater and has plenty of parking with such facilities as toilets and an ice cream

The pier at Aberdovey.

shop near the prominent aerial. It is used for surfing, best on the top third of the tide. It has two churches of historical importance. St Cadfan's was founded in 516, St Cadfan apparently being a French missionary who came to Christianize the region. It contains St Cadfan's stone, the 7th century text which is thought to be the oldest writing in Welsh. One translation reads 'the body of Cingen lies beneath' but another arrives at the entirely different conclusion that it mourns the loss of three ladies carried off in the 6th century by Irish invaders, enough to leave one wondering if both translators read the same stone. Also to be seen are excellent effigies of a 14th century knight in armour and a priest from Edward II's reign. Archbishop Baldwin and Gerald of Wales spent a night here in *The Journey through Wales*.

Just beyond is the terminus of the 12km Talyllyn Railway which has been operated since 1865 to carry slate. It was built by James Swinton Spooner (whose family were involved with development of the Festiniog Railway) for Lancashire cotton baron William McConnell but never reached its intended destination of Bryn Eglwys quarry or Tal-y-llyn or Aberdovey. It was built to a 686mm gauge, the narrowest permitted by the enabling Act. In 1951 it was rescued from dereliction and restored, the first of many lines to be taken over by preservation societies. The Narrow Gauge Railway Museum is at Tywyn Wharf Station.

Inside the narrow mouth of the Afon Dysynni is a large tidal lake, Broad Water. This stores a significant quantity of water. Gerald located it incorrectly in *The Journey through Wales*.

Behind Tonfanau, 178m high Tal y Gareg ends abruptly with Bwch Head Beacon, an 11m white pole on top and a felsic tuff quarry below. Stretching away into the distance are mountains leading up to Cader Idris. The other way, Sarn-y-Bwch runs out 6km from Pen Bwch Point as a subsea ridge.

Rhoslefain beach was once used by smugglers to land salt but the activity these days is of a more innocent nature as climbers swarm over the cliffs, which run from here to Fairbourne. Oystercatchers are not the only wildlife on the rocks as seals like to clamber onto them to sunbathe.

Llangelynin church of St Celynin dates partly from the 12th century and is built on the site of an older church. An unusual item of equipment is a two horse bier which was used to collect the dead from outlying farms.

The cliffs pull back to leave a low shoreline at Borthwen Point with reef breaks. Behind Llwyngwril (grove of green leaves) is an Iron Age hill fort, Castell y Gaer. There is a 17th century burial ground on the

The Afon Dysynni drains Broad Water, right of Tal y Gareg with its quarry while the mountains run away to Cadair Idris beyond.

Pont Abermaw, Cymru
Barmouth Bridge, Wales

way from the beach to Llwyn Du farmhouse which the Quakers used for meetings.

Various standing stones, cairns and homesteads dot the lower slopes of Pen y Garn as the coast arcs into Barmouth Bay. As it approaches Friog, the Cambrian Coast Railway is protected from rock avalanches by a 60m x 300mm thick reinforced concrete roof slab. The 520,000,000 year old folded mudstones contain quartz sulphide veins from the Dolgellau gold belt in a 2km long wave platform.

Fairbourne is built on a low area of land which projects into the estuary of the Afon Mawddach. This resort has a beach which is said to be the finest and safest in North Wales, retaining the Second World War tank traps which were felt necessary. Behind it runs the 310mm gauge Fairbourne & Barmouth Steam Railway of 1916, based on a former 381mm horse tramway of 1890 serving the estate of McDougall, the flour merchant. This is the smallest Welsh narrow gauge line but it is one of the few places where new engines are being built, replicas of famous narrow gauge engines. There are four steam engines and two diesel engines and during the centenary it became the only line with a scheduled horsedrawn tram service. The line also carried the last narrow gauge boat train as it connects with the passenger ferry to Barmouth. Passengers have to hold out their tickets for the driver to see before he will stop the train at stations for them. Other features include a Victorian style station. The estuary is noted for its birdlife in the winter.

Crossing the estuary behind Penrhyn Point is the timber Barmouth Bridge that carries the Cambrian Coast Railway. The viaduct is built on rocks only at the northern end where there were two 12m spans, the navigable channel being crossed by a span which tilted and drew back over the track. These have been replaced by a 41m swinging span and a 36m fixed span, both hogback trusses on cylindrical piers instead of the original cast iron screw piles. There are a further 113 spans of 5.5m which are encased in GRP reinforced concrete sleeves to resist attack by marine borer which threatened to close the viaduct and, hence, the northern end of the Cambrian Coast Railway. This is the longest bridge in Wales.

Between 1750 and 1850 318 vessels were built on the banks of the Afon Mawddach, an estuary the approach to which is said to resemble that to Gibraltar. Barmouth also developed on woollen cloth.

Jasper Tudor, uncle of Henry VII, is said to have planned Richard III's downfall here.

The bar is dangerous with strong westerly winds. There is an RNLI lifeboat museum by the causeway which connects Ynys y Brawd to the mainland.

Above the A496 is Dinas Oleu, the National Trust's first property in 1895. Barmouth harbour is used for fishing and sailing boats and is the headquarters of Merioneth Yacht Club. Ty Crwn is a restored 1834 lockup for drunken sailors while the Grade II★ Ty Gwyn yn Bermo is a restored 1460 townhouse with an exhibition on the quay. HW Tilman lived near Barmouth although he rarely brought his boats here. His journeys by Bristol Channel pilot cutter to Greenland and the Southern Ocean for climbing are recalled by the Three Peaks Yacht Race to Fort William with runs up Snowdon, Scafell Pike and Ben Nevis. Groynes protect one of the finest beaches in Britain and **Barmouth** sees water skiing and surfing, best on the ebb. This resort has an art exhibition in the summer and an arts festival in September with the Dragon Theatre as an important venue.

Low sandhills continue to Llanenddwyn, overlooked by frequent large caravan sites.

Huge concrete blocks connected by chains protect the railway at Llanaber but damage to the seawall in January 2014 storms closed the railway for several months. The 13th century Grade I church of St Mary & St Bodfan is one of the best examples of the Early English style in North Wales. In the 18th century its tombs not only contained the legitimate spirits but also the contraband kind, placed by the local smugglers.

An ancient homestead site is lost among the holiday caravans at Tal-y-bont but the Afon Ysgethin is not too obvious, either.

A historic wreck lies off Bennar beach but landmarks can be a little confusing. There is a carpark reached by a footpath through the dunes (and through a couple of difficult gates) but the footpath can be hard to spot from the water, being near a red and white striped pole and one of several rescue rings.

Distance
57km from Llanrhystud to Llanenddwyn

OS 1:50,000 Sheets
124 Porthmadog & Dolgellau
135 Aberystwyth & Mychynlleth

Tidal Constants
Aberaeron:
HW Dover −0320
LW Dover −0240
Aberystwyth:
HW Dover −0320
LW Dover −0230
Aberdovey:
HW Dover −0250
LW Dover −0210
Barmouth:
HW Dover −0250
LW Dover −0140

Sea Area
Irish Sea

Connections
River Dovey – see RoB p48
Afon Mawddach – see RoB p51

Barmouth Bridge across the mouth of the Afon Mawddach.

Lleyn Peninsula

An iron ring
of castles
and a
backdrop of
Snowdonia
peaks

Men of Harlech, on to glory!
See, your banner famed in story
Waves these burning words before ye,
'Britain scorns to yield!'
Thomas Oliphant

Leaving Llanenddwyn, the coast runs past the dunes of Morfa Dyffryn with their unusual plants and a busy naturist section. Hidden beyond them is Llanbedr Airport, formerly an RAE airfield from which flew some unusual aircraft, including early drones. As well as for civilian use, the site could be used for further drone testing and airliner dismantling and it was shortlisted as the UK spaceport. There is also a mountain rescue post at Llanbedr while Maes Artro has memorabilia from RAF Llanbedr during the Second World War, a Spitfire, an Avro Anson, an air raid shelter under simulated attack, a village of yesteryear, an old farm implements exhibition, an aquarium of local marine life, children's play area and giant draughts set. Canoeing, pony trekking, hill walking and orienteering are catered for with a watersports centre at the old wharf in Pen-sarn. There is a craft centre in **Llanbedr**, formerly a slate village.

Shell Island is noted for over 200 varieties of shells, especially after stormy weather, and is good for lobsters which could be included as shellfish. A tent campsite is one of Europe's largest at 1.2km². Mochras Point was formerly an island of morainic deposits until the Earl of Winchelsea diverted the Afon Artro early in the 19th century to reclaim the land, creating a saltmarsh. The river now exits through a lagoon and can have surf at its mouth, especially on the ebb. Gerald located it incorrectly in *The Journey through Wales*.

Sarn Badrig, St Patrick's Causeway, stretches out for 22km from the point and dries for several kilometres at low water. It probably consists of moraine from the Snowdonia glaciation ice sheet. There can be overfalls when there is 3m of water over Sarn Badrig and at other states of the tide with strong winds but these can be avoided by taking the East Passage on the inside. South of Sarn Badrig flows start north at HW Dover +0530 and south at HW Dover −0030. North of Sarn Badrig flows start northeast at HW Dover +0400 and southwest at HW Dover −0030. Maximum flow is only 2km/h except over shoals. Streams are weak in Tremadog Bay which is an area of accumulation of beach material because of the prevailing southwesterly winds. Shifting dunes have buried half of Llandanwg, including St Danwg's 13th century church on a site probably used since the 5th century with a couple of 6th century inscribed stones.

From Llanfair with its slate caverns, homesteads and settlements dot the hillside across to Harlech.

Harlech is dominated by Harlech Castle, built in 1283–9 by James of St George for Edward I, one of an iron ring of fortresses built to contain the Welsh in the mountains. The high point in medieval castle building, it was located on a cliff rising directly from the sea. It is unusual in that its twin towered gatehouse is the strongest part rather than the keep. Walls are 2.7–3.7m thick. During the rebellion of Madoc ap Llywelyn in 1294 it was held by 37 men and supplied by sea from Ireland, the sea now having receded because of deposition. It was captured by Owain Glyndwr after a siege in 1404 and used for his court until it was retaken by the English in 1409. It was held by the Lancastrians in the Wars of the Roses in a siege from 1461 to 1468, the longest in British

history, ending in their surrender and commemorated in *Men of Harlech*. The Royalist surrrender in 1647 marked the end of the Civil War. The castle now has jousting while the Royal St David's golf course has hosted the British Ladies' Championship where supply ships once sailed. Harlech is a resort with some surf and has a nature trail. *Branwen Daughter of Llyr* in *The Mabinogion* is based around Harlech while Robert Graves describes family holidays here in *Goodbye to All That*.

Morfa Harlech dunes have uncommon plants and edge a saltmarsh. There is now a reserve with a rabbit warren and numbers of wading birds. The winter proliferation of birds and the interesting plants spill over into the estuary of the Afon Dwyryd and Afon Glaslyn. A 2.9m leatherback turtle weighing 961 kg was found washed up in 1988. This is the end of the Snowdonia National Park but that does nothing to depreciate the panorama of peaks behind the estuary.

From Borth-y-Gest in the 12th century Prince Madog, the son of Owain Gwynedd, is said to have sailed to discover America. The drying harbour had four shipyards. **Porthmadog**, however, is named after William Madocks who built Porthmadog Cob in 1808–11 to gain 2.8km² of farmland which turned out to be of poor quality, the boatbuilding town being built a decade later. The Cob, a 1.3km long embankment, carries the A487 and the Ffestiniog Railway, which was opened in 1836, across the Glaslyn estuary. Running from Blaenau Ffestiniog to Porthmadog, this 597mm gauge

Castell Harlech Castle

Harlech Castle, now separated from the water by a golf course and an expanse of dunes.

Criccieth Castle is built upon a distinctive hump in front of the low lying town.

St Tudwal's Islands stand off Machroes.

line has old steam and diesel engines hauling modern observation coaches. The line is linked through the streets of Porthmadog to the Welsh Highland Railway to create a 64km narrow gauge line to Caernarfon. Hidden to the southeast is the Italianate village of Portmerion.

The estuary is used by yachts and small fishing vessels although it was used by vessels to carry slate around the world. Waves break over the bar if the wind is above 30km/h from the south or southwest. The bar's position is likely to change with southwesterly gales. Ynys Cyngar has a Coastwatch lookout.

Morfa Bychan belonged to the Cistercians of Strata Florida. It has surfing but the surf is mediocre. Black Rock Sands are crowded in the summer, cars park on the beach and ice cream vans drive up and down on the beach, serenading the boater for some distance out. At the west end are caves in Graig Dhu, beyond which is another beach with a burial chamber near the Criccieth end.

Prominent at **Criccieth** on the A497 is the mound which stands in front of the town, topped by the ruined Criccieth Castle. It was founded in 1230 by Llywelyn ap Iorwerth and finished with a strong main tower and high outer wall in 1260 by Llewelyn the Last. In 1283 it was captured by Edward I and incorporated into his defensive system, a lozenge shaped inner bailey being built between 1285 and 1292 with high twin towered gatehouse and polygonal curtain wall without towers. The Engine Tower on the north side was built to house a siege engine to bombard attackers. It was captured, sacked and burned in 1404 by Owain Glyndwr, the final uprising of the Welsh against the English, and the scorch marks on the Leyburn Tower and heat cracks in the doorway stones probably date from this time. Inside the remains of the castle are exhibitions of castles of the native Welsh princes and of Gerald of Wales.

Dating from the 6th century is St Cybi's Well. The Victorian resort of Criccieth is today protected by groynes. There is the Criccieth Festival of musical arts and in 1980 part of the *Life & Times of Lloyd George* was filmed here.

The Afon Dwyfor flows quietly down from Llany-

stumdwy, the village where David Lloyd George lived until 1890 and to which he retired in 1944, dying here a year later. The Liberal Prime Minister from 1916 to 1922 and one of the most colourful holders of the office, he was known as the Welsh Wizard for his oratory. There is a memorial here and a museum which has gold and silver caskets, deeds of freedom and other honours and gifts to him.

The ancient Tomen fawr site is unnoticed, unlike the Butlins holiday camp which has become the Hafan y Môr caravan park although this does not seem to upset the seals and cormorants. The location has been developed from a wartime military camp.

Pwllheli, salt pool, is the biggest, busiest and capital town of the Lleyn Peninsula, given its charter in 1355 by the Black Prince. This fishing and shipbuilding port, also a market town, has now become a holiday resort with a marina at the terminus of the Cambrian Coast Railway. The harbour is at the confluence of the Afon Erch and Afon Rhyd-hir but has suffered badly from silt brought down by them. The inner harbour formerly silted up and was no longer used while the outer harbour mostly dried. Part of the harbour has now been dredged to a reasonable depth for Hafan Pwllheli and the lifeboat station is to be replaced. There is an oddly shaped Carreg yr Imbill or Gimblet Rock off the harbour.

Behind the beach of Marian-y-de are toilets, telephone, beach café and children's swings beside a stone circle.

From Pwllheli to Trwyn Llanbedrog the shoreline is mostly of low sandhills. Traeth Crugan may have poor grade amethyst pebbles on it. Oyster Bank lies offshore. Streams up to 1km/h begin northeast at HW Dover +0340 and southwest at HW Dover −0400.

Below St Petrog's church is the 1850s Grade II Gothic style Plas Glynyweddw, mostly used as an art gallery except for a spell with Land Army girls during the Second World War. The coastline is interrupted at Llanbedrog by the 132m high bulk of the granite porphery Mynydd Tir-y-cwmwd with its Tin Man statue and conspicuous remains of quarrying operations.

The Warren with its caravans leads to **Abersoch** at the end of the A499, a former pilgrim departure point and fishing village with boatyards, around which bass are still to be found in the clear water. St Tudwal's Road forms a large mooring for this resort for yachting, windsurfing, jet skiing and powerboating which is fronted by a prominent club building but the waters can be subject to heavy seas in southerly and easterly winds and it can produce surf when other nearby beaches are not suitable. The old lifeboat station at Penrhyn Du is no longer used. Between

Abersoch and Machroes are beach huts. A golf course is based on dunes and it is protected at the front by groynes with a coastal marsh behind.

Off the coast lie the two

St Tudwal's islands. St Tudwal's Island East has a natural spring and the remains of an 800 year old priory and chapel built by Tugdual, Bishop of Treguier, who fled from Brittany to avoid religious persecution following the collapse of the Roman Empire. Since then the island has been inhabited until a century ago. A chapel was built on the site of Tugdual's sanctuary in the 13th century and Edward I possibly visited it in 1284 when the island was inhabited by secular canons associated with Bardsey. A priory of Augustinian canons was present in 1410 but by the 16th century it was the haunt of pirates, including Morgan Irish. In the 18th century it was being farmed. Father Henry Bailie Hughes tried to revive the religious aspects in 1887 by founding a monastery in a converted barn, without success. It was last used, unofficially, during the Second World War as a bombing target. There is a monument on the east side.

Puffins and rabbits are no longer harvested from the 11ha of the two islands and landing is not allowed. The islands, of Ordovician sedimentary rock, have grassy tops and low craggy cliffs with colonies of seabirds, particularly kittiwakes and fulmars, while the deep sea caves are inhabited by grey seals.

St Tudwal's Island West is similar to its neighbour but with a disused lighthouse redesigned as a private house.

St Tudwal's Sound on the inside flows

A sea kayak version of Chicken at St Tudwal's Island East.

Porth Ceiriad during a sea kayak symposium lunch stop.

at up to 6km/h with HW slack 3 hours before Dover. Porth Ceiriad can produce surf when Porth Neigwl is flat, being best in the northeast corner where the break is fast and steep. From here run 5km of cliffs with no landing point. This distance is extended if the surf is up. A settlement and burial chamber have been sited on the top in earlier times and the location suits cormorants and oystercatchers.

Trwyn Cilan is the point at which the northerly tide stream divides to circulate in Tremadog Bay or flow past the end of the Lleyn Peninsula and on northwards. There is a tide rip and the water ebbs at 6km/h. From Trwyn Cilan to Braich y Pwll streams are parallel to the coast, starting west towards the west shore of Porth Neigwl at HW Dover +0300 and east towards the west side of Trywn Cilan at HW Dover −0300, both sets being stronger with southerly winds.

Porth Neigwl's English name of Hell's Mouth comes from the threat it posed to sailing ships. The best known North Wales break, it produces the best surf after northwesterly winds, particularly at the southeast end where many boards will be found. During southwest winds the sea is heavy. Boulder clay cliffs at the back have been sculpted into peculiar shapes by the elements.

A conspicuous chimney is located by a former settlement in Llanengan, which had lead and copper mines. The Grade II St Cian's church, not visible from the water, has twin naves and a 17th century bell, probably from the abbey on Bardsey, and was founded 1,400 years ago by St Einion, King of Lleyn. A stone carved in the 5th century to Melus the Doctor, son of Martinus, is the first to a doctor in Wales and the only early gravestone in Britain to give a profession. It also has a beautiful carved rood screen, solid oak coffer and sacred vessel from the abbey on Bardsey Island.

Mynydd Rhiw forms 304m of mountain ending the beach, topped by two aerials and covered lower down by assorted artefacts, a holy well, long cairn, Iron Age hillfort and hut circle. A granite standing stone and another lying were said to be two robbers who stole money from St Maelrhys church in Llanfaelrhys. Plas-yn-Rhiw is a small manor house, part Tudor with Georgian additions and organic gardens.

Rust coats the cliff face before Trywyn Talfarach, the start of Porth Ysgo, which is backed by the gentler colours of ferns, gorse and foxgloves in season and by a 19th century manganese mine used until 1945. It has the Fisherman's reef break.

Maen Gwenonwy bears the name of King Arthur's sister. Above Porth Cadlan is one of the places reputed to have been the site of the Battle of Camlan, Arthur's final fight against Mordred, Arthur being related to three of the local saints.

Offshore, Ynys Gwylan-fawr and Ynys Gwylan-bâch total 8ha with interesting plants, seals, cormorants and puffins breeding, hence their English name of Seagull Islands. They stand on one limb of a Y-shaped ridge which runs out from Ebolion and the boils, swirls and eddies caused by this are an indicator of what is to come.

Aberdaron Bay has heavy seas with a southerly wind and surf in southerly or southwesterly winds but it tends to dump at high water and there are rocks close in. Wave size decreases going westwards along the beach towards Aberdaron at the end of the B4413. A strong eddy stream runs south southwest on the ebb. This fishing village is popular with divers. One 19th century resident could speak 15 languages but could not find employment for them. St Hywyn's church is mainly 12th century, built away from the sea but now with its own wall to check the advances of the water. It has a Norman doorway and some parts are 600 years older still. In 1095 the church officials hid Gruffud ap Cynan and put him in a boat to Ireland to escape the Normans. A decade later they hid the Prince Gruffudd ap Rhys from Gruffud ap Cynan and, after they forbade solidiers to take him from the church, put him on a boat back to South Wales to keep him from being handed to Henry I. Y Gegin Fawr, the big kitchen, is a café and gift shop. Built in the 14th century, it was probably a resting house for pilgrims on their way to Bardsey Island, Porth Meudwy being the pilgrim departure point. The climate here is mild. It is claimed that the sun shone on 316 days one year.

Pen y Cil tiderace leads into Bardsey Sound, the most serious piece of water in North Wales, running at up to 11km/h. When there is wind against tide the whole sound can be a mass of confused and breaking seas and the island can be isolated for weeks when the boat cannot get out from Porth Meudwy. There is an almost continual tide race near Carreg Ddu with strong return eddies close to the mainland.

The violent turbulence around the island leads to a 2km long eddy at each end, perhaps an appropriate place to find the storm petrel.

Bardsey Island is the Isle of 20,000 Saints. One of the white marble Celtic crosses in the churchyard commemorates these saints as this was the best place in North Wales for the Celtic tradition requiring burial to be in the west, hence the burial of so many saints here. Alternatively, it was said those buried there would never go to Hell, possibly because they were pious. Ynys Enlli (the Welsh name) means the island in the currents but other name derivations are from the Norse Bards Ey, the bards being drawn by the religious associations or named after the Norse warrior Bardr, or even Birdsey after the birds. There is a bird observatory.

Hut circles show that there were inhabitants from very early times and the pasture still conforms to an old field system. Breton St Cadfan founded an abbey in 516 and the Pope declared three pilgrimages to Bardsey to be worth one to Rome. Dubricius died here in 612, just

three years before the arrival of the ousted monks of Bangor-Is-Coed after the Battle of Chester. The present St Mary's abbey ruins date from the 13th century. Merlin was also listed amongst the inhabitants. In the 16th and 17th centuries it became a base for pirates. The lighthouse was built in 1821 with a helicopter landing site added more recently. The island had a farming community in the 19th century. At the beginning of the 20th century there were 100 residents and Lord Newborough, one of the owners, proposed they appoint a king to settle disputes, having a crown of brass, a silver casket for his treasure and a painted wooden soldier as his army, a regime which continued until after the First World War. Some 400 Connemara ponies and sheep are raised here. The Bardsey Island Trust took over ownership in 1979. Today there are just three residents. Visitors are welcomed if numbers do not upset the farming or nature reserve purposes.

The schoolroom has been used as an observation post for bird migration since 1953. Mist nets and Heligoland traps are used for ringing, measuring and counting and species encountered range from herring, lesser and greater blackbacked gulls, mallard, pigeon, blackbird, redwing, jackdaw, sand martin, swallow, wheatear, lanceolated warbler and hoopoe to the great white egret. Over 250 species have been recorded and 40 species breed here including chough, 300–400 pairs of razorbill, guillemot, shag, oystercatcher, kittiwake, fulmar, peregrine, 3,000 pairs of Manx shearwater, for which this is one of the major breeding sites, and the 500 puffins for which this is the main North Wales colony. The lighthouse is the worst in Britain for killing migrating birds and every morning the ground around is littered with up to a hundred migratory birds which have flown into the glass. There have been experiments with decoy lights, lighting up a patch of gorse to try to reduce the carnage.

Rat, rabbit, wood mouse, common shrew (but not, unusually, the pygmy shrew), slow worm, palmate newt, fox and hedgehog complete the land fauna while up to 150 grey seals breed in the sea caves and join the porpoises, dolphins, lobsters and mackerel which are present in the sea around the island. Even a fin whale has been seen offshore. Sallow willow shoots used to be cut for lobster pots and other plants include Wilson's filmy fern, sea pea, small flowered buttercup, thrift, bracken, horsetail, 280 varieties of lichen, hops, herbs and European and miniature gorse which was originally grown for horse feed.

The 1.8km^2 rise, like half a pear with the stalk at the south end, to 167m on Mynydd Enlli and consist of large fault breccia in part of the Lleyn complex with gneiss,

metamorphosed grits and shales, pillow lavas and tuffs all crushed into conglomerates and lenticular strips with gabbro and granite intrusions.

A considerable sea with overfalls forms with wind against tide although it is possible to pass inside. The cliffs are bold and steep with concrete foundations of a wartime radar station. St Mary's Well is where pilgrims used to drink before embarking for Bardsey, being fresh despite often being soaked by the sea. A finger dipped in it will grant wishes if allowed to dry in silence. The 160m Mynydd Mawr marks Braich y Pwll from where a tide race runs north over the Tripods, a bank of sand and shells, at up to 6km/h.

The island was said to have been connected to the mainland by the 60 x 30km Lowland Hundred, the main city of Caer Gwyddno being drowned with most inhabitants by flooding during a night feast in the 6th century.

Streams start north northeast at HW Dover +0500 and south southwest at HW Dover –0100 at up to 4km/h in Caernarfon Bay. The North Wales coast produces semiprecious pebbles of agate, jasper and serpentine but from here to Trywyn Porth Dinllaen it is mostly bold and rocky.

The first reliable landing site is Porth Oer, where there is a beach café and it is a surf beach. It is also known as Whistling Sands Bay as the dry sand can squeak when walked on. Beyond the beach some of the rocks are bright purple in colour and there are stacks with sharp points at the top.

Porth Iago is a surfing inlet although earlier residents have left earthworks and the remains of St Merin's Church.

Off the entrance Maen Mellt looks like a tugboat with light superstructure and dark hull when viewed from further down the coast. Far more real are the jets on training flights from RAF Valley but some residents do not object to the sound intrusion, seeing them as a link with civilization which can seem a long way away at times.

The clear waters of Traeth Penllech are popular with divers. However, not too far away at Porth Ysgaden there are still grains of coal dust in the sand from when coastal colliers used to land coal for customers.

Porth Towyn has surf which works after northerly winds but some low tide rocks need to be watched. On top of the cliffs, caravans look across to Holyhead Mountain.

The insignificant looking Aber Geirch is an inlet where many submarine cables were landed.

Trwyn Porth Dinllaen has the remains of a prom-

Porth Towyn, one of the small inlets on the north side of the Lleyn Peninsula.

Ynys Gwlan-fawr and Ynys Gwlan-bâch off Pen y Cil. The eddies around them were on a day of spring tides.

Reefs of Borth Wen seen from above Porth Dinllaen.

inently positioned building on top, perhaps taking over the role of an earlier fort, and a National Coastwatch lookout. It also has a blowhole as an unsual obstacle for a golf course. Quiet approach on the water to the rocks of Carreg Ddu and Careg y Chwislen with its cone shaped metal beacon may be rewarded by the sight of numbers of seals basking, not being in too much of a hurry to move provided there are no quick movements to worry them. Below the surface seagrass is the only underwater flowering plant in the UK. There is a small tide race and an eddy in Dinllaen Bay, especially on the flood. The lifeboat station was rebuilt in 2013. A 15km/h speed limit is imposed within 100m of the coast in the summer and a flag indicates when firing is taking place in Caernarfon Bay. A quiet resort with silver sands, it is overlooked by **Morfa Nefyn** and **Nefyn** on the cliff tops. Like the Lleyn peninsula, Porth Dinllaen is named after early Christian Irish colonists, the Laigin of Leinster. At one time the village had a herring fleet and built boats. In 1800 there was an ambition to make this the ferry port for Ireland but Holyhead was chosen instead. Undeterred, the idea was launched again in 1837 with the coming of railways and a company was formed in 1844 to build a line but it never happened, other than the straight approach road intended to continue to London, and the bay remains unspoilt although the GWR later planned a broad gauge line from Worcester. Otto, the pirates' mate in Richard Hughes' *A High Wind in Jamaica*, had worked on slate boats out of Porth Dinllaen. Nefyn has moved on from fishing and boatbuilding to surfing. St Mary's church tower has a very large ship weathervane on top. It is now a maritime museum. Archbishop Baldwin and Gerald of Wales spent a night here in *The Journey through Wales*. In 1284 Nefyn was chosen by Edward I as the venue for a contest to celebrate the downfall of Llywelyn the Last and the conquest of North Wales. In 1355 it became one of the ten royal boroughs in North Wales.

Streams start north at HW Dover +0500 and south at HW Dover −0100 at up to 3km/h from Trwyn Porth Dinllaen to the Menai Strait. As far as Trwyn Maen Dylan

the coast is at the foot of mountains, which slope down to the sea.

The church of St Beuno, possibly dating from the 6th or 7th century, at Pistyll on the B4417 was a stopping place for pilgrims going to Bardsey Island. It includes a window for lepers to watch services. Hop vines and danesberry remain from the medicinal herb garden of earlier times.

On Penrhyn Glas, where cliffs rise 120m almost vertically, the remains of a disused quarry can be seen. A further disused granite quarry follows at Porth y Nant with more workings on the 150m cliff at Trwyn y Gorlech. The workers' village at Porth y Nant was abandoned in 1959. Nant Gwrtheyrn was named after Vortigern, who fled here after losing his kingdom to the Saxons or avoiding his subjects. An unusually large skeleton was found in a coffin at Bedd Gwrtheyrn in 1750. When three monks came from Clynnog to convert the heathens they were driven out so they placed three curses, that no residents would be buried in consecrated ground, that no couple from the village would marry and that the village would die. Residents generally drowned or fell over the cliffs, the only girl to attempt to marry within the village died in a hollow oak tree after becoming trapped during the traditional pre-marriage hide and seek and the village became derelict after mining ceased. Above is Yr Eifl (the fork but anglicized to the Rivals) with three peaks reaching up to 564m only 2km from the coast, a mountain with an aerial, cairns, hut circle and settlement along with choughs, puffins, guillemots and feral goats on the acid soils and a view to Ireland. Below are the remains of three piers.

At Trwyn y Tâl there are a marvellous collection of caves, including one which is horseshoe shaped, and rhizostoma jellyfish float about at the foot of the vertical cliffs in which the caves are formed.

The wooden pier was built for loading granite for northwest England and beyond it a short wall protects Trefor's tiny harbour, served by a quarry railway until the 20th century. There is a toilet at the end of the carpark.

Porth Dinllaen with the recent lifeboat station at the end.

Penrhyn Glas with Yr Eifl beyond, both dropping steeply to the sea.

Another dramatic set of peaks are formed by Gyrn Ddu, Gyrn Goch and Bwlch Mawr with more evidence of quarrying on Gyrn Ddu.

A four legged cromlech burial chamber at Clynnog-fawr may be over 3,000 years old. St Beuno's or St Winifred's holy well was believed to have curative powers for eyes but the treatment had to be completed by spending a night on the saint's tomb. Winifred escaped from the advances of Prince Caradoc so he cut off her head, which rolled to the altar where St Beuno was preaching. The well burst forth and he placed the head back on the body, which revived Winifred. About 620, St Beuno built a wattle and daub chapel as a stopping place for pilgrims going to Bardsey Island. The site is also used for the 16th century Perpendicular church which is one of the best known in Wales, an amazingly grand piece of architecture for this remote hamlet. Inside the church is St Beuno's chest, a wooden trunk made from a single log to hold money paid by the owners of lambs or calves born with the saint's mark, a notch in the ear. Also relating to the local animals are a pair of tongs for the removal of dogs during services.

Bass live in the waters around Gored Beuno off Aberdesach. *Math Son of Mathonwy* in *The Mabinogion* describes how Gwydyon follows a bolting sow from Pennardd up the hill and sees where she goes to feed and her disgusting diet. The Afon Llyfni enters and the Afon Llifon follows soon after below a prominent aerial.

Caer Arianrhod, a low tide rock, is the only visible sign of a village marked on a map of 1573 and described in *Math Son of Mathonwy* as a fortress with a causeway to the land. Here lived Arianrhod, daughter of Don, one of the three most beautiful ladies in Britain. She had a son, Lleu Llaw Gyffes, by her brother, the warrior wizard Gwdion. Lleu received a strange wife, Blodeuedd, made of flowers of oak, broom and meadowsweet. Unlikely though the story is, a mound of stones in 7m of water shows unnatural regularity, suggesting it may have been parts of buildings. An 18th century Spanish galleon was lost here, Spanish coins being washed up and the cannons now being at Fort Belan.

The 31m high Iron Age hill fort of Dinas Dinlle, later with a Roman fortification, probably a signalling station for Caernarfon, looks notably out of place on this low shore. The present community next to it is a holiday village which is a possible surfing venue, being best at mid tide, dumping at high water. It was where Lleu Skilful Hand was brought up in *The Mabinogion*.

The low lying shingle shore of Morfa Dinlle is edged with large stones and a bank which protects against flooding. Sandhills run down the edge of the peninsula. The landing strip is now known as Caernarfon Airport. During the Second World War it was RAF Llandwrog and it was here that the first RAF mountain rescue team was formed. In 1989 the Caernarfon Airworld Aviation Museum was opened with aircraft over which visitors may climb, the former RAF Varsity simulator, displays of the Dambusters Squadron, Welsh flying VCs, aviation history in Gwynedd and aviation stamp first day covers, the Astra cinema with aviation films and an aviation adventure playground for children. Flights are available to Beaumaris, Caernarfon, Llanddwyn Island and Snowdon.

The Bar has claimed its share of vessels over the years and a large mussel bank in the main channel presently gives problems for approaching boats but an old breakwater runs along to Abermenai Point to protect against the worst ravages of the sea in Caernarfon Bay. *The Mabinogion* makes references to Abermenai, including as a departure point for Ireland.

Tide movements in the Menai Strait are amongst the most complex anywhere on our coastline. At Menai Bridge the tidal flow reverses 1½ hours before the tide reverses its vertical movement. Surface flow may be in the opposite direction to the flow deeper down. The slack flow at Menai Bridge is over an hour before that at either Puffin Island or Caernarfon as tides flow into the strait from both ends, meet near the bridge and drain out again from this point. Here, the tidal range is some 2.7m larger than at the southwest end of the strait. The tide race at Menai Bridge can be 15km/h, the fastest on the Welsh coast, and so it is vital to work out timings correctly. To get the roughest water at the Swellies the mid-tide period should be used but there is no point in trying to travel too far in this case. It is reported that there has been a decline in the intensity of the Swellies since the 1990s.

The southwest end of the Menai Strait is guarded by two arms of sand dunes enclosing two large sand bays. Traeth Melynog drains the Afon Braint and is crossed by footpaths to Abermenai Point. Until the 13th century there was a causeway across to the mainland. Foryd Bay, between a golf course and Fort Belan, drains the Afon Gwyrfai, teems with wildfowl and waders and conceals some treacherous quicksand. The large area of shallows is conducive to bass, tope and flatfish and there are clam, mussel and oyster fisheries. The Grade I St Baglan's church on the east side, restored in 1993 but now redundant, is one of the oldest and smallest in North Wales.

Caernarfon is a strategic town. In *The Mabinogion*, *The Dream of Maxen* tells how Macsen Wledig, alias 4th century Romano-British emperor Magnus Maximus, dreamed of a girl whom he subsequently found in Gwynedd and married, her requested wedding gift

Caernarfon Castle by the mouth of the Seiont.

being three forts, including one here. The Romans built their rectangular Segontium fort in 78 for a cohort of 1,000 men but its current name comes from Edward I's fort opposite Anglesey, Y Gaer yn Arfon, Wales' most famous fortress. *The Mabinogion* uses the name Caer Seint yn Arvon. With its single wall in banded stone modelled on Istanbul (as seen during the Seventh Crusade) and seven main towers, Caernarfon Castle was begun in 1283 by enlarging the 11th century Norman motte and bailey castle of Hugh d'Arranches to emphasize English domination over the Welsh and has been owned continuously by the Crown ever since, a centre for English government over North Wales and Wales' nearest building to a royal palace. Hourglass shaped, it is extended by the town walls. Madog ap Llywelyn attacked and damaged it badly in 1294. There were several attempts on it during the Glyndwr Rising in the early 15th century, the one with French support nearly being successful.

The Royalists resisted three attacks during the Civil War. Edward II was born here in 1284 and introduced as a 'native-born prince who could speak no English', being made Prince of Wales in 1301. The tradition has continued. George V invested Prince Edward in 1911, when Winston Churchill read the Letters Patent. Prince Charles was invested Prince of Wales in the castle in 1969 by the Queen. The 13 year old Princess Victoria and her party were greeted by an immense crowd and a salute. Other royal visitors have

included George VI and Queen Elizabeth the Queen Mother. The Chamberlain Tower has an exhibition of castles of Edward I and the Queen's Tower, named after Queen Eleanor, is the home of the Royal Welch Fusiliers Museum. The King's Gate is said to be the mightiest in the land. The castle has been built on a peninsula between the now culverted Afon Cadnant and the Afon Seiont, crossed by a modern swing footbridge.

The harbour used to ship slate. Constable of the Castle at one time was David Lloyd George, the Welsh Wizard, one of Britain's most colourful Prime Ministers and Member of Parliament for Caernarfon for 56 years. Part of the *Life and Times of Lloyd George* was filmed here in 1980. Beyond the castle is the terminus of the restored Welsh Highland Railway to Porthmadog. Doc Victoria almost backs onto the castle.

The town has an open air market for Anglesey and the Lleyn Peninsula on Saturdays. It also has the church of Llanbeblig although St Peblig was probably no other than Publius, son of the Roman emperor Magnus Maximus, a throwback to the Segontium days.

After Waterloo Port, Plas Menai is the Welsh Sports Council's National Watersports Centre. The complex of buildings is large and modern with a concrete slipway running down from the boat storage area into the water. The centre has won both a Civic Trust Award and a European Community Award.

The muddy bottom of the strait appears to be covered with a carpet of dead leaves but closer examination shows that they are an unbroken coating of brittle stars in assorted colours, writhing about on the floor of the

The Welsh Sports Council's National Watersports Centre, Plas Menai.

Y Felinheli is the old slate exporting Port Dinorwick, now with many waterfront houses.

Distance
*131km from
Llanenddwyn to
Menai Bridge*

OS 1:50,000 Sheets
*(114 Anglesey)
115 Snowdon
123 Lleyn Peninsula
124 Porthmadog
& Dolgellau*

Tidal Constants
*Barmouth:
HW Dover −0250
LW Dover −0140
Criccieth:
HW Dover −0300
LW Dover −0150
Pwllheli:
HW Dover −0300
LW Dover −0200
St Tudwal's Roads:
HW Dover −0310
LW Dover −0200
Aberdaron:
HW Dover −0300
LW Dover −0200
Bardsey Island:
HW Dover −0320
LW Dover −0230
Porth Ysgaden:
HW Dover −0210
LW Dover −0130
Porth Dinllaen:
HW Dover −0200
LW Dover −0120
Trefor:
HW Dover −0200
LW Dover −0100
Fort Belan:
HW Dover −0120
LW Dover −0100
Caernarfon:
HW Dover −0120
LW Dover −0040
Portdinorwick:
HW Dover −0110
LW Dover −0040
Menai Bridge:
HW Dover −0030
LW Dover*

Sea Area
Irish Sea

Connection
*Afon Dwyryd − see
RoB p54*

strait. Fish life includes bass and flounders and winkles are picked up at low tide. Herons fish and the curlew calls distinctively as it sweeps over the water.

Y Felinheli was used before the Romans and then by the Vikings in the 8th century but saw most of its development as the outlet for the Dinorwic slate quarries in the 19th century. With an old chimney there is much new housing and the Vaynol Dock marina contains berths for pleasure craft. Because the Nant y Garth valley was so steep Archbishop Baldwin and Gerald of Wales had to dismount here in *The Journey through Wales* but thought it good practice for the third Crusade which they were to undertake. The sides of the strait become increasingly steep and wooded and the channel steadily narrows.

The Pont Britannia was the first box girder bridge. Built in 1850 by Robert Stephenson and William Fairburn, trains ran through the wrought iron tubes. At 420m, it was the world's longest railway bridge and stood 30m above the water, arguably the greatest Victorian engineering triumph of its time. In 1970 a schoolboy set fire to it. It was rebuilt with arches and also an upper deck to take the A55. Anglesey stone surfaces the towers. The great stone lions that used to guard the ends of the bridge now squint along steel girders running past their ears. The clearance of the bridge has been retained but craft using the Menai Strait now have to be smaller because of power transmission cables crossing the strait below bridge level.

The Menai Bridge carried the last public turnpike road in Britain. Thomas Telford built his bridge in 1826, possibly influenced by Pickering's design for the Chain Bridge of 1817 near Llangollen. At 521m long with a 176m main span suspended from 16 wrought iron bar chains and a 30m high water clearance, it was the world's longest bridge, the world's first iron suspension bridge and the longest suspension bridge in Britain for 150 years, being rebuilt in 1938–40. Telford claimed it was the longest it was possible to build a suspension bridge as the weight would become excessive. Brunel disputed this and later proved Telford wrong. Lewis Carroll's *Upon the Lonely Moor* proposed boiling it in wine to prevent rust. It was used in filming *The Voyage of Dr Doolittle*.

The Menai Bridge with peaks of Snowdonia rising behind.

52 Isle of Anglesey

A stepping stone from Britain to Ireland

Aloft in air at giddy height upborne
Carried with navigable road; and hung
High o'er Menai's Strait the bending bridge:
Robert Southey

Anglesey or Ynys Môn includes the Mona Complex, the most extensive tract of pre Cambrian rocks in the British Isles, and occupies most of the low plateau which lies to the north of the Snowdon range, the highest mountains in Wales. Its geology is the most complex in southern Britain. It is a windy area with moderate rain but few severe frosts and was said by Gerald of Wales in *The Journey through Wales* and *The Description of Wales* to grow enough grain to supply the whole of Wales if crops failed elsewhere. As well as being old geologically, its human history is extensive and it was home to the Druids. *The Annals of Imperial Rome* mentions them and attacking Anglesey and its barbarous superstitions.

The Menai Strait was formerly three separate valleys with a watershed between the two bridges prior to a postglacial sea level rise. If the watershed at Hendre had been cut 20m lower then Anglesey would have been two islands with a second strait between Malltraeth and Red Wharf bays.

Menai Bridge has the Oriel Tegfryn gallery and has hosted Ffair Borth every October for four centuries, one of the largest local fairs in Wales. A more recent festival has been the Menai Strait regatta fortnight.

Carreg Iago is said to be a corruption of Carreg yr Archjagon, where Archbishop Baldwin stood to preach in *The Journey through Wales*. The Belgian Walk was built by refugees during the First World War. The Grade II★ St Tysilio church on Church Island is reached on a low tide causeway and was built in the 14th century on the site of the 7th century original built by St Tysilio. Before the bridge was built, cattle were swum across the Menai Strait by drovers but bass, codling, conger eels, flatfish, pollack and whiting are the main swimmers now until the Swellies are reached.

The Swellies lie between the bridges and are one of the more popular sea rapids we have, reaching Grade 3 if the conditions are right, although intensity has been reported to have declined since the 1990s. A standing wave over Swelly Rock sometimes breaks into a stopper, a bedrock rapid forms to the south of Ynys Gored Goch on the flood and a standing wave is located to the north of it on the ebb. Ynys Gored Goch, the island of the red weir, is actually two islands joined by a causeway. There was a commercial fishery from the 13th century until 1915 and it was owned by the Bishop of Bangor until 1888 and supplied fish for the monasteries of Anglesey. The eastern island, Tern Island, has a herring smoking tower and a matey

Telford's historic bridge spans the Menai Strait at Menai Bridge, the narrowest point on the strait.

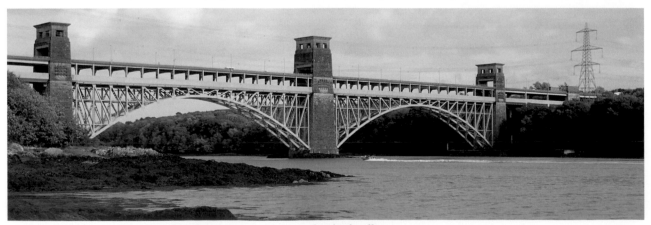

The rebuilt Pont Britannia, now carrying road and rail traffic.

toilet with a double seat. The fish traps still exist with a number of dangerous projections which could trap those playing on the rough water thrown up by the weir.

The village on the right is Llanfair Pwllgwyngyll or Llanfair PG, short for Llanfairpwllgwyngyllgogery-chwrndrobwllllantysiliogogogoch, the church of St Mary in the hollow of the white hazel over the rapid whirlpool and the church of St Tysilio by the red cave, two long names having been added together to produce a tourist pulling combination which the mere name of Swellies could never hope to emulate.

A statue of Nelson stands by the water with his 'England expects that every man will do his duty' speech inscribed on the front, not the most appropriate item for this distant part of Wales.

A 160m high Anglesey marble column built at the top of Craig-y-Dinas in 1816 carries a statue of the 1st Marquess of Anglesey, the second in command to Wellington at Waterloo, a battle in which he had his right leg hit by a cannon ball. It was replaced by a wood, metal and leather device known as the Anglesey Leg and for his remaining 39 years he joked about having one foot in the grave. Plas Newydd, built in the 18th century of Moelfre marble by James Watt, houses Rex Whistler's largest wall painting, a collection of military uniforms and relics of the first Marquess of Anglesey and the Battle of Waterloo. Princess Victoria stayed for two months, with salutes, bands and speeches but also being able to ride her pony, Rosa, and to sail the *Emerald*, the tender of the royal yacht.

Moel-y-don was once a thriving shipbuilding port with a ferry across to Y Felinheli.

St Nidan's church tower is just visible over the trees at Brynsiencyn. The Grade II★ old church was founded 1,300 years ago. A stone in the rear porch still traps water which is supposed to have healing properties. Llanidan Hall hides behind a wall.

Foel has a pier by the former Mermaid Inn at the end of the B4419, used for the ferry to Caernarfon after it was moved from the silting Tal-y-Foel harbour, the route from 1425 to 1849. The Anglesey Sea

Zoo is now located nearby with masses of sealife, a walk through a shipwreck with conger eels, tanks where lobsters can be touched, tide and wave tanks, radio controlled model boats, a playboat in a sea of bark, an adventure playground and cooked or takeaway seafood.

The southwest end of the Menai Strait is guarded by two arms of sand dune enclosing two large sand bays. Traeth Melynog drains the Afon Braint and is crossed by footpaths to Abermenai Point. Until the 13th century there was a causeway across to the mainland. This is the best point to view the splendour of the highest peaks in the Snowdon range which come into view beyond Caernarfon. Foryd Bay, between a golf course and Fort Belan, drains the Afon Gwyrfai, teems with wildfowl and waders and conceals some treacherous quicksand. The large area of shallows is conducive to bass, tope and flatfish and there are clam, mussel and oyster fisheries.

Tides out in the bay are rather easier, following the coast at up to 3km/h on spring tides.

Llanddwyn Bay has extensive sands at low tide but these have made their greater mark on land. Newborough was set up by Edward I to take the people he displaced from Beaumaris to build his castle. Rhosyr was surrounded by rich farmland until the whole village was buried in violent sandstorms in 1331 which created the largest area of sand dunes on the west coast of Britain, Newborough Warren. The warren, a National Nature Reserve, was named after its rabbits, 80,000 to 100,000 being taken each year until 1954 and the introduction of myxomatosis. Marram grass, planted to comply with laws made by Elizabeth I, resulted in a mat, rope and basket making

Lord Nelson looks down the Menai Strait.

The Menai Strait looking north from Moel-y-don.

navigation mark was built on the end of the island in 1800, being replaced by a lighthouse in 1873. There was a lifeboat from 1840 to 1907 and a cannon on Gun Cliff was used to call out the lifeboat crew from Newborough. Surf is likely to be found on the west side and the wreck of a large fishing boat can be seen close inshore at low water. Pilot boats were kept in Pilots Cove where the cottages have now been restored to have traditional interiors. It is still used for an overnight stop for yachts and £1,000,000 worth of marijuana was taken off a boat here some years ago.

Sometimes known as the Island of Love, it was here that St Dwynwen, the patron saint of Welsh lovers, built a convent in the 6th century after a broken love affair. A well was dug, two crosses erected and a church built on the site of her oratory a thousand years later, a place to

The end of Llanddwyn Island can have both a dramatic and a mystical atmosphere.

Llanddwyn Island with the peaks of Snowdonia beyond.

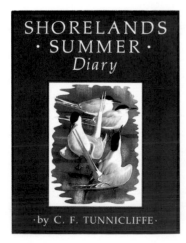

industry which flourished until the 1930s. Corsican pine planting to fix the sand dunes began in 1948, producing Newborough Forest. The Forestry Commission have built a road into the forest and provided a large parking area although this can become very congested.

Off Newborough Forest surf is unexceptional but safe. Llanddwyn Island is not an island except on very high spring tides because of a partly artificial isthmus at Gwddw Llanddwyn. The situation has faced many a boat coming from the Menai Strait and wrecks litter Llanddwyn Bay, one being a boat chartered by a group of divers who intended to use it as a base from which to dive to a wreck. A stone

which pilgrims flocked. A split rock was said to have been for her to use as a seat while watching her last sunset.

It has an old lighthouse. These days it has been claimed as a bird sanctuary and nature reserve. Shags, guillemots and gulls are likely to be seen on Ynys yr Adar.

A rather larger national nature reserve is Malltraeth Sands which occupy the estuary of the Afon Cefni. Greenshanks, redshanks, lapwings, sandpipers and other waders use the sands as a migration staging post. Malltraeth was the home from 1947 to 1979 of Charles Tunnicliffe, the bird artist, who described his life in the area in *Shorelands Summer Diary*. Earlier visitors were the Vikings who sacked Malltraeth. The village was the centre of the Anglesey coal mining industry and had shipbuilding in the 18th and 19th centuries. Across the head of the estuary is Malltraeth Cob, an embankment built by Telford to reclaim land for farming.

The western corner of Malltraeth Bay is marked by Pen-y-parc, a headland with a promontory fort, and there are several wrecks scattered around the bay.

Dunes front Aberffraw with its packhorse bridge over the Afon Ffraw and perhaps surf. *The Journey through Wales* and *The Description of Wales* say that that the village had one of three royal castles in Wales and was the capital of the princes of Gwynedd from Rhoderic the Great in 870 until the 13th century when Llywelyn the Last was defeated and killed by Edward I. The only reminder of their palace is a Norman style arch in St Beuno's church, said to have come from it. The Great Storm of 1331 silted up the river entrance. *Branwen Daughter of Llyr* describes the feasting here when Mallolwch, king of Ireland, arrives to request the hand of Branwen, the most beautiful girl in the world.

Most of the headlands on this coast seem to have rocky islets off them but Braich-lwyd at the northwest end of Aberffraw Bay has none. Instead it offers gently sloping rock slabs which result in a confused sea close inshore.

St Cwyfan's church between Porth Cwyfan and Porth China is strikingly placed on an island with a wall all round. Based on 7th century foundations, it was restored in 1893 and approached on a causeway at low water, services being arranged to suit the tides.

Inland from Ynys Meibion is Anglesey Circuit for racing on former RAF ranges, sandwiched between two SSSIs.

Porth Trecastell funnels in to a small beach which can produce excellent surf but which has a strong rip along each side, especially the south. Its English name of Cable Bay comes from the fact that it is the landing point for a transatlantitc telephone cable. The Welsh name derives from the fort on the headland. Barclodiad y Gawres, the giantess' apronful, is a chambered cairn with five Stone Age carved stones, now covered by a protective concrete dome.

The Oyster Catcher is a prominent and popular restaurant and bar complex built by the Timpson Foundation, used for training reformed young prisoners.

Surfing can also be good at **Rhosneigr** (rhos-y-neidr means viper moor) on the A4080, the only large village on the coast. Cerrig-y-brain rocks form an extensive area at low tide. A tide rip can form over Cerrig-y-Gwyr to the southwest of Ynys Feirig. It was this rock-strewn shoreline which was used by the wreckers of Crigyll, active for thirty years in the 18th century, one of whom was hanged in 1755 after the wife of the owner of the sloop *Charming Jenny* was murdered while getting ashore when the boat was wrecked in a storm. Even without the wreckers, the occasional boat still comes to grief in Cymyran Bay, where the most notable loss was the tea clipper *Norman Court*. Once a shipbuilding centre, it now caters for more modern transport needs.

Across the Afon Crigyll, between the sand dunes and the golf course, is the main runway of RAF Valley, home of SAR helicopters whose pilots have included Prince William, a fast jet flying school, the headquarters of the RAF Mountain Rescue Unit and Anglesey Airport. There is constant activity from all kinds of aircraft, the noise being heard all over the district, accompanied by the smell of kerosene when the wind is in the right direction.

The name Valley dates from 1822 when Thomas Telford cut through a small hill for the A5.

The west coast of Anglesey floods northwards and ebbs southwards. The exception is inside Holy Island. The Inland Sea fills and empties from both ends. Slack water is nearly three hours after Holyhead while flows can be strong.

Entry into the shallow, meandering, sandy channel is from Cymyran Bay past a prominent white house at Cymyran. Other obvious landmarks are the chimney of the former aluminium smelter at **Holyhead** and Holyhead Mountain.

Bryn-y-bar from Cymyran.

Striking orange and green lichens at Carnau.

Looking southeast from Four Mile Bridge.

The single arch of Four Mile Bridge with the last of the ebb.

Inland Sea at low tide with the mill on the skyline.

A medium sized fishing boat lies abandoned on the beach at Bryn-y-bar. The headland to its right and Ynys-las both bear notices banning landing from this irregular channel with its hillsides of heather and cattle.

Jets pass low overhead on final approach to RAF Valley or maybe a curlew sandpiper swoops over.

Occasional outcrops of rock break up the scenery here as farmland slopes down to the water. Local farmers cross on foot at low water and at Ford a track runs along the high water mark of one of the inlets which lead out from the main channel.

At low tide the channel is reduced to the proportions of a small river while at high tide the sandbanks lurk as hidden shallows.

Timing depends on the tides at the Inland Sea. Entry and exit are only possible near slack water. It is possible to paddle a kayak against the flow for half an hour after the tide turns. Four Mile Bridge has only a single arch which carries the B4545 and produces a jet. This was the point at which the water was forded at low tide before Holy Island was connected to the main island by a bridge. If the tides have been missed it is possible to portage across the road at the northeast end of the bridge.

The south end of the Inland Sea is very shallow. It is overlooked by a prominent disused windmill. Just north of the inlet on the west side stands a wooden building which could be an ornithologist's hide or a summerhouse.

The 1.2km long Stanley Embankment was built by Telford in 1823. Unfortunately, he only built one small arch through it and didn't think to leave room for anyone on foot. If the flow through the bridge is in the right direction the shoot can be quite exhilarating, a favourite playspot despite notices banning navigation because of dangerous currents. The tunnel is 3m wide by 1.5m high and a stopper forms inside on the flood. The embankment can be portaged with difficulty in the east corner of the Inland Sea, a portage which involves the A55, the railway, the A5 and passing the remains of a kayak which obviously didn't make it.

South of Penrhos is a nature reserve near where turf from the drowned forests of West Wales were once dug for fuel. Beddmanarch Bay is shallow with a bed of black organic silt which emits a smell of hydrogen sulphide if disturbed. On the other hand, this coast can throw up semi precious stones, agate, jasper and serpentine.

Branwen Daughter of Llyr tells how broken hearted Branwen was buried on the bank of the Afon Alaw.

Penrhyn has some pieces of building which resemble relatively recent fortifications, now wrecked, matched by a wrecked boat in Porth Penrhyn-mawr.

Porth Tywyn-mawr or sandy beach can have surf after a northwesterly.

An inshore eddy runs on the ebb from Church Bay to Carmel Head from an hour after high water to an hour before low water, the tide thus running north for nine hours in every twelve close inshore.

Porth Swtan (Swedes' cove, possibly a Viking raider landing place) is flanked by a windmill without sails at Crugmor-fawr and a church with slender spire at Pen y foel, the latter seeming rather formal for this rugged landscape and being noted in the name of Church Bay. Swtan is a 16th century thatched cottage.

Gradually the cliffs build up to maximum height at Carmel Head, the northwest corner of Anglesey, with its jagged rocks, occasional caves, waters bearing mackerel, pollock, rays, skate and tope and flocks of razorbills and fulmars which glide in for close inspection, sometimes passing within a metre.

It was also the first sighting point for inbound ships in the days of sail and messages were passed from here to Liverpool in about five minutes by semaphore.

The waters off the point are the location of the Carmel Head Gap Race which flows strongly between the head and the Skerries (Ynysoedd y Meolrhoniaid or isle of porpoises although seals are more likely to be seen today). In 1716 William Trench of Dublin erected a lighthouse on the Skerries, consuming 100t of coal per year, the last privately owned lighthouse in the country, to which passing ships had to pay a toll until the 19th century. The present lighthouse dates from 1981. There has been concern about the possibility of disturbance to birds, a warden being resident part of the year to protect them.

On the north side of Carmel Head are the White Ladies, a pair of 10m high beacons which line up with another on the West Mouse and Coal Rock which lies close to the main shipping channel. An inshore eddy runs between Carmel Head and Hen Borth on the flood, giving an almost continuous westerly flow.

Mynachdy (monk's house) on the hillside above is on the site of a monastery and there is said to be an

The Inland Sea empties through the Stanley Embankment.

The White Ladies, a pair of markers to the east of Carmel Head, point to West Mouse. The Skerries lie to the left of the picture.

underground passage to one of the caves where the monks were believed to have hidden their treasure. The church beyond Hen Borth is Llanrhwydrys, founded in 570.

There are overfalls outside Harry Furlough's Rocks, sometimes said to be a misspelling of furlong from the length of the rocks. A lifeboat was stationed in Cemlyn Bay from 1828 to 1919 and there is a monument but now the bay is left to the birds, being a sanctuary with a strange arm reaching nearly across the bay at the inshore end.

A former mill stands by Porth-y-Pistyll.

Dominating this part of the coast is the Wylfa nuclear power station, the largest and last working Magnox type but one of the world's least efficient, closed in 2015. An Advanced Boiling Water Reactor is now being built here. This is the beginning of the powerline which crosses the Menai Strait next to the Britannia Bridge.

Cemaes Bay has eddies on both the ebb and flood and is fringed with low cliffs topped by a nature trail. Samples of rock from different geological ages on posts form a geopark. Cemaes was a shipbuilding and smuggling centre, the little 19th century harbour with its fishing boats emptying completely with the tide. A submarine cable lands nearby and adjacent facilities include a parking area, toilets and a café.

Moving out of Cemaes Bay past cliffs with occasional caves, Middle Mouse or Ynys Badrig comes into sight. It is here that St Patrick was said to have been shipwrecked on his way back from converting Ireland to Christianity and he is believed to have built St Patrick's church at Llanbadrig in 440 in thanks for his survival.

The ruins of the china clay industry are visible as a porcelain works and stone chimney at the head of Porth Llanlleiana. Llanlleiana Head, the most northerly point in Wales which it is possible to reach on foot, is often the most difficult point to round on the north coast. This might have been a criterion in its choice as the site of the Dinas Gynfor hill fort.

Hell's Mouth has an eddy on the flood so that the current usually flows westwards, the coast generally flooding clockwise and ebbing anticlockwise. The cleft to the east of the headland can produce fierce gusts during southerly winds.

Graig Wen, a white topped hill, continues down to the sea as Torllwyn, a headland with two prominent masts which mark the start of a measured nautical mile. Porth Wen has the remains of the Cemaes Brick Works on the west side with a prominent brick chimney and cylindrical structures in brick.

The A5025 runs past Bull Bay which has eddies on both the ebb and the flood, producing surf with the added interest of a rock garden at high tide. Other amenities include a golf course and, from earlier times, Roman baths. Formerly a shipbuilding centre and base for four oared pilot boats, it now houses only fishing boats, these waters having codling and flatfish.

The unusual barrel shaped Grade II★ Roman Catholic church of Our Lady, Star of the Sea & St Winefride at the back of the bay is in reinforced concrete with prominent hoop ribs on the outside and was built in 1930.

Amlwch Port became world famous for exporting copper from Parys Mountain, visible to the south with an armless windmill. First worked by the Romans, it was employing 1,500 people by the beginning of the 19th century and producing 80,000t of top grade ore per year. When the country ran short of small change at the end of the 18th century the Parys Mountain Copper Co minted 250t of pennies and 50t of halfpennies for public use. The

Wylfa nuclear power station with Middle Mouse beyond.

The harbour at Cemaes Bay at low tide.

The lighthouse on Point Lynas outside Porth Eilean.

Copper Kingdom Centre explains everything to visitors and there is also the Sail Loft Heritage Centre. The harbour was built in 1793 and the ruins of warehouses, offices, smelting shops and shipbuilding yards and slipways are still visible. The end of the harbour wall has been slid back a metre by wave impact and has had to be bolted down to its base. Another industry was the tobacco trade which made Amlwch Shag, chewing tobacco soaked in rum. The harbour could be closed with timbers in rough weather and there was a dry dock blasted out of the rocks, no longer in use, like the chemical works. Liverpool pilots operate from here.

East Mouse has rocky ledges under the water which produce difficult water and here the long brown belts of *Laminaria saccharina* become the prominent seaweed. An eddy on the flood passes Porthyrychen and Porth Eilean so the flow is westwards for most of the time.

The stumpy square 12th century church spire which lies before the caravan site between the two inlets is that of the 15th century Grade I St Eilean's church which had been founded in the 5th century and which possesses a range of interesting artefacts including a studded chest and tongs for separating fighting dogs. A painted skeleton has the motto 'The Sting of Death is Sin' in Welsh. The chapel is entered through a small door in the chancel. There is a panel missing from the wooden base of the panelled shrine inside and anyone able to squeeze in and turn without touching the sides is said to have good luck.

Point Lynas brings the mountains of the Snowdon range back into view again. The white castellated lighthouse, signal and telegraph station were built in 1835 by the trustees of Liverpool docks. Six oar pilot boats were stationed at Porth Eilean, possibly to sneak inside the tide race which forms off the point on the flood. Weak eddies run on the flood in Freshwater Bay and Porth Helygon so the current is northwards for nine hours of each tide cycle.

Although not so high now, the strata of the cliffs dip towards the sea, making it difficult to find places to climb out in an emergency.

Ynys Dulas (the appropriately named Seal Island with inquisitive seals often coming very close to kayak paddlers) has a prominent 19th century refuge beacon tower in the centre for shipwrecked mariners, many of whom lost their ships on the island in the days of sail. There are tide rips off Ynys Dulas and Ynys y Charcharorion and a tide race can run right the way across between the two.

Dulas was the home of the Morris brothers who were patrons of the arts and attempted to promote the bard Goronwy Owen, publishing hundreds of letters giving an insight into the attitudes and social life of the times.

The church contains fine 15th and 16th century

Ynys Dulas is marked by its prominent shelter for shipwrecked sailors.

Flemish glass and also the font, oak screen and brass from St Gwenllwyfo church, the remains of which lie to the northeast of the village.

Traeth Dulas is a sandy inlet which drains completely except for the small flow from the Afon Goch. There is a rip through the entrance, especially on the ebb.

Traeth Lligwy may have surf when the atmospheric pressure is high.

The ridge behind Lligwy Bay has a caravan site and is prominently built on although some buildings go back many centuries. Din Lligwy consists of a 4th century chieftain's fortified house and two circular and seven rectangular huts with thick walls. Hen Capel Lligwy is a roofless chapel with a rough font. Finally there is a 4,000 year old burial chamber which revealed 30 bodies when excavated in 1908.

According to the tide, Y Swnt inside Ynys Moelfre (Rat Island) contains a small tide rip, an area of shelter from the waves or both. The lifeboat station, established in 1830, has had a distinguished history and saved nearly 1,000 lives on a coast notorious for its wrecks. One of the most notable was the *Royal Charter* which came to grief on October 24th 1859 with only 45 saved of 464 gold prospectors returning to Liverpool from Australia, one of 114 ships lost in the storm. A dozen people were rescued after a sailor swam ashore with a line. Two thirds of the £500,000 in gold aboard was later recovered and looting of the bodies was said to have contributed to the prosperity of Moelfre. In 2012 a 97g gold nugget, Britain's biggest ever, was found 40m from the wreck site. Two months after the wreck the site was visited by Charles Dickens, who used the story as the basis of the opening tale in *The Uncommercial Traveller,* and Robert Westall used it as the basis for the wreck of the *Hoplite* in *The Watch House.* A century later to the day, coxwain Richard Evans earned his second gold medal by rescuing eight crew members from the *Hindlea. The Journey through Wales* records how a fleet called to meet Henry II at Rhuddlan or Deganwy went instead to Moelfre and attacked local churches. It was the home of Davey Evans in *A Liverpool Lass.*

In the 18th century this coast produced great quantities of herrings but mackerel are more likely to be caught today. Moelfre, at the end of the A5108, is also a sailing and waterskiing base.

Traeth Bychan, small beach, was a loading point for quarries but is now one of the most popular sailing venues on Anglesey with a sailing club slipway.

Sedimentary cliffs studded with fossils stand above deeply pitted and very abrasive coral rocks on the approach to **Benllech**, the birthplace of Goronwy Owen, who died in 1770 in obscurity in Virginia. Benllech has a beautiful beach.

Caravans, beach huts and chalets lead down to Trwyn Dwlban, a point where the turnstone might be found in winter. Beyond is Red Wharf Bay from which the tide

withdraws for 2km. The name is from the blood after a Viking battle in 1179. On the bay's near corner is a large block of rock which looks like a castle from the distance and was the site of Castell-mawr, an early British fortress. Red Wharf Bay used to build ships for the copper trade. Although the bay is a popular mooring for pleasure craft it can be exposed to strong southwesterly gusts. These could not have been blowing on the day when a tribe of witches landed in a boat with no oars, rudder or sail and stayed to terrify the locals. The most likely explanation is that they were Irish cast adrift for their crimes, a common form of punishment, and washed up here.

Llanddona, with its church incorporating parts of the 7th century St Dona's church, is located on the ridge to the south of Red Wharf Bay and pinpointed by two prominent aerials. Less obvious is the fort site further

Dickens

Lifeboat helmsman sculpture outside Meolfre's lifeboat museum.

Great Ormes Head and Puffin Island, seen across Red Wharf Bay from Benllech at dawn.

Puffin Island at Anglesey's most easterly point.

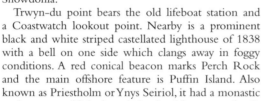

PUFFIN *Fratercula arctica*
19P
RSPB 1889-1989

along on Bwrdd Arthur although the conspicuous remains of quarry buildings and waste tips stand desolately at the foot of the cliffs below it.

Turning the corner brings the Great Ormes Head into view. The horizontal cliff strata are draped with vegetation and the area is alive with gulls, shags, cormorants, guillemots, oystercatchers and shelducks.

The cliffs provide shelter from the prevailing wind although the converted windmill above at Mariandyrys was sited for maximum benefit.

Quarry workings and a jetty beyond the rock outcrop at Trwyn Dinmor are the last signs of human activity before arrival at Trwyn-du with its lighthouse and red conical buoy and the long hump of Puffin Island, all with the backdrop of the mountains of Snowdonia.

Trwyn-du point bears the old lifeboat station and a Coastwatch lookout point. Nearby is a prominent black and white striped castellated lighthouse of 1838 with a bell on one side which clangs away in foggy conditions. A red conical beacon marks Perch Rock and the main offshore feature is Puffin Island. Also known as Priestholm or Ynys Seiriol, it had a monastic settlement established on it in the 6th century by St Seiriol. He also had a chapel at Penmaenmawr, 9km away across Conwy Bay, and there is supposed to have been a former low tide route across the sands connecting the two. It was also known as Ynys Lannog after the legendary 6th century Prince Glannog whose lands became innundated to form the Lavan Sands. The island has more recently had a telegraph station, a former link in the Holyhead to Liverpool chain. The puffins themselves have been decimated by rats.

Weather permitting (and it frequently doesn't), there is a view of the magnificent sweep of mountains on the far side of the bay from Great Ormes Head to the northeastern part of Snowdonia, Tal y Fan, Llwtymor, Bera Mawr, Foel Grach and other peaks forming a high ridge with just the occasional cleft carved by a river.

Penmon is dominated by its quarrying operations which provided limestone for Beaumaris Castle and the two bridges. The disused stone wharf once had a jetty. Many of the building, though, related to Penmon Priory which Maelgwyn Gwynedd allowed St Seiriol to build in the 6th century. The church was rebuilt in the 12th century and some of its Norman architecture remains, together with 13th and 16th century buildings including parts of the dormitory, refectory, prior's house and two Celtic crosses. A hermit's cell is believed to have been used by St Seiriol when baptizing pilgrims. It was not unusual for St Seiriol to spend a day meeting St Cybi from Holyhead in the middle of the island. St Seiriol was known as the Pale because he made both legs of the

journey with the sun on his back while St Cybi the Dark always had the sun on his face.

The domed roof is that of a dovecot built in about 1600 to hold 930 birds to supply the table of local landowner Sir Richard Bulkeley. A more prominent landmark to him is the Bulkeley Memorial pillar above Beaumaris although tall aerials at Llangoed and Llanddona are more noticeable these days.

Llanfaes on the B5109 is marked by its prominent lifeboat station and long slipway, just south of which is

Gallows Point and the Menai Strait from Beaumaris.

Beaumaris at the end of the A545 is the castle, built in 1298 by James of St George for Edward I in response to Prince Madog's 1294 attack on Caernarfon. It completed Edward's defensive chain, closing the strait and cutting the Welsh off from their vital grain supplies on Anglesey. Built in four concentric rings inside a 5.5m moat with 14 obstructions covered by arrow slits, the outer curtain wall had 16 towers and the inner walls were 13m high and 4.8m thick with three towers. Incomplete, it is the most technically perfect of Britain's medieval castles and had a jetty, allowing it to be supplied by sea, the mooring ring still in place for vessels to 40t. In the 15th century it resisted a rebellion by Owain Glyndwr and the town was then walled. In the Civil War in 1642 Anglesey backed the king and the castle held out until 1646. Once a thriving port and shipbuilding centre, the town has many old buildings, the Grade I church of St Mary & St Nicholas (14th century), the Grade II★ Tudor Rose (1400) and Grade II Olde Bull's Head (1472), used as a headquarters by Cromwell and visited on occasions by Johnson and by Dickens. The courthouse (1614) and gaol (1829) include a treadmill water pump, Britain's only one still in its original position, and a ramp leading to the gibbet over the street. The Museum of Childhood Memories with its toys and games has one of Britain's largest collections of moneyboxes. One of the more recent buildings is the *Blue Peter II* inshore rescue boat station by the pier, the latter now reduced to only half its former width but operating a ferry service to Menai Bridge in the summer. The town is very much a yachting centre with a boatyard at Gallows Point.

an old fish weir. Fishing is mostly for mussels now but cormorants and razorbills occupy Fryars Road and the extensive Lavan Sands, catching an assortment of fish. It was at Llanfaes that Egbert of Wessex beat the Welsh in 811. In 1237 Llewelyn founded a Franciscan friary in the village.

The oil pipeline to Stanlow passes under the strait at Mountfield.

Beau marais in Norman French meant beautiful marsh, now the Green. The most important building in

Distance
The Isle of Anglesey is 38km long and lies 200m off Bangor with road access

OS 1:50,000 Sheets
114 Anglesey
115 Snowdon

Tidal Constants
Menai Bridge:
HW Dover −0030,
LW Dover
Port Dinorwic:
HW Dover −0110,
LW Dover −0040
Caernarfon:
HW Dover −0120,
LW Dover −0050
Fort Belan:
HW Dover −0120,
LW Dover −0100
Llanddwyn Island:
HW Dover −0200,
LW Dover −0120
Porth Trecastell:
HW Dover −0120,
LW Dover −0100
Trearddur Bay:
HW Dover −0120,
LW Dover −0100
Holyhead:
Dover −0050
Cemaes Bay:
HW Dover −0030,
LW Dover −0010
Amlwch:
HW Dover −0040,
LW Dover −0020
Moelfre:
HW Dover −0030,
LW Dover −0010
Trywyn Dinmor:
HW Dover −0300,
LW Dover −0010
Beaumaris:
HW Dover −0030,
LW Dover

Sea Area
Irish Sea

Connection
Afon Cefni – see RoB p56

53 Holy Island (Ynys Gybi)

In the midst of fast currents

Lo here I sit at holy head
With muddy ale and mouldy bread
All Christian vittals stink of fish
I'm where my enemyes would wish
Convict of lyes is every sign,
The Inn has not one drop of wine
I'm fasnd both by wind and tide
I see the ship at anchor ride
The Captain swears the sea's too rough
He has not passengers enough.

Jonathan Swift

Around Holy Island is some of the most popular sea kayak paddling in Britain with a number of testing tide races and some striking scenery.

Timing of a circumnavigation is critical, not so much to make the maximum use of tides and tide races on the west coast as to make the Inland Sea possible. As the tides flood north and ebb south in the Irish Sea they are constricted by Anglesey and, in particular, by Holy Island and so very swift currents occur on the west coast with several tide races. The Inland Sea is all but cut off to north and south with the narrowest of exits through which it fills and empties, usually being a couple of hours behind the tide outside and requiring levels in the top third of the tide in the Inland Sea to avoid problems with shallows. Exits to the Inland Sea work outwards or inwards together and unless levels are fairly well balanced the flow at exits is too great to paddle against. Under Stanley Embankment a holding stopper can form over the strongest part of the ebb. Taking all these factors together, one option is to start from Cymyran Bay an hour after low tide, allowing five hours to run north with the flood, arriving at the Stanley Embankment at the top of the tide, crossing the Inland Sea with a good depth of water, passing under Four Mile Bridge when the levels are not dissimilar and running back to Cymyran Bay with the ebb. Cymyran is approached down a track leading southwest from the northwest end of Valley airfield.

Moving out into Cymyran Bay brings a rocky coastline, low at first, dotted with numerous islets. Silver Bay is passed immediately, a beach belonging to part of an estate owned by Bulmer's and reserved for their employees in the cider trade.

Borthwen is the natural harbour for Rhoscolyn with its lifeboat station still standing as a grim reminder of December 1920 when five men were lost from the Rhoscolyn lifeboat, *Ramon Cabrera*, while attempting to rescue the Whitby steamer *Timbo*. Five of the thirteen lifeboat crew were lost during what was officially recorded as 'no service'. The male population of the village, who had been involved in the marble quarrying and oyster catching industries, did not recover and the lifeboat station was closed in 1929. The women and children were subsequently moved to Holyhead where they could be better cared for. Today the houses are used as holiday homes.

Rhoscolyn Beacon stands on Ynysoedd Gwylanod, overlooked by a National Coastwatch lookout point. St Gwenfaen's Well on Rhoscolyn Head was credited with the power of curing mental disorders. With Maen Piscar tide race in full force the boater might consider stopping for a drink.

Into Penrhos Bay the large and poisonous lion's mane jellyfish sometimes floats with the warm tides of summer. Cormorants spread their wings to dry them, oystercatchers and gulls move to a safe distance and sunbathers start up motors and power off to points where others' eyes will not fall upon them.

Cracks and caves gradually begin to appear in the cliffs which have been grey so far except where coloured by marine life and topped by the tiny purple flowers of spring squill but are now able to show nougat shades of pink and white at times.

Turning into Trearddur Bay on the B4545 brings first views of Holyhead Mountain and the chimney of the former aluminium smelter.

Trearddur Bay is dotted with islets. The beach has a number of old tree stumps just below the high water mark. Whitewashed houses surround the bay with a large white

The sweep of Trearddur Bay.

hotel above Porth-y-post, one of the inlets popular with divers. Windsurfers and sailing boats load Trearddur Bay to capacity at times in the summer and inflatable pillars mark their race courses as the regular boom of a gun starts successive races.

Redshanks are seen and herring gulls check closely for edible flotsam.

Approaching Penrhyn Mawr, a fort nestles in a gap in the cliffs, peering out like an owl that has been disturbed in its daytime hideaway. After the corner, South Stack and its lighthouse come into view although the Penrhyn Mawr tide race is likely to be of more immediate interest.

Ellin's Tower, on the clifftop beyond Abraham's Bosom, is a 19th century castellated structure, now used as an information centre. Behind it lies Cytiau'r Gwyddelod, also known as the Irishmen's Huts. These 20 hut circles date from the late Iron Age or the early Roman period and one of the few things known about them is that they are not Irish.

At South Stack the cliffs rise to 120m, highly folded and intensely altered metamorphic rocks of the Mona complex. These are some of the oldest rocks in Wales and so among the oldest in the world. They contain caves, arches and flying buttresses, being well marked with guano and forming an RSPB sanctuary where puffins, guillemots, razorbills, choughs and a handful of other birds nest, for which reason climbers are not allowed to use the rocks in the breeding season. The cliffs are also home to the rare annual rockrose and spathulate fleawort.

A footpath is carried down the cliff face by 365 steps and across a flimsy suspension bridge to South Stack with its lighthouse constructed in 1808 by David Alexander. Passing under the bridge avoids the Holyhead Race but presents water which can offer quite a technical sea rapid in itself.

The cliffs of Gogarth Bay are the seaward extremity of 220m high Holyhead Mountain with some of the hardest rock climb routes in Britain, climbs with evocative names like Dream of White Horses. Holyhead Mountain is the highest point on Anglesey, from the top of which can be seen Ireland, Cumbria, the Isle of Man and Snowdon. This relic of a former plateau bears on its summit Caer y Twr, an ancient fortress, and a set of more modern radar dishes.

The ruggedness can have its problems, though, and the purple heather and yellow gorse can become tinder dry in the summer and, once ignited, can burn for days as the steep slopes prevent the fire brigade getting access.

The best of the caves are in the vicinity of North Stack.

Ellin's Tower near South Stack.

So is a signal station and a tide race which cannot be avoided on the ebb. On the floor of one cave can be seen cannon from a fort built above at the end of the 18th century and there is also a large navigation buoy wedged inside. It was an identification point for inbound shipping in *A Pair of Blue Eyes* and Elizabeth Gaskell's *Mary Barton* claims that Liverpool pilots would come this far to pick up inbound ships.

South Stack with its lighthouse.

Running out from Soldiers' Point is the massive breakwater, its 2.4km completed in 1873 as the world's longest after 28 years of construction, followed in 1880 by the rebuilding of the harbour. The breakwater was built using railways leading down from quartzite quarries on Holyhead Mountain. The New Harbour houses the coastguard station which doubles as a mountain rescue post. **Holyhead** Maritime Museum is in Wales' oldest lifeboat station.

Rounding the end of the breakwater can reveal an oily calm on the water ahead but the water becomes clearer after the harbourmouths which have to be crossed with an eye open for large and fast traffic.

A trestle pier extends from Salt Island and carries a conveyor belt leading off towards the former aluminium smelter. The Holyhead lifeboat is stationed on Salt Island. Ynys Gybi, as it once was, had a salt house to extract salt from sea water. Queen Anne gave permission for rock salt to be handled, too, but the works had ceased operation by 1775.

Vehicle ferries operate from Holyhead's inner harbour at the end of the A55 to Dublin and Dun Laoghaire. The first Irish packet boat commenced operation in 1573 and it is this strategic position at the end of the A5 which has resulted in Holyhead's importance. Thomas Love Peacock's *Headlong Hall* opens with the Holyhead mail coach. In Evelyn Waugh's *Decline & Fall*, Philbrick had already departed by train for Holyhead when detectives arrived at Llanabba Castle to arrest him.

Holyhead's Welsh name of Caergybi is a reminder that

Soldiers' Point breakwater protects Holyhead harbour.

St Cybi was permitted by Maelgwyn Gwynedd to found a monastery and church here in the 6th century inside a 3rd century Roman fort, the church still standing. Another church dating from the 15th to 17th centuries has windows by Burne-Jones and William Morris.

That most English of establishments, the Women's Institute, actually began in 1911 after a meeting organized by a Canadian, Mrs Alfred Watt, in Holyhead's former Station Hotel. Dawn French of comedy duo French & Saunders was born here. According to *Harry Potter & the Deathly Hallows* the Holyhead Harpies were an all witch Quidditch team.

Holyhead is the most populous part of Anglesey and has the bulk of its industry, located by the prominent aluminium smelter to the southeast of the town. Closed in 2009, it was a 260MW plant, making it the UK's largest single consumer of electricity, which was supplied from Wylfa. It is to become a biomass plant and eco park. The bay facing it is guarded by Ynys Peibo with the remains of fortifications while other ruins are seen on the shore near Penrhos.

The rest of the circumnavigation was described, starting at the southern end, in the previous chapter although many craft treat the two islands as one and ignore the Inland Sea.

The channel inside South Stack.

Gogarth Bay with its cliffs stretching towards North Stack. The Skerries are visible in the distance.

Distance
Holy Island is 12km long and lies 60m off Cymyran with road access

OS 1:50,000 Sheet
114 Anglesey

Tidal Constants
*Trearddur Bay:
HW Dover −0120,
LW Dover −0100
Holyhead:
Dover −0050*

Sea Area
Irish Sea

54 North Wales

They rowed her in across the rolling foam,
The cruel crawling foam,
The cruel hungry foam,
To her grave beside the sea:
But still the boatmen hear her call the cattle home
Across the sands of Dee.
Charles Kingsley

The A5 leads over the Menai Bridge towards the restored 1896 Bangor pier, retaining most of its Victorian design. At the landward end is a building with a penny farthing on the gable and a helter skelter next to it.

Porth Penrhyn is the dock for **Bangor**, developed to export slate and now handling mussels and yachtsmen. The town's cathedral, founded by St Deiniol in 548, is probably the oldest in the British Isles and the most abused, restored by Sir Gilbert and Oldrid Scott in the 19th century. It has a 15th century font, 1518 carved oak Mostyn Christ and the *Bangor Pontifical* compiled about 1310 by Bishop Anian II with services only a bishop could take. Every plant mentioned in the Bible which will grow in Wales and also those associated with festivals and saints are to be found at Gardd yr Esgob, the bishop's garden. Archbishop Baldwin preached here and he and Gerald of Wales spent a night here in *The Journey through Wales*. As well as the Museum of Welsh Antiquities the town houses Bangor University, of which the narrator speaks disparagingly of her linguistics professor in *Bridget Jones's Diary*. The Canorion group, formed in the college in 1906, began the work of collecting Welsh folksongs. In the Sherlock Holmes story *The Adventure of the Priory School* the Duke of Holdernesse was claimed to have one of his addresses as Carston Castle in Bangor.

Streams rotate clockwise in Conwy Bay, which is dominated by Lavan Sands and Dutchman Sands. Lavan Sands were claimed to be the innundated lands of the legendary 6th century Prince Glannog. These are up to 5km wide in places and reach nearly to Puffin Island at low water. Before the bridges were built, travellers had to walk across the sands and try to attract the attention of boatmen in **Beaumaris** before the rising water made them retreat. Salmon weirs run out 1km over the sands with a black beacon at the north end of the west weir, but the fish traps are very dilapidated and there are more bass than salmon in these waters now. There are also mussel banks and a good selection of birdlife from plovers to terns. The sands share with the Conwy estuary some 18,000 waders and wildfowl including 1,000 curlew of national importance and 6,000 oystercatchers, 5,000 dunlin and 1,500 redshank, all of international importance.

Behind Bangor Flats is Penrhyn Castle's square shape. Neo-Norman, dating from 1820 to 1845, it contains mock Norman furniture, panelling and

plasterwork by Thomas Hopper, fine pictures and a Victorian walled garden. It was built for the Pennant family with the profits of the West Indies sugar trade and Bethesda slate quarries and includes a Grand Staircase, Great Hall with polished sandstone floor based on Durham Cathedral, billiard table, some fireplaces and a bed all in slate, together with a display of industrial locomotives in the stables including some from the slate quarries. A doll museum contains over a thousand dolls.

Slate slab fences are features of the area. There is a sweep of 300m mountains to the Great Ormes Head from the northeastern part of Snowdonia. Tal y Fan, Llwytmor, Bera Mawr, Foel Grach and other peaks form a ridge with just a couple of clefts carved by the Afon Ogwen and Afon Rhaeadr-fawr. In the estuary of the former is a nature reserve. Beyond the latter Gwynedd gives way to Conwy.

The shoreline approaching **Llanfairfechan** past the Bryn-y-neuadd Hospital is well protected by a sea wall built in 1953, over which there is no obvious route from the resort to the beach. On the east side of the Afon Maes-y-bryn is a carpark with toilets, café and children's playground.

Llanfairfechan is a long established village with an ancient settlement although the most conspicuous feature is the one which is to dominate much of this coast, the A55 North Wales Expressway. It is a coast which throws up agate, jasper and serpentine along its length and is a popular holiday coast because of its proximity to Liverpool and Manchester. There is a small sailing club in the village.

Home to bass, Conwy Bay's eastgoing stream runs southeast towards Penmaen-bach Point. First, however, comes Penmaen-Mawr Point, a high peak above a bold headland which pushes right to the sea and constricts communications, as shown by the headland's viaducts and tunnels. A major engineering success in 1850 was the opening of the Chester & Holyhead Railway. This was an important part of the connection between England and Ireland,

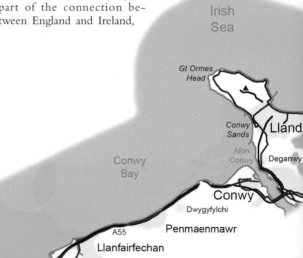

which had to overcome many difficulties. Heavy coastal protection was needed for 70km of the route. This was the most exposed point and engineer in chief Robert Stevenson watched 12m waves destroy a section of the 500m solid masonry wall in 1846. He

Distinctive pierhead structures at Bangor.

replaced it with the Penmaenmawr Sea Viaduct, a 170m open viaduct of 13 spans protected by an apron with large boulders set in concrete and protected by piles. Brick arches superseded the timber and cast iron deck in 1908 but it still serves its purpose of dissipating energy as the sea surges through and around the piers. It feeds into the 230m Penmaenmawr tunnel which is extended at each end by avalanche shelters to protect against rockfalls. The danger remains and a series of unsightly fences have been strung across the slope to protect the new road.

There are disused quarries above, formerly served by a jetty for loading the stone, and the site dates from the Stone Age when there was an axe factory with axes exported as far as London and Ireland.

Penmaenmawr means large stone head. The village was the favourite holiday resort of Gladstone and attracts present day bathers, waterskiers and sailors.

The railway is protected by a 6m wall which was partly destroyed in 1945 and rebuilt in reinforced concrete.

Tyno Helig was a 6th century kingdom 3km out from the present coast, allegedly drowned for the sins of King Helig ap Glannawg. A 1939 investigation of 2ha of undersea ruins showed them to be natural rock.

The Afon Conwy emerges between golf courses and discharges across the extensive Conwy Sands which have mussel banks in places. Behind the Conwy Morfa golf course is the town of **Conwy** and its castle of 1283, which replaced Deganwy Castle, the destruction of which in 822 was the last major achievement of the Mercians. Not visible is the A55 river crossing in

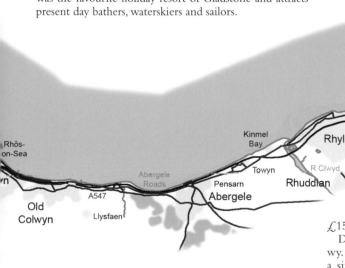

Beyond Dwygyfylchi is Penmaen-bach Point, capped by a fort site on Alltwen, the northern extremity of the Snowdonia range and the end of the Snowdon National Park. Again, the cliffs forced the coaching road and railway builders to use cliff shelves and tunnels. There now three tunnels including a conspicuous new one carrying the westbound carriageway of the A55.

Britain's first immersed tube tunnel, environmentally hidden by the estuary instead of using a bridge which would have been £15,000,000 cheaper.

Deganwy was Dinas Conwy, the fortress on the Conwy. The castle was built between 1244 and 1254 on a site which had been fortified since at least the 9th century. It was fought over and destroyed many times, once by lightning, abandoned in 1263 and reoccupied in 1277. The two hillocks formed natural mottes, the east one being defended by a large open backed U-plan tower while its counterpart formed an inner bailey with curtain wall, hall and large round tower. Between them was a large irregular oval bailey with curtain wall and gatehouse.

303

The remains of old fish traps on Bangor Flats.

Tidal streams flow up to 9km/h into the channel from HW Dover –0500 and ebb from HW Dover –0030. A floating pontoon moored in the estuary is marked 'Rescue'.

Llandudno, Wales' largest seaside resort, was built in the mid-19th century by Edward Mostyn and Owen Williams on a tombolo joining the former island of Great Orme to the mainland. They transformed the marshland into gracious terraces of Victorian elegance which still have some of the best shops in North Wales, the many large hotels proving popular for conferences.

On the West Shore are a putting green, children's playground, paddling pool and statue of the White Rabbit, unveiled in 1933 by Lloyd-George as a reminder that Henry Liddell's family had a holiday home here and that it was on this beach that Lewis Carroll used to stroll with Alice while composing *Alice's Adventures in Wonderland*.

Running across the throat of the Great Ormes Head is a raised path which passes through an aviary and semitropical gardens, drawing attention to the mild climate, and past dozens of benches donated by or in memory of people who have enjoyed holidays in the town.

The final building on the West Shore is the Gogarth Abbey Hotel, the remains of the bishop's palace itself being a little further along at the hamlet of Gogarth where the most conspicuous feature now is a tower on the shore, approached by a walkway from on top of the cliffs.

Near the end of the Great Ormes Head are half a dozen gun emplacements, approached on the landward side down a long flight of steps. They face towards the Gwynt y Mor offshore windfarm, the world's second largest with 250 turbines. The cliff itself can be subject to fierce downdraughts.

The Great Ormes Head is a country park with Carboniferous mountain limestone cliffs up to 120m high and a limestone pavement. A copper mine in use from 1900 to 900 BC removed some 200t of copper from 5km of passages to 70m deep, some so small that they would have needed to have been worked by children, and included two large halls with smelting and drainage facilities. The grass here is rich in unusual plants and is inhabited by feral goats, descendants of a royal pair from Windsor released in 1900, and the grayling thyone and silver studded blue butterflies which are unique to the Great Orme, as is the wild cotoneaster. The limestone is sculpted and on the north side of the head are several caves including Hornby Cave, a sanctuary for sealife of all kinds with grey seals here and common seals further east as far as the Dee estuary. Pigeon Cave has a way out to the cliffs above. St Tudno built a chapel on top of the head in the 6th century, replaced by the present church in the 12th century, restored in 1855. Nearby is his well.

There is a tide race off the head on springs with

The tunnels, viaducts and fences of Penmaen-Mawr Point.

The Conwy estuary seen from the Great Ormes Head with the West Shore in the foreground and Snowdonia peaks rising behind.

large waves in opposing winds and clapotis up to 100m offshore but useful eddies close in to the cliffs if the flow is adverse. Marine Drive runs precariously round the cliff and new benching had to be cut in 1990 after a cliff fall. The top can be reached by Victorian tramway or cable car. Below the disused Great Ormes lighthouse are steep cliffs with row upon row of guillemots.

Happy Valley has an open air theatre. The ornate Llandudno Pier runs 900m out into Ormes Bay. Built in 1876 by John Dixon to a James Brunless and Alexander McKerrow design, it has an 18m T-shaped pierhead and 11 kiosks with an arm connecting along the shore with the pavilion. The 1902 Great Orme Railway, Britain's only rope hauled road tramway, climbs up to the 207m summit. With a hotel on top, from here it is possible to see the Isle of Man and Cumbria on a clear day plus a lot of the Welsh coast nearby. Also running up it is the Cabin Lift, Britain's longest cablecar railway at 1.6km. This small headland is dotted with many features of interest, a burial chamber, Stone Row, St Tudno's Well and an aerial to name but a few.

Water skiing, sailing and sometimes surfing take place in Ormes Bay or Llandudno Bay where tidal streams are negligible. From here to Point of Ayr streams generally run up to 6km/h, starting east at HW Dover −0610 and west from HW at Dover, protected from the north by the Constable Bank.

In Arnold Bennett's *The Card* Denry Machin established a lucrative operation to take trippers out to the wreck of the *Hjalmar* in the former *Llandudno* lifeboat, with associated photographic and confectionery businesses. It was the nearest shopping town for Llanabba Castle in *Decline & Fall*.

The bay ends with the Little Ormes Head, another Carboniferous limestone cliff and pavement block with rich grassland and unusual plants but this time with a conspicuous disused brown quarry. The vertical cliffs are actually higher than on the Great Orme and attract guillemots, razorbills, puffins, fulmars and climbers.

Penrhyn Bay was formerly the mouth of the Conwy until it was diverted by the Irish Sea ice sheet in the Ice Age, dredging up marine shells which can be seen in the subsequent boulder clay cliffs.

Off the shallow boulder strewn beach there are bass, conger eels, flounders, mackerel, mullet, plaice, prawns and rays. At low tide the remains of triangular walls built as fish traps by monks can be seen at Rhôs-on-Sea. On the shore are the remains of the 16th century chapel of St Trillo, a mere 3.6m x 1.8m, also associated with the monastery.

Great Orme Tramway car at the terminus.

Marine Drive runs around Great Ormes Head.

Llandudno Pier with a wind farm beyond.

A wreck lies off Rhos Point while boats generally shelter behind a detached breakwater of stone which forms a makeshift harbour at this waterskiing and bathing venue. In *The Card* the first lifeboat rescue was of a schooner here by the Prestatyn lifeboat. Just south of the harbour is the landing point for submarine cables from Heysham and the Isle of Man. The village is overlooked by the hilltop sites of an ancient settlement and Llys Euryn but its most notable building is the Harlequin Puppet Theatre, built in 1958 by Eric Bramall and employing 1,000 puppets in a season of plays, operas, musical comedies and cabarets. Productions have ranged from *The Mikado* and *The Nutcracker Suite* to *Alice's Adventures in Wonderland*.

Colwyn Bay has negligible tidal streams. Notable is an air dome building near the civic centre. Less obvious from the sea are the promenade miniature railway, Eirias Park's amusements, the indoor pool or the fact that **Colwyn Bay** was the proud holder of the Royal Mail award for being the most successful twin town in the UK at improving world harmony (however that was assessed). Harmony cannot have been improved by the busy transport corridor which separates this resort from the beach with its bathing, waterskiing and sailing, the A55 running along the shore as far as Abergele and the railway following the coast to Flint.

An arc of footbridge rises, Le Mans style, over the road as the Denbigh Moors reach the coast at **Old Colwyn**. Mynydd Marian was formerly the site of Llysfaen Telegraph Station and remains the site of limestone quarrying operations from where stone is loaded onto ships up to 3,000t at 900t/h from the 220m Raynes Jetty and 200m Llysfaen Jetty. There have been frequent landslips at Llysfaen and this section of A55 is protected by a slope of rock pieces up to 1t each topped by 22,000 5t dolos units which make landing extremely difficult. The A547 on top of the cliff is supported by a great concrete arch which appears to be a bridge which does not clear a gap, there being only solid rock visible below the arch.

There was a terrible railway accident in 1868 when a string of railway wagons loaded with paraffin rolled down from the quarry into the path of the Irish Mail. At that time the carriages were lit by gas and passengers were locked into the compartments for safety. No fewer than 33 people died and were buried in St Michael's churchyard, **Abergele**. As a result, until recently, railway carriages were no longer locked, for the safety of passengers.

The cliff pulls back behind Abergele Roads where it is topped by a prominent tower with more fortifications down below. Much larger, however, is the 1815 Grade I folly of Gwrych Castle with its 18 towers, possibly to be converted to a hotel. Offshore is a worm reef.

Seaside amusements and donkey rides are available at Pensarn, the beach where Captain Matthew Webb trained to become the first person to swim the English Channel in 1875.

Belgrano and Towyn seem to be one large static caravan site hiding behind the railway embankment, the Cob. Some 1.8km of shingle beach and groynes are followed by the 1.3km Rhuddlan Marsh wall, first embanked in 1800 by the trustees and improved in 1880 when the LNWR took over. In January 1990 the embankment was breached during a storm and Towyn flooded to a considerable depth. Eventually the water was mopped up and houses redecorated, only to discover subsidence setting in. Meanwhile, embankment protection work was undertaken and in technical circles there was hot debate as to whether such embankments (of which there were plenty in Wales) should remain the responsibility of British Rail or whether they should be managed by councils or the Environment Agency, the latter seeming to have drawn the greatest support.

In quieter times Towyn has harness racing, swimming and other seaside amusements. Swimming and donkey rides are also popular at Kinmel Bay, which has a funfair at each end.

The River Clwyd, which follows the strike faulting of the Vale of Clwyd and forms the Conwy/Denbighshire border, emerges inconspicuously past the Marine Lake in **Rhyl**. It discharges between a sewer running out to a buoy on the west side and revetment on the east side, producing dangerous currents as it leaves the Grade II Foryd Harbour. Sea defences have been upgraded to reduce the risk of flooding of low lying areas. The Marine Lake has waterskiing, windsurfing, pedaloes, sailing dinghies and a minature railway round the outside. Rhyl is made for holidaymakers, ever since Liverpool residents were brought by paddle steamer, but the wreck of the *City of Ottawa* shows it can be less welcoming, as does a plaque recording where Deputy Prime Minister John Prescott punched somebody who threw an egg at him. Poet Adrian Henri attended the grammar school after his family moved out of Liverpool. The Sports Centre has a heated pool and there is a paddling pool. There is a roller skateboarding rink, Superbowl tenpin bowling, Pavilion Theatre, a 76m Sky Tower overlooking the town imported from the Glasgow Garden Festival, and Botanical Gardens and still they have to take shopping trolleys on the beach and abandon them in the intertidal zone. There is a helicopter landing site on the promenade near the hospital. A Rhyl confectioner was used in producing the chocolate featured in Arnold Bennett's *The Card*.

Behind the groynes of Ffrith beach is a golf course which produces a break in the buildings before further coastal protection work and the holiday camps of **Prestatyn**. Another holiday resort, Prestatyn has a large amusement park with vintage cars, motorboat pool and go kart and motorcycle tracks.

The station is particularly interesting as one of the few remaining single storey prefabricated station buildings produced at Crewe at the end of the 19th century. In 2m panels, the timber frame was faced with rusticated boarding, canopies with valances cantilevered out over the platform on timber beams and brickwork used for footings, fireplaces and chimneys. When it was rebuilt in 1979 the style was retained.

Prestatyn is located at the northern end of the Clwydian Hills (with their radio masts) and is at the end of the Offa's Dyke Long Distance Path. Nova Prestatyn is claimed to be North Wales' premier venue for leisure and entertainment. Carol Vorderman was brought up in the town and John Prescott was born here.

Behind the dunes to the east of the town is a river which eventually seeps away into the sand as it crosses the Denbighshire/Flintshire border and nears another holiday camp. The Warren continues to Point of Ayr where there is a conspicuous disused lighthouse on the beach at Talacre, a wreck, sandpipers and often a flock of cormorants drying their wings.

Unlike the days when sailing ships used to travel up the estuary of the River Dee to Chester, silting has resulted in the whole area largely drying at low tide, West Hoyle Bank drying up to 10km from the entrance. Pilots are picked up at Dee south cardinal lightbuoy, northeast of Point of Ayr on the far side of the Welsh Channel. At the east end of the Welsh Channel the flood runs northeast, becoming easterly at HW Dover −0530, reaching 5km/h at HW Dover −0240 and turning northerly at HW Dover −0015. Near springs it runs up to 7km/h between HW Dover −0330 and −0130. The ebb begins at HW Dover +0015, west northwest, becoming northwest at up to 4km/h. Above Point of Ayr the streams run in the channels when the banks are exposed, otherwise running directly in and out. The navigation difficulties keep the estuary empty for the birds and it is mostly a SSSI.

The North Hoyle windfarm is conspicuous in Liverpool Bay. Windfarms include the 40km² Burbo Bank Extension farm with the world's largest turbines, sporting 80m long blades.

To the south of Talacre was Point of Ayr Colliery, one of the last two pits in North Wales. Workings ran out under the sea for 2km and it was the scene of investigations for making oil from coal. A gas terminal has been proposed for Point of Ayr, causing consternation to the RSPB. Natterjack toads live on the dunes.

Wild Road runs past Mostyn Bank off Ffynnongroyw to Mostyn Quay, the last harbour in the estuary which can be reached by seagoing ships, resulting in its selection as a windfarm service port and for transferring Airbus

The disused Point of Ayr lighthouse with the North Hoyle windfarm on the horizon.

A380 wings, brought by barge from Broughton, to a ferry for the onward journey to Toulouse. A 650m training wall is adjacent to a recent Irish Ro Ro terminal. Ironworks have been replaced by small factories and workshops. The quay imports wood products, clay, fertilizer and animal foods and exports steel and cement. Several cranes surround the quay and it has pillbox defence arrangements on the training wall.

A coarse seawall leads to Llannerch-y-môr, a small creek dominated by what was planned as the Fun Ship, the former cruise ship *Duke of Lancaster*, now beached high and dry. The dock has been considered for a yacht marina but nothing has come of it. On the west side of the stream is a craft centre with a large carparking area and parking may also be possible on the east side in an open air market site. Unless the tide is high enough to reach the railway bridge it would pay to disembark on the east side of the creek to avoid the security defences around the ship.

The Duke of Lancaster *at Llanerch-y-môr.*

Distance
75km from Menai Bridge to Llanerch-y-môr

OS 1:50,000 Sheets
115 Snowdon
116 Denbigh & Colwyn Bay

Tidal Constants
Menai Bridge:
HW Dover −0030
LW Dover
Beaumaris:
HW Dover −0030
LW Dover
Llandudno:
Dover −0010
Colwyn Bay:
HW Dover −0010
LW Dover +0010
Mostyn Quay:
Dover

Sea Area
Irish Sea

Connection
Afon Conwy – see RoB p60

55 Merseyside

Silted estuaries given over to the birds

Now no more the big cranes lie idle
the ships are fast turnin' round,
they're buildin' new docks up at Seaforth
all part of our own holy ground.
Now Liverpool is on the move
the sleepin' giant awakes,
the greatest port in all the world
and we've got what it takes.
So when I die, don't bury me
in Anfield or in Ford,
just lock me in a container
for the crane to lift on board,
for the crane to lift on board.

JB Jaques

From Llannerch-y-môr the main channel follows the southwest side of the estuary to Greenfield. Cenwulf died at Basingwerk in 821, possibly preparing to harry the Welsh. Basingwerk Abbey was founded about 1132 but acquired an unusual reputation for an abbey in the 15th century when there were many guests, fine wines and good food served in two sittings. Archbishop Baldwin and Gerald of Wales sampled the hospitality in *The Journey through Wales*. Owain Gwynedd took up position here while his sons Dafydd and Cynan prepared an ambush of Henry II in the Battle of Coed Eulo in 1157.

One of the ugliest pieces of seawall anywhere is of very broken reinforced concrete, the whole resembling a mass of giant, rusty wirewool. In better days the site imported Anglesey copper for sheeting ship hulls and served pilgrims. Water was retained for flushing out the harbour at low water. At Holywell Bank the flood starts at HW Dover −0445 and lasts for five hours. Conditions in the estuary should not be underestimated although the estuary is much used by small boats and an army of cockle collectors may be seen humping sacks of shells around on the Holywell Bank before returning to points such as Bagillt, where there are three disused wharves.

Flint has housed chemical works at various times. Flint Castle stands nearby. The first of Edward I's chain of castles in North Wales, it was built between 1277 and 1286 on the edge of the sea for replenishment. With a square inner bailey with curtain wall and three round towers, it was unusual in that the three storey round keep was detached from the rest of the fortifications and surrounded by its own moat, now dry. It also has the stoutest walls in the UK, 7m thick. This is where Shakespeare claims Bolingbroke forced Richard II to surrender although Conwy Castle is more likely. The town's dock and approach channel have now silted up.

The River Dee proper emerges under a striking cable stayed bridge between the power station at Connah's Quay and the former Shotton steelworks. To travel along the northeast shore of the estuary needs careful attention to tide levels as most of the estuary dries, leaving wastes with just curlews, terns and other birds.

A large area of marsh at the head of the estuary is a danger area because of Sealand Ranges but it should not be a problem anywhere deep enough to float a boat.

The shore crosses from the Welsh county of Flintshire briefly into the English county of Cheshire & W Chester as it approaches **Neston**, the birthplace of Lady Hamilton, where the Grade II church of St Mary & St Helen has notable Edward Burne-Jones stained glass windows. It had a coal mine at one time.

Perhaps nowhere illustrates the change in the estuary better than at Parkgate. When Chester silted up in the 18th century this shrimping village became the embarkation point for Irish packet boats after Neston was used for a time and suffered the same problem but it also had a shipyard. Today it is fronted by up to 2km of spartina grass marsh, even at high water, and water is not even visible across Gayton Sands for much of the time.

Dawpool Bank performs a similar function for Heswall, the next major place on the Wirral peninsula after crossing from Cheshire & W Chester into Merseyside. **Heswall** Hill is red Keuper sandstone with gorse. Along its foot, behind the sewage works on the shore, is the 19km long Wirral Country Park on a former railway line.

Thurstaston Common is the same sandstone and gorse, acid heath rich in insect life, including Thor's Stone, a 7.6m pinnacle of weathered sandstone. The area is used for orienteering and the major building is Thurstaston Hall.

The sandstone and gorse continue to Caldy Hill with its two radio masts, off which lie Caldy Blacks sands, and

Flint Castle, the start of Edward I's chain, looks out over the waters of the Dee estuary.

the land finally drops away at **West Kirby** with Tell's Tower, the Grange Monument and the War Memorial all visible. Along the front is the 13ha Marine Lake with sailing dinghies, sailboards, rowing boats and canoes. The village at the end of the MerseyRail line and on the A540 was the setting of the film *Letter to Brezhnev* in 1984.

Offshore is a Bunter sandstone ridge which gets bigger as it runs out from Caldy Blacks through Seldom Seen Rocks, Lime Wharf, Tanskey Rocks, Little Eye and Little Hilbre Island to Hilbre Island itself, all of which are accessible on foot for half of the tide cycle and have many Ordovician, Silurian and Carboniferous fossils. The last two islands have 17m cliffs on the southwest side. An idea of the rate of erosion is given by the fact that the islands were all linked and covered 3km^2 in the 17th century, having provided camping space for 4,000 soldiers and 200 cavalry on their way to Ireland a century before. Today Hilbre Island covers 4ha, Little Hilbre Island 1ha and Little Eye 2,000m^2 at high tide.

The Devil's Hole cave on Little Hilbre Island was used by smugglers while Lady's Cave on Hilbre Island takes its name from a shipwrecked woman fleeing her father, living here until she died. There was a small religious community before the arrival of the Norsemen in 905. After the Norman Conquest it was given to the Abbey of St Evroul, who maintained a small cell and shrine to St Hildenburgh, and there was a small order of Benedictine monks until 1541 when the parent abbey at Chester was suppressed. The buildings of a former telegraph station are now used by the keeper and staff of what is an important nature reserve. Most of the Dee estuary is a grade 1 SSSI and Special Protection Area under the EU Birds Directive. The RSPB claimed that the 100,000 wildfowl and waders, including 30,000 oystercatchers, 5,500 shelducks, 4,200 teal, 7,200 pintails, 1,800 grey plovers, 17,000 knots, 14,000 dunlin and 7,000 redshanks, were threatened with immediate and permanent damage because of waste tipping, port expansion, road development, pollution and recreation. The bird observatory is one of the finest sites in England for observing and photographing overwintering waders with over 1,000 birds ringed annually and 221 species recorded, including large flocks of curlews, ringtailed plovers, bartailed godwits and sanderlings. A number of hides include one in the stonework of the building which formerly acted as the lifeboat station at the top of its slipway. A wooden building houses Mersey Canoe Club, Britain's second such club, no longer active as a sports club but with some early canoes stored inside.

On the West Hoyle Bank opposite the island is a favourite spot for grey seals to sun themselves, often 100–200 at a time, their presence clearly audible as well as visible.

The golf course of the Royal Liverpool Club, the first to host the British Amateur in 1885, International Amateur in 1902 and English Amateur Championships in 1925, leads to Hilbre Point which ends with Red Rocks, the end of the Dee estuary and start of Liverpool Bay. The disused lighthouse in **Hoylake** (lake by the hillock) is followed by a bathing pool using seawater. The East Hoyle Bank forms a 3km wide beach where sand filled Hoyle Lake as the Dee silted up.

Leasowe lighthouse is also disused. Initially, the shifting sand was not firm

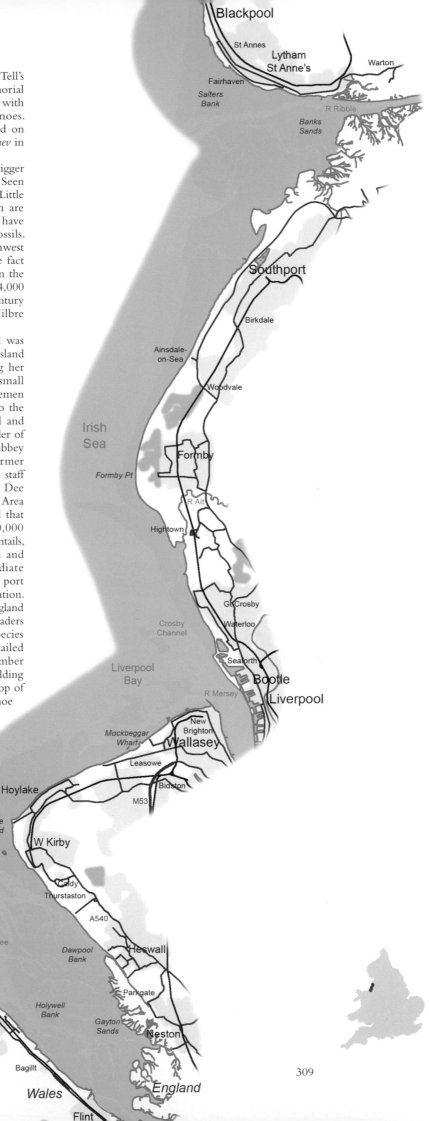

enough to support a tower but a wreck in 1760 deposited cotton bales on the beach. These were left to rot and the ensuing vegetation formed the sand into a base strong enough to support the tower.

Mockbeggar Wharf is sinking at 9mm/year and has caused concern that the Mersey might cut another exit, with all the problems that would cause for the port of Liverpool. To prevent this happening and to keep the sea from the low central part of the Wirral the Wallasey Embankment was started in 1794. The sand, clay, silt and peat structure was only partly successful so in 1829 2.7km of Old Embankment was built, 600mm of clay overlain with 200mm to 500mm sandstone blocks. In 1894 the 3.6km New Embankment extended it and a toe wall was added to prevent undercutting. In 1941 it was faced with 150mm of concrete in 4m squares which have since broken up, requiring a major rebuild to be started in 1973. The fight against the sea goes on.

Behind the wall is the North Wirral Country Park and four golf courses surrounding **Wallasey**, which takes its name from the Old English for island of the Welsh. Leasowe Castle, built four centuries ago by Ferdinand, the second heir to the throne, is now a hotel. The tree covered Bidston Hill, another outcrop of red Keuper sandstone, is 40ha of heathland with a windmill, a former lighthouse and an observatory famous for its tidal predicitions and research. At the foot of the hill is Bidston Moss, on which is Bidston Moss Interchange at the northern end of the M53, its elevated structures built on the longest piles in Europe. In the 1960s St George's school in Wallasey became the world's first heated by solar power.

New Brighton has a breakwater of dolosse units, one of several breakwater structures scattered about this section of the coast. Groynes run out into the sea but that was clearly not all, the smell of sewage being particularly strong and all too clearly visible until the Mersey estuary sewerage scheme was undertaken. A bathing pool allowed visitors an alternative. A marine boating

lake was the scene of a double murder in the haze in *The Adventure of the Cardboard Box*. As lifer is Old English for sludge, it seems that Liverpool had not benefitted from clean water for some while.

New Brighton grew in prosperity on the ferry connection to **Liverpool** from its former pier. Its most prominent features are tower blocks with the 52m spire of Grade II St James' church nestling between them, the tallest spire on the Wirral. The New Brighton Tower of 1898 was even more notable, the tallest building in Britain until it fell into disuse and was demolished in 1921. Perch Rock bears the former Rock Lighthouse and Fort Perch from 1826, now the Museum of the War Plane Wreck Investigation Group with associated tea rooms and nature trail. Indeed, wrecks seem to be the general feature of the area, the Brazil Bank and Great Burbo Bank being littered with them. Powerboat racers try to add more and there is a significant tide race past the end of Perch Rock. The night time land breeze can be stronger than might be expected.

The Crosby Channel of the River Mersey is edged by training banks. Streams flow in the channel when the banks are dry but take a direct line when they are covered. Flood flows in the channel set eastwards while the ebb set is northwest, both strong on springs. At Perch Rock the flow is up to 9km/h. The river is used by tankers up to 200,000t and the *Mersey Channel Collision Rules* need to be read as the penalties for causing an accident are heavy. There is least traffic in the river at low tide. Among the commercial traffic are passenger ferries for Dublin and Llandudno and vehicle ferries for Belfast, Dublin and Douglas, the passing landmarks towards which were ticked off in *Anna of the Five Towns*.

The Mersey used to discharge via the Dee at Shotton but the present channel was possibly opened up by an ice sheet. Crossing the rivermouth from the Wirral to Sefton it is possible to see up to Birkenhead and Liverpool with the Royal Liver Building and the Cunard Tower. The tall ships have also left from here.

Ten kilometres of docks end at **Bootle**. Despite the

Anthony Gormley's Another Place and the Royal Seaforth Docks and Port Radar Station seen from the Crosby Channel.

loss of trade from Liverpool, this is still our seventh busiest port, not least because of the Royal Seaforth Docks with over 3km of quays, including the Seaforth Container Dock Terminal which handles ships up to 75,000t. This revolutionized Liverpool as a port with the world's first computer controlled container operations. There are roll on roll off facilities and berths for bulk liquids, meat and grain. Six wind turbines lead to the Port Radar Station, a striking mushroom shaped tower at the northwest end.

Waterloo was the place wealthy Liverpool merchants chose to build their houses in the Regency and Victorian eras. Its largest feature is a 24ha marina with sailing and canoeing, a model boating lake, children's playground, heated indoor pool and bowling and putting greens.

To the north is Great Crosby. In Norse days Crosby meant place of the crosses. These days it has Anthony Gormley's Another Place or the Iron Men, a hundred cast iron statues of naked men, moulded off himself, on the beach facing out to sea over a wide extent of beach from the docks to the River Alt, popular with the locals. They do form hazards to small boats operating within the intertidal zone.

The present day settlement ends abruptly with a golf course and then the coast seems more rural but this does not mean that it is time to relax. At Hightown on the River Alt are the Altcar ranges, firing at surface targets up to 2.4km from the coast. Notwithstanding, it seems an acceptable place for little gulls which are present all year round in the vicinity of Crosby Beacon.

Wrecks litter the shoreline from Formby Bank to Mad Wharf and out onto Taylor's Bank which reaches out to form the northern side of the Queen's Channel at low tide. Beyond this are the Douglas, Hamilton, Hamilton North and Lennox oil and gas fields. Tides flood straight in and ebb straight out.

The coastline has become entirely of sand dunes by Formby Point and 7km² of these, dotted with SSSIs, continue to Southport. As Mesolithic and Neolithic silt layers are eroded away they briefly reveal lines of prehistoric footprints. Near another beacon can be found the remains of the first lifeboat station, in use from 1776 to 1916. The sea has been encroaching for 700 years and Mad Wharf sands dry up to 2km offshore, welcomed by many waders including oystercatchers and sanderlings. A line of tide poles run out from the point. A screen of trees, home of red squirrels, block out **Formby**, a commuter town for Liverpool after the railway arrived in the 19th century. The name is derived from the Norse man Forni. It has been used for filming *Hilary & Jackie*.

Formby Golf Club has hosted the British Amateur Championship.

Ainsdale Sands beyond Woodvale Airfield have black-headed gulls on the beach and a National Nature Reserve behind the dunes which have developed since the 16th century with rich flora, sand lizards, natterjack toads and red squirrels. For all that, there is plenty of human activity. Pontin's holiday park at Ainsdale-on-Sea is housing Edge Hill University students during term time, a sensible use of the premises during quiet periods. There is waterskiing and a 16km/h speed limit on the beach, dating from the time when the sands were used as a road, the speed limit not being applied when motor races take place on the sands. Indeed, the sands at Southport were used for world record speed attempts. Birkdale Sands have an aircraft runway marked out below the high tide area and the sands are also used for training racehorses. The Trans Pennine Trail with horses at a more sedate pace follows to its terminus at Southport. Behind are the Birkdale Hills, the location of the Royal Birkdale golf course, which has hosted the British Open.

A length of road along the shore holds a lesson for road builders. This road was built across a former rubbish tip, was underdesigned and went into a switchback shape. At the legal speed limit its undulations give an interesting but not uncomfortable ride without damaging suspensions but, thereafter, the ride quickly becomes unpleasant, the ideal hump solution that was discovered by accident.

Southport is claimed to be the golfing capital of England. It is a mainly Victorian and Edwardian watering hole. Author Nathaniel Hawthorne lived here while American Consul in Liverpool. The Parisian look of the main street is spoiled only by the many posters proclaiming that entertainers and pop groups last heard of several decades ago are alive and well and performing the summer season here. Harvey Preston, on the German side in *The Eagle Has Landed*, had earlier been in rep at Southport. Behind the 35ha Marine Lake with powerboats, sailing, rowing and jet skis, is the heart of Southport's life. Pleasureland has over 50 attractions. There is a Blue Planet Aquarium, 1:12, Floral Hall with one of the country's major flower festivals (the Southport Flower Show in August), botanic gardens, 6.7 x 4.9m Lakeside Inn next to Southport Theatre and golf courses. The pier was the first true pleasure pier and was the longest in the country at 1.1km when it opened in 1860, extended to 1.3km in the first decade of its life but subsequently shortened after repeated storm damage. The original tramway has been replaced with a miniature

The remains of the very first lifeboat station on Formby Point.

railway and there are modern amusement facilities, bar, café and shops. Now, back to its original length, it is still the second longest pier in Britain and the longest over land. Sadly, however, there is no approach channel and at low tide the sea is 3km away across Southport Sands.

The flat sands spawn a profusion of unlikely vehicles in addition to the hovercraft making trips to St Anne's. Shrimpers use tractors in the sea or lorries with raised flat beds and large cabs with noticeably fewer windows than might be expected. These lorries seem almost sinister as they move slowly and quietly across the sand before driving into the sea and trailing their nets. Taken with diggers and dump trucks working to extract aggregate from the sands, the area can be more like a construction site on a wet day than the sea.

The Ribble estuary at high tide is a 10km long triangle penetrating inland, its southeast side edged by up to 3km of Banks Marsh with its many drainage channels and its northeast side edged by Lytham St Anne's. At low tide, however, it is totally different, an almost straight coastine, the river discharging and flooding in the Gut Channel between two irregular training walls at up to 3km/h. At this stage the estuary is an almost unbroken expanse of sandbanks which are a Special Protection Area under the EU Birds Directive.

Crossens roost may have 150,000 waders present. The estuary is one of the top five European wildfowl areas and has the second largest British group of pinkfooted geese (10,000), the fourth largest concentration of common terns and the fifth largest blackheaded gullery. Numbers include 470 Bewick's swans, 290 whooper swans, 12,000 oystercatchers, 2,700 grey plovers, 12,000 bar tailed godwits, 35,000 knots, 2,200 sanderlings, 1,600 redshanks 4,000 shelduck, 60,000 wigeon and 4,800 teal, The RSPB claimed the estuary was in immediate danger of permanent damage to the bird colonies by marinas, land reclamation, waste disposal and recreation. Birds which sit unperturbed on the sands or continue squabbles already in progress as fighter aircraft thunder overhead on low level training flights up the estuary seem to suggest that it will take quite a lot to upset their present way of life.

It is an area with few features although there is a wreck off Horse Bank and numerous stakes on Marshside Sands. Over the course of Banks Sands the sand gives way to mud and Sefton gives way to Lancashire as the estuary tapers down to the river proper.

Used by the Typhoon or Eurofighter, Warton Aerodrome's main runway is angled over the estuary at Warton Bank, just above the entry point of the Main Drain, the eastern limit of **Lytham St Anne's**. The most prominent feature on the north shore is a white windmill set amongst the churches of Lytham. Although it looks pristine its machinery was destroyed in 1929 when a gust of wind spun the sails the wrong way. It contains a display of milling and bread. Lytham takes its name from the Old English hlith, slope, although the whole area is notably flat.

The north shore is Lancashire but the refined nature of Lytham St Anne's is out of character for all of this part of the coast. There is a lack of brashness and the coastal entertainments are more conservative. Lowther Gardens and Fairhaven Lake between them offer flower beds, bowling greens, tennis courts, indoor pool, yachting, motor boating, rowing, canoeing, water skiing, launch trips, paddling and a model yacht pool. Royal Lytham & St Annes Golf Club has hosted the Open and the first Ladies' Championship.

The 140m St Anne's Pier of 1885 has a mock Tudor entrance, added last century, and has also suffered the loss of some of its structure. It faces onto Salter's Bank which leads out to Stanner Point, 5km away at low tide. The waters can be difficult. A monument close by relates to an incident in 1816 when the lifeboat and its 13 crew plus 14 of the 16 crew of the Southport lifeboat were lost while trying to reach the barque *Mexico* and, as a result, improvements were made to lifeboat design.

St Annes is the quieter and more reserved end of the town, predominantly Victorian and Edwardian villas. There is parking at North Hollow although this beach is used as a sand yachting centre with the national championships and other major events being held here. The beach runs the risk of being a racecourse at these times and it is not the ideal occasion to try to cross.

Distance
79km from Llanerch-y-môr to Lytham St Anne's

OS 1:50,000 Sheets
102 Preston & Blackpool
108 Liverpool
116 Denbigh & Colwyn Bay
117 Chester & Wrexham

Tidal Constants
Mostyn Quay: Dover
Connah's Quay: HW Dover +0020 LW Dover +0400
Hilbre Island: Dover
New Brighton: Dover
Formby: HW Dover LW Dover −0010
Southport: Dover
Blackpool: Dover

Sea Area
Irish Sea

Ranges:
Sealand, Altcar

Connections
River Dee – see RoB p64
River Mersey – see RoB p71

The windmill at Lytham.

Morecambe Bay

There's a famous seaside place called Blackpool,
That's noted for fresh air and fun,
And Mr. and Mrs. Ramsbottom
Went there with young Albert, their son.

They didn't think much to the Ocean:
The waves, they was fiddlin' and small,
There was no wrecks and nobody drownded,
Fact, nothing to laugh at at all.
Marriott Edgar

Weak tide streams are found between the Ribble and Morecambe Bay although the coast is affected by the wind. Lytham St Anne's ends suddenly with a golf course and Blackpool Airport, the country's first commercial airport, at Squires Gate. Aircraft take off out to sea, flying fast and low over the holiday camp at the west end of the main runway.

Lancashire becomes Blackpool. The town of **Blackpool** lies entirely to the east of the A584 which runs along the top of cliffs with a seawall at their foot. The beach, until recently 500m wide at low tide but disappearing at high tide, has had its straight seawall rebuilt in 2011 with five wavy headlands, the first major use of concrete reinforced with GRP rather than steel to prevent corrosion staining the surfaces. Large precast concrete pebbles act as seats. The town, which has the oldest population in the UK at average age 43.2, has had to develop other more reliable attractions than the beach.

The cliff road is also the line of the Blackpool–Fleetwood tramway which runs from Starr Gate to Fleetwood Ferry Terminal. It opened in 1885 as the world's first electrical street tramway with standard 1.435m gauge, taking power from an underground conduit. In 1899 overhead lines were introduced and other routes were added until 1920. Closures began in 1936 and now only this one remains. Two of the early vehicles can be seen in the Crich Tramway Museum.

Despite its Old English name, Blackpool didn't develop seriously until the railway came in 1846 but it has gone on developing ever since, the emphasis being on pure unashamed pleasure. It has more Victorian and Edwardian entertainment features than anywhere else. The playground of the north of England and Britain's largest holiday resort, it is Britain's leading tourist attraction and draws over 10,000,000 visitors per year. Blackpool is synonymous with rock, the largest stick of which was 430mm in diameter and weighed 410kg. The town was the home of the precursor of Jaguar cars. It has meant illuminations with 1,000,000 lights, lasers, animated displays and tableaux, extending the season, and claims to have had the world's first electric street lighting since 1879. The station searchlight is compared with Blackpool in *Nil Carborundum*. It is also one of the small number of towns which benefit from being on the conference circuit. It has ice and roller skating rinks, a boating lake, a model village, donkey rides, boat trips, Punch & Judy shows and much more.

This peaks at the Pleasure Beach on the South Shore, opened in 1896 and claimed to be Europe's greatest amusement park. Here are the Revolution, Sir Hiram Maxim Captive Flying Machines, Avalanche, Big Dipper, Grand National, first 360° loop the loop rollercoaster in Britain, mirror maze, shows and restaurant and Big One, Europe's tallest rollercoaster at 71m and fastest

at 137km/h. Sandcastle Waterpark claims to be one of Europe's largest indoor entertainment complexes with the world's longest indoor rollercoaster waterslide in the 250m Masterblaster and the world's only indoor Sidewinder. Here are the highest outdoor climbing walls in the UK. Between the Swimming Bath and a rather unlikely windmill is the South Pier and its theatre, opened in 1893, and the UK's only purpose built bungee tower. Blackpool is the only British resort to have three piers. In JK Rowling's *Harry Potter & the Philosopher's Stone* Neville had been pushed off one of the piers by great uncle Algie in the hope of forcing him to do some magic but he had nearly drowned. Denry Machin came here in *The Card* but probably only to mingle in the crowds while he grew a beard. Painter Tom Meadows in *Borstal Boy* was from Blackpool.

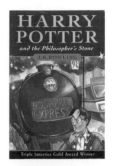

The 460m Central Pier with its theatre was opened in 1868 and has a 33m big wheel on the pier itself.

The Golden Mile has amusement centres, discos, bars, restaurants, waxworks, dome and craft centre and a Sea Life centre with one of Europe's largest shoals of tropical sharks swimming around viewers. Chiefly, though, it has the Blackpool Tower and circus. At 158m high and built 1891–4 with 980t of steel and 250t of cast iron, it was modelled on the Eiffel Tower in Paris although only half the size. It has an aquarium, circus, zoo, ballroom, educational heritage exhibition, bars and restaurants. Adjacent is the 1,900m² Comedy Carpet of precast concrete slabs with comedy writing.

The Grade II North Pier is the oldest of the three piers, being constructed in 1863, 326m long and again with a theatre. After four years a 144m steamer jetty was added and the pierhead enlarged to take a pavilion after a further decade. Some 12,000t of metal was used in its construction but it now has a damaged appearance.

Off the North Shore there is an isolated intertidal rock which seems out of character with the rest of this coast. Groynes begin at Norbreck and continue to the River Wyre. There are a couple of wrecks close inshore at Little Bispham.

Cleveleys began to grow after a 1906 architectural competition. It offers picnic sites, gardens, amusement centres, miniature railway and boating lake. Entertainment came in 2008 in the form of the ferry *Riverdance* beaching on top of the long sea outfall and crushing it. Blackpool gives way again to Lancashire.

Fleetwood is a town designed by Decimus Burton for local squire Sir Peter Hesketh in 1836. The town is much less intrusive than those further south and initially the shoreline is more conspicuous with its groynes and the occasional deep pool between them, perhaps being dredged for fallout from the Rossall Oyster Grounds which lie off the coast. Rossall Point looks out across North Wharf which can be 3km wide at low tide with at least four wrecks dotted across it. The safe course into Fleetwood for ships is up the River Wyre past the disused Wyre light. The lighthouse, designed by Burton and Captain HM Denham, was built in 1840 and was the first structure to use Mitchell & Sons 910mm diameter malleable iron screwed piles. In the same year the Beach Lighthouse or Low Light was opened. Of sandstone with a square colonnaded base, square tower and octagonal top, it was lit by gas, later replaced with electricity. The Pharos Lighthouse or High Light is similar but has a slender column with two lights on a leading line up the channel. Anti-collision rules in the river need to be studied. Streams run in the fairway at low tide but across

313

Blackpool Tower, the most famous landmark in northwest England.

the banks at up to 6km/h once they are covered. The Victoria Pier, destroyed by fire in 2008, was by the Low Light in front of the North Euston Hotel, at the end of the former railway line from Euston. A building with four radar scanners on top belongs to Blackpool & the Fylde College. Round the corner is a survival training platform belonging to the college with several items from a lifeboat to an aircraft fuselage suspended from davits. The docks are a kilometre up the estuary, incoming ships bringing chemicals, fruit, vegetables, timber, grain and general cargo and taking out chemicals, scrap metal and general cargo. It is an oil and gas exploration supply base and has 30% of the England–Ireland drive on ferry traffic and a service to Douglas. There are also pleasure cruises and a passenger ferry across the estuary to add to the confusion. Most of all, however, Fleetwood is known for its fishing fleet. Until the Cod War with Iceland it was the third largest fishing port in the British Isles with middle and distant water trawlers, the premier west

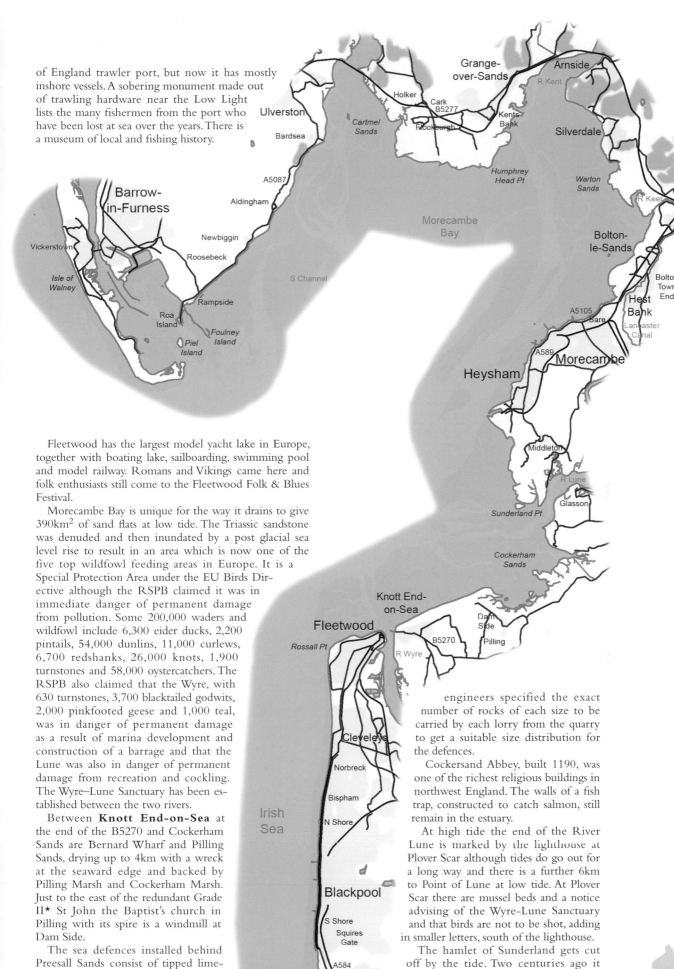

of England trawler port, but now it has mostly inshore vessels. A sobering monument made out of trawling hardware near the Low Light lists the many fishermen from the port who have been lost at sea over the years. There is a museum of local and fishing history.

Fleetwood has the largest model yacht lake in Europe, together with boating lake, sailboarding, swimming pool and model railway. Romans and Vikings came here and folk enthusiasts still come to the Fleetwood Folk & Blues Festival.

Morecambe Bay is unique for the way it drains to give 390km^2 of sand flats at low tide. The Triassic sandstone was denuded and then inundated by a post glacial sea level rise to result in an area which is now one of the five top wildfowl feeding areas in Europe. It is a Special Protection Area under the EU Birds Directive although the RSPB claimed it was in immediate danger of permanent damage from pollution. Some 200,000 waders and wildfowl include 6,300 eider ducks, 2,200 pintails, 54,000 dunlins, 11,000 curlews, 6,700 redshanks, 26,000 knots, 1,900 turnstones and 58,000 oystercatchers. The RSPB also claimed that the Wyre, with 630 turnstones, 3,700 blacktailed godwits, 2,000 pinkfooted geese and 1,000 teal, was in danger of permanent damage as a result of marina development and construction of a barrage and that the Lune was also in danger of permanent damage from recreation and cockling. The Wyre–Lune Sanctuary has been established between the two rivers.

Between **Knott End-on-Sea** at the end of the B5270 and Cockerham Sands are Bernard Wharf and Pilling Sands, drying up to 4km with a wreck at the seaward edge and backed by Pilling Marsh and Cockerham Marsh. Just to the east of the redundant Grade II★ St John the Baptist's church in Pilling with its spire is a windmill at Dam Side.

The sea defences installed behind Preesall Sands consist of tipped limestone coming from a quarry at Burton-in-Lonsdale. It is usual to specify materials with a grading curve which states the percentages of material passing successively smaller sieves. This doesn't work for large rocks so the consulting

engineers specified the exact number of rocks of each size to be carried by each lorry from the quarry to get a suitable size distribution for the defences.

Cockersand Abbey, built 1190, was one of the richest religious buildings in northwest England. The walls of a fish trap, constructed to catch salmon, still remain in the estuary.

At high tide the end of the River Lune is marked by the lighthouse at Plover Scar although tides do go out for a long way and there is a further 6km to Point of Lune at low tide. At Plover Scar there are mussel beds and a notice advising of the Wyre-Lune Sanctuary and that birds are not to be shot, adding in smaller letters, south of the lighthouse.

The hamlet of Sunderland gets cut off by the tide. Two centuries ago it was a port for the West Indies, which might help to explain Sambo's Grave. Construction was said to have been with stone from the abbey at Plover Scar. It made ropes, sails and anchors but lost trade to Lancaster and Glasson.

Low Light, High Light and college building in Fleetwood.

The survival training rig on the River Wyre at Fleetwood.

Behind Heysham Lock, Sunderland Bank and Middleton Sands may be sprinkled with stakes or jellyfish depending on the state of the tide. Middleton's holiday camp and caravan parks have the unusual backdrop of an oil refinery and chemical works, an aerial and **Heysham** nuclear power station, a pair of Advanced Gas Cooled Reactors, around which guided tours may be taken. Heysham 1 holds the world record for the longest run without a shutdown. Alongside the power station is a grey container with two slots in the side, presumably for use as an ornithological hide. The South Jetty runs out from the lighthouse. A section has disappeared at the shore end and is crossed by a bridging section which sags disconcertingly. Also disconcerting is the warm water, quite a respectable bath temperature as it leaves the power station cooling water outflow.

Another form of energy is based around Heysham's artificial harbour where British Gas have an office and use the harbour as a support base for the Morecambe Bay Gas Field. The 300m of quays also serve container traffic, a roll on roll off vehicle ferry to Douglas and passengers and freight to all parts of Ireland. Westerly winds cause a steep and awkward sea near the entrance and yachts are only permitted to enter in an emergency. One person said to have landed here with difficulty was St Patrick when shipwrecked in Morecambe Bay. On the outside of the harbour at Near Naze is a disused lighthouse while submarine cables to Colwyn Bay and Roosebeck run from the apex of Half Moon Bay.

In Heysham Lake the streams run in the direction of the channel.

Throbshaw Point is unusual for the area in being rocky. The ruined St Patrick's Chapel to the east is one of the oldest churches in Lancashire. At 8.5m x 2.7m it is the only surviving Saxon church in England with a simple rectangular shape, not even a porch. Three 1,200 year old clifftop tombs are carved down into the rock itself. St

Silt has to be hosed off the slipway at Knott End before ferry passengers may disembark.

Peter's is another ancient church, founded in the 7th or 8th centuries and rebuilt about 967, with a Saxon west doorway and window, early Norman chancel arch, 17th century bellcote and 1864 north aisle. A carved stone inside shows a bear biting each side and Viking figures along the sides. The village developed from a 7th century village and brews a notable non-alcoholic nettle beer.

Morecambe developed from three fishing villages in Victorian times as a boat train terminal for Scotland and Ireland and became the resort it is today but, among the pleasure craft, yachts and waterskiers, some fishing boats still go out for cockles, codling, shrimps and whitebait and fish weirs can still be found in the sands. Morecambe actually displayed the pioneering seaside illuminations with 7km of candles in coloured glass jars in 1919. Surprisingly, most of the hotels along the front are quite small. There was shipbreaking in the early 20th century. The two piers have been lost to disasters but there are two seawater pools and the modern amusements begin towards the Stone Pier with its lighthouse. Happy Mount Park offers Punch & Judy shows and marching band displays. The Tern project has cormorant, gannet and razorbill sculptures along the front and there is a notable statue of Eric Morecambe.

Fishing boats and leisure craft use Poulton-le-Sands. Morecambe & Heysham Yacht Club have a race control cabin on piers on the shore. Streams flow along the Grange Channel at up to 6km/h when the banks are dry but across the channel when they are covered. The Grange Channel becomes the Kent Channel and, when tides are suitable, the Kent bore can be met well out into Morecambe Bay.

The A589 gives way to the A5105 at Bare and the coastline now becomes peaceful again except for the inevitable low jets. There is a nature reserve at **Hest Bank** near where the Lancaster Canal comes close to the shore and at times, it is possible to see 50,000 birds from here.

In February 2004 21 Chinese cocklers were drowned one night when overtaken by the rising tide, leading to legislation for gangmasters.

The most prominent feature of Bolton Town End and **Bolton-le-Sands** is the cliff which gives Red Bank Farm its name. Further back is an aerial and the green dome of the folly built in Williamson's Park by Lord Ashton, visible from the Lune estuary and coming back into view here.

Off the red bank is Priest Skear, an island of stones before the Keer Channel drains the River Keer. In the 19th century a sea wall was begun to reclaim land as far as Arnside but it was subsequently abandoned.

Jenny Brown's Point was named after an 18th century resident. A stone chimney is a reminder of the local copper smelting industry but the environment is so improved that the local grass is sought after for gardens and bowling greens. Elizabeth Gaskell used to live in Lindeth Tower at Silverdale and Charlotte Brontë stayed in the village when she was young.

An indication of how the channels in the estuary can change, often overnight, is given by the fact that steamers from Morecambe used to call at **Silverdale** until the 1920s. The Arnside–Silverdale Area of Outstanding Natural Beauty remains attractive, the salt marshes being backed by low limestone cliffs with fossils, fields of daffodils in the spring and a nature trail in **Arnside** Park below Arnside Knott. Even a caravan site is quite well hidden.

This area is known as Cumbria's Riviera, the county boundary from Lancashire being crossed after Silverdale, and it was the scene of much smuggling.

A low tide footpath runs from Hest Bank across Warton Sands to Kents Bank but it is dangerous to use without local knowledge, especially as the tides sweep in. An official guide is still appointed for pedestrians but in

Plover Scar lighthouse on the River Lune.

Heysham nuclear power station, a prominent landmark.

Victorian days this was the stage coach route to the Lake District and his workload was more onerous. **Grange-over-Sands** was a watering place and at one time the residents used to cast lots for the belongings of people about to be engulfed, so frequent were the drownings. Named after the granaries or grange built by the monks of Cartmel Priory, it developed in the 16th and 17th centuries on the coastal coal trade and became a

resort in 1857 with the arrival of the Furness Railway, now the Cumbrian Coast Railway which follows the B5277. It has an open air pool, tennis courts and bowling greens and is ideal for ornamental gardens because of its mild climate and shelter from westerly winds. Tractors still cross the estuary in the vicinity of one of the fish traps below Kents Bank and cockles, flukes, mussels and shrimps are still taken from here.

Humphrey Head is 53m high with such rare plants as spiked speedwell and goldilocks aster. Its other contribution towards rarity is that it is said to be the place where the last wolf in England was killed by John Harrington. The ridge also has a cave and St Agnes Holy

Well which was supposed to cure ague, gout and worms, making it a place of pilgrimage and resulting in phials of its water being sold in the markets of Morecambe.

Wraysholme Tower behind the head is an 800 year old pele tower. It was used as a defence against sea raiders and belonged to the wolf exterminating John Harrington.

Whether the landward features are distinguishable will depend on the tide as Cartmel Wharf dries for 10km to Yeoman Wharf at low tide, probably the widest beach in Britain. Cark Airfield is at Flookburgh. Care needs to be taken at the west end of the peninsula where a number of concrete posts stand in the sea, several having shed their concrete and bent over to leave just loops of reinforcing wire sticking up.

Flookburgh is home to Lakeland Miniature Village in Coniston slate. Behind Cartmel Sands is the 300 year old Holker Hall which takes its name from the Old Norse hol kiarr, hollow fen. Built on land owned by Cartmel Priory, it has a newer wing following a fire in 1871 with a notable cantilevered staircase having each baluster carved with a different design. The former home of the Dukes of Devonshire for 300 years, it has paintings by Van Dyck and Sir Joshua Reynolds, a screen embroidered by Mary, Queen of Scots, distinctive furniture and one of the finest libraries in the north of England with over 3,500 books. Set in 10ha of gardens by Paxton, the designer of the Crystal Palace, it has a limestone cascade, formal, woodland and rose gardens, azaleas, rhododendrons, rare and unusual shrubs and trees and a fallow, sika and red deer park. The trees include the oldest monkey puzzle tree in the UK, dating from 1796. It blew down in a gale in the 19th century but with the assistance of 7 horses it was pulled back up again and now stands 24m high. There are a quilting shop, baby animal farm, large model railway, car and boat shows, hot air ballooning and tethered balloon rides, various archery championships, model bus rides, parachute displays, model aircraft, horse driving trials, adventure playground, Punch & Judy, gift shop, cafeteria and restaurant, to name a few.

Roudsea Wood and Mosses are an oakwood ridge on Carboniferous limestone with raised and valley bogs and saltmarshes, acidic soil on Silurian Slate with peat and a fine selection of flora, some quite rare.

The River Leven has a bore and was formerly a slave trading route to Windermere. The railway crosses the River Leven estuary on the Leven Viaduct to **Ulverston**. This is a delightful market town with a Tudor St Mary's church and Quaker associations. It has the Laurel & Hardy Museum as it was the birthplace of Stan Laurel. It is seen at its worst from the estuary, industrial chimneys and tipped waste to the fore. The tower on Hoad Hill is a memorial to Sir John Barrow, founder of the Royal Geographical Society, and is a copy of the Eddystone lighthouse. Further back, three aerials top the ridge to the north of Dalton-in-Furness.

Chapel Island takes its name from the old chapel located on it. Facing it on the west side of the estuary is Conishead Priory, founded in the 12th century by Gamel de Pennington. It was rebuilt in the 1820s in Gothic style but this bankrupted its owner who had to sell it to pay his debts. Had he but known that there were rich veins of iron ore under his estate which would have resolved his financial problems he would not have needed to sell it. It has been a convalescent home and is now the Buddhist Manjushri Kadampa Meditation Centre. It is noted for its fine decorative plaster ceilings, marble fireplaces and wood panelling, including an oak room with wood from Salmesbury Hall. It is set in 28ha of gardens and woods containing a 12th century lake, grotto and hermitage, nature trail and craft shop.

Behind Ulverston Sands with its fish trap is Bardsea Country Park and some stone circles as the A5087 follows the shore.

At high tide there is a straight run down the coast to Rampside but at low water it is necessary to move into the South Channel to avoid Mort Bank or even Lancaster Sound which feeds out past Yeomans Wharf, some 9km from the coast. All this material has to come from somewhere and one source is the coast at Aldingham which has been progressively claimed by the sea, the 12th century church of St Cuthbert now being just above the high water mark. Both a moat and a motte remain on this rural coast between here and Newbiggin.

The submarine cable from Heysham lands at Roosebeck. Another fish trap is located on Rampside Sands. The Grade I Rampside Hall, built 300 years ago, has a row of chimneys known as the 12 Apostles. More prominent, however, is a brick navigation pillar which was used with another similar one at the end of Foulney Island. The island is connected to the causeway to Roa

Roa Island with its lifeboat station.

The Walney Channel leads down towards Roa Island.

Island by a rubble embankment which is awash at high water springs but may also appear to give a clear passage to Roa Island lifeboat station at other times because of mirage effects.

All around Foulney Island are mussel beds while further out are numerous structures littering the sea and related to the exploration activity.

Roa Island has a nesting colony of terns in the spring and summer. The island was fortified in the 12th century to guard the harbour and has a watch tower. A railway was added along a causeway in 1847 with a pier for boat trains to Fleetwood but the pier has since been lost after storm damage and the railway replaced by a road although stone railway sleepers remain on the causeway embankment. A makeshift jetty serves the Piel ferry. It is a popular sailing and windsurfing centre in the summer with moorings and a brick and flint former boathouse.

Piel Channel is relatively narrow, cutting between extensive sandflats, flanked by saltmarsh, particularly around Haws Bed. The northeast end of the channel has been edged by training walls in order to retain a deep channel suitable for use by large ships. Streams at up to 5km/h set northeast at the outside of the bend in Piel Harbour. The northwestgoing stream turns at high water. Westerly winds increase the duration and rate of the northwesterly stream and reduce the southeasterly stream, easterly winds having the opposite effect.

The Morecambe Bay Gas Field pipeline crosses from Snab Sands to Westfield Point.

In the 19th century the ships traded to Ulverston but silting up of the Leven estuary resulted in the loss of the trade to Barrow.

Off Ramsden Dock the stream flows at up to 3km/h, the northwesterly stream turning at HW +0130. Cormorants sit on posts on the training wall and watch the water flow past.

Barrow's docks were built in 1867–1881. The main industry in Cumbria's largest and main industrial town is shipbuilding, especially naval ships, and the skyline is dominated by the hammerhead cranes in the yards of Vickers, now part of BAE Systems. Ships have been built here since 1852. The expression 'Barrow-built' is used with pride in the town to refer to the shipbuilding tradition which has resulted in many fine craft sailing out down Piel Channel, including the Royal Navy's sixth *Invincible*, their first anti submarine warfare carrier.

Barrow has been involved with submarines for more than a century. Builders in Barrow were approached by Swedish industrialist Thorsten Nordenfeld in 1884 to produce an improved version of his first submarine. The *Nordenfeld* was launched two years later and led to the development for the Admiralty of the Hollands, of which *HM Submarine No 1* was launched in 1901. Improvement of this 'damned un-English weapon' followed through the D, H, L, T, K, A, 500, Dreadnought, Oberon, Valiant, Churchill, Swiftsure and Trafalgar classes. Trident nuclear submarines were launched from insignificant looking slipways on the mainland just before the bridge.

The docks themselves are entered via a large dock with double gates although some vessels do operate directly from the Walney Channel. Barrow is the deepest port between Liverpool and the Clyde. It has 3.4km of quays, handles roll on roll off traffic and exports limestone. It is used for building oil and gas industry structures in addition to ships.

The town grew up around Furness Abbey in 1127 with the monks smelting iron on Walney and having their own fleet of trading ships. Local furnaces were built in the 18th century and the steelworks were the world's largest by 1870. The Furness name, however, comes from Fouldray Island promontory, a Norwegian island, the name being brought by Viking invaders from Barra in the 10th century, hence Barrow.

Barrow Island with its shipyard.

The bridge across to the Isle of Walney.

57 Isle of Walney

Ruled by the King of Piel

And this huge Castle, standing here sublime,
I love to see the look with which it braves,
—Cased in the unfeeling armour of old time—
The lightning, the fierce wind, and trampling waves.
William Wordsworth

For such a narrow, flat island, believed to have been the inspiration for Thomas the Tank Engine's island of Sodor, Walney offers a remarkable variety of conditions. Situated adjacent to Barrow-in-Furness, it is reached

over a bascule bridge carrying the A590 across the Walney Channel to Vickerstown, a dormitory town built by Vickers in the 19th century on an island which was then unoccupied except by a few farmers and fishermen. The opening bascule bridge replaced ferries early in the 20th century and there were also low tide footways across.

Just beyond the Ferry Hotel, north of the west end of the bridge, is a convenient slipway, access to the water being difficult from the mainland.

The channel around the northern end of the island dries out on the lower part of the tide. The shallowness is emphasized by a public footpath and a public bridleway crossing Walney Channel from North Scale to the mainland.

The area around the slipway acts as a small boat mooring.

As the built up area is left behind, the channel widens. Walney airfield, home of the Lakes Gliding Club, is

The world's largest windfarms is sited off Walney.

Piel Island with Piel Castle and the Ship Inn. Sir George Beaumont's painting of the castle inspired Wordsworth's poem.

passed on the left and then the coastline becomes marshy, protecting a nature reserve. The area abounds with rabbits, foxes, shrews, weasels and stoats and is the major haunt of the rare natterjack toad, distinguished by the yellow stripe down its back.

Sand dunes gradually become the prominent coastal feature.

The 19km long west beach is an alternating pattern of sand and cobbles but is popular with holidaymakers in the season. A caravan site and then houses reintroduce civilization at North Walney.

The dominant building, though, is the four storey brick tower battery observation post, the remaining part of Fort Walney, now a private residence in the centre of the golf course. This was occupied by the coastguard who had fine views of the water around the island. A rather grand pavilion like building with circular walls by the beach at Vickerstown is no more than the Round House Chinese restaurant.

The world's largest windfarm, with 189 turbines 190m high, is sited off the coast, covering 145km^2. Between Biggar and South End the gas pipelines from the Millom and North and South Morecambe fields make their landfall.

The southern end of the island, too, is a nature reserve, this time laid out with nature trails. The 90ha reserve has

three hides for watching the birdlife. This reserve houses the largest colonies of herring and lesser blackbacked gulls in the British Isles, 10,000 pairs of each. Also present are cormorants and oystercatchers and numbers of eider ducks winter here. The eider drake has distinctive black and white markings and in flight the head and bill form a squat triangle slightly nose down, reminiscent of the RAF's Gnat trainer, as he sweeps past at low altitude.

The lighthouse at the southeast end of the island marks the Piel Bar, an area of shallows with a confused sea breaking over it. Rounding the corner, it seems most direct to cut between Piel Island and the Snab Sands but appearances can be deceptive and it is only possible to leave the north end of Bass Pool at the higher end of the tide as Piel Island is connected to Walney at most times.

Its large ruined castle was built in the 13th century as a defence for Piel Harbour and a warehouse for the monks of Furness Abbey. In 1487 Lambert Simnel landed and declared himself king. Henry VII did not agree and informed him in the manner of the times. However, the title King of Piel is still retained by the landlord of the Ship Inn which also had the distinction of being open 24 hours every day even when nowhere else was. The inn stands at the top of a stairway up from the water, this acting as a landing point for the passenger ferry which operates from Roa Island in the summer.

Distance
Walney Island is 13km long and lies 200m off Barrow-in-Furness with road access

OS 1:50,000 Sheet
96 Barrow-in-Furness & South Lakeland

Tidal Constants
Barrow (Ramsden Dock): Dover +0030
Duddon Bar: Dover +0020
Haws Point: Dover +0020

Sea Area
Irish Sea

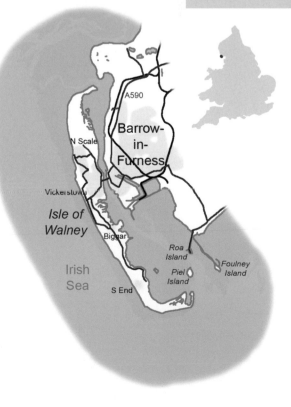

58 Lake District

There was an old man of St Bees,
Who was stung in the arm by a wasp.
When asked, 'Does it hurt?'
He replied, 'No, it doesn't.
I'm so glad it wasn't a hornet.'
Sir William Schwenck Gilbert

At first the surroundings in the Walney Channel leave a little to be desired. Cliffs on the east side are of slag, accumulated over many years. Barrow had steelmaking as one of its two main industries with the world's largest ironworks in the 19th century.

Beyond is the Dock Museum, opened in the Victoria ship repair dock, giving the story of steel shipbuilding

Black Combe seen across the Duddon estuary at low water from the dunes of Sandscale Haws.

Windfarm behind the beach at Kirksanton Haws.

322

with displays, theatre, shop and café. New factories stand back from the bank.

Heaps of scrap cars add to the dereliction, some resting in the water, their roofs forming islands of metal as they project above the surface.

Lowsy Point is marked by a community of shacks. The area can be difficult and a hole forms in the water, having taken down three youths in a boat.

Duddon Mouth largely drains to leave Duddon Sands, drying up to 3km from the entrance. The flood begins at HW Dover −0600 and the ebb at HW Dover. The estuary can have 31,000 waders and wildfowl including 1,300 pintails, 5,200 knots, 6,900 oystercatchers, 2,100 curlews and 1,500 redshanks in addition to gulls. The estuary has been declared an EU Birds Directive Special Protection Area which the RSPB claimed was threatened with immediate danger of permanent damage by tidal barrage and road developments. The barrage idea is not new. George Stevenson planned to build embankments across the Duddon, Leven and Kent estuaries as part of

On the beach at Kirksanton.

bricks, the town having had four blast furnaces and a brickworks. Birdwatching is good here. A low tide footway crosses the estuary.

Millom quarried red haematite iron ore under the sea bed until 1968, some of the purest in the world. The mine was, in the 19th century, had 11 shafts and was the busiest in Brit-

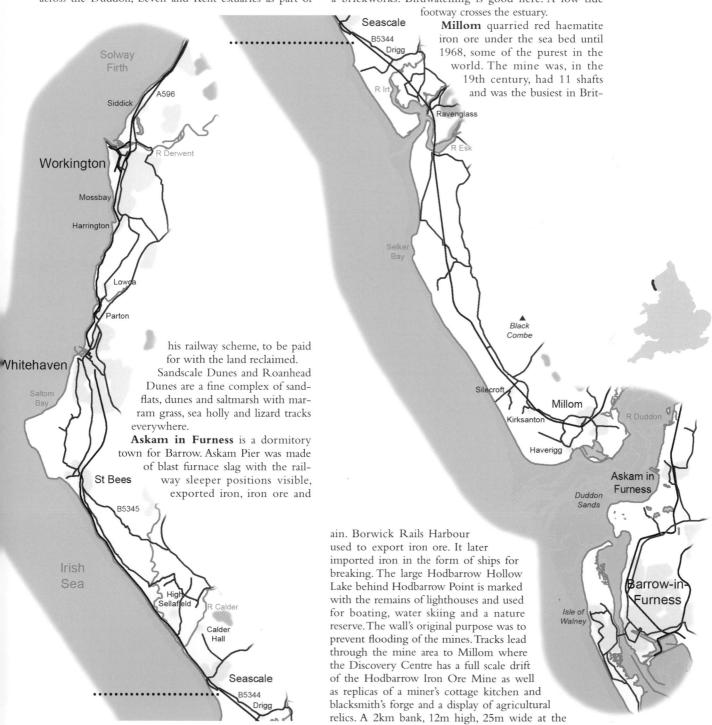

his railway scheme, to be paid for with the land reclaimed.

Sandscale Dunes and Roanhead Dunes are a fine complex of sand-flats, dunes and saltmarsh with marram grass, sea holly and lizard tracks everywhere.

Askam in Furness is a dormitory town for Barrow. Askam Pier was made of blast furnace slag with the railway sleeper positions visible, exported iron, iron ore and

ain. Borwick Rails Harbour used to export iron ore. It later imported iron in the form of ships for breaking. The large Hodbarrow Hollow Lake behind Hodbarrow Point is marked with the remains of lighthouses and used for boating, water skiing and a nature reserve. The wall's original purpose was to prevent flooding of the mines. Tracks lead through the mine area to Millom where the Discovery Centre has a full scale drift of the Hodbarrow Iron Ore Mine as well as replicas of a miner's cottage kitchen and blacksmith's forge and a display of agricultural relics. A 2km bank, 12m high, 25m wide at the

Black Combe towers above the beach at Silecroft.

High sand dunes to the north of Annaside.

The sand dunes drop away at Selker Point while, further inland, the fells retreat from the coast.

The important nuclear power, fuel reprocessing and research plant at Sellafield.

top and 64m wide at the bottom, runs from Hodbarrow Point and was built in 1900–05 to protect the mine.

The skeleton of a wooden ship is embedded in the sand at the point where one of Lakeland's most active rivers meets the energy of the Irish Sea while Borwick Rails was chosen as a ship breaking site.

Overlooked by the spire of the church of St George in Millom, Haverigg is a fishing harbour with more dunes which run westwards and reach 20m in height at Haverigg Point, hiding the open prison there.

The beach at Kirksanton Haws is next to a windfarm and there is a derelict building on the beach. The area has several signs of earlier use, the five Bronze Age stone circles on a hill at Lacra having been a religious centre, perhaps with two approaching avenues. The Giant's Grave is found south of Kirksanton village with two standing stones, one with cup marks.

From Kirksanton Haws, high red sand dunes and sandstone cliffs run northwest to Selker Head. Flows follow the coast to St Bees Head but only at up to 2km/h although strong westerly winds produce heavy seas. The fells reduce and fall back going northwards but at this point the coast is only a kilometre from the foot of the magnificent Skiddaw slate bulk of 600m high Black Combe. Not surprisingly, the coast immediately becomes part of the Lake District National Park, here taking the form of a golf course surrounded by standing stones, all hidden behind the dunes.

A submarine cable from Douglas lands at Silecroft, a beach which has surfing except for the top four hours of the tidal cycle when it dumps.

Gutterby Spa never became a spa and now even the mineral spring is no more. In fact, there is more to see at Annaside where there are, at least, many rockpools.

Selker Point with its mussel beds and perhaps a heron signals the start of the 12km Eskmeals army gunnery range around the mouth of the River Esk. The coastline is marked by several towers, assorted concrete block structures and two brilliant white geodesic domes. The beach is often covered with spent shells. There is a tide gauge at one point.

The River Esk gives access to Ravenglass and has been used by both Romans and smugglers in their turns. The flood in the estuary begins at HW Dover −0600 and the ebb at HW Dover.

The Drigg Dunes & Gullery on Drigg Point contains one of the largest colonies of blackheaded gulls in Britain, four species of tern, many waders and shore birds plus natterjack toads, none of which seems to be unduly

The heavily carved doorway of the priory church in St Bees, including sculpted heads.

The Dragon Stone, showing a sea monster.

disturbed by the fact that they live in the middle of a firing range. A permit is required for entry.

The nature reserve is on a peninsula created by the River Irt which runs parallel to the coast for 2km from the far boundary of the national park. A site at Drigg used to discharge low level radioactive waste into a trench and thence into the river but it now goes into an outfall directly into the sea. While the outfall was being installed, live shells from Eskmeals before 1940 were found all over the sea bed. Rhizostoma jellyfish are now more likely to be found on the beach.

Seascale on the B5344, at the beginning of a shooting spree in 2010, is separated by golf links from the complex which has also been known over the years as Calder Hall, Windscale and now Sellafield, one of the most important nuclear sites in the world, located at the mouths of Newmill Beck, the River Calder and the River Ehen, the latter following the coast closely for 2km. In 1951 the nuclear fuel reprocessing plant was opened, to be followed in 1956 by the world's first commercial nuclear power station, now being dismantled. In 1958 there was a serious nuclear leak and this is still recalled by those concerned with the high frequency of childhood leukaemia in the area. The site is one of the most controversial locations in the country for conservationists and Sellafield try hard to promote a better image for themselves. The Irish Sea is already the most radioactively polluted sea in the world, much of the blame being laid at Sellafield's door. The outfall from Sellafield used to be marked by a buoy but this made it too easy for environmentalists to find and block up and now there are two buoys, the outfall being between them, rather nearer No 2 buoy. An exhibition explains nuclear power, looks at world energy needs, radiation and safety and has computer games, a fission tunnel, a walk in model of a reactor core, a shop and guided tours with the possibility of seeing operations close up by prior arrangement. This is the preferred site for an underground low/intermediate level nuclear waste repository with as much excavation as in the Channel Tunnel. A series of 250m x 25m caverns would be dug 800m down, the radioactive waste mixed with concrete and stored in drums in the caverns and then the caverns backfilled with concrete. Research work has even considered the effect of a 70m drop in sea level and another Ice Age. A silver sphere holds an Advanced Gas Cooled Reactor, facing across to Starling Castle. Sellafield is also the site of a combined cycle gas turbine power station of just 170MW.

Sand dunes continue, among which are two caravan sites at Braystones and a line of beach shacks.

St Bees takes its name from St Bega, an Irish princess who took a childhood religious vow and fled to avoid an arranged marriage with a Norse prince. She asked Lord Egremont for land to build a convent and received the generous reply that she could have all the land covered by snow on mid summer's day, an answer which needs to be seen in the context that this coast is normally free of snow even in the depths of winter because of the mild climate. Having friends in high places helps, however, and on the appointed day a snowstorm duly appeared. Her Benedictine convent was established in 650 and owned land, mines, salt pans and quarries, including the one which was to supply stone for St George's Chapel at Windsor. The convent was destroyed by the Vikings and subject to many Scottish raids, rebuilt by the Normans in 1120, dissolved in 1538 and restored in the 17th and 19th centuries. The church was restored as the Priory Church of St Mary and St Bega with the best 12th century deeply notched Norman arch doorway in the area although the church was much altered in the 19th century. Another notable item is the Dragon Stone, a 12th century door lintel carved with a sea monster. The neighbouring stone buildings were Archbishop of Canterbury Edmund Grindal's school of 1583.

The shore area now has caravan sites, playground, toilets, beach shop, café and Seacote Hotel. Off the beach is a wreck site. A ruined coastguard station is located on the head with another coastguard station by the lighthouse. It is a popular place with walkers, not least because St Bees Head is one end of the Coast to Coast Walk. The head is the only significant set of cliffs in Cumbria, the red St Bees sandstone rising vertically to the 98m high flat summit with its white lighthouse, from where the Isle of Man can be seen. St Bees sandstone was used for the Maughold Village Cross on the island. Access is forbidden to the RSPB reserve but the 10,000 cormorants, fulmars, razorbills, 5,000 guillemots, puffins, kittiwakes and other gulls which breed on the cliffs can be viewed better from below, the largest seabird colony and the only cliff nesting site in northwest England. It is the only English nest site for the black guillemot. There are three RSPB observation points.

Fleswick Bay between South and North Heads is a cove which was probably used by smugglers.

St Bees Head, described in *The French Revolution* as a 'sapphire Promontory', is, effectively, the start of the Solway Firth. Tide streams in the entrance to the firth are generally anticlockwise with E–W movement up to 3km/h and north–south movement up to 1km/h. The flood into the firth begins at HW Dover –0500 and the ebb starts at HW Dover +0100. In addition, there may be ripples and eddies from HW Dover –0540 for an hour as the eastgoing stream meets the ebb from the firth.

Despite the oyster grounds, Saltom Bay signals another change in the coastline, now high, composed largely of slag and topped with industrial complexes, often derelict. The plants include the former large chemical works of Albright and Wilson, based on Triassic anhydrite. This firm were permitted to discharge 500t of zinc, chromium, copper and nickel per year into the Irish Sea, the largest such discharge around the British coastline.

Much of the industrial activity was founded on the now declined Cumberland Coalfield, such as the Duke Pit of 1747 with a shoreline fan house built to look like a ruined castle, the elaborate Wellington Pit of 1840 and the Haig Colliery which ceased production in 1987. Mining took place up to 6km offshore.

Whitehaven is a derivative of the Old Norse for

North Head at St Bees.

white headland haven. It consisted of six fishermen's cottages in 1566 but the Lowther family developed it as a shipbuilding and coal exporting port. It lies where the B5345 joins the A5094 and was the first planned town since the Middle Ages. In its heyday it was the second port to London, only declining as Liverpool grew. It was the centre of the British rum trade. The Brocklebank Line, now part of Cunard, was formed here and one of the better known trainee seamen from the port was John Paul Jones, the founder of the American navy. He put his knowledge to good use in 1778 during the American War of Independence when he raided the harbour, setting fire to some ships, mentioned in *The French Revolution*, and capturing the fort but failing to capture the town, the last direct invasion of English soil by a foreign power and the only American attack. In 1805 the schooner *Hooton*, sailing from the port, was wrecked on the Isle of Man, a box of hedgehogs it was carrying being the ancestors of all the hedgehogs on the island. The artificial tidal harbour with its lighthouse and a column at the root of the harbour wall has 920m of quays, used for importing phosphates which have to be brought ashore in barges as silting restricts the harbour to ships of 1,500t. A heavy sea forms across the harbour entrance in westerly gales and the flood stream normally sets east across the entrance with eddies off it.

The Beacon is Copeland's museum and the Rum Story features the UK rum trade which was centred on the town. There are a sports centre and swimming pool in the town. Another famous son was Jonathan Swift, author of *Gulliver's Travels*, perhaps the inspiration for the town's Biggest Liar in the World Competition.

The prominent St Bridget's church to the north of Parton is close to the site the Romans chose for their fort of Gabrosentum on the banks of a small river.

On top of the cliffs at Lowca are a disused mine and a brickworks, the derelict buildings clearly roofless against the skyline. Meanwhile, the railway snakes along the foot of the cliffs on an embankment which has been reinforced, none too beautifully, with a variety of tipped hardware. Some 3km off Cunning Point is a magnetic anomaly, probably resulting from the dumping of slag from Workington.

Heaps of white slag are prominent on the shoreline at Harrington which had an ironworks and shipbuilding. The small harbour exported coal to Ireland and limestone to Scotland. A blockship was sunk across the entrance during the Second World War when magnesium was made here. The slag increases to form cliffs past the extensive former works at Mossbay although the final kilometre to Workington has been landscaped.

Workington is located around the mouth of the Derwent but does not present its best face to the sea. The 460m South Pier ends in a line of rocks and a small race can form out to sea past these on the ebb with eddies at times.

The town developed on rich pockets of very pure haematite although the name is nothing to do with industry but is Old English for Weorc's farm. They used to ship coal to southern England and made railway tracks in the steelworks. Now the ironworks and steelworks are disused and even the chapel on the summit of Chapel Hill is in ruins. On the south side of the harbour is a disused shipyard, yet all is not dead. Some 1.6km of quays include a liquid sulphur terminal, the dock importing chemicals and petroleum products and exporting coal and railway track materials. A battery of small cranes are in use on the quay and fishing boats come and go, emulated by a flotilla of small boats taking out anglers.

It seems to have been a favourite destination for people making less than happy crossings from Scotland. Mary, Queen of Scots crossed to here with 30 others in an open boat after losing the Battle of Langside in 1568.

There is another mine to the south of Siddick, sea dyke. Between it and the Burrow Walls Roman fort is Siddick Pond, a favourite spot for winter wildfowl. Beyond Siddick are two large Iggesund Paperboard factories and the only practical exit for some distance lies between them, located by a small green cone beacon on the end of an outfall. The shore is of boulders, slag and pieces of brick but at least there is a right of way across the railway, if not actually a level crossing. Beyond a high flood embankment is a track with plenty of parking space, alongside a field used by microlights. They now have to make their final approaches over the A596 and turn sharply into the field to avoid the chimneys of the new factory which, inconsiderately, have been placed in the way.

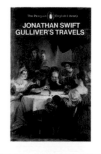

Distance
76km from Vickerstown to Siddick

OS 1:50,000 Sheets
89 West Cumbria
96 Barrow-in-Furness &
South Lakeland

Tidal Constants
Barrow (Ramsden Dock): Dover +0030
Duddon Bar: Dover +0020
Tarn Point: Dover +0020
Whitehaven: Dover +0020
Workington: HW Dover +0040 LW Dover +0030

Sea Area
Irish Sea

Range
Eskmeals

Connection
River Duddon – see RoB p75

59 Solway Firth

'I long woo'd your daughter, my suit you denied;–
Love swells like the Solway, but ebbs like its tide–
Sir Walter Scott

From Siddick the coast is low. This probably accounts for nearly 30 Roman forts and fortlets between here and the end of Hadrian's Wall at Bowness-on-Solway, intended to keep the Picts from landing behind the line of the wall.

A windsock just before **Flimby** indicates an airstrip. Off the coast there are frequent floats marking lobster pots.

Maryport with its hollow pier leading out from an area of excavation was formerly a mining town at the nrpthern end of the Cumberland coalfield. Its disused cast iron lighthouse is one of the world's earliest. Maryport harbour, sheltered by a bar, was silted up but now has a marina. Situated at the mouth of the River Ellen, it was named after Mary, wife of Humphrey Senhouse who built the harbour and docks in the 18th century and whose eldest daughter gave her name to Elizabeth Dock. Crew members from Maryport visited the Tyne and married into Catherine Cookson's family, as she describes in *Our Kate*. By the harbour is the Lake District Coast Aquarium. Maryport Maritime Museum has displays on Christian Fletcher, who was born locally in 1764 and who was to lead the *Bounty* mutineers, and on Thomas Ismay, who founded the White Star Line, whose best known ship was the *Titanic*. Captain WA Nelson's voyages under sail at the turn of the 20th century were made from here and the port also initiated the broadside launch, a procedure devised because of the limited space in the harbour. Senhouse Dock itself was used for loading railway lines made in Cumbria. The town has a carnival with procession and field events in July. *The Lazy Tour of Two Idle Apprentices* describes Maryport as having 'a bit of waterside Bristol, with a slice of Wapping, a seasoning of Wolverhampton, and a garnish of Portsmouth'.

The Senhouse Roman Museum and a house with a turret top high ground beyond the town. Begun about 1550 and one of the most important collections of Roman antiquities in Europe, it is located at the Alavna Roman Fort, a naval base used to defend against attacks from across the Solway. Alongside the parade ground were a whole series of altars to the emperor Jupiter Optimus Maximus, found buried here. The Roman road leading northeast from it is paralleled by the Allerdale Ramble, which reaches the coast here, and by the Cumbria Cycle Way, which uses the B5300. The high ground ends with a golf course.

Allonby Bay has negligible current from HW +0200 to HW −0200 but the banks and shoals move frequently. There is a conspicuous triangular hill at Heatherbank but the views inland to the mountains of the Lake District are largely unrestricted. There may be the odd jet ski about but conditions are generally quiet, appreciated by curlews, snipe, oystercatchers, blackbacked gulls and perhaps a sunstar floating on the surface.

Ponies graze freely on the green at **Allonby**, a whisky smuggling centre where Harry Bertram went to earth in Scott's *Guy Mannering*. *Redgauntlet* had Allonby Tom as one of the smugglers. Francis Goodchild found Allonby the British Isles' most delicious piece of sea coast in *The Lazy Tour of Two Idle Apprentices*. Magdalen Vanstone also hid here briefly in Wilkie Collins' *No Name*. Two centuries ago it became a resort. Christ Church at the south end of the village has a memorial to Joseph Huddart who was born here in 1741 and became a surveyor of unknown Far East coasts and harbours. After watching a cable snap at sea he invented a new method of making ropes and set up business in London to manufacture this vital commodity.

Stepped defences and cribwork lead to Dubmill Point.

Silloth's silos stand by the harbour.

East Cote lighthouse faces the Solway Firth.

the railway in 1856, a notable attraction being some of the finest sunsets over the sea in England, even if most of the scenery visible is Scottish. Today it offers the Lido Residential Park, swimming, tennis, squash and a carnival.

Ingoing flows start at HW Dover −0345 and outgoing flows at HW Dover +0115 at up to 7km/h, particularly by the mouth of the basin, off which there is also a westgoing flow from HW −0040. At first the grassed parkland area with its tea, coffee and snacks café is fronted by groynes and then a stepped sea wall, from the toe of which air bubbles along its length as the tide floods. East Cote lighthouse, built in 1864, was the rear one of a pair of leading lights to mark the channel to Silloth. As this moved, the lighthouse was built on rails so that it could be repositioned as necessary.

Inland from the lighthouse is a holiday camp on the edge of a disused airfield. Most of the rest of the south side of the firth is nature reserve and an

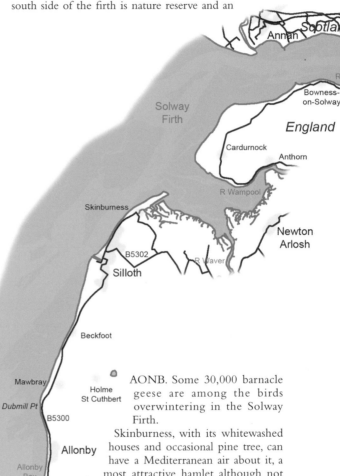

Sandhills follow from the point to Silloth and the coast is low lying right round to Southerness Point. The first serious sandbanks come off Mawbray, the Beckfoot Flats drying up to 2.5km off Mawbray Bank at the high water line and then tapering in to the Lees Scar light structure off the golf course at Silloth.

Silloth's most conspicuous landmark are silos by the harbour which imports grain and oil. Following winter storm damage to the lock gate across the entrance in 1879, another basin was constructed inland of a further protective lock gate. The name comes from the sea laths or granaries of the Cistercian monks of Holme Cultram Abbey. Cobbled streets are set around the Green, leading to the B5302, but the town is essentially Victorian. With a promenade to Skinburness, it became a resort after the arrival of

AONB. Some 30,000 barnacle geese are among the birds overwintering in the Solway Firth.

Skinburness, with its whitewashed houses and occasional pine tree, can have a Mediterranean air about it, a most attractive hamlet although not everyone thought highly of it. Edward I chose it as his base for attacking Scotland, earning it special hatred. Skinburness was nominated by Nanty Ewart as an alternative when Bowness was not available for landing contraband in *Redgauntlet*. Large rocks placed around some of the houses come as a reminder that most of the village was swept away in a flood in 1303, resulting in a general exodus to set up **Newton Arlosh**.

Grune Point, probably Point of Carne in *Redgauntlet*, now with its pillbox, is notable for its birds and plants while sheep and cattle graze on the saltings of Skinburness Marsh and Newton Marsh. These surround Moricambe, the combined estuary of the rivers Waver and Wampool that are mentioned at times in *Redgauntlet*, which largely drains at low tide to leave a large area of sandbanks. Three disused airfields surround the inlet which was used for bombing practice during the war. A structure in the middle used to carry a target but

Cormorants nest on the former bombing target in Moricambe.

A section of aircraft lying in the estuary.

Remains of the railway viaduct on the English side.

The Anthorn radio masts, seen across Moricambe from Grune Point.

now supports a colony of nesting cormorants, alongside a bright blue canvas box which has apparently been provided for their use but which they ignore. Lying on the sand are sections of aircraft wing and undercarriage.

Dominating all and the whole upper end of the Solway Firth are a forest of radio masts of Anthorn Radio Station on a former airfield. These used to be part of the communication link with our submarine fleet but have been superseded by satellites. Even so, they have not been dismantled, are brightly lit at night and, among other functions, provide the Radio 4 time pips. The 13 masts form a six pointed star, all linked with interconnecting wires. Around the perimeter at intervals are brick buildings.

The coast from Cardurnock to Bowness-on-Solway had pairs of ditches connecting towers and fortlets to Hadrian's Wall. Cardurnock Flatts widen as the Solway Firth narrows, pushing the entering River Eden's deep channel against the Scottish shore.

Construction of a barrage has been considered. Herdhill Scar has the remains of a railway bridge with a corresponding embankment on the Scottish side of Bowness Wath at Seafield. The Solway Viaduct was built in 1869 to carry a direct railway route from the iron ore mines of Cumbria to the smelting furnaces of the Clyde but never carried heavy traffic as it was vulnerable to the weather. The longest bridge in Europe at 1.76km, it had 181 piers but none of the spans opened so it completed the closure of Port Carlisle by obstructing shipping which was already having difficulty with silting. James

Brunlees' design suffered from water freezing in the piers in 1875, cracking them, and in 1881 ice floes damaged 45 piers and 37 spans, making two breaks in the viaduct. Trains ceased in 1921 but the bridge then began its most popular period as it was used by **Annan** men to walk to English public houses on Sundays, those in Scotland being closed on the Sabbath. It was dismantled in 1935.

The shoreline has peat bog or fine turf on top of marine clays. A parking area at the west end of Bowness is convenient for reaching the water when the tide is up but not when there is just mud. Clegs can be a nuisance. It was the final departure point for Prince Charlie in *Redgauntlet*.

The far corner of the Roman empire.

Distance
43km from Siddick to Bowness-on-Solway

OS 1:50,000 Sheets
*85 Carlisle &
Solway Firth
89 West Cumbria*

Tidal Constants
*Workington:
HW Dover +0040
LW Dover +0030
Maryport:
HW Dover +0040
LW Dover +0030
Silloth
HW Dover +0050
LW Dover +0100
Annan Waterfoot:
HW Dover +0110
LW Dover +0300*

Sea Area
Irish Sea

Connection
River Wampool – see RoB p77

Index

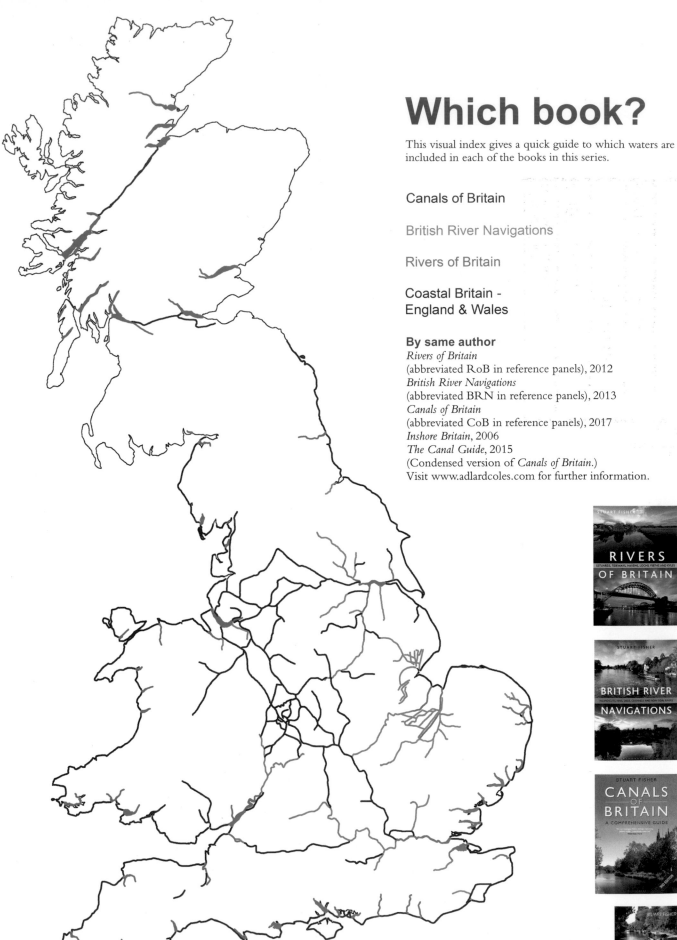

Which book?

This visual index gives a quick guide to which waters are included in each of the books in this series.

Canals of Britain

British River Navigations

Rivers of Britain

Coastal Britain -
England & Wales

By same author
Rivers of Britain
(abbreviated RoB in reference panels), 2012
British River Navigations
(abbreviated BRN in reference panels), 2013
Canals of Britain
(abbreviated CoB in reference panels), 2017
Inshore Britain, 2006
The Canal Guide, 2015
(Condensed version of *Canals of Britain*.)
Visit www.adlardcoles.com for further information.

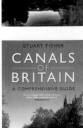